WAR AND PEACE

Gallimard | Fondation Martin Bodmer

31e Année. — N° 11116

LE NUMÉRO CINQ CENTIMES

Tarif des Abonnements
Seine et Oise   6 fr.   10 fr.   20 fr.
France et Colonies   6 »   11 »   20 »
Étranger   9 »   19 »   35 »

RÉDACTION & ADMINISTRATION
2-4-6, Boulevard Poissonnière
TÉLÉPH. : Gutenberg 5-09 — 5-08 — 15-00
Adresse Télégraphique : MATIN-PARIS

Mardi 4 Août 1914

Le Matin

Stéphane LAUZANNE, Rédacteur en chef   Jules MADELINE, Président

L'Allemagne déclare la guerre à la France

La guerre sainte de la civilisation contre la barbarie

L'agression germanique se développe selon une logique implacable. Chaque jour apporte à l'Allemagne un déshonneur, en attendant les jours qui lui apporteront la défaite.

Samedi 1er août, quelques heures après que la Russie eut accepté la proposition que l'Allemagne lui avait formulée, d'accord avec elle, l'Allemagne déclare la guerre à la Russie.

Le dimanche, elle viole la neutralité du Luxembourg ; sans déclaration de guerre, elle viole la frontière française ; sans déclaration de guerre, elle commet des actes de guerre.

Hier lundi, en envoyant dans la nuit à la Belgique un ultimatum qui expirait à 7 heures du matin, elle viole la neutralité de la Belgique.

Ainsi se continue la série des coups de force contre les faibles, commencée par l'attentat de l'Autriche sur la Serbie, d'une nation de 50 millions d'hommes sur une nation de 5 millions d'hommes.

Il est désormais acquis à l'Histoire que l'Allemagne ne peut vivre que par l'oppression des faibles.

Le mépris que les Allemands témoignent pour les droits, pour les libertés des petites nations, comme il explique, comme il illustre l'histoire et l'Alsace-Lorraine ! Ont-ils dû souffrir assez, nos frères de là-bas, sous le joug de ces Germains qui fabriquent des juristes, mais ne comprennent pas le droit ; qui croient que le progrès ne se fait à la machine, qu'une supériorité s'exprime par les coups, et que le dernier mot de la civilisation, c'est les forces.

Laissons-les dans leur erreur ; qu'ils continuent à croire à la force : mais qu'ils ne comptent plus sur elle ; ils ne l'ont plus. D'insolences en insolences, de menaces en menaces, ils ont lassé la patience de l'Europe.

La catastrophe à laquelle on ne croyait plus, devant laquelle tous les pays reculaient d'horreur, ils l'ont rendue visible. Tout ce qui avait été fait depuis cent ans pour garantir aux hommes leurs libertés, aux peuples leur souveraineté, ils l'ont effacé en trois jours. Pour eux il n'y a plus de lois, plus de droit international, plus de traités. L'Allemagne envoie aux peuples des ultimatums pour les obliger à renier sa propre signature.

L'empereur Guillaume demande aux autres nations de le déshonorer ; c'est qu'il ne peine : il s'en charge.

Il n'est pas jusqu'au prétexte ridicule invoqué hier par l'Allemagne pour déclarer la guerre à la France qui ne doive révolter tout ce qu'il y a dans l'univers d'êtres pensants.

Alors la mort de milliers et peut-être de centaines de milliers d'hommes, le sang qui va couler sur la terre, la misère, la faim, à travers les nations, c'est parce que deux aviateurs... O peuple menteur ! O criminel empereur !

Allons ! La guerre qui commence est une guerre sainte.

Les Anglais passent pour perdre rarement leur calme, et cependant les voyageurs arrivés hier de Londres à Paris, et qui se sont trouvés dans des wagons chargés de soldats anglais, nous racontaient que là-bas aussi l'enthousiasme est immense. On acclame la France, on hue l'Allemagne.

Il semble que l'Angleterre entière pousse un hymne de délivrance.

Les Anglais, comme les Français, ne songent pas à ce qu'ils risquent. Ils songent que c'en est fini de l'hégémonie factice de l'Allemagne en Europe.

Si en France les trains qui emportent le peuple mobilisé retentissent de tant de « Marseillaises », si d'un bout à l'autre du territoire, en dépit des femmes qui pleurent, tous les hommes chantent, c'est qu'ils ont la certitude de servir une cause sacrée : la cause de la civilisation humaine.

Ils défendent les conquêtes de la civilisation contre les reprises de l'absolutisme, le vingtième siècle contre le retour au moyen âge, l'humanité contre la barbarie, l'intégrité du territoire, des droits et des libertés nationales contre la nation qui viole tous les territoires, tous les droits, toutes les libertés.

× × ×

Le préfet de police, par ordre du gouvernement, fait connaître officiellement à la population :

1° Des violations de frontière avec réquisitions de bestiaux ont eu lieu sur quelques points par des détachements allemands, notamment aux environs de Belfort ;

2° Le gouvernement italien a notifié officiellement au gouvernement français la déclaration de neutralité de l'Italie.

L'ambassadeur d'Allemagne a demandé ses passeports à 5 h. 45 et a quitté Paris à 10 h. 10 du soir

L'AMBASSADEUR DE FRANCE QUITTERA BERLIN AUJOURD'HUI

LA CONVERSATION DE M. VIVIANI AVEC M. DE SCHOEN

A 5 h. 45 du soir, M. de Schœn, ambassadeur d'Allemagne à Paris, s'est rendu au ministère des affaires étrangères.

Il a été reçu par M. Viviani, président du conseil et ministre des affaires étrangères, en présence de M. de Margerie, directeur politique.

M. de Schœn s'est montré très ému.

Il a commencé par dire qu'il constatait avec le plus vif regret l'échec de ses efforts qui avaient eu pour but, pendant de nombreuses années, d'améliorer les relations de la France et de l'Allemagne.

Il a déclaré avoir consacré à cette œuvre le plus grand dévouement et la plus sincère activité.

Il a ajouté éprouver une grande douleur à constater que la situation à Paris était devenue impossible.

Son gouvernement l'avait chargé de déclarer au gouvernement de la République que des aviateurs français avaient survolé la Belgique, que d'autres aviateurs français avaient survolé l'Allemagne, fait tomber des bombes jusqu'à Nuremberg, et que ces faits constituaient un acte d'agression, de violation du territoire allemand.

— Le passage des aviateurs français et leurs actes au-dessus de la frontière allemande et belge obligeaient l'Allemagne, a dit formellement l'ambassadeur,

à se déclarer en état de guerre avec la France

M. de Schœn a ensuite dit qu'il tenait à porter à la connaissance du président du conseil un fait d'ordre personnel.

Comme il se rendait au ministère, deux individus étaient montés sur le marchepied de son automobile et l'avaient injurié.

M. Viviani et M. de Margerie ont écouté en silence les déclarations de l'ambassadeur d'Allemagne.

Lorsque M. de Schœn eut terminé, M. Viviani a répondu qu'il était entièrement faux que des aviateurs français eussent survolé l'Allemagne et la Belgique et fait tomber des bombes.

Il a rappelé à M. de Schœn que, dans la note qu'il lui avait remise hier, le gouvernement de la République avait protesté contre la violation du territoire français, à laquelle s'étaient livrés, en plusieurs endroits, des détachements allemands, commandés par des officiers allemands, et contre le meurtre d'un caporal français.

Il lui a rappelé que, de plus, le gouvernement français, dans le but d'éviter des incidents de frontière, avait donné l'ordre à ses troupes de rester à dix kilomètres de la frontière allemande, que des détachements allemands, s'étant livrés à des actes d'agression sur les troupes françaises, avaient franchi cet intervalle de dix kilomètres et pénétré jusqu'à onze kilomètres en territoire français. Ces faits-là étaient précis, exacts, incontestés, et constituaient nettement une agression allemande sur territoire français.

M. de Schœn, toujours extrêmement ému, a pris congé de M. Viviani et de M. de Margerie, qui l'ont conduit jusqu'au perron du ministère des affaires étrangères.

L'ambassadeur d'Allemagne salua à plusieurs reprises le président du conseil et le directeur politique des affaires étrangères. Puis il monta dans l'automobile qui le ramenait à l'ambassade d'Allemagne.

Immédiatement après cette entrevue, M. Viviani a fait télégraphier à M. Jules Cambon, l'ambassadeur de France à Berlin, et l'a chargé de demander immédiatement ses passeports au gouvernement allemand et de consigner dans une note que M. Cambon remettrait, en même temps que la demande de passeports, la protestation de la France contre la violation du Luxembourg, occupé par l'Allemagne sous le prétexte que la France avait l'intention d'envahir le Luxembourg. M. Viviani a invité également notre ambassadeur à Berlin à protester contre l'ultimatum envoyé à la Belgique, par lequel le gouvernement impérial demandait des facilités pour les opérations militaires en territoire belge, opérations qui étaient « dirigées contre la France », parce que, d'après le gouvernement allemand, la France avait l'intention d'occuper Namur et d'autres endroits du territoire belge.

M. Cambon quittera Berlin aujourd'hui.

L'Allemagne a donc déclaré la guerre à la France le 3 août, à 5 h. 45 du soir.

Note officielle

L'ambassadeur d'Allemagne a remis au gouvernement français une note dans laquelle son gouvernement l'avait chargé de déclarer à la France qu'il la considérait comme en état de guerre.

L'ambassadeur d'Allemagne n'a invoqué que des faits mensongers pour donner une raison à la détermination de son gouvernement, entre autres que quelques aviateurs français auraient survolé Nuremberg.

BELGIQUE --- FRANCE --- ALLEMAGNE

BRUXELLES, 3 août. — Hier soir, à sept heures, le ministre d'Allemagne a remis au gouvernement belge un ultimatum disant que l'Allemagne avait appris que des masses françaises importantes se disposaient à opérer vers Givet et Namur et qu'elle se considérait dans l'obligation de prendre des mesures défensives, et priait le gouvernement belge de faire connaître avant sept heures du matin si la Belgique était disposée à lui faciliter les opérations.

Le gouvernement belge a répondu qu'il était très surpris de ces affirmations, ayant reçu, concernant la neutralité de la Belgique, des assurances formelles de la France. Il a ajouté que la Belgique avait trop le sentiment de sa dignité et de ses intérêts pour accéder à une pareille mise en demeure. La Belgique refuse nettement de faciliter les opérations allemandes et proteste contre toute violation de son territoire. Elle est résolue par tous les moyens en son pouvoir à défendre énergiquement sa neutralité, garantie par les traités et par le roi de Prusse. (Havas.)

Les mesures « défensives » que l'armée allemande va prendre sur le territoire des nations voisines feraient sourire, si les jours n'étaient pas si tragiques. Les professeurs de droit allemand nous avaient déjà prodigué les formules bizarres ; ils viennent de découvrir « l'invasion défensive ». Ils ne feront pas fortune avec cette nouveauté.

La Belgique a répondu dans cette manière réelle où elle excelle : une manière bon enfant, candide et si ferme ! La surprise qu'elle a manifestée au sujet des intentions françaises est charmante. La France allait l'envahir. Allons donc ! A quoi cela se voyait-il ? Justement, la France avait pris la précaution quelques jours auparavant de l'assurer du contraire.

Quant à la dernière phrase, avec quel soin supérieur elle distingue le roi de Prusse et les traités avec lesquels il est en effet le roi de Prusse n'a aucun rapport.

Parce que la signature de la France était au bas du traité de Prusse, bien que cette signature eût été arrachée par la force, la République française s'est résignée, quarante-quatre ans, à ce démembrement séparé des provinces qu'on lui avait prises.

Devant sa signature donnée et qui garantit la Belgique sa neutralité, le roi de Prusse n'hésite pas un instant. Il a la renie. (Havas.)

Bruxelles, 3 août. — Nous sommes en mesure d'affirmer qu'en cas d'hostilités contre la Belgique, la France s'est déclarée prête à remplir les obligations incombant aux puissances garantes de la neutralité de la Belgique.

Le conseil des ministres a décidé qu'il ne ferait pas actuellement appel à la garantie des puissances, et qu'il agira selon les circonstances. Le gouvernement affirme que jusqu'à présent les Allemands ne sont pas entrés en Belgique. (Havas.)

Les premiers actes d'hostilité

Les Allemands ont fusillé M. Samain, l'ancien président du Souvenir français, et emprisonné tous les membres du Souvenir français

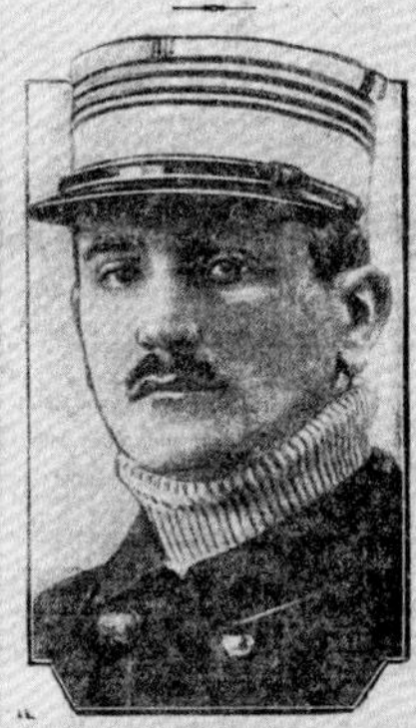

ALEXIS SAMAIN

Les Allemands ont bien débuté. Ils ont fusillé Alexis Samain, président du Souvenir français en Alsace-Lorraine et emprisonné tous les membres du Souvenir français.

Comme leur premier acte donne tout de suite sa signification à la guerre ! Il faut que l'Alsace meure, n'est-ce pas ?

— Qu'elle vive française... Elle vivra.

* *

Petit-neveu de cette femme de Metz que M. Maurice Barrès dans Colette Baudoche, appelle Mlle Aubertin la France, Alexis Samain avait fondé à Metz en 1909 une société de gymnastique « Lorraine sportive ».

La création de cette société déplut vivement aux autorités. L'uniforme des jeunes groupés par Alexis Samain avait un aspect trop français.

« Lorraine sportive » donna un grand concert à l'hôtel Terminus de Metz le 8 janvier 1911. Conformément à la loi allemande les invitations avaient été faites par écrit, deux personnes y étaient considérées comme invitées de droit, routinés. A peine le concert avait-il commencé qu'un commissaire de police pénétrait dans la salle et ordonnait aux exécutants de cesser de jouer.

Alexis Samain expliqua au commissaire que la réunion était privée et le pria de se retirer. La musique salua la sortie du trouble-fête par la marche du Sambre et Meuse.

A la suite de ces incidents, Alexis Samain fut arrêté. On l'accusait d'avoir incité, la foule à la rébellion contre la force armée. Cette mesure causa une vive indignation à Metz.

Les autorités se résignèrent à mettre Samain en liberté. Bientôt Alexis Samain et « Lorraine sportive » étaient mêlés à un autre incident. La « Lorraine sportive » et son président sont mis en accusation. On leur reproche d'entretenir une agitation subversive. Alexis Samain est condamné à six semaines de prison.

Le 11 février 1911, Alexis Samain et son frère Paul se trouvaient de nouveau impliqués dans une grave affaire. Pris à partie par un sergent nommé Maasch, dans une rue de Metz, Paul Samain fut atteint par lui. Alexis Samain, voulant faire retenir d'un coup de poing Alors, l'un de ses amis, nommé Martin, fut tué par le sergent et lui.

Les deux frères Samain furent arrêtés. Enfin on reconnut qu'ils n'étaient pas pour rien dans la mort de Maasch. Le 22 mars suivant ils étaient acquittés.

Un aviateur allemand survole Lunéville et jette trois bombes

DÉGÂTS MATÉRIELS SEULEMENT

M. Malvy, ministre de l'intérieur, a reçu, dans la soirée, du préfet de Meurthe-et-Moselle, le télégramme suivant :

LUNÉVILLE, 3 août. — Un aéroplane allemand a survolé Lunéville, ce jour avant 18 heures, à une hauteur de 1.500 mètres environ. Il a laissé tomber sur la ville trois bombes qui ont fait une violente explosion, mais n'ont causé que des dégâts matériels.

L'une est tombée dans une rue centrale, endommageant la chaussée ; une autre est tombée à dix mètres de la sous-préfecture, éventrant le sol et l'autre sur le toit d'un vaste hangar et en brisant toutes les vitres.

La population, un instant un peu inquiète, a repris immédiatement son calme. (Havas.)

Dans les Balkans

Neutralité de la Bulgarie de la Roumanie et de la Grèce

SMYRNE, 3 août. — Dépêche particulière du « Matin ». — La Bulgarie est tombée d'accord avec la Roumanie pour observer la neutralité. Une déclaration en ce sens doit paraître demain.

× ×

ATHÈNES, 2 août. — Le conseil des ministres, sous la présidence du roi, a examiné minutieusement la situation créée par la guerre européenne. Il a décidé de persévérer dans l'attitude qu'il a observée jusqu'à présent. La Grèce ne serait pas entraînée dans un conflit.

Néanmoins, le conseil des ministres a décidé qu'au cas où quelque État balkanique voudrait profiter de la situation actuelle pour modifier le statu quo créé par le traité de Bucarest, la Grèce, d'accord avec les États intéressés au maintien de ce traité, s'y opposerait. (Havas.)

LA JOURNÉE DIPLOMATIQUE

Ultimatum de l'Allemagne à la Belgique

MOBILISATION DE L'ARMÉE ET DE LA FLOTTE ANGLAISES

Déclarations de sir Edward Grey garantissant au nom de l'Angleterre la protection des côtes françaises et la neutralité de la Belgique

D'après les nouvelles qui nous parviennent, l'Allemagne a 100.000 hommes dans le Luxembourg.

Ses armées n'ont pas encore envahi la Belgique.

Elle a commis quelques violations nouvelles de territoire en France.

Elle n'a pas encore engagé la bataille.

Résumons la journée d'hier.

Dans la nuit, l'Allemagne demande à la Belgique de lui faciliter le passage de l'armée allemande sur son territoire. La Belgique étant faible, l'Allemagne donne à sa prière, la forme de l'ultimatum. La Belgique le repousse.

A l'heure où l'on apprend l'ultimatum allemand, on apprend en même temps la mobilisation générale de l'armée et de la flotte anglaises.

<center>~~~~</center>

A 5 h. 45 du soir, M. de Schœn, ambassadeur d'Allemagne, porte à M. Viviani, président du conseil des ministres de France, la déclaration de guerre de l'Allemagne.

Sir Edward Grey, ministre des affaires étrangères d'Angleterre, a fait hier à la Chambre une déclaration dont on peut conclure avec certitude :

1° Que l'Angleterre ne laissera jamais violer, même provisoirement, la neutralité de la Belgique : « EN CAS DE LA NEUTRALITÉ VIOLÉE, L'ANGLETERRE REMPLIRAIT SES OBLIGATIONS. » (Edward Grey).

2° Que l'Angleterre est prête à la flotte. LA MOBILISATION DE L'ARMÉE CONTINUE. NOUS SOMMES PRÊPARÉS A ENVISAGER LES CONSÉQUENCES QUI SUIVRAIENT L'EMPLOI DE TOUTES NOS FORCES. NOUS FERONS FACE A CETTE SITUATION SI ELLE SE DÉVELOPPE, COMME IL SEMBLE PROBABLE.

3° Il résulte en outre des déclarations du ministre des affaires étrangères anglais, que la flotte anglaise garantira la France contre la flotte allemande.

La Chambre des communes a voté sans discussion le bill de M. Lloyd George, mettant un milliard et quart à la disposition du gouvernement. Ce bill a reçu hier soir la sanction royale.

LE DISCOURS de sir Edward Grey aux Communes

LONDRES, 3 août. — Dépêche particulière du « Matin ». — Depuis trois jours, l'intérêt se porte surtout ici sur les nouvelles de France, chaque attitude apportant une nouvelle sensation.

Aujourd'hui, une question extrêmement importante : l'attitude de l'Angleterre devant la crise — la séance de l'Assemblée était attendue anxieusement. La Chambre des communes était bondée. L'émotion générale était vive.

Après le vote d'un moratorium présenté par M. Lloyd George, chancelier de l'Échiquier, sir Edward Grey demande à la Chambre d'envisager la crise au triple point de vue des intérêts, des obligations et de l'honneur de la Grande-Bretagne. Il déclare qu'il est impossible de sauvegarder la paix de l'Europe en raison du manque de temps, et les dispositions montrées dans certains milieux — l'attitude de l'Allemagne — l'obligent à précipiter le résultat en déposant les efforts faits pour certaines grandes puissances en vue du maintien de la paix.

Au sujet des obligations de l'Angleterre, sir Edward Grey assure l'Assemblée que dans la crise actuelle le gouvernement n'avait jusqu'à hier promis à aucune puissance autre chose que son appui diplomatique.

La France est impliquée dans la guerre actuelle par son alliance définie avec la Russie, mais cette obligation ne s'applique pas à nous de la même façon, nous ne sommes pas parlementaires dans l'alliance franco-russe.

La flotte française est concentrée dans la Méditerranée, par suite de l'ami-

(Voir en deuxième page les autres tentatives allemandes.)

Le Petit Journal

ADMINISTRATION
61, RUE LAFAYETTE, 61

Les manuscrits ne sont pas rendus

On s'abonne sans frais
dans tous les bureaux de poste

5 CENT. SUPPLÉMENT ILLUSTRÉ 5 CENT.

26ᵐᵉ Année — Numéro 1.278

DIMANCHE 20 JUIN 1915

ABONNEMENTS

SIX MOIS UN AN
SEINE et SEINE-ET-OISE .. 2 fr. 3 fr. 50
DÉPARTEMENTS .... 2 fr. 4 fr. »
ÉTRANGER .... 2 50 5 fr. »

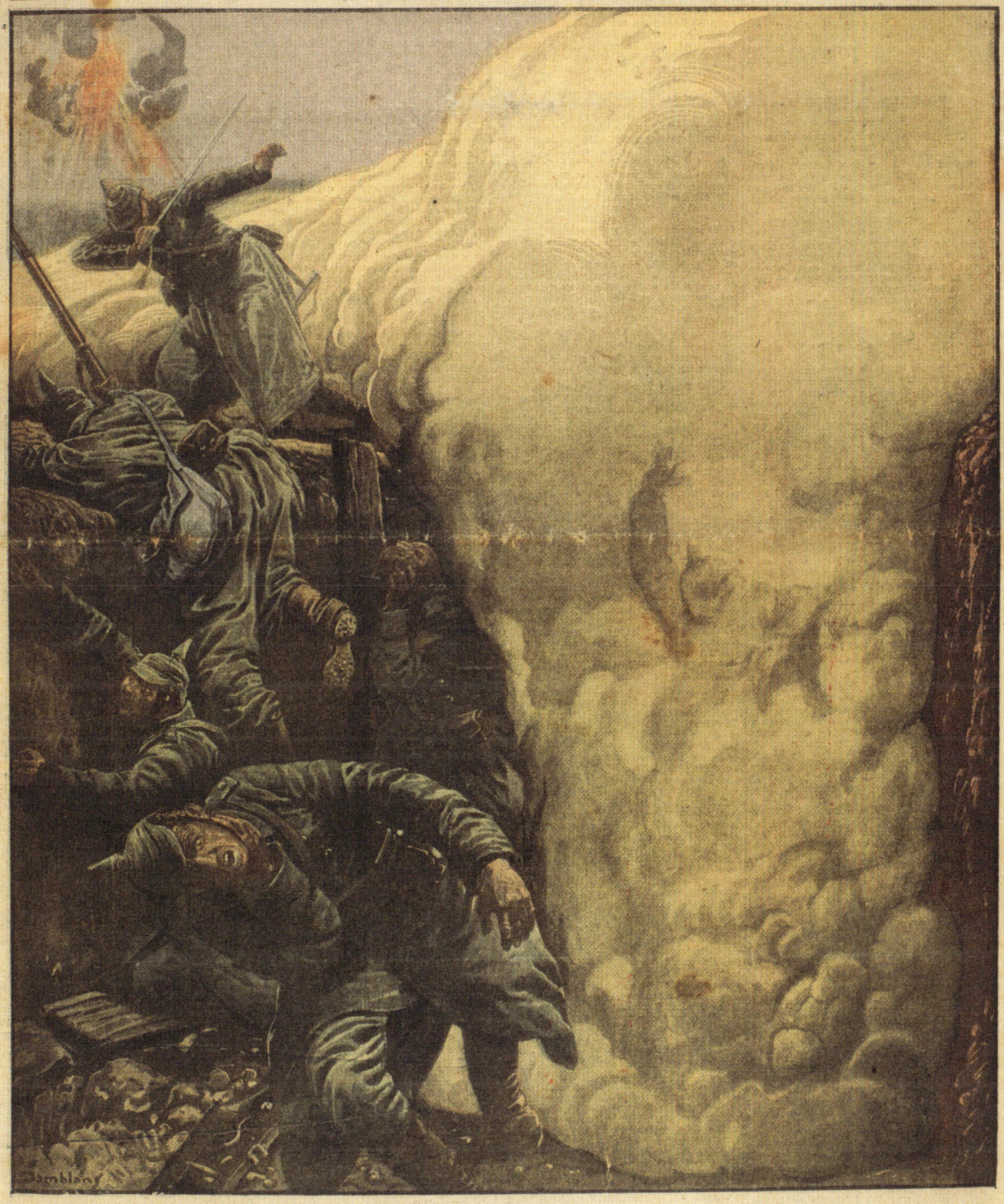

Victimes de leur propre barbarie

Soldats allemands asphyxiés par les gaz qu'ils avaient lancés contre les Russes
et qu'un coup de vent rejette sur leurs tranchées

L'Amérique en Guerre

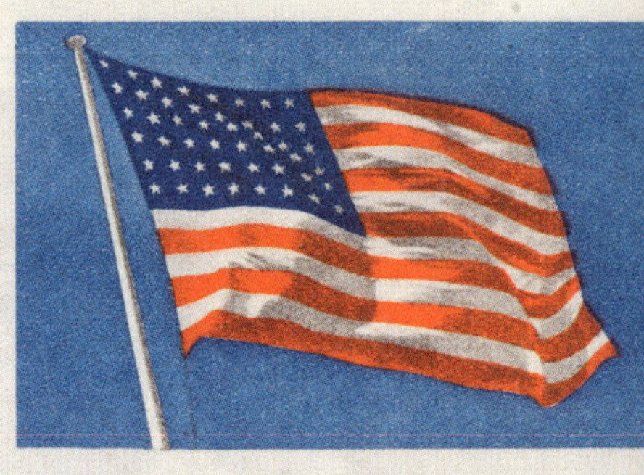

LES ALLIÉS SONT SUR LA TERRE D'EUROPE

Alger, 13 juillet.—Le samedi 10 juillet à 3 h. du matin, à la lumière d'un croissant de lune, des troupes américaines, britanniques et canadiennes débarquaient sur la terre d'Europe, en Sicile.

18 heures plus tard, dans la nuit de samedi à dimanche, le Q.G. du général Eisenhower pouvait annoncer officiellement: "Les opérations se poursuivent selon l'horaire prévu."

Et après quarante-huit heures, lundi à midi le communiqué allié annonçait la capture de Syracuse et de 9 autres villes de la côte sud-est, et de 2.000 prisonniers.

Mardi, Ragusa et Augusta tombèrent à leur tour.

Par l'importance des moyens employés, comme par la multiplicité des objectifs qui s'offrent aux Alliés, le débarquement en Sicile constitue dès maintenant, une des opérations combinées les plus grandes qui se soient jamais effectuées. L'importance des effectifs engagés ne peut naturellement pas être encore révélée. Mais le Q.G. allié a déjà annoncé qu'une flotte de 2.000 navires de tous types avaient à l'origine participé à l'affaire.

Le premier communiqué

C'est à six heures, samedi matin, que le Q.G. allié a donné au monde la première nouvelle du débarquement en Europe. Voici le texte de ce document:

"Des troupes alliées, sous le commandement du général Eisenhower ont entrepris des opérations de débarquement en Sicile de bonne heure ce matin. Les débarquements ont été précédés par une attaque aérienne alliée. Des forces navales alliées ont escorté les troupes de choc et ont bombardé les défenses côtières pendant l'attaque."

Samedi soir un second communiqué donnait les premières précisions. A 7 heures, soit quatre heures après le début du débarquement, les troupes étaient maîtresses de 160 kms. de plages. L'artillerie était débarquée et mise en position sous la protection du tir des grosses pièces navales des unités alliées—britanniques, américaines, indiennes, hollandaises, polonaises et grecques—qui participaient à l'opération.

Les troupes avancent

Dimanche, à midi, le communiqué allié commençait ainsi:

"Toutes les plages sont solidement occupées et les troupes avancent." Durant toute la journée les flottes alliées continuèrent de débarquer des troupes avec leurs voitures, leurs canons, leur essence, leur matériel et leur ravitaillement. La tâche principale de la flotte, qui est d'amener l'armée à terre, disait encore le communiqué, se poursuit sans relâche.

Il fallut attendre lundi pour obtenir quelques précisions sur la nature des opérations et l'importance des premiers succès. On savait déjà que les débarquements s'étaient opérés sur de nombreux points s'échelonnant

(Suite à la page 4)

Eisenhower s'adresse aux Français

De bonne heure samedi matin, le général Eisenhower, Commandant-en-Chef allié en Afrique du Nord, adressait au peuple français l'avertissement suivant:

"Les forces armées des Nations Unies ont aujourd'hui déclenché une offensive sur la Sicile. C'est la première étape de la libération du continent européen. Il y en aura d'autres. Je demande au peuple français de rester calme, de ne pas se laisser prendre aux fausses rumeurs que l'ennemi pourrait faire circuler. La radio alliée vous tiendra au courant des événements militaires.

"Je compte sur votre sang-froid et sur votre sens de la discipline. Ne commettez pas d'imprudence, car l'ennemi vous guette. Restez à l'écoute de la radio alliée et ne suivez jamais les rumeurs. Contrôlez soigneusement les informations qui vous parviennent.

"Vous nous aiderez matériellement en restant calmes et en évitant de vous exposer aux représailles par des actions prématurées. Lorsque l'heure d'agir arrivera, nous vous le dirons. Jusque-là, aidez-nous en observant nos recommandations, c'est-à-dire restez calmes, réservez vos forces. Nous répétons: lorsque l'heure d'agir arrivera nous vous le dirons."

LE PRESIDENT ROOSEVELT
et le Quatorze Juillet :

LE QUATORZE JUILLET EST, POUR TOUS LES PEUPLES DU MONDE épris de liberté, une fête. Nous la fêtons cette année-ci, en Amérique avec une ferveur particulière. La France—notre alliée et notre amie—est maintenant à nouveau entière dans la guerre. La France immortelle affirme une fois de plus, dans les circonstances les plus héroïques, sa grandeur et sa gloire.

"En ce jour anniversaire de la conquête par les Français de leurs libertés je veux rappeler encore une fois que c'est à l'époque de la révolution américaine et de la révolution française que furent établis les principes fondamentaux qui régissent nos démocraties. La base de notre édifice démocratique est le principe qui place la source de l'autorité gouvernementale dans le peuple et dans le peuple seul.

"Les Français ne peuvent avoir qu'un point de ralliement—la France elle-même. Son rayonnement surpasse tous les partis, toutes les personnalités et tous les groupes qui ne peuvent vivre que dans la gloire de la nation française.

"Un de nos buts de guerre, exprimés dans la Charte de l'Atlantique, est de rendre à nouveau maîtresses de leur destinée les populations aujourd'hui sous le joug de l'envahisseur. Il ne doit subsister aucun doute, nulle part, quant à l'inébranlable décision des Nations Unies, résolues à rendre aux peuples opprimés l'exercice de leurs droits sacrés. La souveraineté française réside dans le peuple de France. Aujourd'hui ce peuple est bâillonné par une oppression barbare. Dans la liberté de demain, quand les Français et leurs frères d'armes des Nations Unies auront chassé l'ennemi du sol français, le peuple français regagnera ses libertés en érigeant un gouvernement de son propre choix.

"Vive la Liberté, l'Egalité et la Fraternité! Vive toujours la France!"

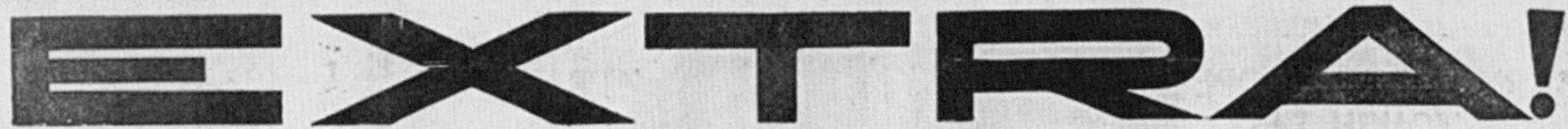

ALL THE NEWS ALL THE TIME
Largest Home Delivered Circulation
Largest Advertising Volume

Los Angeles Times

EQUAL RIGHTS
LIBERTY UNDER THE LAW   TRUE INDUSTRIAL FREEDOM

IN TWO PARTS

PART I — GENERAL NEWS

Times Office: 202 West First Street
Los Angeles 53, Cal.
Times Telephone Number MAdison 2345

VOL. LXIV   ★★★   WEDNESDAY MORNING, AUGUST 15, 1945   DAILY, FIVE CENTS

PEACE!

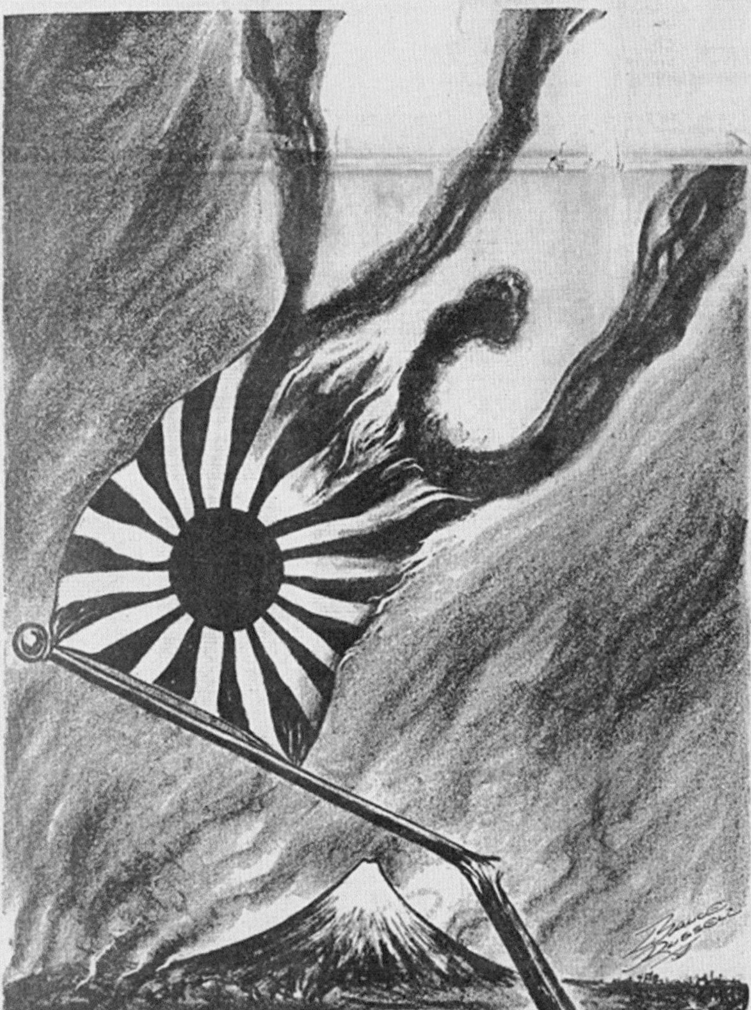

Japs Accept Allies' Terms Unreservedly

WASHINGTON, Aug. 14. (U.P.)—President Truman announced tonight that the Japanese government has accepted the surrender terms without qualifications.

He made the announcement at a press conference. He read a statement which said:

"I deem this reply a full acceptance of the Potsdam declaration which specified the unconditional surrender of Japan. In the reply there are no qualifications."

The President also revealed that he had named Gen. Douglas MacArthur the supreme commander to receive the Japanese surrender.

Meanwhile, he said, Allied armed forces have been ordered to suspend offensive operations.

VJ-Day will not be proclaimed until after the formal signing of the surrender terms by Japan.

The three Allies in the Pacific war—Great Britain, Russia and China—will be represented at the signing by high ranking officers.

The Japanese government's message accepting the Allied terms said that Emperor Hirohito is prepared "to authorize and insure the signature" by the Japanese government and the imperial general headquarters of the necessary terms for carrying out provisions of the Potsdam declaration.

Hirohito Will Obey Allies

"His Majesty is also prepared to issue his commands to all the military, naval and air authorities of Japan and all the forces under their control wherever located to cease active operations, to surrender arms and to issue such other or-

Air Onslaughts Continue Around Clock on Japan

GUAM, Aug. 15. (AP)—Allied aerial onslaughts on Japan continued in nonstop around the clock fury today with bombing, strafing and rocketing planes accentuating Allied demands for acceptance of surrender terms laid down for Nippon.

More than 800 Marianas-based superfortresses have dropped 6000 tons of demolition and fire bombs into the home islands in the past 24 hours.

The B-29 raids were under way even as Tokyo radio yesterday said an answer to the Allied note of Saturday was en route, and the raids continued into the early hours today. Two hundred two-based fighters gave escort.

Gen. Douglas MacArthur's communique from Manila today reported the strongest Japanese interception attempt over Korea seen in weeks by Pacific Air Forces pilots.

The communique said 16 were downed and two probably by more than 40 Thunderbolts on the Korean mission Monday. The interception was over Meijo on the west central coast, where an important airdrome is located. One Thunderbolt was lost.

Headquarters of the Army Strategic Air Forces indicated

Turn to Page 2, Column 7

President Declares Two-Day Holiday--Wednesday and Thursday

WASHINGTON, Aug. 14. (AP)—President Truman tonight declared a two-day holiday, tomorrow and Thursday, for all Federal employees in Washington and throughout the country.

He told a press conference that the reason for two days was the employees had not had a chance to celebrate the last surrender on VE-Day.

ders as may be required by the supreme commander of the Allied forces of the execution of the above-mentioned terms."

The President did not say where the surrender terms will be signed but it has been reported ceremonies will take place aboard a battleship or at Okinawa.

Truman did say that arrangements are now being made for the formal signing at the "earliest possible moment."

The President, attired in a blue double-breasted suit, blue

Turn to Page 2, Column 3

LA VANGUARDIA

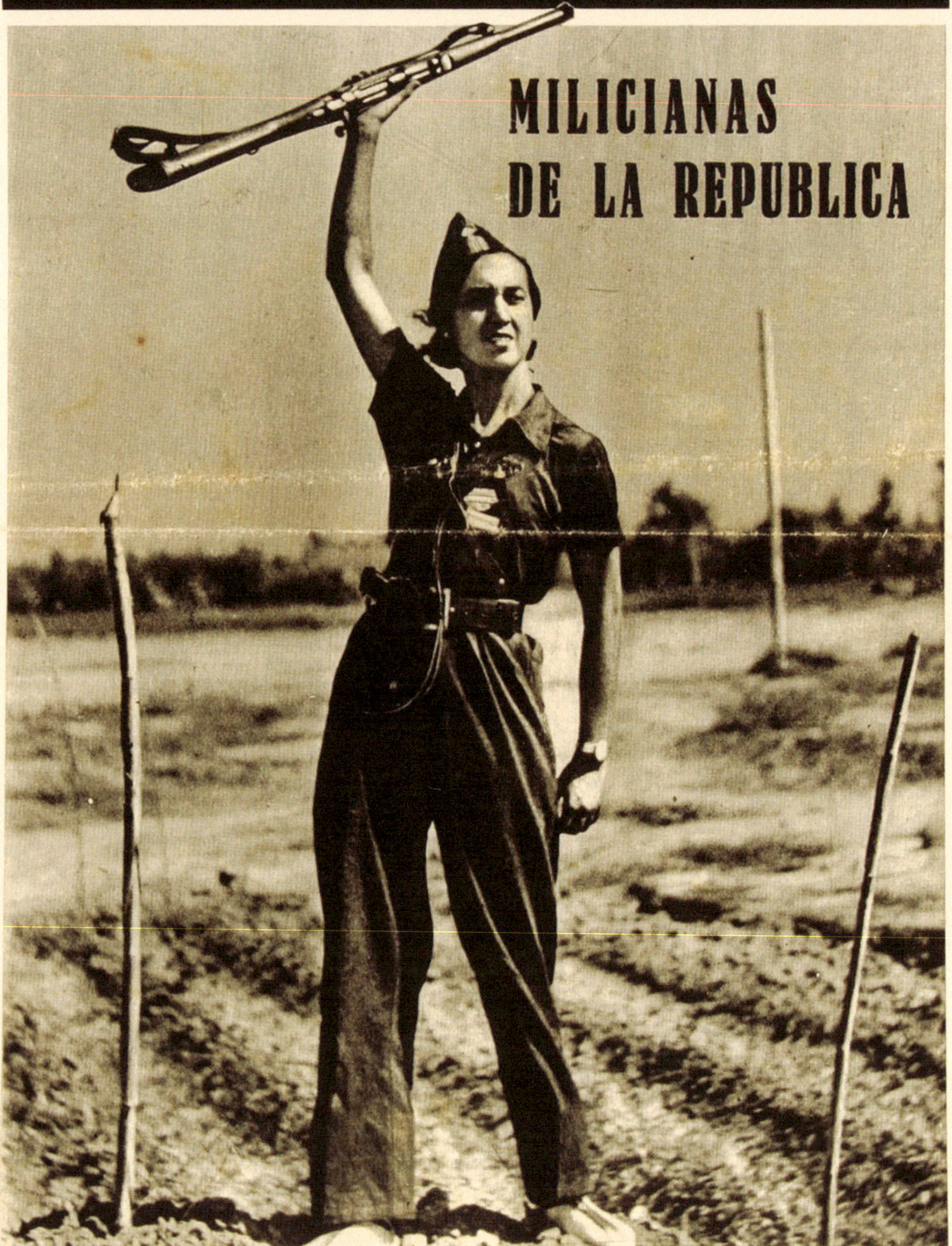

Pilar Pérez Llopis, sargento del Batallón «Pablo Iglesias», de Valencia

(Véase en nuestras páginas tipográficas la crónica de nuestro enviado especial, Roldán-May.)

NEW YORK

Herald Tribune

CITY EDITION

Vol. CV No. 36,059

Copyright, 1945, New York Tribune Inc.

TUESDAY, AUGUST 7, 1945

THREE CENTS
In New York City

First Atomic Bomb Smashes Japanese City;
New Weapon Equals 20,000 Tons of TNT;
Truman Tells Foe to Quit; Shorter War Seen

Target Area Obscured by Smoke Cloud

Results at Hiroshima, Japanese Army City, Are Not Yet Appraised

He Reports Attack, Silent on Damage

Special Crews Are To Be Trained for Atomic Bomb Runs on Japan

By The Associated Press

WASHINGTON, Aug. 6.—Hiroshima, first enemy city to feel the American atomic bomb, was a major military target. Whether it hit anything important now cannot be determined until the smoke and dust clear.

The text of a War Department memorandum:

"In response to questions as to the damage accomplished by the atomic bomb dropped on Hiroshima, the War Department announced that it was as yet impossible to make an accurate report.

"Reconnaissance planes state that an impenetrable cloud of dust and smoke covered the target area. As soon as accurate details of results become available, they will be released by the Secretary of War."

Was Major Army City

The War Department describes Hiroshima as "an army city."

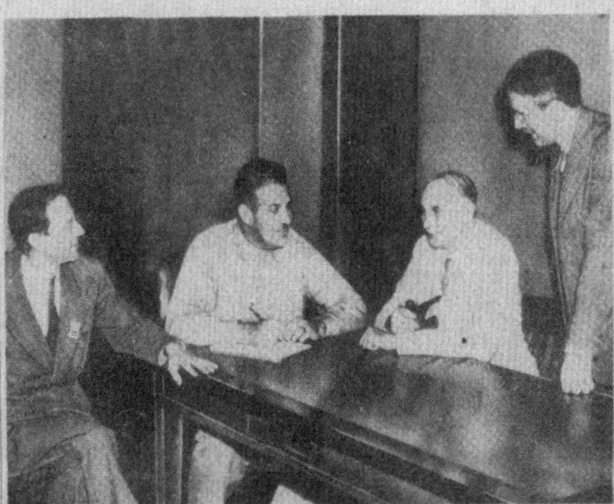

A conference at Oak Ridge, Tenn., of four scientists who helped develop the atomic bomb. Left to right, Sir James Chadwick, England; Major General Leslie R. Groves, in charge of the project; Dr. Richard C. Tolman, of Office of Scientific Research and Development, Washington, and Dr. H. D. Smyth, of Princeton, N. J., who served as a consultant on the project

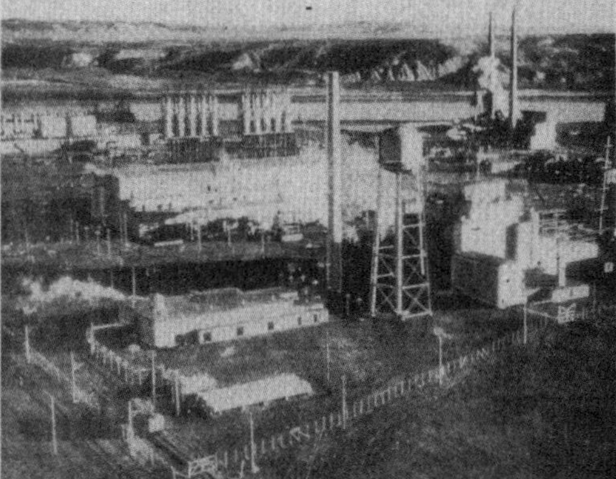

A view of one of the production areas for the atomic bomb at the Hanford Engineering Works at Richland, Wash., near the town of Pasco. The other production plant was at Oak Ridge, Tenn., near Knoxville, while a testing laboratory was located at the Alamogordo, N. M., Army air base, where the first tests of the devastating new bomb were made by scientists   Associated Press wirephoto

Kyushu City Hit In Biggest Raid Of Fire Bombs

100 Fighters and Bombers Blast Tarumi Two Hours; Smoke Rises 12,000 Feet

By The Associated Press

MANILA, Aug. 7 (Tuesday).— More than 400 fighters and bombers subjected the southern Japanese port of Tarumi on Sunday to the greatest fire raid yet staged by the Far East Air Force, leaving Tarumi engulfed in flames and wrapped in smoke billowing 12,000 feet high.

A communique issued by General Douglas MacArthur today announced that bombers and fighters of all categories, operating from Okinawa, poured jellied gasoline bombs, rockets and bullets for two hours into munition dumps and storage centers for aircraft parts clustered in the Kyushu Island city.

Mitchells and Invader attack bombers thundered in at low level with fire bombs, while Liberators, Thunderbolts and Mustangs supported with precision bomb strikes at wharves on Kagoshima Bay. Returning pilots said the entire *(Continued on page 2, column 6)*

Tokyo Tells of Raid

SAN FRANCISCO, Aug. 6 (P).— Tokyo radio announced the bombing of Hiroshima, target of the American atomic bombing announced by President Truman, raided at 8:20 a. m. Monday (7:20 p. m. Sunday, United States Eastern war time).

The President said that the new and powerful bomb was dropped at that time but the Tokyo broadcast, recorded by the Federal Communications Commission, made no mention of any unusual destruction.

It reported only that "a small number" of American B-29s attacked Hiroshima, a city on southern Honshu, with incendiary and explosive bombs.

Train Special Crews

PEARL HARBOR, Aug. 6 (UP).— Specially trained air crews will fly the new atomic bombs to Japan, it was understood today. There was no information available on the types of planes which would be used. It was said, however, that the terrifying blast which is expected to engulf even the plane dropping them was one of the problems solved before the bomb could be used.

Informed sources here said full *(Continued on page 14, column 6)*

Jobs for Men

There are many other excellent opportunities listed in today's Classified Section.

Truman's Statement Reveals Terrible Warning to Japan

Disclosure of Atomic Bomb Underscores Potsdam Warning That Prompt and Utter Destruction Is Tokyo's Alternative to Surrender

By The Associated Press

WASHINGTON, Aug. 6.—Following is the complete text of the statement by President Truman announcing the use of an atomic bomb for the first time in history:

Sixteen hours ago an American airplane dropped one bomb on Hiroshima, an important Japanese Army base. That bomb had more power than 20,000 tons of TNT. It had more than 2,000 times the blast power of the British "Grand Slam," which is the largest bomb ever yet used in the history of warfare.

The Japanese began the war from the air at Pearl Harbor. They have been repaid many fold. And the end is not yet. With this bomb we have now added a new an revolutionary increase in destruction to supplement the growing power of our armed forces. In their present form these bombs are now in production and even more powerful forms are in development.

It is an atomic bomb. It is a harnessing of the basic power of *(Continued on page 8, column 2)*

Truman Visits Ship's Messes To Tell of Bomb

Personally Informs Entire Crew of Augusta at Sea, Doesn't Hide Jubilation

By The United Press

ABOARD U. S. S. AUGUSTA, Aug. 6.—President Truman personally told the entire crew of this cruiser today about the success of the atomic bomb used against Japan, and he happily agreed with the sailors that it would shorten the war.

"Send some more of 'em over Japan and we'll all go home," was the universal reaction.

The President was lunching with the crew. He rose from the chow table and told the sailors about it, then he walked to the second enlisted mess and announced it again. Next, he walked *(Continued on page 8, column 4)*

Cavern Below Columbia Was Bomb's Cradle

Atom Was Split There in January, 1939, and Race With Germans Was On

By Robert S. Bird

The atomic bomb that has opened for mankind a fateful door to a new era was born under the campus of Columbia University, in the rock-hewn vaults beneath the Physics Building in a corner of The Green, facing 120th Street, near Broadway.

There, in January, 1939, Dr. John R. Dunning, assistant professor in the physics department, and Dr. Enrico Fermi, Noble prize winner of Italy, who had recently joined the Columbia staff, successfully performed an experiment—perhaps the most momentous in all history.

In their deep cavern laboratory they split the uranium atom and unlocked the basic energy of the universe. Unbeknown to them, this experiment had been performed in Berlin two weeks before, but the Dunning discovery paved the way for the development in this country of the complex processes that resulted in the bomb that was dropped on Japan yesterday.

Within a year and a half the tremendous significance of their experiment had engaged the attention *(Continued on page 4, column 1)*

A Description of the First Blast In New Mexico Desert July 16

Scientists in an Ominous Rainstorm Unloose a Flash Brighter Than Brightest Sunlight, Then a Tremendous Roar; Steel Tower Is Vaporized

From the Herald Tribune Bureau

WASHINGTON, Aug. 6.—The War Department's official description of the first test, conducted in New Mexico, of the history-making—and history-changing—atomic bomb follows in full:

"Mankind's successful transition to a new age, the atomic age, was ushered in July 16, 1945, before the eyes of a tense group of renowned scientists and military men gathered in the desert lands of New Mexico to witness the first results of their $2,000,000,000 effort. Here in a remote section of the Alamogordo Air Base, 120 miles southeast of Albuquerque, the first man-made atomic explosion, the outstanding achievement of nuclear science, was achieved at 5:30 a. m. of that day. Darkening heavens pouring forth rain and lightning immediately up the zero hour heightened the drama.

"Mounted on a steel tower, a revolutionary weapon destined to change war as we know it, or which may even be the instrumentality to end all major wars, was set off with an impact which signalized man's entrance into a new physical world. Success was greater than the most ambitious estimates. A small amount of matter, the product of a chain of huge specially constructed industrial plants, was made to release the energy of the universe locked up within the atom from the beginning time. A fabulous achievement had been reached. Speculative theory, barely established in pre-war laboratories, had been projected into practicality.

"This phase of the atomic-bomb project, which is headed by Major General Leslie R. Groves, *(Continued on page 14, column 2)*

Atomic Bomb's Warhead Is Put At 25 Pounds

A New Chemical Element, Pluto, May Be a Part of Uranium-Energy Missile

By John J. O'Neill

A new chemical element, Pluto, was created by science to produce a super atomic energy source. The new element never existed in nature. It was created entirely by artificial processes and was found to have explosive properties even greater than those of Uranium 235 which was the original source through which tremendous amounts of atomic energy were released from matter—3,000,000 times as much as is released from equal weights of T. N. T. That is the nature of the energy unleashed against Japan.

Pluto is the heaviest element in existence. It has an atomic weight of 239, one unit heavier than Uranium 238 which is the heaviest natural element. It is created by shooting a neutron, a subatomic particle of matter, into Uranium 238.

Pluto and uranium provide a *(Continued on page 30, column 6)*

Senator Hiram W. Johnson Dies; Foe of League and Charter, 78

California Republican and Isolationist Was Last of Irreconcilables of 1919

By The Associated Press

WASHINGTON, Aug. 6.—Senator Hiram W. Johnson, seventy-eight, died of thrombosis of a cerebral artery at 6:40 a. m. today in Bethesda Naval Hospital.

The Republican Senator from California, a national political figure since early in the century, had been under treatment there for two and a half weeks. He was in a coma when he died.

One of his last official acts was to cast the one vote in the Senate Foreign Relations Committee against ratification of the United Nations charter for a world organization of nations.

Even after the onset of his fatal illness his vote was recorded against final ratification through a pair with two charter supporters *(Continued on page 18, column 3)*

Senator Hiram W. Johnson   Harris & Ewing

Basic Force Of Universe Is Unleashed

Truman Tells How Allied Science Yoked Atom at $2,000,000,000 Cost

125,000 Helped U. S. On War's Top Secret

New Power Age Forecast, World Prosperity Aided, After Japan Is Crushed

Secretary Stimson's history of the bomb—Page 12

By Jack Tait

WASHINGTON, Aug. 6.—The mightiest explosive force ever devised by man—an atomic energy bomb possessed of the terrific power of more than 20,000 tons of T. N. T.—has hit Japan, President Truman announced today in a statement released by the White House.

Sixteen hours before the statement was issued the bomb was sent plunging down on Hiroshima, an important Japanese army base. Today Washington military authorities were convinced that this historic development of American and British scientists will shorten the war and that it marks the beginning of "the atomic age," the future benefits of which to civilization can only be guessed at present.

Even more powerful forms of the bomb are being developed, President Truman said. "It (the bomb) is a harnessing of the basic power of the universe," he said. "The force from which the sun draws its power has been loosed against those who brought war to the Far East."

War Seen Shortened

Henry L. Stimson, Secretary of War, in another statement, asserted that this greatest secret weapon in history will prove a "tremendous aid" in shortening the war against Japan.

Both he and President Truman told how civilization will be enriched after the war through the harnessing of atomic energy to supplement coal, oil and water as basic sources of power in industry. Secretary Stimson said: "We are at the threshold of a new industrial art which will take many years and much expenditure of money to develop."

The War Department, in a series of releases today, told how $2,000,000,000 was expended on the project to develop the bomb, known by the Army code name of "Manhattan Engineer District." It told of the tireless efforts to top American and British scientists who outraced German scientists in developing the bomb; of two cities erected by the government at production sites, of 125,000 workers who took part in the vast project.

Test Explosion Described

The first test of the first man-made atomic explosion took place at 5:20 a. m. July 16 in a pouring rain near Alamogordo air base of Albuquerque, N. M. Plate glass windows were shattered 100 miles away. The blast shook the entire southern portion of New Mexico, western Arizona, and the El Paso district of west Texas.

This is an official description of the explosion "at the appointed time, there was a blinding flash lighting up the whole area brighter than the brightest daylight. A mountain range three miles from the observation point stood out in bold relief. Then came a tremendous sustained roar and a heavy pressure wave which knocked down two men outside the control center five and a half miles away from the explosion. Immediately thereafter, a huge multi-colored surging cloud boiled to an altitude *(Continued on page 14, column 2)*

Major Bong Killed as Jet Plane Explodes on Test Flight in West

By The Associated Press

BURBANK, Calif., Aug. 6.— Major Richard Ira Bong, America's leading fighter pilot in the South Pacific area before he was returned to the United States and assigned to test flying duty, was killed today in the crash of a jet-propelled P-80 plane.

Major Bong, who had forty Japanese planes to his credit, was killed at 2:30 p. m., the Army's Western Procurement Office announced, about four minutes after he left the Lockheed air terminal.

Witnesses said the plane exploded with a terrific roar and disintegrated—parts were hurled in small bits over a wide area at a spot within a few miles of the airport.

"A piece fell from the plane," said Mrs. J. B. Villarino, who was attracted to the plane because it seemed to be flying so low. "It might have been the engine wing. The the plane started straight down and crashed with a tremendous burst of smoke. Huge flames swelled up, plainly visible from my house, although it is about two miles from the scene of the crash."

After returning from overseas service, the former Poplar, Wis., *(Continued on page 28, column 6)*

The Washington Post

98th Year ·· No. 146 ··   ©1975, The Washington Post Co.   WEDNESDAY, APRIL 30, 1975   Phone (202) 223-6000   Classified 223-6300.   20c Beyond Washington   15c
                                                                                                        Circulation 223-6100   Maryland and Virginia

Saigon Surrenders to Vietcong; Withdrawal Ends Role of U.S.

By Haynes Johnson
Washington Post Staff Writer

The American evacuation from Vietnam, which took place amid scenes of chaos, panic and suffering, is over.

It came only hours before the government in Saigon that it had long supported finally fell, surrendering unconditionally to North Vietnam, which had fought for this ultimate triumph for 30 years.

The final act of American involvement that had lasted for a generation, took the lives of 56,737 military personnel, cost more than $160 billion and affected virtually every aspect of national life occurred in the early morning hours of Wednesday.

As the last helicopters were taking to the air with U.S. Ambassador Graham Martin and other survivors of the once overpowering American presence, President Ford issued a statement. He said the evacuation "closes a chapter in the American experience" and called upon the nation "to close ranks, to avoid recrimination about the past."

In the final, desperate 24 hours about 6,500 persons were evacuated by American helicopters protected by Navy F-4 Phantom jets to carriers waiting in the South China Sea. Of those, about 1,000 were Americans, the rest South Vietnamese, Secretary of State Kissinger said.

The end to America's bitter Vietnam experience came suddenly. Shortly after 6 o'clock Monday night, Washington time, a general brought a whispered message to Mr. Ford, who was presiding over a meeting of his energy advisers. Panic was growing, evacuation was becoming more difficult hourly, and two U.S. Marines had been killed in a rocket attack at Saigon's Tansonnhut airport.

Within hours the President had ordered the evacuation of the remaining Americans.

The final departure triggered panic among Vietnamese soldiers and civilians. At the U.S. embassy Marines and American civilians used pistol and rifle butts to smash the fingers of Vietnamese trying to claw their way over a 10-foot wall.

Others fended for themselves as best they could. What appears to be about one-third of the South Vietnamese air force, one of the largest in the world, left for the security of an American base in Thailand.

As the evacuation proceeded, in darkness and poor weather, one figure starkly evoked memories of the most divisive, longest war in American history. In the last few days about 55,000 South Vietnamese have been evacuated from their homeland—almost exactly the number of Americans who died there on their behalf.

These refugees are now strung out across the Pacific, from the Philippines to Guam to Wake Island where American soldiers fought and died in World War II, and on into California. They are huddled together in hastily constructed tent cities awaiting a new life in the United States.

In Washington, where the end was played out on a chill, rainy April day, Defense Secretary James R. Schlesinger told America's armed forces that their sacrifices in Vietnam had not been in vain. "In combat you were victorious and you left the field with honor," he said.

Hanoi 'Changed Signals'

Kissinger Says North Sought Armed Victory

By Murrey Marder
Washington Post Staff Writer

Secretary of State Henry A. Kissinger said yesterday that North Vietnam kept escalating its demands for a political settlement in Saigon and on Sunday night "changed signals" to "a military option."

Kissinger said that "the impatience of the North Vietnamese to seize power" brought demands that were "escalating literally with every passing day."

By tightening military pressure on American access routes, Kissinger somberly told a televised news conference, the Communists shifted from a political to a military course, ending the bargaining so far as the United States was concerned.

That process appeared to be completed last night for the South Vietnamese as well, with Gen. Duong Van (Big) Minh's announcement of unconditional surrender.

Before that announcement came, all that the United States could claim was that it had gained a week's time to evacuate remaining Americans and some 55,000 South Vietnamese, with, possibly, as Kissinger put it, some contribution to "a sort of negotiation" in South Vietnam once the Americans were all out.

It is "too early to judge" Kissinger said, "whether it is possible to avoid a battle for Saigon," which he said "is basically unnecessary" because the South Vietnamese government is prepared "to correspond to the demands of the Communist side."

Kissinger sought to soften, as much as he could the final frustration of the United States for its hope of achieving even a token of political satisfaction for all the American anguish in Vietnam. American diplomacy, he said, may have contributed to "a political evolution" in Saigon that may "preserve a vestige of other forces than the Communist forces." But he acknowledged that "it is clear that what is being aimed at is a

See DIPLOMACY, A16, Col. 8

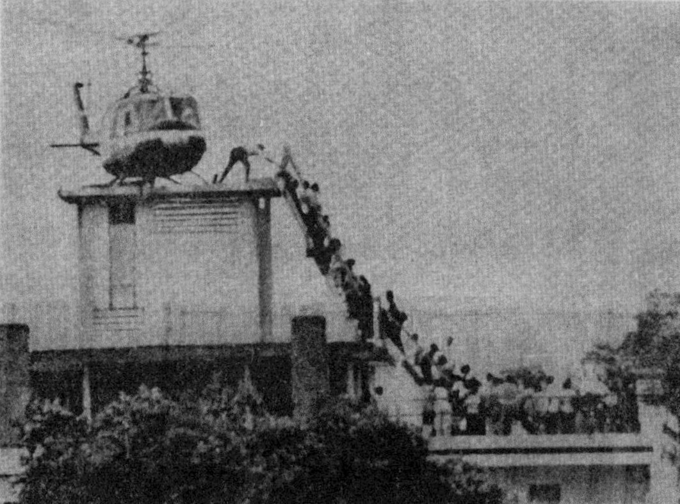

A crewman for an Air America helicopter helps evacuees up a ladder on top of a building in Saigon as craft waits.
—United Press International

Deciding on the Final Withdrawal

By Lou Cannon and Michael Getler
Washington Post Staff Writers

The end began with a brief, whispered conversation.

Shortly after 6 p.m. Monday, Lt. Gen. Brent A. Scowcroft slipped into the Cabinet room of the White House where President Ford was presiding over a meeting of his energy advisers. Scowcroft, the President's deputy national security adviser, handed Mr. Ford a note and then conferred with him in whispers about the death of two U.S. Marines in a Communist rocket barrage at Saigon's Tansonnhut airport.

Panic was growing, Mr. Ford was told. Evacuation was becoming more difficult hourly.

Without interrupting the meeting the President whispered instructions to Scowcroft, who left the room. He returned a few moments later for another whispered conversation. The President's action at that moment set in motion an emergency National Security Council meeting and triggered a chain of events that was to lead to the final American withdrawal from Vietnam.

Mr. Ford had been aware for the past several days that there was impatience, both at the Pentagon and in Congress, with what seemed to be the slowness of the U.S. evacuation. Now, as an aide recounted it later, he realized that time was running out.

This was the sequence of events in the next 12 hours as 14 years of American involvement in the Vietnam war reached its conclusion:

7:12 p.m.—President Ford ended the energy meeting without making any decision on whether the administration would seek to reimpose oil import tariffs. He left the Cabinet room and walked across the hall into the Roosevelt Room where his National Security Council already was gathering.

National security adviser Henry A. Kissing-

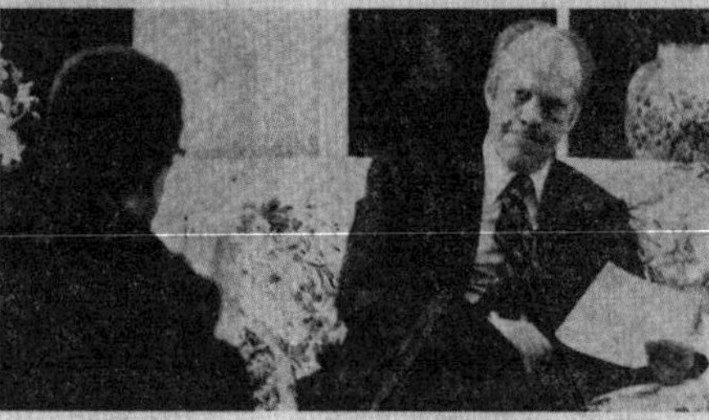

White House Photo via United Press International
President Ford and Secretary Kissinger discussing evacuation at meeting Monday night.

er was there along with Scowcroft. So were Defense Secretary James R. Schlesinger, Central Intelligence Director William E. Colby and Gen. George S. Brown, chairman of the Joint Chiefs of Staff.

7:23 p.m.—The NSC meeting began. The only topic of discussion was whether it was

See DECISION, A29, Col. 1

"This action closes a chapter in the American experience. I ask all Americans to close ranks, to avoid recrimination about the past, to look ahead to the many goals we share and to work together on the great tasks that remain to be accomplished."   —President Ford.

Minh Orders All Forces to End Fighting

Panic in City   VC Take Over

By John Saar
Washington Post Staff Writer

Leaving scenes of chaos and mass panic behind them, Americans fled the embattled and collapsing city of Saigon Tuesday in an armada of helicopters guarded by U.S. Marines, fighter-bombers and gunships.

The American exodus from South Vietnam to ships of the waiting U.S. 7th Fleet was accompanied by danger, difficulty and delay as Communist forces and bitter South Vietnamese soldiers turned their weapons on helicopters swooping in to extricate Americans from the roof of the American embassy and 12 other landing zones.

Two U.S. Marines died in a predawn bombardment of Tansonnhut airport and two pilots were missing and presumed dead after their helicopter plunged into the South China Sea.

In Washington, President Ford said panicky South Vietnamese had threatened to clog Tansonnhut's runways and delay the evacuation a full day. That persuaded the U.S. government to use helicopters rather than planes, he said.

The carefully planned evacuation—code-named Operation Talon Vise and using a force of 800 Marines and 81 giant helicopters —began at 11 a.m. (11 p.m. Monday EDT) and became progressively slower and more hazardous as the day wore on.

When the 19-hour airlift ended early Wednesday, 6,400 Americans and South Vietnamese had been evacuated to a task force of more than 40 ships reported cruising 25 miles off-shore.

See EVACUATION, A12, Col. 1

From News Dispatches

SAIGON, April 30 (Wednesday) — South Vietnam's President Duong Van (Big) Minh announced an unconditional surrender to the Vietcong Wednesday, after his second attempt in two days to achieve a cease-fire was rebuffed.

Shortly after noon Saigon time (12:10 a.m. Wednesday EDT) about 20 tanks carrying green-clad Vietcong troops entered the presidential palace grounds. Moments later an explosion rocked the palace area. President Minh reportedly had left the palace in the company of North Vietnamese troops.

Saigon radio went off the air and the Vietcong flag was raised over the palace.

In the city's streets, some people watched and others cheered as grinning Vietcong and North Vietnamese soldiers arrived in trucks and jeeps.

A jeep flying the Vietcong flag drove along a street about a block from the abandoned U.S. embassy. The eight cheering men in the vehicle were in civilian clothes but carried an assortment of rifles.

One of the men was sitting on the fender holding the flag. He beckoned to an American newsman and said in English, "Go home, go home."

At the Defense Ministry building, about a dozen North Vietnamese soldiers talked with a South Vietnamese army colonel and several junior officers. There was no apparent resistance to the Communist forces as most of the city's defense force simply lay down their arms and melted into the general population.

The full text of Minh's

See VIETNAM, A6, Col. 1

On Capitol Hill, the Reaction Is Muted

By George Lardner Jr.
Washington Post Staff Writer

The end was barely discernible on Capitol Hill. The Senate was preoccupied with speeches about inflation and recession. The House indulged in a brief spate of preliminary sparring over control of the Navy's petroleum reserves and then closed its doors for the day.

For America, the war in Vietnam was over. In Congress, it was accepted quietly, numbly, as an American tragedy that would best be forgotten but for the lessons to be learned. But if there were lessons to be learned, they had been enunciated, on all sides, long ago.

"I don't think the country's ever been torn apart so much since the war between the states," Rep. F. Edward Hebert (D-La.), until recently chairman of the House Armed Services Committee, reflected in the House lobby. "Let's forget it, but don't forget to learn."

Hebert paused, then smiled over the impracticality of his own injunction. "The tragedy," he said, "is that we never learn from history. We never learn."

The muted reaction was reflected in the Senate as well. There was a sense of relief, but it came in soft voices, in remarks coaxed by the press. There were no grand speeches, no cries of consolation and no shouts of recrimination.

The only way to redeem anything from the whole nightmare is not to repeat it," said Sen. George McGovern (D-S.D.) "That's the only consolation I can draw from it."

It was, like Hebert's, an uncertain consolation at best. Nearly three years ago, in the midst of his futile campaign for the White House, McGovern had matter-of-factly predicted that if he became President, the Thieu regime would fall and North and South Vietnam would eventually reunite as one nation.

McGovern got little thanks for the prophecy then. He gets little thanks now. Most of his Vietnam mail in recent days has been from critics, people who blame the unhappy end of the war on the opposition to it, who tell McGovern, "You must be happy now, you must be celebrating."

"I'm not doing any dancing or celebrating," McGovern said fervently. He said he thought most people would be "content to drop the issue now." But

See MOOD, A16, Col. 1

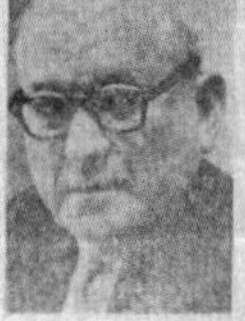

Rep. Hebert

"The tragedy is that we never learn from history. We never learn."

U.S. Embassy Plundered

By James Fenton
Special to The Washington Post

SAIGON, April 30 (Wednesday)—The American evacuation of Saigon ended Wednesday shortly after first light.

The crowd of South Vietnamese which had besieged the embassy all night then entered and looted the whole place while American Marines sent in to provide security were still on the roof.

At 6 Wednesday morning a group of Koreans who had been trying to leave the city said that the Americans had called for the evacuations after making sure that there were no Americans left outside the gate.

I went up to the roof of the Hotel Caravelle and watched the dawn breaking over the city. The large Caravelle helicopters were still arriving and figures—presuma-

bly the last of the Marines could be seen boarding them on the embassy roof.

But on the nearby Alliance Francaise building another group of people was waiting hopelessly for the choppers to arrive. Yesterday Air America had been evacuating people from that point.

There was no visible sign of fighting at any point. Looting was still going on in the Brinks Building, a former U.S. officers' billet a block from the Caravelle. A lone mattress could be seen falling from the third floor into the street below.

Just after 7, I walked up to the U.S. embassy, and witnessed a scene of extraordinary pillage. Office equipment was lying all around the street, and the crowd was milling around picking up whatever it could.

See SAIGON, A8, Col. 1

LE COURRIER

L'ESSENTIEL, AUTREMENT.

ABONNEMENTS (022) 809 55 55 fax (022) 809 55 67 • RÉDACTIONS GENÈVE (022) 809 55 66 VAUD (021) 683 08 85 VALAIS (027) 455 09 81 • PUBLICITÉ (022) 308 68 78
E-MAILS abo@lecourrier.ch • redaction@lecourrier.ch • lecteurs@lecourrier.ch   N° 32 • 135ᵉ année • Fr. 1.50 • LUNDI 10 FÉVRIER 2003

REFUSEZ LA GUERRE!

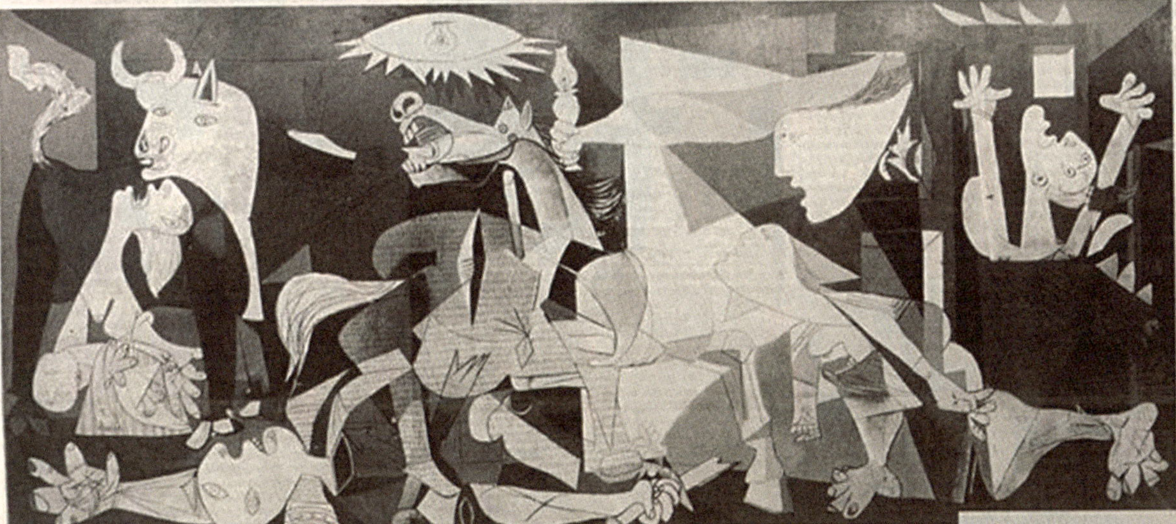

Guernica, la fresque antiguerre de Pablo Picasso, exposée au Conseil de sécurité de l'ONU, a été masquée par un rideau bleu et des drapeaux, le 5 février, pendant que le secrétaire d'Etat étasunien Colin Powell présentait ses «preuves» contre l'Irak. KEYSTONE

Manifestation samedi 15 février à Berne, 13h30, Schützenmatte, comme à Paris, New York, Rome et partout dans le monde...

Le Courrier s'associe aux très nombreuses organisations qui appellent à manifester pacifiquement et appuie leurs revendications:

• Non à la guerre contre l'Irak et sa population: quelles que soient les instances qui la décident (USA, ONU) et ses buts officiels, cette guerre ne sert qu'à satisfaire les intérêts pétroliers et stratégiques des USA.

• Levée immédiate de l'embargo contre la population irakienne. Arrêt des bombardements en cours actuellement.

• C'est au peuple irakien de décider de son avenir. Ni le dictateur Saddam Hussein, ni un régime de pantins mis en place par les USA ne garantiront les droits fondamentaux des femmes et des hommes vivant en Irak. Nous soutenons les forces sociales qui se battent en Irak pour les droits sociaux, démocratiques, économiques et culturels de la population.

• Droit à l'autodétermination pour tous les peuples de la région, y compris pour les peuples kurde et palestinien. Halte à l'occupation des Territoires occupés par l'armée israélienne.

• Arrêt immédiat des atteintes aux droits démocratiques fondamentaux perpétrées au nom de la «guerre contre le terrorisme». Nous soutenons les mouvements de protestations qui se développent partout dans le monde contre cette guerre.

• Elimination partout dans le monde de toutes les armes de destruction massive, dont les Etats-Unis sont les principaux détenteurs.

• Le Conseil fédéral doit se prononcer à l'ONU clairement contre une guerre contre l'Irak. Nous exigeons qu'il refuse tout appui aux Etats-Unis et à leurs alliés dans leurs préparatifs de guerre, qu'il leur refuse en particulier le droit de survoler l'espace aérien suisse. Nous demandons qu'il interrompe toute collaboration en matière d'armement avec les Etats-Unis et Israël.

Des transports vers Berne sont organisés depuis plusieurs villes de Suisse romande. Il est nécessaire de s'inscrire avant mercredi. Une participation financière est demandée.

SION, rendez-vous à 10h30 rue Matthieu Schinner, Sion. Halte possible à **MARTIGNY**. Inscription: 079/451.01.88 ou mpsvs@hotmail.com

GENÈVE. Départ Place Neuve 10h. Inscription: SSP-vpod. Tél. 022/741.50.80 ou sspge@vtxnet.ch

NEUCHÂTEL. Rendez-vous à 12h30 dans le hall de la gare CFF.

LA CHAUX-DE-FONDS. Départ 11h à la gare CFF. Inscription 032/889.84.46 ou nonalaguerrecdf@yahoo.com

NYON. Départ devant la gare CFF à 10h.

MORGES. Départ devant la gare CFF à 10h30.

LAUSANNE. Départ devant le stade de la Pontaise à 11h. **VEVEY**. Départ du giratoire du Grévier (sortie autoroute) à 11h15.

YVERDON. Départ devant la gare CFF à 11h30. Inscription: 079/620.69.29 ou suzanne.peters@bluewin.ch.

Plébiscite pour les droits populaires

VOTATIONS • Les Suisses ont largement accepté, par 70,3%, l'extension des droits populaires. Tous les cantons du pays ont dit oui à ce texte qui introduit l'initiative populaire générale et permet à 100 000 citoyens d'influencer la Constitution ou une loi. ● 4/5

Un oui massif pour les frais hospitaliers

VOTATIONS • Le plan de paiement élaboré par le parlement pour les frais hospitaliers a été accepté par 77,35% des votants. Un vrai plébiscite, mais les objets en votation ce week-end n'ont pas déplacé les foules: la participation s'élève à 28,2%. ● 4/5

Bâtir un «autre monde» dans les favelas

BRÉSIL • Reportage à Sambinha, l'une des 600 favelas de Rio de Janeiro, où des bénévoles cherchent à bâtir un «autre monde possible», alors qu'ils vivent dans les abîmes de celui-ci. Par ailleurs, l'Etat reste encore totalement absent de ces lieux. ● 2

La peine capitale se porte toujours bien

ÉTATS-UNIS • Le ministre de la Justice étasunien John Ashcroft a contraint des procureurs fédéraux à demander la peine de mort dans 28 cas où ils n'en avaient pas l'intention. Près de 70% des Etasuniens ne jugent toujours pas la peine capitale comme un procédé barbare. ● 11

Des gardiens de prison à La Clairière

GENÈVE • Dès le 1ᵉʳ mars, des gardiens de prison surveilleront les jeunes délinquants en détention à La Clairière. Une mesure qui permettra de mieux définir les rôles éducatif et répressif au sein de l'institution, selon son directeur Jean-Michel Gottardi. Entretien. ● 3

WAR AND PEACE

Edited by

PIERRE HAZAN

and **JACQUES BERCHTOLD, NICOLAS DUCIMETIÈRE**

CHRISTOPHE IMPERIALI

Gallimard | Fondation Martin Bodmer

CONTENTS

MULTILATERALISM:
THE BACKBONE OF LASTING PEACE

I t is a pleasure to contribute to this publication on the three coordinated exhibitions at the Martin Bodmer Foundation, the United Nations Office at Geneva and the International Committee of the Red Cross. The exhibitions showcase exceptional documents on the evolution of international cooperation, and inspire timely reflection about the future of international relations and the role of the United Nations in a world of constant change. It is appropriate that this initiative takes place in Geneva, the birthplace of peace diplomacy and a key hub of the United Nations.

These exhibitions come at a pivotal moment. For nearly seventy-five years, the multilateral arrangements established after the Second World War have saved lives, expanded economic and social progress, upheld human rights and, not least, helped to prevent a third descent into global conflagration. From the articulation of international law to the advancement of gender equality, from protecting the environment to limiting the proliferation of lethal weapons and deadly disease, multilateralism and diplomacy have a proven record of service to people everywhere.

Yet today we are living with a paradox: no country alone, no organization alone, can provide the solutions we need for today's global challenges, but multilateralism is under attack. The world is threatened by global warming, but also by a heating up of global political tensions. We are seeing an increasing deficit of trust in governments and political establishments, and the rising appeal of nationalist and populist voices that demonize and divide. This is very dangerous at a time when collective action is essential.

The world is increasingly multipolar, a positive evolution. But as history tells us, multipolarity alone does not guarantee peace. Europe was multipolar a hundred years ago, but multilateral frameworks for cooperation and problem-solving did not exist. The result was a catastrophic world war.

Today, it is vital that the world has strong and effective multilateral institutions and architecture, and that international relations are based on international law. At the same time, we need new forms of cooperation with other international and regional organizations – a networked multilateralism – as well as closer links with businesses, civil society and other stakeholders – an inclusive multilateralism.

But it is not enough to proclaim the virtue of multilateralism; we must prove its added value by responding to global anxieties and delivering lasting peace and a fair globalization that lifts all. Strengthening multilateralism also means strengthening our commitment to achieving the Sustainable Development Goals, the internationally agreed blueprint for building a better world for all by 2030. The United Nations Charter points the way, with its vision of people and countries living as good neighbours, defending universal values and recognizing our common future.

The United Nations marks its seventy-fifth anniversary in 2020. I want that observance to be the launchpad for a discussion on the future of multilateralism and on our direction as a human family. As a committed multilateralist but also as an engineer fond of evidence and facts, I see no other way forward than to address our challenges together, in solidarity, leaving no one behind. In that spirit, I commend these exhibitions to a wide global audience and express my gratitude to the close partners that have made them possible.

ANTÓNIO GUTERRES
Secretary-General of the United Nations

WHAT THE HISTORY OF WAR AND PEACE CAN TEACH US ABOUT THE FUTURE OF HUMANITARIAN ACTION

The ICRC is delighted to be participating in this exhibition of unique works on the theme of war and peace, alongside the Martin Bodmer Foundation and the United Nations, and with the support of the Swiss Confederation. The inseparable notions of war and peace are as old as civilization itself. For centuries, societies across the globe, from the Babylonians with the Hammurabi Code to the ancient Greeks at the time of the Peloponnesian War to the tribes of Papua New Guinea, have sought to establish various forms of customary norms and rules around combat and warfare.

Some of these rules evolved through custom and tradition. For instance, the Somali *Biri-ma-geydo* is a set of practices governing armed conflict, derived from both traditional and sharia law, which aim to protect those not taking part in combat. Similarly, in medieval Europe, the notion of chivalry created an obligation for knights to respect those who could not defend themselves. In some cases, norms were set down in texts, such as the *Viqayet*, written by the Arabs when they ruled Spain. This document, dating from the thirteenth century, established a veritable code of warfare.

A critical moment for the modern age came about in 1859, when a citizen of Geneva named Henry Dunant felt compelled to act after witnessing large-scale suffering on the battlefields of Solferino. He did so by seeking broad agreement to humanize warfare through the provision of neutral assistance and protection to the wounded and sick.

What followed was the advent of modern humanitarianism, with the signing of the First Geneva Convention in 1864, the founding of the International Committee of the Red Cross (ICRC) and the repositioning of humanitarian issues at the centre of great-power politics.

No longer solely the domain of religious authorities and charities, as it had been for centuries, humanitarian intervention became an issue of public policy, international cooperation and, over time, professionalism and expertise. Today, the Geneva Conventions and their Additional Protocols form the core of international humanitarian law, the body of laws that regulates the conduct of armed conflict and seeks to limit its effects.

It was the philosopher Jürgen Habermas who first theorized the concept of "private people coming together as the public" to create the public sphere through critical discourse. He posited that politics could be brought out of the hidden corridors of power by moving the debate into this new, public political space. In a similar way, through diplomacy and advocacy, private citizens acting to advance social issues came together to found the ICRC. Martin Bodmer's legacy can also be viewed in this light: he felt compelled to act and to contribute to the common good by furthering intellectual and historical discourse.

Soon after the outbreak of the Second World War, Martin Bodmer, a deeply humanistic man, offered his services and resources as a volunteer member of the ICRC board; he went on to serve as the organization's vice-president for seventeen years (from 1947 to 1964). He was responsible for what became known as "intellectual aid", which involved distributing more than a million books to prisoners of war. The importance of this form of relief was recognized by the Third Geneva Convention, which stipulates a legal obligation to provide prisoners of war with intellectual, educational and recreational activities.

Over several decades, Martin Bodmer amassed one of the most important private collections of documents tracing the human experience of war and peace through the ages.

The lens of the past can teach us much about the world of today. History is a patient teacher: it asks that we pause and reflect, taking a long view of the circumstances and experiences of those who have gone before us in order to observe, learn and adapt, for the present and for the future.

As a historian by training, I have often looked back in order to look to the future, to understand where and how we might best carry forward the legacy of modern humanitarianism, a legacy in which the ICRC has played a critical role.

The ICRC's history stretches back more than 150 years, and its institutional memory offers many lessons that are relevant to conflicts and situations of violence today.

While the ICRC's mandate and status as a neutral, impartial and independent organization have not changed much over the decades, the environment and the dynamics of violence and conflict have undergone a rapid and deep transformation, especially in the last few years, which has changed the organization itself.

Today, the ICRC operates in over eighty countries around the world. We bear daily witness to the suffering of individuals and communities, especially those caught up in war and violence. We are currently experiencing a singular period of growth, similar to the one that followed the First World War. During the last six years, the ICRC's annual budget has doubled, reflecting growing humanitarian needs: it currently stands at over two billion Swiss francs. In recent years, our headcount has increased from just over 10,000 to more than 17,000.

We are guided by the principles of humanitarian action and seek to find practical and pragmatic solutions for people; we negotiate humanitarian spaces to deliver aid and gain access to people affected by conflict and other forms of violence. We urge belligerents to comply with humanitarian law everywhere it applies: in conflict regions in Africa and the Middle East, but also in Myanmar, Afghanistan, Ukraine and elsewhere. We represent humanitarianism and form part of a social movement, incorporating both the Red Cross and the Red Crescent, that mobilizes more than seventeen million volunteers throughout the world and enables millions of people to witness the true meaning of solidarity.

Today, more than two billion people are affected by a lack of security, armed conflict or other forms of violence. By 2030, half of these people will be living in extreme poverty. Last year, a record 68.5 million people were displaced and more than 120 million currently depend on some form of humanitarian aid. Scientific estimates indicate that the cost of violence and war today account for more than ten per cent of the total global gross domestic product.

However, these figures do not tell the whole story: more than eighty per cent of people displaced by violence come from the fifteen countries where the ICRC's largest operations are located, and they account for an equivalent share of humanitarian aid. That explains the paradox facing us today: although, overall, the global population is now healthier, better educated, better connected and wealthier than ever before, many regions and countries still remain fragile in the long term, affected by a lack of development, violence and governance problems on a massive scale.

The following six trends relating to contemporary conflicts are most relevant to our work, and point to the fundamental changes described below.

First, wars are growing increasingly protracted. The ICRC has recognized the changing needs of affected populations and adapted its operations to continue to work in post-conflict and fragile environments. Indeed, in the countries hosting its ten largest operations, the ICRC has been on the ground for an average of thirty-six years.

Second, the impact of urbanization means that wars are increasingly fought in densely populated, urban areas, such as the Gaza Strip, Mogadishu, Mosul or Aleppo. Meanwhile, the weapons used are often designed for open battlefields. The deployment of weapons that scatter explosive munitions over a wide area, such as large air-delivered bombs and missiles, artillery, mortars and multi-barrel rocket launchers, put civilians at great risk of incidental death and injury, in addition to damaging or destroying critical infrastructure essential to their survival, including water-supply and electricity networks. The destruction they cause to markets, workplaces and schools is also long-term.

Third, the root causes of conflict are becoming increasingly complex and difficult to tackle, often consisting in a tangled web of politically motivated violence, terrorism, social violence and white-collar crime. Violence breeds violence, and its various forms are more and more difficult to separate, which is also a challenge for our traditional legal systems, namely international humanitarian law, human rights law and international criminal law.

Fourth, armed groups have become more numerous and radical, but also more fragmented. Our research indicates that more armed groups have formed during the last six years than over the previous sixty. Today, only a third of all conflicts involve two sides, while more than a fifth involve ten or more parties. This makes our core work – promoting respect for international humanitarian law and negotiating access to victims – far more complicated.

Fifth, wars often involve partners and allies, organized in new constellations; this carries the risk of diluted responsibility, complicates the chain of command and leads to an unchecked flow of weapons. Moreover, there is a tendency for belligerents to deny responsibility for violations of humanitarian law, or to try to shift the blame onto others. This only increases the climate of impunity and ultimately causes further suffering.

Sixth, we are poised on the threshold of a fourth industrial revolution. The technological advances it will spawn may well be used to create increasingly sophisticated and deadly weapons. However, these new technologies will no doubt also be harnessed to find new ways to provide humanitarian aid and to create new development opportunities for fragile societies.

These developments are taking place on a stage where longstanding social problems are creating a perfect storm: developmental deficits and injustice, climate change and failed governance at all levels are an expression of these multilayered threats.

The ICRC is a daily witness to the humanitarian impact of the convergence of these dynamics. It is all too easy to feel discouraged in the face of this bleak picture of human suffering. Nevertheless, I see many reasons to be hopeful. During my visits to South Sudan, Yemen, Syria and many other places, I have met countless people who display great resilience despite the immense suffering they are experiencing; they want nothing more than to continue with their lives, earn an income, send their children back to school and look to the future with hope once again. And the ICRC is working to support them and to lay the foundations for stability and peace.

Every day, in conflict zones around the world, the ICRC shields vulnerable communities by supporting the structures they depend on. Humanitarian action bolsters health systems, shores up electricity and water supply, and supports livelihoods and cash grants for small businesses. Millions of people are able to survive and to return to their former, stable lives thanks to sustained and long-term humanitarian support for water and waste infrastructure and health systems, and investment in community-building and livelihood support.

Frontline humanitarian action is a vital stabilizing factor in fragmented environments and a building block for peace. But we cannot stop at responding to the impact of violence; we must also focus on how wars are conducted and the limits that must be placed on armed belligerents and their conduct in order to reduce the suffering and the needs of those who are caught in the middle.

As a neutral humanitarian organization, the ICRC talks to all parties: states, non-state armed groups, partners and allies – in short, anyone who can influence the conduct of hostilities. Where there is humanity and respect for international humanitarian law, there is a better chance for peace. Today the ICRC fulfils a variety of requests to act as a neutral intermediary in situations of conflict. We are called on to prevent relations from deteriorating and conflicts from escalating, or to suggest ways of building mutual trust in order to advance peace.

International humanitarian law, be it conventional or customary, is designed to be non-political and to ensure a measure of humanity in the worst circumstances.

The value proposition, the inherent benefit, of international humanitarian law, however, is to insist on behaviours that not only prevent the worst human suffering and devastation from occurring during war, but also, precisely by doing so, enable reconciliation to take place after the war has ended.

I often wonder how history will judge the period we live in. I firmly believe that, despite the many horrors and failures of the present time, the record will show that we have drawn the lessons of the past, that we have strengthened humanitarian norms and laws, and that we have left a stronger legacy for the generations to come.

PETER MAURER
President of the International Committee
of the Red Cross

THE PEN AND THE SWORD

Libraries and arsenals, reading rooms and barracks are not wholly separate worlds. To achieve excellence in the fine arts requires *exercitum*. Among the educated elite, military training was long ranked as the art that encouraged exercise *par excellence*. War is a pervasive theme in music, painting and literature, but so are indignation and resistance in the face of war. Moreover, it is an oft-remarked yet bitter truth that times of war seem conducive to the emergence of exceptionally powerful masterpieces.

Composed in the nation that was the cradle of both Europe and democracy, the epic war poem the *Iliad* celebrated the years-long siege of Troy by the Greeks. This great masterpiece grounded the many city-states of ancient Greece in a common culture, just as the campaign to recapture the adulterous Helen had once united their armies. The *Iliad* acknowledges the deep connection between two basic instincts, sexual desire and bloodlust, and transposes them into a great work of literature. Attempts to depict what war is like and to explain the urge to fight spring from the same source. Thinkers, artists and soldiers alike have contributed to reflections about war and peace. Recognizing the foundational importance of Homer, Martin Bodmer (1899–1971) chose the epic poet as the cornerstone of his library (papyrus PB 1), the first of five major works that have decisively illuminated the history of the human spirit.

Around the mid-fifteenth century, another cradle of European humanism – Cosimo de' Medici's Florence – became keenly aware of the importance of searching out ancient manuscripts, as well as more recent ones. This significantly expanded the scope of spiritual knowledge, and resulted in the founding of the Laurentian Library, Europe's first truly cosmopolitan public library. The groundwork laid by the Florentines served as the inspiration for the enlightened world tirelessly promoted by Martin Bodmer. A member of the International Committee of the Red Cross, Bodmer was convinced that a library of *Weltliteratur* would help advance the cause of peace. However, it was in the heyday of Florentine bibliophily that Uccello painted his breathtaking tribute to the warrior ethos, *The Battle of San Romano* (1456; it hangs in the Louvre), whose three giant panels glorify and exalt the military exploits of the *condottiere*.

Sigmund Freud, a contemporary of Martin Bodmer, was struck by the extent to which nations had turned a blind eye to signs of danger in the run-up to the assassination of Archduke Franz Ferdinand in Sarajevo. After the outbreak of the First World War, he observed that "the primitive, savage and evil instincts of mankind have not disappeared from the structure of individuals; they continue to exist, suppressed beneath the surface, just waiting for an opportunity to reappear." With the benefit of hindsight, he understood that the life and death instincts carry out a complex dialectical game within each individual. He analysed human beings' predisposition to express aggressive and destructive instincts more fully in an epistolary discussion with Albert Einstein, published under the title *Why War?*. In 1931, the League of Nations, taking the view that war was too grave a subject to be left to the generals and hoping to prevent a second world war, supported a proposal from the Permanent Committee on Arts and Letters of the International Committee on Intellectual Cooperation inviting Freud, the founding father of psychoanalysis, and Einstein, the discoverer of relativity and an ardent pacifist, to debate the philosophical and anthropological question "Is war inevitable?". Their correspondence was published simultaneously in English, French and German, in 1933.

The League of Nations, again through the International Committee on Intellectual Cooperation, also sponsored an international symposium on Goethe, in Frankfurt, in 1932. The Nazi party, recently defeated at the ballot box, resorted to threats and refused to recognize the League's legitimacy. Led by Romaine Rolland, European intellectuals were nevertheless determined to honour the centenary of Goethe's death and ensure Europe reaped the benefit of recent progress towards peace. Martin Bodmer (for whom Goethe and his tolerant, global vision of supranationalism acted as a beacon) did his part, helping his friend Paul Valéry draft a highly political anniversary speech, which he delivered at the Sorbonne (and later in Frankfurt, under the aegis of the League). Bodmer and Valéry sought to present an optimistic view of Europe as open to reconciliation and affirmed the reality of friendly Franco-German relations, illustrated by the allegory of Napoleon's friendship with Goethe.

On the long road to a world at peace, ideas about war have always intersected with initiatives directed at overcoming the intractable human urge to go to war. It is worth recalling these constant and persistent efforts in the right direction. Although the end goal – a world where equitable multilateralism is permanently established and recognized as just – still lies on the horizon, comparing archival documents and testimonies from many different times and places, by contributing to a better understanding of the various stages of war, can help us keep a clear head and encourage us to persist. With that in mind, the Martin Bodmer Foundation, Museum and Library are delighted to join forces with the United Nations and the International Committee of the Red Cross in organizing this *War and Peace* exhibition.

JACQUES BERCHTOLD
Director of the Martin Bodmer Foundation

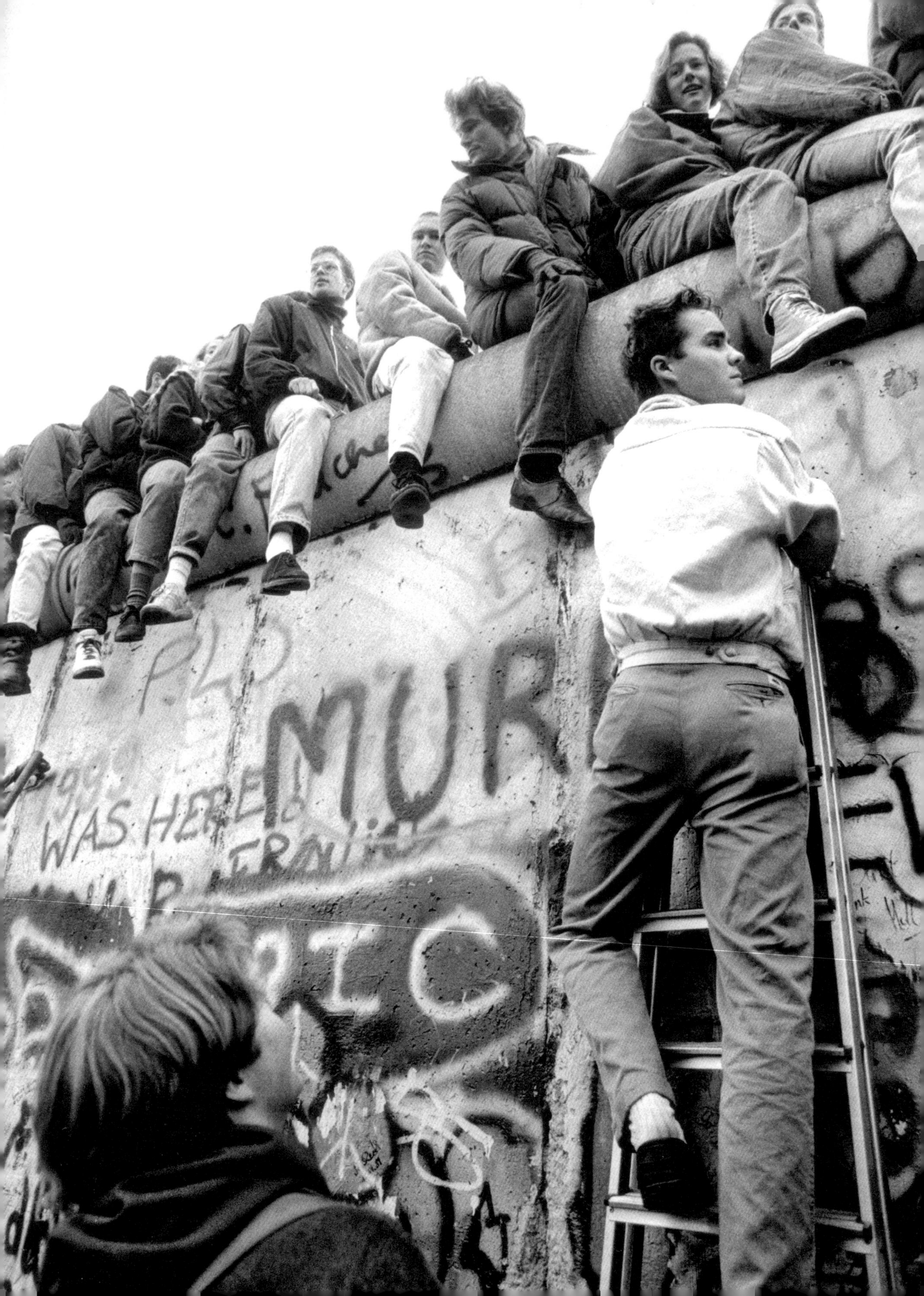

IS WAR THE FUTURE OF HUMANITY?

Is war the future of humanity? Down through the ages, human beings have never ceased to think about, justify, prepare for, wage and glorify war. Nor have they ever ceased to attempt to curb its worst excesses, condemn its ravages, and imagine – and work to build – a more just and peaceful world. In every twist and turn of history, as rebuilding follows tragedy, and in the many ways humans have addressed the issue of war and peace, a centuries-long dialectic has emerged, in which human beings are torn between their most destructive passions and their noblest desire: to live and share with each other. That constant dialectic is what Sophocles, in *Antigone,* calls δεινός (*deinós,* terrible), a word that designates at once the evil genius and the goodness in humankind, what Jacques Derrida terms the "human enigma".

The exhibition *War and Peace* is the outcome of a partnership between the Martin Bodmer Foundation, the United Nations and the International Committee of the Red Cross (ICRC). Its purpose is to connect past and present, to take a step back from the anxiety aroused by the challenges of today and examine it with the benefit of hindsight. The international system inherited from the post-Second World War period is crumbling. And in several areas of the world, in a context of growing inequality and populism, we are witnessing the rise of illiberal, authoritarian regimes, not to mention the spread of fake news, a migration crisis that is sowing division in an ageing Europe and tempting it to fashion itself into a fortress, and, lastly, climate change, which is sparking fresh conflict in Africa over the control of resources.

Human history has been one long date with destiny. Since Antiquity, authors have written beautifully and powerfully about the inherent tension between the need for peace and the inevitability of war. Their production spans religion, philosophy, military strategy, literature, memoirs of soldiers and civilians caught up in the misery of war, hate-filled pamphlets and pleas for reconciliation. The *War and Peace* exhibition is an invitation to take a breathtaking view through the centuries and across different cultures. It features the Sumerian creation myth, in which Marduk kills the goddess Tiamat by cutting her in half with his sword, thus creating the sky and the sea; the exhortations of Roman senator Cato the Elder to destroy Carthage; the despair of Immanuel Kant, who, after lamenting that "Out of the crooked timber of humanity, no straight thing was ever made", went on to write his *Perpetual Peace,* the expression of his firm conviction that the forces of reason and universal moral law would triumph in the end; and Victor Hugo's solemn appeal for amnesty for the Communards after the "Bloody Week" of May 1871, because "the wound must be closed. All hate must be extinguished". Looking back over such a long period of time provides ample food for

The fall of the Berlin Wall on Potsdamer Platz, 10 November 1989, photograph.

thought, but also inspires us to take action to address the challenges of the present. And those challenges are considerable. If this exhibition had been organized just thirty years ago, it would have radiated an extraordinary optimism. Demonstrators in East Germany were knocking down the Berlin Wall, spelling the end of the Cold War. It was a time to celebrate the "dividends of peace", the victory of democracy and liberalism. Copies of Francis Fukuyama's *The End of History and the Last Man*, which proclaimed the messianic dawn we were then experiencing, were selling by the million. Multilateralism reigned supreme. With his "Agenda for Peace", Secretary-General Boutros Boutros-Ghali was breathing new life into the founding principles of the United Nations Charter, emphasizing preventive diplomacy and urging the world to keep the peace – or to impose it when necessary.

Three decades later, the outlook has brutally changed, and we are now in the throes of a social, political and identity crisis. What makes a nation? What makes a society and an "international community" in a world so fragmented, unequal and violent? That is the crucial question posed by the exhibition *One Hundred Years of Multilateralism in Geneva* at the United Nations, inviting us to take a step back and examine the past, the better to shape the present. Whereas the twentieth century had more than its share of murderous, totalitarian ideologies claiming to have resolved the great enigma of history, the twenty-first century has begun with a question: how can we, in all the rich diversity of our identities, adapt to an environment experiencing such tremendous upheaval?

Artificial intelligence, robotization, information and communications technology – the digital revolution is mapping out new spaces and drawing new frontiers, at once physical, virtual, political, economic, social and cultural. What potential does this brutal paradigm shift hold? What hope does it offer, and what setbacks? What forms of violence might it enable? As always, this transformation of our world entails a new relationship to the law. That is the focus of the exhibition at the International Red Cross and Red Crescent Museum, *150 Years of the International Review of the Red Cross*.

The fact that these three exhibitions are being organized in Geneva is neither neutral nor coincidental. The city of Geneva, which for hundreds of years was spared the scourge of war, is where the first international arbitration took place; where the initial Geneva Convention was drawn up, in 1864, although at the time the laws of war were destined solely for "civilized peoples"; where the League of Nations sat, although the British delegation felt affronted that such a small, dull city had been chosen to host the organization; where the Nansen passport for stateless persons – and later the international Refugee Convention – were first conceived; and where so many texts whose implementation transformed the lives of millions of men, women and children were negotiated, discussed and drafted.

It was in Geneva, too, that Martin Bodmer lived during the Second World War, having been invited to join the executive of the ICRC, before becoming its vice-president in 1947. He was fully informed of the enormity of the destruction and suffering endured by civilians, and therefore able to gauge the ensuing loss of faith in the idea of progress, a main tenet of the Enlightenment. Towards the end of the war he became firmly convinced that culture held the key. To counter the "narrow-minded rigidity" of "national" literatures, Bodmer, inspired by Goethe, argued vigorously in favour of rehabilitating the concept of *Weltliteratur,* or world literature, a vibrant, dynamic, open-minded body of work that is constantly evolving, in a perpetual dialogue with the world. In his notebooks, he made a case for the "cosmopolitanism" that the Nazi and Stalinist regimes had designated as the enemy. In his biography of Martin Bodmer, Jérôme David remarks that for him "*Weltliteratur* had become the cultural equivalent of Kant's right to unconditional hospitality", that is, "cosmopolitanism as an ideal – the ideal of a peaceful global society".

Martin Bodmer's thinking on the idea of "open culture" was profoundly modern. But how can that aspiration to a cosmopolitan culture be squared with the deep sense of dispossession felt by so many in the world today? The most serious challenge at present is undoubtedly the fact that so many men and women feel that they no longer belong, that they are part of a vast voiceless cohort, the playthings of forces beyond their control, dispossessed of their very selves, the future closed off to them forever. Confronted with a heartbreakingly brutal world, in which truth and falsehood are increasingly harder to tell apart, is it any wonder that some find refuge in identifying closely with a particular community, nation or religion? Symbolically, it is striking that one of Africa's most feared armed groups chose to call itself Boko Haram – literally, "ban books" – as if in direct refutation of Martin Bodmer's dream. While violence can never be excused, it, too, is fuelled by despair. In 1948 Albert Camus observed: "No worthwhile life is possible without projection onto the future, without promise of development and progress. To live with one's back to a wall is a dog's life."

In many parts of the world, a rising rumble of anger can be heard. History has taught us what disastrous consequences may follow. Memories of injury are very often exploited by warmongering ideologies, wreaking all-too-familiar devastation. We thought war had been banished from Europe following the death of fifty million people in the cataclysm of the Second World War, yet it has come back to haunt us, first with the implosion of the former Yugoslavia and later in the former Soviet territories. It is a sign of the times that defence budgets are as large as they have ever been since the end of the Cold War,[1] and that in 2017 the total number of refugees and displaced persons worldwide swelled to over 68 million.[2]

In this fractured twenty-first century world, how can we redefine the cosmopolitanism that Martin Bodmer aspired to? To realize a culture of openness and a world at peace we need to recognize otherness, by guaranteeing access to a forward-looking education for all and ensuring a minimum level of protection for the most vulnerable. Hannah Arendt expressed this principle as "the right to have rights", by which she meant that every person possesses a set of inalienable rights regardless of their particular situation or the prevailing political and economic circumstances.

More than seventy years ago, on 8 August 1945, Albert Camus penned an editorial in the daily newspaper *Combat*. The atom bomb had just been dropped on Hiroshima and commentators around the world were enthusiastically saluting the fact that it was now possible to wipe out an entire city with a bomb the size of a football. Speaking out against this chorus of approval, Camus warned: "Our technical civilization has just reached its greatest level of savagery. We will have to choose, in the more or less near future, between collective suicide and the intelligent use of our scientific conquests." The context has changed, but the challenge remains, and our responsibility is, as much as ever, to choose between war and peace. That is what is at stake, and therein lies the implicit question posed by *War and Peace*.

PIERRE HAZAN
Curator of *War and Peace* and
Transitional Justice advisor to the Centre for Humanitarian Dialogue,
expert on armed conflict mediation

Notes

[1] According to SIPRI, in 2017 global defence spending reached US\$ 1.74 trillion, https://www.sipri.org/sites/default/files/2018-04/sipri_fs_1805_milex_2017.pdf

[2] UNHCR, see https://www.unhcr.org/globaltrends2017/

Is war part
of human nature?

Can we avoid war
by preparing for it?

How should we read
calls to **VIOLENCE
IN SACRED TEXTS?**

Who writes history?

THE ORIGINS OF WAR

WHEN HUMAN CULTURES THINK ABOUT WAR

GILAD BEN-NUN

Leipzig University
Centre for Area Studies

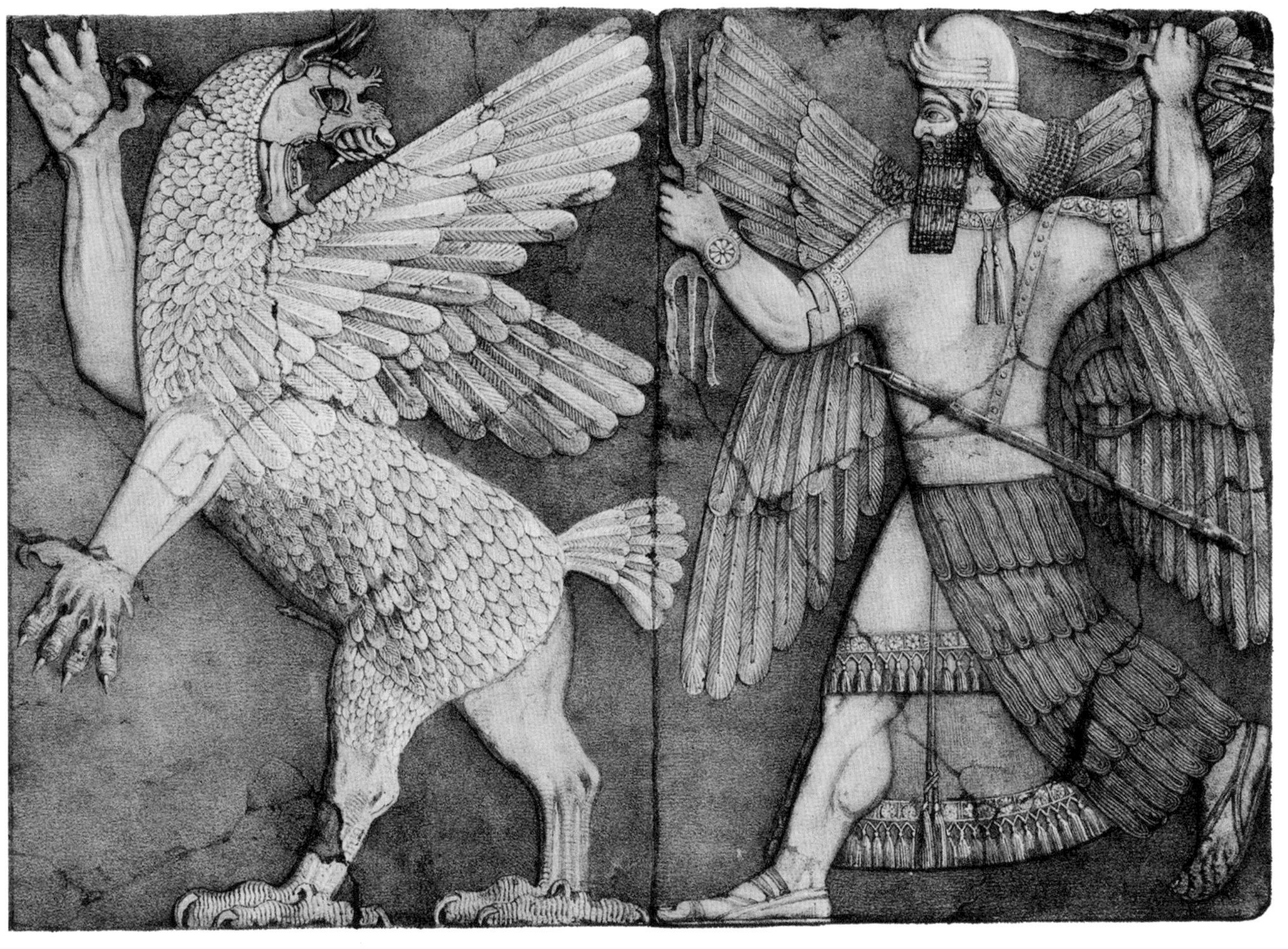

Marduk, the Babylonian sun god, set out with his lightning dagger to defeat the goddess Tiamat, keeper of the tablet of destinies. Relief, second millennium BC, Niniveh, ancient Assyrian city of Upper Mesopotamia, located in the outskirts of present-day Mosul, Iraq.

s war the habitual condition of man? Are intervals of peace in the history of humanity little more than exogenous exceptions to the permanence of war? Or are peace and stability the natural human state, and war its exceptional nemesis? This perennial dilemma has perplexed humanity since the dawn of time.

To begin with, war forms an integral part of the world's creation myths. The separation of the heavens was explained by the ancients of Sumer (Babylon) as the result of a battle between the female goddess Tiamat, and her male adversary, Marduk. In the Sumerian myth of Enûma Eliš (1700 BC), Marduk's slaying of Tiamat by severing her body in two created the sky and the waters of today's Persian Gulf. While Egyptian and Jewish mythologies borrowed from this cosmology, it was the Greeks who adopted the Sumerian notion of warring elements in their creation myth. Hesiod's *Theogonia* (700 BC) recounts how the blood of the slain sky-god Uranus landed on the earth and created the Furies, the female deities of vengeance. Uranus' wife, Gaia (Mother Earth), watched in horror, as her slain husband's body brought war and suffering into the world.

The association of war with the creation of the world was not exclusive to the Near East. The gods Izanagi and Izanami from Japanese mythology are said to have dipped their *naginata* (a long Japanese war-blade) into the sea. When they pulled it out, three drops of saltwater fell back into the ocean, creating the Japanese archipelago. For Sumer, Greece and Japan, war was thus integral to the basic construct of the world.

China stands in contrast to the warring ethos of the Near East and Japan. In Chinese mythology, peace was the natural order of things and war the exception. According to the Confucian cosmology (500 BC), benevolence, peace and, especially, order flowed from the emperor, to whom all the lands in the world were initially awarded. He then entrusted these lands to his vassals in descending order of virtue. War – understood as disorder and chaos – was juxtaposed to the natural, normative procession of life, which, by the providence of the emperor, was always restored to tranquillity after the end of the necessary military campaign. Throughout human history, China was virtually always in a state of demographic superiority vis-à-vis other cultures. The idea that, during most of that time, somewhere between a quarter and a third of humanity subscribed principally to a peaceful rather than a bellicose worldview is rather comforting.

Glorifying war, belittling peace

History, or rather its writing, could hardly escape the mythical aspect of war. Joshua's violent conquest of Canaan would serve as the primary blueprint for "the people of the covenant", from returning Babylonian Jews in the third century BC to Northern Irish Protestants marching in the Orange Order. To readers of Herodotus across the ages, the suicidal stance of Leonidas and his three hundred Spartans at the Battle of Thermopylae stood as the epitome of virility, devotion to a cause and purposefulness. Nietzsche, a classical philologist by training, even posited war as a necessary precondition of human artistic creativity in his *Birth of Tragedy* (1872).

Peace, on the other hand, gradually came to be associated with cultural boredom, creative decay and moral and political debacle. Ibn Khaldun postulated that it was domestication and peaceful agricultural prosperity that weakened the bellicosity of Middle-Eastern nomads, once they settled in the freshwater oases they conquered. This military weakening meant they could not fend off the next wave of marauding nomads coming to the same freshwater source. The author of the

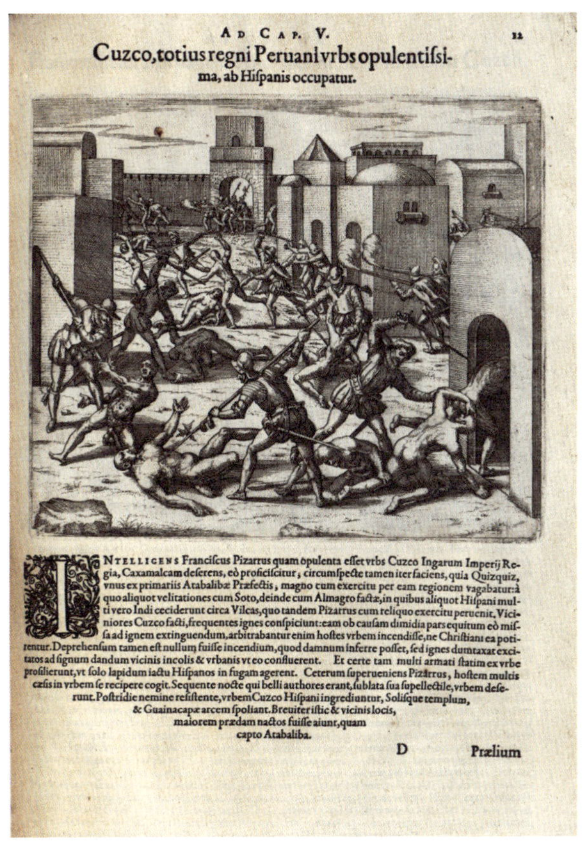

NTELLIGENS Franciscus Pizarrus quam opulenta esset vrbs Cuzco Ingarum Imperij Re-
gia, Caxamalcam deserens, eò proficiscitur, circumspecte tamen iter faciens, quia Quizquiz,
vnus ex primariis Atabalibæ Præfectis, magno cum exercitu per eam regionem vagabatur: à
quo aliquot velitationes cum Soto, deinde cum Almagro factæ, in quibus aliquot Hispani multi vero Indi ceciderunt circa Vilcas, quo tandem Pizarrus cum reliquo exercitu peruenit. Vici-
niores Cuzco facti, frequentes ignes conspiciunt: eam ob causam dimidia pars equitum eò mis-
sa ad ignem extinguendum, arbitrabantur enim hostes vrbem incendisse, ne Christiani ea poti-
rentur. Deprehensum tamen est nullum fuisse incendium, quod damnum inferre posset, sed ignes dumtaxat exci-
tatos ad signum dandum vicinis incolis & vrbanis vt eo confluerent. Et certe tam multi armati statim ex vrbe
prosilierunt, vt solo lapidum iactu Hispanos in fugam agerent. Ceterum superueniens Pizarrus, hostem multis
cæsis in vrbem se recipere cogit. Sequente nocte qui belli authores erant, sublata sua supellectile, vrbem dese-
runt. Postridie nemine resistente, vrbem Cuzco Hispani ingrediuntur, Solisque templum,
& Guainacapæ arcem spoliant. Breuiter istic & vicinis locis,
maiorem prædam nactos fuisse aiunt, quam
capto Atabaliba.

D Prælium

The Storming of Cusco, in
Girolamo Benzoni, *Americae pars sexta,
siue, historiæ ab Hieronymo Bezono
Mediolanese scriptæ, sectio tertia*,
Frankfurt, Theodor de Bry, 1596.
Cologny, Martin Bodmer Foundation.

Muqaddimah's – who, in its elaboration, invented sociology – also impregnated this new academic discipline with its affinity for war-like thinking. Bismarck's borrowing of Max Weber's ideas for his "blood and iron" unification of Germany could partly be premised on sociology's potential for bellicosity, especially given its infatuation with the nation-state's defining feature: its monopoly over the means of violence and coercion. The Third Reich's administrative apparatus certainly drew upon Weber's theory of the state.

Yet not all periods of history succumbed to the bellicose order of things. In retrospect, the Middle Ages appear largely peaceful in comparison to other eras of world history. To the Stoics, peace was the *ultima ratio* of politics. The Church Fathers' adoption of Stoicism meant that Christianity was positively imbued with the idea of world peace. Thanks to the thinking of the Catholic Fathers from Augustine to Aquinas **[cat. 4]**, the idea of a "just war", based on late Roman jurisprudence, became an explicit part of official Church doctrine. War was seen as the tragic result of man's banishment from the heavens; temporal and religious leaders had a duty to limit its waging to a minimum, and only as a last resort. To this end, the upholding of treaties (*pacta sunt servanda*) became a duty whose breach would be considered a serious religious offence. And while Christianity often conditioned its upholding of this principle when dealing with non-Christians (as in Spain's conquest of Latin America), it was Islam that first extended *pacta sunt servanda* to all mankind: monotheists and polytheists alike "fulfil the treaty with them [the polytheists] to the end of its term", because "Allah loves the righteous" (Quran, sura al-Tawbah, v. 4). Charlemagne exchanged gifts with his Muslim counterpart, Harun al-Rashid, and marvelled at his scientific and philosophical knowledge. Salah ad-Din promised King Richard the Lionheart safety and sanctuary for Christian pilgrims to Jerusalem. Following the partition of the Promised Land (1192), unarmed Christians could pray in Jerusalem without fear. The sanctity of the treaty would be scrupulously guarded by the great Ayyub himself. The Lionheart could return to England. In a rare episode in human history, it was as *peacemakers* that Salah ad-Din and King Richard endured in the collective memory, while treaty-breakers like Renaud de Châtillon were swiftly forgotten.

Historians did not always contribute to peace. In the worst cases, the historical record was simply fabricated, as in Sophronius of Jerusalem's account of the Arab conquest of the city (AD 637). Far from his tale of horror, recent archaeological surveys of Israel, Palestine and Jordan have failed to yield a single chemical trace of carbon that might substantiate Sophronius' claim that the Arabs burned many churches during their conquest. Instead, modern excavations reveal that an entire new wing of Jerusalem's Church of the Holy Sepulchre was erected *after* the Arabs had taken control of the city. As Gideon Avni has pointedly noted, Sophronius "embellished" his history of the Arab conquest with false horror stories for his own political ends. For historians at least, fake news is old news. Fifteen centuries would pass before Sophronius' literary sins came to light. Meanwhile, the myth of Arab bellicosity continued to thrive unabated. Destabilized by the new, archeologically proven facts put forth by Avni, some in the scholarly establishment still refuse to let go of their unwarranted opinions.

In other instances, peace was simply forgotten. Medievalists aside, few people today are familiar with the partitioning of Jerusalem, in 1229, between Sultan Al-'Kâmil and Frederick II, under the terms of the Treaty of Jaffa Tel-Ajul. One would assume that this historical precedent of a voluntary partitioning of the holy city, with guarantees of worship and a multi-communitarian administration, could serve as an example for modern-day peacemakers. Instead, readers searching for this treaty in the English version of Wikipedia will come up empty-handed. Lacking the drama of war, Al-'Kâmil and Frederick's determination to sue for peace *prior* to the commencement of war was simply not exciting enough to be remembered.

Necessity, the state, and the birth of modern international law

The rise of the centralized state in the fifteenth century signalled a new era in the annals of war and peace: the emergence of *political necessity* as a harbinger of conflict. Stressing their political imperatives, European leaders supplanted the just war theory of Augustine and Thomas Aquinas with naked Machiavellian realism, before subscribing to Hobbes' vision of *raison d'état* **[cat. 9]**. In its infancy, the state's ferociousness was directed against archetypal "others". Long before it launched its Armada against England, Spain began by expelling all indigenous Jewish and

Muslim inhabitants from Al-Andalus. The slaughter of the indigenous peoples of Latin America under Cortés and Pizzaro followed soon after. Spain's defeat against England in 1585 was merely a prelude to the Thirty Years War, during which a third of Europe's population was traumatically annihilated. Scorched-earth policies, which had largely been abandoned in medieval times (Godfrey of Bouillon's 1099 razing of Jerusalem being the exception) experienced a resurgence. French armies in the Palatinate emulated Cato the Elder's repeated calls for the destruction of Carthage. Seventeenth-century French generals now preferred Tacitus' accounts of the Romans "spreading salt on Carthage", so that nothing would ever grow there again, over Augustine's vision of perpetual peace in chapter nineteen of his *City of God*. Louis XIV's instruction to his generals that "the Palatinate should be made a desert" resulted in the flattening of Heidelberg.

It is against this background of the *return* of total war to the fore that one must understand the rise of modern international law. For Grotius **[cat. 8]**, the aspiration was not to consolidate peace, but, more modestly, to establish a minimal threshold that would hopefully help to prevent war. As Sir Michael Howard's aptly notes, while Kant was the first to give peace a truly modern legal garb, he drew heavily from an illustrious lineage of jurists who preceded him. From Al Farabi and Maimonides to Marsilius of Padua and Sir Thomas More, and from Erasmus of Rotterdam **[cat. 100]** to Bartolomé de la Casas **[cat. 101]**, peace has always had its share of eloquent defenders who remained unabatingly vocal in their quest to rein in bellicosity and promote non-violent alternatives.

The age of extremes and "treaties after trauma"

Few periods in human history have been as bellicose as the twentieth century. The rise of the individual in the nineteenth century, and the consecration of *his* (as opposed to *her*) fetish for masculine self-expression, enabled war to reach unprecedented heights of destruction. What united male combatants in the First World War was their enthusiasm at the thrilling prospect of combat. Yet the realities of modern warfare soon hit home. Destruction was carried out on an industrial scale. The means of killing now included aerial bombardment and chemical weapons. Against the voices of peace who established international multilateralism and the League of Nations, and opted to outlaw wars of aggression (in the 1928 Kellogg-Briand Pact **[cat. 130]**), fascism and extremist nationalism responded with a renewed impetus for violent conquest. Georg Cohn's articulation of the principle of non-recognition of territorial acquisition by force (the so-called "Stimson Doctrine") was answered by Carl Schmitt's *Grossraum* theory **[cat. 12]**, which served as the ideological bedrock for Hitler's empire. Of the 17,000 synagogues that served European Jewry in 1933, only 762 remained standing by the end of the Second World War. Hiroshima would resemble Dante's inferno.

Treaties invariably come after trauma: Westphalia after the Thirty Years War **[cat. 122]**, The League of Nations after the First World War, The Fourth Geneva Convention for the protection of civilians after the Second World War, the Responsibility to Protect after Rwanda and Srebrenica. In a single instance of human exception, however, the Treaty on the Non-Proliferation of Nuclear Weapons *did not* follow trauma – a trauma that could have come about during the Cuban Missile Crisis, but was ultimately avoided. Suddenly, it was *peace* that was an absolute necessity and *war* that could be done without. International multilateralism miraculously prevailed. Realists could afford to become optimists – but only so long as they could rely on the multilateral system to help them save the day.

THE GREEKS AT WAR

ANDRÉ HURST
University of Geneva

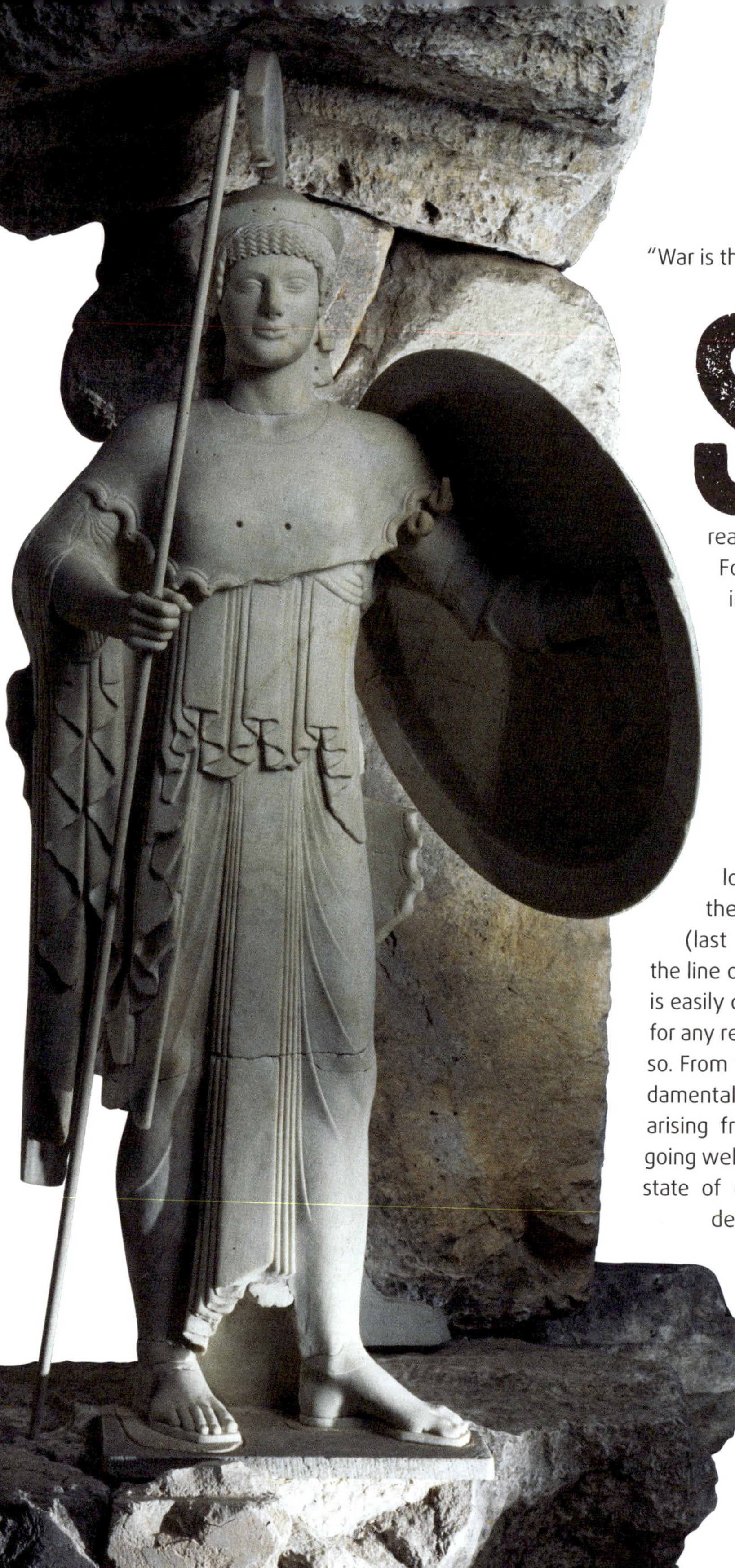

So said Pericles himself, according to Thucydides **[cat. 119]**.[1]

The context is of course important. If the Athenian general, who left his mark on the fifth century BC, did indeed pronounce those words, it was because he had good reason to do so:

For those of course who have a free choice in the matter and whose fortunes are not at stake, war is the greatest of follies. But if the only choice was between submission with loss of independence, and danger with the hope of preserving that independence – in such a case it is he who will not accept the risk that deserves blame, not he who will.[2]

Pericles had just embroiled his fellow-citizens in what, for Athens, would be the misadventure of the Peloponnesian War (last thirty years of the fifth century BC), and the line of defence attributed to him by Thucydides is easily discernible: it would be stupid to go to war for any reason other than that one was forced to do so. From this point of view, there are thus two fundamentally distinct situations: a state of happiness arising from a kind of equilibrium (everything is going well and one's decisions are one's own) and a state of constraint in which one risks becoming dependent on others. Only in the second situation is war is justifiable; in the first, it is "the greatest of follies".

Pericles was not alone in thinking this way. According to Herodotus, Croesus, when defeated by Cyrus, said to the latter: "No one is so foolish as to choose war over peace."[3] Having entered into war against Cyrus,

Croesus excused himself by saying that a god had swayed him: Apollo had impelled him to go to war. No man would otherwise be so foolish.

Is war folly? Was that the general feeling among the ancient Greeks? There is room for doubt. Think of the popularity of Homer: doesn't the *Iliad* celebrate warriors **[cat. 68]**? Yes, but a closer look reveals a more nuanced message, and the glorification of warriors such as Achilles or Hector is not necessarily synonymous with the glorification of war itself:

> [S]o the battle broke, storming chaos, troops inflamed,
> slashing each other with bronze, carnage mounting,
> manslaughtering combat bristling with rangy spears,
> the honed lances brandished in hand and ripping flesh
> and the eyes dazzled now, blind with the glare of bronze,
> glittering helmets flashing, breastplates freshly burnished,
> shields fiery in sunlight, fighters plowing on in a mass.
> Only a veteran steeled at heart could watch that struggle
> and still thrill with joy and never feel the terror. [4]

It is hard not to perceive a kind of pleasure in the "generic" description of this battle, even if it ends with the assertion that only a heart of steel could thrill with joy at the sight of war.

In fact, wasn't war the normal state of affairs between the Greeks and their neighbours? If we believe the poets who wrote from the point of view of the soldiers engaged in battle, there were conflicting perspectives on war. The first expressed the predominating theme that war confers glory. In the seventh century BC, the Spartan poet Tyrtaeus celebrated soldierly valour, writing that it was glorious to die on the front line, and that the young man fallen in combat was beautiful (whereas the fall of an older man, "with head already white and grizzled beard", was disgraceful). [5] The soldier must at all costs avoid offering his back; he must stand against the foe and, covered by his "broad shield", "feet set firmly apart, bite on his lip". [6] Others, such as Callinus, echoed that sentiment, as did the tragedians (Aeschylus' *Perseus* immediately springs to mind). The need to fight was not called into question.

The second theme that emerges as a counterpoint is that of the wretched warrior. Around the same time, the poet Archilochus of Paros struck a sarcastic tone, directed first and foremost at himself: did he or did he not flee during a battle, dropping his shield, the better to cut and run? No one knows, but "I'll soon find another one that's no worse", [7] he scoffs. Elsewhere, he mocks the so-called exploits of warriors: "Seven

Figure of Athena from the west pediment of the temple of Athena Aphaia in Aegina, marble, *c.* 500 BC. Archaeological Museum of Aegina.

x x x x x x x x x x x x x x x x x x x x x x x x x x x x x x x x x x x x x x x x x x x x x x x x x x x x x x x x x x x x x x x men fell dead when we overtook them at a run, though we the killers are a thousand."[8] He boasts of a slaughter that was not even the outcome of hand-to-hand combat, describing most of the pathetic braggarts as liars to boot. Not everyone, it would seem, agreed that warriors were glorious.

There were those who lionized war, but also those who vaunted the benefits of peace. One example is the lyric poet Bacchylides (fifth century BC), Pindar's illustrious rival. In one well-known fragment, he describes the visible signs of peace: wealth, feasting, dancing and singing, the welcome rest of morning, and "the webs of red-brown spiders … on the iron-bound handles of shields".[9] Another example is Euripides, who, in his lost tragedy *Cresphontes*, had the Chorus sing a hymn to peace, which is preserved in a text by Stobaeus: "Peace, with your depths of wealth, fairest of the blessed gods … I fear old age may overwhelm me with hardships before I can look upon your graceful beauty".[10]

What about the comedies? Aristophanes was a poet of peace: in the oldest of his surviving comedies (*The Acharnians,* 424 BC) he mocks a swaggering general; in *Lysistrata* **[cat. 71]**, he has the soldiers' womenfolk – who want an end to war – withhold sexual privileges. In *Peace*, he goes so far as to imagine that the gods are so disgusted with war that they decide to live far away from humans, leaving the field clear for Polemos, the god of war. Polemos having locked Peace in a cave, the peasants join forces to rescue her – successfully, of course. During this scene, the chorus evokes, in its celebration of peace, a sorry picture of life in the rear-guard: "I am happy, so happy, to be rid of helmets, of cheese and onions".[11] Being in the army was decidedly not all lightness and joy.

Since the gods themselves are involved, let us see what Homer and Hesiod, the two poets credited with having "taught the Greeks the descent of the gods", have to say.[12]

In the *Iliad* (5.889–898), the god of war, Ares, complains to his father, Zeus, that a mortal has wounded him in the battle before Troy (admittedly, with the help of Athena). Zeus makes no bones about his feelings:

> No more, you lying, two-faced …
> no more sidling up to me, whining here before me.
> You – I hate you most of all the Olympian gods.
> Always dear to your heart,
> strife, yes, and battles, the bloody grind of war.
> You have your mother's uncontrollable rage – incorrigible,
> that Hera – say what I will, I can hardly keep her down.

× ×

> Hera's urgings, I trust, have made you suffer this.
> But I cannot bear to see you agonize so long.
> You are my child. To me your mother bore you.
> If you had sprung from another god, believe me,
> and grown into such a blinding devastation,
> long ago you'd have dropped below the Titans,
> deep in the dark pit. [13]

Clearly, even though the worldview of the *Iliad* is marked by war, the god of war did not enjoy the favour of the supreme deity.

The elderly Phoenix even brings up the misfortunes that war causes during the embassy to Achilles. His tale of the war between the Aetolians and the Curets – a true *mise en abyme* of the *Iliad* as a whole, with names and situations changed – ends with the return to the battlefield of Meleager. Like Achilles, Meleager has stayed away from the fighting. His mind is changed, however, after hearing his wife's description of the fate in store for his family: "all the griefs that fall to people whose city is seized and plundered – the men slaughtered, citadel burned to rubble, enemies dragging the children, raping the sashed and lovely women. How his spirit leapt when he heard those horrors." [14]

It is not so simple, however, for the same supreme god sired Athena, without any help from Hera (and the war god Ares' resemblance to his mother is one of the main reproaches made to her). Athena was unquestionably a divinity of war, but her field of action was not limited to war, and sanctuaries were built in her name, unlike Ares.

In Hesiod, it is Athena who is described at greater length as a goddess of war, whereas Ares is simply listed as one of the children of Zeus and Hera (*Theogony*, 921–26).

If there is a lesson to be drawn from these seminal texts about how war was perceived, it is that the gods of war were not among the highest ranked in the pantheon.

For all that, no one placed war on a higher pedestal than the philosopher Heraclitus of Ephesus (sixth to fifth century BC): "War is father of all and king of all; and some he manifested as gods, some as men". [15]

No one can claim that Heraclitus was ignorant of what war meant in terms of everyday, real-world brutality. His city, Ephesus, had witnessed military clashes with the Persians. That being said, for him war was part of a worldview based on constant opposition: "God is day and night, winter and summer, war and peace, satiety and hunger". [16]

× ×

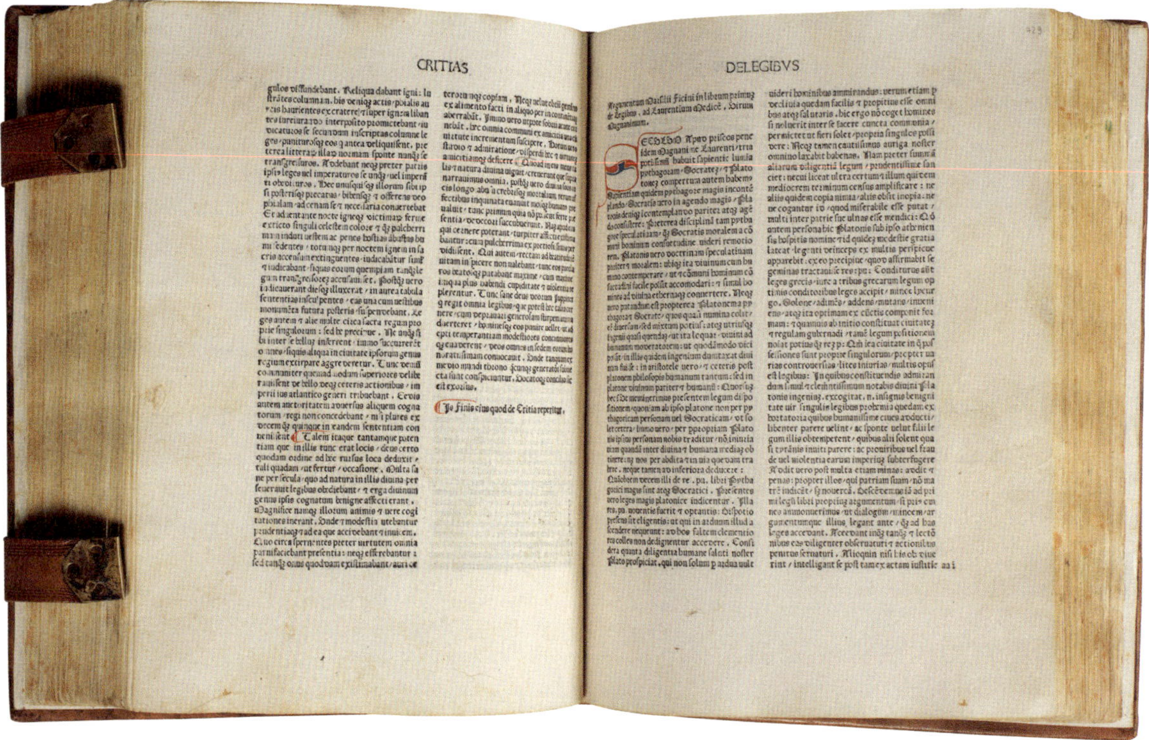

Indeed, in the same fragment, Heraclitus says that the divinity changes, just as fire does when it is mingled with spices, and is named according to the flavour of each. War, the origin of all things, is thus part of a broader concept based on the idea that fire is the most important of the traditional four elements (water/fire/air/earth). It is necessarily accompanied by its opposite, peace, and is part of the fundamental human condition: "There is a harmony in the bending back, as in the case of the bow and the lyre."[17]

War is thus seen as a fact of life; and although he concedes its primacy, nothing Heraclitus says can be construed as praising war.

In the following century, Plato, in a text in which he states that he wants to organize life in human society (*The Laws*), tackles the question of war from the outset. The three old men engaged in dialogue represent the concepts of society espoused in Athens, Sparta and Crete, respectively. In response to the Athenian's first question, about the laws of his state, the Cretan replies that they are ordained with an eye to war; peace being nothing more than a name – given that war, even when informal, is constant – a good constitution must be predicated on war. In reply to which the Athenian points out that risks creating the conditions for a civil war, and states that the goal of the wise legislator is to procure social peace.[18]

Plato, *De Legibus*, in *Opera*, Latin translation and commentary by Marsilio Ficino, Florence, Lorenzo di Alopa, [1484–85], editio princeps. Cologny, Martin Bodmer Foundation, Inc. B 196.

Notes

[1] Thucydides, *The History of the Peloponnesian War*. 2.61. In Richard Crawley's English translation. The text dates from the end of the fifth century BC.

[2] *Ibid.*

[3] Herodotus, *The Histories*, 1.87. In A. D. Godley's English translation (1920). The text dates from the second half of the fifth century BC.

[4] *The Iliad*, translated by Richard Fagles, Penguin Books, London, 1990, v. 13.337–344.

[5] Tyrtaeus, Fr. 10, in M.L. West, *Greek Lyric Poetry*, Oxford University Press, Oxford, 1993, p. 24.

[6] *Ibid.*

[7] Fr. 5; *ibid.*, p. 4.

[8] Fr. 101; *ibid.* This is the fragment of Archilochus that Federico Fellini used for the Greek lesson in his film *Amarcord*.

[9] Fr. 4; *Bacchylides: The Poems and Fragments*, ed. Sir Richard C. Jebb, Cambridge University Press, Cambridge, 1905, p. 62.

[10] Stobaeus, *Anthologium*, 4.14 .1-2; 5-7. *Euripides: Fragments* trans. Christopher Collard and Martin Cropp, Loeb Classical Library, Harvard University Press, Cambridge, 2008.

[11] Aristophanes, *Peace*, Ian Storey, Bloomsbury Academic, London, 2019, v.1127-1129, p. 36.

[12] Herodotus, *op. cit.*, 2.53.

[13] *Iliad, op.cit.*, 5.998 ff. "Deep in the dark pit" is a reference to the Tartarus, the prison of the Titans.

[14] *Iliad, op.cit.*, 9.591–595.

[15] Heraclitus, fr. B53 DK: πόλεμος πάντων μὲν πατήρ ἐστι, πάντων δὲ βασιλεύς, καὶ τοὺς μὲν θεοὺς ἔδειξε τοὺς δὲ ἀνθρώπους (literally "… the father of all things").

[16] Heraclitus, fr. B67 DK: ὁ θεὸς ἡμέρη εὐφρόνη, χειμὼν θέρος, πόλεμος εἰρήνη, κόρος λιμός.

[17] Heraclitus, fr. B51 DK: παλίντροπος ἁρμονίη ὅκωσπερ τόξου καὶ λύρης.

[18] Plato, *The Laws*, 624a–628a.trans. R.G. Bury, Harvard University Press, Cambridge, 1961, 624a–628a.

[19] Plutarch, *On the Fortune or the Virtue of Alexander*, Loeb Classical Library Vol. 4, 1936, 329 A-B.

[20] Euripides, *The Trojan Women*, trans. Gilbert Murray, George Allen, London, 1905, v.95-97, p. 16.

[21] The English translation is from A. T. Willis, "Euripides' Trojan Women: A 20th-Century War Play In Performance", D. Phil. Dissertation, Balliol College Oxford, 2005, p. 117.

That objective was reiterated a century later by the founder of Stoicism, Zeno of Citium. In a book that was especially well known and admired in Antiquity, Zeno lay the groundwork for a global utopia that would mark the end of war in all its forms. Plutarch reflects his point of view:

> Moreover, the much-admired *Republic* of Zeno … may be summed up in this one main principle: that all the inhabitants of this world of ours should not live differentiated by their respective rules of justice into separate cities and communities, but that we should consider all men to be of one community and one polity, and that we should have a common life and an order common to us all, even as a herd that feeds together and shares the pasturage of a common field. This Zeno wrote, giving shape to a dream or, as it were, shadowy picture of a well-ordered and philosophic commonwealth. [19]

The alternative to this utopian vision is crudely affirmed in Euripides' tragedy *The Trojan Women* (415 BC), in which he relentlessly denounces the misfortunes of war. At the end of the prologue, the god Poseidon cries out:

> How are ye blind,
> Ye treaders down of cities, ye that cast
> Temples to desolation, and lay waste
> Tombs, the untrodden sanctuaries where lie
> The ancient dead; yourselves so soon to die! [20]

This same threat continues to hang over humanity, as Jean-Paul Sartre underscored in his adaptation of Euripides' play (*Les Troyennes*, 1965). He makes Poseidon's cry the closing words; on the page, they take the shape of a bomb falling to earth:

> Pallas! Pallas Athena! To work!
> You will all pay now.
> Make war, stupid mortals,
> Ravage the fields and the towns,
> Violate the temples, the graves,
> And torture the defeated:
> It will be the death of you.
> All of you. [21]

× ×

FAKE NEWS: A WEAPON OF MYTH DESTRUCTION

JEAN-PAUL MARTHOZ
UC Louvain

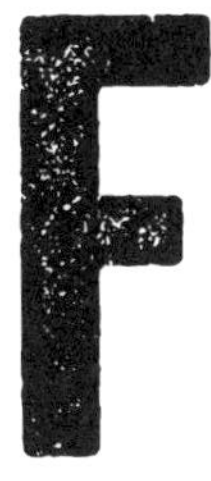ake news, alternative facts, post-truth, conspiracy theories: the terms sound freshly minted, linked as they are to very recent events comprising, in quick succession, Brexit, Donald Trump's election, the yellow vest movement in France and, more generally, mounting populism and extremism, from the Philippines to Brazil. They are brandished by governments voicing their determination to fight the hostile actions of foreign autocrats they accuse of weaponizing the Internet, manipulating social networks and interfering in the internal affairs of their countries.

We've come a long way from the "end of history", the triumph of reason and moderation heralded by the American political scientist Francis Fukuyama after the fall of the Berlin Wall. New fault lines have opened up new fronts. In this battle-scarred landscape, misinformation reaches farther than ever, strikes closer to home and has a breathtakingly immediate impact, thanks to the profound changes in the public sphere wrought by new technologies, digital platforms and social networks, although that isn't the only reason.

False information conceived for the strategic purpose of harming ideological and geopolitical adversaries has emerged against the more general backdrop – at times political (the West's hegemony called into question by new powers), at others economic (globalization), social (rising inequality) or cultural (migration and social diversity) – of growing insecurity and uncertainty, a breeding ground for identity-related tension. It provokes anxiety, because it foreshadows rifts that expose underlying threats to democracy and freedom.

To come to grips with the feeling of things moving far too fast, however, we have to reconsider the phenomenon of fake news from a historical perspective. Misinformation has been a political tool and a weapon of war since time immemorial. Every historical upheaval has been accompanied by monstrous lies, a cynical truth echoed by the authors of the UNESCO Constitution, in 1945, when they wrote in the preamble, a few short months after a conflict stirred in the hate-filled cauldrons of totalitarian ideologies: "since wars begin in the minds of men, it is in the minds of men that the defences of peace must be constructed".

Lies are the common thread running through Barbara Tuchman's masterful work, *The March of Folly: From Troy to Vietnam*. Lies that come in myriad forms, depending on the strategy of misinformation or concealment, but also on the need to find a moral justification and popular backing for policies that are likely to be disputed. In the Middle Ages, Philippe Le Bel, for example, did not hesitate to lie to consolidate his power. To break the Knights Templar, he accused them of the worst crimes of sodomy, idolatry and blasphemy.

State deceit is often conflated with dictatorship and totalitarianism. It is certainly deployed in such despotic regimes. In the Soviet Union, Stalinism saturated society with false information: accusations of treason to execute opponents, blatant fabrications to hide failures or crimes, such as the Great Famine in Ukraine in the early 1930s. Nazism rose on the stepping stones of falsehood, conspiracy theories in particular, asserting that France – the age-old enemy – Jews and Bolsheviks were plotting against the German nation. Joseph Goebbels was shameless about the rules of the game – "When you lie, lie big" on which is exactly what the *Protocols of the Elders of Zion* did. The *Protocols* were a violently anti-Semitic tract fabricated in the early twentieth century by the Tsar's police and exploited by Nazism to foment hatred and support for the policy to exterminate the Jews.

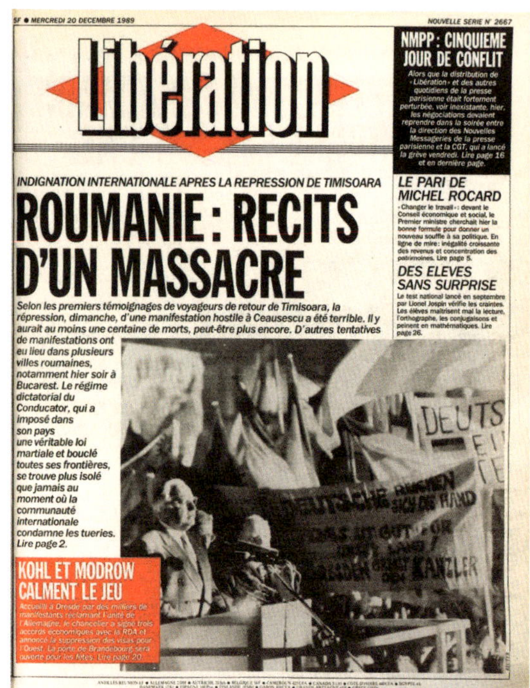

During the Cold War, the Kremlin launched numerous disinformation campaigns against the United States. These "active measures", as the KGB called them, were intended, for example, to convince international opinion that Martin Luther King's assassination had been planned in the corridors of power in Washington, or that the AIDS virus was the product of an American military lab. Relayed by political commissaries eager to mislead and by fellow travellers just as eager to be misled, these "big lies" poisoned, for decades, the wells of information from which one segment of global opinion drank.

Democracies also lie, at the risk for their governments that their falsehoods will eventually come back to haunt them when the current shifts. During the Great War, in the United Kingdom and in France, fake news flirted with censorship, ultimately and famously brainwashing the public with atrocity propaganda. In the words of Philip Gibbs, correspondent for the *Daily Telegraph*, "The job was to hide the truth, not from the enemy, but from the nation."

During the Second World War, democracies were more careful with the truth. "If there's a disaster, we announce it before the Germans claim victory," said one BBC official. "That way, when the tide turns and we start winning, we'll be believed." That pledge was only partially honoured, however, for the military censors were ever watchful, "blue pencil" at the ready, and bits of disinformation were released in staggered fashion to mislead the Germans, in particular about the place and date of the Allied landings in continental Europe.

× ×

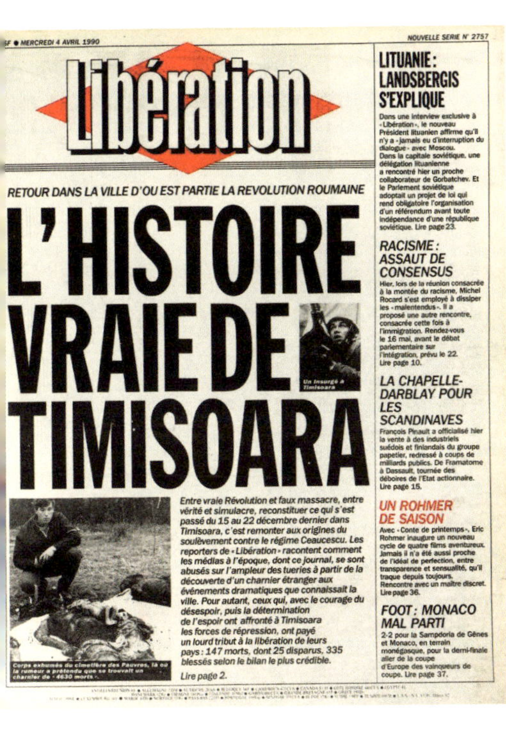

Front page of the French daily *Libération*, 20 December 1989 and 4 April 1990.

Later, to defend the "free world", the United States invented communist plots wherever its power was contested by nationalists, as in the case of Mohammad Mossadegh in Iran (1953) and Jacobo Arbenz Guzman in Guatemala (1954). Both were overthrown with the help of the CIA and its "psyops" (psychological operations, ingenuously renamed "military information support operations" in 2010).

The Vietnam War was a tissue of lies, to the point that war correspondents in Saigon referred to official press briefings as the "Five O'Clock Follies", "the longest-playing tragicomedy in Southeast Asia's theater of the absurd", according to Associated Press Bureau Chief Richard Pyle. As Hannah Arendt bitterly noted in her essay, *Lying in Politics,* "The … policy of lying was hardly ever aimed at the enemy but chiefly if not exclusively destined for domestic consumption, for propaganda at home and especially for the purpose of deceiving Congress."

The fall of the Wall did not change anything. In Romania, the 1989 uprising against Ceausescu went hand in hand with one of the most outrageous fabrications in history. Romanian secret service agents hostile to the Tyrant of the Carpathians "invented" the existence of a mass grave in Timisoara. Journalists who visited the "martyred" town's morgue said they "saw nothing", yet the fabrication, peddled by careless media, spread like wildfire around the world.

Later, during the two Gulf Wars, misinformation was part of the American arsenal. In 1990, the United States claimed that the Iraqis had removed the incubators from a Kuwaiti maternity clinic. In 2003, it claimed that Saddam Hussein had a huge stockpile of weapons of mass destruction. Both claims were false, but they were relayed by a largely credulous – when not downright slavish – press.

In the past few years, attention has focused on more sophisticated methods of misinformation. In this most recent episode, suspicion is centred on Russia, which stands accused not just of fibbing but rather of attacking the very architecture of the global information system. In Russian army doctrine, information war is everything. Concocted by intelligence services, it is waged on platforms offering some degree of "deniability", be they troll factories, "citizen-run" alternative fact sites or state media simulating newsworthiness the way ketchup claims to be a vegetable. The aim is to create confusion, sow doubt and erode trust in the political or media institutions that are the backbone of democracy.

Donald Trump's America is no exception. The occupant of the White House rattles the expression "fake news" to attack media that are critical of him and to mask the stupefying number of untruths, approximations and lies in his Twitter feed. But he is only one element in a much larger toxic environment that is grounded in a populist webosphere where emotions and "alternative facts" – to quote the already legendary term coined by his adviser Kellyanne Conway, in 2017 – reign supreme.

The case of the United States reminds us that misinformation falls on especially fertile ground in polarized societies, with groups of people hunkered down in their ideological silos. For decades, General Franco's partisans persuaded themselves that the Basque town of Guernica was demolished by the "Reds", whereas it had in fact been destroyed in an air raid led by Nazi Germany's Condor Legion and Mussolini's Legionary Air Force. Until the late 1980s, the Kremlin stubbornly blamed the Nazis for the Katyn massacre, near Smolensk (Russia), whereas it was the Soviet political police that had executed nearly 20,000 Polish army officers and members of the intelligentsia in the spring of 1940.

For democracies, spreading misinformation is not without risk. As the "dissident" American journalist I.F. Stone put it, "All governments lie, but disaster lies in wait for countries whose officials smoke the same hashish they give out." Thus, during the Great War, the very real atrocities committed by German troops against Belgian civilians were exploited for propaganda purposes by the Allied democracies, in particular to convince the United States, which remained neutral until 1917, to enter the war against "Prussian savagery". After the Armistice, however, some of the most horrific stories were called into doubt or qualified, and public opinion became deeply mistrustful – to such an extent that, when information started circulating about Nazi barbarity, the sceptics and cynics were able to invoke "the rubbish about German atrocities during the Great War" to mask their complicity or justify their failure to act.

Today, fake news carries unprecedented weight, not only because of its ability to go viral, but also because of the surveillance, profiling and targeting techniques used in this age of big data, as revealed by the Cambridge Analytica affair during the 2016 American elections. Fake news is also alarming because, as it appeals to entire swathes of public opinion, it expresses the defeat of the thinking and discernment on which democracy is supposedly predicated. "Post-truth and the rise in populism go hand in hand", Alexis Brocas and Aurélie Marcireau warn in *Le Nouveau Magazine Littéraire*.

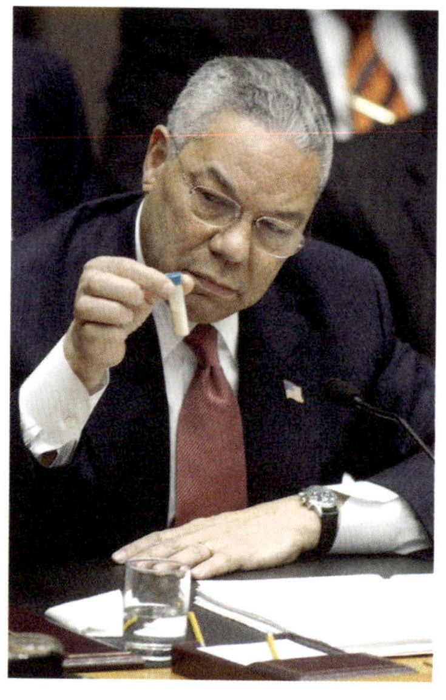

Secretary of State Colin Powell, appearing before the United Nations Security Council on 5 February 2003, holds up a vial of anthrax as proof of Iraq's continued defiance of Security Council Resolution 1441 as well as its previous resolutions.

Can we stem the tide? Worldwide, governments are trying to inoculate themselves against fake news – although in dictatorships the vaccines they use tend to be directed at real but troublesome facts. Some governments, as in France and Germany, are adopting legislation targeting "poorly maintained" digital platforms that allow hateful or misleading posts. Serious media engage in endless fact-checking exercises, and everyone is talking about media education, the new Holy Grail of truthful information. We'll be tilting at windmills, however, if we attempt to neutralize fake news without taking account of influences outside the specific sphere of information, in the "moral atmosphere of a time", as Stefan Zweig wrote in *The World of Yesterday*, shortly before taking his own life. At certain key moments, misinformation is not an exception, a hiccup in democracy. It is a sign of, and exacerbates, the collapse of values and social dislocation. Its encroachment on the public sphere must therefore be viewed with alarm, as history has taught us that it is the harbinger of tragedies, bloodshed and pogroms.

"A people ... deprived ... of its capacity to think and to judge ... with such a people you can then do what you please", Hannah Arendt warned. Shortly after publishing his dystopian novel, *1984*, George Orwell exhorted: "The moral to be drawn from this dangerous nightmare situation is a simple one: Don't let it happen. It depends on you."

WAR AND PEACE IN POSTERS

JEAN-CHARLES GIROUD
Bibliothèque de Genève, Geneva
and Centre d'iconographie genevoise

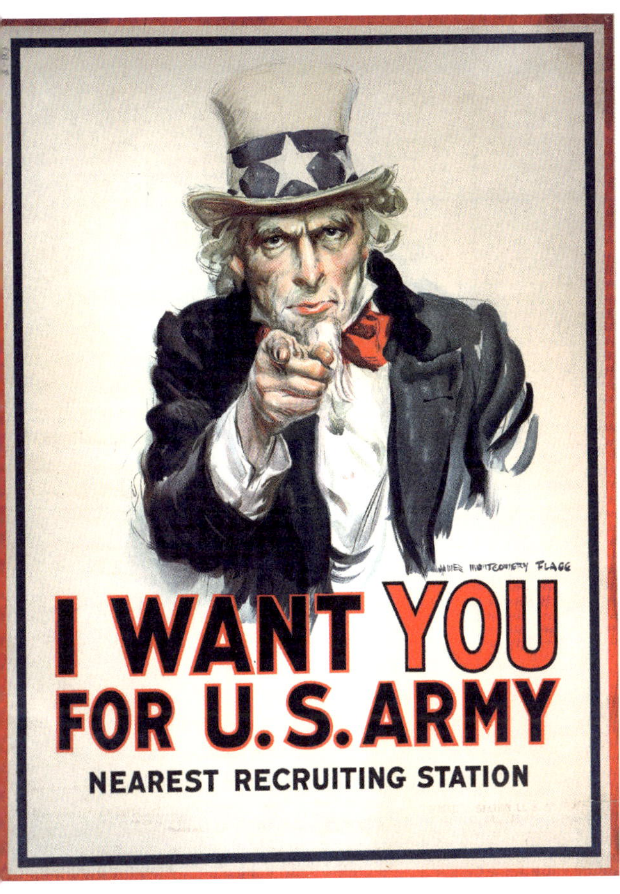

I Want You for U.S. Army, recruitment poster featuring the figure of Uncle Sam, by James Montgomery Flagg, 1917.

The purpose of a poster is to inform and influence, and different kinds of posters do more or less of each. When it comes to propaganda – the vast category to which posters about war and peace belong – influencing takes precedence over informing. To get its message across fast, a good poster has to make its meaning as simple as possible. According to common morality, one should mobilize against war and for peace. To mobilize for war, therefore, a propaganda poster must switch these values around and make war seem both desirable and just. It achieves this by deploying instinctive – even primitive – devices to undermine reason. Mobilizing against peace involves a different approach: while stressing that the cause of peace is a noble one, the poster must appropriate it discreetly and press it into service on the side of war. Posters of this kind thus resonate at the very foundations of a society. In propaganda, the stakes are high; to understand these posters, therefore, it is crucial to identify who is producing them and what their intentions are.

A war of images

The use of posters in support of war goes far back in history. Under the Ancien Régime they were the sole preserve of the authorities, who exercized this power by posting official placards in specially reserved spaces in well-frequented areas. These large, text-only sheets publicized the government's decisions, its wars and sometimes its peace treaties. It was in First World War that the war poster truly came into its own. In most of the belligerent countries, they were at their most compelling in 1914. Their impact amplified tenfold by images, they soon demonstrated their appalling effectiveness in announcing and advocating for war. The most famous posters date from this period: in the first year of the war, the British government called for volunteers with a recruiting poster that featured the minister for war, Lord Kitchener (1850–1916), pointing a finger at the viewer, alongside the message "Britons, [Lord Kitchener] wants you". Never before had a poster taken such a direct, commanding tone. Its fame spread, and it inspired other warring nations, including Italy and the United States, where the 1917 poster of Uncle Sam saying

"I Want You for U.S. Army", by James Montgomery Flagg (1877–1960), went on to become an enduring icon.

Making up an entire chapter in the world history of poster art, these thousands of designs were a constant presence during the war. In France and Germany, they were produced mainly by the state, and were displayed in prominent places, such as banks and organizations that backed the war. The powers that be spoke with one voice. For artists, this was an opportunity both to demonstrate their patriotism and to underline the need for everyone to rally to the cause. These spectacular posters reflect a propaganda effort on a scale never before seen or experienced in modern societies. At times, they even came to be regarded as a weapon in themselves.

Political propaganda posters

That these posters would have a lasting influence became evident immediately after the war, as exemplified by the images produced in the Weimar Republic, Hungary and France, among others. In Switzerland, they inspired a new wave of illustrated political posters, which adopted the same combative tone. From now on, all (or nearly all) wars would come with their quota of propaganda posters, but also, it must be stressed, posters condemning war, produced by the opposition and often illegally posted in public spaces.

The arrival to power of the Bolshevik regime in Russia, in 1917, ushered in a new category of propaganda posters. This time it was about defending not a country, but a political party. Bolshevik posters emerged in – and were strongly influenced by – a situation of unprecedented violence. In their avant-garde creations, artists frequently (although not invariably) depicted the new struggle against the enemies of the people. These warlike scenes often drew on the iconographic vocabulary of monstrousness (octopuses, rats, dragons or snakes) perfected during the Great War. In Russia, this movement survived in various forms until the end of the Soviet regime, in 1990. As "socialist realism" became the norm, the style changed; later posters feature a greater diversity of subjects, and peace makes a frequent appearance.

This movement spread to countries within the Soviet sphere of influence, starting in Europe, all of which adopted its codes and style. As of the 1950s, Maoist China offered a striking contrast between propaganda posters celebrating the country's happiness under the Party's leadership and more warlike images depicting the ongoing fight to the death against bourgeois forces. This same pattern appears in Vietnam, in constant reminders of the victory of 1975 and the conflict with China over disputed islands. In Cuba, this once highly original art form is dying out, while in North Korea it is enjoying its hour of glory, in the form of particularly hostile attacks against enemies of the state. All these posters are linked to authoritarian political regimes with a penchant for pointing the finger publicly at their enemies. They are also a way of reminding citizens of who is in charge, propaganda being intended primarily for internal consumption.

The ambiguity of peace posters

It is usually easy enough to work out who is behind pro-war posters and what their message is, but those calling for peace (which are far fewer in number) can sometimes conceal ulterior motives. To ascertain their true meaning and purpose (often far from peaceable), one needs to find out who funded them. In the aftermath of a war, peace posters may appear in the victorious country, as was the case after the First World War with French loan posters. Also in France, the peace movement experienced a revival during the interwar period. Among the most striking images from that time are the peace posters designed by Jean Carlu (1900–97) between 1932 and 1937. In 1932, under the umbrella of the Office for Peace Propaganda, of which he was the driving force, Carlu created his most famous poster, *For the Disarmament of Nations*. Using photomontage, the poster denounced the threat of war and the rise of Nazism. Although Carlu himself was a leftist, he intended his poster to be apolitical. The ambiguity of his position, however, and the poster's similarity to Soviet designs, caused so much confusion that it sparked a political dispute between the right and the left, thus blurring his message. Carlu's adversaries were quick to point out this doublespeak. Undeterred by the controversy, Carlu continued to design posters every bit as passionate as this one.

Similarly, between 1947 and 1960, against the political backdrop of the Cold War, the peace posters of André Fougeron (1913–98), Pablo Picasso (1881–1973) and Hans Erni (1909–2015) were regarded by the left as prophetic and by the right as a veil for rampant Soviet militarism. In 1950, *The Dove that Goes BOOM* parodied Picasso's 1949 poster for the World Congress of Partisans for Peace, in which his famous dove of peace made its first appearance. Intended to mock the doublespeak of the USSR, this poster was produced by Peace and Liberty, an organization founded by Jean-Paul David (1912–2007), and was quietly subsidized by the United States. Peace was thus a paradoxical issue during the

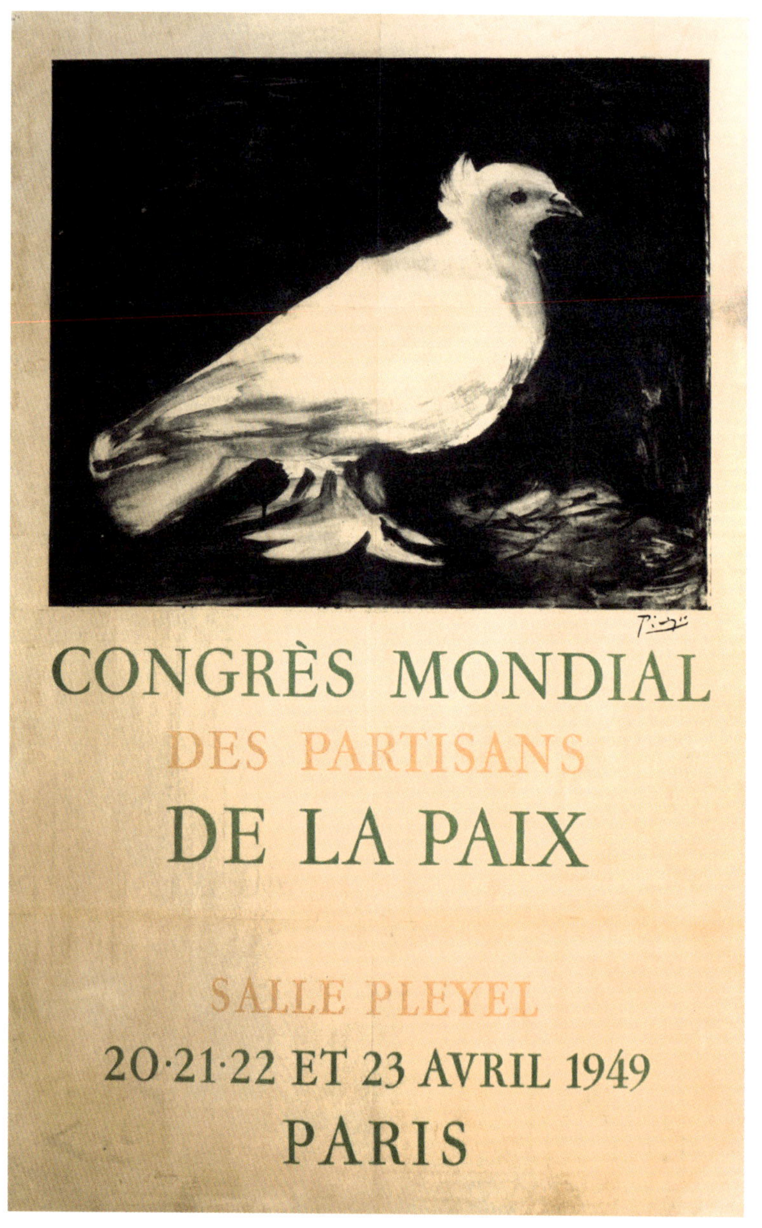

Cold War. In the wake of the 1950 Stockholm Appeal for nuclear disar-mament, Swiss artist Hans Erni designed one of the most significant social posters of the twentieth century, *Atomkrieg Nein (No to Nuclear War),* for the Swiss Peace Movement, to coincide with the 1954 Geneva Accords on Indochina. Its purpose was to ensure a frosty reception for the American delegation (the United States stood accused of consider-ing the use of the atom bomb in Indochina), in order to weaken its position and strengthen that of the Democratic Republic of Vietnam, then under Soviet influence. Erni's poster outraged the right and was

Pablo Picasso's poster
for the first World Congress
of the Defenders of Peace, 1949.
Private collection.

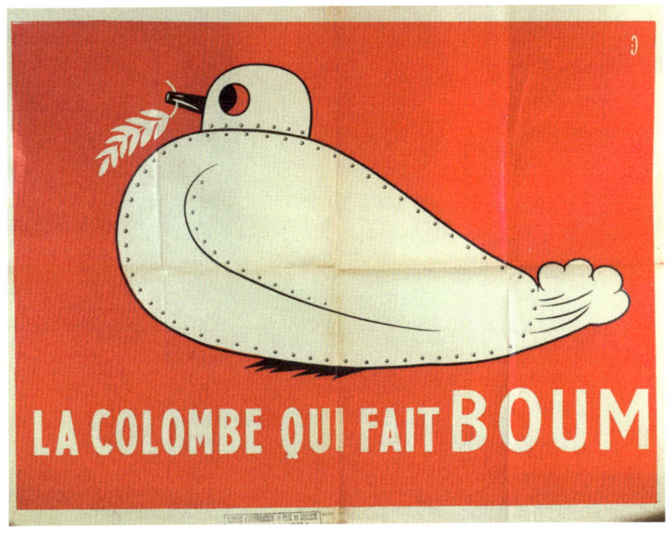

The dove that goes BOOM,
first poster published by
the "Peace and Liberty" movement,
1952–53, colour lithograph.
Private collection.

eventually banned, while on the left it bolstered the arguments for peace. The peace posters of this era thus reveal the constant presence of the frontline in public discourse at that time.

One of the greatest eras for peace posters began in the 1960s, in California, where young people were protesting against nuclear weapons and the war in Vietnam. Hippies were the heart and soul of the "Peace and Love" movement, and psychedelic posters celebrated these values, in an atmosphere fuelled by drugs and rock 'n' roll. These peace posters, proudly springing from the margins of society, had a worldwide impact. In many countries, posters against the Vietnam War – in particular the US military intervention – abounded. Official, large-format and colourful in communist countries, small, monochrome, cheap and often fly-posted in the West, they showed that American pacifism did not travel well across the Atlantic. During the conflicts that raged between 1960 and 1970, unauthorized posters in Western Europe systematically supported anti-imperialism and the left, displaying a fighting spirit, to say the least, on the question of Indochina first, and then of Chile, Greece, Spain, Iran and the Middle East, where they invariably championed the Palestinian cause against Israel.

UN and ICRC posters

Two major international organizations, the UN and the ICRC, have produced large numbers of posters on war and peace. Their output is unwaveringly consistent with their values and comes across as straightforward, devoid of any desire to manipulate, and conveying ideals shared by people the world over.

In Red Cross posters – the sheer number and variety of which is bewildering – peace is not a subject in itself, although it is often implicit. War, on the other hand, features regularly. It is often shown as the backdrop to the work the Red Cross is, or should be, doing. Unlike the posters described above, they make no moral judgement about war, treating it merely as a fact of life that justifies the work of the Red Cross. They are unusually sensitive, and display great political shrewdness. In 1922, for example, a fund-raising poster by Jules Courvoisier for the Swiss Red Cross depicts war merely as a dark, tragic background, which can be recognized as Geneva, thus precluding more problematic associations. Likewise, the posters designed in 1943 by Otto Baumberger (1889–1962) for distribution in Switzerland (the ICRC was present on all fronts) show utterly unidentifiable scenes of war.

Since their founding, the UN and its agencies have been actively promoting peace through the medium of posters. Many of these are produced for celebrations such as United Nations Day, on 24 October. On such occasions, a poster depicting the organization's main objectives is often distributed all over the world, in many languages. Their iconography is typical of the subject: a dove, Planet Earth, an outstretched hand, flags fluttering in the breeze. The International Day of Peace was celebrated for the first time in 1982, prompting several remarkably successful international poster competitions and giving graphic artists from a wide variety of backgrounds a chance to show what they could do. These contests offer a great opportunity to design original posters, often focusing on the image of the dove. In a different context, in 2003, the Italian graphic artist Armando Milani designed a poster so original, yet so breathtakingly simple and ingenious, that it has become an icon in its own right (*War Peace. United Nations: Translating War into Peace*).

Posters and propaganda

These countless images may seem derisory when measured against the serious issues they illustrate. One may also wonder how effective they are. More than most, they presuppose a receptive viewer, one who is uncritical when presented with simplistic assertions or exaggerations verging on the grotesque. Although they may seem over the top, their cumulative ability to influence people should not be underestimated. They take on their full significance only in the broader context of propaganda that activates all the levers in a society: the media, schools, political parties and businesses. That is when they come into their own: simplifying complex issues, reducing them to slogans that echo far and wide and, in this way, playing their part in a general onslaught whose impact is nothing short of formidable.

Translating War into Peace,
2003, poster, designed by Armando Milani
for the United Nations, New York.

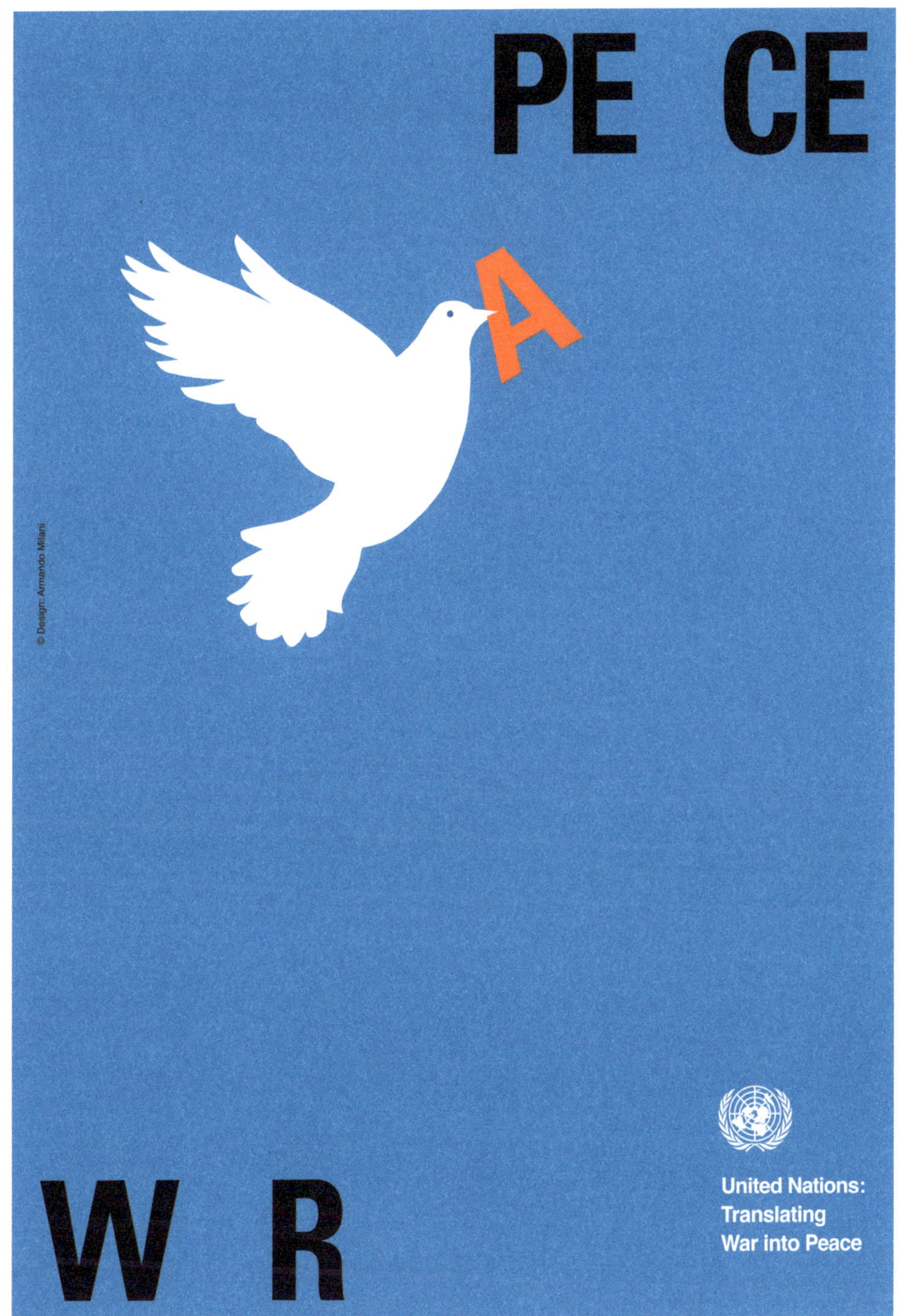
PE CE
A
W R
United Nations:
Translating
War into Peace
© Design: Armando Milani

**When all three Abrahamic faiths call for a just war,
and philosophers justify or, conversely, attempt to limit war.**

1

Torah, Oxford, Nathan Forster, 1750, unpunctuated edition

Cologny, Martin Bodmer Foundation

The Hebrew Torah, the oldest and most foundational of the Abrahamic texts, comprising the law of Moses (Genesis, Exodus, Leviticus, Numbers and Deuteronomy), has provided a powerful blueprint for the way human beings have dealt with war ever since. Characteristically, the Hebrew God was both male and warlike: "The Lord is a man of war" (Ex. 15:3). Yet even in this early age, war, in the Jewish tradition, could not be conducted without restraint. For one, it could not begin abruptly: "When you march up to attack a city, make its people an offer of peace." (Deut. 20: 10) The Torah's legal restrictions on war prefigured the modern idea of *jus ad bellum* (the conditions under which states may lawfully resort to the use of armed force). Similarly, war was no excuse to exempt oneself from the laws of humanity, what today we call *jus in bello:* laws regulating conduct during warfare. Women and children (the "non-combatants" of ancient times) were to be spared: "thou shalt smite every male thereof with the edge of the sword, but the women and the little ones ... shalt thou take ... unto thyself" (Deut. 20:13–14).

Of special relevance to us today is the absolute prohibition against sexual enslavement and violence against women: "When you go to war against your enemies… and you notice among the captives a beautiful woman… thou shalt not sell her at all for money, thou shalt not deal with her as a slave" (Deut. 21: 10–14). The decision to award the 2018 Nobel Peace Prize to Nadia Murad, a courageous young Yazidi woman who was sexually enslaved by ISIS, stands as a stark reminder of the enduring relevance of one of the world's oldest legal and religious codes.

G. B.-N.

* *

2

Bible in German, with illustrations by Gustave Doré, Stuttgart, Eduard Hallberger, 1867

Cologny, Martin Bodmer Foundation

Images of war in the Christian Bible (the New Testament) are associated primarily with Jesus' disciples, particularly the Epistles of Paul and Timothy. Jesus, for one, certainly did not shy away from the idea of armed conflict. In Luke 11:21, Jesus states: "When a strong man, fully armed, guards his castle, his property is safe." His most famous warlike exhortation radically challenges peace: "I did not come to bring peace to the earth; I did not come to bring peace but a sword." (Matt. 10:34) Nevertheless, when compared with the combativeness of Moses in the Jewish Torah, or the warring ethos of Muhammad in the Quran, Jesus comes across as the least belligerent, the most pacific, of the three founding fathers of the Abrahamic religions. With St Paul, Christianity took a partial step back from the peaceful message of Jesus, introducing theological arguments for war: "be afraid, for he does not bear the sword in vain. For he is the servant of God, an avenger who carries out God's wrath on the wrongdoer." (Rom. 13:4) The image of the soldier became a central theme of Christianity, as in Timothy's "good soldier of Christ Jesus" (2 Tim. 2:3). With terrible historical consequences: from the Crusades to the conquest of Latin America by Cortés and Pizarro, from the American slave trade to colonialism, wars fought in the name of the cross have caused unfathomable human suffering.   **G. B.-N.**

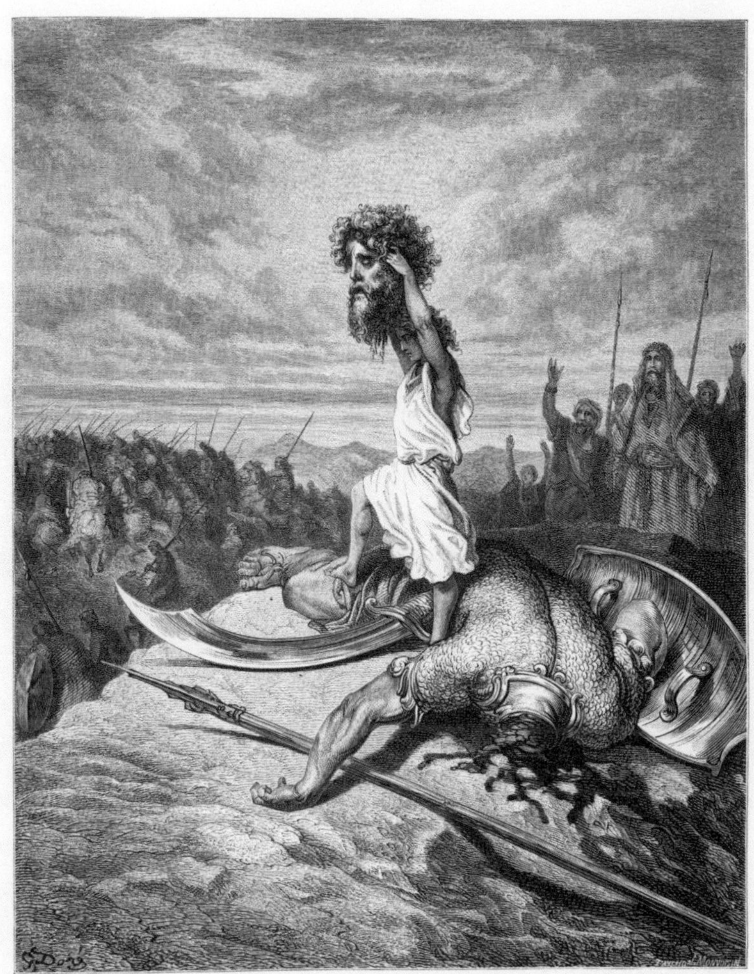

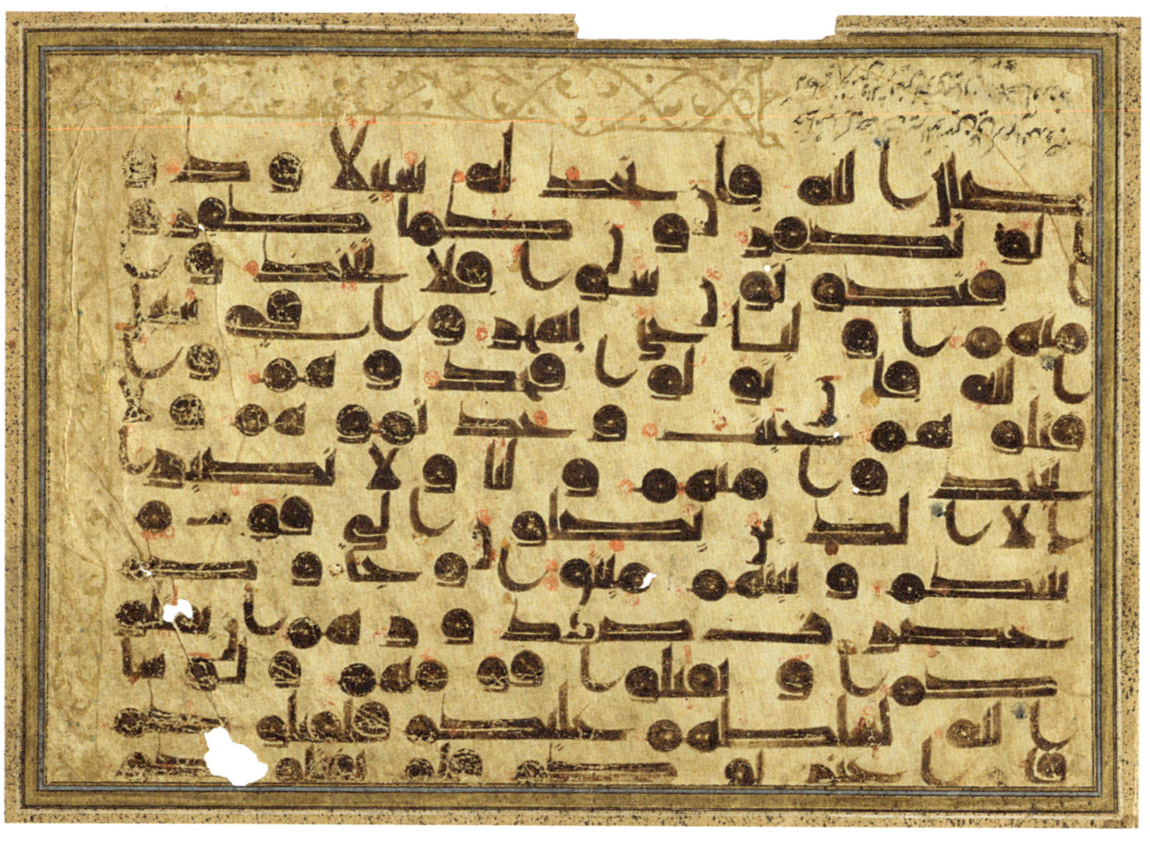

3
Quran, Sura 62, 6–10 and 63, 4–8, 8th–9th century, page in Kufi script

Cologny, Martin Bodmer Foundation, CB 539

As with the other Abrahamic faiths, the legitimation of war was intrinsic to the worldview of Islam. The unification of religion and state, faith and political power under a single contemporaneous ruler (*Amir al-Mu'minin*) required that the Islamic state be built on solid legal foundations. The ultimate objective of Islam was to unite the entire world under God's word, as expressed through his Prophet in the Quran. *Jihad* (and the verb *jahada*) denotes the exertion of believers in the service of God's word, their efforts to advance the faith.

In the Prophet's early Quranic suras from Mecca, *jihad* is associated with the internal, psychological struggle for control of one's own mind: "Those who exert themselves (*jahada*) do so for their own benefit." (Quran 29: 5-6) Only in the later suras from Medina does the word acquire its more bellicose association with war and strife: "Have faith in God and His Messenger and struggle (*jihad*, wage war) for his cause." (Quran 61: 11) Muslim scholars later divided the various meanings of *jihad* into four categories: *jihad* of the heart, *jihad* of the tongue, *jihad* of the hands and, last only, *jihad* of the sword. Due to Islam's preoccupation with the law, *jihad* of the sword became inseparable from the

Islamic law of nations: war could be fought only if certain legal requirements were met, a concept similar to the Roman *bellum justum*.   **G. B.-N.**

4
Thomas Aquinas
(1224/25–1274)

Summa Theologica,
Latin manuscript on parchment,
Paris, *c.* 1280

Cologny, Martin Bodmer Foundation, CB 161

The writings of St Thomas Aquinas stand at the pinnacle of the 1,300-year-long elaboration of the just war doctrine (*bellum justum*). First formulated by Cicero in his *De officiis* (first century BC), this Roman legal concept was formally incorporated into Christianity in the fifth century AD by Augustine, who directly quoted Cicero in his *City of God* (xix, 21). Aquinas' full and comprehensive rendition in the *Summa Theologica* (1265–74) brought the just war doctrine to its most perfect textual climax.

Aquinas systematically defined the preconditions for a just war, setting down the three criteria that justified conflict on legal, ethical and moral grounds: it had to be declared by a recognized ruler (not bandits or pirates); be pursued for a just cause (*justa causa*), primarily in defence of a commonwealth; and be motivated by legally and morally sound intentions (not the sudden rage or whim of rulers). Remarkably, this allowed for the uprising of oppressed peoples against their rulers: "Tyrannical government is unjust because it is directed not to the common good, but to the private good of the ruler." (*Summa...* 2, li. qu. 42) Much of contemporary legal thinking on the crime of aggression (first prosecuted in Nuremberg in 1945–46), the legitimacy of anti-colonial insurgencies for self-determination, and even the questionable justification of nuclear weapons as a deterrent, all draw from St Thomas' ideas. **G. B.-N.**

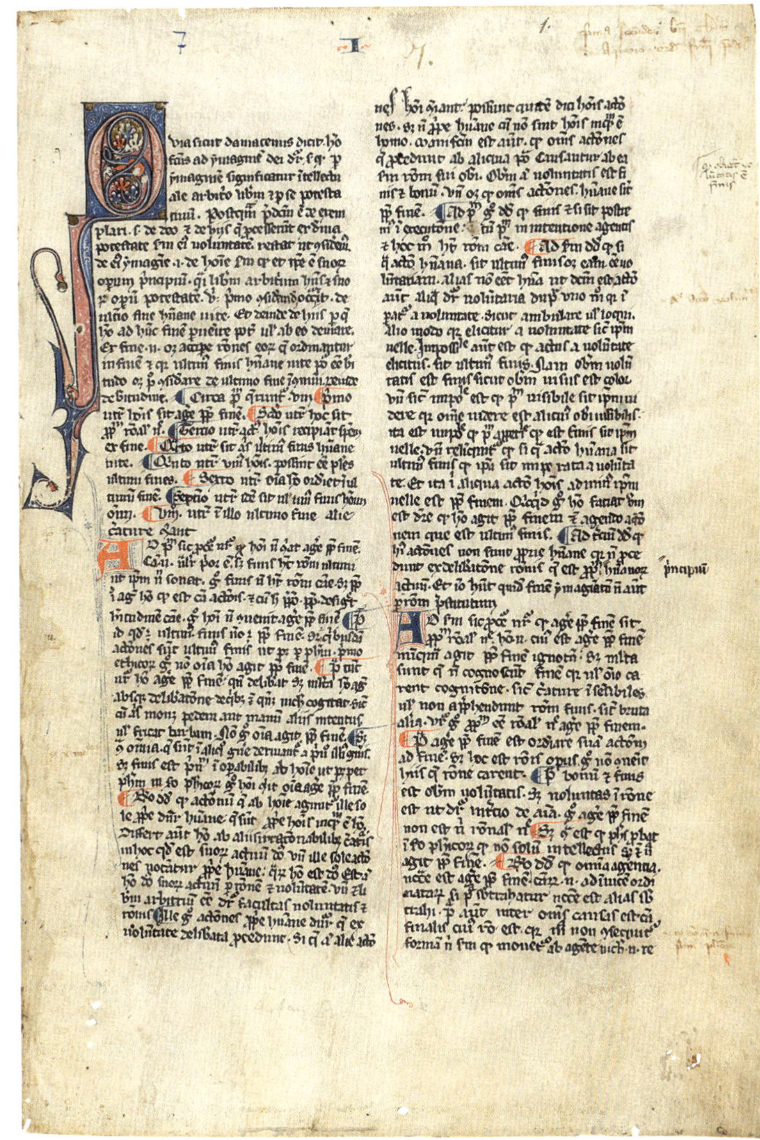

Martin Luther (1483–1546)
Von wetlicher Obrigkeit [Semlar Authority], Bonn, 1523, first edition

Cologny, Martin Bodmer Foundation

Few eras in European history were as volatile as the Protestant Reformation, which "officially" began in 1517, when Martin Luther aired his *Ninety-five Theses* against the corruption of the Catholic Church. With no faith in Rome's willingness to undertake meaningful reform, Luther immediately sided with the nobility in its opposition to the temporal power of the pope, thus securing its political support. In 1523, Luther published *Secular Authority*, the main argument of which was that political stability could best be achieved through submission and obedience to rulers, provided they were just. Borrowing from Augustine's *City of God*, and Jesus' own words, "render unto Caesar" (Math. 22:21), Luther's doctrine rested on the separation of the two estates of Christianity, the spiritual and the secular.

Crucially, in *Secular Authority*, Luther supported a sovereign's right to wage war against internal dissent – to target his own citizens, in other words: "We must firmly establish secular law and the sword, that no man doubt it is in the world by God's will and ordinance." This advice seemed vital at the time when Luther was writing, which coincided with the outbreak of the German Peasants' War (1524–25). Given the Reformation's potential for social revolution, all civil strife had to be forcefully quelled. Luther therefore called upon the nobles to "kill rebel peasants like mad dogs". Given that Lutheranism became the state religion of Prussia, which in turn would come to control much of Germany, the willingness of the people to submit to an autocratic regime, and to remain silent as the state targeted its own citizens, would have dire historical consequences.

G. B.-N.

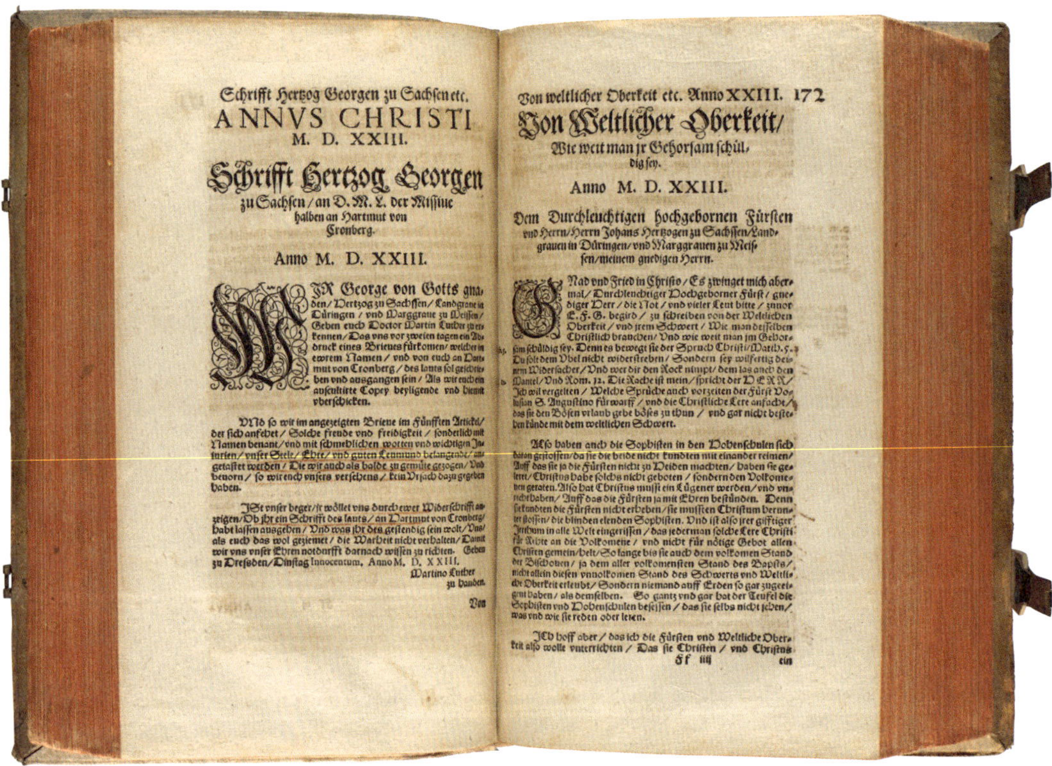

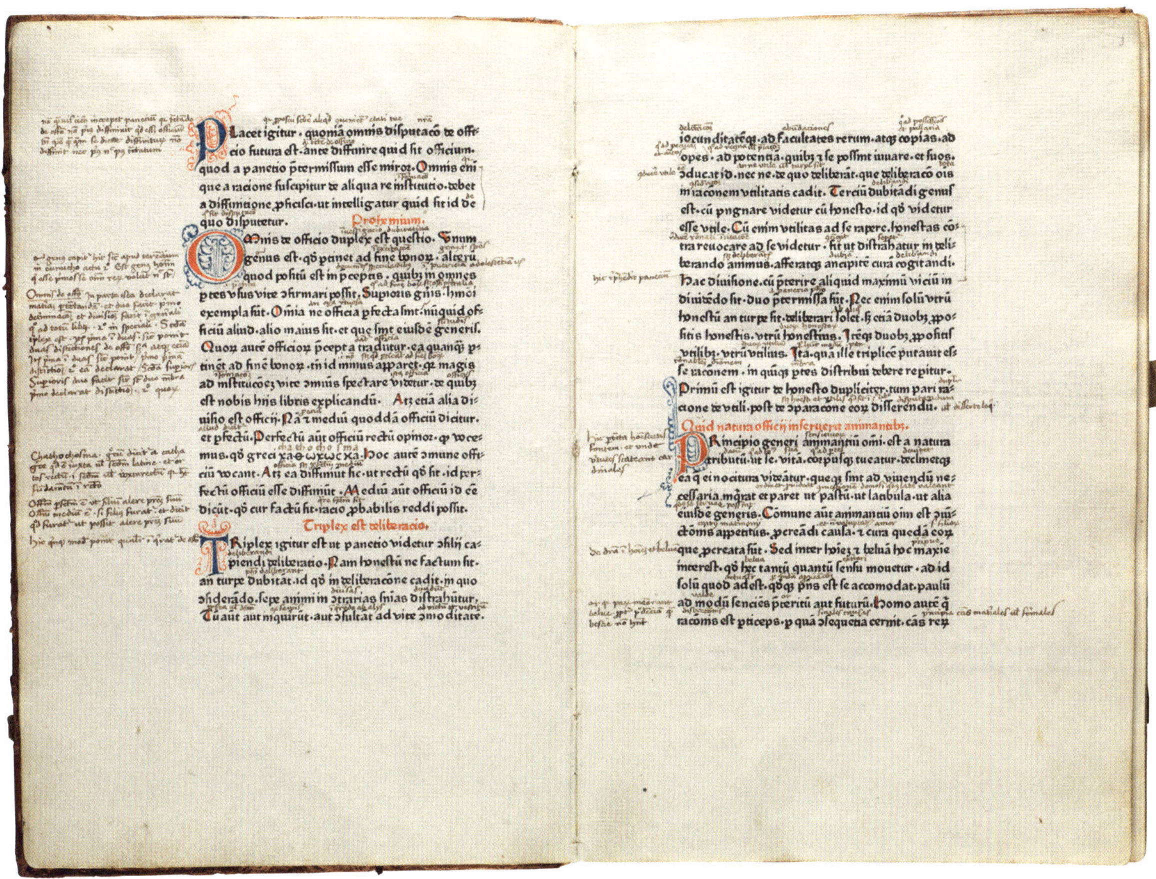

6
Marcus Tullius Cicero
(106-43 BC)

De Officiis, [Mayence], Johann Fust and Peter Schöffer, 1467, editio princeps

Cologny, Martin Bodmer Foundation, Inc. Bodmer 73

Few historical figures have influenced our image of the Roman Republic, its statesmanship and its statecraft more than Marcus Tullius Cicero (106–43 BC). The speeches of this greatest of Roman orators, the "Lion of the Senate", have profoundly shaped notions of republicanism for well over two millennia. For Cicero, the ultimate justification for war was to secure peace: "Wars then are indeed to be waged for this reason, that without wrong, life may be lived in peace." (*De officiis*, I, ii. 34–35) Treaties were inviolable. The spreading of "salt on Carthage" to ensure its permanent devastation was justified by the fact that the Carthaginians were "breakers of treaties" (*De officiis*, I, xii, 38). Yet at the end of the day, "What we want is peace", since often "from victory there will come many evils" (*Letters to Atticus*, vii, 5). Cicero's idealized exposition of Rome's tradition of just war (*bellum justum*) still forms the bedrock of our global code of conduct in international affairs today. The Roman senate is reminiscent of the United Nations in New York; when the UN Security Council debates intervention under Chapter VII of the UN Charter, it is executing Ciceronian ideals. When the Council is paralyzed, as permanent members cast that most Latin of words, *veto*, it is following the procedures of the Roman senate. For Cicero, debate was key. Caesar's decision to "go it alone" in the first century, or the United States' impulse to do so in the twenty-first, threaten to destroy entire systems of governance and, more often than not, trigger further war and suffering.

G. B.-N.

The writings of Niccolò Machiavelli, widely considered the father of modern political thought, ranged from the naked realpolitik of what *is*, in *The Prince*, to the morally preferable what *ought* to be, in *The Discourses*. In *The Art of War* (*Dell'arte della Guerra*), this great precursor of modernity presciently foretold the rise of national armies. Medieval and early-modern armies often depended on foreign mercenaries. The problem with these soldiers-for-hire was their corruption and tendency to flout the rules of war, especially with regard to civilians and non-combatants: "military institutions have become completely corrupt and far removed from the ancient ways", Machiavelli observed in the preface to *The Art of War*. This drawback became acute when rulers failed to pay mercenaries' salaries. Under such circumstances, they would often seize what they felt they were owed directly from their employer's subjects, including through hostage-taking and ransom. Macchiavelli's solution was to return to the ways of ancient Rome by restoring national armies. His premise – that an army of conscripts would be more disciplined than an army of mercenaries – proved largely correct. Yet a disciplined national army can become even more brutal than a mercenary one, if its leadership is bent on obliterating civilians. The destruction of Warsaw by the Nazi Wehrmacht and razing of Manila by the Japanese in 1945 painfully demonstrate this point. **G. B.-N.**

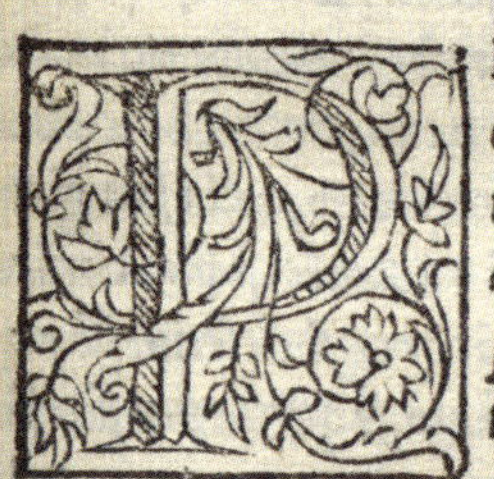

LIBRO PRIMO DELL'ARTE DELLA
guerra di Niccolo Machiauegli cittadino et
Segretario Fiorentino à Lorenzo di
Filippo Strozzi Patritio
Fiorenti
no.

4

PERCHE IO CREDO che si possa lodare dopo la mor-te ogni huomo sança carico, sendo mancata ogni cagione, & sospetto di adulatione, non dubiterò di lodare Cosimo Rucellai nostro. Il nome del quale non sia mai ricordato da me sança lagrime. Hauèdo conosciute in lui qlle parti, le quali in uno buono amico dagli amici, in uno cittadino dalla sua patria si possono disiderare. Perche io nõ so quale cosa si fusse táto sua, nõ eccettuando nõ ch'altro l'anima, che p gli amici uolētieri dal lui nõ fusse stata spesa. Nõ so quale impresa lo hauesse sbigottito, doue qllo hauesse conosciuto il bene della sua patria. Et io confesso liberamente non hauere riscontro tra tanti huomini, che io ho conosciuti & pratichi, buomo nel quale fusse il piu acceso animo alle cose grandi & magnifiche. Ne si dolse con gli amici d'altro nella sua morte, se non di essere nato per morire giouane dentro alle sue case, & inhonorato, sança hauere potuto, secondo l'animo suo, giouare ad alcuno. Perche sapea che di lui non si poteua parlare altro

a iiij

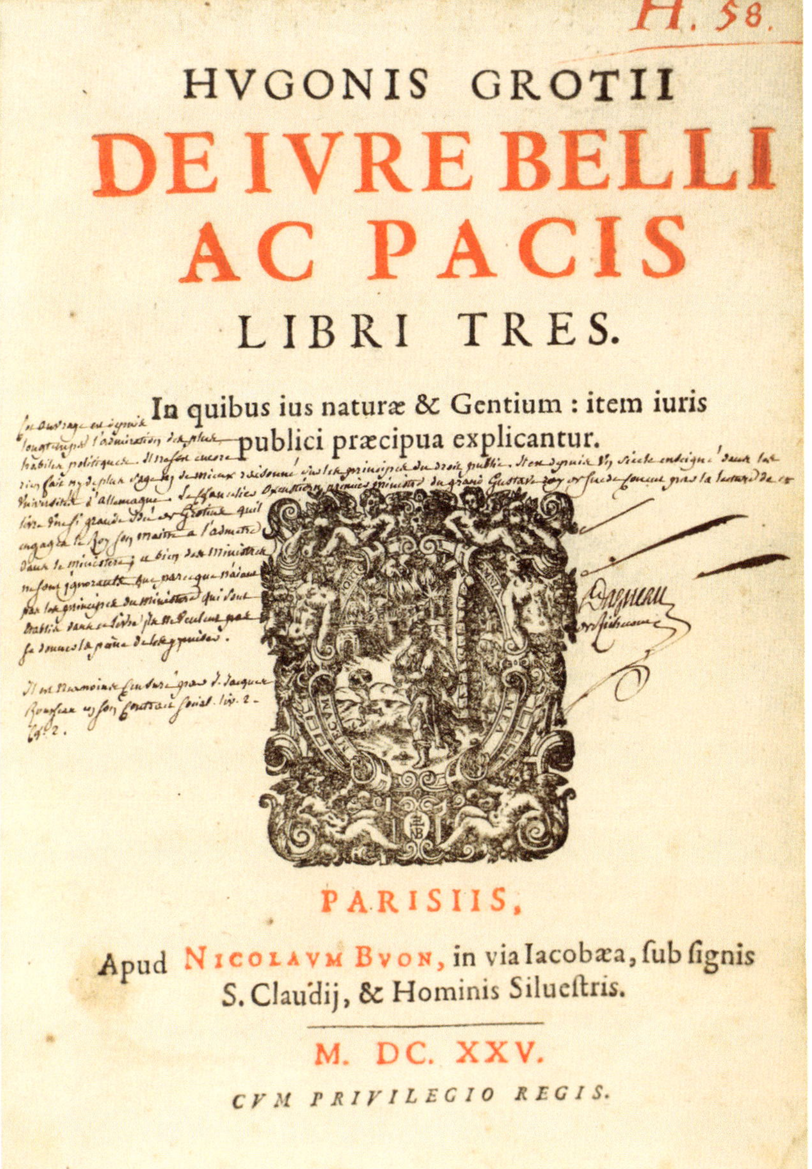

8

Hugo Grotius (1583-1645)
De jure belli ac pacis [On the Law of War and Peace], Paris, Nicolas Buon, 1625, first edition

Cologny, Martin Bodmer Foundation

Grotius' crucial contribution to the theory of war and peace can be reduced to four central notions. First, he defined the state as an independent subject of law. Second, he posited that this called for the development of a distinct field of law applying exclusively to states. Third, he fleshed out the just causes of war (*justa causa*) which Aquinas had left somewhat undeveloped. And fourth, he provided the international law of the high seas with a firm juridical grounding.

Writing in the midst of the collective trauma of the Thirty Years War (1618–48), in which a third of Europe's population was annihilated, Grotius was the first to grasp the positive potential inherent in the idea of mutual respect for the inviolability of state sovereignty. His proposal for a system of laws to govern equable relations between states was embraced as the epistemological foundation that would enable a solution to end the conflict. That solution consisted in the Peace of Westphalia, which was premised on the principle of non-intervention in the domestic affairs of other states. Grotius saw only three legitimate reasons for a state to resort to war: to defend itself against an ongoing wrong, to recover a debt owed by another state, and to inflict punishment for past infractions. Grotius' international legal system would continue to serve as a solid foundation for thinking about war and peace for the next three centuries.

G. B.-N.

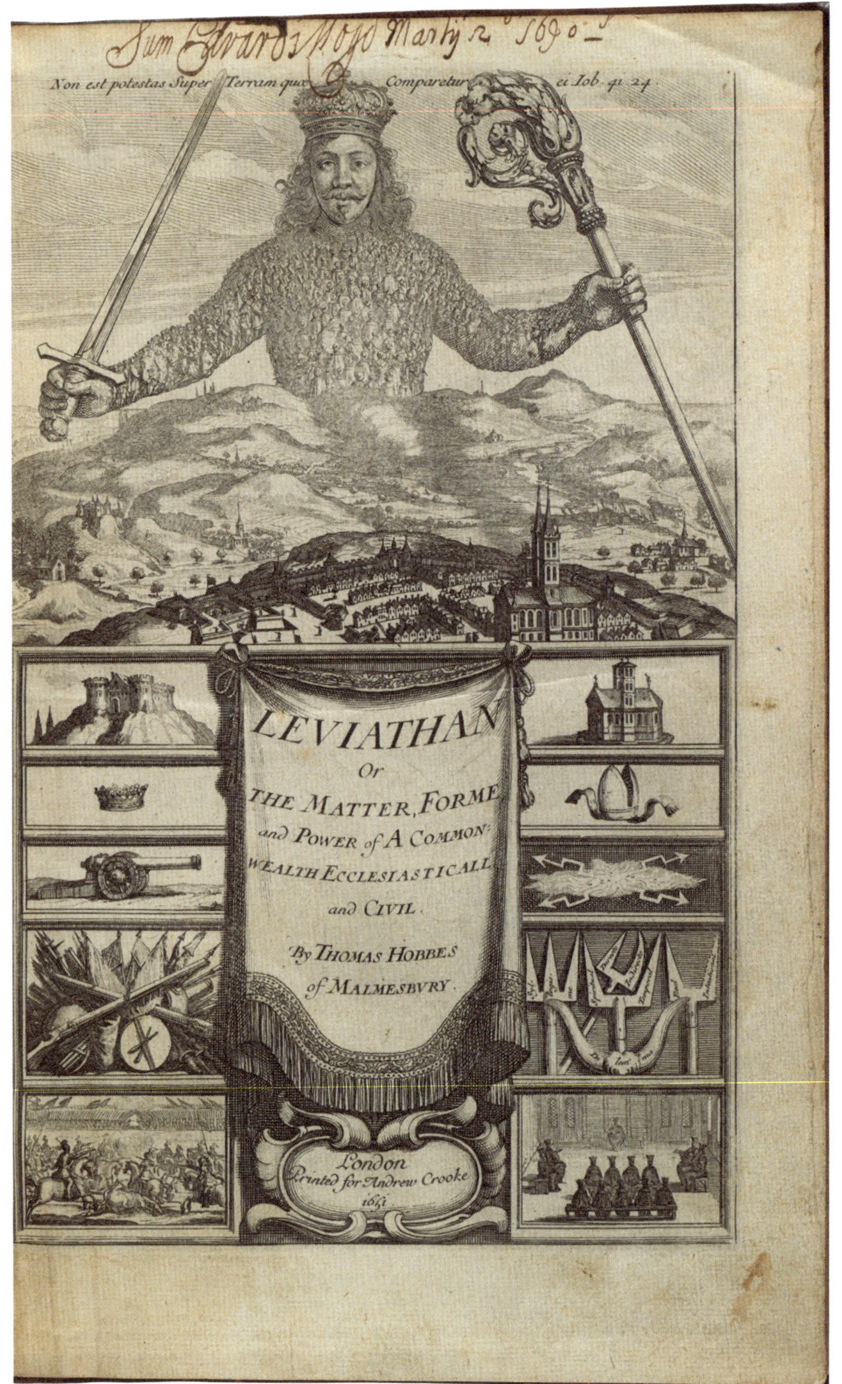

9
Thomas Hobbes (1588–1679)

Leviathan, London, Andrew Crook, 1651, first edition

Cologny, Martin Bodmer Foundation

After witnessing the wholesale destruction of Europe in the Thirty Years War (1618–48), Thomas Hobbes posited that: "during the time men live without a common Power to keep them all in awe, they are in that condition which is called War; and such a War, as is of every man, against every man." (*Leviathan*, chap. 1, 13). For Hobbes, the behaviour of states was not fundamentally different from that of individuals. When the international environment was chaotic, fear was the central motivator for action. States went to war when they feared for their security. In such an unpredictably violent world, was there any law that could be applied to all states? To Hobbes the answer was obvious: the law of self-preservation. States needed to consider whether their actions infringed on the vital interests of other states. For the sake of their own survival, they had to remain on high alert at all times and assume that war was intrinsic to international affairs. For example, modern nuclear deterrence, is profoundly Hobbesian.

Hobbes' naked justification of vile power politics has never ceased to captivate minds. From the pre-emptive destruction of Heidelberg by the French in 1688 to Carl Schmitt's arguments in favour of Hitler's violent subjugation of the Eastern Europeans, Hobbes' unapologetic vindication of war has long been the *bête noire* of non-aggressive concepts of the international order. Nevertheless, his theory contains a measure of truth that remains painfully evident today.   **G. B.-N.**

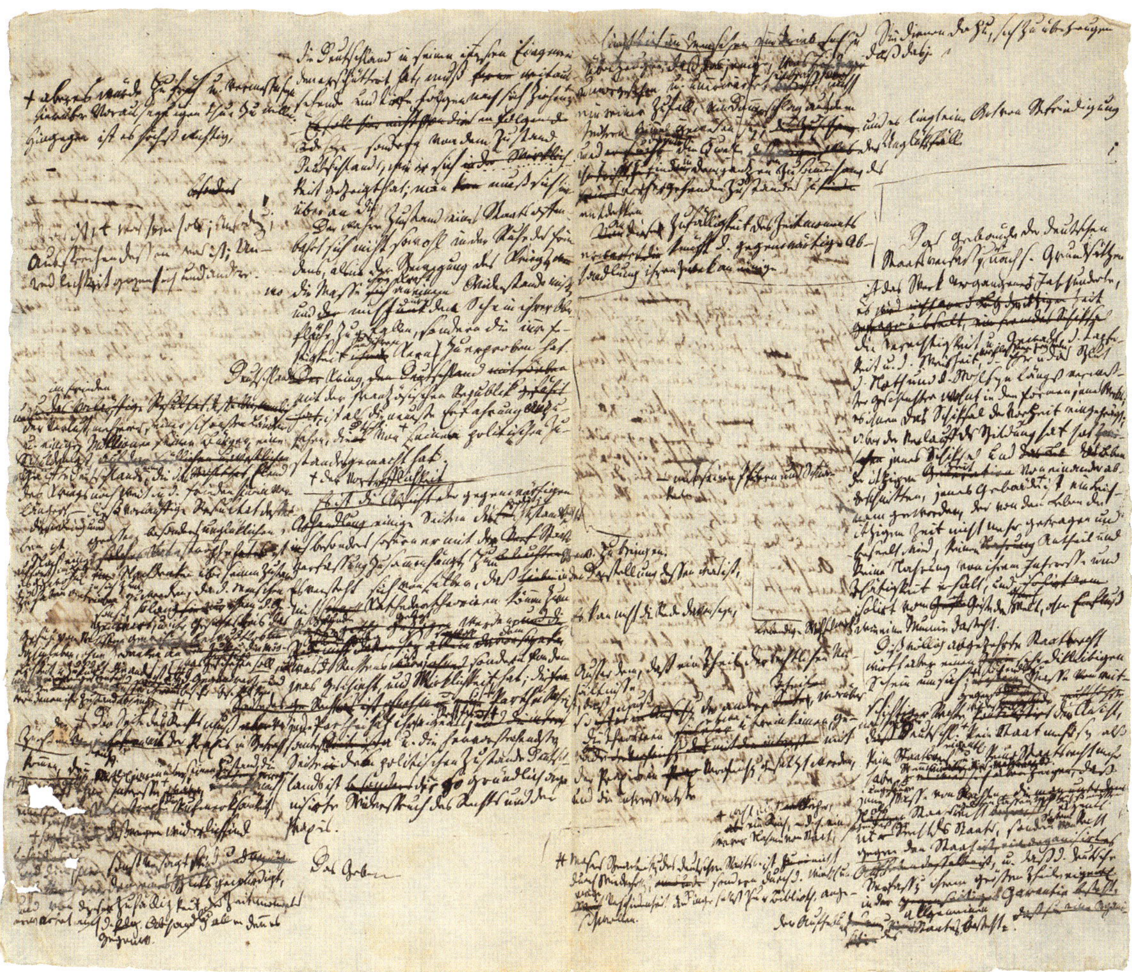

10

Georg Wilhelm Friedrich Hegel (1770–1831)

Autograph manuscript, fragment appended to *Über die Reichsverfassung [On the Constitution of the Empire]*, 1801

Cologny, Martin Bodmer Foundation, Aut. H 27.1

Spring 1801: Hegel has just moved to Jena, where he has obtained a post at the university, under the aegis of his master, Schelling. The Treaty of Lunéville – Napoleon Bonaparte's first great success as first consul – was signed on 9 February of the same year, to the detriment of Germany, which lost sizeable territories as a result.

It was in that context that the young Hegel was driven to question the nature of what was known as Germany. Could it be fairly described as a state? Comparing its constitution to that of the French Republic and other European models (in particular Britain and Italy), Hegel ruminated on the concept of the state. The influence of Rousseau, and above all Montesquieu, can be seen in his thinking; also discernible in this text are the lineaments of his philosophy of law and history. By coming to grips with the concept (the word and the thing), he laid the foundations upon which he would later expand his examination of the state. His dialectical philosophy would give full weight to something that he was the first to observe and for which ample evidence exists, namely the mismatch between law and prac-

tice, between the spirit of the times and the institutions that embody it.

Hegel explicitly situated his observations in the context of Germany's military defeat. It is not in times of peace, he wrote, that one asks the most penetrating questions about one's condition. War lays bare truths without which history cannot move forward.

The document presented here is an isolated fragment, the authenticity of which is documented by a handwritten note from one of Hegel's students, Eduard Gans. It was belatedly appended to other fragments relating to the draft of a book that Hegel never submitted for publication, but which appeared, long after his death, under the title *Über die Reichsverfassung*.   **C. I.**

69

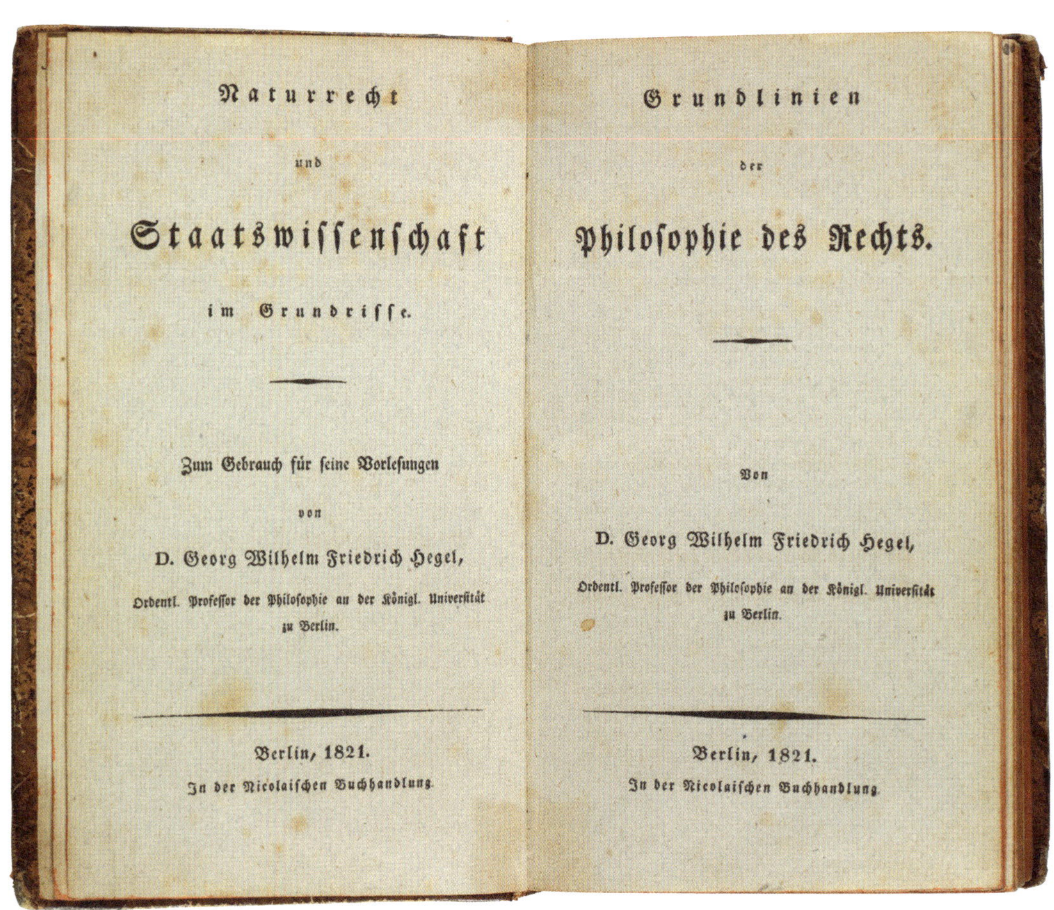

11
Georg Wilhelm Friedrich Hegel (1770–1831)
Grundlinien der Philosophie des Rechts [*Elements of the Philosophy of Right*], Berlin, Nicolaischen Buchhandlung, 1821, first edition

Cologny, Martin Bodmer Foundation.

The evolution of Georg Wilhelm Hegel's thinking on the subjet of war is characteristic of the European idealism that followed in the wake of the French revolution and the birth of its brainchild, nationalism. As a young teacher in Tübingen, Hegel was fascinated by the French people's attack on the Bastille, in 1789. After Napoleon crushed Prussia's forces in Jena, in 1806, and violently subjugated its citizens, Hegel began to ponder how an emergent, strong and centralized state (like France) could harness the collective will of the people to the benefit of the country and its inhabitants.

For Hegel, the state was much more than the sum of its individual parts. As the embodiment of the collective spirit of its people, war was one of the key channels through which a state's citizens could express their gallantry: "The true courage of cultured nations is the readiness to sacrifice oneself in the service of the state" (*Philosophy of Right & Law*, art. 327). Hegel's idea here – that war could be an arena for individual valour and self-expression – would captivate young people across Europe in the run-up to the First World War, thus explaining their enthusiasm to fight "the war to end all wars". Only in the trenches of the Western Front and on the beaches of Gallipoli would their Hegelian idealism clash with the harrowing realities of war. By then, the sacrifice of Europe's "lost generation" was well underway.   **G. B.-N.**

12
Carl Schmitt (1888–1985)
Völkerrechtliche Großraumordnung [*The Großraum Order of International Law*], Berlin–Vienna, 1939, Deutscher Rechtsverlag, first edition
Cologny, Martin Bodmer Foundation

Throughout history, conquest had invariably led to territorial appropriation, while the trauma of war has prompted the signing of territorial treaties. According to this historical logic, the tragedy of the First World War resulted in the creation of the League of Nations, the central purpose of which was to outlaw wars of conquest. Yet aspiration and reality soon parted ways, as France and Britain swiftly invented substitutes for annexation, imposing international mandates, as Britain did in Palestine, or indefinite military occupation, as France did in the German Rhineland.

Enter Carl Schmitt, international law's "prince of darkness". A native of the Rhineland, Schmitt understood that mandates and military occupation were mere surrogates for good old-fashioned conquest. Conceptualizing these new forms of territorial appropriation, Schmitt argued for an international order of "great spaces" (*Grossraume*), dominated by hegemons that violently subjugated all peoples under their purview. To Japan, East Asia. To the United States, the Americas (as per the Monroe Doctrine). To Britain, the high seas. To Russian Slavs, Central Asia. Europe, finally, would be Germany's Grossraum. Three weeks after Schmitt aired this concept, in 1939, Hitler adopted it as his own. Under Nazi occupation, all ethnic groups that were unwanted in the German *Grosssraum* – namely, Jews, Gypsies and Slavs – would be either removed or exterminated.   **G. B.-N.**

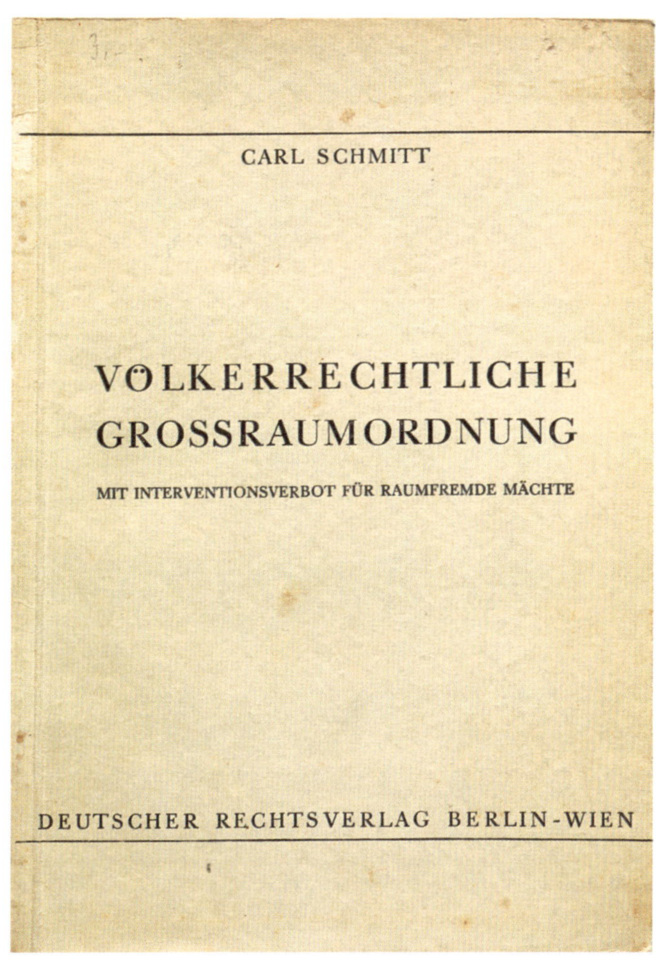

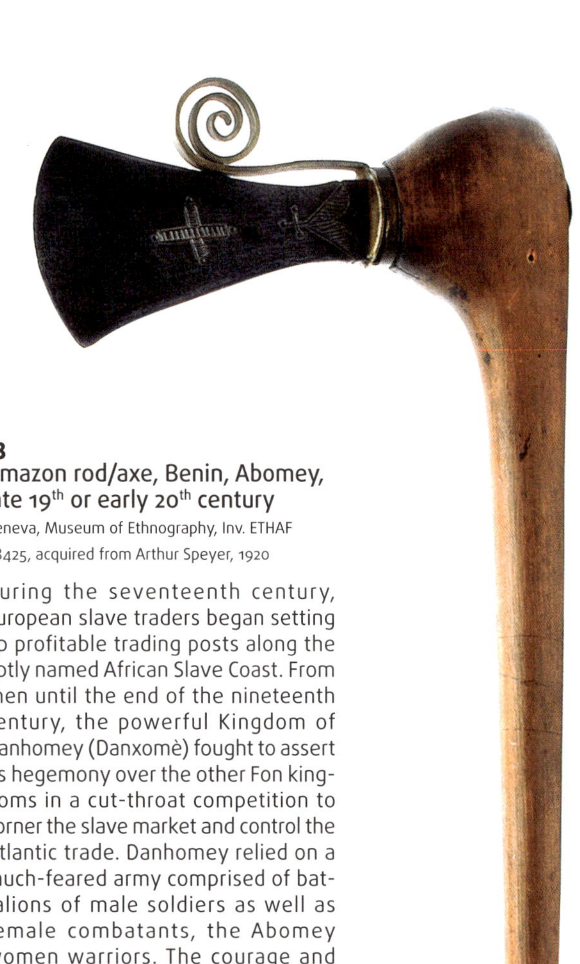

13
Amazon rod/axe, Benin, Abomey, late 19th or early 20th century

Geneva, Museum of Ethnography, Inv. ETHAF 08425, acquired from Arthur Speyer, 1920

During the seventeenth century, European slave traders began setting up profitable trading posts along the aptly named African Slave Coast. From then until the end of the nineteenth century, the powerful Kingdom of Danhomey (Danxomè) fought to assert its hegemony over the other Fon kingdoms in a cut-throat competition to corner the slave market and control the Atlantic trade. Danhomey relied on a much-feared army comprised of battalions of male soldiers as well as female combatants, the Abomey women warriors. The courage and strength of these "amazons" was frequently described by Europeans who witnessed their military parades and the Danhomeans' struggle against the colonizer. In November 1892, the French marched on the capital Abomey. King Béhanzin held out until January 1894, after which the Fon kingdom was annexed by the French.

This axe-shaped rod has a curved blade, engraved with a cross and set in a light-coloured wooden handle with a bulbous head. A spiral of copper wire curls over the blade. A symbol of authority, the rod (in French, *récade*, from the Portuguese *recado*, message) is a staff of command that, in itself, delivers a message. Those shaped like an axe were reserved for women and would have been carried by female warriors in military parades or by princesses performing royal war dances to the sound of Agbadja drums.   **F. M.**

14
Titus Livius (59 BC–AD 17)
Römische History vsz T. Livio [History of Rome since its Founding], Strasbourg, 1507, Johann Grüninger, illustrated with 214 woodcuts

Cologny, Martin Bodmer Foundation

In the martial society that was Ancient Rome, certain symbols marked periods of conflict and peace, and the passing from one of these states to the other. While writing his great history of Rome during the reign of Augustus, Titus Livius (Livy) witnessed an extremely rare event: the shutting of the gates of the Temple of Janus. Built by Numa Pompilius, and one of the oldest in the city, the shrine was dedicated to the two-faced god who, with Saturn, protected Latium, particularly through the success of its armies. The gates were thus kept open during a conflict, so that the god's power could assist the legions. Conversely, "shutting the gates of Janus" was a sign that Rome was officially at peace. This occurred only twice: "once after the first Punic War in the consulship of T. Manlius, the second time, which heaven has allowed our generation to witness, after the battle of Actium, when peace on land and sea was secured by the emperor Caesar Augustus" (*Roman History*, I, 19). Another symbol of the advent of war was the lifting of the battle standards surmounted by Jupiter's eagles (*signa militaria*), which gave legions their marching orders. When, against the advice of the senate, the hot-headed consul Flaminius decided to start the Second Punic War, something unheard-of happened: "the standard could not be moved though the standard-bearer had exerted his utmost strength. He turned to the messenger and asked him: 'Are you bringing a despatch from the senate, also, forbidding me to go on with the campaign? Go, let them dig out the standard if their hands are too benumbed with fear for them to pull it up.'" (*Roman History*, XXII, 3).

N. D.

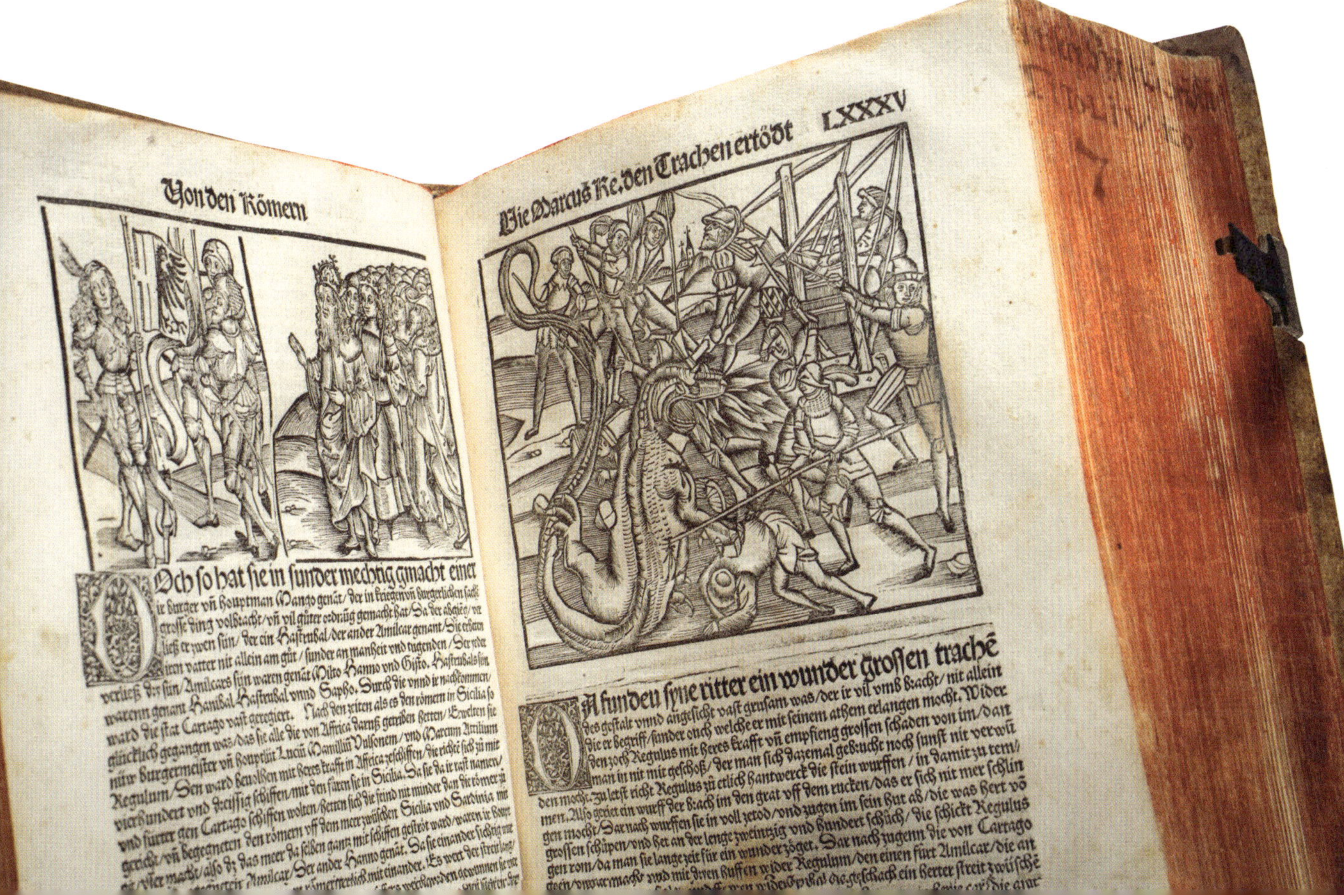

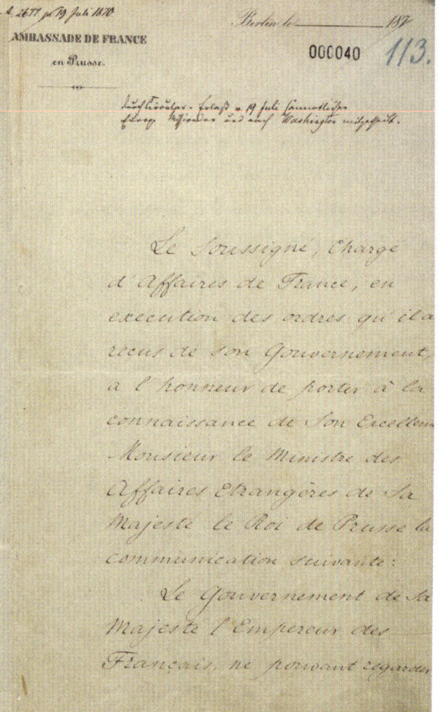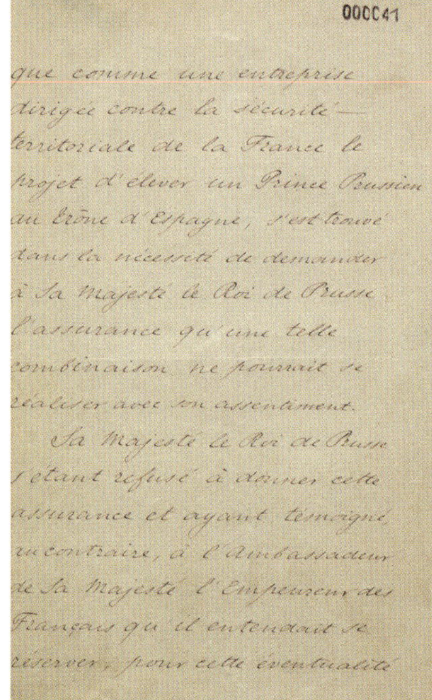

France's Declaration of War on Prussia, 19 July 1870

Berlin, Auswärtiges Amt, Politisches Archiv, R 6196

On 19 July 1870, a French chargé d'affaires in Berlin, Georges Le Sourd, delivered France's declaration of war on Prussia to the German Foreign Office. His acting ambassador, Count Vincent Benedetti, had abruptly returned to Paris, several days earlier, to relate to the minister in person the serious events that, according to him, explained the situation in which the two nations found themselves.

The seeds of the war had been sown in 1866, but, over the course of a few days, events had suddenly gathered pace. Since its victory over Austria, at Sadowa, on 3 July 1866, Prussia had loomed as a threat to the French Empire. In fact, the minister president of Prussia, Otto von Bismarck, was looking for a pretext to goad Paris into declaring war on Berlin, as a means of achieving German unity.

He found it in the vacancy of the Spanish throne. When the government of Napoleon III learned, in early July 1870, that Madrid had chosen a Hohenzollern prince and cousin of the king of Prussia, the crisis came to a head. France initially obtained a stunning victory when the prince's renunciation to the throne was accepted by the king of Prussia, much to the chagrin of Bismarck, who considered resigning. But in short time the situation deteriorated anew, Paris demanding, under pressure from the Bonapartist authoritarians, Berlin's guarantee that no Prussian prince would ever be a candidate for the throne of Spain.

When the French ambassador, himself under pressure from his government, insisted, the king of Prussia, who was on a *cure* in Ems at the time, politely refused, and then turned down a fresh request for an audience. Bismarck seized the opportunity to write up the event in a manner that, while not untrue, was deliberately humiliating for France – Benedetti was informed that his request had been turned down by a mere aide de camp – and had what history would refer to incorrectly as the "Ems dispatch" distributed throughout Europe.

In that charged atmosphere, and without Benedetti, who was in Paris, even being given a hearing, the Corps législatif (Legislative Body) bowed to the French government and voted to approve war credits, on 15 July.

Four days later, the declaration of war on Prussia was notified to Berlin. It was justified in the text on the grounds of both interest and honour. France had not obtained the guarantees it had demanded and had been humiliated by the king (in reality by Bismarck). Europe would look on France as the aggressor, and France would find itself without allies, whereas all of Germany rallied behind Prussia.

E. A.

16
Aristide Briand (1862–1932)
Telegram about the Greek–Bulgarian incident, 27 October 1925

Geneva, United Nations Archives

Following an incident on the border with Bulgaria on 19 October 1925, the Greek army advanced a few kilometres into Bulgarian territory. Three days after the start of the hostilities, Sofia placed the matter before the League of Nations. French statesman Aristide Briand, the acting president of the Council, immediately telegraphed the Greek and Bulgarian governments, informing them that the Council would convene a special session to examine the matter. He urged the two parties to suspend their military operations in the meantime, and reminded them of their "obligations as League Members". On 26 October, a week after the incident, the Council adopted a resolution calling for a ceasefire and for the withdrawal of Greek troops. Having observed that its decisions were being executed, the Council approved the establishment of a commission of enquiry to determine responsibility for the incident and how to prevent a reccurrence. While the "Demir-Kapu conflict" is generally seen as a minor episode, the League of Nations intervention was a success, demonstrating that the Geneva-based organization could prevent an escalation of hostilities by taking rapid and resolute action. Briand's telegram nipped a major offensive by the Greek army in the bud. A few hours more, and the conflict might have taken another turn. As the commission of enquiry observed in a report, "the saving of a few minutes can prevent a catastrophe".

P.-E. B.

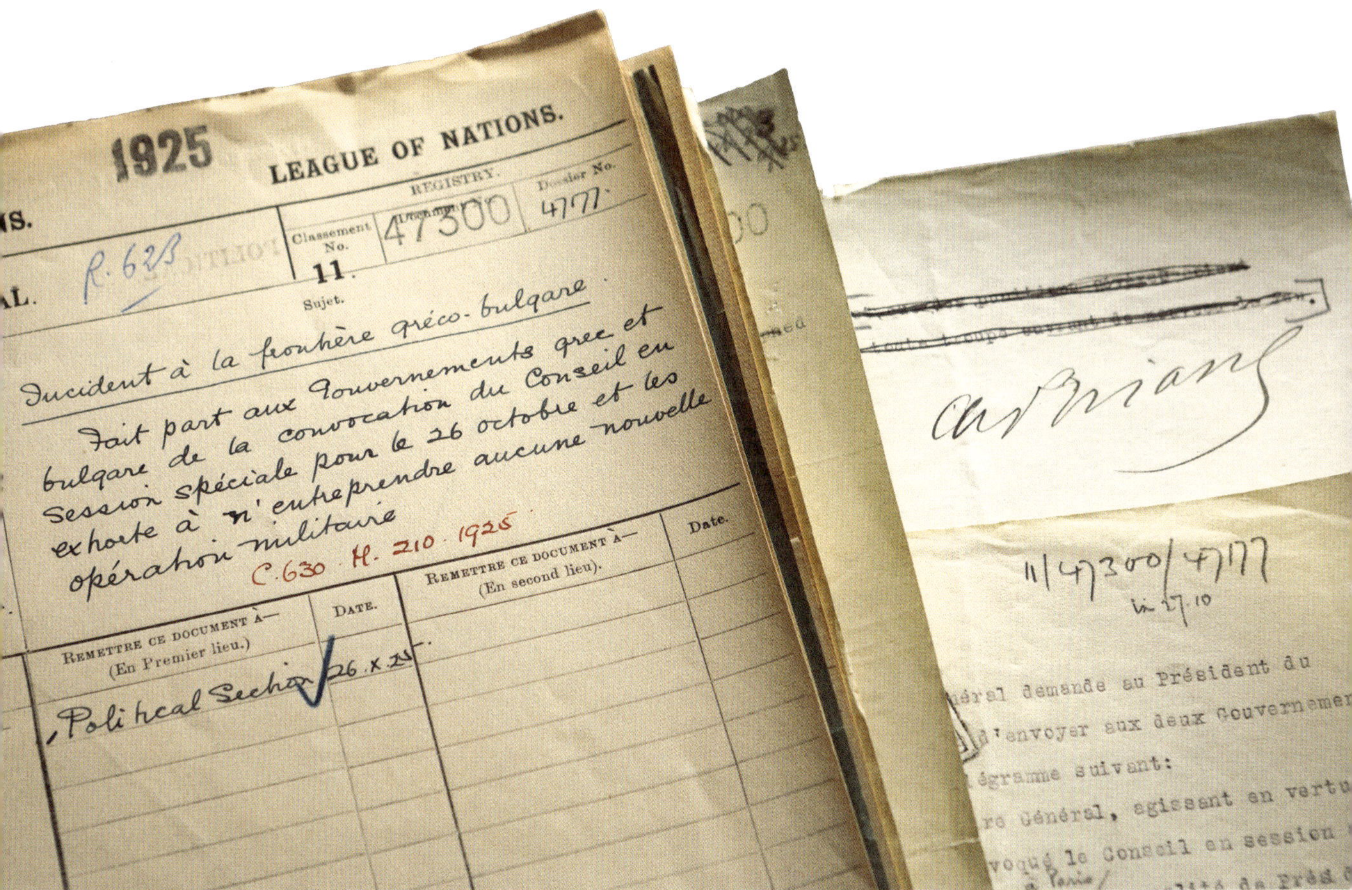

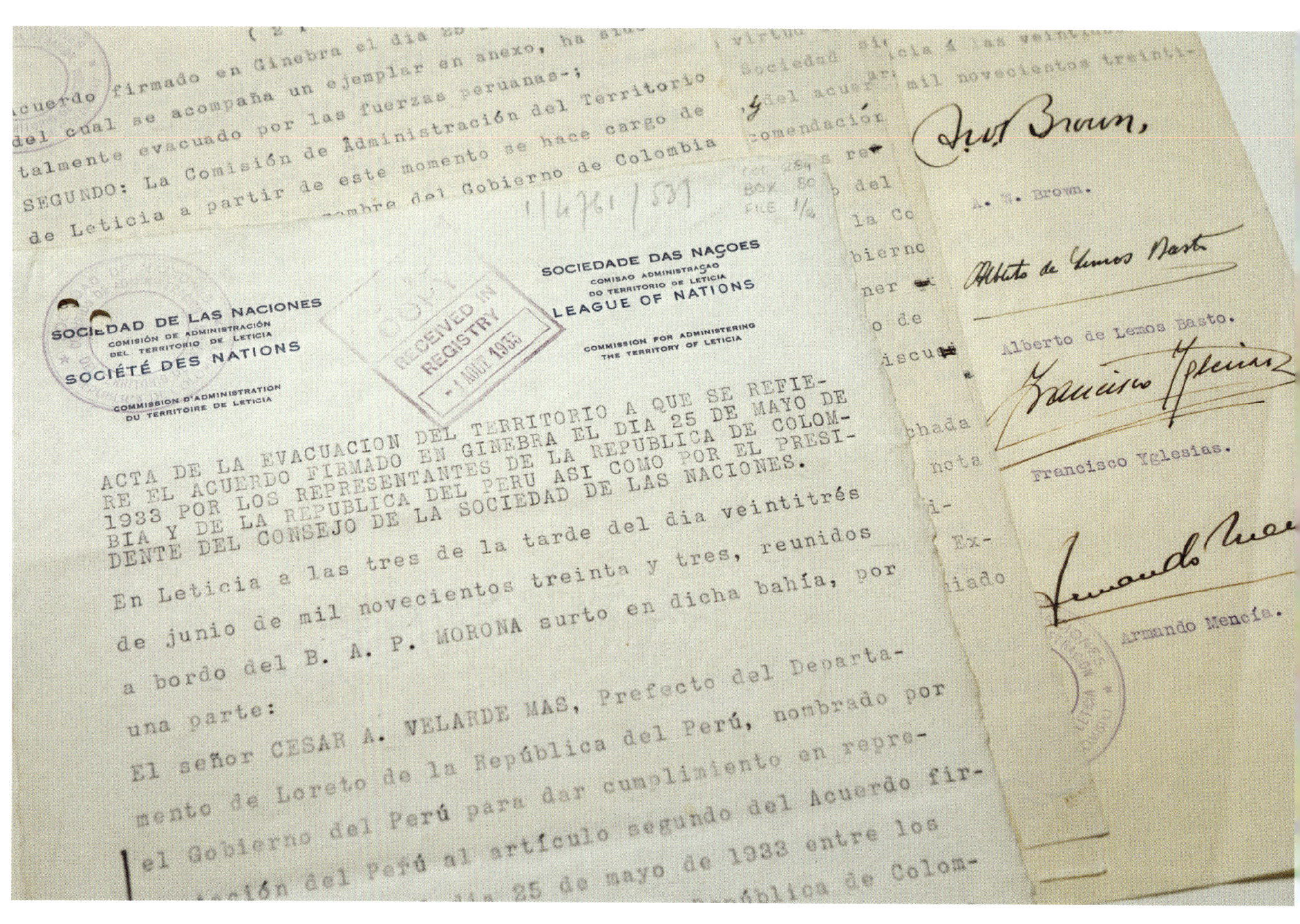

17
Evacuation decree for the territory of Leticia, 23 June 1933

Geneva, United Nations Archives

The dispute between Peru and Colombia over Leticia erupted in September 1932, when irregular Peruvian troops occupied this small Colombian port on the banks of the Amazon, in an act of force that triggered an escalation of tensions between the two countries. Clashes broke out, prompting fears of a major conflict. Eventually, on 25 May 1933, in Geneva, the League of Nations managed – not without difficulty – to broker an agreement, whereby Peru would withdraw and the administration of Leticia would be temporarily transferred to an international commission appointed by the League. The League's aim, in intervening, was not to resolve the dispute but rather to create the conditions for the two governments to reach a definitive agreement. On 23 June 1933, the members of the international commission – an American, a Brazilian and a Spaniard, together with a League official – signed a document with the representative of Peru defining the terms of the evacuation of Leticia. The commission then took office and administered the territory for one year, with the support of a military contingent placed at its disposal by Bogotá. Finally, on 18 May 1934, Colombia and Peru signed an accord in which Peru agreed to return Leticia to Colombia. The commission's mandate expired a month later. The "Leticia Affair" is a little-known instance of successful peacekeeping by the League of Nations in the 1930s. **P.-E. B.**

18

Germany's withdrawal from the World Disarmament Conference, 14 October 1933

Geneva, United Nations Archives

When the Conference for the Reduction and Limitation of Armaments opened in Geneva, in February 1932, it kindled great hope among the public, despite the looming tension and uncertainty. The global economic crisis was starting to bite. The representatives of the participating nations arrived individually, and several plans were presented. One of the main obstacles was Germany's demand for "equality of rights". Berlin considered the military provisions of the Treaty of Versailles unfair and demanded that it be allowed to rearm – a prospect that was utterly out of the question for France, which viewed any rearmament by Germany as a direct threat to its security. After the German delegation first exited the talks, in September 1932, the great powers agreed to pursue the discussions, which would include recognition of "equality of rights in a system which would pro-vide security for all nations". However, the rise to power of Adolph Hitler, in early 1933, made any agreement impossible. Ultimately, on 14 October 1933, the Nazi minister of foreign affairs, Konstantin von Neurath, informed the Conference in a telegram that, given the participating states' "lack of willingness" and their "failure to abide by their commitments", his country was "obliged" to leave the Conference. Several weeks later, Germany notified its withdrawal from the League of Nations. **P.-E. B.**

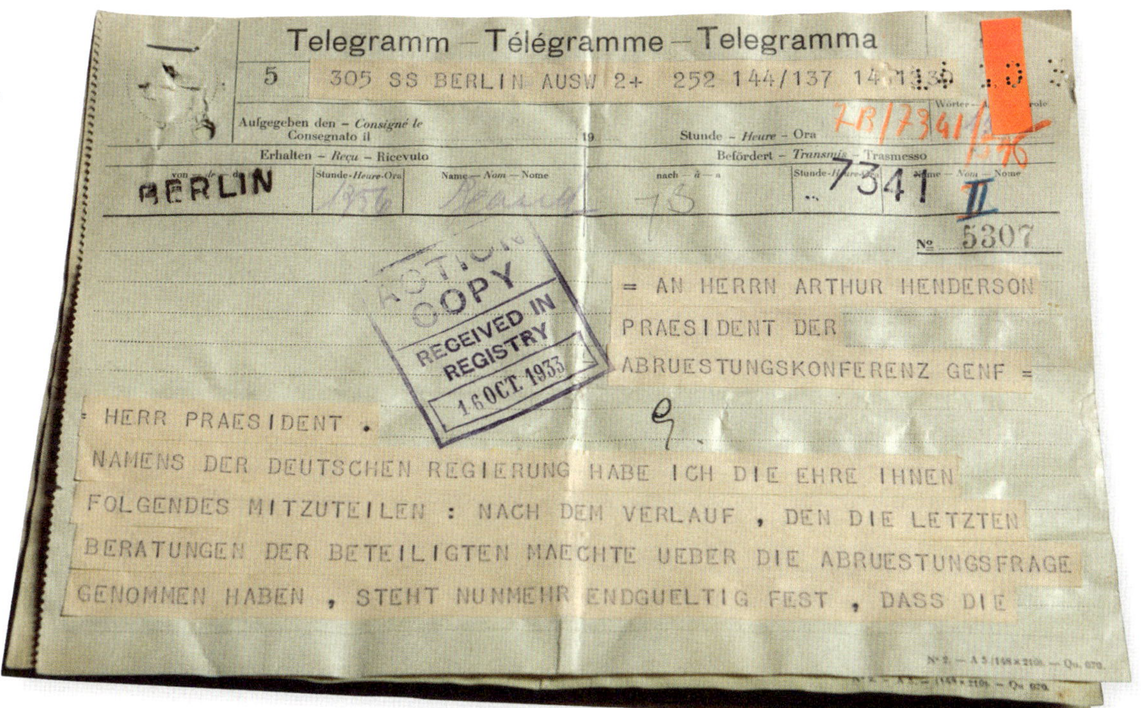

19
Map associated with the German-Soviet Treaty of Friendship, Cooperation and Demarcation, 28 September 1939

Berlin, Auswärtiges Amt, Politisches Archiv,
BILATR SOW Nr. 56

This map of Eastern Europe bearing the signatures of Stalin and von Ribbentrop is one of the direct outcomes of the Hitler-Stalin Pact agreed in Moscow on 23 August 1939. It was appended to the Pact's second secret protocol. Signed by the two foreign ministers, von Ribbentrop and Molotov, the Pact included a non-aggression treaty, which was made public and was applicable immediately, and also a secret protocol, which marked out the two countries' respective spheres of influence. Finland, Estonia, Latvia, eastern Poland and Bessarabia were returned to the USSR, which would either annex them or occupy them in the months to come. On the basis of the pact, the German army invaded much of Poland on 1 September 1939, whereupon the Red Army occupied the rest of the country. All the same, in areas around Lublin and Warsaw the Wehrmacht advanced farther than the secret protocol provided for and, on 28 September, von Ribbentrop was recalled to Moscow to set the final boundaries in a treaty of friendship and delimitation. A second secret protocol allowed for an exchange: the USSR would have a free hand in Lithuania in return for the status quo in occupied Poland. The new demarcation line was drawn on a map which von Ribbentrop and Stalin signed as a sign of mutual trust. The metre-long map is kept in the archives of the Auswärtiges Amt in Berlin. In Poland and the Baltic states, 23 August 1939 is a date that stands out in the collective memory. In 1989, to mark the fiftieth anniversary of their loss of independence, almost two million people formed a 600-kilometre human chain from Tallinn to Vilnius via Riga: the Baltic Way.   **F. W.**

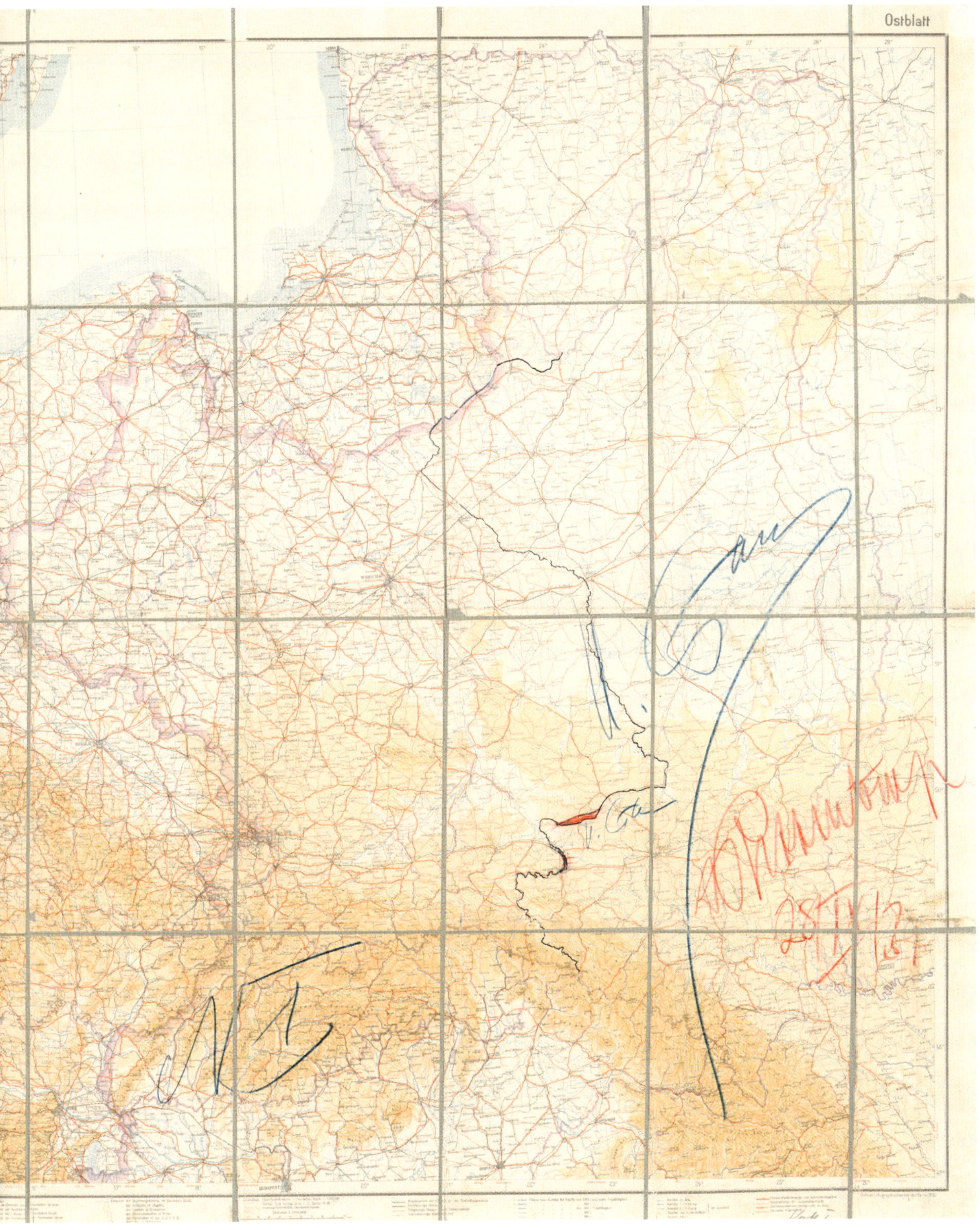
Ostblatt

War starts in the mind,
encouraged by propaganda.

20
Demosthenes (384–322 BC)
Philippicae, in *Demosthenis orationes duae and sexaginta,* Venice, 1504, Aldo Manuzio, Greek editio princeps

Cologny, Martin Bodmer Foundation

The term "philippic" has entered common parlance to mean a speech attacking a specific person. That is a measure of the seminal importance of the four harangues delivered by Demosthenes in Athens between 351 and 341 BC and collected under precisely that title, *The Philippics.* Their target was Philip II of Macedon, who at the time was gradually expanding his dominance over a large area of Greece. In the face of this threat, Demosthenes deployed his considerable eloquence to denounce the spinelessness and defeatism of the Athenians and invite them to react to an increasingly worrying situation. For ten years, he adapted his speeches to the fluctuating political and military situations of the Greek city-states – with mixed results from a practical point of view.

At another level, however, his harangues were a notable success. They soon came to be regarded as unsurpassable models of an art that, having established itself in the fifth century, was now at its peak. The art of rhetoric probably emerged first in a legal context, but before long it had become a political tool of the utmost importance, especially in the context of Athenian democracy, where what mattered was winning the support of an assembly by the power of one's voice.

It can even be said that Demosthenes fashioned words into weapons. Using all the tricks of the art to maximize its effectiveness, rhetoric was now accorded a special place in the military arsenal. Convincing a deliberative assembly and shaping public opinion: these were the victories that a good speech was expected to deliver.

This art of speech would be added to subsequent centuries by thousands of voices, reinforcing its spread and impact. However, it was the type of political rhetoric exemplified by *The Philippics* that engendered the various forms of propaganda that today invariably accompany the clash of weapons.

C. I.

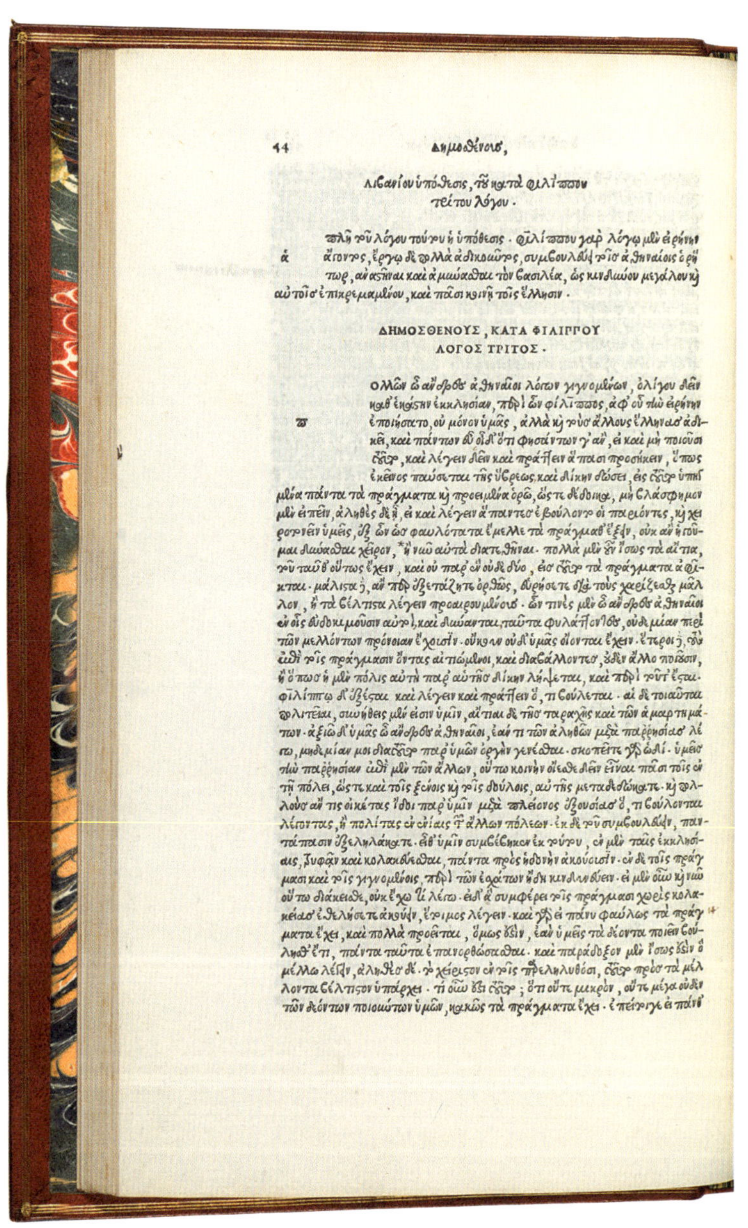

21
Napoleon Bonaparte
(1769–1821)
[À mes soldats...], Rivoli,
18 January 1797, autograph
manuscript

Cologny, Martin Bodmer Foundation, Aut. N-4.3

"We were thirty thousand barefoot against eighty thousand Austrian bullies, all fine men, well set up. I see 'em now! But Napoleon – he was still only Bonaparte then – he knew how to put the courage into us! We marched by night, and we marched by day; we slapped their faces at Montenotte, we thrashed 'em at Rivoli, Lodi, Arcole, Millesimo, and we never let 'em up." So does Balzac, in the words of one of his characters, sum up the victory at Rivoli, the two-day long battle (13–14 January 1797) that brought the siege of Mantua to an end and marked a decisive stage in the Italian campaign. From his headquarters in Verona, on 18 January, Bonaparte sent the Directory a celebratory account of individual exploits (first and foremost those of Massena, the "darling of the victory") and collective triumphs: "The Roman legions, it is said, covered twenty-four miles each day; our brigades cover thirty, and fight while under way". This valuable manuscript, entirely in Bonaparte's hand, is a first draft of the official correspondence, in the form of a proclamation addressed directly to the troops to lift their spirits.   **N. D.**

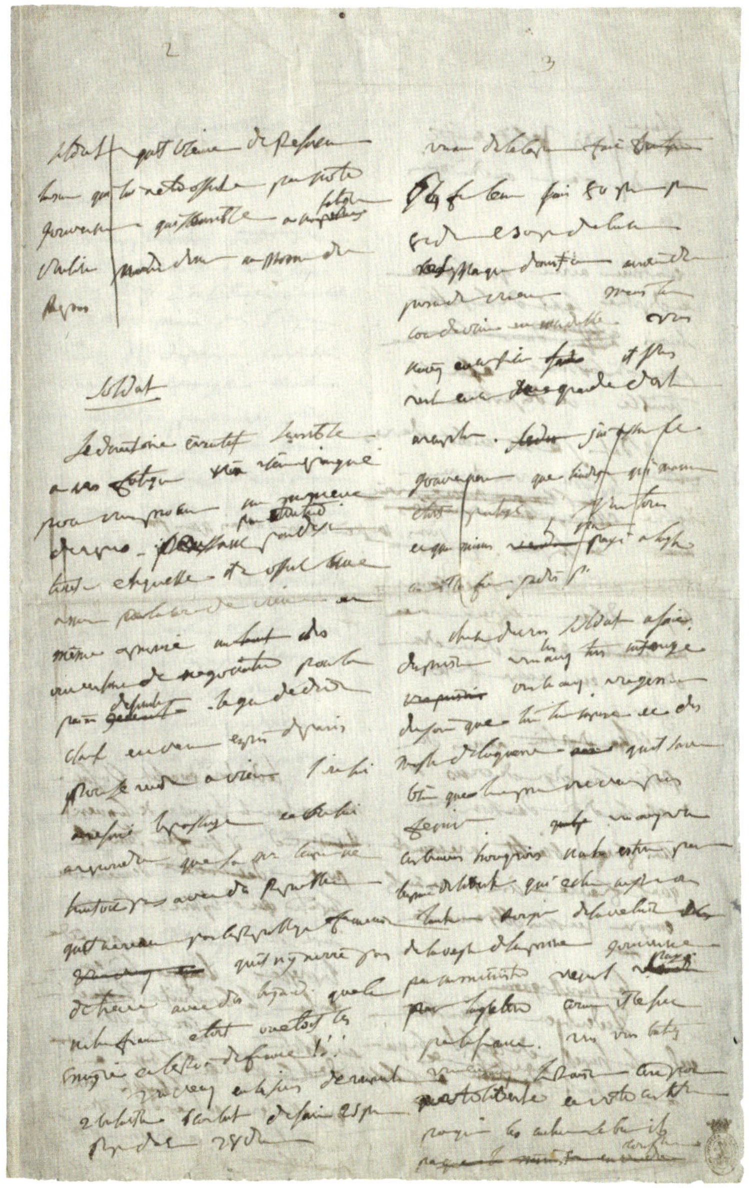

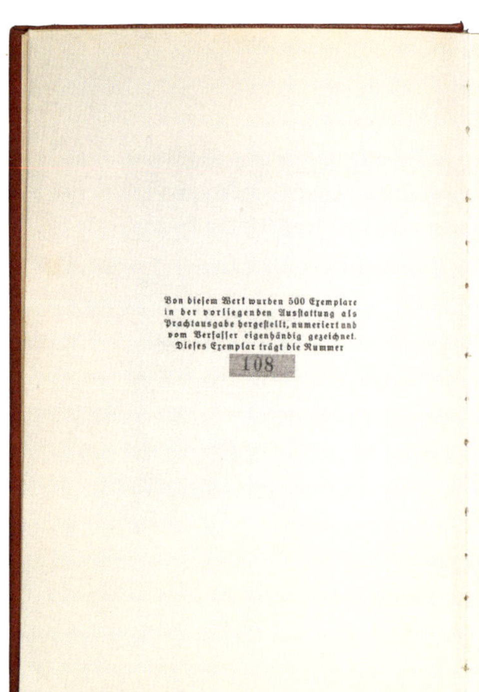

22
Adolf Hitler (1889–1945)
Mein Kampf [My Struggle],
Munich, Franz Eher Nachfolger,
first edition, one of 500 numbered
deluxe copies (No. 108),
with an autograph dedication
to Hermann Kriebel
Cologny, Martin Bodmer Foundation

On 1 January 2016, seventy years after
the death of Adolf Hitler, *Mein Kampf.
Eine Abrechnung (My Struggle: Settling
Accounts)* entered the public domain.
The possibility of its being reprinted
sparked heated controversy. This work
of propaganda was written by Hitler
between November 1923 and 20
December 1924, in Landsberg Prison
(where he was held after the failed
putsch to overthrow the German government, on 8 November 1923). He
took advantage of his incarceration to
write a manifesto laying down the Nazi
ideology.

Mein Kampf recounts Hitler's life journey
and provides his analysis of the situation
in Germany, followed by his programme
for the National Socialist movement. In a
pamphleteering and often rambling
style, peppered with lengthy digressions,
he writes of the importance of uniting
German communities into a single
empire, the need for the country to
re-arm and expand its "living space", the
superiority of the Aryan race and the
obligation for society to rid itself of dis-
abled people. He also vituperates against
those he calls his enemies (Jews,
Bolsheviks, the press and democracy),
and expresses his aim to establish a racist, elitist regime in Germany. The success
of this first book encouraged him to write
a second volume in 1926. Circulation
soared in the 1930s and, as of 1936, every
newlywed couple received a copy of
Mein Kampf from the government as a
wedding gift. By 1945, some ten million
copies had been printed.   **P. H.**

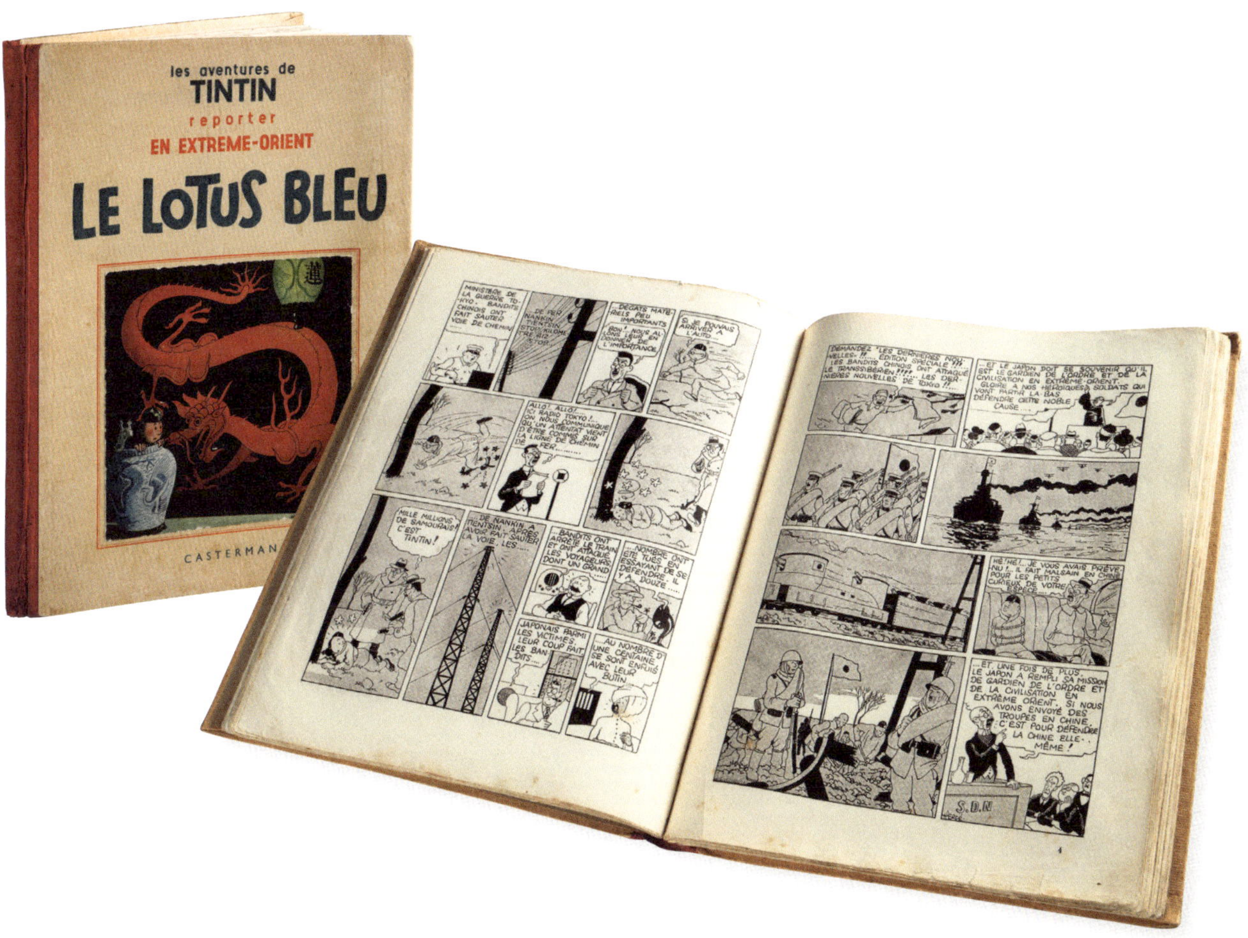

© Hergé / Moulinsart, 2019.

23
Hergé (1907–1983, Georges Rémi, known as)

Les Aventures de Tintin, reporter en Extrême-Orient. Le Lotus bleu [The Adventures of Tintin, a Reporter in the Far East: The Blue Lotus], Paris–Tournai, Casterman, 1936, first edition

JPD private collection

After *The Cigars of the Pharaoh*, Tintin's crusade against international opium traffickers takes him to China. Abandoning the cartoonishness of the early albums (especially *Tintin in the Land of the Soviets* and *Tintin in the Congo*), Hergé researched this album with the thoroughness that was to characterize the rest of his work. *The Blue Lotus* offers a realistic, politically astute depiction of the complexities of 1930s China. Hergé addresses several "hot topics" in international current events of the time, such as the "Mukden Incident", which took place in September 1931, when the Japanese army used the pretext of the sabotage of a railway line in Southern Manchuria, orchestrated by them but attributed to the Chinese, to justify military intervention. A few months later, the Japanese created the nation of Manchukuo, ruled by the former emperor of China, Puyi, but in fact a vassal state. In two vivid pages, Hergé lucidly renders the story of this disinformation and propaganda operation, designed to lend legitimacy to what was in reality a campaign of territorial expansion. The action has shifted to a place near Shanghai, but the tricks and exaggerations of the propaganda machine, the nationalist rhetoric of the politicians and the soothing justifications of the Japanese diplomats at the League of Nations (while troops mobilize in the background), are portrayed both accurately and in a manner accessible to young readers. **N. D.**

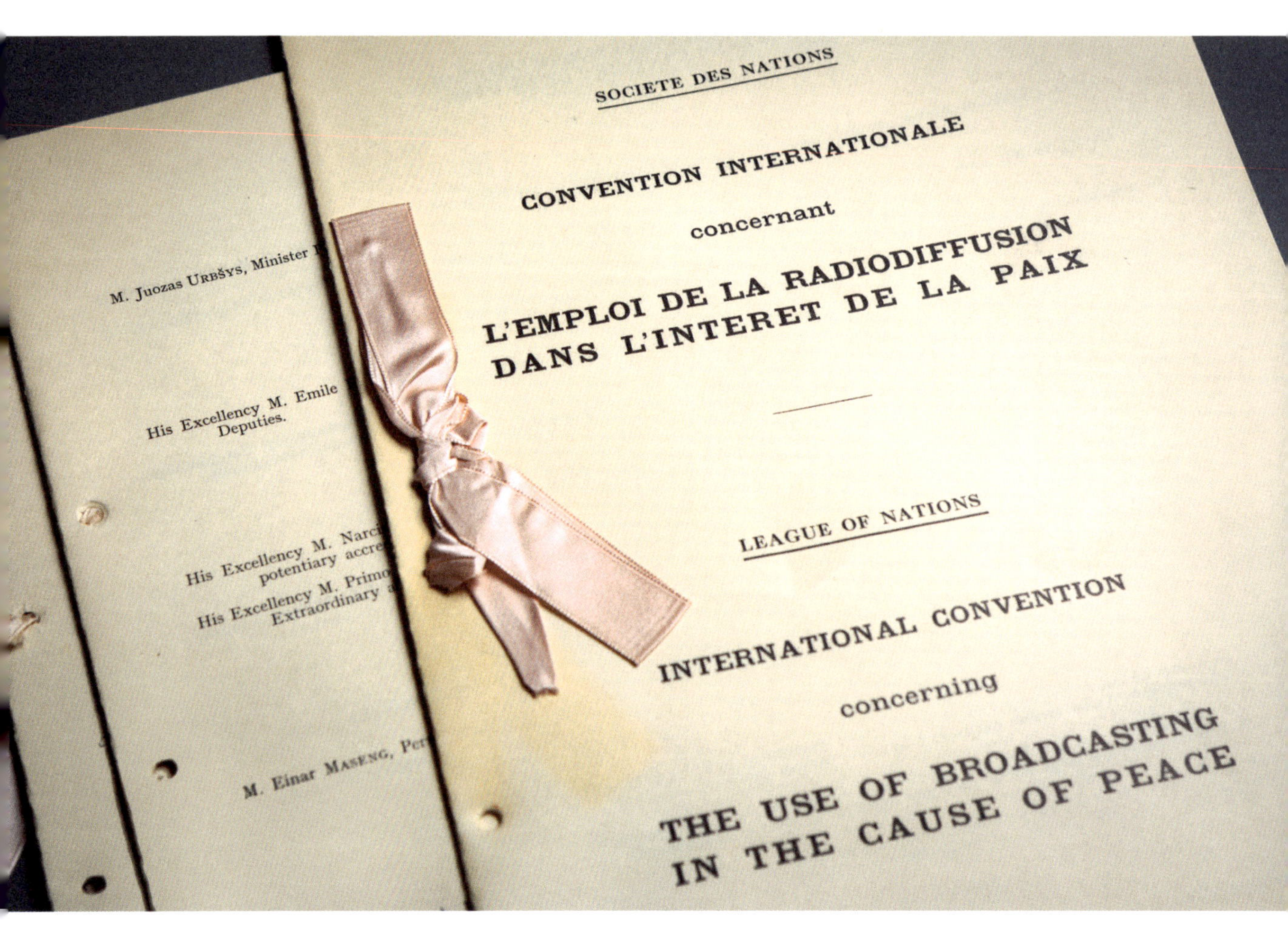

24
International Convention concerning the Use of Broadcasting in the Cause of Peace, 1936

Geneva, United Nations Archives

In the interwar period, radio rose to prominence as a powerful means of communication. As its reach grew, it became clear that, in addition to bringing peoples closer together by helping them learn about each another, radio could be used to incite or fuel conflict. The signatories to the International Convention concerning the Use of Broadcasting pledged to ensure that radio broadcasts in their countries did not "constitute an incitement either to war" or "to acts likely to lead thereto". They also undertook to stop without delay any transmission "likely to harm the good international understanding by statements the incorrectness of which is or ought to be known to the persons responsible for the broadcast". The terms of the Convention, which was signed by around twenty states in the following years, now seem particularly forward-looking, especially with regard to the measures proposed so as to limit the spread of misleading information. However, its implementation was limited in the run-up to the Second World War, as none of the authoritarian regimes of the time signed it.

P.-E. B.

25
Edmond-François Calvo
(1892–1957)
La Bête est morte! La Guerre mondiale chez les animaux [The Beast is Dead! World War Among the Animals], Paris, **1944–1945, first edition**
Cologny, Martin Bodmer Foundation

Children, too, experience the tragedy of war. Yet making war understandable for a child can be tricky: how should one explain the horror and suffering? In the summer of 1944, as the Allied troops were nearing Paris, a group of children's authors and cartoonists took up the challenge, creating this iconic album, with drawings by Calvo (in a style influenced by Walt Disney) and text by Jacques Zimmermann and Victor Dancette (creator of the Bibliothèque Rouge et Or, a famous French children's book imprint).

This beautifully drawn comic book tells the story of the main episodes of the war in a way that is accessible to very young readers. The belligerents are portrayed as animals: the wolves of "Barbary" (Nazi Germany) have invaded their squirrel and polar bear neighbours (France and Russia, respectively), with the help of their friends the hyenas (Italy). Fortunately, an alliance of bulldogs (Britain) and bisons (United States), assisted by the Great Stork (De Gaulle), sound "the death knell for the dominance of the Big Bad Wolf. The Wild Beast – whose reign was meant to last a thousand years! – has finally been flattened after five years of struggle, suffering and sacrifice by all peace-loving animals." Printed "between Le Vesinet and Ménilmontant, in the teeth of the Big Bad Wolf [Hitler], in the snout of the Decorated Pig [Goering], and without

permission from the Garrulous Skunk [Goebbels]", the first volume appeared "in the third month of the Liberation" (August 1944). Particularly impressive is the two-page spread depicting the Wolves' attack on the "Livarot Line" (Maginot Line). Volume II, *Quand la bête est terrassée (The Beast is Flattened),* was "printed in June 1945, in the hope that the Beast is well and truly dead". Bedtime reading for an entire post-war generation, this book has since been the subject of numerous dissertations and theses, and was hailed by the Institute of Contemporary History as "a must-read" of wartime literature. **N. D.**

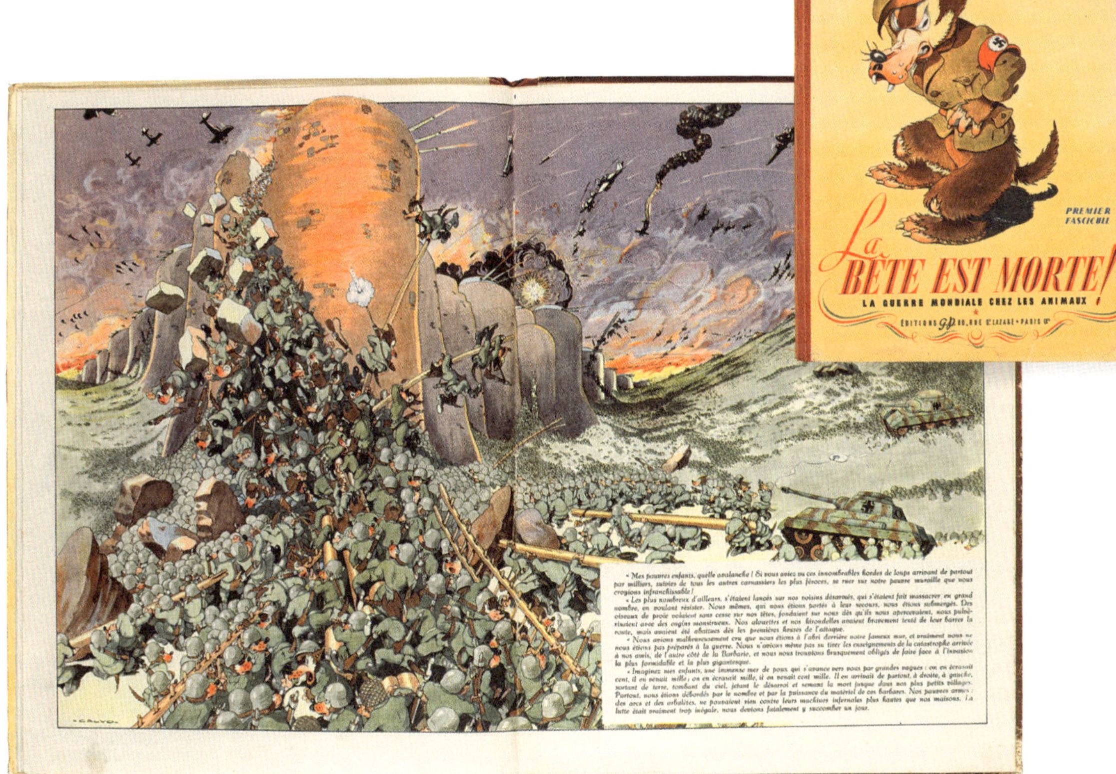

Is there an "Art of War"?

Can law
restrain
barbarity?

*Is peace
without freedom
preferable to
arms violence?*

**Do video games trivialize
the act of KILLING?**

THE TIME OF DESTRUC-
TION

THE ROLE OF EMOTIONS IN THE DESTRUCTION OF CULTURAL HERITAGE

DAVID SANDER

University of Geneva

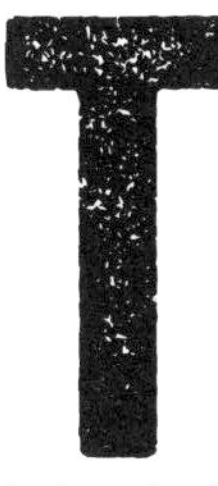here is a good deal of research to suggest that our emotions play an important role in the emergence of conflicts, and also in how they are sustained, resolved and revived.[1] Whether the situation is one of attack or defence, emotions are involved.[2] Armed conflicts are harmful to the lives of individuals; they can be carried to the extremes of war crimes, or crimes against humanity, and they often go hand in hand with the destruction of the enemy's cultural heritage.

In 2017, the United Nations Security Council adopted Resolution 2347, which states that "directing unlawful attacks against sites and buildings dedicated to religion, education, art, science or charitable purposes, or historic monuments may constitute, under certain circumstances and pursuant to international law, a war crime". One of the reasons for this resolution is undoubtedly to be found in the strategy of the Islamic State of Iraq and the Levant, aimed at the wholesale destruction of the cultural heritage of the regions under its control, an example being the Temple of Bel at the Palmyra site, one of the most emblematic and best conserved in Syria. What emotions drive an individual – or a group, or even a state – to destroy a cultural heritage?

The Convention on the Prevention and Punishment of the Crime of Genocide states that genocide can be carried out by a series of acts committed "with intent to destroy, in whole or in part, a national, ethnic, racial or religious group". The emphasis is on causing "serious bodily or mental harm" to members of the group. Thus, although the Convention seems to focus in particular on the physical destruction of individuals in the biological sense, it does not appear to preclude the concept of destruction of cultural heritage, over and above genetic heritage, when such destruction is considered to cause serious harm to a person's mental integrity.

Cultural heritage is far more than the context in which a person develops: it represents a memory extrinsic to the group he or she identifies with, and it is also a source for the internalization of values and norms that help us all, during our socialization process, to understand others and their behaviours. Destroying the tangible or intangible heritage of an individual or a community ultimately harms their socialization process and, more generally, their well-being, with repercussions both for their memory of past generations and for the attachment of future generations to the culture in question.

It is thus understandable that, when coining the term "genocide" in 1944, Raphael Lemkin felt that "ethnocide" could be used to express

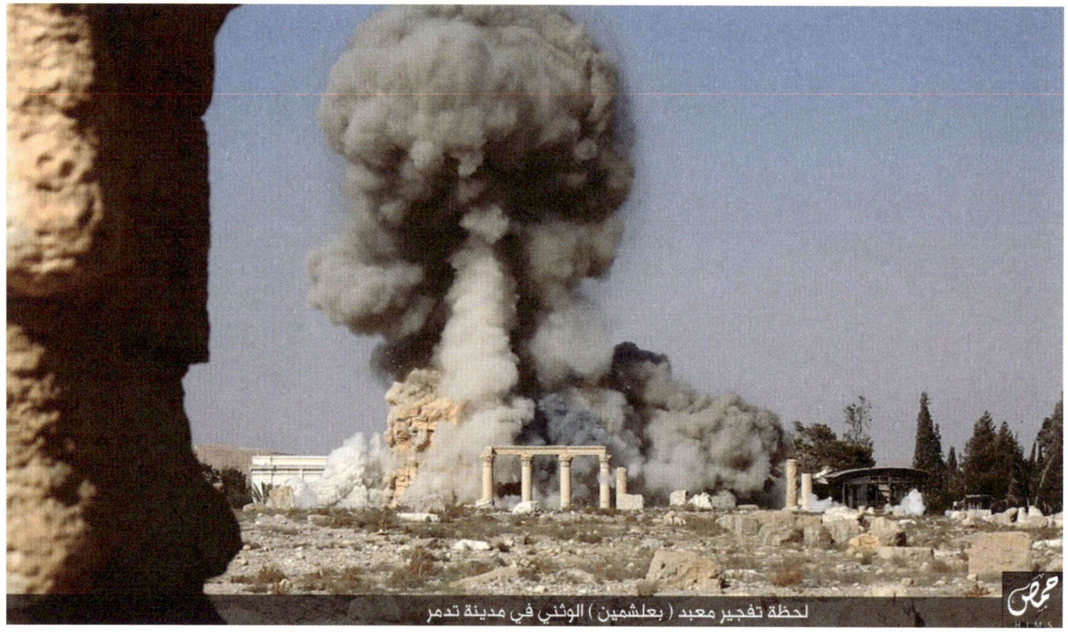

the same idea **[cat. 41]**. According to Rabinbach, the aim of this idea was "to build a bridge between two very different subsets of crimes: mass murder and national and cultural annihilation",[3] the destruction of cultural models being, in Lemkin's eyes, an act that could be considered genocidal. In recent decades, however, it is harm to physical rather than mental integrity that has typically come to be understood when we speak of genocide. Pierre Clastres writes: "In short, genocide murders peoples' bodies, while ethnocide kills their spirit."[4] While it would appear that the terms "ethnocide" and "genocide" have, over time, ceased to be used interchangeably, Lemkin's linking of the motivations behind physical and cultural destructiveness is striking. More recently, the concept of "cultural genocide", or sometimes "cultural crime", has been used, mainly in cases where only the cultural heritage has been destroyed.

In the past twenty years, the disciplines that study the emotions in the humanities, social sciences, behavioural sciences and natural sciences have come together in an academic field that goes by the name of "affective sciences".[5] This new academic discipline analyses the various natures and functions of affective phenomena. Our emotions are triggered when we are confronted with an event that we appraise

The destruction of Palmyra, Syria: this undated image appears to be a screenshot from a video broadcast on 25 August 2015 by ISIS of Homs province, in central Syria. It shows smoke rising from the Baal Shamin Temple in the ancient city of Palmyra. News of the reported destruction of the temple by Islamic extremists was met with international condemnation.

× ×

subjectively as being important. If the event is favourable to our well-being, our values or our interests, we feel positive (pleasant) emotions, while if it is unfavourable to them, we feel negative (unpleasant) emotions. Research indicates that although our emotions may sometimes be dysfunctional, they are essential to our well-being, to good cognitive functioning and to good social relationships.[6] Definitions of what an emotion is have varied widely throughout history, depending on the theoretical approaches adopted, but in recent decades a consensus seems to have emerged whereby it has multiple components.[7] An emotion is said to consist of five parts: (1) a cognitive evaluation (appraisal) of an event relevant to our well-being (e.g. interpreting a phrase as a compliment), (2) its expression (e.g. smiling), (3) a peripheral response (e.g. a quickening of the heartbeat), (4) an action tendency (e.g. wanting to draw closer to the person who has complimented us) and (5) a feeling (e.g. feeling proud).

Conflicts involve at least three types of emotions: individual, "intergroup" and collective. Individual emotions are triggered when our well-being, our values or our *personal* interests are affected by an event. Intergroup emotions are triggered when the well-being, values or interests of the *group* we feel we belong to are affected, especially by an action carried out by a member of another group, to which we do not feel we belong. Thirdly, what are known as the collective emotions are those that come to the fore when we belong to a social whole. They are felt by crowds attending sports events or commemorations; they are given mass expression (in social media, for example) when they accompany collective movements; and they may be reinforced by processes of emotional contagion even where there is no identification with a group. It has been suggested, for example, that the emergence of rules of punishment and exclusion are underpinned by the collective emotions of indignation and contempt.[8]

In the context of destructive emotions, two components have been particularly studied: appraisal on the one hand, and action tendencies on the other. This is because they are the two that correspond, respectively, to the *causes* of an emotional response and to their potential *behavioural consequences*. These components can thus shed light both on the reasons why one emotion is triggered rather than another (e.g. anger as opposed to fear) and what kind of behaviour is facilitated by that emotion (e.g. hostility as opposed to protection).

When it comes to appraisals, the emotions that are believed to drive someone to hurt their enemy in a conflict situation are, typically, those that entail a subjective judgement whereby the enemy's action is deliberately immoral, insulting, offensive, disgusting, humiliating or malicious and, generally speaking, highly prejudicial to our well-being, our values or our interests. The three emotions typically involved in condemning another person on the basis of these appraisals are anger, contempt and disgust. They may generate destructive behaviour, as they are associated with action tendencies of rejection and hostility.

The ways in which individuals appraise a situation can vary enormously. If attacked, for example, one person may feel anger, while in the same situation another may feel fear, depending on whether or not they feel capable of handling the attack. These variations in appraisal go a long way towards explaining the subjectivity of emotions. Once a particular emotion has been triggered, other factors will determine whether the action tendency will be translated into behaviour; for example, different emotional regulation strategies may lead a person to alter their emotional responses and, therefore, their subsequent behaviour.

Strategies for regulating emotions may be intra-individual (if the individual decides to modify their own emotion) or inter-individual (if they modify the emotion of another person, as in some mediation methods). Other emotions, linked more to appraising danger, can also prompt aggression and destructiveness. Fear, for instance, which is characterized by a tendency to protective action, does not necessarily lead to flight behaviour – it could also lead to a decision to attack the source of the threat. Emotions linked to a feeling of inferiority can also be destructive: this has been suggested for malicious envy, where the action tendency would be to harm the envied group. [9] Another, related emotion is what is known as *Schadenfreude* (a word more familiar than the rarely used English term "epicaricacy"), which means pleasure at other people's misfortune – a pleasure we relish even more when we have negative feelings about them.

Hatred – unlike anger, for example – is thought to be based on an appraisal not of the other person's actions, but of their nature. [10] In hatred, the theory goes, it is not an action by another person that is judged to be disgusting, immoral or dangerous, but *the other person*, as a member of a cultural group, who is judged – irrationally – as being disgusting, immoral or evil by their very nature. Posters or speech accompanying hate crimes often use analogies representing the victims as disgusting individuals (rats or cockroaches, for example), as a

L'*Étonnement avec frayeur*
[*Amazement with Fear*],
in Charles Lebrun's album,
head from the "Diagrams" series,
17th century, black ink and
graphite. Paris, Louvre Museum,
Department of Prints and
Drawings.

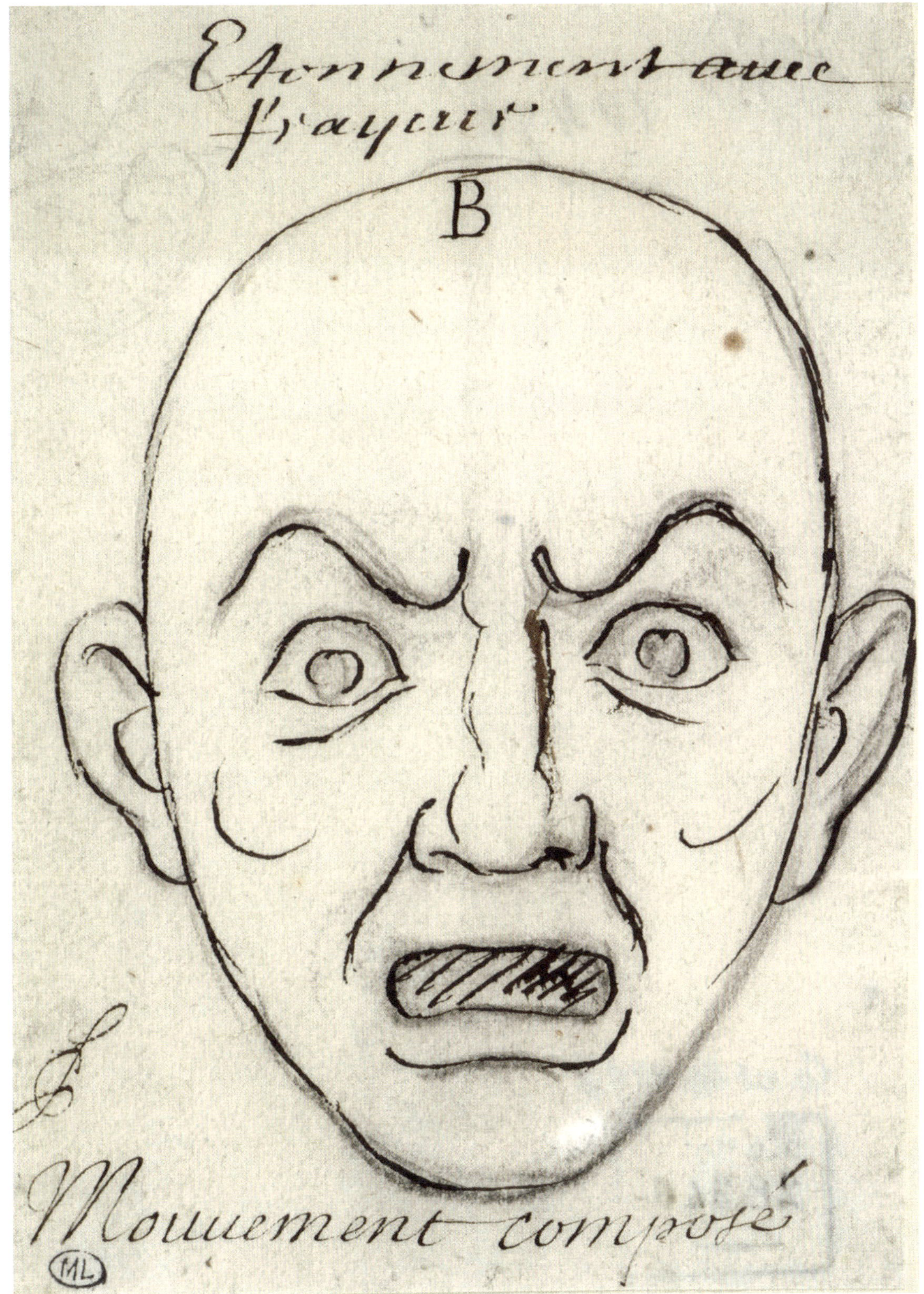
Etonnement auec
frayeur
B
Mouuement composé

way of illustrating their evil or demonic nature (for example, Islamist terrorism often uses names associated with Satan to describe targets to be destroyed).

According to this theory, the genetic legacy present in children and the potentially timeless cultural heritage are thus possible targets of the tendency to act from hatred. Cultural heritage represents longevity and a form of cultural memory that is therefore detested, and on which the tendency to destructive action can vent itself. It is important to underline the distinction between anger and hatred. Anger towards someone is typically triggered by the judgement that that person has committed an injustice or, at any rate, that their behaviour has deviated from the norm, and that one can – must, even – correct it. Correcting may generate a tendency to punish, but it may equally, as the work of Eran Halperin suggests, prompt a desire to change the other's behaviour through education, negotiation or compromise. For anger to prove constructive, it must not be associated with hatred towards the individual in question, or their group, because hatred leads to destructive action against a group as a whole, through a generalization akin to that made by the Wolf, in La Fontaine's well-known fable, before he decides to eat the Lamb:

> "Then 'twas your brother held me up to scorn."
> "I have no brother." "Well, 'tis all the same;
> At least 'twas some poor fool that bears your name."

With Staub, we may take it that the more strongly a destructive group adheres to rigid values and inflexible traditions, the more likely it is to develop intergroup hatred. [11]

In genocide, therefore, this psychological process of intergroup hatred is believed to be complementary to other processes, such as dehumanization [12] or desensitization to mass suffering. [13] Although, by definition, the process of dehumanization applies to human victims, it is conceivable that the destruction of cultural heritage may in itself be a dehumanizing process, by which the target group is stripped of its typically human attributes – the cultural ones – in order to make its members appear less human. The existence of these psychological processes not only requires the introduction of international measures to protect victims and their cultural heritage, and the adoption of appropriate sanctions, it also calls for research aimed at understanding these processes in at-risk groups, and perhaps intervening to prevent them.

If emotions prompt our individual and collective decisions and actions, they are probably fundamental to the establishment, maintenance and modification of the values and norms that govern our societies. As human responses to what is good or bad, just or unjust, emotions play a role in the collective establishment of rules and laws. Although, as we have said, they may contribute to the destruction of cultural heritage, they can, in other circumstances, also be decisive in building it, when founded on a desire to promote philanthropic values, for example. And it is unlikely that our emotions are completely divorced from our political decisions, or from how we make laws to protect cultural heritage.

Notes

[1] Halperin, E., *Emotions in Conflict: Inhibitors and Facilitators of Peace Making*, Routledge, New York, 2016.

[2] Cernadas Curotto, P., Halperin, E., Sander, D. and Klimecki, O., "Emotions in Attacker-Defender Conflicts." *Behavioral and Brain Sciences,* (in press).

[3] Rabinbach, A., "Raphael Lemkin et le concept de génocide", *Revue d'Histoire de la Shoah*, 2,189, 2008, pp. 511–54.

[4] Clastres, P., "De l'Ethnocide", *L'Homme*, 3/4, 1974, pp. 101–10.

[5] Sander, D. and Scherer, K.R. eds, *Oxford Companion to Emotion and the Affective Sciences*, Oxford University Press, New York and Oxford, 2009.

[6] Sander, D., "Psychologie des émotions", *Encyclopædia Universalis*, 2016.

[7] *Ibid.*

[8] Minner, F., "L'Indignation, le mépris et le pardon dans l'émergence du 'cadre légal' d''Occupy Geneva'", *Revue européenne des sciences sociales*, No. 56, 2, 2018, pp. 133–59.

[9] Lange, J., Weidman A.C. and Crusius, J., "The Painful Duality of Envy: Evidence for an Integrative Theory and a Meta-Analysis on the Relation of Envy and Schadenfreude", *Journal of Personality and Social Psychology*, 114(4), 2018, pp. 572–98.

[10] Fischer, A. et al., "Why We Hate", *Emotion Review*, 10(4), 2018, pp. 309–20.

[11] Staub, E. *The Roots of Evil*, Cambridge University Press, New York, 1989.

[12] Harris, L. and Fiske, S., "Dehumanized Perception: A Psychological Means to Facilitate Atrocities, Torture, and Genocide?", *Zeitschrift für Psychologie,* 219(3), 2011, pp. 175–81.

[13] Slovic, P., "'If I Look at the Mass I Will never Act': Psychic Numbing and Genocide." *Judgment and Decision Making*, 2(2), 2007, pp. 79–95.

THE SAMURAI WARRIOR AND THE IDEOLOGY OF BUSHIDO

PIERRE-FRANÇOIS SOUYRI
University of Geneva

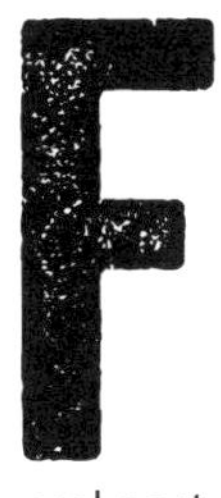rom popular novels to Hollywood films and from martial arts to cartoons, the world of the Japanese samurai has captured the imagination of contemporary society **[cat. 26]**. *Bushidō,* the "way of the warrior", is just one of the concepts that can provide some insight into the true nature of those long-ago warriors, or so we are led to believe. But *bushidō* is not merely an innocuous word with an exotic aura. It was an integral part of the apparatus that shaped a national Japanese mystique during the early twentieth century and played a role in triggering the outbreak of imperialist violence.

The concept of the "way of the warrior" took hold gradually in Japan, emerging between early medieval tales and later narratives. Towards the end of the classical and the start of the medieval period, the Japanese warrior class constructed a new cultural world for themselves, a world very different from that of the court in Kyoto, centring as it did on practices of combat that called for special physical and psychological training. This world, which was known from the eleventh century as the "way of the horse and bow", prompted disgust, criticism and, occasionally, empathy. The tension between values considered alternatively repulsive and fascinating eventually gave rise to the great works of medieval Japanese "warrior literature", such as the *Heike Monogatari (The Tale of the Heike)*. At the time, personal glory, courage and honour were understood as relative values; they were always linked to victory, on which depended the survival of the warrior, his lands and his lineage. This approach to combat, which involved training in horse riding and archery, gradually incorporated other values, such as self-denial, that became the hallmark of a particular social group: the samurai.

The word *bushidō* appears only in the sixteenth century. It was associated with values – loyalty, courage, a sense of honour – that were all the more strongly espoused that they rarely matched the more prosaic reality of actual power relations, in an age when suspicion and betrayal were everyday features of military alliances.

With the peace of the Tokugawa period (1603–1867), and the relative bureaucratization of the warrior class, the samurai elites came to reject *bushidō* as associated with barbarism – retrograde and rather uncouth. They preferred the Chinese-style "way of the gentleman scholar" (*shidō*), a code of behaviour that promoted restraint, culture, self-sacrifice and compliance with the rules. Now, rather than military service, a samurai's main responsibility was to assist his lord in an administrative, managerial capacity. Maintaining order and peace was the lord's concern. Rather than a good fighter, a warrior must be a good administrator, first and foremost. This definitively brought to an end to the incessant feudal wars that had characterized the preceding centuries. The sword, which the samurai wore as a badge of honour, became more a social status symbol than a weapon, thereby further heightening its significance.

The aim of the Tokugawa shoguns was to help these warriors transition from the medieval model to a new one, founded on law and lawfulness; the samurai now had to be careful to follow procedures. This represented a step forward in the bureaucratization of the warrior class, while the dissemination of Chinese Confucian thought can be understood as a process of civilizing behaviour.

The transformation of samurai into officials, however, aroused resentment among some (admittedly a small minority), who were keen to revive the warrior ethic in a world by then devoid of bellicosity. Those who cultivated a certain nostalgia for a less polished society found themselves torn between the obligation to observe the new principles of governance, which they had to comply with out of fealty to their lord, and the feeling that they were somehow betraying their former status.

This contradiction was most strongly expressed by the author of the *Hagakure* (*In the Shadow of Leaves*). Following the demise of Nabeshima Mitsushige, daimyo of Saga, one of his samurai, Yamamoto Tsunetomo, unable to follow his master in death, decided instead to impart his vision of the way of the warrior to one of his own disciples. The *Hagakure*, which he composed between 1710 and 1716, is thus written from the point of view of a samurai confronted with a rapidly changing world and attempting to restore the world of the warriors of old as he sees it – albeit without questioning its legality – rather than adjust to the new social order, in a kind of anachronistic illusion. It is a work of edification, a manifesto against the softening of the samurai as a result of pacification. The title perhaps alludes to the fact that Yamamoto Tsunetomo had decided to retire from the world and live as a recluse, because committing suicide to accompany one's lord into death was by then officially forbidden.

It opens with a striking thought: "The way of the samurai is found in death. When it comes to either/or, there is only the quick choice of death."[1] Serving one's master had to come before everything else, including life. Death could arrive at any moment, so one must be prepared, to avoid covering oneself with shame when the time came. In

Portraits of two **yakunin** *(samurai) in full regalia*, photo 7 *in* Stillfried & Andersen, *Views & Costumes of Japan*, Yokohama, a collection of 101 photos of old Japan from negatives taken by Felice Beato and the Stillfried & Andersen studio, 1877–80, colour pencil, albumen print. Musée national des arts asiatiques Guimet, Paris.

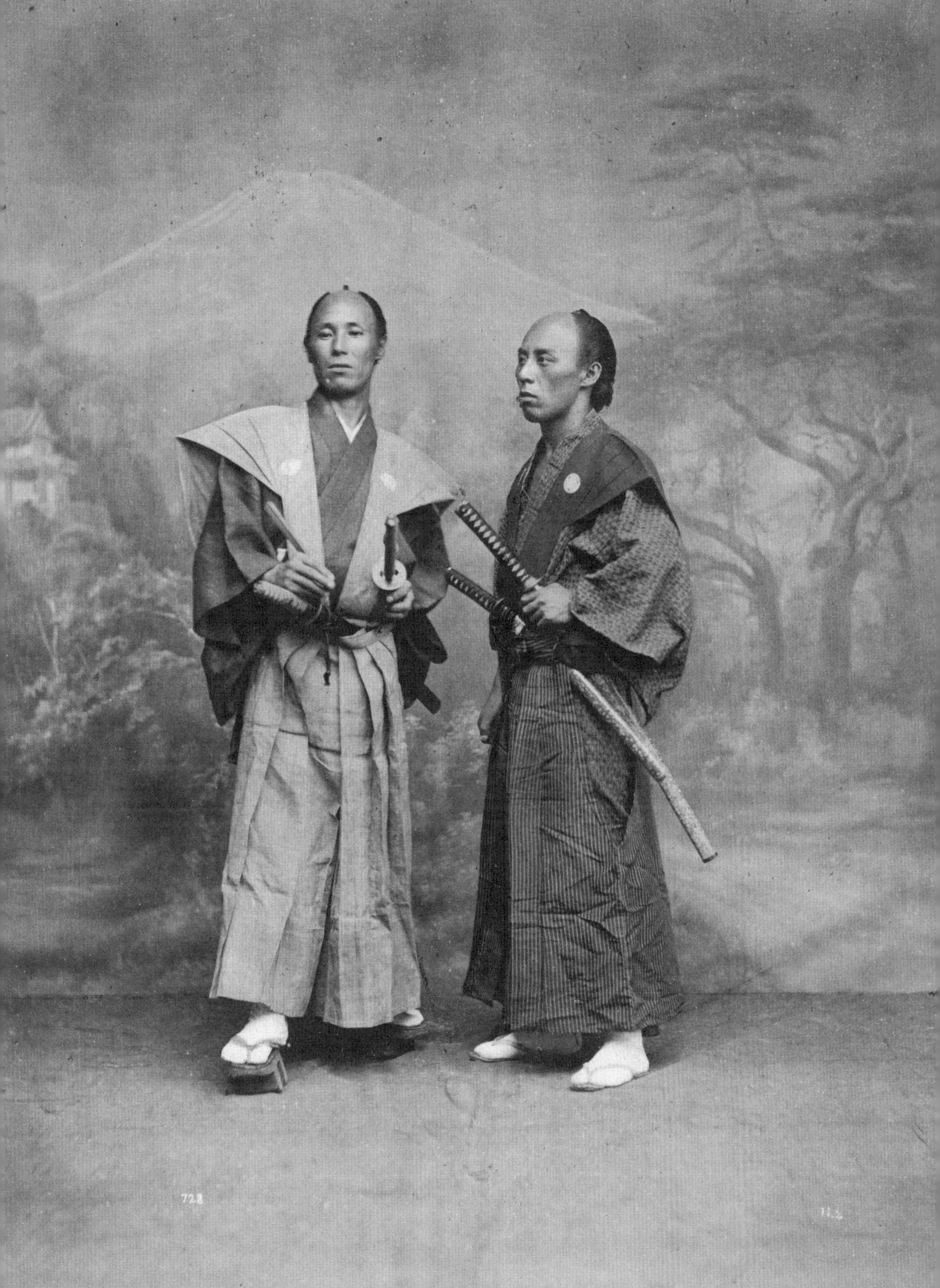
728

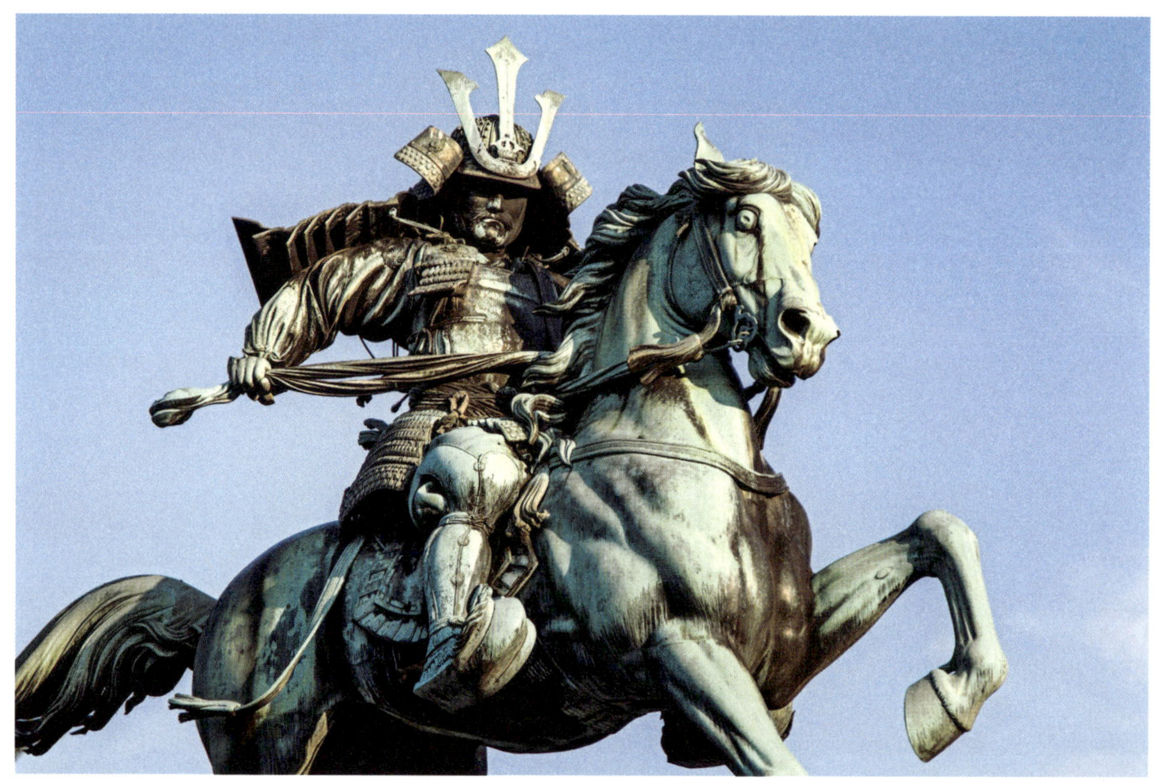

Statue of a samurai
by Masashige Kusunoki, bronze,
14th century. Japan, Tokyo, Kokyo
Imperial Palace Garden.

his text, which stands as a latent criticism of the intelligentsia's neo-Confucianism, Yamamoto refers to concepts such as the impermanence of things and the vanity of the world. The warrior must abide by an ethic of service and death (albeit one that had never really held sway, even at the peak of the medieval wars). That meant devoting oneself entirely to serving one's master:

> Only a samurai whose ideal is nothing less than to sacrifice his life for his lord, to die in an instant and transform himself into a spirit, whose constant concern is the fortunes of his daimyo …, only he truly deserves to be called the samurai of his lord. [2]

Yamamoto's stance – that *bushidō* had been aestheticized and taken out of context – seemed so incongruous to his contemporaries that they regarded his book as the work of a death-obsessed eccentric, a fanatic whose precepts could only lead to suicidal violence, whose writings were both iconoclastic and heretical in relation to the orthodoxy of the time, to put it bluntly. The daimyo himself forbade it to be read or published.

And there the matter might have ended. But the manuscript of the *Hagakure* was rediscovered in 1906 and, in the period leading up to 1945, became a publishing success, especially in nationalist and militaristic circles. An attempt was made to pass it off as a good-conduct guide for soldiers, who would learn from it to scorn death, on the model of the samurai of old. Under the American occupation, it was banned. In 1967, the novelist Yukio Mishima devoted an essay to it, *Introduction to Hagakure*, in which he confessed that he had made Yamamoto's work his "spiritual guide" in the post-war years, at a time when it was again generally disregarded. Mishima says he found in it "freedom and passion": "During the war, the *Hagakure* was like a luminescent object exposed to broad daylight, whereas it was in deepest darkness that it showed its true splendour."[3] In the Jim Jarmusch film *Ghost Dog* (1999), the character played by Forest Whitaker similarly keeps the *Hagakure* by his bedside.

In the nineteenth century, *bushidō* became an element of an essentialist, and subsequently nationalist, discourse, which contrasted the dominant, Chinese-derived Confucianism with the supposedly intangible Japanese way of thinking. Indeed, by then China could no longer be held up as a model in the face of a domineering, conquering West. Around 1900, however, the Japanese tradition also came to be understood as the product of a history that was thought by many to resemble Chinese history less and less and European history more and more. The Japanese increasingly viewed their world as rooted in a feudal past, like Europe. The samurai became the knights of old Japan, and *bushidō* a kind of chivalric code.

In *The Book of Tea* (1906), the art critic Okakura Tenshin lamented the craze for *bushidō*, the art of death, in both Japan and the West, advocating instead the friendly, peaceful " way of tea" (*sadō*), which he likened to an art of living. It was true, he added, that Westerners only began calling Japan "civilized since she began to commit wholesale slaughter on Manchurian battlefields".[4]

In sharp contrast to the medieval "way of the horse and bow", the modern "way of the warrior", as reinterpreted by the thinkers of the Meiji period, was transformed into a new, ready-made concept of a timeless Japanese essence, which encompassed values of abnegation, fealty to one's lord (who in the meantime had become the sovereign, that is, the emperor) and contempt for death. This new ideology, born out of a reinvention of the past, was harnessed in the service of the new nation-state – that is to say, of a modern army directed at the conquest of Asia. The *Hagakure* became bedside reading for militaristic army officers in the 1930s, and the Japanese people began to dream of a modern nation of fighters, devoted body and soul to the cause of the state and the emperor – something the samurai of old, whose overriding concern was the survival of their fiefdom, had never been.

The official ideology of the time thus sought to persuade the nation as a whole to believe that the samurai, who never accounted for more than five per cent of the population, embodied the very essence of the Japanese people, a quasi-mystical ideal. Schools began to teach stories of exemplary samurai who, more often than not, chose a heroic death over life without glory. The Japanese heroes celebrated at that time were most often tragic figures who achieved greatness only in defeat and death.[5] Their life had been a failure, but their death was magnificent, theatrical, the crowning glory of their career. In the West, a hero is endowed with certain qualities (he is a righter of wrongs, loyal, likeable, magnanimous and so on) and undergoes all sorts of trials before emerging victorious in the end. In Japan, the hero fights in accordance with the Japanese conception of loyalty and justice (fealty to his lord, emperor and country), but he does not always win. Rarely does the tale have a Hollywood ending. Yet though he does not always succeed in his cause, the hero prevails in an uncertain future, beyond death; he gives his life for his ideal, and his death overwhelms his opponent.

That, in a nutshell, is the story of the fourteenth-century warrior Kusunoki Masashige, which was much embellished in the Meiji period. In the years leading up to the Second World War, he came to be considered one of the great faithful heroes of Japanese history, as attested by the imposing statue erected in 1900 in front of the imperial palace in Tokyo. Kusunoki Masashige had been one of the staunchest supporters of the emperor Go Daigo. In 1336, he agreed to enter battle against the emperor's main opponent, the general Ashikaga Takauji – he became shogun in 1338[6] – knowing full well that it was madness and that he could not win. But the emperor had ordered him to fight, and so he did, despite the inequality of the contest. He prepared for death and, on the evening following his defeat, he committed suicide, serene in the knowledge that he had obeyed to the last. If he had refused to fight and waited to do battle at a more favourable time, he would have lived, but he would have disobeyed. By dying courageously, Masashige redeemed his defeat. His heroic death as a loyal vassal would hang like a millstone around the necks of his adversaries forever. His enemy, the victorious general, thus appears as the villain of the story. Defeat is nothing; death alone has value. So what if Go Daigo's partisans were overcome in the battle of Minatogawa? Masashige, the faithful vassal, had fulfilled his duty to the end and died a dignified death. That was all that mattered.

The fact that heroes like Masashige were held up as examples to Japanese children of the early twentieth century helps explain the seemingly suicidal behaviour displayed by Japanese soldiers during the Pacific War. The formation of kamikaze units makes more sense when one understands that victory was not their main motivation: they sought the glory of dying, not the glory of winning. American soldiers felt trapped in an asymmetrical war, in which the enemy were driven not by the need to emerge victorious from combat, but by a desire to impress their adversaries with their determination in the face of death. This approach to combat, which the American troops regarded as irrational fanaticism, had a profound impact on the conflict throughout 1944 and 1945. On the Japanese side, it resulted in appalling losses, while it caused the Americans such anxiety that the use of any means available seemed justified if it could bring the war to a swift end.

Through a series of shifts, the values of the samurai who fought fiercely for their lords in the civil wars of the late twelfth century thus came to embody the values of the expansionist Japanese state in the early twentieth. After the Second World War, however, the *bushidō*-inspired ideology of militarism fell victim to the censorship imposed by the American occupying forces, and the discourse surrounding the values symbolized by the samurai suddenly appeared as a precipitating cause of the disaster of 1945.

In response, Japan developed a different form of nationalism to account for its greatness. Japan was a remarkable country not because it had once possessed a social group known as the samurai and had built an impressive military force – that had been crushed, and was now understood to have been the cause of the nation's defeat. Rather, it was great because its culture was centuries old. Following the post-war reconstruction, it is that culture – presented as one of peace – that has been promoted, through the so-called traditional arts, from print-making to the arts of tea, flowers and ceramics, as well as more modern ones, such as manga, video games, J-pop and cosplay. With the idea of "Cool Japan" – the antithesis of the *bushidō* ideology – Japan has become a "soft power" nation.

The Americans'aim in the post-war period was undoubtedly to eradicate the culture of militarism. By a curious twist of history, however, it has been partly rehabilitated in several major works of contemporary American cinema (*Star Wars, Ghost Dog, Kill Bill, The Last Samurai*, to name only a few). That said, any success the Americans achieved in eradicating militaristic ways of thinking was possible only because, to rebuild their country on new foundations, the vast majority of Japanese turned their backs on the old ideologies and embraced the new, peace-oriented constitution of 1946. Since the 1950s, Japanese conservatives have been trying to change the constitution, proposing – so far without success – the abolition of Article 9, by which the Japanese state renounces the right of belligerency. Even if the current Abe government were to succeed in passing this reform, *bushidō*, now outmoded in the eyes of the vast majority of Japanese, will most likely be relegated to the storeroom of outdated ideological props.

Notes

[1] Yamamoto Tsunetomo, *Hagakure, The Book of the Samurai*, trans. William Scott Wilson, Kodansha International, Tokyo, New York and London, 1979, p. 23.

[2] *Hagakure,* quoted in Yukio Mishima, *Le Japon moderne et l'éthique samouraï,* Arcades Gallimard, 1985, pp. 105–6 (published in English in 1981 as *Hagakure: The Samurai Ethic and Modern Japan*).

[3] *Ibid.* p. 15.

[4] Okakura Tenshin, *The Book of Tea*, Putnam, London and New York, 1906, p. 3.

[5] Ivan Morris, T*he Nobility of Failure: Tragic Heroes in the History of Japan,* Martin Secker & Warburg Limited, London, 1975.

[6] For an appraisal of this historical figure in context, see Pierre-François Souyri, *Histoire du Japon médiéval. Le monde à l'envers*, Éditions Perrin, Paris, 2013, pp. 220-38.

POLITICAL POETRY DURING THE WARS OF RELIGION (1562–1598)

NICOLAS DUCIMETIÈRE

Martin Bodmer Foundation

uring the reign of the Valois, France experienced
a hundred-year long age of gold and steel, a
period marked by the advent of a cultured and
literate society in which humanism spread its
light, and by the torment and heartbreak of civil
and religious wars. At the time, poetry, a prime
example of a noble genre, was as likely to
address religion and politics as it was to sing of love and
death. It is hardly surprising, therefore, that it was turned
to account for the warring interests, and often looked
beyond the boundaries of the kingdom for the source of
those misfortunes. Discernible from the 1560s onward,
poetical involvement reached its pinnacle during the eighth
and last War of Religion, when Henry IV, the Huguenot
prince who would become king of France, reconquered the
kingdom and peace by force, but also thanks to a skilfully
deployed propaganda policy.

Poetry joins the battle (1560–88)

In 1560, following the accidental death of Henry II, the
crown passed to his son, Francis II, a puppet in the hands
of his mother, Catherine de' Medici, and, more importantly,
of his wife's uncles, the Guise clan. The Reformation, which
in France had gained followers even among princes of the
blood (first and foremost the prince of Condé), appeared
more threatened than ever by that ultra-Catholic clan.
Protestant humanists such as Théodore de Bèze were
already choosing exile. To remove the young sovereign
from his relatives' influence, a group of Huguenots tried to
abduct him, but the attempt failed, further exacerbating the hatred
between the two communities. A young boy at the time, the future
poet and soldier Agrippa d'Aubigné was taken by his father to the
foot of the castle walls at Amboise, where they looked on as their
fellow Protestants were hanged, and swore to avenge them: that
grisly sight would mark d'Aubigné for life. To defuse the situation,
the Queen Mother turned to the Court's best poet, Pierre de Ronsard,
who composed an *Elégie sur les troubles d'Amboise*. In this humanist
poem, Ronsard called on the adversaries to engage in conciliation and
interreligious dialogue, appealing to their reason in moderate, highly
modern terms:

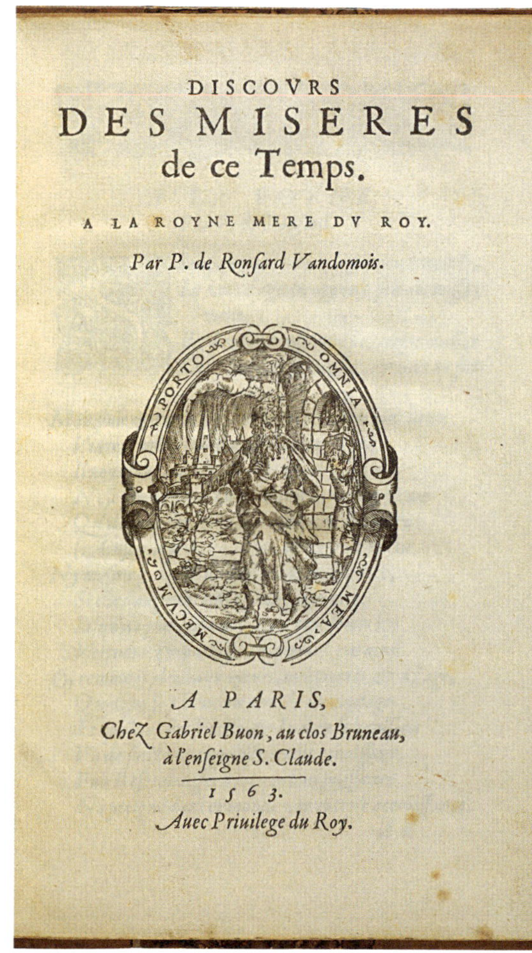

**Pierre de Ronsard, *Discours des
Misères de ce Temps**, [*Discourse
on the Miseries of These Times*]
Paris, Gabriel Buon, 1563.
Cologny, Martin Bodmer Foundation.

> Car il faut désormais défendre nos maisons,
> Non par le fer tranchant, mais par vives raisons,
> Et courageusement nos ennemis abattre
> Par les mêmes bâtons dont ils veulent nous battre.
> Ainsi que l'ennemi par livres a séduit
> Le peuple dévoyé qui faussement le suit,
> Il faut en disputant par livres le confondre,
> Par livres l'assaillir, par livres lui répondre. [1]

Unfortunately, two years later, a skirmish between the Duke of Guise's escort and Huguenots at worship in the village of Wassy degenerated into a massacre, provoking an uprising by the entire Reformed party. A short time later, when his poem was reissued, Ronsard replaced the *livres* (books) of the last line with *armes* (weapons): "Par armes l'assaillir, par armes luy respondre". The first of the eight Wars of Religion had just broken out – they were to hold the Kingdom of France in their bloody grip for thirty-six years.

In that onslaught of violence, both camps made adroit use of their weapons and their quills. The 1560s thus witnessed the outbreak of literary hostilities within the armed conflict, in the form of the *Querelle des Discours*, a rhetorical war of sorts between Ronsard and the Reformation poets. [2] In his *Discours des Misères de ce Temps*, Ronsard, the Queen Mother's champion, lamented that such an atrocious war should be born of "a pestilential opinion of humankind", "Within the cabinet of Theologians, / Of these new rabbis". He lashed out at the Reformation, "the error of a foreigner [Luther]", and the internecine fighting it spawned:

> Ce monstre arme le fils contre son propre pere.
> Et le frere (ô malheur) arme contre son frere.
> La sœur contre la sœur, & les cousins germains,
> Au sang de leurs cousins veullent tremper leurs mains. [3]

These words, written at Catherine's behest, did not, of course, go unanswered. [4] From Geneva and Orléans (the Reformation bastion in France), vengeful pamphlets attacked the official poet of the Valois, accusing him of having traded his poet's laurels for a priest's robes. Close friends of Condé and Calvin, such as the pastors Antoine de Chandieu and Bernard de Montméja, wrote brilliant diatribes in iambic pentameter. Ronsard returned the compliment with impish reason:

× ×

Tu m'estimes méchant, & méchant je t'estime,
Je retourne sur toy le mesme fait du crime:
Tu penses que c'est moy, je pense que c'est toy:
Et qui fait ce discord? notre diverse foy. [5]

Even some of Ronsard's disciples turned in acrimony against him. In his anonymous 1563 *Réplique* to Ronsard's response, for example, Louis des Masures refers to Ronsard as "formerly a poet and now a priest", and informs us that Bèze cared about Ronsard "[a]s much as for a pot he'd shatter at his feet". The literary nation was being split asunder: as on the actual battlefield, clashes in the world of writing pitted brother against brother, friend against friend.

As one battle followed another, many officers in both camps put quill to parchment, if only to report on the horrors of the hostilities and man-to-man combat:

Se disant, il l'enfonce [the blade] & joignant le costé
A double coup roidit l'estoc ensanglanté
Au defaut de l'harnois: ja, la playe ruiselle
Un sang noir & caillé, le pouvre homme chancelle
Regardant de travers son vaincœur odieux:
L'ame s'enfuit du corps loin, bien loin dans les Cieux. [6]

The most talented of those soldier-poets was undoubtedly Agrippa d'Aubigné. Recovering from a serious wound, the celebrated Huguenot captain started writing *Les Tragiques* in 1577 **[cat. 77]**, providing a detailed account of the daily lives of warriors and the din of battle, but also describing his horror at the succession of atrocities inflicted on the people, howling his rage in this anathema:

J'appelle Dieu pour juge, & tout haut je deteste
Les violeurs de paix, les perfides parfaicts,
Qui d'une salle cause amenent tels effects:
Quel œil sec eust peu voir les membres mi-mangez
De ceux qui par la faim estoient morts enragez? [7]

Reconquering the land and soul of France (1589–93)

The assassination of Henry III in August 1589 marked the end of the Valois dynasty. Henry was succeeded by his distant cousin, Henry of Bourbon, who was king of Navarre, but above all leader of the Protestant

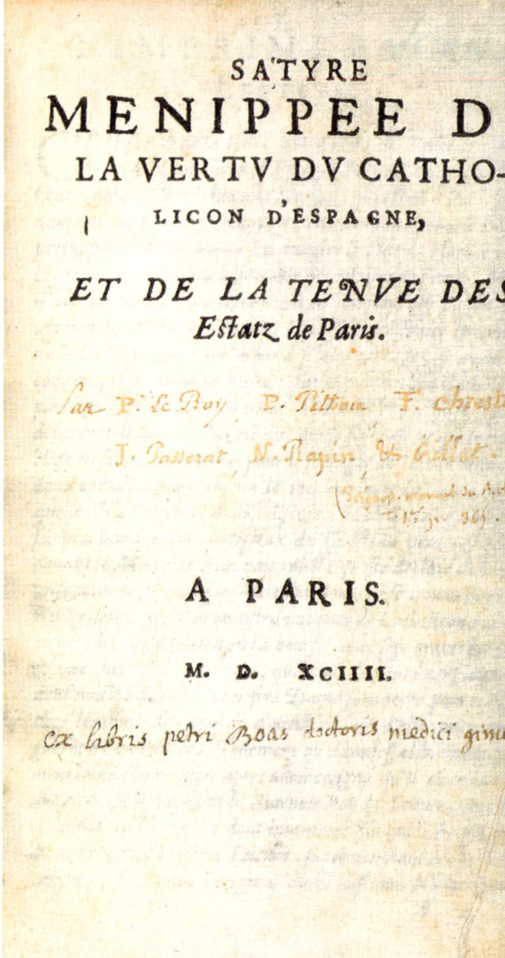

Collective edition of *Satyre Ménippée*, s. l. n. n. [Tours or Paris, Jamet Mettayer], 1593 [i.e. 1594].
Nicolas Ducimetière Collection.
According to the historian Charles-Jean-François Hénault, "the *Satyre Ménippée* was likely no less helpful to Henry IV than the battle of Ivry: ridicule is more powerful than one might think".

party. Like a recurrent disease, the civil war resumed, caused by the same afflictions, according to Salluste du Bartas:

> Mais las! une gangrene, une lepre, un peste
> Occupe tant ce corps, une torche funeste
> Cendroye nostre Gaule, & sans ce que ta main,
> De ce brouchant estat tient de si court le frein,
> Nostre Sceptre jadis reveré de tant d'hommes
> Voleroit en esclas, ou plustost en atomes.
> Le prestre est le fuzil, le noble est le soufflet
> De ce brasier ardent, le sot peuple se plait
> A leur voir flamboyer, & d'une rage extreme
> Y jette volontiers au lieu de bois soi-mesme. [8]

Many were the poets who had recourse to the metaphor of illness, of gangrenous cankers infecting the body of France. The king's personal physician, Gérard François (the author of a long medical-political poem[9]) was one; another was the magistrate Pierre Boton, who, giving a voice to France on her deathbed, denounced the dubious treatment inflicted on her by political quacks:

> Qui par leur fer n'ont fait qu'agrandir & germer
> L'escarre de l'Eglise au lieu de le fermer.
> Par leur guerre civile, ils m'ont si mal traictée,
> Par leur fer violant ils m'ont tant agittée,
> Ils m'ont ouvert le corps par tant d'incisions,
> Il m'ont tant travaillé par tant d'extorsions,
> Le fer, le feu, le sang, estant les medecines,
> Qu'ils m'ont faict avaller par leurs dextes mutines,
> Que j'en reste debile, & sans force, & vigueur,
> N'ayant plus rien d'entier, & de sain, dans le cœur ... [10]

Faced with widespread revolt, the new king set off to reconquer his kingdom, but also his subjects, most of whom were hostile to the Reformed monarch. While good king Henry is remembered above all for his appreciation of the finer things in life and was not a greatly learned man, he was not without humanist culture. Like his close advisers, he knew that he would have to spread his political message through books. To a man, the Protestant poets welcomed his first and unexpected victories over the armies of the Catholic League. The pastor Pierre Poupo, a refugee in Geneva, greeted the victory at Arques in strongly bellicose terms, rejoicing in the enemy casualties:

> Gloire, gloire au Seigneur, la Ligue est escornee,
> Tous ces felons sont morts, bruslez, ou pris,
> Et des mesmes couteaux dont ils nous ont meurtris,
> On void de jour en jour leur race exterminee. [11]

Reconciliation through war (1593–98)

The King's conversion to Catholicism, on 25 July 1593, brought most of the French over to his side. One town after another pledged allegiance to him, and the territory was reconquered in a kind of genuine liberation, during which the foreign occupiers allied with the rebels were kicked out of France. The retaking of Paris, in March 1594, marked a turning point and was enthusiastically praised by many poets. Alexandre de Pontaimery evoked the Spanish occupation in anaphoric terms reminiscent of a certain well-known Gaullist speech pronounced at a more recent liberation of the capital:

> Paris desespéré, des-peuplé, des-uni
> Qui n'est que d'Espagnols, & de Lorrains muny,
> Paris, qui de Paris à fait un corps de garde
> D'où l'Espagnol tousjours en la France regarde,
> Paris, qui de Paris n'a que le bastiment
> Paris, qui de Paris a le nom seulement ... [12]

Whether Protestant or Catholic, the official poets could now unabashedly celebrate the military triumphs of Henry IV, whom they repeatedly described as the "French Hercules". Other poets put him on a par with Achilles or Alexander the Great, when he led the charge wearing a helmet topped with a "large white feather from an African ostrich". [13] And they never failed to accentuate the good king's clemency towards his subjects, including the former rebels among them. What better way to win hearts and minds?

This legendary hero, this demi-god, had formidable adversaries, first and foremost among them the multiple and constantly regenerating heads of the Hydra, the monster to which the rebel League, the enemy from within, was readily assimilated:

> Là est dessous le char l'Hydre de nos miseres,
> La Ligue au mol cerveau composé de chimeres,

> La peste des Françoys, le funeste flambeau,
> Qui en cendre a reduit ce Royaume si beau:
> Ce serpent venimeux, porte cent mille testes,
> Il surpasse un Prothee en formes & pretextes ... [14]

As more and more people rallied to the king's side and the threat was reduced to pockets of opposition (such as Brittany, controlled by the Duke of Mercœur), the royal propaganda machine turned its guns against an even more daunting enemy, one able to reunite the French and muster them under the federating white flag of the monarch. The adversary, the aggressor who had been working for years to undermine the kingdom and fatherland was easily identified: Spain. No attack could be too strongly worded or too insulting. Many poets stressed the country's suspect proximity to the land of Islam; the Spanish "demons" were presented as the "demi-Moors of Castile [15]", the "olive-skinned Spaniards [16]", "partly cooked Iberians [17]", "swarthy men of the Tagus[,] rogue Rodomonts [or] negroid Castilians [18]". In countless poems, the personification of France railed at the foreign invaders:

> Las! j'ay veu dessus moy ces Marrans bazanez,
> Ces Mores insolens, Bisognes effrenez,
> Lasches à la besongne, & prompts à la parolle,
> Non point formez de pierre, ainsois de terre molle,
> Desireux de plonger dans mon sein leur fureur:
> Et sans avoir du cœur vouloir percer mon cœur. [19]

By nature a corrupting influence, the "wily Spaniard" was said to have procured many a devoted servant by scattering "all around the golden apple / Lacquered with Indian gold". [20] At the head of an empire on which the sun never set, proud Philip II did not merit his title of "Most Catholic Majesty":

> Ce grand Roy du Peru qui contrefaict si bien
> Le zelé Catholique & reformé Chrestien,
> Tient dans Tolede ecole ouverte de magie,
> (Abominable erreur, pire que l'heresie)
> Le Sarrazin, le Juif, & l'Atheiste fol,
> Vivent paisiblement dessous cest Espagnol.
> En Flandre, il entretient toutes sectes diverses,
> Les schismes, l'heresie, & les erreurs perverses ... [21]

It was thus against a denatured, almost monstrous enemy that the poets called on the French to fight, united under the banner of their sovereign and finally setting aside their quarrels. That just war was intended to enable the rebirth of a kingdom drained of its blood: "The lily shall blossom again, the sacred banner / Shall be seen to fly in triumph over all"[22]. Charging from victory to victory at the head of his people, the triumphant king would outdo Alexander by subduing "the Brahman of India", who were as willing as all other peoples to "Admire [his] wisdom, adore [his] worth, / Proclaim [his] clemency, & prize [his] gentleness".[23] In less bellicose terms, most poets congratulated Henry – not so much the king as the father of the nation – above all for having restored peace twice over, once with the Edict of Nantes (30 April 1598) **[cat. 121]** and again with the Peace of Vervins (2 May 1598), the former putting an end to the civil war, the latter to the conflict with Spain:

> Entre tant de malheurs, durant l'intelligence
> De tous les estrangers avec nous contre nous,
> Henry, non tant le Roy, que le père de tous;
> O miracle du Ciel!, a mis la paix en France.[24]

Portrait of Henry IV as Hercules slaying the Lernaean Hydra, French School, c. 1600, oil on canvas. Paris, Louvre Museum.

Notes

[1] Pierre de Ronsard, "Elégie sur les troubles d'Amboise", in *Œuvres*, Paris, Buon, 1560, Vol. III, ff. 215v–216r.

[2] See Jean Paul Barbier-Mueller, *Bibliographie des Discours politiques de Ronsard*, Geneva, Droz, 1996.

[3] P. de Ronsard, *Discours des misères de ce temps*, Paris, Buon, 1562, ff. 4v–5r.

[4] See, for example, *La Polémique protestante contre Ronsard*, presented and annotated by Jacques Pineaux, Paris, Didier, 1973.

[5] P. de Ronsard, *Responce … aux injures et calomnies, de je ne sçay quels Predicans, & Ministres de Geneve…*, Paris, Buon, 1563, f. 15r.

[6] Alexandre de Pontaimery, *La Cité du Montelimar, ou les trois prinses d'icelle…*, s.l.s.n., 1591, p. 178.

[7] A. d'Aubigné, *Les Tragiques*, [Maillé], s.n., 1616, p. 15.

[8] Guillaume de Salluste du Bartas, *Cantique de la victoire d'Ivry…*, Lyon, Tholosan, 1594 [1590], pp. 17–18.

[9] Gérard François, *De la Maladie du grand corps de la France, des causes et premiere origine de son Mal: Et des remedes pour le recouvrement de sa santé*, Paris, Mettayer and L'Huillier, 1595.

[10] Pierre Boton, *La France divisée – Poème contenant l'histoire tragique de la Ligue…* Paris, Morel, 1595, pp. 12–13.

[11] Pierre Poupo, *La Muse chrestienne…*, Paris, Le Franc, 1590, sonnet LXX.

[12] A. de Pontaimery, *Le Roy triomphant…*, Lyon, Ancelin, 1594, p. 37.

[13] Nicolas Le Digne, *Description du medaillon d'Alexandre le Grand…*, Paris, Périer, 1601, f. 8 v.

[14] P. Boton, *Le Triomphe de la liberté royale, et la prinse de Beaulne…*, Paris, Morel, 1595, p. 7.

[15] Jean Godard, *Les Trophées de Henry quatriesme, tres-chrestien et tres-victorieux Roy de France, & de Navarre…*, Lyon, Dauphin, 1594, p. 99.

[16] Claude Expilly, *Les Poëmes…*, Paris, L'Angelier, 1596, p. 126.

[17] A. de Pontaimery, *La Cité du Montelimar…*, op. cit., p. 59.

[18] P. Boton, *Le Triomphe de la liberté royalle…*, op. cit., p. 20.

[19] Pierre Davity, *Les Travaux sans travail…*, Rouen, L'Oyselet, 1609 [Tournon, 1599], pp. 298–305.

[20] Claude Binet, *Les Destinées de la France…*, Paris, Mettayer et L'Huillier, 1594, p. 33.

[21] P. Boton, *La France divisée…*, op. cit., pp. 24–25.

[22] P. Davity, *Les Travaux sans travail…*, op. cit., pp. 298–305.

[23] *Ibid.*

[24] Jean du Nesme, *Le Miracle de la Paix en France…*, Paris, Nivelle, 1598, p. 24, sonnet (39).

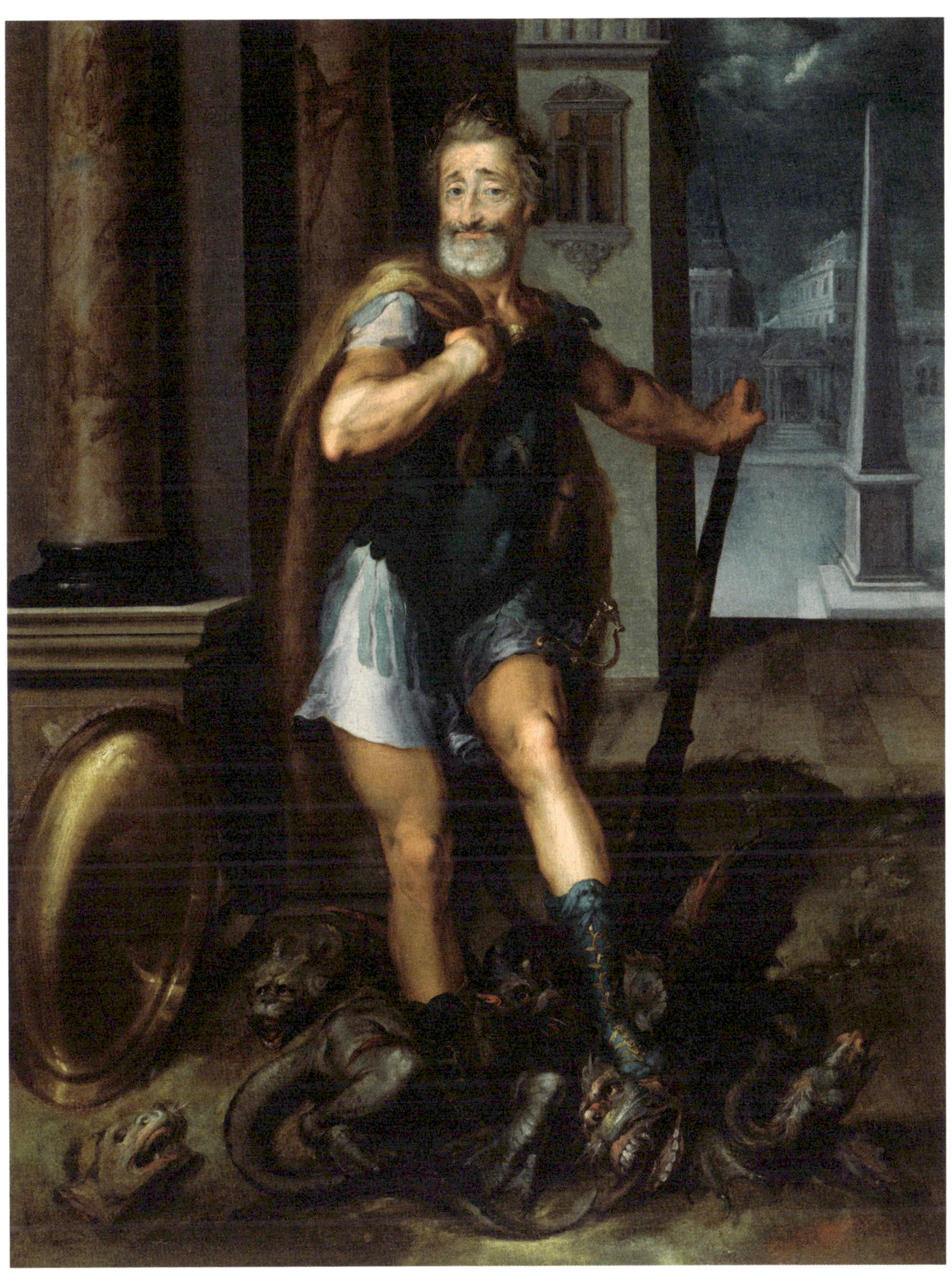

THE FIRST WORLD WAR NOVEL IN FRANCE

JEAN KAEMPFER
University of Lausanne

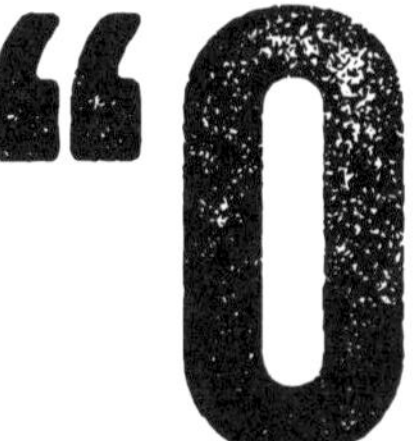

"Of all the possible accounts of the war, those of the men in the trenches are the most insignificant."[1] That, in essence, is what Jean Norton Cru referred to as the "paradox attributed to Stendhal". The famous passage at the start of Stendhal's *The Charterhouse of Parma* **[cat. 78]**, in which Fabrice wanders the battlefield at Waterloo, lost, disoriented and powerless to understand what is happening, is a scene that has become emblematic of the modern war narrative. At the time when Cru's book was published, in 1929, the soldier's drastically restricted viewpoint no doubt appeared to some – historians especially – as a weakness. For Cru, however – and, according to him, for Stendhal as well – the only way to understand the true nature of war was through such first-hand accounts of soldiers' experiences. That conviction informs *Témoins*, a collection of several hundred stories, novels and memoirs by soldiers who had experienced the crucible of battle, published by Cru in the decade following the end of the hostilities.

The memoir – a narrative written in the first, sometimes the third, person, but always exclusively focused on the experience of a specific soldier or squadron – is also the starting point of this essay. It defines the dominant, even hegemonic, narrative mode of the genre known as the First World War novel, a heuristic artifact that I shall use to draw out some of the common characteristics and themes of the vast body of writing about the war produced over the past hundred years.[2] For reasons of convenience, these comments are limited to French writers, but a cursory exploration suggests that they are equally valid for German- and English-language authors.

Jean Galtier-Boissière's *La fleur au fusil*, published in 1917, is a prime example of the war memoir.[3] Cru held it in very high regard, in large part due to its diary form, which allowed the author to relate events as they occurred, in unvarnished terms. The book covers the brief period – the first two months of the conflict – between mobilization and the German retreat in September 1914. Two sharply contrasting moments stand out, both of which would become commonplaces of the genre. There is at first the heady atmosphere of the day of departure: Galtier describes the exuberant joy of the conscripts boarding "the excursion train for Berlin, there and back!", on 6 August, as "a singular inebriety ... that mixed patriotic enthusiasm with a taste for adventure and a thirst for blood".[4] But then come the exhausting marches under the sun, the first volleys of gunfire and the baptism of battle: "The sneering of the shells is hideous. It's as though they were laughing at our anguish before smashing into us."[5] This is followed by the first wounded soldiers and the sight of villages going up in flames at night, prompting this assessment from a corporal: "Mate, if I'd had any idea *their war* was going to be like this..."[6] Galtier took note: he described in detail the tortured world created by the war, the growing numbers of appallingly wounded men it spat out, the black, swollen corpses it left in its wake, the wretched convoys of civilians it forced onto the roads.

The first-hand account, a key narrative condition of the genre, thus converged with one of its central themes, the familiar trope of the topsy-turvy world, which the reality of war forced these authors to explore anew. Indeed, the war produced a sort of counter-culture, turning to rubble a landscape of fields and villages that had evolved over thousands of years since the Neolithic revolution. It created a paradoxical economy, in which productive forces were placed in the service of destruction. It reversed the generational order by ordaining the death of masses of young men. And lastly, by legitimizing slaughter, it brutalized and undermined the slow and gradual progress of civilization.

As action at the front ground to a standstill and the soldiers retreated to the trenches, this denatured world developed a humanity all of its own. Henri Barbusse was the first to explore this theme in *Under Fire*, which won the Goncourt Prize in 1916 **[cat. 84]**. Mired in the trenches, the *poilus* were condemned to a life that was both physically and morally diminished. Plagued by fleas and rats, surrounded by decomposing bodies, their moral existence was reduced to fear, boredom and "an animal passivity that will accept anything".[7] The camaraderie born of this shared feeling of abandonment was precious, but, in its own way, also animal in nature; it could not replace the friends or lovers chosen in time of peace.

The unusual concurrence in the First World War novel of a theme and a form – namely, the topsy-turvy world and the first-person narrative – leads the writer to an impossible moral crossroad: must I accept, and can I justify, the dehumanizing experience I am being forced to undergo? The question of judgement cannot be evaded: such is the *ethical* constraint of the Great War novel. Galtier, for his part, hesitated. Though he accepted the omnipresence of death with fatalism, he also experienced the euphoria of battle: "My comrades drink from the same potent cocktail as I do. All eyes are shining with ferocious joy."[8] He does not explicitly judge the war: it simply is, and it provokes in him a variety of feelings, alternating between despondency and excitement. The war undoubtely developed a culture all its own, which the soldiers understood as such, and from which they drew the strength they needed to consent to the inhumane circumstances imposed upon them. For Barbusse, on the other hand, it was more a matter of constraint than consent, the necessary corollary of which was that one must "kill war[9]". The wisdom of war is short-lived, a truth that Jules Romains, in his *Prelude to Verdun*, forcefully expressed in the words of Lieutenant Jerphanion, writing from the front to his friend Jallez:

What we see, both at the front and behind the lines, is horrible … *Nothing is worth this*. Nothing = all the reasons we can think of. This = the life we're leading (with the threat of what manner of death hanging over our heads!). That is the final word of the wisdom of war. Everything else is literature.[10]

To have seen war is enough – case closed! This shortcut would become the rule: the overwhelming majority of Great War novels conclude with an unappealable call for pacifism.[11]

This is especially true of the second wave of First World War stories that followed in the wake of the personal histories collected by Jean Norton Cru. This second wave, which can be described as a "literature of re-creation",[12] takes the raw material of the war, by then widely available, and transmutes it into the singular world of the writers who appropriated it. I will briefly discuss two of these works: Giono's *To the Slaughterhouse* (1931) and Céline's *Journey to the End of the Night* (1932). Each espoused a particular brand of pacifism. Giono's was principled and sincere, whereas Céline took the view that pacifism was born of violent trauma and resulted in a morality of cowardice. Both, however, grounded their denunciation of war in another denunciation: employing a widely used strategy, they reproduced the heroic, epic style traditionally applied to war in their own writing, thereby revealing it as fraudulent. This dialogism is inherent to the Great War novel: there can be no war story without a war of stories. As if the personal account, confined within its subjectivity, could only be enhanced by setting it against a contrasting backdrop, thus avoiding the "paradox attributed to Stendhal" – the suspicion of inconsistency.

In Céline's *Journey*, the devaluation of heroic virtues proceeds from a two-pronged attack. Heroism, usually viewed as a prerogative of men at war, is claimed, in Céline's account, by a pleasant young woman working far the front, the American nurse Lola, who is "in charge … of a special service, whose mission it was to supply the Paris hospitals with

Following pages
Voyage au bout de la nuit
[*Journey to the End of the Night*],
written by Louis-Ferdinand Céline,
graphic novel by Jacques Tardi,
Futuropolis, Gallimard, 1991.

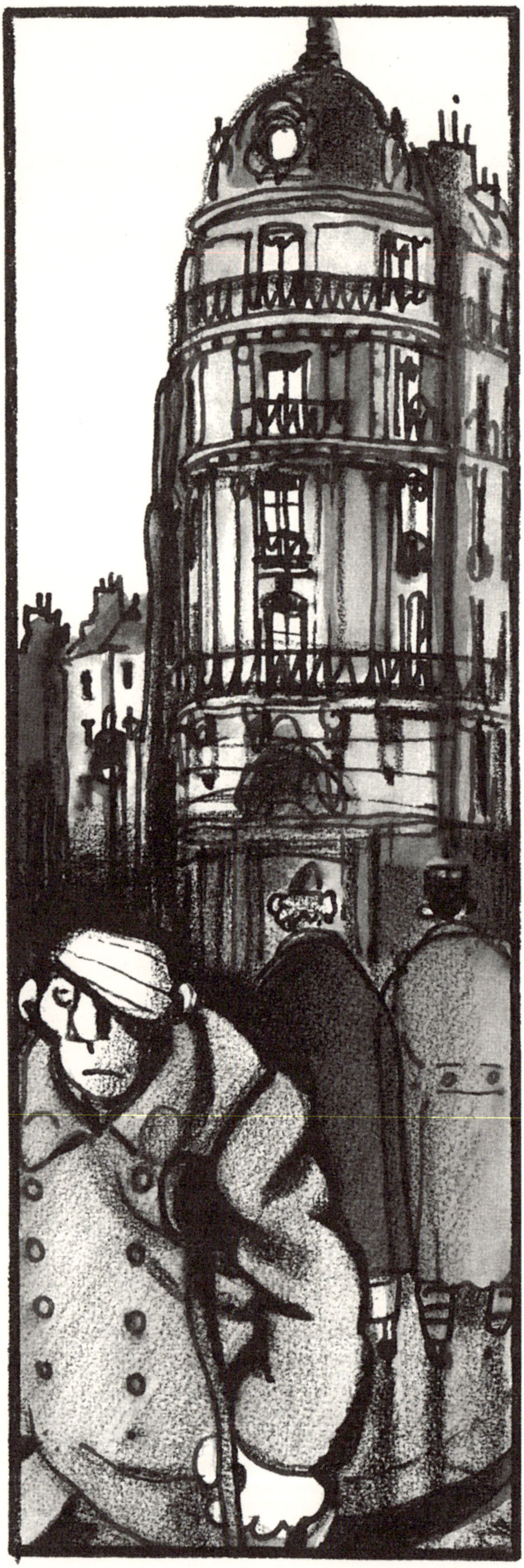

Tout marchait parfaitement en somme et nous étions bien en train de gagner la guerre, quand un certain beau jour, à l'heure du déjeuner, je la trouvai bouleversée, se refusant à toucher un seul plat du repas. L'appréhension d'un malheur arrivé, d'une maladie soudaine me gagna. Je la suppliai de se fier à mon affection vigilante.

D'avoir goûté ponctuellement les beignets pendant tout un mois, Lola avait grossi de deux bonnes livres ! Son petit ceinturon témoignait d'ailleurs, par un cran, du désastre. Vinrent les larmes. Essayant de la consoler, de mon mieux, nous parcourûmes, sous le coup de l'émotion, en taxi, plusieurs pharmaciens, très diversement situés. Par hasard, implacables, toutes les balances confirmèrent que les deux livres étaient bel et bien acquises, indéniables. Je suggérai alors qu'elle abandonne son service à une collègue qui, elle, au contraire, recherchait des « avantages ». Lola ne voulut rien entendre de ce compromis qu'elle considérait comme une honte et une véritable petite désertion dans son genre. C'est même à cette occasion qu'elle m'apprit que son arrière-grand-oncle avait fait, lui aussi, partie de l'équipage à tout jamais glorieux du *Mayflower* débarqué à Boston en 1677, et qu'en considération d'une pareille mémoire, elle ne pouvait songer à se dérober, elle, au devoir des beignets, modeste certes, mais sacré quand même.

Toujours est-il que de ce jour, elle ne goûtait plus les beignets que du bout des dents, qu'elle possédait d'ailleurs toutes bien rangées et mignonnes. Cette angoisse de grossir était arrivée à lui gâter tout plaisir. Elle dépérit. Elle eut en peu de temps aussi peur des beignets que moi des obus. Le plus souvent à présent, nous allions nous promener par hygiène de long en large, à cause des beignets, sur les quais, sur les boulevards, mais nous n'entrions plus au Napolitain, à cause des glaces qui font, elles aussi, engraisser les dames.

Jamais je n'avais rien rêvé d'aussi confortablement habitable que sa chambre, toute bleu pâle, avec une salle de bains à côté. Des photos de ses amis, partout, des dédicaces, peu de femmes, beaucoup d'hommes, de beaux garçons, bruns et frisés, son genre, elle me parlait de la couleur de leurs yeux, et puis de ces dédicaces tendres, solennelles, et toutes définitives. Au début, pour la politesse, ça me gênait, au milieu de toutes ces effigies, et puis on s'habitue.

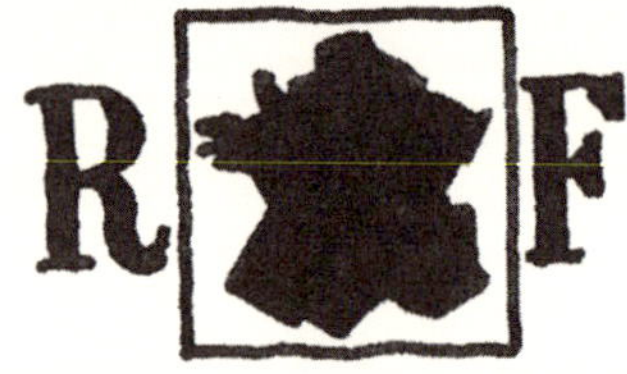

Dès que je cessais de l'embrasser, elle y revenait, je n'y coupais pas, sur les sujets de la guerre ou des beignets. La France tenait de la place dans nos conversations. Pour Lola, la France demeurait une espèce d'entité chevaleresque, aux contours peu définis dans l'espace et le temps, mais en ce moment dangereusement blessée et à cause de cela même très excitante. Moi, quand on me parlait de la France, je pensais irrésistiblement à mes tripes, alors forcément, j'étais beaucoup plus réservé pour ce qui concernait l'enthousiasme. Chacun sa terreur. Cependant, comme elle était complaisante au sexe, je l'écoutais sans jamais la contredire. Mais question d'âme, je ne la contentais guère. C'est tout vibrant, tout rayonnant qu'elle m'aurait voulu et moi, de mon côté, je ne concevais pas du tout pourquoi j'aurais été dans cet état-là, sublime, je voyais au contraire mille raisons, toutes irréfutables, pour demeurer d'humeur exactement contraire.

Lola, après tout, ne faisait que divaguer de bonheur et d'optimisme, comme tous les gens qui sont du bon côté de la vie, celui des privilèges, de la santé, de la sécurité et qui en ont encore pour longtemps à vivre.

Elle me tracassait avec les choses de l'âme, elle en avait plein la bouche. L'âme, c'est la vanité et le plaisir du corps tant qu'il est bien portant, mais c'est aussi l'envie d'en sortir du corps dès qu'il est malade ou que les choses tournent mal. On prend des deux poses celle qui vous sert le plus agréablement dans le moment et voilà tout ! Tant qu'on peut choisir entre les deux, ça va. Mais moi, je ne pouvais plus choisir, mon jeu était fait ! J'étais dans la vérité jusqu'au trognon, et même que ma propre mort me suivait pour ainsi dire pas à pas. J'avais bien du mal à penser à autre chose qu'à mon destin d'assassiné en sursis, que tout le monde d'ailleurs trouvait pour moi tout à fait normal.

Cette espèce d'agonie différée, lucide, bien portante, pendant laquelle il est impossible de comprendre autre chose que des vérités absolues, il faut l'avoir endurée pour savoir à jamais ce qu'on dit.

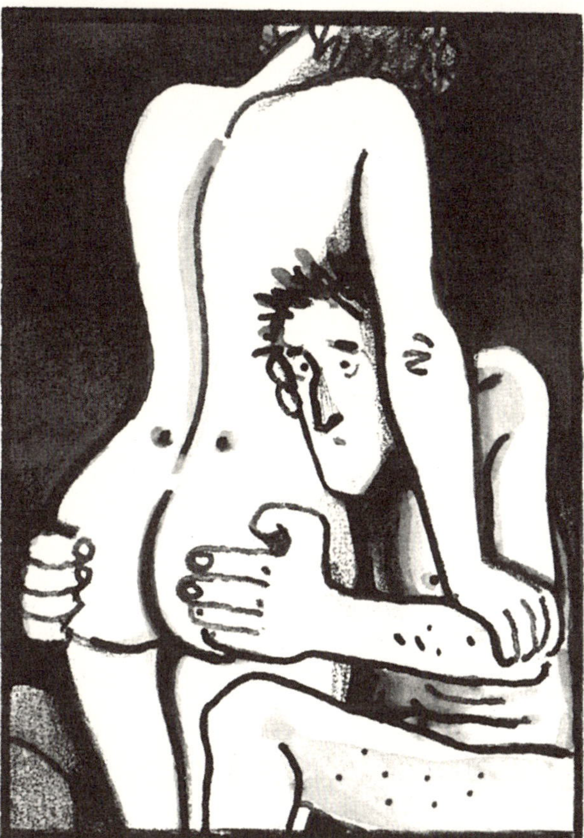

En somme, il était salement mauvais, le moral. Si je lui avais dit ce que je pensais de la guerre, à Lola, elle m'aurait pris pour un monstre tout simplement, et chassé des dernières douceurs de son intimité. Je m'en gardais donc bien, de lui faire ces aveux. J'éprouvais, d'autre part, quelques difficultés et rivalités encore. Certains officiers essayaient de me la souffler, Lola. Leur concurrence était redoutable, armés qu'ils étaient eux, des séductions de leur Légion d'honneur. Or, on se mit à en parler beaucoup de cette fameuse Légion d'honneur dans les journaux américains. Je crois même qu'à deux ou trois reprises où je fus cocu, nos relations eussent été très menacées, si au même moment cette frivole ne m'avait découvert soudain une utilité supérieure, celle qui consistait à goûter chaque matin les beignets à sa place.

Cette spécialisation de la dernière minute me sauva. De ma part, elle accepta le remplacement. N'étais-je pas moi aussi un valeureux combattant, donc digne de cette fonction de confiance ! Dès lors, nous ne fûmes plus seulement amants mais associés. Ainsi débutèrent les temps modernes.

Son corps était pour moi une joie qui n'en finissait pas. Je n'en avais jamais assez de le parcourir ce corps américain. J'étais à vrai dire un sacré cochon. Je le demeurai.

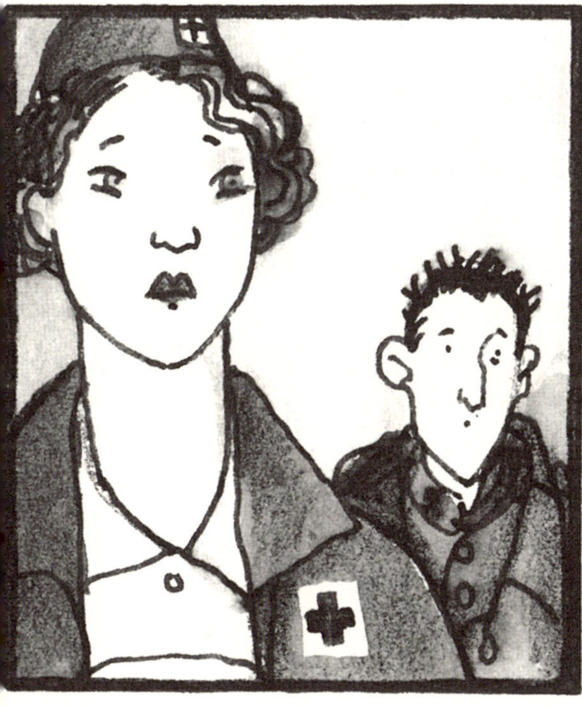

Ma conclusion c'était que les Allemands pouvaient arriver ici, massacrer, saccager, incendier tout, l'hôtel, les beignets, Lola, les Tuileries, les Ministres, leurs petits amis, la Coupole, le Louvre, les Grands Magasins, fondre sur la ville, y foutre le tonnerre de Dieu, le feu de l'enfer, dans cette foire pourrie à laquelle on ne pouvait vraiment plus rien ajouter de plus sordide, et que moi, je n'avais cependant vraiment rien à perdre, rien, et tout à gagner.

On ne perd pas grand-chose quand brûle la maison du propriétaire. Il en viendra toujours un autre, si ce n'est pas toujours le même, Allemand ou Français, ou Anglais ou Chinois, pour présenter, n'est-ce pas, sa quittance à l'occasion... En marks ou francs ? Du moment qu'il faut payer...

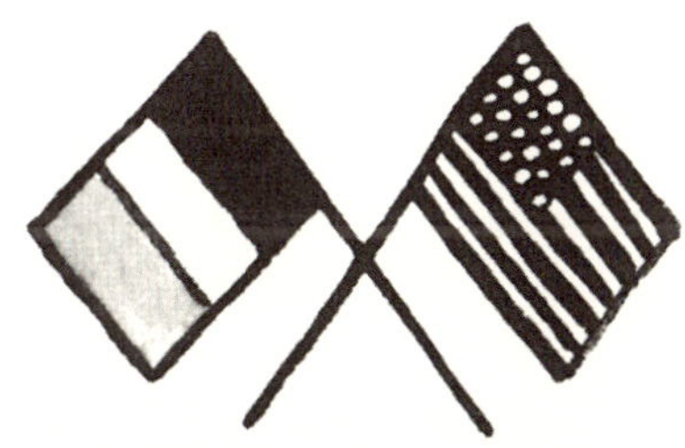

49

apple fritters."[13] Feeling duty-bound to taste the fritters every day, Lola gains two pounds in a single month. Faced with that disaster, "soon she was as afraid of fritters as I was of bullets", writes the protagonist, Bardamu. He suggests she turn her job over to someone else, but she won't hear of it, regarding this as a shameful compromise, akin to desertion: "She couldn't dream of shirking her fritter duty, which may have been humble but was nevertheless a sacred duty." Céline gives the story a burlesque twist: by applying the lofty vocabulary of heroism to a situation not designed for heroics, he discredits it. Worse slights are to follow, forcing the reader to the inescapable conclusion that no situation ever deserves to be described as heroic and that heroism is by nature indecent, intrinsically obscene.

Giono's *To the Slaughterhouse* invalidates the idea of heroism by describing at length the horror of death under shellfire. It contains one episode of hand-to-hand fighting, towards the end of the novel. In a farmyard, Olivier, one of the main characters, happens upon the corpses of a young woman, her head split open by a piece of shrapnel, and of a small child, who is being devoured by a huge sow. Olivier doesn't think twice: he lunges at the animal with his knife, striking at its throat and stomach. Though "blinded by blood, covered with blood, deafened by growls and snarls", he stands up in the end as the "sow's gut and blood emptied into the ground".[14] This struggle between the hero and the monster is not without precedent: Giono offers up a deliberately vile version of the classic scene – of which there are many examples in Ariosto – where a valiant knight saves an innocent victim from the clutches of a dragon or villain. But where Céline adds a dash of comedy, Giono's judgement is unappealable, the savagery of the scene definitively sweeping away the memory of the epic glories it debases.

After flourishing during the inter-war period, the First World War novel understandably ran out of steam after 1945, as historians and

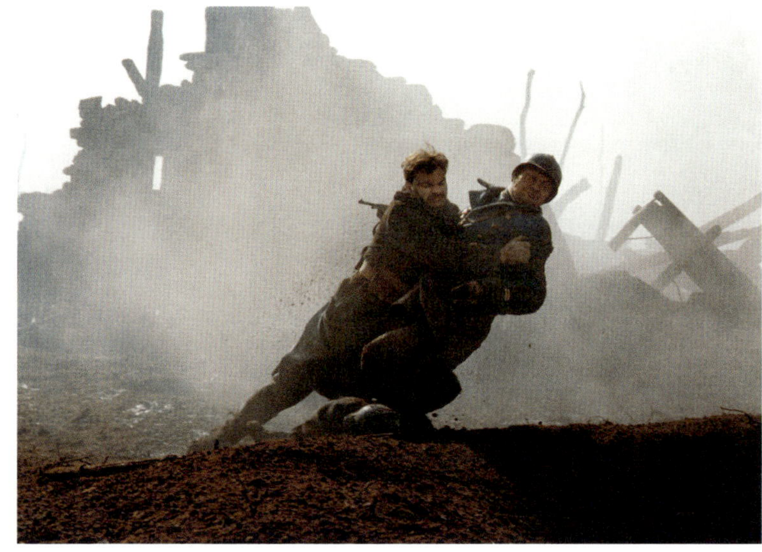

Un long Dimanche de fiançailles
[*A Very Long Engagement*],
film directed by Jean-Pierre Jeunet
after Sebastien Japrisot's novel
of the same name, 2004.

Notes

[1] Jean Norton Cru, *Témoins, Essai d'analyse et de critique des souvenirs de combattants édités en français de 1915 à 1928*, Paris, Les Etincelles, 1929, p. 15.

[2] Some of the thoughts in this essay were first presented in a talk at the thirty-fourth Congrès de la Société française de littérature générale et comparée (see http://sflgc.org/acte/jean-kaempfer-le-roman-de-la-grande-guerre-jalons-pour-lhistoire-dun-genre-seculaire/).

[3] Jean Galtier-Boissière, *La fleur au fusil* [1917], Paris, Vendémiaire, 2014.

[4] *Ibid.,* p. 114.

[5] *Ibid.,* p. 134.

[6] *Ibid.,* p. 135.

[7] Gabriel Chevallier, *Fear: A Novel of World War I* [1930], trans. Malcolm Imrie, Profile Books Limited, London, 2011.

[8] Galtier-Boissière, *op. cit.,* p. 151.

[9] Henri Barbusse, *Under Fire: The Story of a Squad* [1916], trans. Fitzwater Wray, The Floating Press, 2009.

[10] Jules Romains, *Prélude à Verdun* [1938], *Les Hommes de bonne volonté*, Paris, Robert Laffont, collection Bouquins (1988), Vol. 3, p. 100.

[11] Consent or constraint? Both points of view were debated. For a helpful summary, see: https://www.lemonde.fr/societe/article/2006/03/10/1914-1918-guerre-de-tranchees-entre-historiens_749539_3224.html (consulted on 24 August 2018).

[12] The term was coined by Maurice Rieuneau. See *Guerre et révolution dans le roman français de 1919 à 1939*, Paris, Klincksieck, 1974.

[13] Louis-Ferdinand Céline, *Journey to the End of the Night* [1932], trans. Ralph Manheim, New York, New Directions Books, [1983] 2006: https://books.google.ch/books?id=jd7EAgAAQBAJ&printsec=frontcover&hl=de&source=gbs_ge_summary_r&cad=0#v=onepage&q=apple&f=false.

[14] Jean Giono, *To the Slaughterhouse* [1931], trans. Norman Glass, London, Peter Owen Publishers, 1969: https://archive.org/stream/ToTheSlaughterhouseJeanGiono/To+the+-Slaughterhouse+-+Jean+Giono_djvu.txt.

novelists turned their pens to more urgent matters. Yet it experienced a spectacular revival in the 1980s, in a third wave that continues until today. This third period is essentially reflective, consisting of well-documented works that converse and play with a longstanding narrative tradition. It includes stories about family relationships, such as Claude Simon's *The Acacia* (1989) and Jean Rouaud's *Fields of Glory* (1990), in which the war appears as the endpoint of a search for identity, pursued through an exploration of family history. It also encompasses critical reinterpretations of the genre, focusing on less well known episodes of the war, such as the 1917 French Army mutinies, the execution of soldiers to set an example, and episodes of fraternization with the enemy. Many of these narratives are written in the investigative style familiar from detective fiction – an example that springs readily to mind is Sébastien Japrisot's *A Very Long Engagement* (1991).

What explains this renewed popularity? Perhaps the fact that the First World War defies all explanation. It has causes, which historians have discussed at length (imperialism, Prussian militarism and so on), but no justification. One would be hard put to say the same of the Second World War, which was fought under the banner of anti-fascism. The axiological approach to the Second World War is grave and measured: it is a war that can be discussed. A war that had no redeeming features beyond its scope was thus followed by a just war. Later, the end of the Cold War and the advent of globalization gave rise to a belief in "the end of history". From that perspective, the First World War novel is sometimes viewed as a sort of place of remembrance, buttressing pacifist convictions. What was the Great War? Why, nothing but a monstrous illustration of the absurdity of mass violence, fortunately long obsolete – that is the basic idea. But this optimistic and somewhat naïve summation cannot fully account for the recurrence of the genre. That is because it is also powerfully demystifying. It is a reminder to all those who enthusiastically endorse military interventionism that every war contains a bit of the Great War, and is in some way or other closed off and inhospitable to whatever humanizing forces of honour and heroism it may contain.

THE GENEVA CONVENTIONS: 150 YEARS OF CODIFICATION OF THE LAWS OF WAR

LINDSEY CAMERON
International Committee of the Red Cross

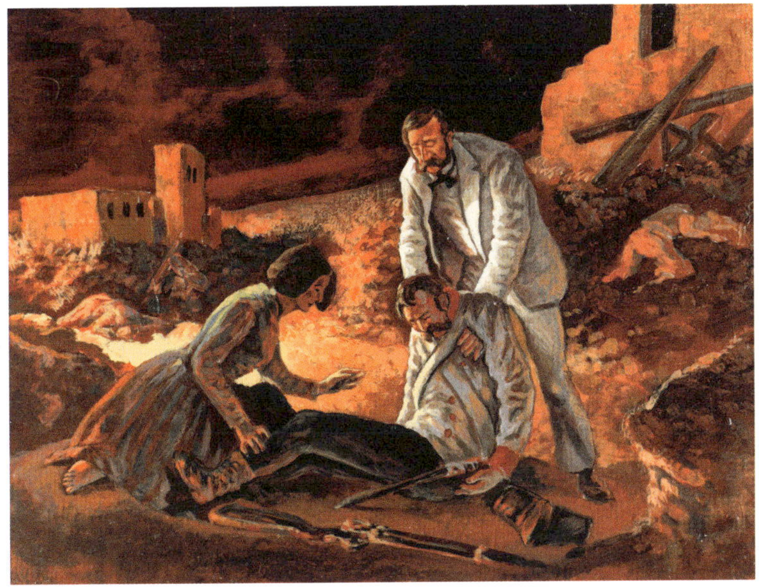

Henry Dunant (1828–1910),
Swiss philanthropist, founder
of the Red Cross in 1863 and first
recipient of the Nobel Peace Prize
in 1901, oil on canvas, artist
unknown.

The story of Henry Dunant is well known. A Genevan business-man, Dunant visited Solferino during the battle between the Austrian and French forces on 24 June 1859, and tended the tens of thousands of wounded and sick soldiers in the days that followed. It is also well known that the observations and proposals stemming from that experience, which Dunant recorded in his little book, *Un Souvenir de Solferino*, published in 1862, helped to provide the impetus for the adoption of the Geneva Convention of 1864, titled Convention for the Amelioration of the Condition of the Wounded in Armies in the Field **[cat. 35]**. The seventieth anniversary of the 1949 Geneva Conventions **[cat. 42]** is an opportunity to reflect on the legacy of the 1864 Convention for international humanitarian law today.

In all times, all around the world, war has been subject to certain customs, practices or specific understandings between the fighting parties. However, the 1864 Geneva Convention is widely recognized as being the origin of international humanitarian treaty law: binding agreements between states that protect of the victims of armed conflict and regulate the means and methods of warfare.

The 1864 Geneva Convention was short, containing only ten articles. Seven of these laid down substantive rules regarding the protection of the wounded and sick and those who cared for them. Article six defined the fundamental rule so familiar today but novel at the time: "Wounded and sick combatants, to whatever nation they may belong, shall be collected and cared for." Articles one and two prohibited attacks against "ambulances" (which at the time meant field hospitals), as long as they were not being defended militarily, as well as against on-duty medical and religious personnel. Article seven proposed that "A distinctive and uniform flag shall be adopted for hospitals, ambulances and evacuation parties" and "An armlet may also be worn by personnel enjoying neutrality, but its issue shall be left to the military authorities." That flag was of course the red cross emblem, as the article went on to specify. Finally, article nine left the Convention open for states not present at the adopting conference to join subsequently. A relative novelty in international treaty law at the time, this provision set a precedent for future conventions by allowing for universal ratification. Today, every country in the world is party to the Geneva Conventions of 1949, which form the core of modern international humanitarian law.

Regarding the protection of the wounded and sick in the armed forces, the fundamental concepts set down in 1864 have remained unchanged for 150 years. At the same time, some of the more technical aspects of the rules have changed over time, through revisions of the 1864 Convention in 1906, 1929 and 1949, as well as the Additional Protocols of 1977 and 2005. From a historical perspective, the adoption in 1864 of a convention to protect the wounded and sick in armed conflict may seem unremarkable: the time was perhaps ripe for clear rules on the subject. The presence during the Crimean War (1854–56) of journalists who were able to describe the suffering of combatants in almost real time had made the public (and governments) more sensitive to the plight of wounded and sick combatants – including, or rather especially, those of their own side. This climate was likely an important catalyst, which made it possible for Dunant and his partners, chief among them Gustave Moynier, to mobilize public and private support for their initiative. Moynier – sometimes referred to as "the builder" – was the legal mind behind the Geneva Convention of 1864 **[cat. 135]** and a member of the "Committee of Five" (alongside Dunant, Henri Dufour, Louis Appia and Théodore Maunoir) who promoted the idea of a Convention.

The 1864 Convention also emerged at the beginning of an era of great significance for the development and codification of international law more generally. Jeremy Bentham had first advocated for codification in the early nineteenth century, but it was only in the 1860s and 1870s that the idea gained traction and attracted more widespread interest. In Europe and America, international lawyers were busy developing their own versions of a code of international law, including rules on armed conflict. One of the most well known among them was Swiss jurist Johann Caspar Bluntschli, whose work was inspired by Francis Lieber's 1863 *Instructions for the Government of the Armies of the United States in the Field*, commissioned by the Union during the American Civil War. In light of the Martin Bodmer Foundation's *War and Peace* exhibition, it is particularly noteworthy that many of those who took a close interest in the codification of international law, including international humanitarian law, had strong pacifist leanings and believed that the foundations of peace must be laid – at least in part – on the humane conduct of war.

The late nineteenth and early twentieth centuries saw a flourishing of conferences and efforts to pursue the codification and development of international humanitarian law. Indeed, as early as 1871, following the Franco-Prussian War, the 1864 Convention was found to be relevant yet insufficient. Work to codify and develop the law at this time included efforts to extend the 1864 Convention to cover naval warfare, which at the time was a significant field of combat; the adoption of the St Petersburg Declaration of 1868 prohibiting the use of expanding ("dum-dum") bullets; the elaboration of key rules and standards at the Brussels Conference of 1874; and the negotiation and adoption of the 1899 Hague Conventions. The 1864 Convention itself was revised in 1906, after the Russo-Japanese War, around the same time as the revision, in 1907, of the Hague Conventions.

Since those early years, and following the First World War (1914–18), the categories of persons protected and the situations to which interna-

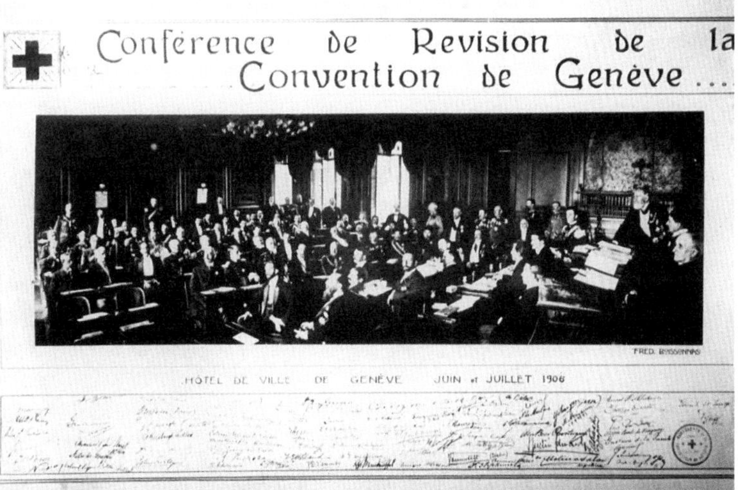

Revision of the Geneva Convention of August 22, 1864, the first international convention aimed at improving the condition of wounded and sick soldiers on the battlefield, July 6, 1906, photograph.

tional humanitarian law applies have continued to expand. This development naturally follows and reflects the course of history. For example, while the Hague Conventions contained some provisions governing the treatment of the millions of combatants captured during the First World War, significant progress was made with the Geneva Convention Relative to the Treatment of Prisoners of War of 27 July 1929, which laid down the principle that prisoners must at all times be treated humanely and defined detailed rules designed to help achieve this.

Drawing on the experiences of the First World War, efforts were also made during the 1930s to adopt a convention that would protect civilians in war, but these were unsuccessful. Subsequently, the Second World War saw civilians and military personnel killed in equal numbers, compared to a ratio of one to ten in the First World War. The ICRC continued its pre-war push to extend the protection of the Geneva Conventions to civilians. In 1949, the international community responded, with states revising and expanding existing international humanitarian law and adding a new Convention specifically for the protection of civilians.

The 1949 Geneva Conventions protect wounded, sick and shipwrecked members of armed forces, prisoners of war and the civilian population. In addition, article three, which is common to the four Geneva Conventions, marked a turning point, by extending for the first time to situations of non-international armed conflicts. The adoption of this "convention in miniature" proved to be highly significant, as more than ninety per cent of armed conflicts nowadays are non-international in nature, meaning they are not conflicts between two or more states, but rather between a state (or group of states) and an armed group, or between armed groups.

Indeed, in the two decades that followed the adoption of the Geneva Conventions, the world witnessed an increase in the number of non-international armed conflicts and wars of national liberation. In response, two Protocols Additional to the four 1949 Geneva Conventions were adopted in 1977. They strengthen the protection of victims of international (Protocol I) and non-international (Protocol II) armed conflicts, and place limits on the way wars can be fought. Protocol II was the first-ever international treaty devoted exclusively to situations of non-international armed conflict.

The extent to which armed conflict has evolved over the past seventy years cannot be underestimated. Contemporary warfare rarely consists of two well-structured armies facing each other on a battle-

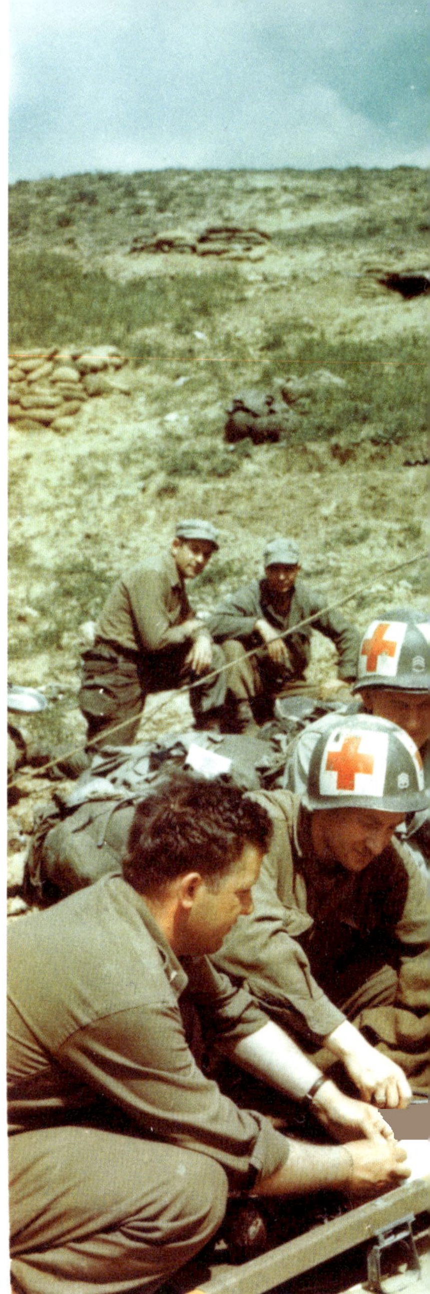

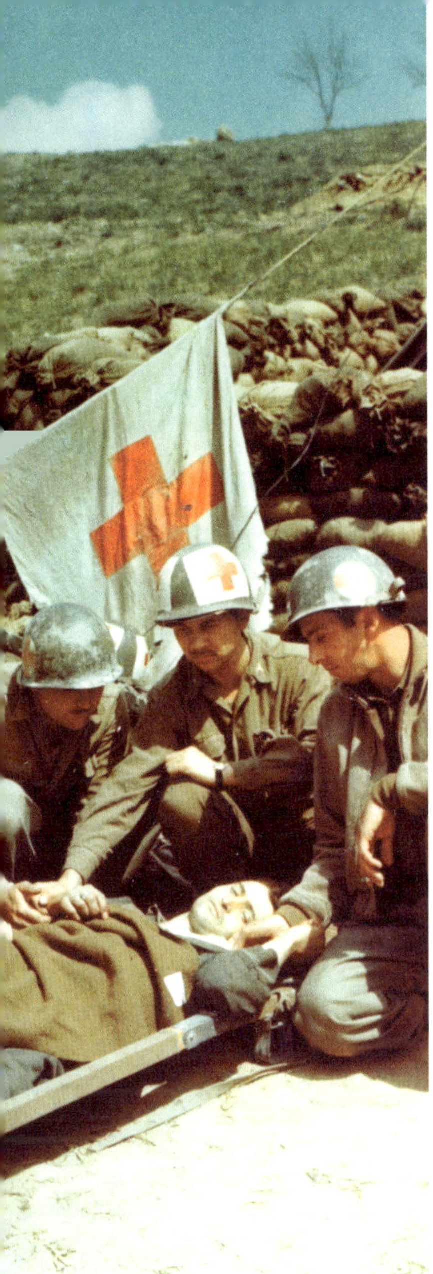

Soldiers of the 10th US Mountain Division tending a wounded soldier, Italy (?), photograph, c.1944.

field, in contrast to the dominant model that sparked the adoption of the very first Geneva Convention more than 150 years ago. As lines have become increasingly blurred between various armed groups, and between combatants and civilians, it is civilians who have increasingly become the main victims. International humanitarian law has necessarily adapted to this changing reality. The adoption of the first two Additional Protocols is just one example; treaties and rules prohibiting or regulating weapons such as anti-personnel mines and cluster munitions, or protecting cultural property in wartime, also illustrate how international humanitarian law has adapted to realities on the ground.

While the framework of rules has grown larger and more detailed over the decades, the difficulty of implementing the law in the midst of armed conflict has remained as acute as ever. While some methods and mechanisms are set down in the Conventions themselves (such as the "protecting power" system, whereby a neutral state is appointed to scrutinize the behaviour of a party to a conflict, or the establishment of an "international humanitarian fact-finding commission", which can conduct enquiries provided certain requirements are met), none have proved fully satisfactory and, as a result, they have rarely been relied upon in practice. They nevertheless remain available as options. At this moment in time, there appears to be no universal appetite for developing another type of mechanism. There have, however, been considerable developments in international criminal law, which represents a major step in the implementation of international humanitarian law in terms of individual responsibility. It is to be hoped that states will muster the political will to honour their obligation "to respect and ensure the respect" of international humanitarian law "in all circumstances", and that all parties to armed conflicts will do their utmost to respect their obligations under international humanitarian law.

WAR IN RUSSIAN LITERATURE FROM TOLSTOY TO SOLZHENITSYN

GEORGES NIVAT
University of Geneva

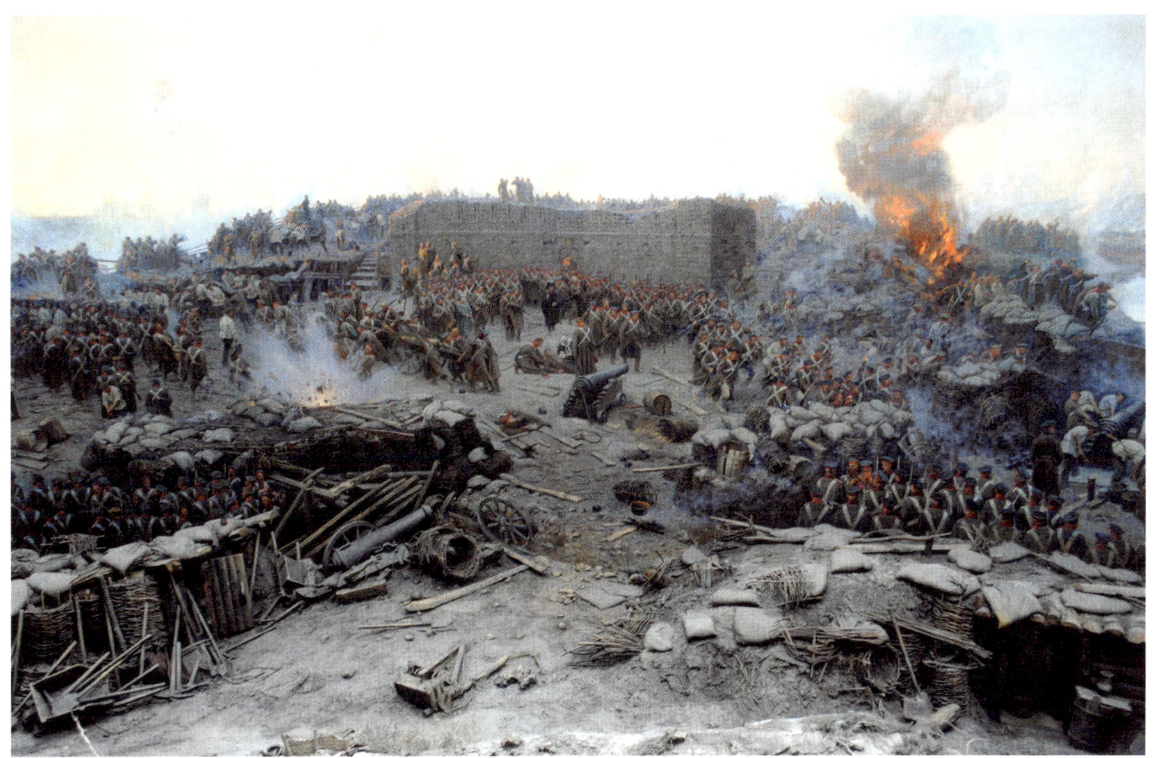

**Siege of Sevastopol, 1854–1855,
during the Crimean War** (detail),
by Franz Alekseyevich Roubaud
(1856–1928), oil on canvas, 1905.
Museum of the Heroic Defence
and Liberation of Sevastopol,
Ukraine.

The origins of Russian war literature can be traced back to the twelfth-century epic poem *The Tale of Igor's Campaign* and its magnificent "lament of Yaroslavna", in which, from the ramparts of Putivl, the princess laments Igor's defeat and his probable death at the hands of the victorious Polovtsians. Stunningly set to music by Borodin in his opera *Prince Igor*, this lament can be said to have set the tone for Russian literature about war: compassion for the victims.

But it was in 1854 that Russian war literature was truly born. Like *The Tale of Igor's Campaign*, it rose out of a crushing defeat: the Crimean war. A coalition of British, French and Turkish armies and fleets landed in Crimea and besieged Sevastopol. There, on 19 November 1854, a young officer arrived. His name was Count Leo Tolstoy, and he had previously served two years in the Caucasus, where he wrote two short stories, "The Raid" and "The Wood-Felling". In early 1854, he was sent to Silistra, Bulgaria, where he witnessed twelve thousand Slavic inhabitants fleeing before the Turks, until only twenty-five elderly men were left in the town. The three *Sevastopol Sketches* mark the emergence of Tolstoy the writer. "Sevastopol in December" still brims with patriotism, although by that time twenty-two thousand Russians had died. "Suddenly there comes a dreadful rumble, engulfing not just your hearing but your whole being," he wrote. In the next story, "Sevastopol in May" (1855), "the angel of death hovers ceaselessly", while in the town centre the military band gives a concert. One goes to the front by rota, the narrator explains, and, while waiting your turn, you quarrel, you read a Thackeray novel, yet always there is fear in your soul and in your gut. "I'm going to be killed today for sure, I can feel it. Especially as it wasn't my turn – I volunteered", he thinks, and "Oh, it's my thirteenth time going there, to that bastion. An unlucky number. I'm going to be killed, I know it." What Tolstoy describes, essentially, is how a soldier lives with death.

Tolstoy had read Plato's *Laches*, in which Socrates puts his companion on the spot by asking him to define courage. Does courage mean never running away? In response, Socrates quotes Homer: Aeneas' horses knew how to flee as well as to pursue – "unthinking perseverance is not courage, and flight may be the braver choice". Tolstoy would recall these horses in *War and Peace* **[cat. 80]**, when describing Kutuzov's decision to retreat. In his depictions of war, he dwells increasingly on the wounded, the amputees, the men suffering of gangrene. Everyone is soaked in the blood of the man next to him. In the bastion's quarantine area there hung a "dense, heavy stench, through which a few guttering candle flames struggled to burn". The correct definition of courage not only cannot be found, it cannot be conceived. Tolstoy even goes so far as to describe death from the inside, as felt by a living person who thinks he is dead: "It's all over, I've been killed", thinks a man who has fallen on his back.

Sevastopol marked the emergence of war as carnage – war that would not budge, that dug its heels in for never-ending slaughter. The whole of Russia raved about the *Sevastopol Sketches*. Not only because Tolstoy had transformed a defeat into a moral victory through literature, but above all because these stories enabled the Russian people to identify not with a victory, but with an ordeal they had experienced collectively and, thereby, to identify with humanity as a whole.

The Battle of Solferino, in 1859, is the direct successor to Sevastopol in the history of war. It resulted in a horrendous massacre: forty thousand men died in the mud. Henry Dunant's contemporaneous book about the battle became a best-seller **[cat. 79]**. Today it makes for uncomfortable reading: Dunant's pro-French bias does not seem to sit well with the idea – still germinating in the author's mind at the time – of the International Red Cross, which he helped found in 1864. Tolstoy, for his part, would go much further than Dunant (to whom we nevertheless owe a debt of gratitude): his rebellion eventually led him to vehemently oppose authority of any kind, including not only that of the army but also that of the state.

× ×

Tolstoy started work on *War and Peace* shortly after the Battle of Solferino. The title was inspired by Proudhon, an ardent socialist and pacifist, whom Tolstoy visited while the former was living in exile in Brussels. The two driving forces of his great masterpiece are peace – in other words, the human family – and war, that vast turmoil that threatens to destroy this same human family. Tolstoy drew on his own experience of battle, but also on the memories of dozens of fighters from the Napoleonic wars, the life of Adolphe Thiers (which supplied details that tarnished the reputation of this great French statesman) and family correspondence. In *War and Peace*, Tolstoy narrates several major battles: Schöngrabern, Eylau, Austerlitz and, especially, Borodino. He was fond of Stendhal's *Charterhouse of Parma* and its hero, Fabrice, adrift on the battlefield at Waterloo. Albert Sorel, in his *Tolstoy: Historian* (1923), admired the "disorder" of Tolstoy's representation of war: "A battle presupposes a plan and an order – Tolstoy claims there is neither." He compared the Russian's philosophy, as a historian, with that of Joseph de Maistre; Tolstoy was a nihilist, de Maistre a theocrat, but both shared a kind of mystical view of necessity.

As day follows day, and one moment follows another, the war between Russia and twelve other nations gradually peters out. Borodino pitted a fencer armed with a light foil against a man with a cudgel. Similarly, the historians of the 1812 campaign were still playing by fencing rules, whereas Tolstoy had moved on to cudgels of the kind depicted in one of Goya's strangest paintings in the Prado.

In a manner worthy of Shakespeare, Tolstoy interweaves scenes set among the officers and among the soldiers. Within the general staff, Kutuzov is the only one who fully understands the courage needed to retreat – "to flee, and live to fight another day", according to the rule of the Scythians. At Schöngrabern, Prince André transitions from a traditional view of the battle – that is, surveyed from above – to the chaotic mêlée of combat. Together with Bagration, he arrives at the top of a mount where little Captain Tushin is tending his cannons. Abandoned soon afterwards, André faces the enemy alone, with no cover at all. A childish joy suffuses him and his twenty-four men, seventeen of whom are killed in the skirmish. His head is suddenly filled with a fantasy: "The enemy cannon were no longer cannon, to him, but the pipes of an invisible smoker amusing himself by sending curls of smoke up into the sky. 'Ah, there goes another puff,' he exclaimed."

This is Tolstoy's favourite device for showing the reader what war is like: regression to childhood. The fighter becomes as cruel and selfish as a child. But the soldier/child thereby also regains his purity and simplicity. André, in a state of undress after an operation without any anaesthetic, experiences a happiness that cancels out the pain: "The best moments of his life – in particular his early childhood, when someone would undress him and lie him down in his little bed, when his nurse would sing lullabies to him, when, his head buried in his pillow, he was happy to feel alive – those moments appeared in his imagination not as the past, but as reality." Beside him lies the groaning Anatole. He had supplanted the prince in Natasha's affections and ruined his life, yet "André remembered everything, and a profound pity, a passionate love, filled his happy heart".

As the Russian soldier personified, Platon Karataev embodies a child-like people. Pierre Bezhukov, a prisoner of the French, sits next to him. A workman accused of raising fires has just been executed. The hut is dim, and in the darkness are two dozen other prisoners. Just as he is thinking that the world is crumbling and turning into a heap of meaningless ruins, Pierre becomes aware of a small fellow smelling strongly of sweat: Platon. "You've seen plenty of trouble, sir, haven't you?" the man asks suddenly. In a sing-song voice, like an elderly peasant nurse, he adds: "There now, my little pet, don't you upset yourself – it's nothing. You'll soon feel better!"

Platon acts on Pierre like a balm. He has an astonishing way of speaking. "Prison and a beggar's bag – two things you can't turn down," he instructs a despairing Pierre. Platon's altruism and goodness are utterly natural, as if war were his home – a home where "everything moves and is transformed, and that movement is God". The army has become the human family, and the Russian soldier lives in profound harmony with this family. "His words and acts came forth from him as spontaneously, as regularly, as necessarily, as perfume from a flower," Tolstoy writes.

In 1877, Russia resumed its lengthy war against Turkey. Volunteers set off for the Balkans to free the Slavs from the Turkish yoke. Among them was another of Tolstoy's fictional characters, Count Vronsky (this is shortly after Anna's suicide), as well as the writer Vsevolod Garshin. While Tolstoy had nothing but contempt for the volunteers, Garshin penned some vivid descriptions of the war in his short stories, especially "Four Days", "A Coward" and "Officer and Servant". The protagonist's monologue in "Four Days" employs the same narrative technique as Tolstoy in *Sevastopol Sketches*. He lies wounded, with next to him the enormous, already putrefied corpse of a fat Turk. Crawling over to the dead body, he takes his gourd, drinks greedily and crawls away. The inner dialogue between the dying soldier and the man who killed him, in which

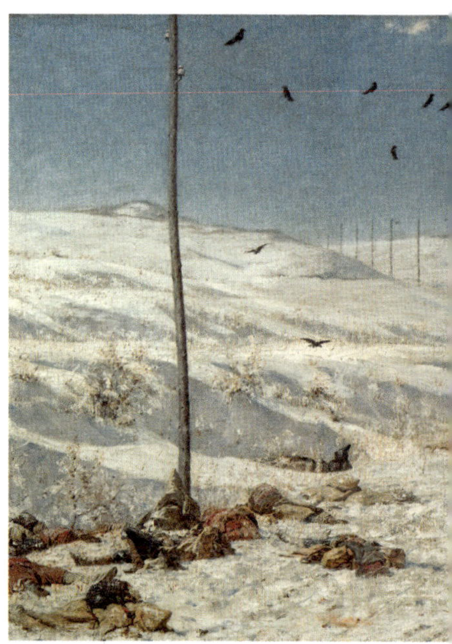

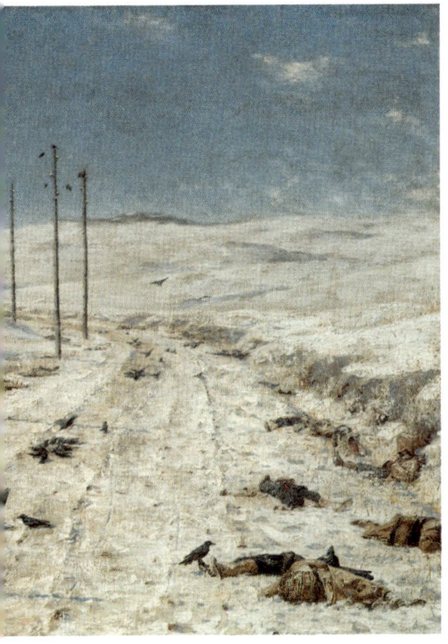

The Road of the War Prisoners,
by Vasily Vasilyevich Vereshchagin,
oil on canvas, 1878–79. New York,
Brooklyn Museum of Art.

only one of the two speaks, perfectly sums up the war. "In front of me is a man I have killed. Why did I kill him? … I'd be happy to change places with him. He hears nothing, feels nothing – no pain where he's wounded, no thirst. The bayonet went straight to his heart." The two trips made by the dying man – a few metres over to the corpse and then back again, to escape the stench – fill the entire four days. Here the monologue on the absurdity of war is intermingled with clear-sighted naturalism: the protagonist has enlisted as a volunteer, he has travelled a thousand kilometres, he has suffered hunger and thirst, all in order to kill this fat Turk.

The absurdity of war, the return to childhood, cruel and pure, would go on to inspire all subsequent Russian war literature, including the work of Astafyev and Solzhenitsyn.

His four legs in the air … how bloated they are. How much fatter a horse gets, in dying! A man, on the other hand, shrivels up. Lying there on his stomach he's so clenched, so small, you'd never think he was the one making all that din, doing all that shooting, the one stirring all those masses now abandoned, thrown over backwards.

This passage from Solzhenitsyn's *The Red Wheel* is particularly dramatic, offering a panoramic vision of maddened teams of half-dead horses dragging remnants of harnesses, and a whole artillery battalion bogged down in a marsh. Solzhenitsyn knew – in a different, crueller way than Tolstoy – that war is not where man belongs, that men at war have strayed far from the human home.

War and Peace takes away the men's home and then gives it back to them, but nothing is restored to the survivors in Viktor Nekrasov's *In the Trenches of Stalingrad*, Viktor Astafyev's *The Damned and the Dead*, Vasily Grossman's *Life and Fate* **[cat. 94]** or Solzhenitsyn's *The Red Wheel*. War bursts onto the scene, kills and – even worse – mutilates. Beyond the Stalinist bards of war, such as Constantin Simonov, beyond the artificial celebration of victory in today's de-ideologized Russia, Russian literature offers a sweeping indictment of war. Even under the Soviet yoke, it remained true to itself. Just beneath the surface it held onto the astonished Socratic portrait of Tolstoy's little "soldier-people" and his ragged hero, the *muzhik* Platon Karataev. On the evening of 22 October 1812, Pierre stumbles, exhausted, into a convoy of prisoners being driven forward in the pouring rain by the retreating French: "He thought he was thinking about nothing, but his soul had sunk deep down into grave, soothing thoughts. Yesterday, he had had a conversation with Platon Karataev…"

BOOKS AND BARBED WIRE: CULTURAL AID FOR PRISONERS OF WAR

DANIEL PALMIERI
International Committee of the Red Cross

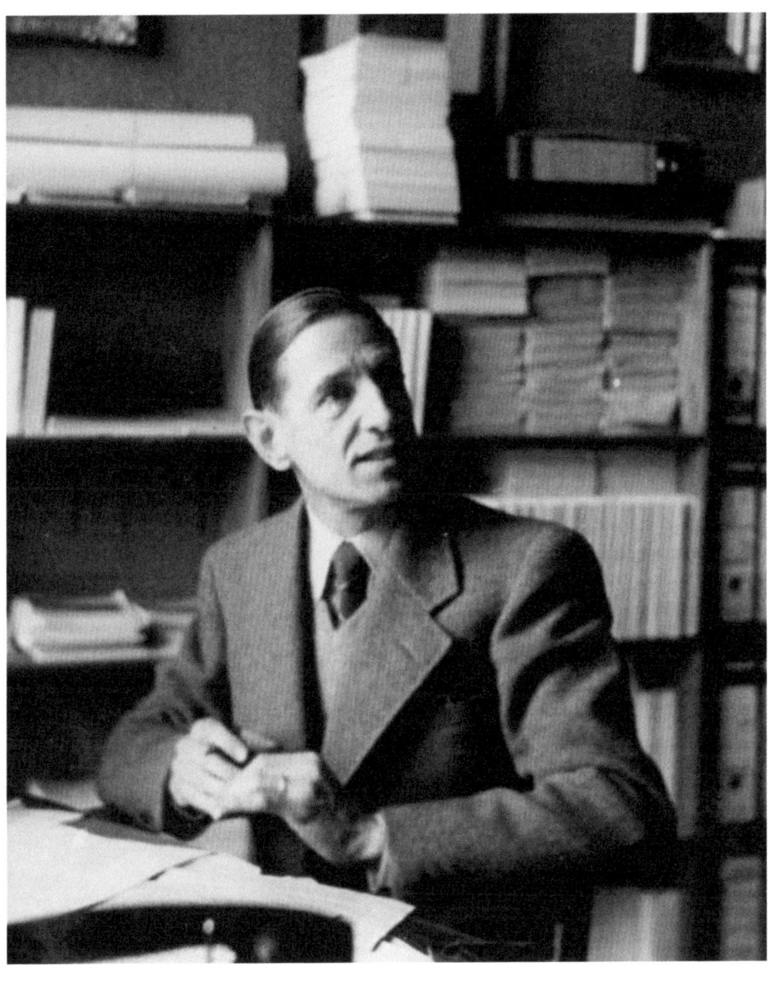

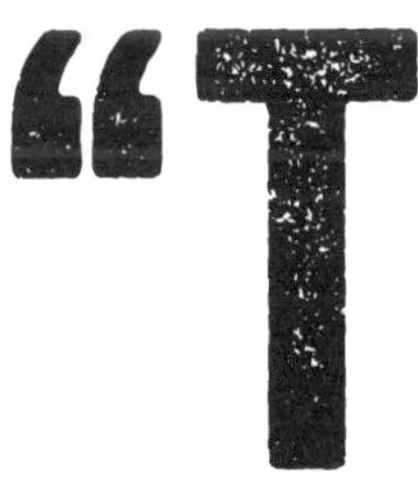

Martin Bodmer in his office
at the International Committee
of the Red Cross (ICRC).

"The ills of the body are the words of the soul, so you should not attempt to cure the body without the soul". Attributed to Plato, this quote still serves as a blueprint for cultural aid to prisoners of war, more than two thousand years later.

It was only in the second half of the nineteenth century, however, that the view that prisoners should be provided with not only material but also spiritual support – in the broadest sense of the term – in order to reduce their suffering in captivity, gained broad acceptance. This realization stemmed from two important factors that emerged during this period.

The first was increased concern for the welfare of military victims of armed conflict, beginning in the 1850s. The upsurge in attention to the suffering of combatants is generally traced back to the Crimean War of 1853–56, although, paradoxically, the majority of deaths during that conflict were due to illness – cholera in particular. British public opinion

x x x x x x x x x x x x x x x x x x x x x x x x x x x x x x x x x x x x x x x x x x x x x x x x x x x x x x x x x x x x x x was outraged by the negligence and inadequacy of military medical services and full of praise for the private initiatives that plugged the gaps, such as Florence Nightingale (1820–1910) and her volunteer nurses. A few years later, the pitifully insufficient care provided to the wounded at the Battle of Solferino (24 June 1859) led to the founding of the International Committee of the Red Cross (ICRC) on the initiative of the "Committee of Five",[1] thereby enshrining the protection of wounded military personnel in international law.[2]

The second was the advent of compulsory education, especially in Western Europe, which was rapidly eradicating illiteracy among large swathes of society. Rooted in the liberal revolutions of the 1830s, the movement to ensure primary education for all gained broad momentum only in the final quarter of the nineteenth century. In France, it was given a major boost by laws enacted in 1881 and 1882 under the leadership of education minister Jules Ferry. No longer reserved for an elite, reading became a popular pastime.

In addition to these two broad social developments, a third factor to come into play was the unprecedentedly large number of soldiers taken prisoner in international conflicts around this time. The Franco-Prussian war of 1870–71 is a case in point, with more than 450,000 French soldiers held prisoner in Germany and occupied France. For those imprisoned in Germany, the shock of capture was exacerbated by the disorientation of being held in a strange, hostile country. Far from their families, friends and workmates, fearful and ignorant of what would become of them, these prisoners endured a "moral suffering"[3] no less acute than any physical pain. That, at least, was how the ICRC described the plight of French prisoners in Germany. To "salve their wounds", the ICRC made unprecedented efforts to enable the exchange of correspondence between prisoners and their loved ones, trace missing soldiers and pass on news to families. In so doing, the ICRC was taking the first steps towards providing cultural aid to prisoners of war, no longer limiting itself to meeting their material needs. Reading would soon become an essential part of this new form of humanitarian aid.[4]

The Franco-Prussian War (1870–71)

The Franco-Prussian war marks the first time that books were delivered to prisoner-of-war camps. To assist wounded military personnel – the ICRC's main group of concern – the organization set up an International Agency in Basel tasked with collecting and distributing aid.[5] The Agency made no distinction between wounded soldiers recovering among their own and those in the hands of the enemy, but its ministrations did not extent to uninjured prisoners, leaving them at a disadvantage compared with their wounded comrades. Following discussions with the ICRC, in November 1870, the International Agency established a "Prisoners-of-war Relief Committee" with the mission of assisting all prisoners. To distinguish this body both from the Agency and from the ICRC, its emblem was a green cross, "the red cross remaining reserved exclusively, under the terms of the Geneva Convention, for use by hospitals and ambulances".[6]

Non-food (and non-clothing) aid began reaching prisoners before the International Agency even had a chance to request it. On 29 August 1870, for instance, the Lausanne-based publisher Bridel sent a "bundle of publications" to Germany, and the Société de publicité in Geneva sent a crate of books.[7] We know nothing about the type of material sent. Was it literature? Science books? It seems safe to assume that it consisted of "quality reading", like the "edifying and interesting books" sent by Msgr Gaspard Mermillod, titular bishop of Hebron, to the "French Catholic sick and wounded [prisoners]."[8]

The First World War

While mass imprisonment had become usual after 1870, a new factor that came to bear during the First World War was the greater length of detention, which made captivity much harder to bear. Held for several years far from home, prisoners of war often suffered from depression or other forms of neurasthenia, popularly referred to as "barbed-wire syndrome". Germany and France agreed in January 1915 to send books to prisoner-of-war camps to prevent "intellectual idleness" among detainees.[9] In parallel, quite a few of these initiatives were led by organizations rather than individuals, as had been the case during the Franco-Prussian War. The Danish Red Cross, which was mainly responsible for matters relating to prisoners of war on the Eastern Front, set up a "books department", which worked with Copenhagen University to send several hundred thousand books to prisoner-of-war camps.[10] A "book service for the victims of war" was established in Fribourg, Switzerland, by the Mission catholique suisse.[11] The Young Men's Christian Associations, which was already heavily involved in promoting reading before the war, emerged as the most dynamic of these cultural and educational aid organizations, thanks to their international network.[12] As in 1870, the ICRC took no part in selecting or collecting books, but helped organize delivery when needed. The ICRC also played an important role in passing on requests from prisoners received during visits to camps in various parts of the world. A section of the reports produced by the ICRC after each inspection addressed the "intellectual occupations"[13] and "recreations" of prisoners.[14] In particular, the ICRC reported on the presence (or, more often than not, the absence) of libraries in the camps and advocated for books to be sent.

The experience of 1914–18 prompted a re-evaluation of the very idea of captivity in wartime. Even before the end of the conflict, the ICRC began planning an international convention focusing on conditions of detention for prisoners of war, including their cultural needs. This issue is addressed in two articles of the Convention adopted in 1929,[15] one of which specifically states that prisoners of war must be permitted to receive books.

The Second World War

The Second World War can be seen as a repeat of the First, but on a scale that was in many respects unprecedented, including in terms of the numbers of prisoners taken. No exact figure is available, but they were certainly many times more numerous than in the preceding conflict, when between eight and nine million people were held in captivity.[16] Needs increased accordingly, requiring better coordination than during the Great War. Many initiatives to provide cultural and spiritual aid had been launched during the "war to end all wars", but these had all been individual or, at best, organized at a local level. When conflict broke out again, in September 1939, the belligerent states themselves requested that the distribution of books be coordinated and centralized.[17] An "Advisory Committee on Books for Prisoners and Internees of War" was set up in Geneva under the auspices of the ICRC, which this time played a leading role.[18] In addition to the ICRC, the committee comprised six international organizations: the World Alliance of Young Men's Christian Associations, the International Bureau of Education, The Ecumenical Commission for the Chaplaincy Service to Prisoners of War, the Fonds européen de secours aux étudiants (European Assistance Fund for Students), the International Federation of Library Associations and the Mission catholique suisse en faveur des prisonniers de guerre (Swiss Catholic Mission for Prisoners of War). The committee was chaired by the ICRC representative, Martin Bodmer (1899–1971). Its purpose was to divide up the work into clearly defined areas of specialized activity, oversee censorship and avoid any gaps or duplication in the distribution of books. Martin Bodmer's chairmanship of the committee comes as no surprise. Having been a member of the ICRC since February 1940 and present in Geneva since the beginning of the war to "support Max

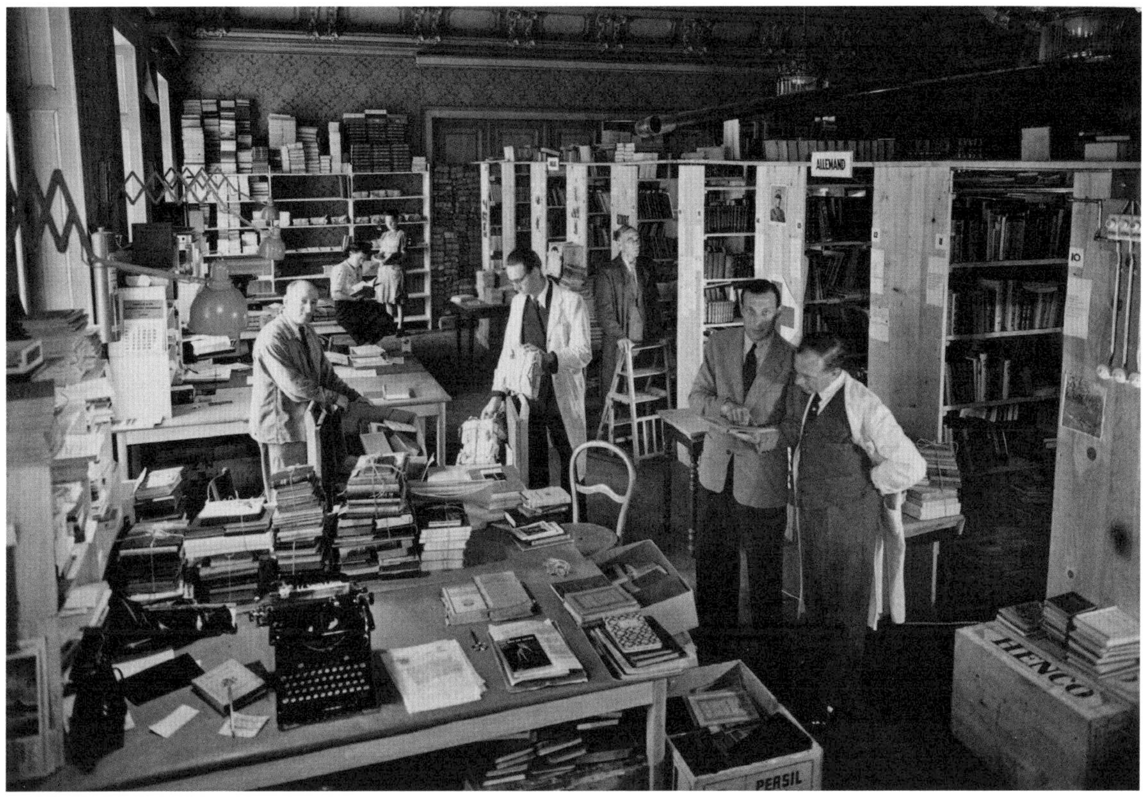

ICRC Headquarters in Geneva:
office of the Intellectual Relief Service, the department responsible for sending books to prisoners of war during the Second World War. ICRC, audio-visual archives, V-P-HIST-03256-09A.

Huber",[19] the president of the ICRC, Bodmer was, as the founder of a "library and archives of exceptional importance", the ideal man for the job.[20] He had also worked for the ICRC previously. At some point – the exact date is not known[21] – Bodmer set up a "Cultural Relief Service" within the ICRC's Central Prisoners of War Agency in Geneva. The Service left no archives, so little is known about its structure and staffing, other than that it employed some fifty people, divided into several departments,[22] and was directed by Martin Bodmer **[cat. 40]**.[23] What we do know is that the Service sent more than 840,000 books to prisoner-of-war camps between 1940 and December 1943.[24]

In the latter area too, the Second World War influenced humanitarian law. In 1949, the Third Geneva Convention (for the protection of prisoners of war) reminded detaining powers of their obligation to encourage "intellectual, educational, and recreational pursuits, sports and games amongst prisoners".[25] For the first time, this policy was extended to include civilian internees.[26] Books had won their place behind the barbed wire.

Notes

1 Founded in Geneva on 17 February 1863 by Henry Dunant and Gustave Moynier. The "Committee of Five" or "International Committee for Relief to the Wounded" is better known as the "International Committee of the Red Cross", the name it adopted in December 1875.

2 Thanks to the Convention for the Amelioration of the Condition of the Wounded in Armies in the Field signed in Geneva on 22 August 1864. This convention is the precursor of modern international humanitarian law.

3 *Actes du Comité international de secours aux militaires blessés*, Imprimerie Soulier & Wirth, Geneva, 1871, pp. 179–80.

4 For the ICRC, "cultural assistance" also included games, sports equipment, musical instruments and supplies for painting, drawing, sculpture, etc.

5 Archives of the International Committee of the Red Cross (AICRC), A PV, meeting of 18 July 1870.

6 AICRC, C AB, 227; Letter from the Basel Agency, 22 November 1870.

7 *Bericht der Agentur in Basel*, No. 1, 13 September 1870, p. 12.

8 AICRC, A AF, 16,4/801. Letter from Gaspard Mermillod to Gustave Moynier, 6 January 1871.

9 *Procès-verbaux de l'Agence internationale des prisonniers de guerre (AIPG)*, edited and annotated by Daniel Palmieri, p. 62: https://shop.icrc.org/les-proces-verbaux-de-l-agence-internationale-des-prisonniers-de-guerre-a-geneve-21-aout-1914-11-novembre-1918.html.

(An English version of this publication is available at the same URL (*Minutes from Meetings of the International Prisoner-of-War Agency, 21 August 1914 to 11 November 1918*), but while it contains the historical background to the minutes it does not include extracts from the minutes themselves, unlike the French original.)

10 ICRC, *Service des Secours intellectuels*, ICRC, Geneva, 1944, p. 5.

11 *Procès-verbaux de l'Agence internationale*, *op. cit.*, p. 62.

12 Théodore Geisendorf-Des Gouttes, "L'Alliance Universelle des Unions chrétiennes de Jeunes Gens et son activité en faveur des prisonniers de guerre", *Revue internationale de la Croix-Rouge*, No. 4, 15 April 1919, pp. 418–34.

13 *Rapport de MM. Les Drs Blanchod & Speiser sur les visites aux camps de prisonniers allemands au Maroc en décembre 1915 et janvier 1916*, Librairie Georg & Cie, Libraire Fischbacher, Geneva, Paris, March 1916, pp. 51–52.

14 *Rapport de MM. Dr A. von Schulthess et F. Thormeyer sur leur visite aux camps de prisonniers de guerre russes en Allemagne, en avril 1916*, Librairie Georg & Cie, Geneva, July 1916, p. 13.

15 Articles 17 and 39 of the Convention relative to the Treatment of Prisoners of War, Geneva, 27 July 1929.

16 https://encyclopedia.1914-1918-online.net/article/prisoners_of_war (accessed on 7 September 2018).

17 AICRC, CR 109-5, 265, "coordination des secours intellectuels et spirituels", note by Martin Bodmer, 9 May 1940, p. 1.

18 According to Bodmer, the creation of the Committee did not go entirely smoothly, and the first meeting had to be adjourned following "heated discussions"; *ibid.*

19 AICRC, A PV Comité, closed session, 20 December 1939.

20 "Nouveau membre du Comité international de la Croix-Rouge", *Revue international de la Croix-Rouge*, No. 254, February 1940, p. 155.

21 The first official mention of the Service appears in 1940; see *Revue internationale de la Croix-Rouge*, No. 262, p. 798. It would appear that the Service was already operational in June and July 1940, and was sending parcels of books to prisoners (p. 800). It may have been set up in order to meet the ICRC's need for a dedicated department to take part in the work of the Advisory Committee on Books for Prisoners and Internees of War, established in May 1940.

22 ICRC, *Service des Secours intellectuels*, *op. cit.*, p. 11.

23 There is a code for the Service in the ICRC's archives (AICRC, B G 30) but no documents.

24 ICRC, *Service des Secours intellectuels*, *op. cit.* p. 13. It also distributed music, musical instruments, board games and stationery.

25 Convention (III) of 12 August 1949 relative to the Treatment of Prisoners of War. Geneva, 12 August 1949. Art. 38.

26 Convention (IV) relative to the Protection of Civilian Persons in Time of War. Geneva, 12 August 1949, Art. 94. It should be noted that civilian internees are under no obligation to participate in intellectual activities.

FROM INFORMATION ENERGY TO CYBER WARFARE

SOLANGE GHERNAOUTI
University of Lausanne

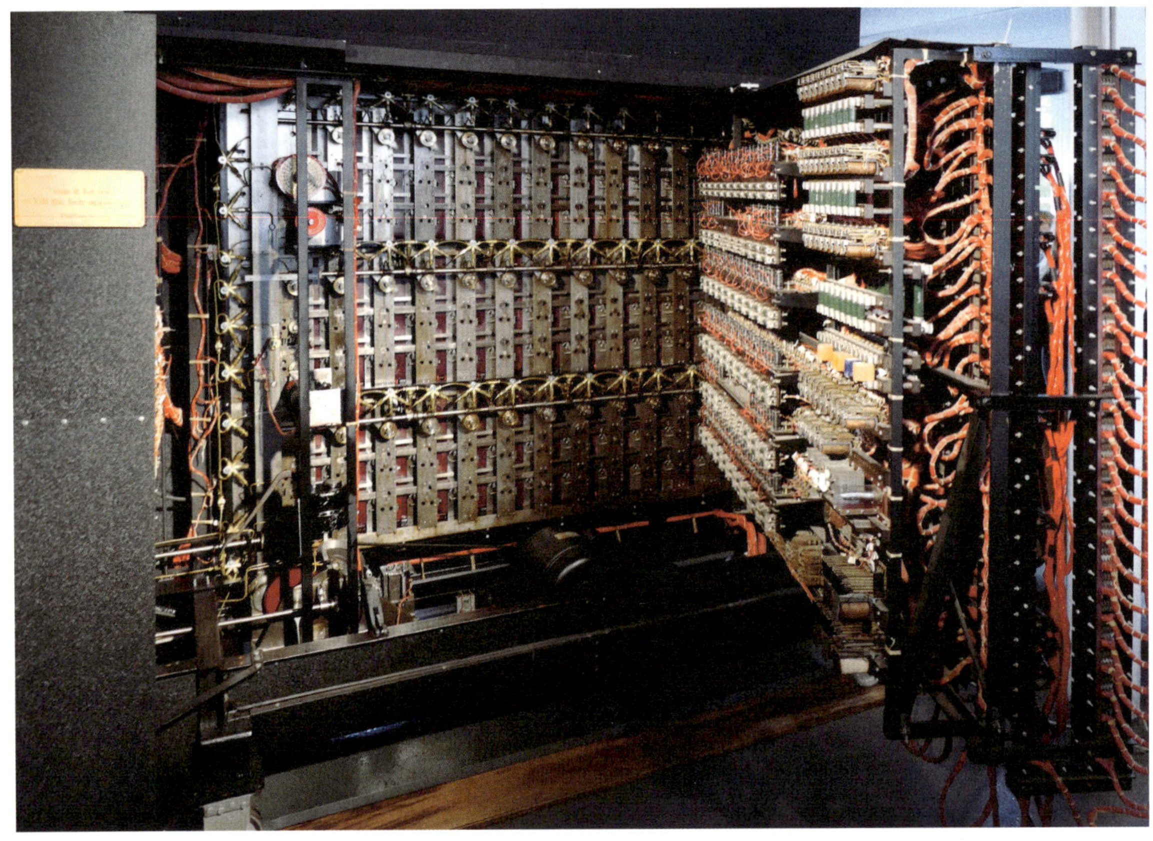

> "Energy, the new spirit. Energy, the new god."
> Pierre Teilhard de Chardin, *The Phenomenon of Man*

Energy as a means of projecting power and dominance

In Greek, *energeia* means "force in action". Energy is generally understood to connote force, power, vigour or efficiency. Since humans gained mastery over fire, our world has developed around the control of energy, but also of science, technology and the means of communication. In the nineteenth century, the ability to transfer energy – and to understand the physics behind it – laid the foundations of the industrial revolution and the arms industry. This marked the beginning of a transformation of both the art of warfare and the reality of the battlefield.

During the First World War, chemical energy appeared on the battlefield in the form of poison gas. The invention of new means of transportation (cars, lorries, tanks, submarines and aircraft) made it easier to move around and provide logistical support, to project force, to engage in surveillance and to gather intelligence.

Rear view of the Bombe machine, at Bletchley Park. This electro-mechanical device, invented in 1939 by Alan Turing and modified by Gordon Welchman in 1940, was used during the Second World War to break German messages encrypted using Enigma machines.

The work of the English mathematician Alan Turing during the Second World War kindled the development of information coding and decoding, computers and programming. The detonation of the first atomic bombs in Japan, in 1945, marked a turning point in the ways the power of destruction was manifested. Mastery of the atom and its physical energy became an instrument of total destruction, effectively erasing the traditional boundaries of the battlefield and the distinction between soldiers and civilians. The potential for the total annihilation of human life brought the prospect of a new type of war – one that, although unlikely, was not impossible – and resulted in the Cold War (1947–91). Combined with the mastery of computer science, these technological advances spelled a decline in conventional warfare, led to the rise of multiple variations of asymmetric conflict (guerrilla warfare, terrorism, etc.) and prompted a technological arms race.

During the Cold War, in parallel with the conquest of space,[1] a US Department of Defense initiative led to the invention of the Internet.[2] And so began the development of the information highway and information energy. Indeed, the conquest of space would not have been possible without computers and telecommunication satellites.

The conquest of outer space and cyberspace

Earth, sea, air, space and cyberspace[3] are where we live, but also where confrontations take place. They are theatres of commerce and military operations. They are arenas in which individuals, organizations and states express their power.

Space is a strategic challenge for countries in terms of building military capabilities and supporting economic development. Additionally, satellites are vectors for the expansion of the Internet and massive data processing, or big data. They are simultaneously instruments of domination and prime targets for attack. Effective management of information technology risks is thus central to both space and cyberspace policies.

Deploying weapons in space and cyberspace, providing security and ensuring the safety of space operations and electronic transactions involves computer code, cyber security and cyber-protection measures that are simultaneously offensive and defensive, proactive and reactive.

Since the first transatlantic telegraph cable was laid, in 1858, the continent-to-continent transmission of information has relied on undersea cables.[4] In times of conflict, these cables have often been cut in order to isolate a country or a whole continent. Controlling this transmission

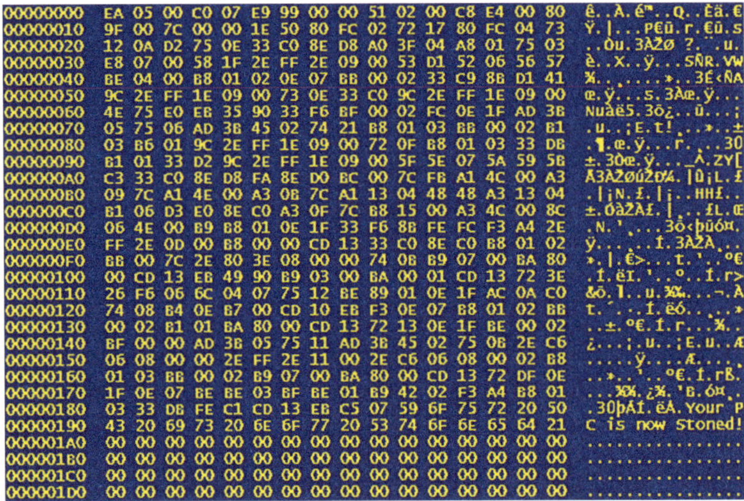

infrastructure is seen as the next logical step after conquering the seas, land and means of communication, according to a logic of domination and the affirmation of political, military and economic power.

Cyber attacks and information and cyber warfare

The Internet enables acts of economic and military warfare. It serves indirect strategies that, even in peacetime, can weaken a business sector, an organization, a critical infrastructure or a country. Information and communication resources can be both targets and instruments of crime and conflict. Cyberspace is a battlefield. And no country is safe from cyber operations intended to harm it. The Internet can help further political, economic, criminal or ideological objectives. It can be used to inflict damage without resorting to physical combat or invasion, by weakening the enemy's economic, scientific or cultural power.

The omnipresence of information technology and telecommunications in military operations and in every aspect of defence, from decision making to military equipment, creates a permanent, structural cyber risk. The more a country's military and economic capacity comes to depend on digital technology, the more vulnerable it becomes to cyber attacks. [5]

Attacks against systems that control critical infrastructure and essential services may be part of an offensive, deterrent or retaliatory cyber war. [6] In combination with conventional military operations, cyber attacks can disable an adversary's defences, destabilize their intelligence gathering, impair their decision-making processes or paralyse their nerve centres, media and communications.

Computer code of the Stoned virus, created in 1987.

All conventional conflicts are now accompanied and amplified by cyber attacks and information or disinformation campaigns. The Internet can be used to carry out sabotage, manipulate public opinion, reveal personal or confidential information, destabilize, influence, justify acts of aggression or defence, and trigger nationalistic reflexes. Not only cyber dissidents, but cyber patriots, too, may attack sites hostile to their cause and orchestrate propaganda campaigns on social networks. Cyberspace is a global sounding board that can be exploited for the purposes of activism, to call for civil disobedience or to promote terrorism, among others. It can also serve the causes of whistle-blowers reporting abuse, crime and injustice.

The damage inflicted by cyber attacks (semantic warfare, the disclosure or manipulation of information, false information, disinformation campaigns, etc.) cannot be observed directly. The relative invisibility of the harm they cause makes them even more dangerous. Their impact on a population, or on political or economic leaders, can facilitate strategies of psychological warfare. It is now possible to undermine a nation's democracy by influencing election results or enabling foreign interference.

In the present situation of digital colonialism[7] imposed upon us by hegemonic providers, which individuals, organizations and states alike have come to depend upon, digital infrastructure and services are central to mass surveillance[8] and espionage. The area of attack includes all Internet-enabled objects and systems, and is steadily expanding, weakening society as whole.

Even as the dependence and interdependence of infrastructure and systemic risks give rise to widespread distrust, while heightening existing vulnerabilities, state power depends on the ability to affirm the nation's cyber power and cyber sovereignty. Over the long term, digitization structurally alters our way of life, our ability to live in peace, the way we protect and defend our countries and guarantee their sovereignty. It creates new risks and helps aggravate existing ones. It is as imperative for a country to have a military cyber force as it is to prepare for major crises. Its stability, sovereignty and economic development depend on its ability to control cyber risks, cyber security and cyber defence holistically.

The Dassault Neuron drone, an experimental unmanned combat aerial vehicle (UCAV) presented at the 47th Le Bourget Paris Air Show, in June 2007.

The invention of the cyber soldier and the normalization of global cyber warfare

On the Internet, there is no direct confrontation. Combatants remain hidden behind multiple technological go-betweens. They are no longer soldiers in the traditional sense: they know nothing of the price of blood, physical courage or the horrors of the battlefield. Their weapons are networked computers, computer code and information. For some, the only requirement may be that they know how to use a computer, while others may be experts in electronics, computer technology, telecommunications, cryptography, artificial intelligence or cognitive science.

The "right" to kill by remote-piloting a drone or activating a computer program is no longer the prerogative of state players, nor is it a male privilege, nor a power limited to a particular timeframe or geographical area. The drive to subjugate the adversary through the use of digital technology is ongoing, global and normalized. To misquote Carl von Clausewitz,[9] technology is the continuation of politics by other means **[cat. 34]**.

Digital dependence falls within the logic of stealth cyber warfare, not just because this new type of war is fast and fleeting, but also because it remains hidden and undeclared. Carried out over a long period of time, it is invisible, real and pernicious. It often relies on the insidious manipulation of Internet users, and on the abuse, misuse or criminal use of digital resources. Now permanent, cyber warfare started with the creation of the technical infrastructure and the adoption of laws (or the lack thereof) that cede power to the entities that control digital technology and services, data, information flows and cyber security.

It is a war without limits, in which it is not easy to determine who the enemy is,[10] who is behind a cyber attack and where it originates from, making retaliation difficult; ensuring compliance with humanitarian law and the law of war is arduous; large-scale cyber operations can be conducted without any military involvement; and the victims are civilians as well as soldiers.

What lies ahead?

Technology can be a lever of both social transformation and organized violence. It can be employed by actors bent on defending their interests, with varying degrees of integrity. Economic and military wars have one thing in common: they aim to annihilate or subjugate the enemy, and to seize power and resources. From now on, the territory to be conquered, exploited and defended is cyberspace.

The militarization of space and cyberspace raises questions about the effectiveness of international regulatory mechanisms, and demonstrates the need to draft, implement and comply with codes of conduct, standards, regulations and confidence-building measures. It raises doubts as to the existence of a genuine willingness to engage in cooperative dialogue at the international level on the role of private entities and civil society, as well as public-private partnerships. A comprehensive, collective approach should also address disarmament, responsibility for sustainable development, and the resilience of both the information and communications infrastructure and the environment (removing and recycling satellite debris and IT waste, electromagnetic radiation, energy consumption, global warming, digital migrants,[11] etc.).

Information technology has immense potential to enable enrichment, control, power and war. As the philosopher Hannah Arendt **[cat. 139]** reminds us, "the banality of evil" defies words and thought, because it is an active, ongoing process. Understanding the challenges of digital energy, and its geopolitical, social, cultural and economic corollaries, may encourage some among us to become cyber-peace warriors, fighting to ensure technical progress is synonymous with social progress, peace and stability for all.

Notes

[1] On 20 July 1969, as part of the Apollo spaceflight programme, American astronaut Neil Armstrong was the first person to walk on the Moon.

[2] The Internet was designed in the 1960s, under the umbrella of the Department of Defense's Defense Advanced Research Projects Agency (DARPA). The Global Positioning System (GPS) was developed a few years later, also for military purposes. This system was launched in 1973, became fully operational in 1995 and was opened up to civilian applications in 2000.

[3] Cyberspace is made up of all the systems connected to the Internet, namely, hardware, software, telecommunication networks, information infrastructure, data and e-services.

[4] The Internet backbone consists of some four hundred intercontinental cables, which, along with communication satellites, must be available for information to circulate.

[5] A cyber attack is carried out remotely using computer code and networks. Its aim is to cause computers to malfunction or to modify, steal or destroy IT resources by violating their security criteria (availability, integrity and confidentiality).

[6] The North Atlantic Treaty Organization (NATO) summit in September 2014 defined massive cyberattacks as acts of war warranting a military response. http://www.nato.int/cps/fr/natohq/topics_110496.htm

[7] Digital colonialism refers to the system used by the parties that own the information infrastructure to to expand their power, developing cyberspace and using it to their own advantage and in their own interest, making users dependent on it while monitoring, exploiting and enslaving them.

[8] Mass surveillance, concomitant with the use of the Internet, was revealed by Edward Snowden in 2013.

[9] General and military theoritician of Prussian origin (1780–1831). His classic book, *On War*, was published in 1832.

[10] In contrast, the enemy knows who the target is, and the data required to exact maximum damage can be obtained via social networks or social engineering, purchased or hacked.

[11] Is there a place in this world where digital migrants, rebels, and those who wish to escape mass surveillance and digital addiction or overwork can find refuge?

*The art of war and the birth and development
of international human rights.*

26
Bagai (horse armour),
bagu (horse tack), *bamen*
(horse mask), *tachidō tōsei
gusoku* (armour),
Japan, late Momoyama period,
1573–1615 (horse armour and
mask); Edo period, 1615–1868
(horse tack and armour)
Dallas, The Ann & Gabriel Barbier-Mueller
Museum: The Samurai Collection

The samurai, or *bushi*, were the elite warriors of premodern Japan. Initially, samurai were armed servants, but later they became experts in warfare. For nearly 700 years, beginning in 1185, Japan was governed by a military government, led by the shogun, ruling in the name of the emperor. Samurai were loyal to individual *daimyo*, provincial lords with large hereditary land holdings.

With the rise of the samurai class, horses came to play an integral part in battle. Historical texts show that warhorses were valued not only for their strength and speed, but also for their bravery and ferocity – characteristics frequently celebrated in their warrior masters. In the relatively peaceful Edo period (1615–1868), the animal's regalia displayed its owner's wealth and status in ceremonies and processions.

The large, red and gold lacquered saddle pads worn by this horse served to protect its flanks from the heavy stirrups. *Abumi* (stirrups), like this set, were made almost entirely of iron and provided a broad platform on which the samurai could stand as he used his bow at a gallop. Body armor for horses emerged around 1600 and was worn by the steeds of high-ranking samurai. Made of small tiles of lacquered leather sewn to fabric, the armor consists of one part covering the neck and shoulders and another protecting the hindquarters. Dynamic *bamen* (horse masks) may have accompanied the armor, giving the horses a menacing presence. This example, created with papier-mâché, gives the horse the appearance of a dragon with distinct horns, bushy brows and gleaming eyes. The rider wears a gold-lacquered armor created with hundreds of small iron and leather scales meticulously laced together with orange silk cord. The helmet, whose bowl is formed with sixty-two iron plates, is adorned with a glowing dragon as the fore crest. Large shoulder guards, styled after those worn by the earliest samurai, functioned as a shield in combat.

J. Bea

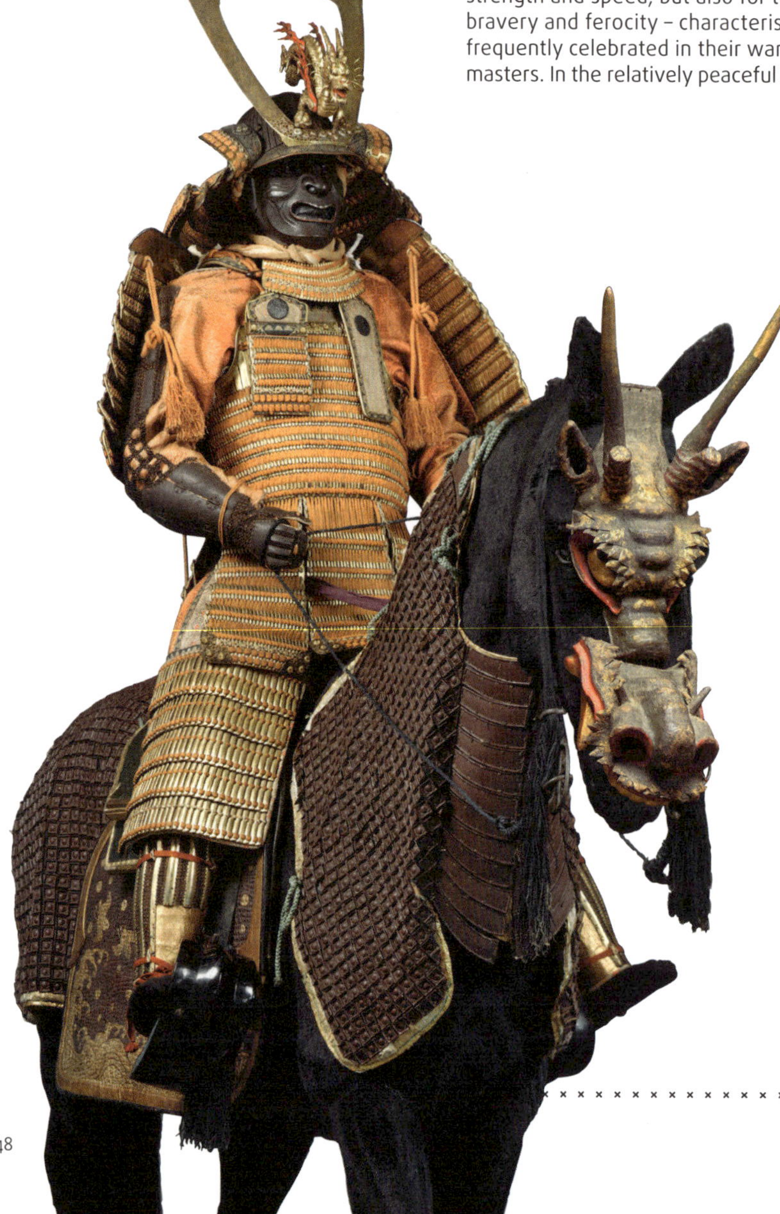

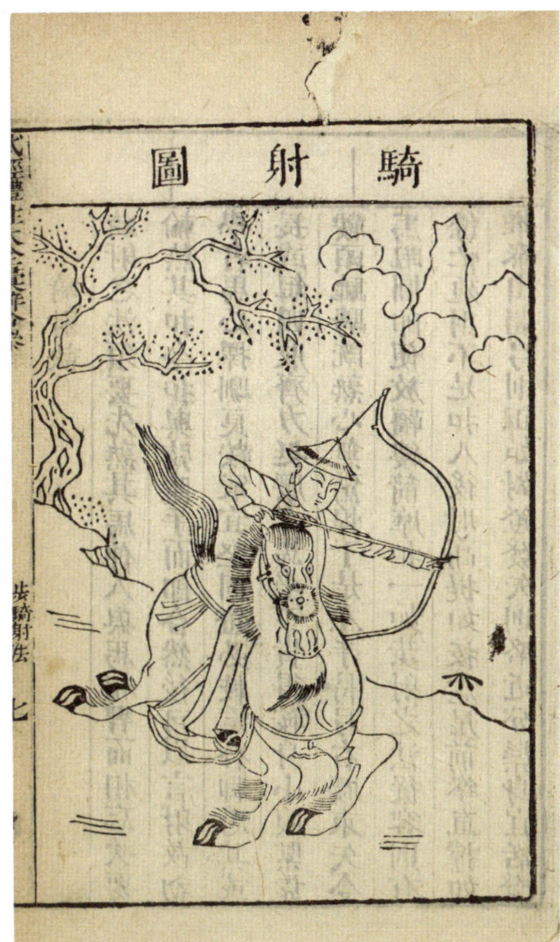
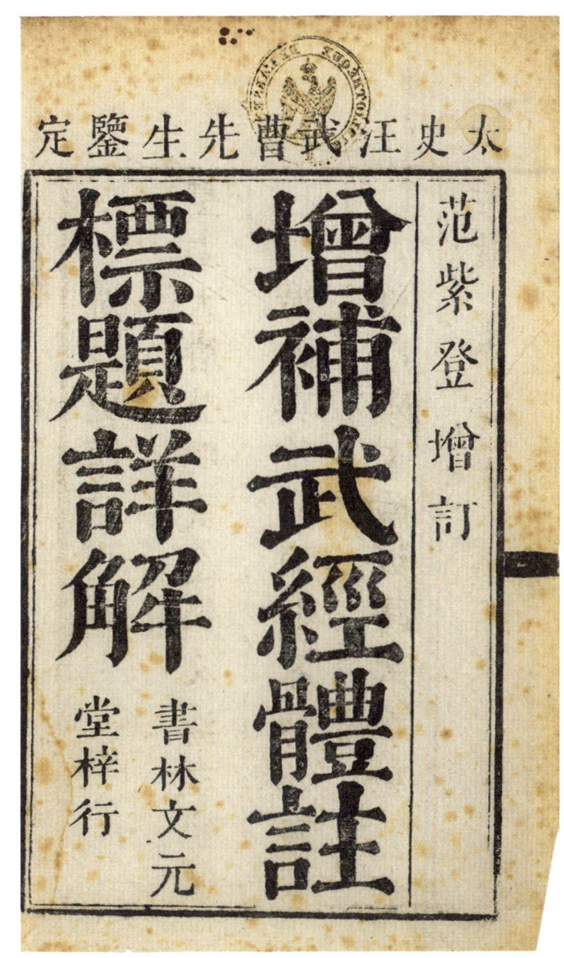

27
Sunzi (6ᵗʰ century BC)
The Art of War, in *Canonical Military Books*, with comments, expanded edition, [China], *c.* 1711

Paris, Bibliothèque nationale de France, département des Manuscrits, chinois 5055

The Art of War (*Sunzi bingfa*) is the first and most famous of the many treatises of military strategy produced in ancient China. Traditionally attributed to General Sunzi (or Sun Tzu), it is today viewed more as a collective work dating to the end of the Warring States period (fourth or third century BC). In 1972, a version written on bamboo strips was discovered in Yinqueshan (Shandong province), in a tomb dating to the second half of the second century BC: this is the oldest known version of the text. The first print editions appeared during the Song Dynasty (960–1279), during which *The Art of War* was canonized as one of the "seven military treatises" of ancient China.

The Art of War comprises thirteen chapters, each on a specific aspect of military strategy: planning, manoeuvres, espionage, etc. The style is succinct, and part of its success lies in the fact that its methodical formulations, many of which have become Chinese proverbs, are applicable in contexts other than war, in particular economics. One of the main ideas espoused – somewhat paradoxically for a treatise of this kind – is that war as such should not exist: a good strategist will best his opponents before entering the battlefield, thanks to his tactics and sound preparations, rendering combat itself pointless. *The Art of War* has been translated into many European languages and did extremely well in the West. As such, it is truly part of our universal heritage.

N. Z.

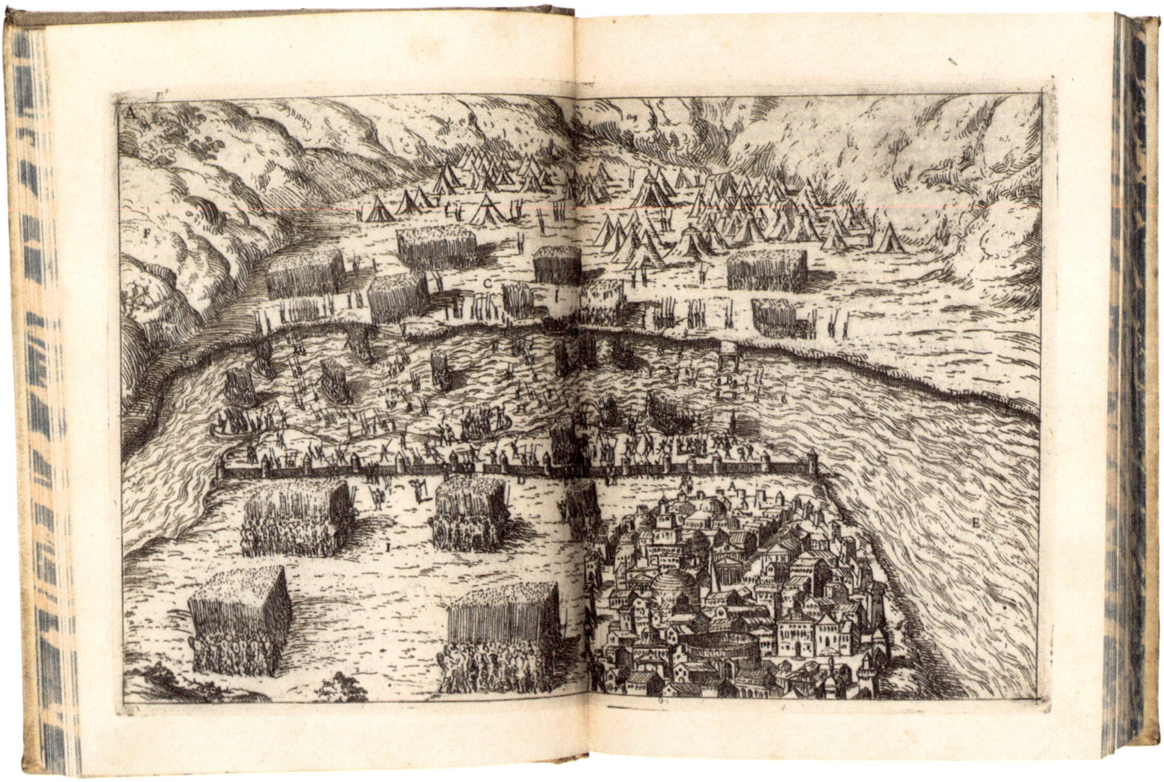

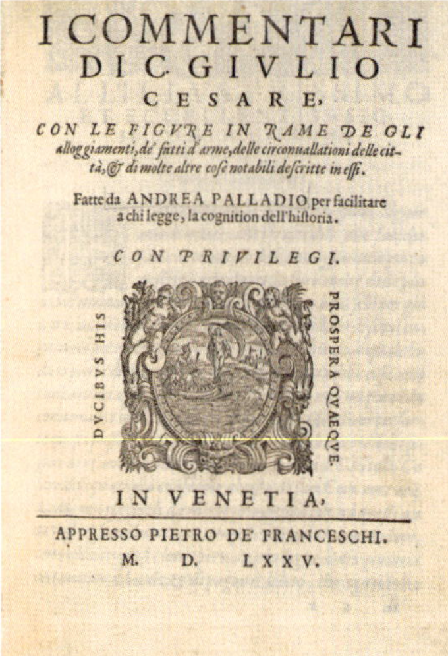

28
Gaius Julius Caesar (100–44 BC)
I Commentari di C. Giulio Cesare… [*The Commentaries of Julius Caesar…*], Venice, Pietro de Franceschi, 1575, with illustrations by Andrea Palladio

Cologny, Martin Bodmer Foundation

Most likely compiled from field notes and reports to the Roman Senate (the reason they were called *commentari*), the seven volumes of Caesar's account of the Gallic War (58–52 BC) were written in a mere three months, at Cesar's secretariat, shortly after the final victory at Alesia. They were intended as propaganda for the great conqueror, who was also proconsul of the Roman republic, in view of his triumphant return to Rome. Consequently, the truthfulness of his account was almost immediately called into question. It was nevertheless admired by contemporaries (including the exacting Cicero) for the purity of its language, and it remains the primary source on the Gallic Wars to this day (Livy's account of the events having disappeared). The *Commentaries* were first printed in 1469, in the original Latin, but they had already been translated into most European languages during the Middle Ages. This Italian edition, containing Francesco Baldelli's translation (first published in 1570), has always been particularly prized for its illustrations: forty-two copperplate engravings by the great architect Andrea Palladio (1508–80), who had a fascination with ancient literature and culture. The various battles and sieges (Gergovia, Alesia) illustrated by Palladio include "Genava", where Caesar's legions destroyed the bridge to the north side of "Lacus Lemannus" and built defensive ramparts to defend the city against the migration of the Helvetians (Book I). Before becoming a symbol of peace, Geneva, too, was a conflict zone. **N. D.**

29
[Pseudo-] Maurice (539-602)
Strategikon, Milan, *c.* 1570–82,
Greek manuscript

Cologny, Martin Bodmer Foundation, CB 115

Like many Roman and Byzantine emperors, Maurice (539–602) began his career as an army officer. Tiberius II Constantine, his predecessor and father-in-law, appointed him commander of the armies fighting the Persians in Armenia, after which he campaigned against the Avars and the Slavic tribes. He donned the purple in 582, and continued throughout his reign to defend the borders of the Empire, from the Levant to the Balkans and from Africa to southern Italy. Although a great soldier, he was also a prudent manager. However, his extreme parsimoniousness alienated his troops, and he was ultimately dethroned by mutineers and beheaded, together with his five sons.

This treatise of military strategy, the fruit of Maurice's reforms of his army, is attributed to him, but may have in fact been commissioned from his brother Peter or another general. It is presented in the introduction as a "modest, elementary handbook" for aspiring officers. In twelve thematic sections, it details Byzantine military tactics, highlighting the role of the cavalry, while also addressing topics such as the infantry, sieges and surprise attacks, supplies, exercises and marches, discipline and punishment, the duties of an officer (to be simple and close to his men), and more. Book XI describes the empire's traditional enemies (the Francs, Lombards, Avars, Persians, etc.). Copied by the scribe Camillo Zanetti from a tenth-century manuscript (Ambrosiana B119), the text shown here is combined with a Byzantine military treatise (*De velitatione*, formerly attributed to Emperor Nicephorus II Phocas) and excerpts from Julius Africanus' *Cestus,* on the art of war.

N. D.

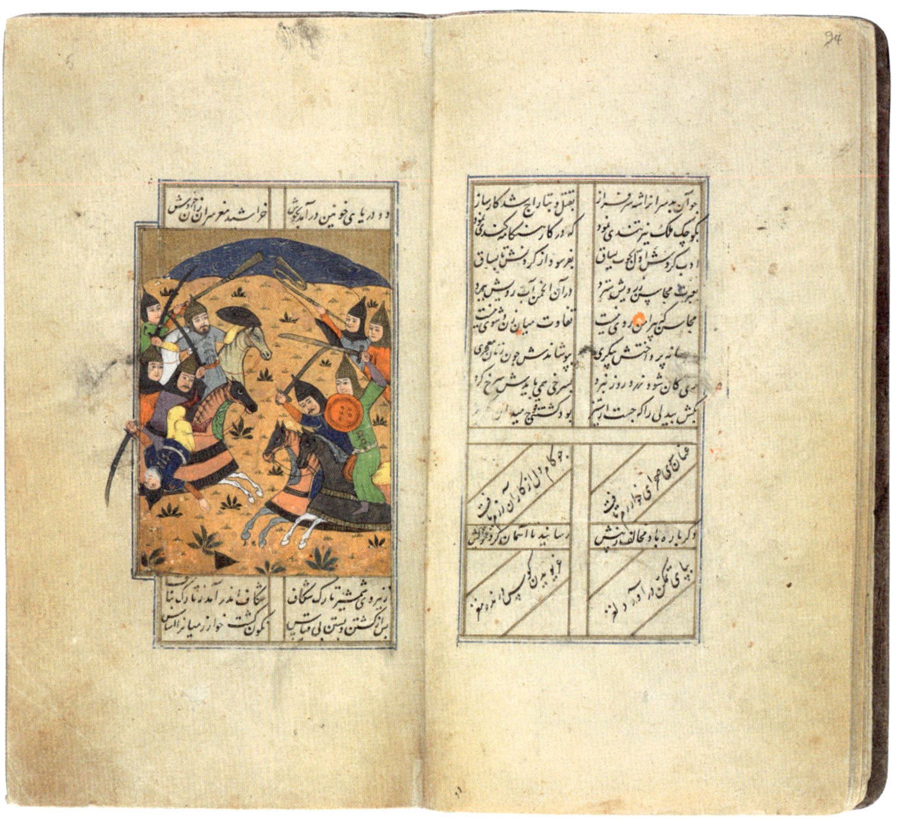

30
Abdallah Hatefi (*c.* 1454–1521)
"Timur-nama" [Song of Timur],
Persian manuscript on paper,
1522; provenance: Fath Ali Qadjar
(1772–1834), shah of Persia

Cologny, Martin Bodmer Foundation, CB 517

Born in Khorasan province (Afghanistan),
Hatefi was one of the leading poets of
the Timurid court. He is known chiefly
for his *Khamsa* (*Quintet*), fame of
which spread beyond the borders of
Persia. The fourth and most famous
poem in the collection is the "Timur-
nama" (Song of Timur), shown here,
sometimes also called "Zafar-nama"
(Song of Victory). It was written in
1498 for the Timurid ruler of
Afghanistan, Babur (1483–1530), a
descendant of Tamerlane and Genghis
Khan, who became the first Mughal
emperor of India. It takes the place
usually occupied by the "Eskandar-
nama" (Song of Alexander [the Great])
in other *Khamsa*, such as Nizami's.
Over the space of thirty years, Timur
Lang (1336–1405, "Timur the Lame" in
Persian, Tamerlane in the West) carved
out an empire stretching from Syria to
the Indus. The son of a Turkic tribal
chief, this fearsome conqueror was
notorious for the cruelty of his troops
and their habit of erecting pyramids of
skulls; their ferocity was deemed "the
synthesis of Mongol savagery" (R.
Grousset). For historian G. Martinez-
Gros, Tamerlane practiced "a kind of
preventive extermination" in territories
he considered indefensible over the
long term. His empire was thus built on
military might and the reign of terror:
approximately ten million people (five
per cent of the world's population at the
time) were massacred in what some
historians have called the "Timurid
disaster". And yet, this ruthless warrior
– who was also a cultured man and a
protector of the arts – was worshiped
by his people and is admired to this day
throughout Central Asia.

Produced just one year after the
author's death, this replica has a pres-
tigious pedigree: it belonged to Shah
Fath Ali Qajar, who reigned from 1797 to
1834, the first sovereign of Persia to
have been forced to endure a British
protectorate in order to stave off
Russian pressure. **N. D.**

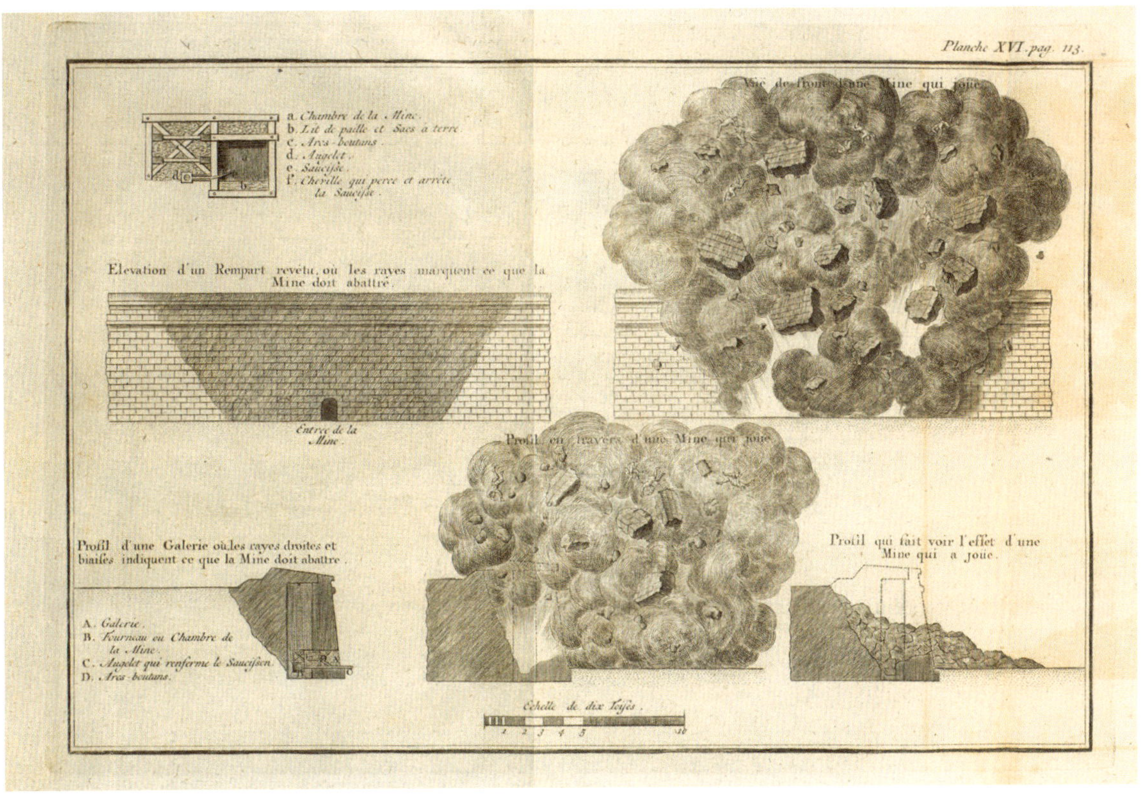

31
Sébastien Le Preste, Marquis de Vauban (1633–1707)

De l'attaque et de la défense des places [*On the Attack and Defence of Strongholds*], The Hague, Pierre de Hondt, 1737, first posthumous edition

Cologny, Martin Bodmer Foundation

Born into the petty nobility of the Morvan (a "minor country gentleman at most", according to Saint-Simon), Vauban distinguished himself very early on in the service of Condé, and was noticed by Mazarin. He became commissioner-general of fortifications in 1678, and was a key architect of the *pré carré* (lit. "square meadow") design so dear to the heart of Louis XIV. Thanks to his genius for the art of defence, the kingdom gained an "iron belt" of a hundred fortresses (whose advantage was not so much that they were impregnable as that they could immobilize an assailant indefinitely with ten times fewer men). It was popularly said that "a town built by Vauban is a town saved, a town attacked by Vauban is a town lost". An indefatigable worker (in 1681, his great year of inspections, he travelled 7,500 kilometres), he devoted his life to the king's service: in the space of forty years, he spent a total of only three and a half with his family. He was made lieutenant-general in 1688, and received the baton of marshal of France in 1703; shortly before his death, however, he fell from grace after penning a treatise advocating for equality of taxation.

The fruit of Vauban's many years of experience, *On the Attack and Defence of Strongholds* was written at the start of the War of the Spanish Succession, by order of the king, for the instruction of the Duke of Burgundy. Not intended for public consumption, it was published only thirty years after its author's death, based on one of the manuscripts in circulation. In discussing first the attack and then the defence of strongholds, Vauban's purpose was to "teach with what art and what wisdom the manoeuvres of a Siege must be conducted, from the moment when the Siege has been decided on until one has gained full mastery over the Stronghold". This edition contains with thirty-six folding plates, illustrated with engravings on copper showing fortifications, examples of attacks, construction profiles and plans, and so on. **N. D.**

32
Napoleon Bonaparte
(1769–1821)

[César], autograph manuscript, with corrections [St Helena, 1818]; provenance: Count Louis Marchand (1791–1876), first valet to the emperor and executor of his will (according to a note in his own hand, dated 15 August 1853)

Cologny, Martin Bodmer Foundation, Aut. N–4.1

St Helena, 1817. Installed in the rustic, windswept Longwood House, Napoleon is bored. For this voracious reader, the three thousand-volume library offers the only respite from monotony. He makes notes in his books, commenting on Plutarch or correcting a battle description. Apart from history, his other favourite pastime is the theatre, of which he has always been very fond. General Montholon mentions in his diary, on 8 January 1817, that the Emperor is reading *La Mort de César (The Death of Caesar)*, a tragedy by Voltaire; and again on 10 September: "after dinner, a reading of *La Mort de César*. 'If I had written this tragedy', said the Emperor, 'I would have written Caesar differently from Voltaire. I wanted to write about him when I was young.'"

A few months later, Napoleon penned this synopsis of the first two scenes of a tragedy about Caesar. Unlike Voltaire, Napoleon adopts a decidedly political and military approach: at the very start, "Anthony reports on the situation in Rome" and on factions hostile to Caesar, who in turn takes stock of the war against the Parthians. The figure of the Roman conqueror fascinated the Little Corporal and, according to Las Cases, "he thought him one of the most attractive characters in history" – although smugly adding: "I gave battle sixty times, Caesar only fifty." This interest was to result in a *Summary of Julius Caesar's Wars*, published in 1836. These pages are hard to read (as always with the Napoleon's hasty scrawl, made even more illegible at

the end of his life by his frequent use of pencil) and contain innumerable corrections. But the emperor's "literary relaxation" (as Marchand put it) did not last long: the synopsis comes to an abrupt end, and the third page is covered with feverish calculations. No more time for literature – back back to war it is. Stranded on a rocky outcrop in the middle of the Atlantic, the fallen Titan tots up figures and shifts around the companies, battalions and divisions of an imaginary army of his elite Old Guard, bringing into play fleets with "30 ships [of the line]" and "40 frigats [sic]". Thoughts of Caesar had roused the ogre and awakened his appetite for conquest. **N. D.**

33
Napoleon Bonaparte
(1769–1821)

[Vie d'Alexandre le Grand],
autograph manuscript, with
corrections and notes, St Helena,
c. 1816

Cologny, Martin Bodmer Foundation, Aut. N–4.6

At the time of his Italian Campaign, Bonaparte told those around him of his admiration for Alexander the Great, whom he considered superior to Caesar in the art of war (he especially admired the Macedonian's ruses against the Persians). During the Egyptian Campaign, he summoned up the memory of the ancient Greek conqueror when haranguing his troops. Yet Alexander's name rarely appeared in his official proclamations, and it was only when he found himself idle, in exile on St Helena, that his passion for this great man truly blossomed. According to Las Cases, "[the emperor] was reading about Alexander's expedition in Rollin … he complained of a tasteless, purposeless account that failed to do justice to Alexander's great vision; he felt the urge to redo this piece" (3 May 1816). Napoleon's own *Memoirs* show him admiring Alexander on three counts, as "[a] great warrior, great politician [and] great legislator", while also criticizing him for yielding to the excesses of power: "he started out with the soul of Trajan; he ended up with the heart of Nero and the habits of Heliogabalus." This document is evidence both of Napoleon's interest in Alexander and of the working methods customary at Longwood House: Las Cases and Generals Bertrand, Montholon and Gourgaud would consult the imposing library and prepare notes according to the emperor's instructions. Ensconced in his own room or in the billiard room, Napoleon would then dictate or correct for hours on end – as he did with this biographical note, which bears copious annotations in pencil. **N. D.**

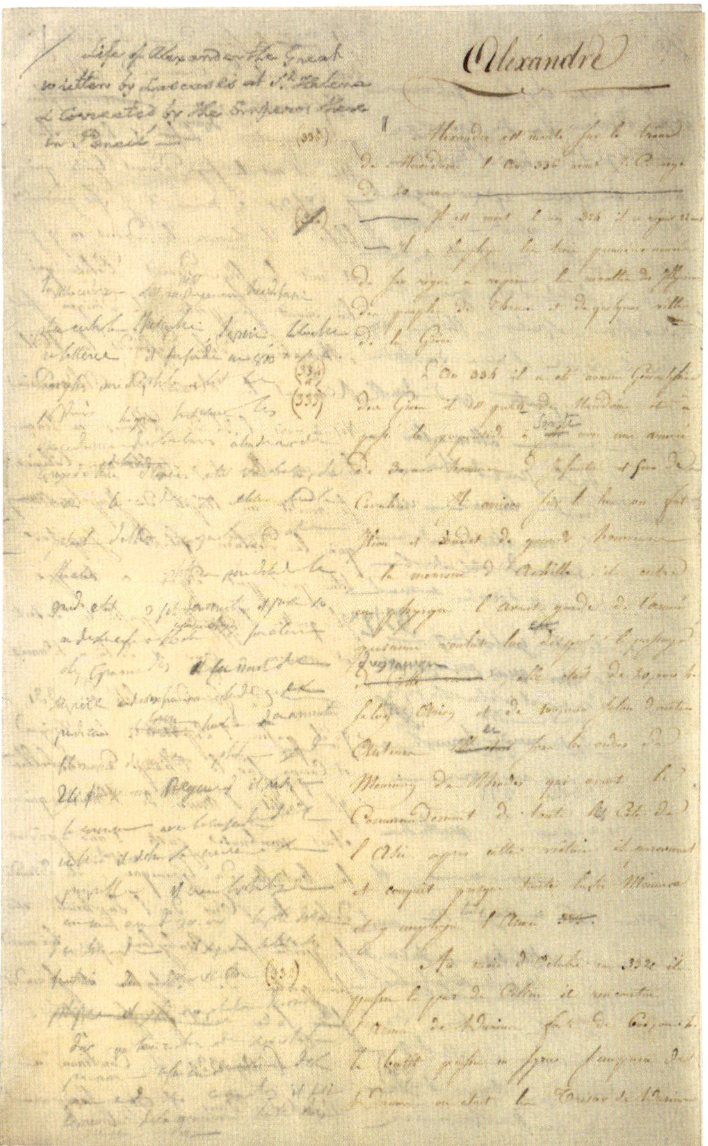

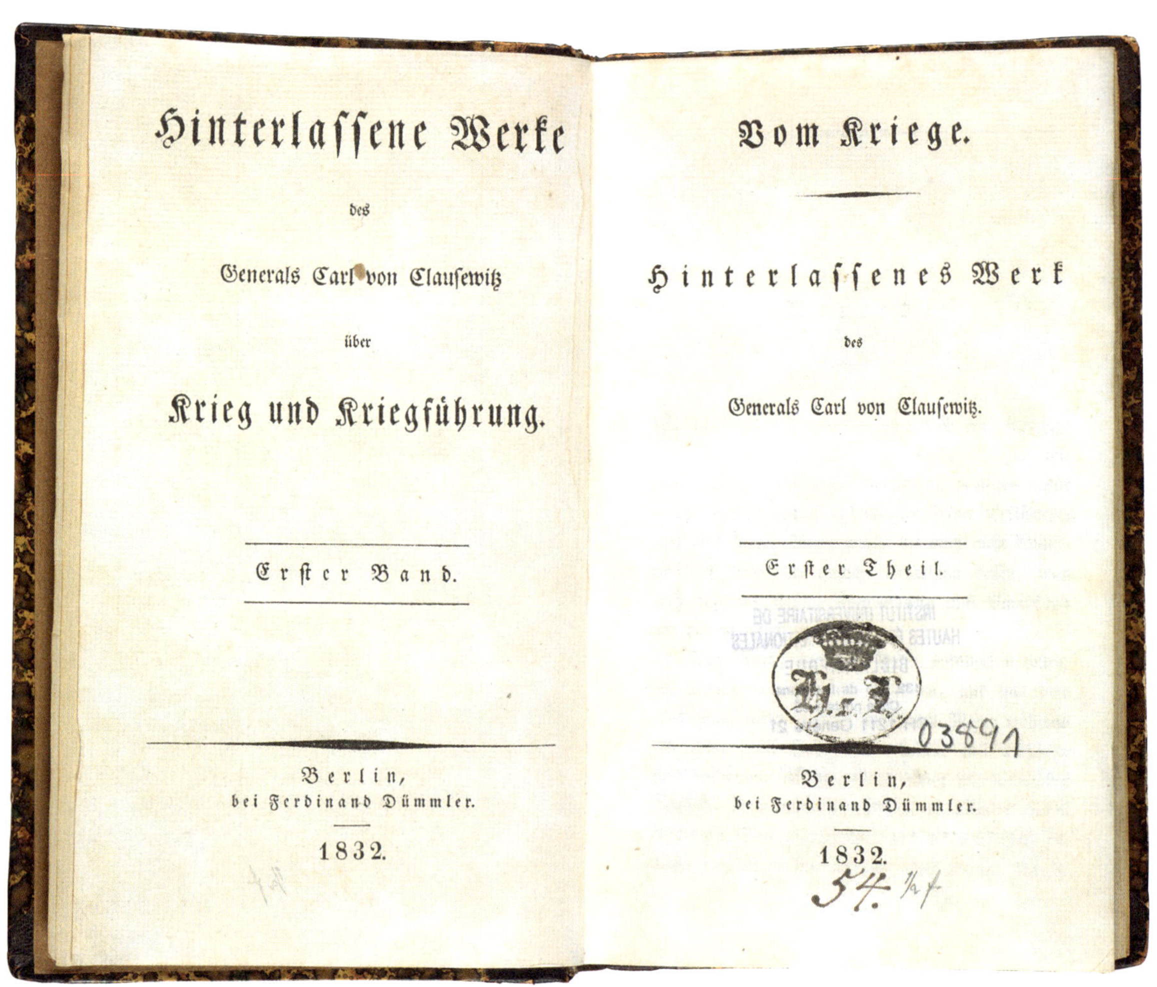

34
Carl von Clausewitz
(1780–1831)
Vom Kriege [*On War*], Berlin,
F. Dümmler, 1832–33

Geneva, The Graduate Institute (IHEID), 355.01

Born in 1780, in Burg, Carl von Clausewitz was a Prussian general. who fought in the Napoleonic Wars, is better known today for his writings than for his military exploits. His treatise of military strategy, *On War*, written between 1816 and 1830 but published only after his death, remains on the syllabus of military academies to this day. Clausewitz defined war as "an act of violence to compel our opponent to fulfil our will". One of his main aims was to show that war was a form of politics between nations, or, as he famously said, "War is a mere continuation of policy by other means." A second key concept is absolute war, which entails "rising to extremes" and annihilating the enemy. Clausewitz was influenced by the transformation of both the nature of war and the conduct of hostilities. Following the French Revolution and the advent of national conscription, limited clashes had been replaced by total war. Clausewitz also drew lessons from Napoleon's campaigns, which exemplified a new conception of war as a series of rapid troop movements. Thanks to its analyses of famous campaigns, *On War* still stands as one of the most influential treatises of military strategy ever written, making a lasting impression on Lenin, Churchill, De Gaulle and Mao Zedong.

P. H.

35
Convention for the Amelioration of the Condition of the Wounded in Armies in the Field, Geneva, 22 August 1864

*Bern, Swiss Federal Archives, K1#1000/1414#2**

This treaty – the cornerstone of modern international humanitarian law – was signed in Geneva on 22 August 1864 by twelve of the sixteen states taking part in a diplomatic conference convened by the Swiss authorities, the first event of its kind organized in Switzerland. Entitled "Convention for the Amelioration of the Condition of the Wounded in Armies in the Field", the text, which was very short, comprising only ten articles, set forth the obligation to care for wounded or sick soldiers regardless of their nationality. It also instructed belligerents to respect the neutrality of medical personnel and facilities, and required the latter to wear a distinctive sign in the form of a red cross on a white background. The convention had been drafted by two private individuals, Gustave Moynier (1826–1910) and Henry Dunant (1828–1910), respectively the president and secretary of the International Committee for Relief to Wounded Soldiers (which later became the International Committee of the Red Cross). Generally known as the first or original Geneva Convention, it was revised, with the inclusion of new articles, in 1906 and 1929. **D. P.**

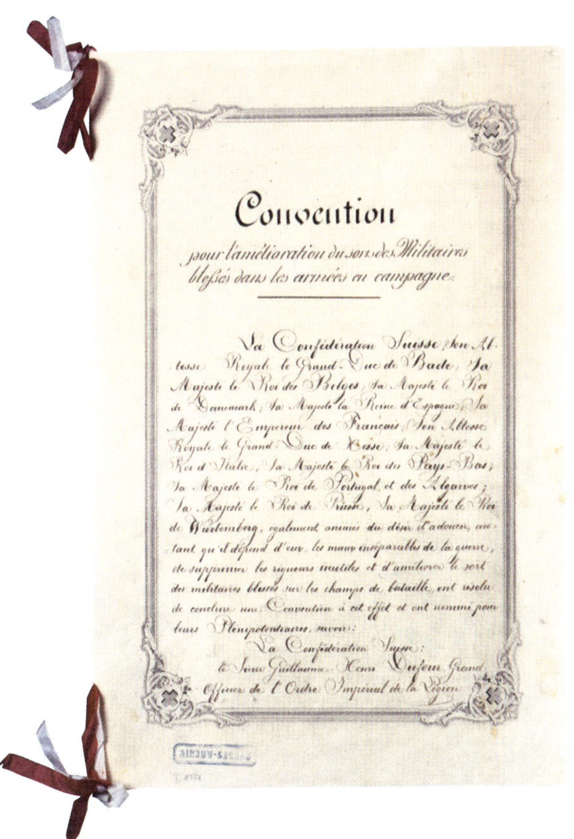

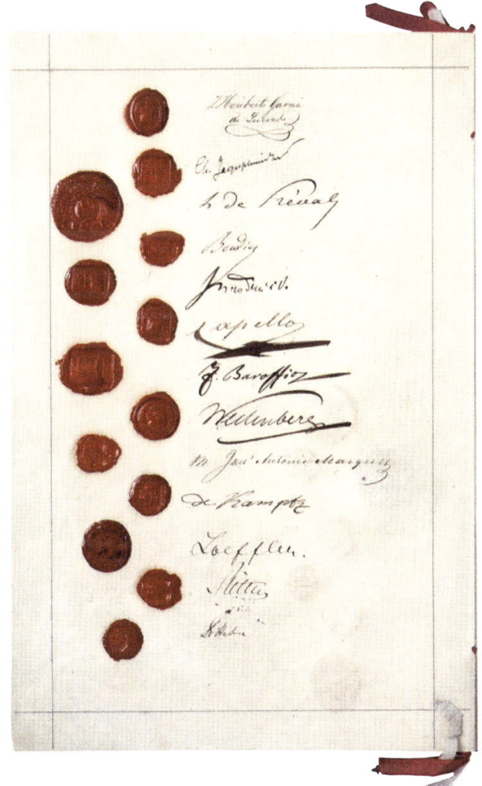

36
Henry Dunant (1828–1910)
Autograph note, 1873

Geneva, Martin Bodmer Foundation, Aut. D-52.1

While he was the one who came up with the idea for the Red Cross – having outlined it in 1862, in his internationally acclaimed book, *A Memory of Solferino* – Henry Dunant had a troubled time in the organization. He was one of the five founders of the International Committee of the Red Cross (ICRC), established in February 1863, but served as its first secretary for only a short time. Legal troubles – he was convicted in 1868 of fraudulent bankruptcy – forced Dunant to leave Geneva in March 1867; he resigned from the ICRC in August. From then on, he led a rootless and often destitute life, returning to Switzerland only in 1887. During his forced exile, and despite being cast out from the ICRC, Dunant continued to claim a key role in establishing the Red Cross – and rightly so, though he was guilty of the occasional misrepresentation. For instance, contrary to what Dunant claims in this note, there is no real proof that he came up with the idea for the organization's emblem, a red cross on a white background. Rather, it seems to have been chosen following a discussion at the international conference organized by the ICRC in October 1863. What is certain is that at no time did the participants use the term "crusade". And lastly, the claim that the emblem was adopted in honour of Switzerland, by inverting the colours of the Swiss flag, is mentioned only in 1906, on the occasion of the revision of the Geneva Convention.　　**D. P.**

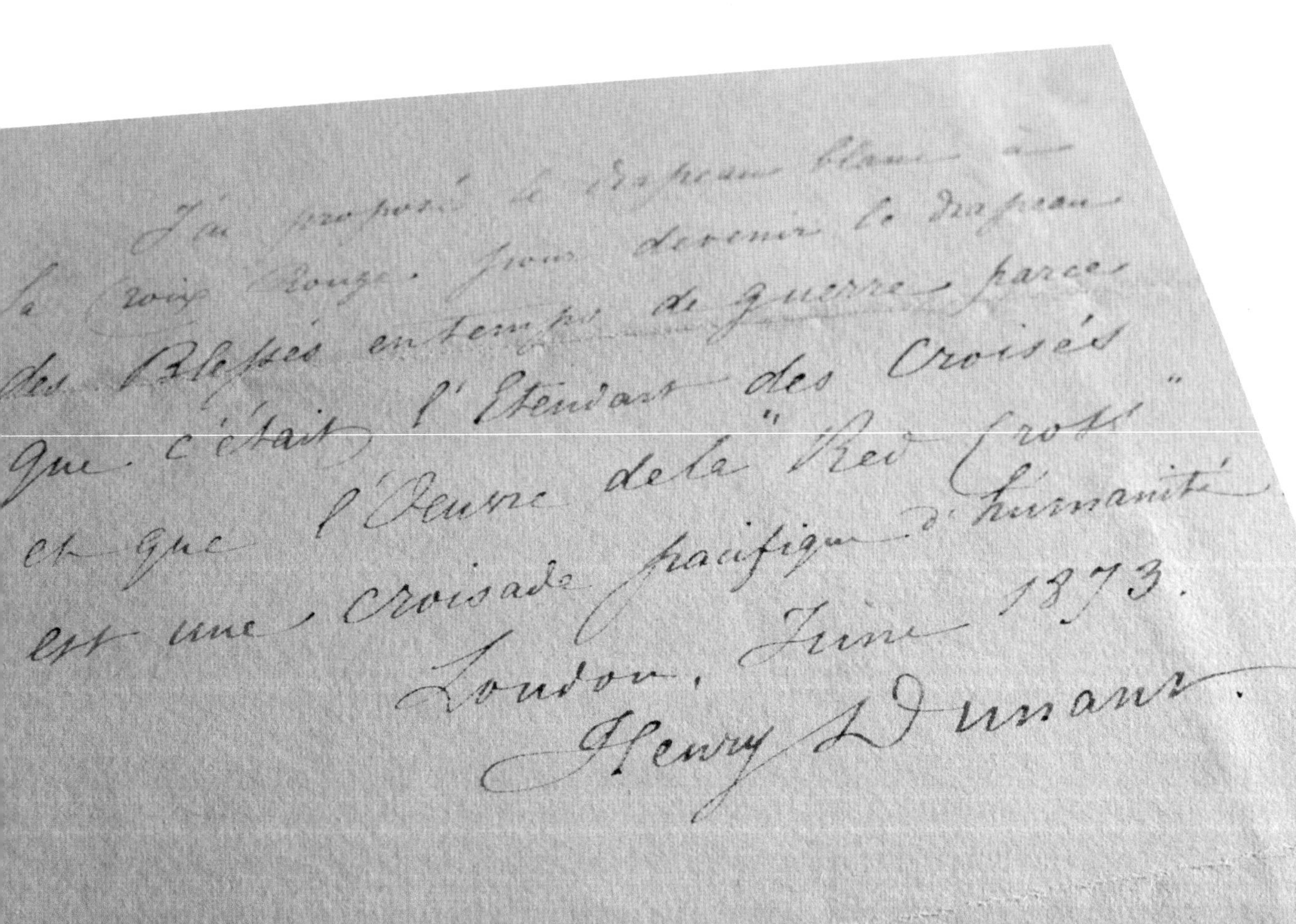

Le titre que nous donnons à cet article pourrait facilement induire en erreur sur son contenu ; aussi convient-il que nous prévenions nos lecteurs de ce dont il s'agit, afin que leur attente ne soit pas trompée.

Aucun État nègre, pas même la République de Libéria, n'a encore adhéré à la Convention de Genève ; il n'est même pas à désirer qu'ils le fassent, car les peuples noirs de l'Afrique sont, pour la plupart, trop sauvages encore pour pouvoir s'associer à la pensée humanitaire qui a inspiré ce traité et pour la mettre en pratique. Les aspirations civilisatrices du roi Jean, le souverain chrétien de l'Abyssinie, et de son vassal Ménélik au Choa, ou celles non moins remarquables du roi de l'Ouganda, le fameux M'tésa, qui a aboli la traite des esclaves dans ses États, pourraient en leur faire adopter la Croix rouge dans un moment d'enthousiasme, s'ils la connaissaient ; mais personne ne le leur a encore proposé, et c'est fort heureux, car ni ces potentats ni leurs sujets [ne so]nt mûrs pour un tel progrès. Quant à des Sociétés de secours, [il est] non moins superflu de dire qu'il n'en existe aucune chez les...

...ne nous proposons ici que de relever quelques...
...sez insignifiant...

THE TIME OF DESTRUCTION

37
Gustave Moynier (1826–1910)
"La Croix-Rouge chez les Nègres" [The Red Cross among the Negroes], *Bulletin international des Sociétés de secours aux militaires blessés, publié par le Comité internationale de la Croix-Rouge*, no. 41, January 1880, p. 5-7
Geneva, ICRC

For many years, the concept of the Red Cross and that of "civilization" were closely linked. Only states that had attained a certain level of development were considered capable of joining this philanthropic enterprise. What made a country "civilized" was of course defined by the same class of people who were behind the International Committee of the Red Cross, that is, the Western European bourgeoisie. This narrow view of who deserved to be part of the Red Cross "family" was compounded by colonialism, which established a new level of discrimination: colonized nations, no matter how "civilized", were not - or no longer - seen as elegible to sign the 1864 Geneva Convention. Only their new Western "masters" were entitled to this privilege. Unsurprisingly, Africa remained something of a *terra incognita* for the Red Cross. According to the ICRC, this was all for the better, as the small number of free "Negro states" were still "too savage" to enforce the Geneva Convention – with the exception of the Congo Free State, which ratified the treaty in 1888. That seems particularly ironic in the light of the massacres perpetrated across the country during the reign of Leopold II of Belgium, in which around half of the population died. The Congo Free State was nevertheless viewed favourably by Gustave Moynier (1826–1910), the president of the ICRC, who happened also to be the country's consul general in Switzerland. **D. P.**

38
Ministers of Wei-Ou-Pan
Ratification by China
of the Geneva Convention
of 1864, Beijing, 3 April 1904

Geneva, ICRC, ICRCA, A AF 3,5/7

The Geneva Convention of 22 August 1864, which aimed to protect wounded and sick soldiers on the battlefield, was the first modern international treaty to clearly define the rules of war. Drafted by the International Committee of the Red Cross (ICRC), it was initially adopted by the European powers at a diplomatic conference in Geneva. The ICRC hoped that, in time, the treaty would become universally ratified by all the "civilized" states of the world. Invitations were therefore sent to Mexico, the United States of America and Brazil to attend the 1864 conference. The ICRC closely followed developments in countries outside Europe and seized every opportunity to promote the Geneva Convention among their sovereigns, such as when the shah of Persia visited Geneva in July 1873. Persia was the first non-European nation to sign the original Geneva Convention in December 1874.

In contrast, some nations were considered too "barbaric" to join the treaty. This was the case of China in the second half of the nineteenth century. China also suffered in the ICRC's estimation as a result of the prestige of its neighbour, Japan, which was deemed to have entered the age of (Western) civilization and modernity since the early 1870s, and which signed the Geneva Convention in 1886. This largely explains the ICRC's lack of interest in China and the fact that the country only ratified the treaty at the beginning of the twentieth century. **D. P.**

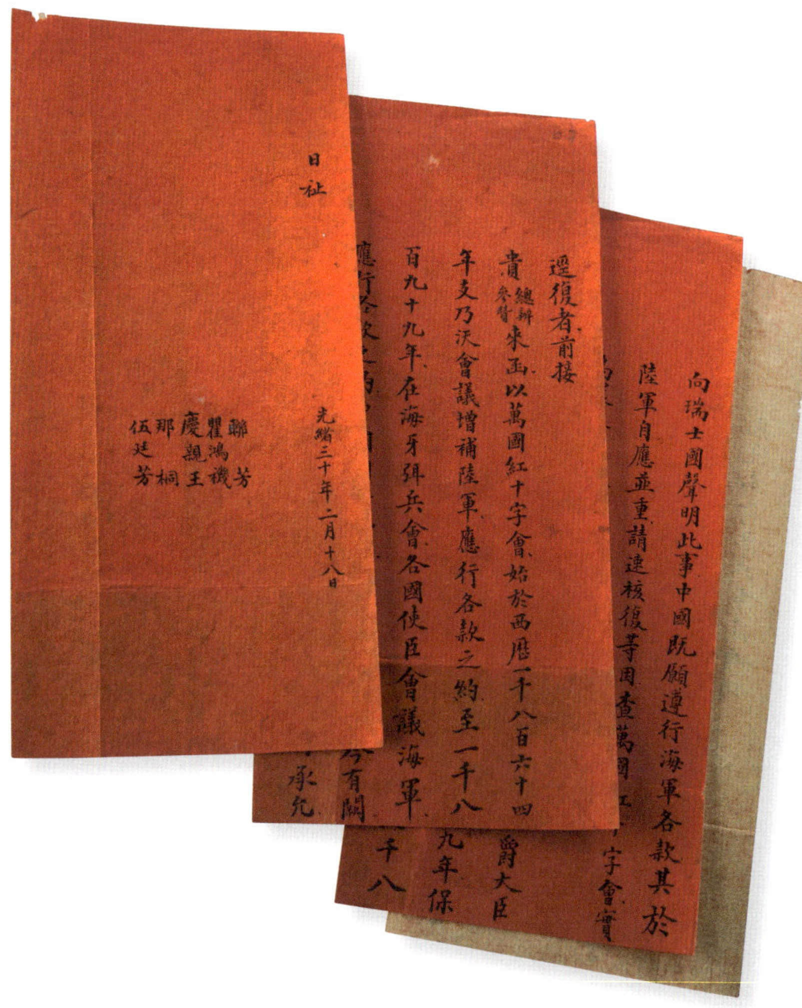

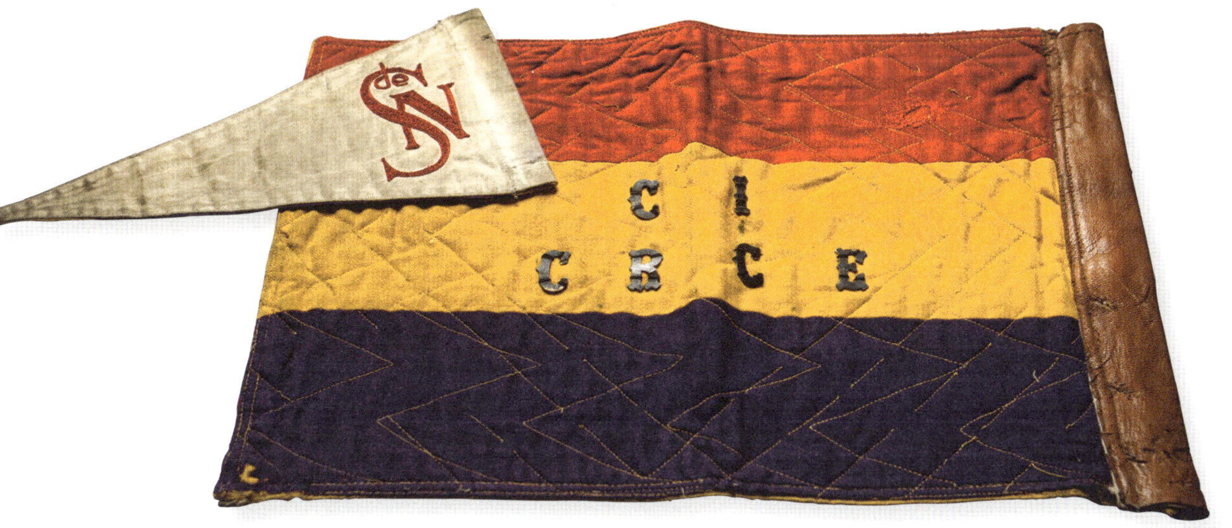

39
Flags of the International Commission appointed for the withdrawal of non-Spanish combatants from Spain
Geneva, United Nations Archives

On 21 September 1938, Juan Negrín, President of the Spanish Council of Ministers, speaking to the Assembly of the League of Nations, announced the unilateral withdrawal of foreign combatants enlisted with the Republican army. The aim was no doubt to bring international pressure to bear on Germany and Italy, so that they would suspend their support for Franco's forces. Negrín asked that an international commission be established to verify the withdrawal. The League of Nations agreed to that request in the following days and set up a commission made up of three commissioners (from Finland, Great Britain and France), four members of the League secretariat and nine adjutant officers from several Member States. In October 1938, the commission started to identify – and supervise the withdrawal of – nearly 12,000 non-Spanish combatants. The League had never had an emblem or a flag: the Member States had no intention of providing it with symbols that might hint at the constitution of a "superstate". The banners adopted by the commission made its members recognizable in the field and allowed them to move about freely as they discharged their duties on the territory controlled by the Republican government.

P.-E. B.

40
Martin Bodmer (1899–1971)
Typed and signed letter to the president of the ICRC, 1 June 1941

Geneva, ICRC, ICRCA, A CL 004-002

During the Second World War, an Advisory Committee on Books for Prisoners and Internees of War was created in Geneva under the auspices of the International Committee of the Red Cross (ICRC), and chaired by the ICRC representative, Martin Bodmer (1899–1971). In addition to the ICRC, the committee involved six other international organizations, including the World Alliance of Young Men's Christian Associations and the International Bureau of Education. The purpose of the committee was to divide up work into clearly defined spheres of activity, in order to oversee censorship and avoid any gaps or duplication in the distribution of books. Martin Bodmer's chairmanship of the advisory committee came as no surprise. Having been a member of the ICRC since February 1940, as well as the founder of a library and archive of exceptional importance, Bodmer was the ideal man for the job. The bibliophile had also worked at the ICRC at some point – the exact date is unknown – creating an "Intellectual Relief Service" within the Central Prisoners of War Agency, established by the ICRC in Geneva. The service employed around fifty people, divided into several teams. What these were called and how the service was organized is unclear – aside for the fact that it was directed by Martin Bodmer – as no records were kept. However, we know that it was responsible for sending more than 840,000 books to prisoner of war camps between 1940 and December 1943. **D. P.**

[...] in Klaren. Es sind eben jene Misstände, dass die Regierungen am liebsten nur mit uns zu tun haben wollen, da der direkte Kontakt mangels an Vertretern an Ort und Stelle aber fehlt, sich an die YMCA halten müssen oder eben jene Leute, die die Interessen besonderer Organisationen vertreten, statt die Gesamtsache und die des Roten Kreuzes, das schliesslich doch die verantwortliche Instanz ist. Diese Frage muss also ernstlich geprüft werden, und ich glaube, wir werden um die Entsendung eines Vertrauensmannes nicht herumkommen, resp. wir dürfen diese relativ kleine Mehrausgabe nicht scheuen, wenn wir die Interessen des CICR und damit die der Kriegsgefangenen so vertreten wollen, wie es nötig ist.

Ich hoffe dass Sie eine recht gute Kur machen und sich wirklich erholen können. Mit sehr herzlichen Grüssen und Wünschen bin ich

stets Ihr ergebener

Martin Bodmer

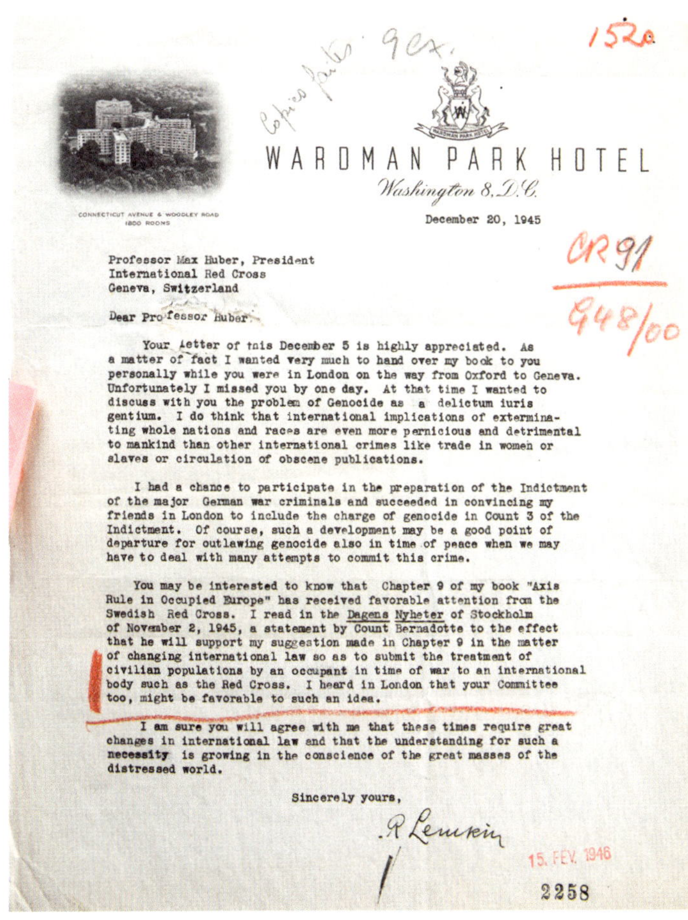

41
Raphael Lemkin (1900–59)
Typed and signed letter to Max Huber, president of the ICRC, 20 December 1945

Geneva, ICRC, ICRCA, B CR 91-8, 1520

The crime of genocide was legally defined only in 1948, even though various events of the first half of the twentieth century clearly fit the bill. Polish lawyer Raphael Lemkin (1900–59) is credited with coining the term, as early as 1944, to refer to the 1915 mass slaughter of the Armenians, as well as the ongoing extermination of European Jews by the Nazi regime and its allies. After the Second World War, Lemkin succeeded in getting genocide recognized as a crime against humanity. The crime of genocide was one of the legal bases for the judgments handed down by the Nuremburg tribunal (1945–46), even though at the time it did not exist as a charge. The international Convention on the Prevention and Punishment of the Crime of Genocide was adopted in December 1948 by the United Nations General Assembly, and entered into force in January 1951.

After the war, Raphael Lemkin contacted the International Committee of the Red Cross (ICRC) about the problem of genocide, at a time when the organization was involved in a major revision of international humanitarian law. In July 1950, Lemkin again turned to the ICRC for help in getting the 1948 Convention ratified, as it had still not come into force. However, the ICRC sent him a deliberately evasive reply, perhaps fearing that the new treaty would overshadow the Fourth Geneva Convention of 1949 on the protection of civilians in wartime, which was due to enter into force shortly. **D. P.**

42
Geneva Convention of 1949, Geneva, 12 August 1949

Bern, Swiss Federal Archives, K1#1822

The scale of the destruction and atrocities committed during the Second World War brought to light the inadequacy of international humanitarian law for dealing with the new reality of global warfare since the mid-1930s. A complete overhaul was needed in order to better serve those the law aimed to protect. Until then, the focus of international humanitarian law had been on combatants, whether wounded, shipwrecked or imprisoned. By contrast, civilians, who suffered a great deal during the war, were overlooked. To make up for this, as soon as the Second World War was over, the International Committee of the Red Cross (ICRC) set about drafting new conventions and revising the treaties already in force. After a lengthy process, the texts were adopted at a diplomatic conference in Geneva, on 12 August 1949.

In the case of an international armed conflict, the Geneva Conventions afford protection to wounded and sick soldiers in the field (Convention I); wounded, sick and shipwrecked members of the armed forces at sea (II); prisoners of war (III); and civilians in wartime (IV). All four conventions also contain a common Article 3 – a sort of "mini convention" within the convention – that enjoins the parties to extend humane treatment to people placed "hors de combat" (in French in the original) and to non-combatants during internal armed conflicts. Article 3 also specifices that the ICRC may offer its services in such situations. **D. P.**

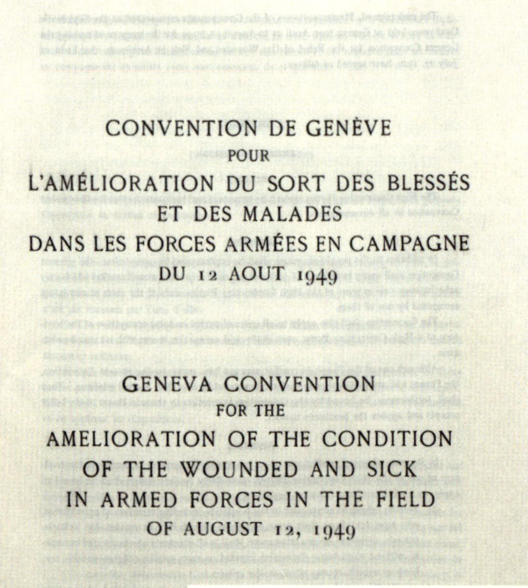

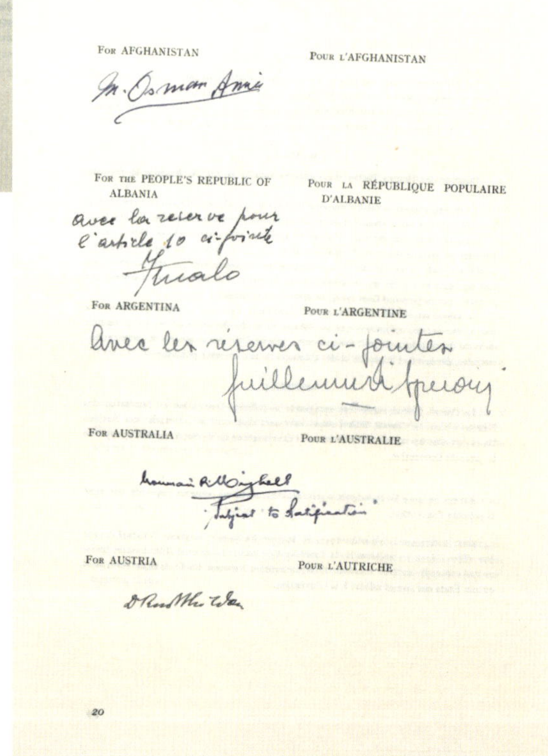

[...] nuestros delegados [...] heridos [...] enemigos de ser o

[...] nuestros mortificados sanitarios necesarios para una

[...] de todas las [...]

humildes.

[...] que, mientras aquí se respetan todas las leyes de la guerra

[...] con el sentido de humanidad posible en las condi-

[...] enemigos con el sentido de humanidad posible en las condi-

[...] lucha, el Ejército enemigo viola sistemáticamente estas le-

[...] las bandas Masferreristas asesinaron instituían el comer-

[...] traían para la Sierra. Larga sería la exposición de crímenes

[...] conocerán internacionalmente otros quedarían en el ámbito na-

[...] que puede contribuir a humanizar esta guerra, unilateralmente

[...] to de puestos permanentes de la Cruz Roja Internacional en el

[...] que ofrecemos queda a discreción del Comité Internacional de la

[...] sición de no reconocidos como beligerantes, recibiendo sola-

[...] "bandoleros", "forajidos", etc. nos impiden hacer tramitaciones

[...] o enemigo.

[...], cúmpleme felicitar a esa humanitaria Institución por la [...]

[...] que cumpliera su misión

Por el Comandante en Jefe Fidel Castro
Comandante de Columna # 8

43
Ernesto "Che" Guevara (1928–1967)

Typed and signed letter from the Cuban rebels to the ICRC, Sierra Maestra, 24 July 1958

Geneva, ICRC, ICRCA, B AG 200 060-005

The first contact between the International Committee of the Red Cross (ICRC) and the Cuban rebels, led by Fidel Castro, took place in July 1958. The rebels wanted to hand over wounded prisoners from the government forces to the Cuban Red Cross, and Castro approached the ICRC to intervene with the Cuban regime to secure authorization. The ICRC sent two delegates to Cuba to discuss the handover of the wounded prisoners with both sides.

The operation took place on 23 and 24 July 1958 at a military outpost in the rebel-held Sierra Maestra. In total, 253 sick or wounded prisoners trickled in and were handed over by the guerrillas to the Cuban Red Cross and the army, under the auspices of the ICRC. They received first aid on the spot, before being evacuated by helicopter.

During the handover, the ICRC delegates spoke to Ernesto Guevara, known as Che, who was one of the rebel commanders. On 24 July, he presented them with a typed letter asking the ICRC to recognize a delegation in Caracas, which would enable the rebels to convey messages between Geneva and the Sierra Maestra. Behind this request, lay the real purpose of this letter: to obtain official recognition of the revolutionary movement from the ICRC.

D. P.

44
ICRC Delegation to Algeria, Report on the Cinq Palmiers transit and screening centre, 17 November 1959

Geneva, ICRC, ICRCA, B AG 251 008-008

In February 1955, the French government granted the International Committee of the Red Cross (ICRC) permission to visit prisoners detained in Algeria during what at the time was called "the events". A first series of inspections took place at the end of February. Between February 1955 and June 1962, the ICRC organized a total of ten missions to Algeria, visiting some five hundred detention or internment centres. After each visit, the ICRC drew up a detailed, confidential report, which it submitted to the detaining authorities. But on 5 January 1960, French newspaper *Le Monde* published a summary of the reports from the ICRC's seventh mission, conducted between October and November 1959, which had been leaked to the paper.

The article highlighted the poor conditions of detention and cases of torture and forced disappearance recorded by the ICRC. The fact that the ICRC teams included doctors who had examined the marks left by torture on the victims' bodies lent weight to the their findings. These reports also provided "official" confirmation from a neutral source of facts that had been known for some time in French society. The French authorities never blamed the ICRC for the public disclosure of the information: the leak came from the French administration itself. Nonetheless, the ICRC was denied access to detention facilities in Algeria for a year, despite its repeated requests to return. **D. P.**

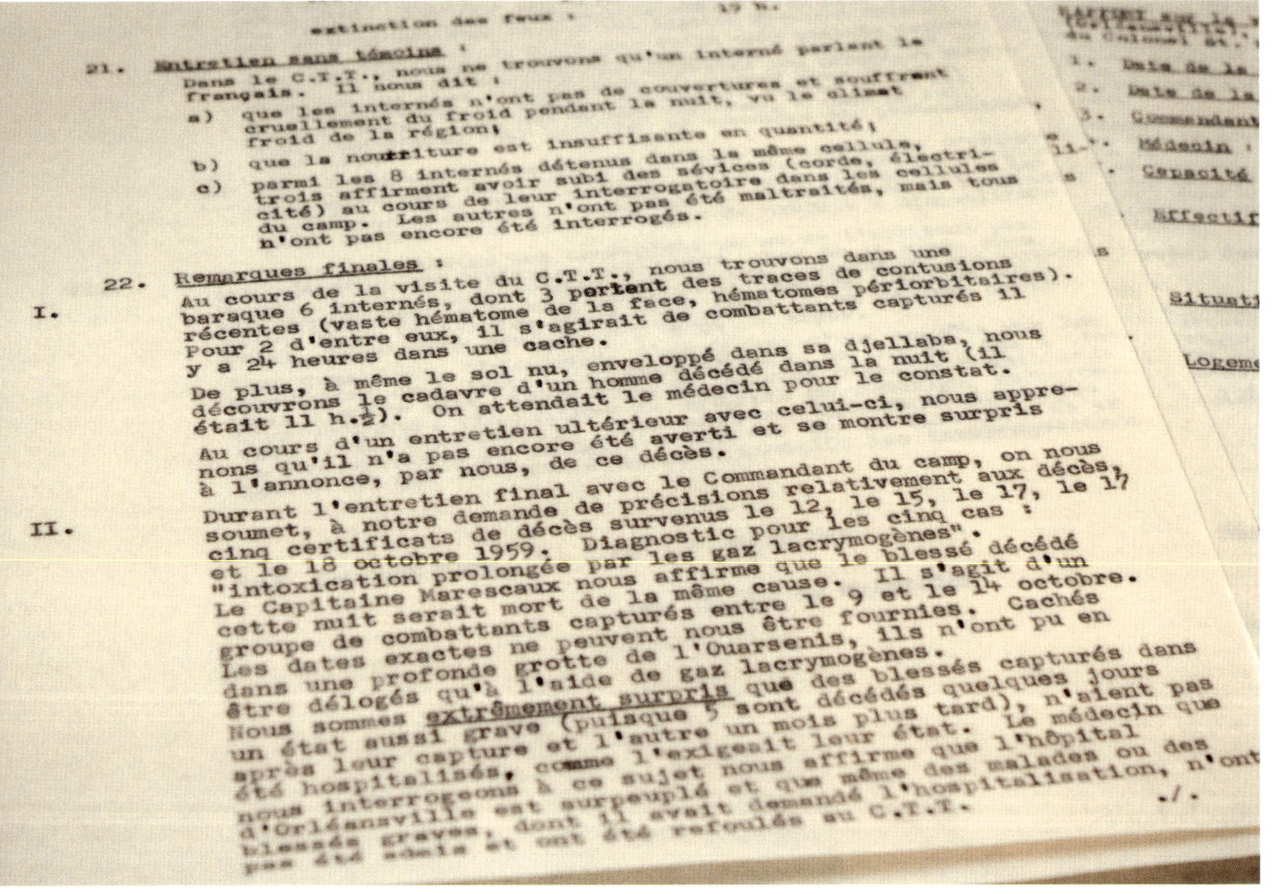

extinction des feux :   17 h.

21. **Entretien sans témoins** :
Dans le C.T.T., nous ne trouvons qu'un interné parlant le français. Il nous dit :
a) que les internés n'ont pas de couvertures et souffrent cruellement du froid pendant la nuit, vu le climat froid de la région;
b) que la nourriture est insuffisante en quantité;
c) parmi les 8 internés détenus dans la même cellule, trois affirment avoir subi des sévices (corde, électricité) au cours de leur interrogatoire dans les cellules du camp. Les autres n'ont pas été maltraités, mais tous n'ont pas encore été interrogés.

22. **Remarques finales** :
Au cours de la visite du C.T.T., nous trouvons dans une baraque 6 internés, dont 3 portent des traces de contusions récentes (vaste hématome de la face, hématomes périorbitaires). Pour 2 d'entre eux, il s'agirait de combattants capturés il y a 24 heures dans une cache.
De plus, à même le sol nu, enveloppé dans sa djellaba, nous découvrons le cadavre d'un homme décédé dans la nuit (il était 11 h.½). On attendait le médecin pour le constat.
Au cours d'un entretien ultérieur avec celui-ci, nous apprenons qu'il n'a pas encore été averti et se montre surpris à l'annonce, par nous, de ce décès.

Durant l'entretien final avec le Commandant du camp, on nous soumet, à notre demande de précisions relativement aux décès, cinq certificats de décès survenus le 12, le 15, le 17, le 17 et le 18 octobre 1959. Diagnostic pour les cinq cas : "intoxication prolongée par les gaz lacrymogènes".
Le Capitaine Marescaux nous affirme que le blessé décédé cette nuit serait mort de la même cause. Il s'agit d'un groupe de combattants capturés entre le 9 et le 14 octobre. Les dates exactes ne peuvent nous être fournies. Cachés dans une profonde grotte de l'Ouarsenis, ils n'ont pu en être délogés qu'à l'aide de gaz lacrymogènes.
Nous sommes extrêmement surpris que des blessés capturés dans un état aussi grave (puisque 5 sont décédés quelques jours après leur capture et l'autre un mois plus tard), n'aient pas été hospitalisés, comme l'exigeait leur état. Le médecin que nous interrogeons à ce sujet nous affirme que l'hôpital d'Orléansville est surpeuplé et que même des malades ou des blessés graves, dont il avait demandé l'hospitalisation, n'ont pas été admis et ont été refoulés au C.T.T.

-./.

45
Geoffrey Cassian Senn
(1898–1981)

Report of a visit to Nelson
Mandela, Robben Island,
8 April 1967

Geneva, ICRC, ICRCA, B AG 225.005-17.01

After making just one visit in September 1963 to the only political prisoner recognized as such by the South African authorities, the International Committee of the Red Cross (ICRC) was granted access to the country's detention facilities in May 1964. There, ICRC delegates met detainees facing charges or serving sentences, who belonged to various political and activist movements fighting against South Africa's apartheid regime. Securing the right to visit prisons and speak in private with the detainees was no mean feat. The ICRC had to wait another three years before being allowed to inspect South African prisons again, in April, May and August 1967. It was during one of these visits – on 8 April 1967 – that the ICRC met Nelson Mandela (1918–2013) for the first time, on Robben Island.

The commander of the armed wing of the African National Congress had been arrested in August 1962, sentenced to life in June 1964 and jailed on Robben Island ever since. Although he was already there when the ICRC delegates visited in 1964, they had not been able to meet him.

Nelson Mandela was interviewed by ICRC delegate Geoffrey Cassian Senn (1898–1981), the organization's representative in southern Africa since 1941. The two men did not hit it off. Mandela felt that Senn was not open-minded and that the years he had spent in Rhodesia – another apartheid regime – had rubbed off on him.   **D. P.**

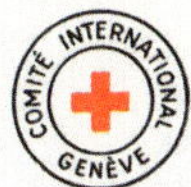

COMITÉ INTERNATIONAL
DE LA
CROIX-ROUGE

Robben Island, 8th April 1967.

Note on Interview with Mr. Nelson Mandela.

His remarks are as follows:
He is living with 30 other political convicts in a
cell block, isolated from the other prisoners, and
these 30 work together in a lime stone quarry.

He describes the work as strenuous - more strenuous than,
e.g., the work in the stone quarry, where the continuity
of work is not of the same intensity, and where short
interruptions always occur. The group of 30 does this work
without break or change since January 1965.

He deems that the physical strength of all has diminished.
The white glare of the lime in the sum affects the eyes
and dark glasses are supplied on application by the Medical
Officer, but they are of a cheap kind and the prisoners
have bought their own of a better kind.

There are weak prisoners in the group:
Govan Mbeki (56; B.A. & B.Econ.) suffering from Hypertension
          and swelling of feet in day time.
Walter Sisulu (54; Estate Agent) suffering from Hypertension.
Raymond Mhlaba (46; trade unionist) suffering from the same.
Ahmed Kathrada (38; official of South African Indian Congress)
          had once broken his leg and is now suffering from dis-
          ability to a degree & pains.
Edward Daniels (36) has a hernia which is often painful, and
          varicous veines and wears often elastic bandages.
Lallo Chiba (32;) complains of pains in testicles and in the
          rhenal region; has often difficulties in walking.
Mlamli Makwetu (36) is often in pains due to an earlier
          spinal injury.
Johannes Dangala (32) crippled (clump-foot), had sinus oper-
          ation about 2 months ago.
Elias Motsoaledi (42; trade unionist) asthmatic.
Leslie van der Heyden (27; B.A., teacher)rheumatoid arthritis
          and probably piles.
All the aforesaid have been treated one time or another at
the hospital, and are receiving treatment as far as needed.

Could the group not be given other work, at least for a
month, to break the monotony and the strain?

Food: could the diet not be improved by adding "samp" with
          beans and some fat? Could some fruit be given?
          -----

17 AVR. 1967   729

Victims' accounts, international denunciation of abuses committed against civilians, and the courage and blindness of the ICRC during the Second World War.

46
Henri Moisan (1894–1985)
Notebook, autograph manuscript, 1915–1916

Cologny, Martin Bodmer Foundation, gift of Annie Moisan

An orphan who had been apprenticed at the age of ten, Henri Moisan eagerly enlisted on 3 August 1914, and was assigned to the infantry. In March 1915, he started a keeping a diary, in which he described the horrors of the front – "a field littered with corpses on which night falls", he wrote, quoting Victor Hugo. For months, he consigned his thoughts and impressions in this notebook, occasionally while on leave behind the lines, but most often at the front, in a neat hand that stands in stark contrast to the daily horror. Death was everywhere: "A few metres from my lodgings, we walked – literally – over a Boche so summarily buried that his posterior physiognomy is exposed for all to see, to all the affronts of the weather, and to everyone's footprints. The lack of respect for the dead was astonishing: "You may think that I'm the only one to feel it: think again, here everyone feels the same." He wrote of mud ("What a disaster!") and slaughter: "To understand the horror of war you have to have lived the life we were living". The shelling was so intense that the spirit, tense to the breaking point, yearned for the peace of annihilation: "Will we go mad? … Those who aren't here cannot image the effect on our bodies of a shell bursting right beside us. The commotion is so violent that it seizes our throats, grips our hearts, stuns us by making the blood rush to our heads and deafens us."

On 29 April 1915, Moisan was seriously wounded: "When the shrapnel struck my head, I was momentarily paralysed. I simply could not move, and I thought I could feel my head emptying. I had seen some of my poor mates badly wounded to the head, their brains spilling out of their injuries. And the only thing I could think of in that instant was that I was going to die." Awarded a military distinction, he was among the last defenders of Fort Vaux, which fell to the Germans in June 1916. Imprisoned until the end of the war, Moisan went on to become an entrepreneur and local politician. During the Second World War, he joined the Resistance; arrested in Amiens, he escaped the firing squad thanks to the bombardment of the prison by the Royal Air Force, during its famous Operation Jericho.   **N. D.**

47
Louis Abelly (1604–91)
*La Vie du vénérable serviteur
de Dieu, Vincent de Paul…*
[*The Life of the Venerable Servant
of God, Vincent de Paul…*], Paris,
Florentin Lambert, 1664

Saint-Mihiel, Benedictine Library, T.399

Libraries have frequently been direct victims of armed conflict. Whether handwritten or printed on papyrus, parchment or paper, books are vulnerable to burning and looting. Some of these autos-da-fé are well known, symbols of the triumph of savagery over culture: the burning of the libraries of Alexandria in Antiquity, of Constantinople in the Middle Ages, and of Louvain (burnt to the ground by the Germans in 1914 and again in 1940) and Sarajevo in modern times. Recent bonfires in Timbuktu and Mosul offer further evidence that books are often viewed as legitimate targets.

The First World War exacted a heavy toll on libraries in France and Belgium. In Saint-Vaast, in July 1915, 50,000 books went up in flames. The Verdun library was hit in October of the same year: a similar number of books were recovered from the ruins, but happily the heritage collections had been evacuated in time. In Reims, the looting of the cathedral in 1914 was followed in May 1917 by the destruction of the 151,000 volumes in the city's library. Even books that survived the attacks more or less intact emerged scarred, like this one, from the Benedictine Library of Saint-Mihiel, roughly thirty kilometres from Verdun (first shelled by the French in October, the building was almost completely destroyed towards the end of the war). The red morocco binding, embossed with the coat of arms of Cardinal de Retz, bears the stigmata of the shrapnel that struck it, leaving a deep, dramatic wound. **N. D.**

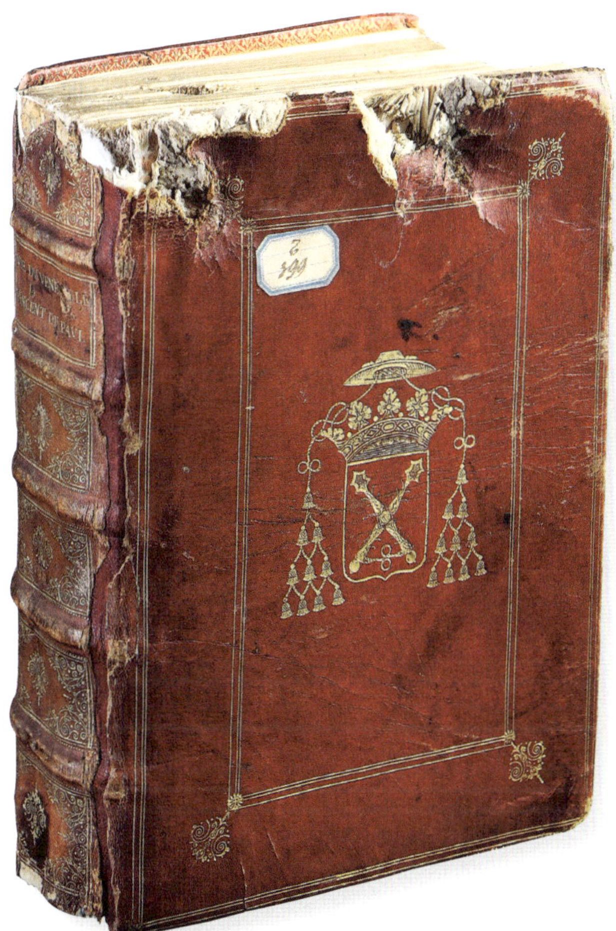

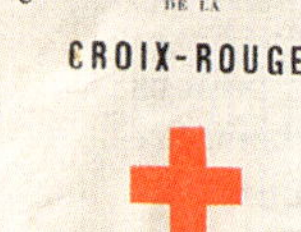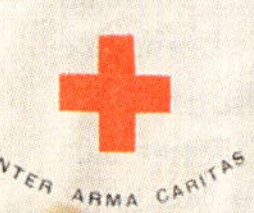

Genève, 6 Février 1918.

Le Comité International de la Croix-Rouge aux Belligérants

APPEL

CONTRE L'EMPLOI DES GAZ VÉNÉNEUX

L'un des caractères les plus douloureux de la guerre qui désole actuellement l'humanité, c'est la violation journalière des conventions les plus solennelles, de ce qu'on a appelé les lois de la guerre, de ces accords par lesquels on espérait en diminuer la cruauté. Bien loin d'atténuer les maux qu'entraîne la guerre, on peut dire que les progrès de la science dans l'aéronautique, la balistique ou la chimie, n'ont fait qu'en aggraver les souffrances et surtout les étendre à toute la population, en sorte que la guerre ne sera bientôt plus qu'une œuvre de destruction générale et sans merci.

Nous voudrions aujourd'hui élever la voix contre une innovation barbare que la science tend à perfectionner, c'est-à-dire à rendre toujours plus homicide et d'une cruauté plus raffinée. Il s'agit de l'emploi des gaz asphyxiants et vénéneux dont, paraît-il, l'usage va aller en augmentant dans des proportions qu'on ne soupçonnait pas jusqu'ici.

Le Règlement, adopté à La Haye, concernant les lois et coutumes de la guerre sur terre contient ce qui suit : « Il est notamment interdit d'employer du poison ou des armes empoisonnées, » et aussi : « d'employer des armes, des projectiles ou des matières propres à causer des maux superflus. » Les

48
Appeal against the Use of Poison Gas, Geneva, 6 February 1918

Geneva, ICRC, ICRCA, A CS-070

The First World War saw the emergence of new methods of combat that enabled wars to be fought not only on land and at sea, but also in the sky, under the oceans, and, lastly, in the air, in the form of poisonous gases. These chemicals grew progressively more effective and toxic, from simple irritants at the start of the war in 1914, to increasingly deadly and widely used chemicals in later years. By 1917, with the introduction of mustard gas, their deployment as weapons had become the norm. Worse, the belligerent nations were building capacity to produce them on an ever-larger scale.

Faced with this alarming situation, in February 1918, the International Committee of the Red Cross (ICRC), which until then had remained relatively silent on the issue, published an appeal against the use of poison gas. The plea garnered considerable public attention, and was met with a "fine and unanimous", but ultimately rather empty, response from the Allies, who agreed to refrain from resorting to "such conduct condemned by human law" on the condition that Germany followed suit. Germany replied in the same vein, and the ICRC's appeal ended up being mainly symbolic. Incidentally, the organization was accused by both sides of playing into the enemy's hands by seeking to outlaw a weapon that could potentially render the adversary incapable of causing any further harm. Nevertheless, the appeal paved the way for greater public awareness and resulted in the adoption, in 1925, of the Protocol for the Prohibition of the Use in War of Asphyxiating, Poisonous or other Gases. **D. P.**

49
Letter of protest to the Ottoman Red Crescent Society, Geneva, 14 September 1915

Geneva, ICRC, ICRCA, C G1 B 04-14

From the end of the nineteenth century, the International Committee of the Red Cross (ICRC) was very concerned about the fate of the Christian population during the numerous political and military crises that roiled the Ottoman Empire. At the time, the ICRC's remit did not extend to the protection of civilians in internal armed conflicts, yet the organization seems to have felt a certain religious solidarity towards Christians in the Middle East. The ICRC also shared the view, common at the time, that the Ottoman Empire was the sick man of Europe, albeit one that might still prove deadly. At the time of the Armenian massacre in Adana, in 1909, the ICRC asked the Turkish Red Crescent Society to intervene "immediately and effectively" to help the victims – to no avail. Following the massacres of 1915, however, the ICRC publicly condemned the "systematic extermination" of Armenian communities, and denounced the Turkish Red Crescent's inaction in the face of such "human slaughter". The concept of genocide did not yet exist, but the wording used by the ICRC show the extent to which these massacres exceeded the ordinary bounds of war and its already plentiful horrors. The vehemence of the ICRC's response, contrasting with its usual reserve, can perhaps be explained by the presence, as vice-president of the organization, of Edouard Naville (1844–1926), who was also a member of various pro-Armenian associations in Switzerland.

D. P.

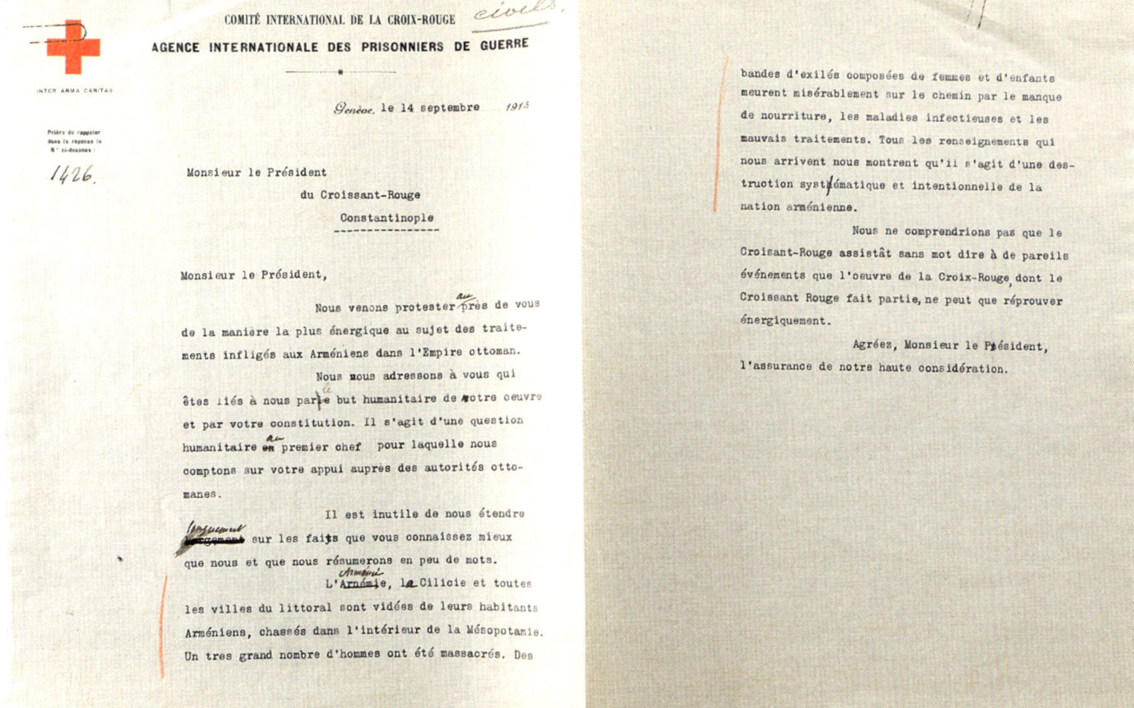

× ×

50
Mrs Bowers
Signed handwritten letter to Fridtjof Nansen, 11 June 1920

Geneva, United Nations Archives

In April 1920, nearly half a million prisoners from the First World War were still waiting to be repatriated. Despite assistance from the International Committee of the Red Cross (ICRC), national Red Cross societies and various private organizations, the situation appeared to be worsening by the month. Some reports estimated that between 120,000 and 200,000 men interned in Russia might not survive the winter.

Faced with this alarming news, the Council of the League of Nations appointed Norwegian diplomat Fridtjof Nansen to coordinate efforts on behalf of the prisoners and oversee their repatriation. Between April 1920 and July 1923, Nansen, in collaboration with the ICRC and other voluntary organizations, succeeded in repatriating over 427,000 prisoners of twenty-six different nationalities.

A report adopted by the League's Assembly in September 1923 praised the work of Nansen, whose "creative genius … managed to improvise everything". To accomplish his mission, the Norwegian diplomat had successfully overcome obstacles of all kinds: political (in particular, lack of trust on the part of the Soviet government), logistical (arising from the lack of transport) and financial (his budget was less than 400,000 pounds).

P.-E. B.

51
Nansen Passport (identity and travel certificate), 1922

Geneva, United Nations Archives

Hundreds of thousands of people were forced to flee Russia in the aftermath of the October Revolution and the civil war. Many found themselves stranded in neighbouring countries, completely destitute and stripped of their nationality by the Soviet government. In the face of this crisis, in 1921, the League of Nations appointed Fridtjof Nansen high commissioner for Russian refugees. A former polar explorer and Norway's representative to the League, Nansen was already responsible for overseeing the repatriation of prisoners of war. Despite ludicrously scant financial resources, and often faltering political support, Nansen worked tirelessly on behalf of refugees right up until his death in 1930.

In 1922, the states participating in the Intergovernmental Conference in Geneva, convened by Nansen, agreed to the creation of a "certificate of identity". What later came to be called the "Nansen passport" was a first step in international refugee protection. It allowed Russian refugees to cross borders and settle in countries that were able to accommodate them. In the following years, the passport was issued to other categories of refugees, such as Armenians, Chaldo-Assyrians and the like. The stamps affixed to the document were purchased by the passport holder on each renewal, and the funds raised were used to assist the poorest refugees. **P.-E. B.**

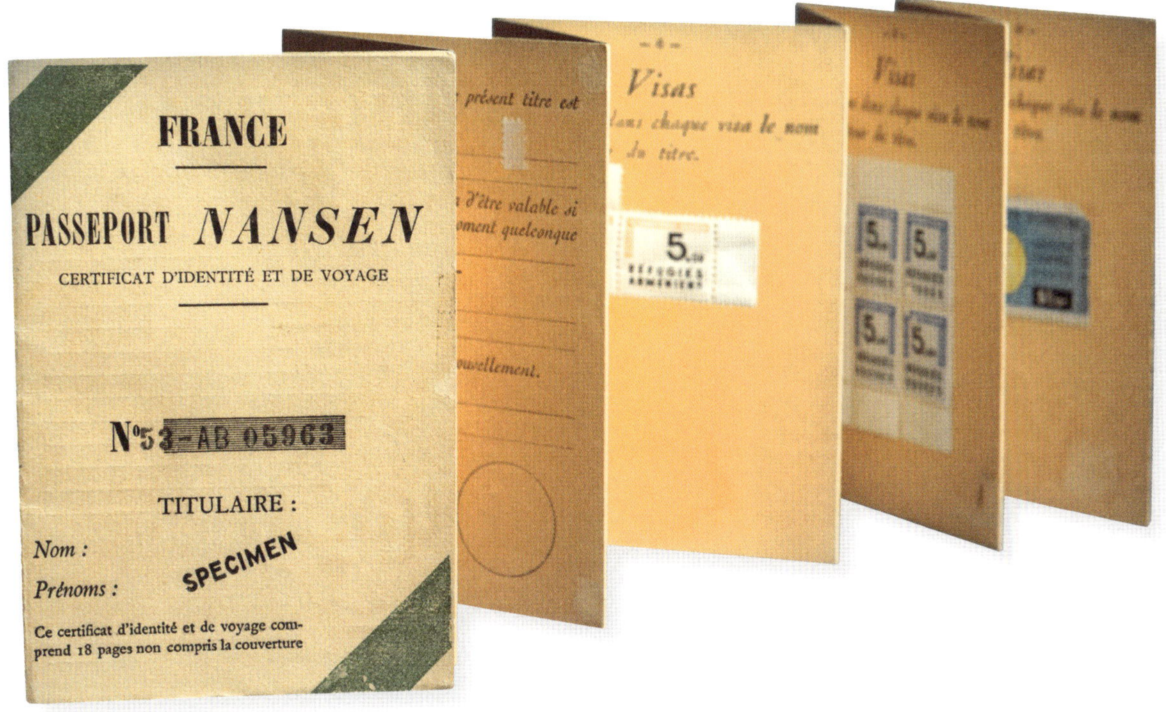

52
**Pacifist petitions delivered
to the League of Nations**
La Bataille des Pyramides
[*The Battle of the Pyramids*],
**cartoon by Alois Derso and Emery
Kelen, 1935**

Geneva, United Nations Archives

When the Conference for the Reduction
and Limitation of Armaments began,
in February 1932, millions of signatures flooded into Geneva in the form
of petitions from around the world,
mostly thanks to the efforts of feminist peace organizations. *The Battle
of the Pyramids*, a satirical cartoon by
Alois Derso and Emery Kelen, depicts
the massive arrival of these petitions. The drawing mirrors the painting of the same name by Antoine-Jean
Gros, which captures the moment in
Napoleon Bonaparte's 1798 Egyptian
Campaign when he harangued his
troops with the famous pronounce-
ment: "From the height of these pyramids, forty centuries look down
upon you." Derso and Kelen replaced
Napoleon with Arthur Henderson, the
British president of the Conference,
showing him pointing at the heaped
"pyramids" of petitions that have
arrived in Geneva. All the main protagonists of the conference are depicted;
at the centre is the American feminist
and peace activist Mary Woolley, who
was in Geneva as part of her country's
delegation.   **P.-E. B.**

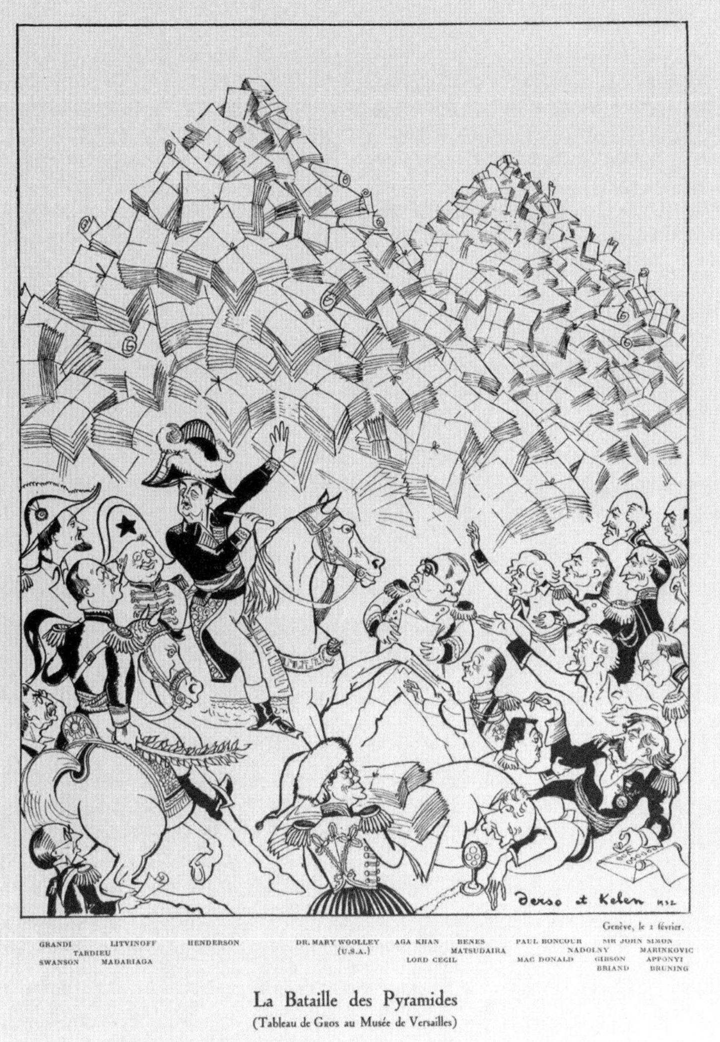

La Bataille des Pyramides
(Tableau de Gros au Musée de Versailles)

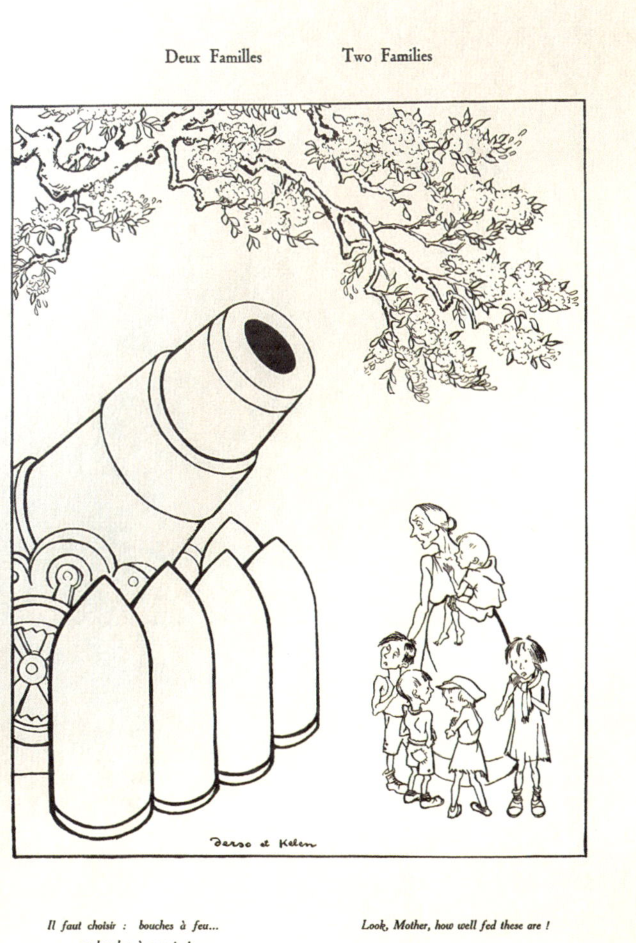

Il faut choisir : bouches à feu...
ou bouches à nourrir !

Look, Mother, how well fed these are !

53
Alois Derso (1888–1964) and Emery Kelen (1896–1978)

"Two Families", cartoon, in *Days of Hope and Glory: Cartoons on the Disarmament Conference*, Geneva, [published by the authors], 1932

Geneva, United Nations Archives

The Hungarian cartoonists Alois Derso (1888–1964) and Emery Kelen (1896–1978) were well known in the corridors of the League of Nations. For nearly fifteen years, they cast a sharp eye on the major political events taking place in Geneva, and drew what they saw; no leading figure escaped the bite of their caustic pencil. Most of the cartoons in *Days of Hope and Glory* (1932) are about the Conference for the Reduction and Limitation of Armaments, which opened in Geneva in February of the same year and was attended by diplomats and military experts from fifty-nine countries. Among others, Derso and Kelen caricatured the grand procession of leaders arriving to take part in the discussions, or parodied British First World War recruitment posters to invite military experts to join the diplomatic corps. "Two Families" alludes to the economic crisis that formed the backdrop to the discussions. The Conference raised the hopes of people all around the world, but in the end it was unsuccessful.

P.-E. B.

54
Appeal by the Chinese Government, Report of the Commission of Inquiry, known as the Lytton Report, 1 October 1932

Geneva, United Nations Archives

This report is named after Lord Lytton, the British president of the Commission of Enquiry set up by the League of Nations to investigate the situation in Manchuria. In September 1931, the Japanese army began to occupy that region of China, after the bombing of a railway line under its protection. The matter was quickly brought before the Council of the League, but the discussions in Geneva were fruitless and pre-vented neither the escalation of hostilities nor the expansion of the Japanese occupation. Finally, in early 1932, the state of Manchukuo was pro-claimed.

The Commission's final report was pub-lished in October 1932. It traced the or-igins of the crisis and laid bare the wrongs on both sides of the dispute. Without going so far as to declare Japan the aggressor, it did state that "a large area of what was indisputably the Chinese territory has been forcibly seized and occupied by the armed forc-es of Japan". It also establishes that the government in Manchukuo was regard-ed locally as "an instrument of the Japanese" and that Manchukuo could not be recognized as an independent state.

On the basis of the Lytton Report, in February 1933, the League's Assembly adopted a resolution recommending the non-recognition of Manchukuo and the withdrawal of the Japanese troops. No sanctions were stipulated, however: deprived of the support of the great powers, the League was unable to respond to what was a blatant violation of its Covenant. Some weeks later, Japan withdrew, unpunished, from the Geneva-based organization. The Manchurian cri-sis had undermined the credibility of the League of Nations.

P.-E. B.

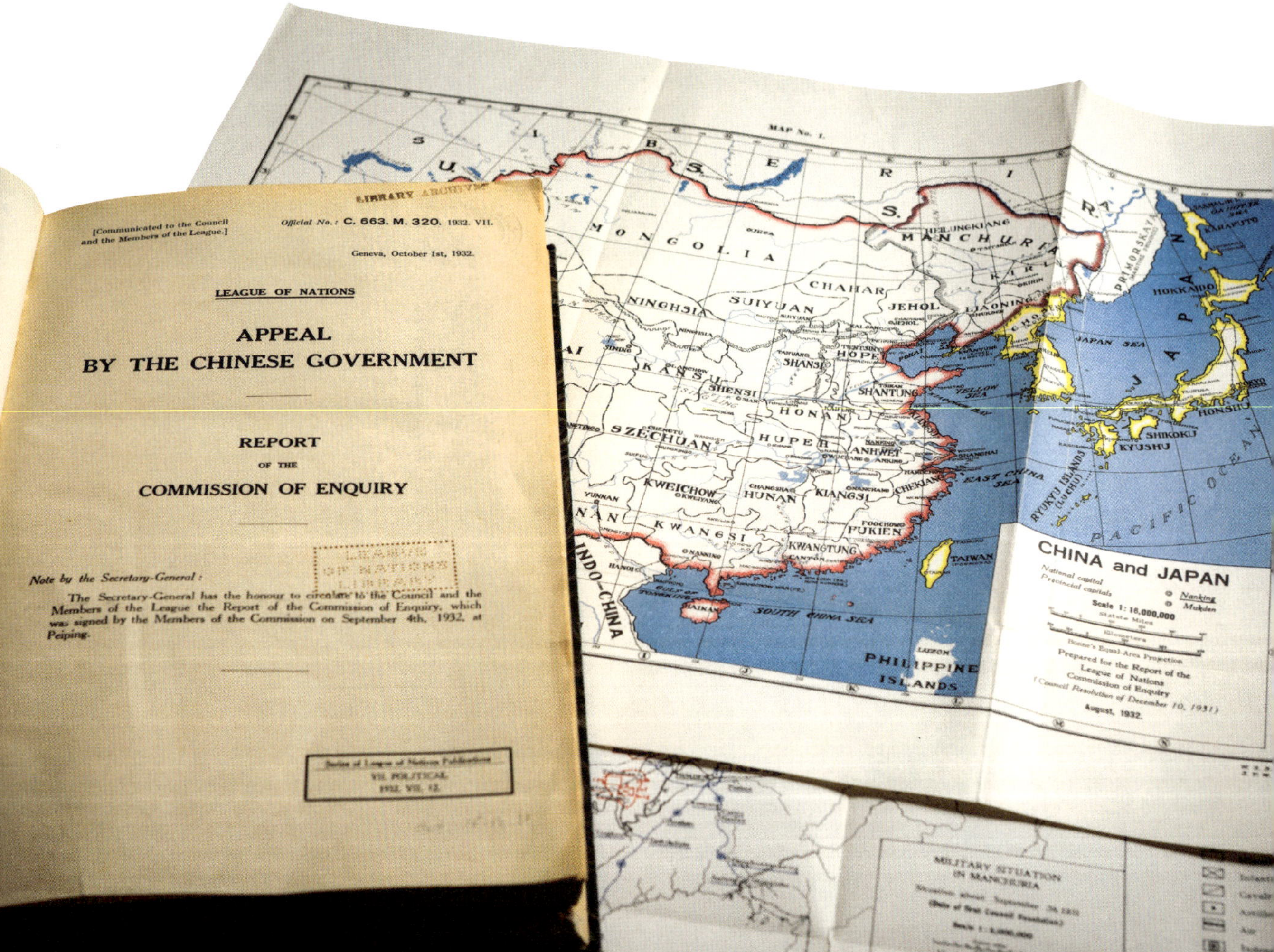

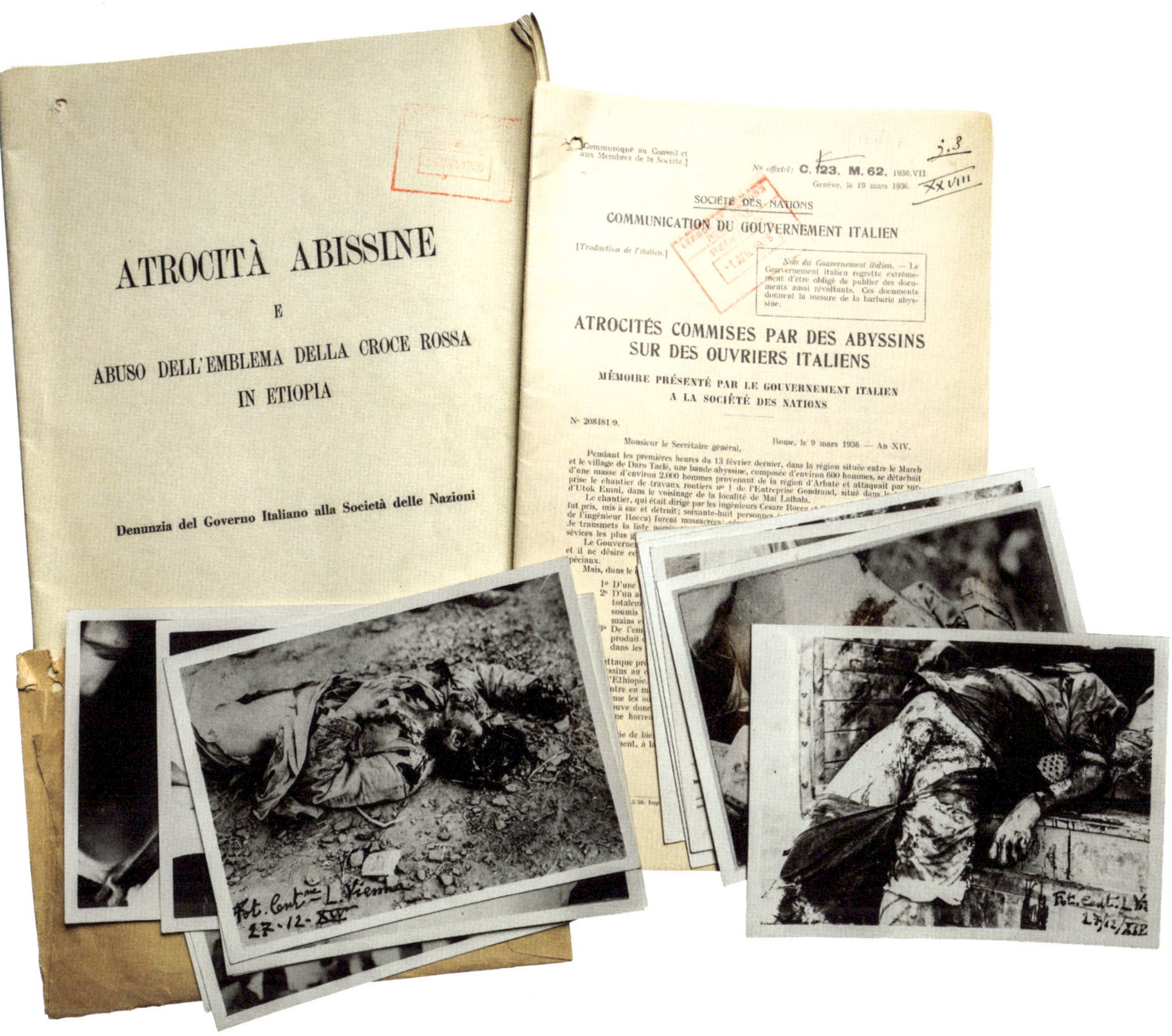

55
Invasion of Ethiopia by Italy
in October 1935
– Photographs sent to the League
of Nations regarding the use
of mustard gas by the Italian air
force, 19 March 1936
– Italian Ministry of Foreign
Affairs, *Atrocità Abissine e abuso
dell'emblema della Croce Rossa
in Etiopia. Denunzia del Governo
italiano alla Società delle Nazioni*
[*Abyssinian Atrocities…*], 1936

Geneva, United Nations Archives

In October 1935, Italy invaded Ethiopia. At the League of Nations, the two governments accused each other of violating the law of war. The Ethiopian authorities denounced the bombing of Red Cross ambulances and the use of mustard gas, prohibited since 1925. Rome, for its part, sent Geneva a report on the "Abyssinian Atrocities and Misuse of the Red Cross Emblem in Ethiopia", pointing in particular to the use of dum-dum bullets, the killing of prisoners and the mutilation of dead or wounded Italian soldiers. Although international public opinion came down largely on the side of Ethiopia, the great powers were reluctant to intervene, fearing that they would push Benito Mussolini into the arms of Adolf Hitler at a time when Germany was rearming. Although the League ultimately imposed sanctions on Italy, they were too weak to have any impact: they did not target oil, and the Suez Canal remained open. Addis Ababa finally fell, in May 1936, and Mussolini annexed Ethiopia. **P.-E. B.**

56
Marcel Junod (1904–1960)
Letter from the ICRC delegation
in Ethiopia, Addis Abeba,
24 March 1936

Geneva, ICRC, ICRCA, B CR 210-15/13

The Abyssinian Campaign (also known as the Second Italo-Ethiopian War), from October 1935 to May 1936, was the first conflict on the African continent in which delegates of the International Committee of the Red Cross (ICRC) were present on the ground.

Despite their military and technological superiority, the Italians met with strong resistance. Fearful that the conflict would get bogged down, Mussolini's regime made widespread use of poison gases against the enemy. The Italian air force also indiscriminately bombed Ethiopian targets, including ambulances and field hospitals, in violation of the 1929 Geneva Convention – signed by both Italy and Ethiopia – which explicitly protected medical facilities.

ICRC delegates Marcel Junod (1904–61) and Sidney H. Brown (1898–?) witnessed these violations of international humanitarian law, and reported them to the ICRC in Geneva. But headquarters seemed little inclined to take decisive action vis-à-vis the Italian aggressor. Indeed, several members of the ICRC made no secret of their admiration for Mussolini, not least Giuseppe Motta (1871–1940), who, in addition to his role within the ICRC, was foreign minister of Switzerland at the time. This attitude meant that the ICRC refused to pass on the information provided by its delegates to the League of Nations, which was just then investigating violations of international treaties during the Ethiopian conflict.

D. P.

que du mardi 17 mars, … brièvement … gramme de Dessié.

Le Mardi 17 à 6 heures du matin, nous étions au champ d'aviation et camouflions notre avion de Croix Rouge pour la bonne raison qu'il avait été bombardé deux fois à Dessié auparavant, malgré les signes. De là, nous nous rendions à Mulet à l'ambulance anglaise et y arrivions à 8 heures. Nous n'étions pas plutôt arrivés, que trois avions de bombardement italiens survolainet la plaine de Kworam, reconnaissaient les avions malgré leur camouflage et commençaient un bombardement en règle. L'avion du Gouvernement, situé à 200 mètres du nôtre, fut atteint le premier et brula comme une allumette. A cette vue, de Mosen et moi décidions rapidement de se rendre à notre avion, d'en enlever le camouflage afin de montrer les signes pour éviter une grave perte. Nous descendîmes de la colline à travers les bombes, nous cachant sous les quelques malheureux arbres ou buissons et vâmes rapidement au bord de la plaine. Là, nous fûmes arrêtés une forte odeur de gaz moutarde et décidâmes de prendre un plus long mais dans un terrain surélevé. Ces trois avions furent renforcés au bout d'une heure par deux autres et à eux cinq jetèrent environ deux cents bombes dont par miracle aucune n'atteignit notre avion. Ayant épuisé leurs bombes, ils repartirent vers le Nord et nous profitâmes de cet instant pour courir à l'avion espérant peut-être avoir le temps de le mettre en marche rapidement. Mais à nouveau, nous fûmes arrêtés par de fortes bouffées de gaz moutarde que dégagaient les bombes tombées autour et par la venue de trois avions de chasse. Ces avions volant en cercle, piquèrent par plusieurs fois sur notre avion et le criblèrent de balles à l'aide de leurs mitrailleuses. Malgré cela, l'avion était toujours debout et vers 11 heures les avions italiens repartirent vers Alagi. Sans perdre de temps, nous courumes à l'avion et constatations que seule les balles et vides de …

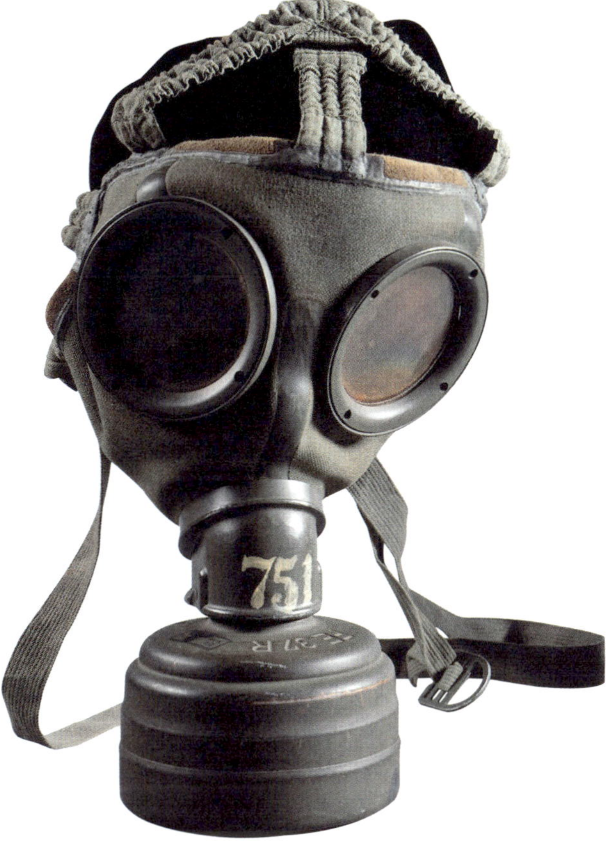
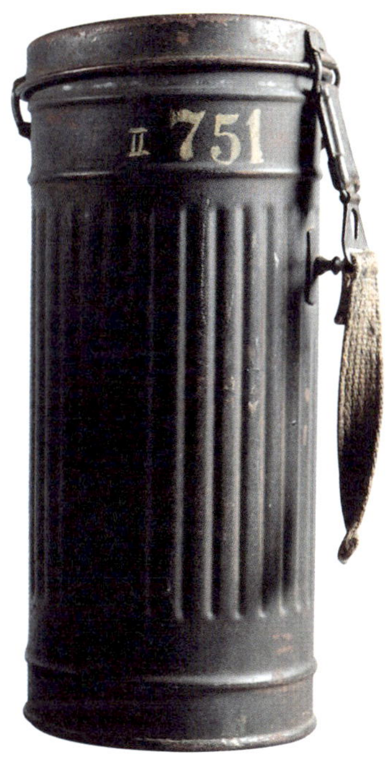

57
**Gas mask used by
the Wehrmacht, 1938 model
with FE 37 R filter, [Berlin], 1941,
green canvas and rubber**
Label with the name of grenadier
Anton Padkowski and the serial
number 751
Private collection

Bacteriological warfare dates from the very earliest of times: the Mongols catapulted plague-ridden corpses into the besieged town of Caffa in what was a harbinger of the fourteenth-century Black Death. Chemical attacks, on the other hand, are the offspring of the industrial age. The first was launched by the German army on 22 April 1915, during the second battle of Ypres, a town that gave its name to the deadly gas yperite, more commonly known as mustard gas. The belligerents subsequently raced to outproduce each other, to the point that, in 1918, a quarter of all shells leaving the factory had a chemical charge (phosgene, arsine, chlorine, hydrogen cyanide, etc.). By the time the Armistice was signed, nearly 150,000 tonnes of gas had been used on the Western front alone, directly killing 100,000 and wounding over a million, in some cases irreversibly (burns, blindness, lung damage or cancer). The horrific nature of the weapons led to a formal ban of their use (Article 171 of the Treaty of Versailles; Geneva Protocol) – but not of their manufacture. Several nations deployed gas attacks between 1920 and 1930 (Spain in Morocco, Italy in Ethiopia, Japan in China). Nazi Germany developed the first neurotoxins (sarin gas) in 1939; France developed a powerful blister and asphyxiating mustard agent, tris(2-chloroethyl)amine. And yet, even though the countries of Europe had stocked their arsenals with chemical weapons and furnished their armies and civilian populations with gas masks, not a single deadly gas attack was launched during the Second World War, perhaps for fear of reprisals and an unstoppable escalation. **N. D.**

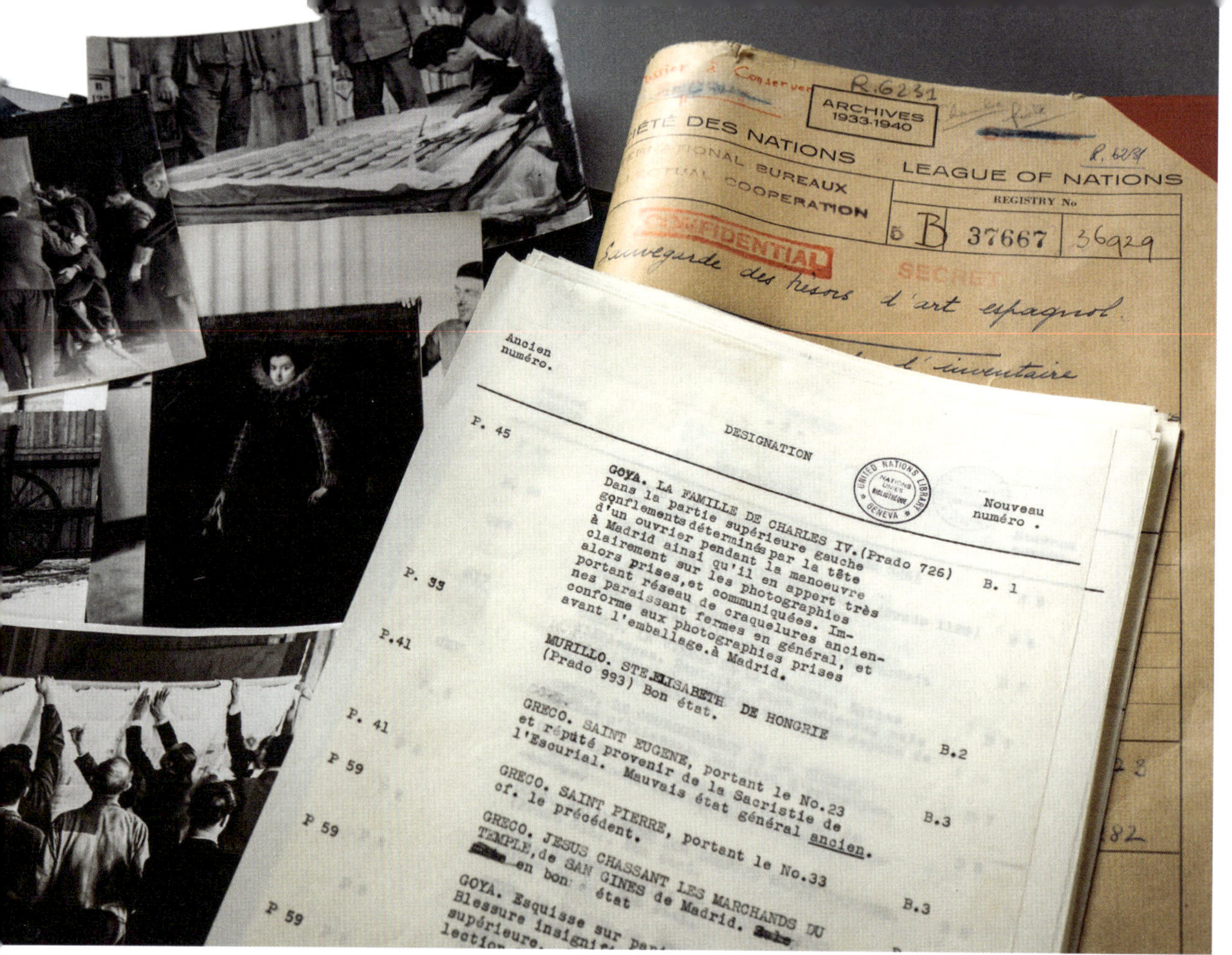

58

Inventory of artworks from Spanish collections transported to the Palace of the League of Nations, 1939

Geneva, United Nations Archives

In February 1939, 1,845 crates containing the collections of several Spanish museums arrived in Geneva by train. This was an attempt to protect Spain's artistic heritage from the civil war that had been tearing the country apart since 1936; with the advance of Franco's troops, and the bombing of the Catalan towns where artworks from Madrid museums had been evacuated for safekeeping, the worst was feared. On arrival, the crates were placed under the protection of the League of Nations and stored at its headquarters, the Palais des Nations. They reached Geneva thanks to an initiative by the International Committee for the Safeguarding of Spanish Art Treasures, an independent body comprised of representatives from cultural associations and from European and American museums. Quietly supported by the secretary-general of the League, Joseph Avenol, the "International Committee" managed both to overcome the financial and logistical obstacles presented by the evacuation, and to obtain the approval of both the Republican government and Franco's minister for foreign affairs. The inventory prepared in Geneva by a committee of experts gives some idea of the treasures involved. From paintings by Velasquez, Goya, El Greco, Titian and Rubens to sixteenth-century tapestries and other remarkable artworks, the list is impressive. Some were later exhibited at Geneva's Art and History Museum, attracting 400,000 admiring visitors. Starting in April 1939, the masterpieces were gradually repatriated to Spain. The little-known story of the evacuation of the "Spanish treasures" is among the earliest examples of the international protection of cultural property during an armed conflict.

P.-E. B.

59
The "non-appeal" of 1942: Minutes of the plenary meeting of the ICRC, Geneva, 14 October 1942

Geneva, ICRC, ICRCA, A PV 6/1942

Following the fiasco of its March 1940 public appeal to the belligerent countries to protect civilians against air raids, in the summer of 1942, the International Committee of the Red Cross (ICRC) considered issuing another appeal, calling for greater humanity. In light of the growing hostilities and reprisals, the ICRC felt dutibound to convey to the warring nations its concerns on several matters, including the repressive measures taken against certain categories of civilians. As to what these measures consisted of, the appeal remained vague, refraining from any explicit reference to the deportation and persecution of Jews. The ultimate aim was that all civilians subjected to such repressive actions should enjoy the same rights as prisoners of war. The wording of the appeal was measured – it was not, strictly speaking, a denunciation. The majority of ICRC members approved the text, although they were not all of the opinion that it should be made public. However, at the Committee meeting of 14 October 1942, they decided to abandon the initiative in favour of confidential bilateral representations to the belligerents. The unusual presence of the Swiss president and member of the ICRC Philipp Etter (1891–1977), who, along with the Swiss authorities, opposed the appeal, may explain why it was dropped. The ICRC is still widely criticized for not speaking out publicly at the time. **D. P.**

PV 7/1942

– 6 –

35

M. BODMER se déclare en faveur de l'appel. On attend du Comité un acte de courage.

Mlle FERRIERE préconise l'envoi de l'appel. Il conviendrait de l'envoyer à titre confidentiel et d'éviter le ton pédagogique.

Mlle ODIER estime que le Comité ne peut rester muet devant l'aggravation de méthodes de guerre qui impliquent de plus en plus la population civile. Cet appel n'indisposera pas les belligérants. En revanche si nous ne faisons rien, nous compromettrons notre action d'après guerre, notre silence pouvant être interprêté comme une acceptation.

Mlle BORDIER, tout en reconnaissant que l'appel n'obtiendra guère de résultats pratiques, estime que le C.I.C.R. ne peut rester silencieux. Elle propose que l'appel soit envoyé de façon confidentielle, sous forme de lettre.

M. ZANGGER estime que la position du Comité est aujourd'hui beaucoup plus instable que pendant la guerre. L'insensibilité des

60
Edward Raczynski (1891–1993)
"The Mass Extermination of Jews
in German-Occupied Poland …",
London/New York/Melbourne,
Hutchinson, 1942

Cologny, Martin Bodmer Foundation

On 10 December 1942, the Polish gov-
ernment-in-exile in London published a
sixteen-page diplomatic note on the
mass extermination of Jews in German-
occupied Poland. Sent to the twenty-six
Allied governments that had signed the
United Nations Declaration, the note –
often incorrectly referred to as the
"Karski report" – was signed by Edward
Raczynski, the Polish minister for foreign affairs in exile. It described the policy of "total extermination of the Jewish
population of Poland and of the many
thousands of Jews that the German
authorities have deported to Poland
from Western and Central European
countries and from the German Reich
itself". Based to a large extent on the
account of Jan Karski, a Catholic Pole and
resistance member who was one of the
first eyewitnesses to the Shoah before
arriving in London, the note contains a
detailed description of the Nazi death
machine, the elimination of the Warsaw
Ghetto, deportations to the death camps
of Treblinka, Belzec and Sobibor, and the
gas chambers. In his diplomatic note,
Raczynski estimated that one-third of
Poland's approximately three million
Jews had already been killed – a figure

that turned out to be an underestimate.
The diplomatic note was the first official
denunciation by an Allied government
of the ongoing extermination of the
Jews and the first official statement
defending all Jewish victims, not just
those of the state concerned. The note
also contains the joint declaration of the
Allied governments denouncing the
extermination of the Jews, with Poland
"the principal Nazi slaughterhouse".
That denunciation ultimately had no
impact, however, as the Allies never
bombed the train lines running to the
Nazi camps. **P. H.**

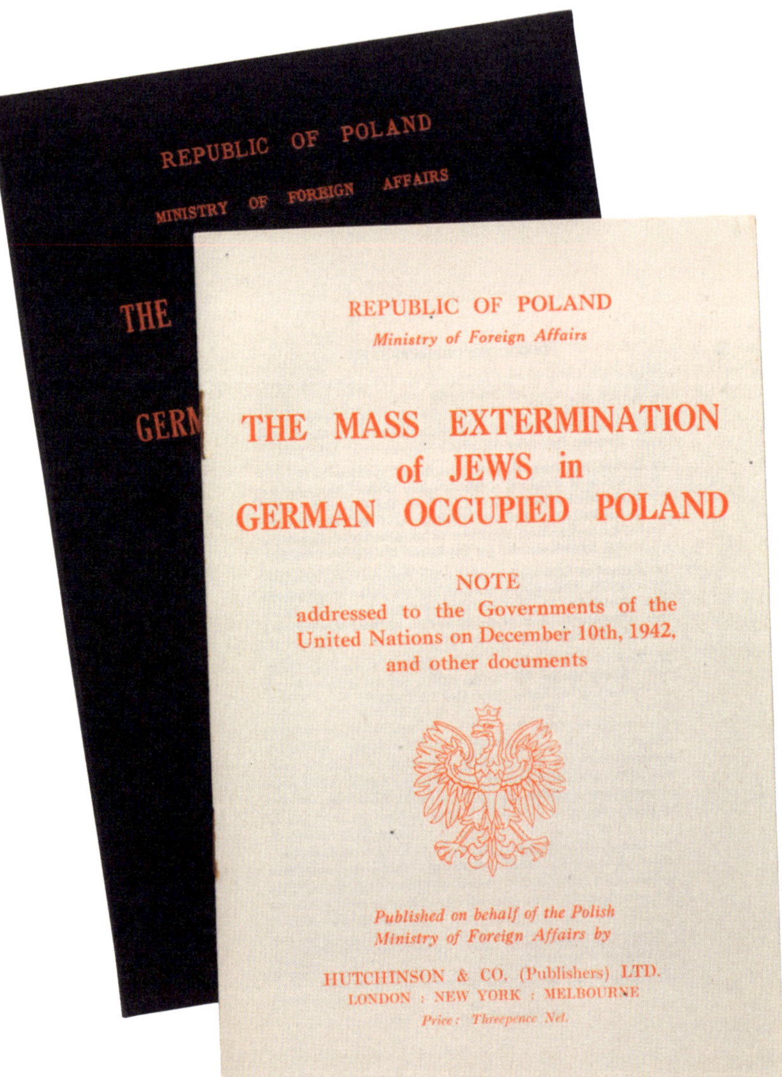

61
Maurice Rossel (1917–2008)
Report on a visit of the ICRC
to Theresienstadt, Berlin,
27 June 1944

Geneva, ICRC, ICRCA, B G 59-12.368.02

The visit of the International Committee of the Red Cross (ICRC) to Theresienstadt (Terezín), in the Protectorate of Bohemia and Moravia, on 23 June 1944, remains to this day a controversial episode in the organization's history. It was the only time during the war that the German government allowed the ICRC to inspect a concentration camp. Almost two years of negotiation were necessary for the ICRC to gain access to the camp, during which German authorities carefully prepared for the visit by transforming Theresienstadt into a model Jewish detention facility.

The conditions under which the ICRC inspection took place were problematic. First, it was led by a young and inexperienced delegate, Maurice Rossel (1917–2008). Second, Rossel was constantly surrounded by SS officers, unable to walk freely around the ghetto or talk to its inhabitants. Not having identified any major problems, Rossel wrote a fairly positive report, which was liberally reused by Nazi propaganda. Rossel was later accused of having closed his eyes to the reality of the situation in Theresienstadt, a ghetto where people were sent to die and a gateway for deportation to the concentration camps.

D. P.

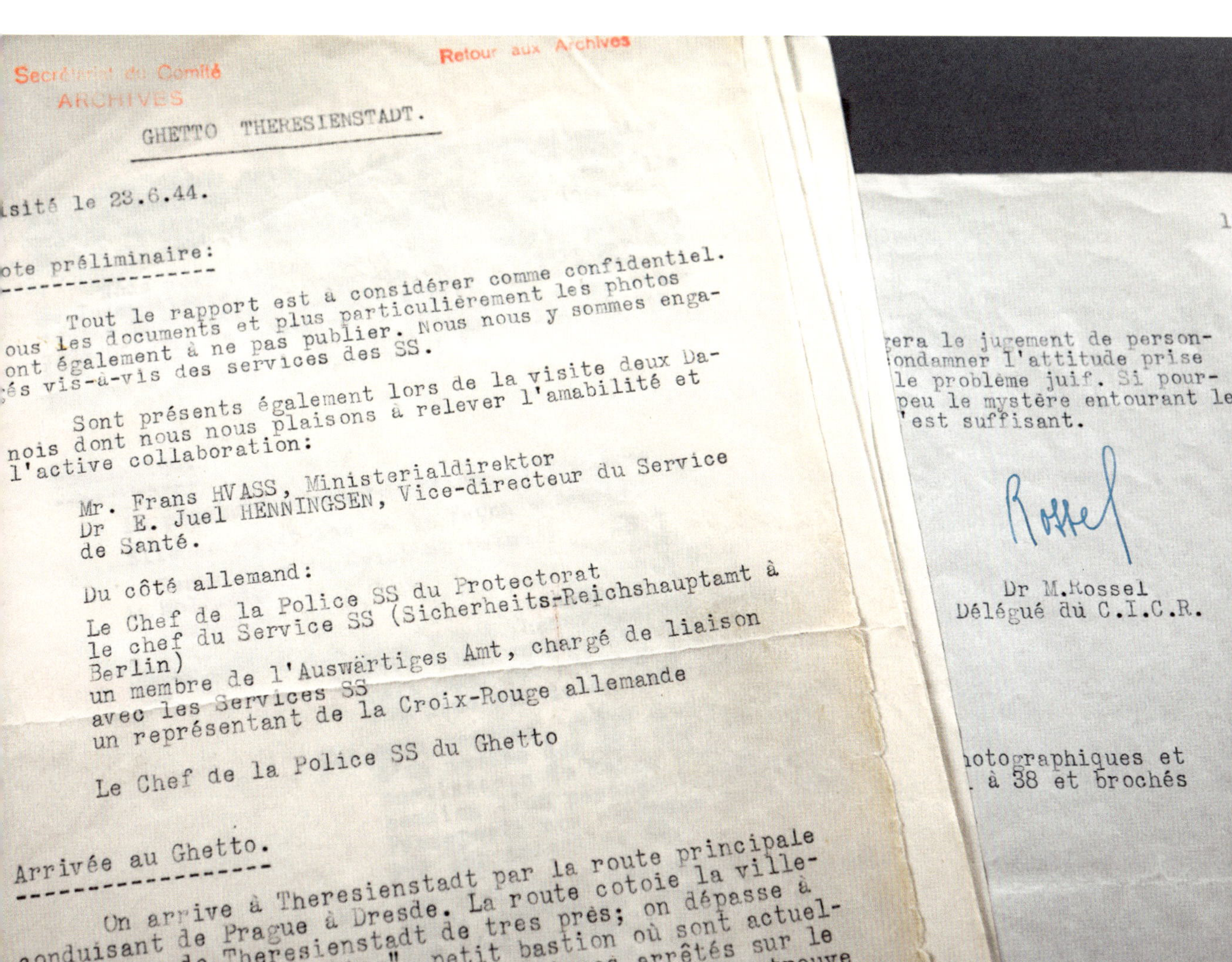

Secrétariat du Comité
ARCHIVES
Retour aux Archives

GHETTO THERESIENSTADT.

visité le 23.6.44.

Note préliminaire:

Tout le rapport est à considérer comme confidentiel. Tous les documents et plus particulièrement les photos sont également à ne pas publier. Nous nous y sommes engagés vis-à-vis des services des SS.

Sont présents également lors de la visite deux Danois dont nous nous plaisons à relever l'amabilité et l'active collaboration:

Mr. Frans HVASS, Ministerialdirektor
Dr E. Juel HENNINGSEN, Vice-directeur du Service de Santé.

Du côté allemand:
Le Chef de la Police SS du Protectorat
le chef du Service SS (Sicherheits-Reichshauptamt à Berlin)
un membre de l'Auswärtiges Amt, chargé de liaison avec les Services SS
un représentant de la Croix-Rouge allemande

Le Chef de la Police SS du Ghetto

Arrivée au Ghetto.

On arrive à Theresienstadt par la route principale conduisant de Prague à Dresde. La route cotoie la ville-forteresse de Theresienstadt de très près; on dépasse à "...ire Festung", petit bastion où sont actuellement ... politiques arrêtés sur le ...

15

... rera le jugement de person-
... ondamner l'attitude prise
... le problème juif. Si pour-
... peu le mystère entourant le
... est suffisant.

Dr M. Rossel
Délégué du C.I.C.R.

... otographiques et
... à 38 et brochés

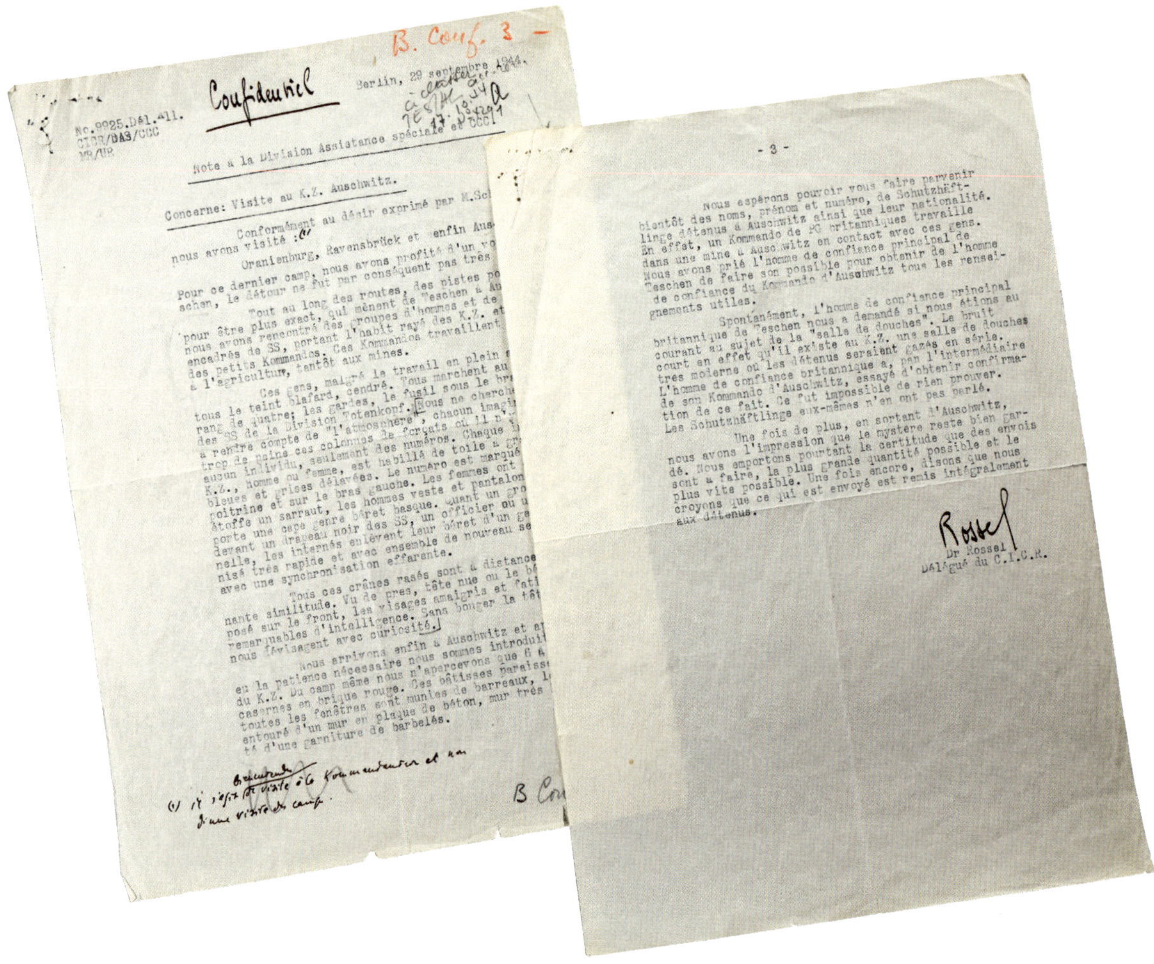

62
Maurice Rossel (1917–2008)
Report on a visit to the Auschwitz I command post, Berlin, 29 September 1944

Geneva, ICRC, ICRCA, B G 059-12.367.01

When visiting a prisoner of war camp in Teschen (Cieszyn), in Silesia, on 26 September 1944, the International Committee of the Red Cross (ICRC) delegate Maurice Rossel (1917–2008) decided, of his own initiative, to make a "small detour" to Auschwitz. This was part of the ICRC's efforts to visit certain concentration camps in the Third Reich, in order to check that its food parcels were being properly distributed or to obtain permission to deliver them. The ICRC delegates were not allowed to visit the camps, and therefore had to resort to talking to SS leaders "on the doorstep" (Jean-Claude Favez), generally at the *Kommandantur* (command post). This was Rossel's experience, too: on 27 September 1944, he was received at the command post of Auschwitz I (Stammalger), located on the edge of the actual camp. Of the camp itself, Rossel could only make out "between six and eight very large red-brick barracks". The conversation mainly focused on the distribution of ICRC food parcels, which Rossel concluded were undoubtedly being handed out to the detainees. He appears not to have realized that the area in which he found himself was just a small part of a vast concentration camp. However, he did leave with a strong impression that the mystery surrounding Auschwitz – about which rumours abounded – remained very much intact. **D. P.**

CONFIDENTIEL

NOTE concernant la déportation d'Israélites
HONGROIS

Le 13 Mai, veille de mon départ de Budapest, j'ai été informé par la Communauté Juive, qu'une conférence ferroviaire devait avoir lieu les 15 et 16 Mai au sujet du transport de 300 à 330,000 juifs sur Kassa et éventuellement la Pologne.

Vis à vis de la population et des autorités ce transport concerne seulement un envoi de main d'oeuvre, mais comme les personnes déportées comprendront des enfants et des vieillards la signification de ce transfert est tout autre. Il m'a été affirmé, non seulement par la Communauté Juive, mais par une haute personnalité hongroise, que la destination de ces transports est la Pologne vers les installations perfectionnées de mise à mort par le procédé du gaz bleu.

La Communauté Juive affirme avoir des preuves de la disparition, par ce procédé, de leurs coréligionnaires polonais.

Jean de Bavier

Genève, le 30 Mai 1944

63
Jean de Bavier (1892–1964)
Confidential note from the ICRC delegate in Hungary, Geneva, 30 May 1944

Geneva, ICRC, ICRCA, B G 59-337

Rumours abounded during the Second World War about what was happening at camps in Poland, where Jews and Gypsies were sent after being rounded up across Europe. Some of the information was based on the first-hand accounts of former detainees. In April 1944, Rudolf Vrba and Alfred Wetzler, who had recently escaped from the Auschwitz-Birkenau camp, published an account of their experience, known as the Vrba-Wetzler Report. However, much of the information about the camps at the time was based on hearsay, and thus difficult to verify.

The note sent to the International Committee of the Red Cross (ICRC) headquarters in Geneva, in late May 1944, by Jean de Bavier (1892–1964), an ICRC delegate based in Budapest, fell in the second category. Bavier was close to the Jewish community in Hungary, and exceedingly worried about what might happen to them. He gathered a lot of information, which he shared with his superiors in Geneva, along with his concerns. He went so far as to suggest that the ICRC make a direct representation to Hitler in order to save the last major Jewish community in Europe. This initiative caused him to be recalled immediately to Geneva.

From the autumn of 1939, the ICRC no longer had access to the former Polish territories occupied by the Third Reich. It was therefore unable to verify the veracity of the information that reached it, often in roundabout ways, and confined itself to obtaining the names of people detained in the Nazi camps and trying to send them food. **D. P.**

64
Rózsa Deák (1924–?)
[Cookbook from Bergen-Belsen],
1944–45

Cologny, Martin Bodmer Foundation

Rózsa Deák's recipe book is a poignant example of a document created under extreme conditions. Born into a Jewish family in Hungary, the twenty-year-old Rózsa Deák was arrested on 16 May 1944, and deported to Bergen-Belsen. Writing materials were prohibited in the camp, yet the young woman managed to write down a hundred and forty-two recipes into an old copybook. The poor quality of the notebook is a reflection of the living conditions in the camps. The majority of the recipes are for traditional Hungarian dishes, reflecting a desire to maintain a link with everyday life and family customs. The notebook also includes recipes from other culinary cultures, such as "Italian food", which bear witness to the solidarity of the deportees in their struggle with a shared obsession: the torture of constant hunger. The recipes are mostly for desserts, revealing an acute need for the comfort that imagination – and writing – could provide. This notebook is not an isolated document: throughout the twentieth century, many cookery manuscripts have been produced in similar situations of detention, violence and persecution.

M. E.

65
Fritz Bilfinger (1901–?)
Telegram following an ICRC visit to Hiroshima, Tokyo, 30 August 1945

Geneva, ICCR, ACICR, B G 003/51-X

Shortly after Japan entered the Second World War, the International Committee of the Red Cross (ICRC) opened a delegation in Tokyo, in January 1942. It was responsible mainly for collecting information about prisoners of war and non-combatants detained by the Japanese authorities. For almost four years, the delegation faced severe obstacles, particularly in the territories occupied by the Japanese army. Not only did the ICRC receive only sporadic information about the prisoners being held by the Japanese, but it was also, in most cases, unable to inspect the facilities where they were detained.

Following the Japanese surrender, on 15 August 1945, the ICRC focused its efforts on the internment camps. It was against this backdrop that the ICRC delegate responsible for the Hiroshima sector, Fritz Bilfinger (1901–?), was sent to assess the effects on the city of the atomic bombing of 6 August, and to determine what could be done to aid the survivors. On 30 August 1945, Bilfinger travelled to Hiroshima; his telegram to the ICRC bears witness to the disastrous situation he found there. Several days later, the ICRC returned to the devastated city with several tonnes of medicines and other medical supplies, which were distributed on the personal orders of General MacArthur.   **D. P.**

-- 2 --

BLOODCELLS AND OTHER INTERNAL INJURIES NOW DYING IN GREAT NUMBERS STOP
ESTIMATED STILL OVER ONEHUNDREDTHOUSAND WOUNDED IN EMERGENCY HOSPITALS
LOCATED SURROUNDINGS SADLY LACKING BANDAGING MATERIALS MEDICINES STOP
PLEASE SOLEMNLY APPEAL TO ALLIED HIGH COMMAND CONSIDER IMMEDIATE
AIRDROP RELIEFACTION OVER CENTER CITY STOP REQUIRED SUBSTANTIAL QUANTITIES
BANDAGES SURGICAL PADS OINTMENTS FOR BURNS SULFAMIDES ALSO BLOODPLASMA
AND TRANSFUSION EQUIPMENT STOP IMMEDIATE ACTION HIGHLY DESIRABLE ALSO
DISPATCH MEDICAL INVESTIGATING COMMISSION STOP REPORT FOLLOWS CONFIRM
RECEIPT   BILFINGER

August 30, 1945

D   GAIMUSHO   TOKIO

6 SUZUKI FOR JUNOD STOP VISITED HIROSHIMA THIRTIETH CONDITIONS
APPALLING STOP CITY WIPED OUT EIGHTY PERCENT ALL HOSPITALS
DISTROYED OR SERIOUSLY DAMAGED INSPECTED TWO EMERGENCY HOSPITALS
CONDITIONS BEYOND DESCRIPTION FULLSTOP EFFECT OF BOMB
MYSTERIOUSLY SERIOUS STOP MANY VICTIMS APPARENTLY RECOVERING
SUDDENLY SUFFER FATAL RELAISE DUE TO DECOMPOSITION OF WHITE

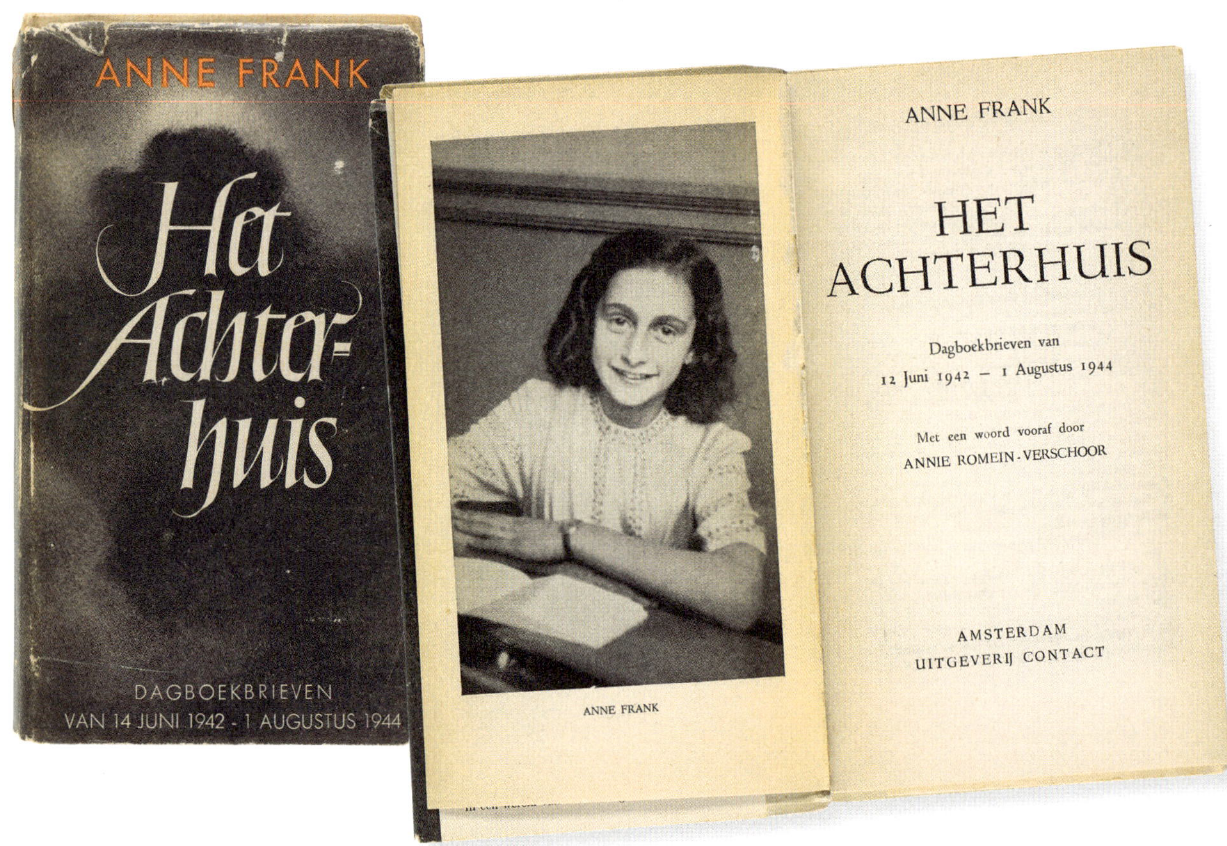

66
Anne Frank (1929–45)
Het Achterhuis: Dagboekbrieven van 12 Juni 1942–1 Augustus 1944 [The Annex: Diary Notes 12 June 1942–1 August 1944], Amsterdam, Contact, 1947, first edition

Cologny, Martin Bodmer Foundation

The Diary of Anne Frank (originally published in Dutch under the title *The Annex: Diary Notes 12 June 1942– 1 August 1944*) is the personal diary of Anne Frank, a German Jewish girl who hid with her family and four others for two years in Nazi-occupied Amsterdam. Anne Frank was thirteen when she received the diary, on 12 June 1942, and she started writing in it that same day.

The entries stop on 1 August 1944, a few days before she and her family were arrested, following an anonymous tip-off. Anne's diary was retrieved from its hiding place by one of their protectors, within hours of the arrest of the eight people in hiding and two of their benefactors. Anne Frank died of typhus in the Bergen-Belsen concentration camp in March 1945. Her father, Otto Frank, was the only member of the family to survive. After the end of the war, he organized the publication of the manuscript. Anne Frank's writing demonstrates an intelligence, sensitivity and depth rare for a girl of her age. She writes about typical teenage concerns, but also about the historical context. We see her trying to find her place in the prevailing atmosphere of brutality and oppression, but also affirming her own identity versus that of the people she was cooped up with for several years until their arrest. The book was translated into seventy languages and has sold some thirty million copies. Primo Levi, the author of *If This Is a Man*, himself a survivor of Auschwitz, said of Anne Frank's diary: "Anne Frank moves us more than the countless victims who have remained anonymous, and perhaps that is how it should be. If we had to show compassion for each of them, if we were even capable of doing so, life would be unbearable." **P. H.**

67
Primo Levi (1919–87)
Se questo è un uomo [*If This Is a Man*], Turin, Francesco de Silva, 1947, first edition
Cologny, Martin Bodmer Foundation

Primo Levi published his first book, *If This Is a Man,* in 1947 (it appeared in the United States with the title *Survival in Auschwitz*). A native of Turin and a chemist by training, Levi had survived the Auschwitz concentration and extermination camp. He described life in the death camps in a sober, almost clinical style. Of the initial print run of 2,500 copies, only 1,500 were sold. Aside from a few admiring reviews, including one by Italo Calvino in *L'Unità*, the book made little impression; the war had just ended, and the public was not yet ready for a book like this. Only as Europe gradually awakened to what had happened at Auschwitz, where over a million people perished, did *If This Is a Man* gain recognition as a major work of concentration camp literature and, more broadly, a chronicle of the evil that human beings are capable of inflicting upon each other.

In this slim book, Levi dissects the process by which the deportees were reduced to nothing: "In a moment, with almost prophetic intuition, the reality was revealed to us: we had reached the bottom. It is not possible to sink lower than this; no human condition is more miserable than this, nor could it conceivably be so. Nothing belongs to us anymore; they have taken away our clothes, our shoes, even our hair; if we speak, they will not listen to us, and if they listen, they will not understand. They will even take away our name: and if we want to keep it, we will have to find in ourselves the strength to do so, to manage somehow so that behind the name something of us, of us as we were, still remains." **P. H.**

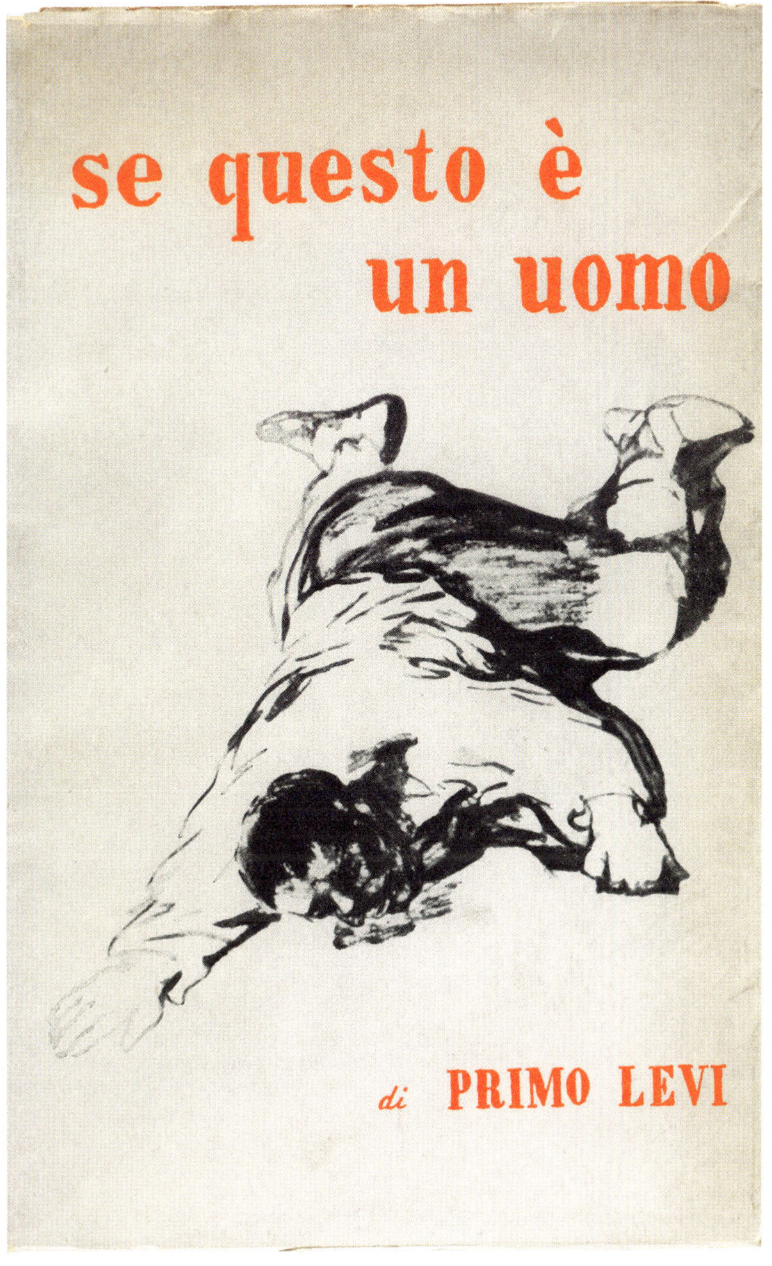

*While some writers glorify war, others portray the suffering
and misery it causes, or campaign for peace.*

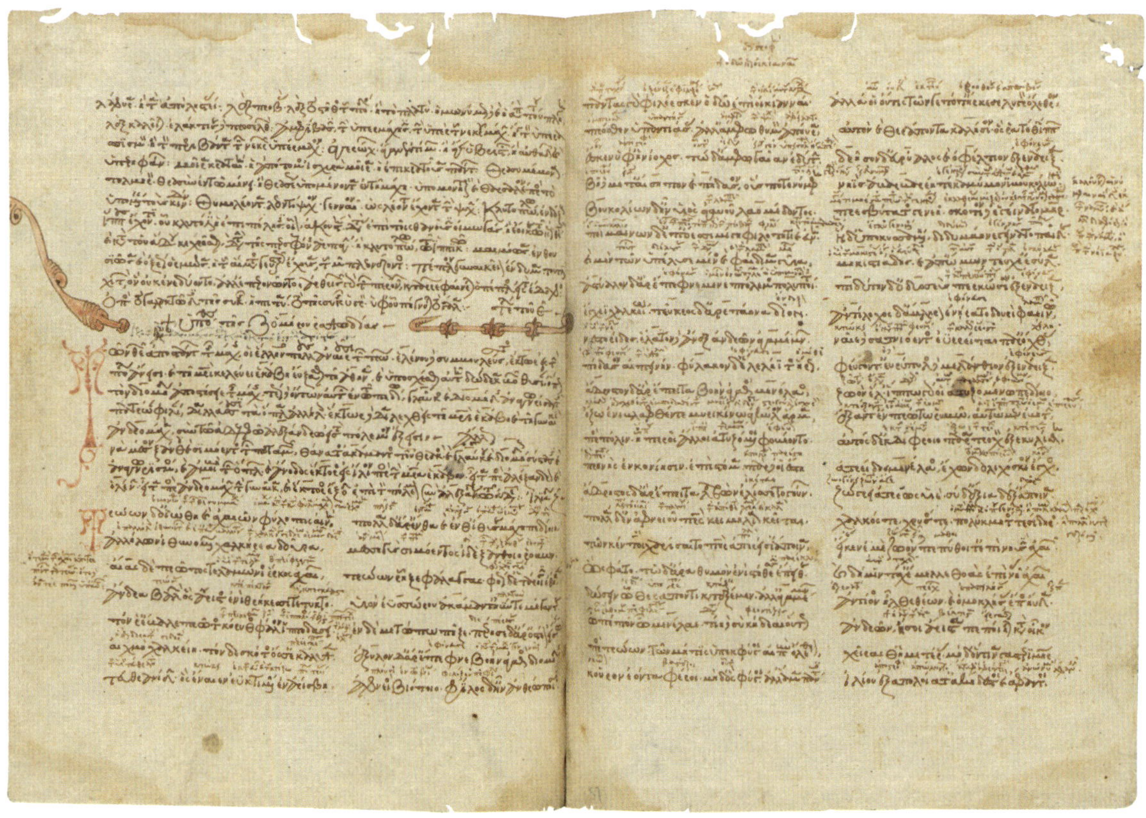

68
Homer (late 8ᵗʰ century BC)
Ilias, Italy, Terra d'Otranto,
13ᵗʰ century, Greek manuscript
on parchment and paper

Cologny, Martin Bodmer Foundation, CB 85

Homer's *Iliad* is the epitome of the epic
war poem. A coalition of Greek armies
lays siege to Troy, in Asia Minor, for ten
years. The cause of the conflict is the
abduction of the queen of Sparta,
Helen, by the Trojan prince Paris. In
ancient Greece, the poem's twenty-four
songs in dactylic hexameter were
recited by heart by singers known as
aoidos. The descriptions of hand-to-
hand combat are among the most striking passages in the *Iliad*. The first of
these pits Menelaus against Paris, and
seems initially to have brought peace.
On Mount Olympus, the god Zeus is
delighted that Menelaus' victory has
resulted in this positive outcome. But
his wife, Hera, wants Troy destroyed
and, with the help of the goddess
Athena, goads the Trojans into breaking
the truce. Hector engages in mortal
combat with Ajax and, later, Achilles. In
the end, a stratagem devised by the
wily Ulysses hands victory to the
Greeks. The fall of Troy is accompanied
by massacres and destruction of
unprecedented violence.   **J. B.**

69
Virgil (70–19 BC)

Aeneas [*The Aeneid*], in *Opera*, Venice, Wendelin von Speyer, 1470, printed on vellum and illuminated

Cologny, Martin Bodmer Foundation, Inc. B 248

The Aeneid, Virgil's epic poem in twelve books (29–19 BC), charts the providential destiny secured for imperial Rome by Julius Caesar's political and military prowess. The poem starts by extolling the apotheosis of Pax Romana and a united and peaceful world. Augustus, Caesar's adopted son, who was crowned emperor in 27 BC and to whom the *Aeneid* is addressed, has closed the gates of war once and for all, imprisoning an enraged Discord within (Kant cited these lines in his *Perpetual Peace*). Like Caesar, the deified Augustus serves as the link between the people and the gods. Virgil emulates Homer throughout. The poem begins from when Aeneas, a citizen of Troy, is forced to leave the city after its sacking (the epitome of destructive warfare, described in the *Iliad*). A traumatized survivor of the night of violence he narrates, Aeneas is given a sacred mission: the cruel defeat of Troy presages the birth of Rome. Aeneas' tribulations take him to Italy, where his victories in Latium enable his descendants to found the city of Rome (an *Odyssey* is thus followed by an *Iliad*) and herald the advent of the new golden age of Augustus' reign. Aeneas accepts the mission, which forces him to look to the future, whereas his grief inclines him to turn to the past. In book VI, he descends to the underworld, guided by the Sibyl, where he receives the prophetic vision of his descendants, Julius Caesar and Augustus, who call on him to establish a powerful and peaceful empire. Dante would remember that passage: visiting the inferno with Virgil, he hears the Justinian emperor praise the "divine" peacemaker Julius Caesar. On arriving in Latium, Aeneas discovers King Latinus and his war trophies (book VII) but is soon brought face-to-face with the young and handsome Rutulian king, Turnus, who objects to the arrival of the Trojans. Turnus had been promised to Lavinia, but Fate intends her for Aeneas (echoing the role of Helen as the cause of conflict in the *Iliad*). One bloody battle follows rapidly on another (books VIII–XII). Venus asks Vulcan to forge a shield for Aeneas, adorned with scenes from the history of Rome, from the birth of Romulus to Augustus' naval victory at Actium (31 BC). The belligerent Turnus displays amentia, mad behaviour. The epigraph of Rousseau's *Social Contract* "of agreement and peace" includes a verse quoting the pacifist Latinus who, unlike the uncompromising Turnus, resorted to laws and treaties in an effort to welcome the Trojans rather than fight them. The war over, the poem concludes with the bloody death of Turnus. The most widely circulated pagan poem during the Middle Ages, the *Aeneid* inspired one of the earliest romances in French, the *Roman d'Énéas* (1160). **J. B.**

PVBLI VIRGILII MARONIS
Æneidorum libri duodecim
Feliciter incipiunt

P Rimus bab& libyca ueniat ut troes i urbem.
E doc& excidium troiç cladéq; secundus.
T ertius a troia uectos canit çquore teucros.
Q uartus item miserç duo uulnera narrat elissç.
M anibus ad tumulum quito celebrant honores.
A eneam memorat uisentem tartara sextus.
I n phrygas italiam bello iam septimus armat.
D at simul çneç socios octauus:& arma.
D aunius expugnat nono noua moenia troiç.
E xponit decimus tuscorum in littore pugnas.
V ndecimo rutuli superantur morte camillç.
V ltimus imponit bello turni nece finem.
D escriptio Primi Libri.

A Eneas primo libyç depellitur oris
V ir magnus bello nulli pietate secundus.
A eneas odiis iunonis pressus iniquç
I taliam querens siculis errauit in undis:
I actatus tandem libyç peruenit ad oras:
I gnarusq; loci fido comitatus achate
I ndicio matris regnum cognouit elissç.
Q uin etiam nebula septus peruenit ad urbem.
E reptosq; undis socios cum classe recepit.
H ospitioq; usus didonis per cuncta benigne
E xcidium troiç iussus narrare parabat.

I Lle qui quondam gracili modulatus auena
Carmen:& egressus siluis uicina coegi
V t quanuis auido parerent arua colono
G ratum opus agricolis.at nunc borrétia martis

E ñ. Liber Primus Incipit

A RMA:VIRVMQVE CANO:
troiç qui primus ab oris
Italiam fato profugus:
lauinaq; uenit
L ittora:multum ille & terris iactatus:& alto
V i superum:scçuç memorem iunonis ob iram.

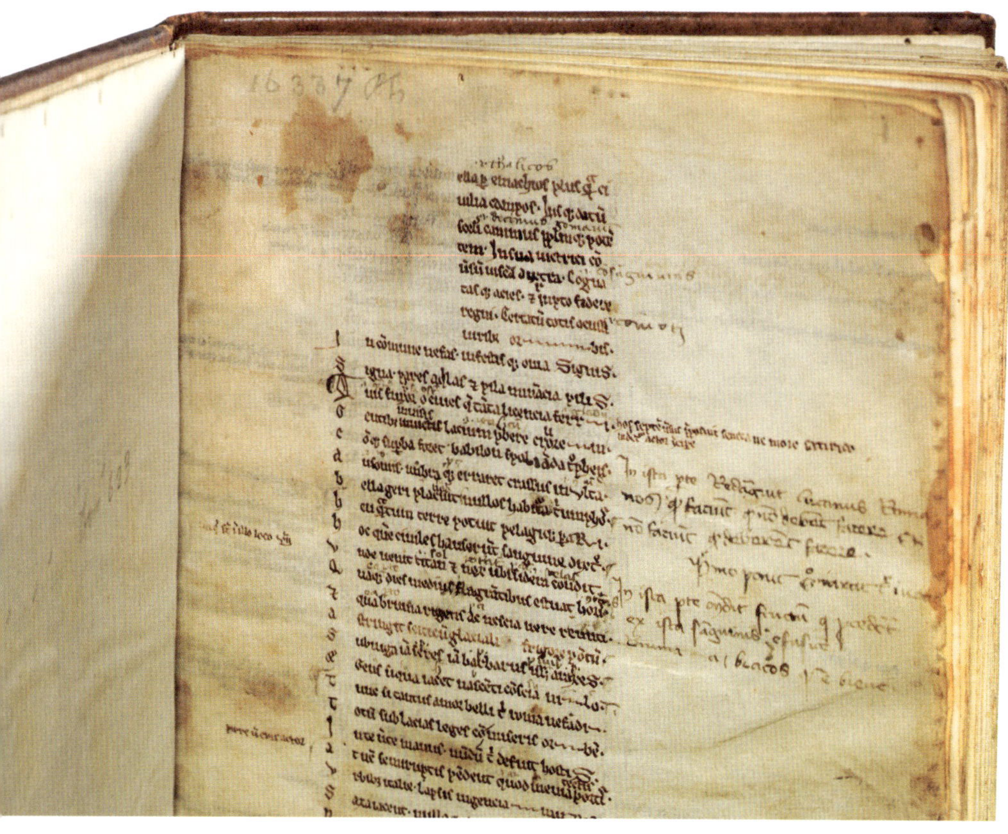

70
Lucan (AD 39-65, Marcus Annaeus Lucanus, known as)
De Bello civili [*Pharsalia*], manuscript in Latin on parchment, 13th century

Cologny, Martin Bodmer Foundation, CB 108

Lucan's brief but intense life was closely entwined with Nero's. Born in AD 39, two years after the future emperor, Lucan achieved fame at an early age, when his *Laudes Neronis* won the poetry prize at the first Neronia, in AD 60. He did not remain long in favour, however: side-lined by Nero, he became an ardent critic of the emperor and even joined in the plotting by Piso to oust him. Convicted of treason, he was made to kill himself in AD 65, at the age of twenty-five, at the same time as his uncle, Seneca, and others.

Although Lucan died before completing his masterwork, *Pharsalia*, the ten songs it comprises were enough to ensure the poem a prominent position in Latin literature, at the juncture between two major genres: the epic and the historical. It was clearly modelled on the *Aeneid*, formally but also in terms of its general outline. Those similarities throw into sharp relief the difference between the two poems: Virgil depicts Aeneas as a civilizing hero, the founder of eternal Rome, whereas Lucan's "heroes" rise up against each other and tear the city apart in a fratricidal civil war. These two protagonists are Caesar and Pompey; *Pharsalia* tells the story of their struggle for power, in 49–48 BC.

The events Lucan related in his poem took place a full century earlier before his time, allowing him to cast a historian's eye on his subject matter.

In a complete break with Virgilian tradition, his epic tale makes no attempt to incorporate the gods and has no recourse to the supernatural. As Voltaire mused in his *Essay on Epic Poetry*: "What sort of figure would Caesar have cut in the plain of Pharsalia … if Venus had descended in a cloud of gold to his aid?" In fact, Lucan, who was intensely curious about the new knowledge of his time, sprinkled his text with facts about geography, astronomy, meteorology and so on. That combination of positive knowledge and epic force, underpinned by vigorous and colourful language, makes Lucan a major figure among epic war poets. Agrippa d'Aubigné was heavily influenced by his work, and both Baudelaire and Huysmans afforded him a place of honour in their literary pantheon.

C. I.

An iconoclastic way of depicting war: humor as a weapon.
Resorting to comedy and satire to denounce warmongering.

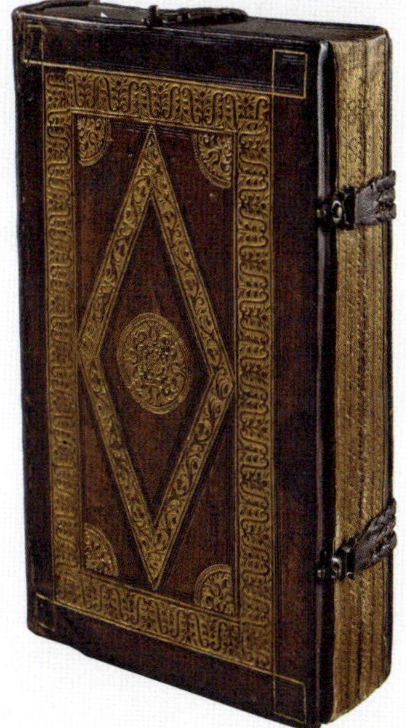

71
Aristophanes
(445–385/375 BC)
Opera [Greek], Basel, Andrea
Cratander, 1532, first collective
Greek edition/editio princeps
of *Lysistrata*

Cologny, Martin Bodmer Foundation

In Aristophanes' bawdy Athenian comedy (411 BC), a cunning, politicized Athenian woman named Lysistrata (litterally, "the one who loosens the army") rebels against the tired clichés of male dominance ("War is men's business! Women's place is the home"). In an attempt to redefine these roles, Lysistrata persuades the Athenian women to withold sex until the men come to their senses and Athens stops waging war against Sparta: "To end the war, withhold your favours from your husbands." The men quickly understand how complementary the realms of Mars and Venus truly are. Women have a great yearning for peace, and only if they engage in politics will it be possible to emerge from a culture of incessant war and to nurture values that promote social harmony in peaceful, happy city-states. **J. B.**

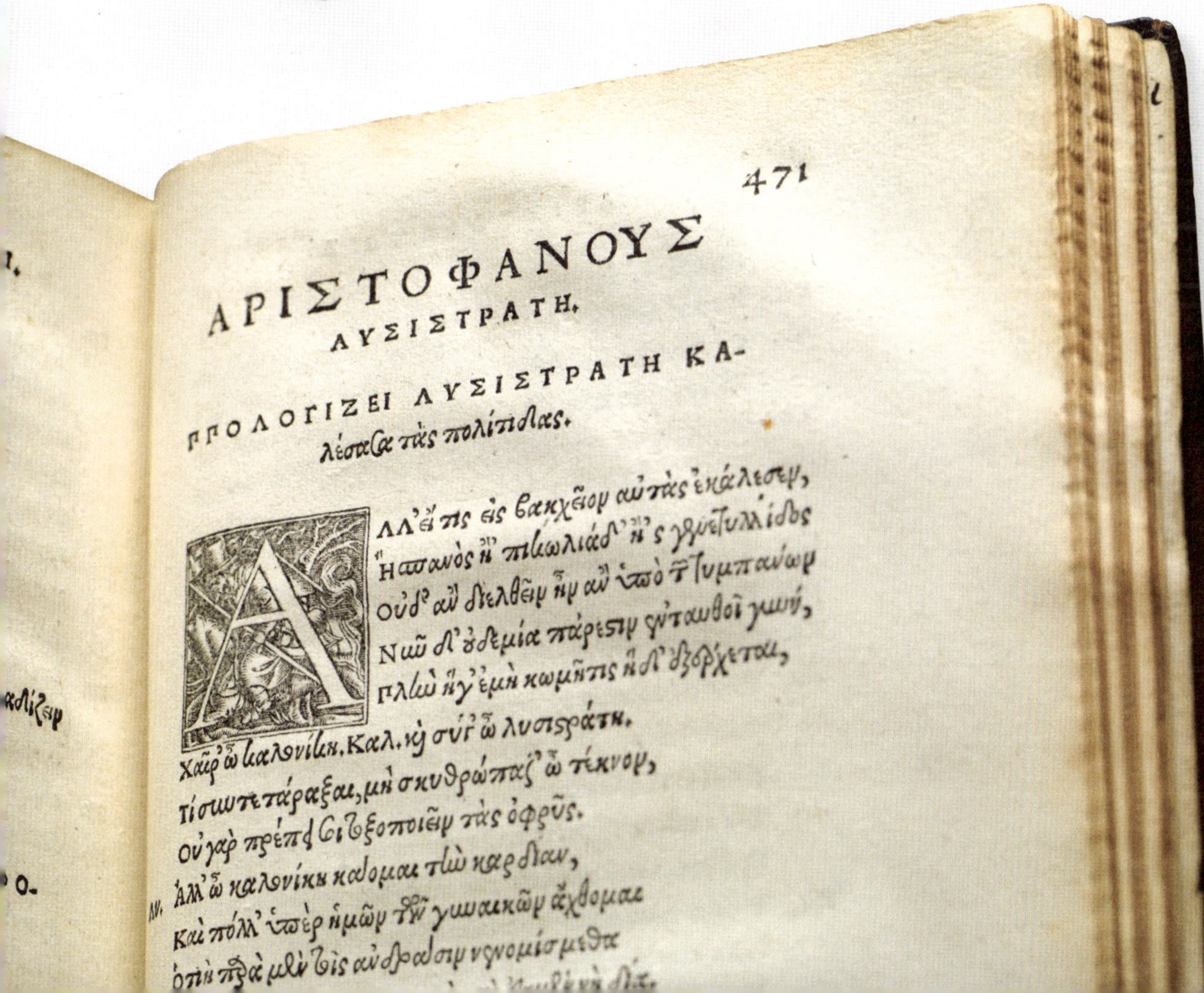

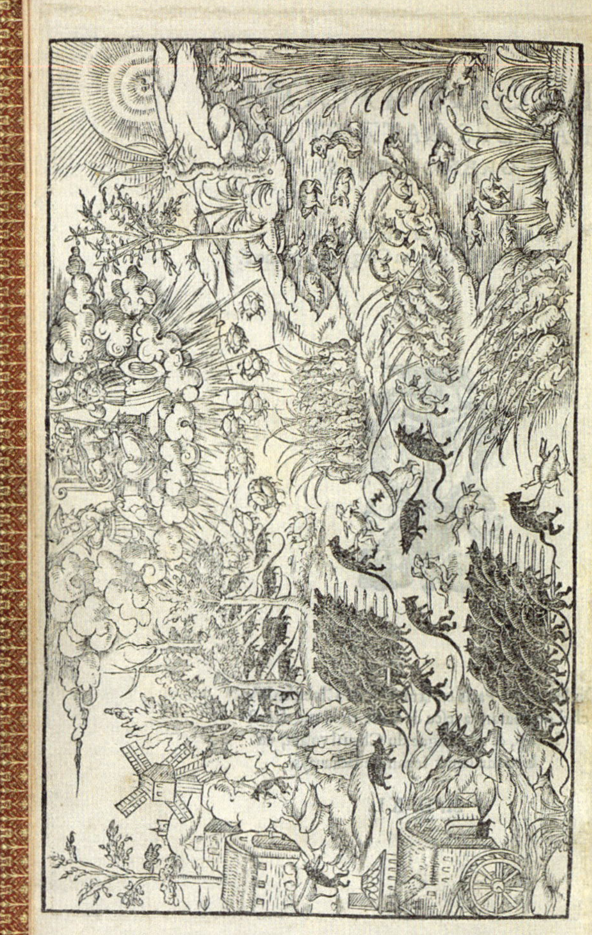

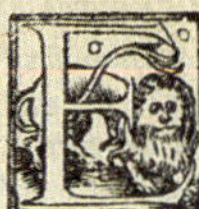

EN voulant commancer loeuure quay entrepris,
O Muses, ie vous pry, descendre en mes espriz,
Du hault mont Helicõ, pour mes chãtz accorder,
Du fier & dur combat, que ie voys recorder.
Oeuure certes de Mars: & guerres non pareilles.
Suppliant aux humains, de mettre en leurs oreilles,
Comment les Ratz, pareilz aux Geantz filz de terre,
On fait (ainsi quon dit) aux Grenouilles grãt guerre:
Dont telle fut entre eulx loccasion & source.

VNg Rat, iadiz, fuyãt les Chatz a plaine course,
De grant soif alter:, vint ses barbes mouyller,
Pour la doulceur de leau, au prochain grenouiller:
Mais dame IOYENMARE, enuyeuse & criarde,
Ceste pauure Souriz soudainement regarde:
Si luy vint dire ainsi, a gueule bee & vuyde.
    Qui es tu mon amy? dou viens tu? qui te guyde?
Diz en la verite: & ne me ments de rien:
Car si ie te cognoys, amy, digne de bien,
Chez moy te meneray: ou bien traitte seras,
Et comme hoste & amy, maint don rapporteras.
De moy: ie suys le roy GROSGOSIER: adore
Des Grenouilles ou lac: & leur chef honnore.
Mon pere BOVRBILLART, me feit soubx ces rouseaux
Par amourettes ioinct a la Royne des eaux,
Quant a toy, ie te voy, beau, fort, preux, & vaillant,
Pour estre vng roy, vng prince, vng duc, vng assaillãt
Sime dy, ie te pry, de ton sang & lignaige.
    A quoy lautre respond: & parle en tel langaige.
    Et comment mon amy? tenquiers tu de ma race?
Quoyseaulx, hõmes & dieux ont veue en toute place?
GRIPPEMYE iay nom: & sappelle mon pere
BRISEMICHE au grant cueur: FRIPPELIPPES ma mere,
Fille au roy RONGELARD: laquelle en vng bucher
Mengendra, & nourreit (comme son enfant ch:r)
De figues & de noix: & toute autre viande.
Mais, veu quentre nous deux la difference est grande,
Commét pourrõs nous estre amyz plusque ne sõmes?
Car ta vie est es eaux: la mienne entre les homm:s,
Ou ie mange comme eulx: Et si nespargne pas

A ij

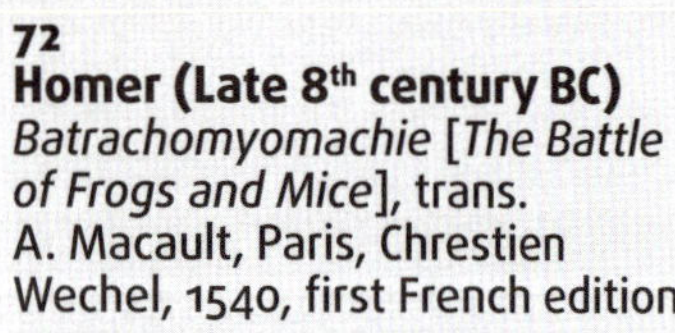

72
Homer (Late 8th century BC)

Batrachomyomachie [*The Battle of Frogs and Mice*], trans. A. Macault, Paris, Chrestien Wechel, 1540, first French edition

Cologny, Martin Bodmer Foundation

Dating from the same late-ancient period as the *Iliad*, the *Batrachomyomachia* (*Battle of Frogs and Mice*) is a parodic poem composed in dactylic hexameter. It was attributed in Antiquity to Homer; the author of the great war epic purportedly also offered his compatriots this comic and satirical take on the same topic. The poem ridicules the warrior ethos (the battle involves the basest of animals); it closely follows the plot of the *Iliad* and is full of Homeric epithets. The epic genre and the animal fable are closely entertwined. Homer frequently resorted to comparisons: Achilles is as brave as a lion, for instance. In shorthand this becomes "Achilles the lion", or "man is a wolf to man". Later, Aesop deployed animals as characters of their own: there is no mention of Achilles in his tale about the lion. The advent of the animal fable and the bestiary as an independent trope was never far removed from the epic.

J. B.

73
François Rabelais (1494–1553)

La Vie treshorrificque du grand Gargantua, père de Pantagruel [*The Very Horrific Life of Great Gargantua, Father of Pantagruel*], Lyon, P. de Tours, 1548, first edition

Cologny, Martin Bodmer Foundation

François Rabelais was the first French-language author to denounce the war-mongering of bad kings with such virulence. In his first satirical novel, *Pantagruel,* he relates how King Anarch is defeated and severely punished for his acts of war. Ever the humanist legal scholar, Rabelais revisits and expands on this theme in the sequel, *Gargantua* (1534), in the person of King Picrochole ("bitter bile"), a quick-tempered, vengeful megalomaniac who rashly attacks the kingdom of Grandgousier. This was Rabelais' way of mocking Emperor Charles V's insatiable – and anachronistic – lust for conquest. The pacifist ideals of Rabelais' good giants are very much in the tradition of Erasmus' *Querela pacis* and Thomas More's *Utopia* ("[The Utopians] detest war as a very brutal thing"), while his caustic portrayal of war makes a mockery of the false and utterly obsolete values conveyed by nationalistic epics and chivalric romances. In French, a *picrocholine* is a quarrel whose root cause is as insignificant as it is absurd. **J. B.**

180

& dist à ses gens Compaignons i'entens le trac de noz ennemis, & i'appercoy aucuns d'iceulx qui viennent contre nous à la foulle, serrons no us icy, & tenons le chemin en bon rang, par ce moien nous les pourrons receuoir à leur per te, & à nostre honneur.

Comment le Moine se deffist de ses gardes, & comment l'escarmouche de Picrochole fut deffaicte. Chapitre.   xliiij.

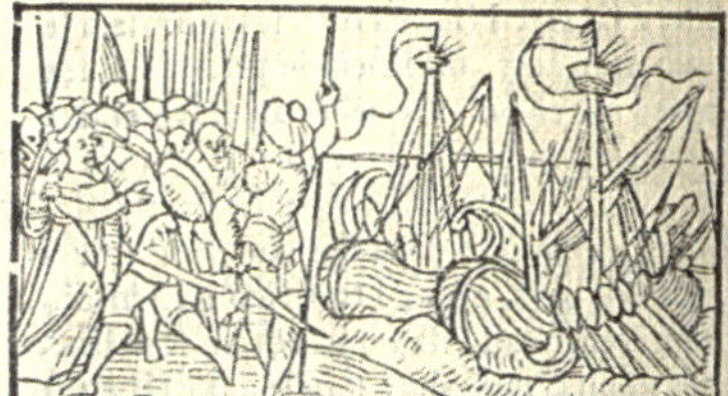

LE Moine les voyãt ainsi departir en des ordre, coniectura qu'ilz alloient charger sus Gargantua & ses gens, & se contristoit merueilleusement de ce qu'il ne les pouoit secourir. Puis aduisa la contenence de ses deux archiers de garde, lesquelz eussent volun tiers

181

tiers couru apres la troupe pour y butiner quel que chose & tousiours regardoient vers la vallee en laquelle ilz descendoient. D'aduantaige sillogisoit disant, ces gés icy sont bien mal exer cez en faictz darmes. Car oncques ne m'ont demadé ma foy, & ne m'ót osté mon braqmart.

Soubdain apres tira sondict bracquemart, & en ferut l'archier qui le tenoit à dextre luy coupant entierement les venes iugulaires, & arteres spagitides du col, auecqs le garguareon, iusques es deux adenes: & retirãt le coup luy en treouurit le mouelle spinale entre la seconde & tierce vertebre, là tomba larchier tout mort. Et le Moine detournant son cheual à gauche cou rut sus l'autre, lequel voiant son compaignon mort, & le Moine aduentaigé sus soy crioit à haulte voix. Ha monsieur le priour ie me rens, monsieur le priour mon bon amy, monsieur le priour. Et le Moine crioit de mesme. Monsieur le posteriour, mon amy, mósieur le posteriour, vous aurez sus voz posteres.

Ha (disoit l'archier) monsieur le priour mon mignon, monsieur le priour, que Dieu vous fa ce abbé. Par l'habit (disoit le Moine) que ie por te ie vous feray icy cardinal, Rançonnez vous les gens de religion? Vous aurez vn chapeau rouge à ceste heure de ma main. Et l'archier cri oit, Mósieur le priour, mósieur le priour, mon-   m 3   sieur

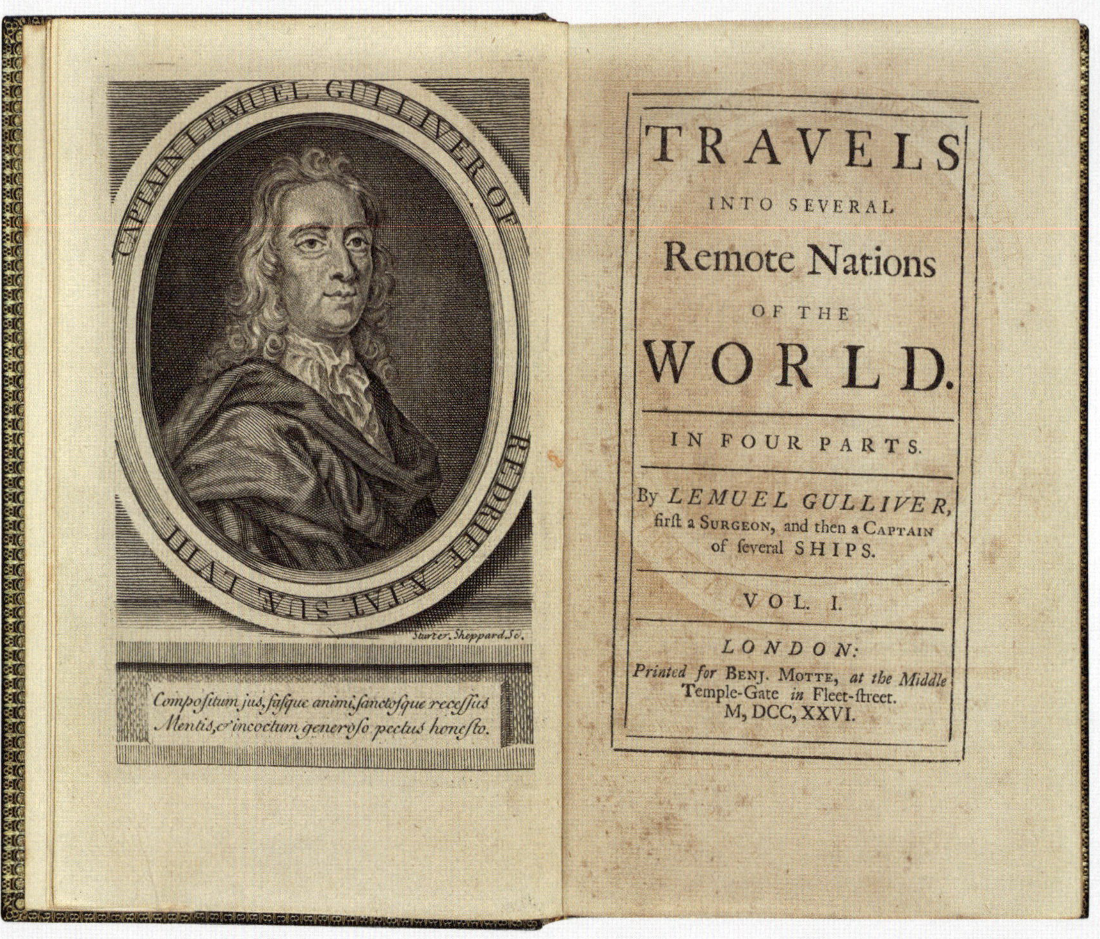

74
Jonathan Swift (1667–1745)
Travels into Several Remote Nations of the World, London, Motte, 1726, first edition

Cologny, Martin Bodmer Foundation

In *Gulliver's Travels* (1726–27), the Irish author Jonathan Swift reflects on topics as wide-ranging as violence, body marking, the origins of war and the many forms that oppression takes. Where one might hope to find Reason on the side of moderation and tolerance, she disappoints by instead dictating aggressive, fanatical behaviour. The law of the jungle triumphs and the powerful are cruel towards the weak, vindicating Hobbes' view of war as the natural state of man. Swift's satirical tale addresses the various forms of collective belligerence, and the many absurd reasons used to justify conflict, more effectively than any dry essay. War is everywhere, and takes many shapes. While casting a critical eye on the devastating and destructive violence we observe in others, Swift also underscores the well-meaning violence deployed on our side to improve and civilize them. Gulliver's intervention helps optimize one party's war effort to the detriment of the other, but the hero lacks the distance necessary to break free of the absurd political framework that contributes to legitimizing state violence, justified on dangerous ideological principles. In one famous example, Gulliver observes that, despite the superiority of their society over that of England, the Lilliputians are engaged in a savage war, the cause of which, he discovers, is an ongoing dispute between the emperors of the islands of Lilliput and Blefuscu over which end of a boiled egg to crack first (big-endians versus little-endians). While visiting the Houyhnhnms (part four, chapter five) the protagonist explains to his master for what reasons the princes of Europe go to war, and how their citizens are constantly at war with each other.

J. B.

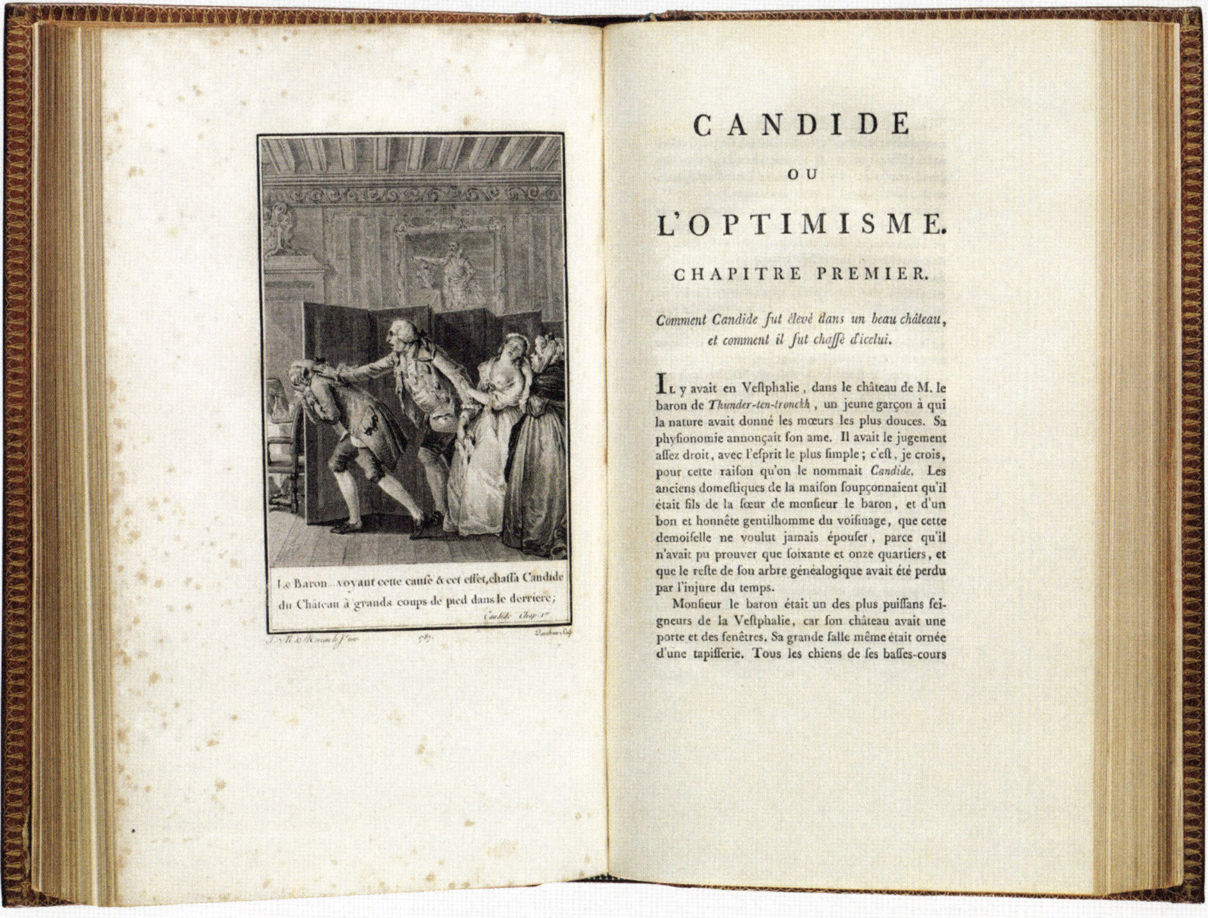

**75
Voltaire (1694–1778, François-Marie Arouet, known as)**
Candide, ou l'Optimisme [*Candide: or, the Optimist*], in *Œuvres complètes*, Kehl, Imprimerie de la Société littéraire typologique, 1785-89 with etchings by J.-M. Moreau le Jeune

Cologny, Martin Bodmer Foundation

Voltaire's philosophical tale *Candide: or, the Optimist* (1759) advocates a life of almost total self-sufficiency, eschewing all things political, as the only way to prevent *libido dominandi*, lust for domination, which leads only to fruitless upheaval. By the final chapter, Candide has come full circle from the beginning of the story, which finds him living in an "earthly paradise" on a baron's es-tate. The young man leaves this garden of Eden to embark on a series of voyages, the first of which teaches him a distressing lesson: people everywhere are tearing each other to shreds. Expelled from Westphalia, Candide is conscripted into the Bulgarian army just as it is about to engage the Abarian forces in battle; chapter two describes his subjection to the showy spectacle of the military drill. Chapter three relates the battle and Candide's desertion after witnessing the atrocities and "heroic butchery" perpetrated by the Abarian and Bulgarian kings – fictional characters in which readers would have easily recognized the rulers of France and Prussia. Having first celebrated the "Prussian drill", the tale then makes an about-face (the art of the *volta*) and turns into a savage critique of military sadism and war – women with their throats slit, girls raped and disembowelled to satisfy a "natural want", brain matter spilling onto the ground. The war witnessed by Candide reads as an allusion to the Battle of Minden, during the Seven Years' War, in which the French and their Saxon allies were roundly defeated by the combined forces of the British and Prussian armies, led by Ferdinand of Brunswick, on 1 August 1759. *Candide* was first published in February 1759, but Voltaire later added the following geographical and historical details pertaining to its fictional author: "Translated from the German of Dr. Ralph with additions found in the doctor's pocket when he died, at Minden, in the year of our Lord 1759." **J. B.**

76
Louis Pergaud (1882–1915)
La Guerre des boutons [*The War of the Buttons*], 1912, signed autograph manuscript
Geneva, Jean Bonna Library

"That'll show 'em we ain't no chickens!" These fighting words addressed by Lebrac to his troops perfectly encapsulate the slang-filled prose of Louis Pergaud, and the declaration of war between the "Longevernes" and the "Velrans", two neighbouring villages that have been rivals for as long as anyone can remember. The author warns the reader from the outset: "If you have sensitive ears and are an easily offended soul, I advise you to skip five or six pages. To come back to Lebrac ...." Everything is fair game in this epic struggle between tough village urchins: not a button, buttonhole, shoelace or suspender escapes unscathed. For generations of readers, the author's frank, sometimes bawdy prose was synonymous with the larger-than-life characters of Lebrac, the Aztec, TiGibus, Tintin, La Crique, Grangibus and Camus, to name only a few. Louis Pergaud, a former schoolteacher and the winner of the Goncourt Prize in 1910, based *The War of the Buttons* on his memories of growing up in Franche-Comté, as well as his experiences in the classroom. As the story progresses, the line between the game and real life blurs, and the war takes a dark and cruel turn. In August 1914, Pergaud left Lorraine to join the war effort, before the harsh reality of the frontline restored him to his pre-mobilization anti-militarism. He died in April 1915, not far from Verdun. This priceless complete manuscript is the one used for the first edition of Pergaud's novel, published on 10 September 1912 by Mercure de France. **V. De D.**

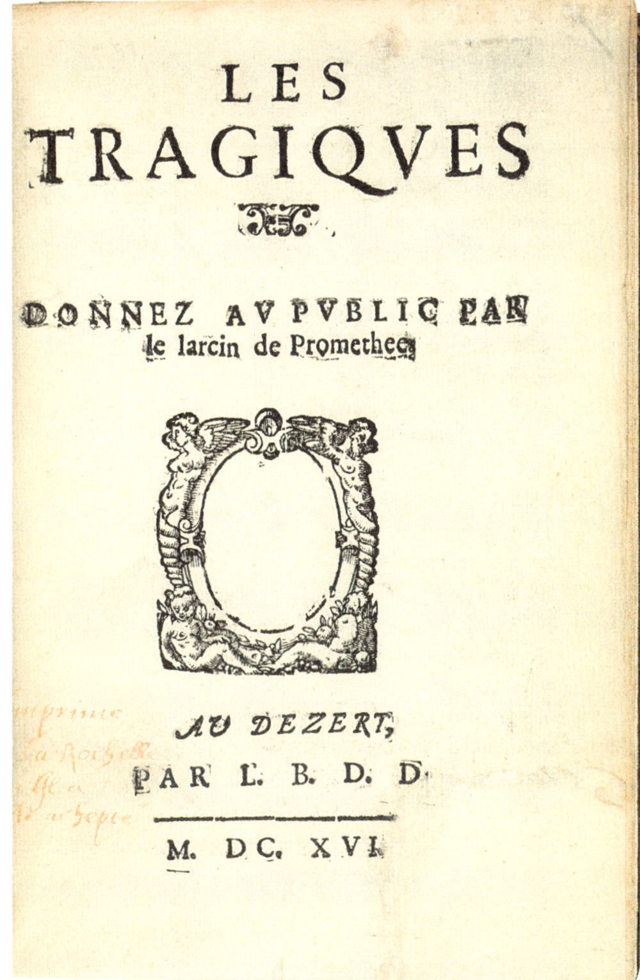

77
Agrippa d'Aubigné (1552–1630)
Les Tragiques, donnez au public par le larcin de Promethee [The Tragedies...], "Au Dezert" [Maillé], "par L.B.D.D.", 1616, first edition

Cologny, Martin Bodmer Foundation

"An abbreviated image of his century," in the words of Sainte-Beuve, Agrippa d'Aubigné was equal parts warrior and writer. A child prodigy (he was translating Plato at the age of seven) and a student of the most renowned humanists, he was confronted with the horrors of war from childhood. In 1560, witnessing a hanging of Huguenots alongside his father, he was adjured by the elder Aubigné: "My child, let not your head, after mine, be spared in order to avenge the deaths of these worthy leaders". He never wavered from that injunction. While still in his teens, he enlisted with nothing more than the shirt on his back, a romantic start to a long military career. Jarnac, Coutras, Arques, Ivry – Aubigné was present at every battle and siege from the third to the eighth and last of the War of Religion. An equerry to Henry of Bourbon-Navarre and one of his most loyal vassals, Aubigné was nonetheless unable to stomach the conversion and *realpolitik* of the newly crowned King Henry IV. Disgusted by too many concessions, the "fierce partisan", as he described himself, retired to his fortress in Poitou before departing for Geneva, where he spent his final years writing.

Aubigné left an extensive and diverse oeuvre, ranging from love poetry and religious verse *(Petites œuvres meslées)* to historical essays *(L'Histoire universelle)* and even a comic novel *(Les Aventures du Baron de Fæneste)*. But his masterpiece remains the great epic poem *Les Tragiques*, in which he denounces the horrors of the civil war and the men responsible for it. The 9000-line poem is divided into seven books, a nod to the seven seals of the Apocalypse. Aubigné began writing this account of the Huguenot resistance against a tyrannical and decadent rule in 1577, while recovering from "wounds sustained in a great battle". It was published only forty years later, in 1616, on Aubigné's private press at the Château de Maillé. The first edition appeared anonymously, purporting to have been published "In the Desert" by "L. B. D. D". Those initials clearly stand for "Le Bouc Du Désert" (the Desert Ram), the epithet by which the uncompromising Aubigné was known to his detractors. The poet claimed ownership of his text on the title page of the second edition, published in Geneva ten years later.

N. D.

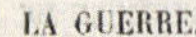

78
Stendhal (1783–1842, Henri Beyle, known as)

La Chartreuse de Parme
[*The Charterhouse of Parma*],
Paris, Ambroise Dupont, 1839,
first edition, with dedication

Cologny, Martin Bodmer Foundation

This masterpiece of Stendhal's later years (1783–1842) was published in the twilight of his life, when he was fifty-six. Fabrice del Dongo, a young Milanese, dreams of military glory. He joins Napoleon's army during the Hundred Days, following the emperor's return from Elba, and ends up at Waterloo. Never before had a novelist described the cacophony of battle with such "immersive", disorientating subjectivity. Until then, following time-honoured convention, war narratives most often presented a generically orderly overview of the battle, as conveyed by historiographers drawing on accounts by senior officers. Stendhal, in contrast, deploys the same lexicon with a sly humour that subtly de-heroicizes combat: the "hero", though proud and ambitious, is not in the least heroic; he notices red uniforms on the ground, and the morning rain; among the dead bodies, he is aware of wounded soldiers who are suffering and dying. Following his revolutionary approach of "internal focusing", Stendhal shows nothing of the battle other than what an inexperienced seventeen-year-old boy might have perceived or felt – his partial, stunned, utterly confused viewpoint. In sharp contrast to great epic tableaux, the battle is narrated from the perspective of a protagonist who understands it no better than the dazed horse beside him. Stendhal himself fought under Napoleon (and, on 11 November 1808, was very distressed by the spectacle of war in Ebersberg, the scorched city and burned bodies. What he depicts here is the ghastly absurdity of battle. Fabrice goes on to make a name for himself outside of the military arena.

J. B.

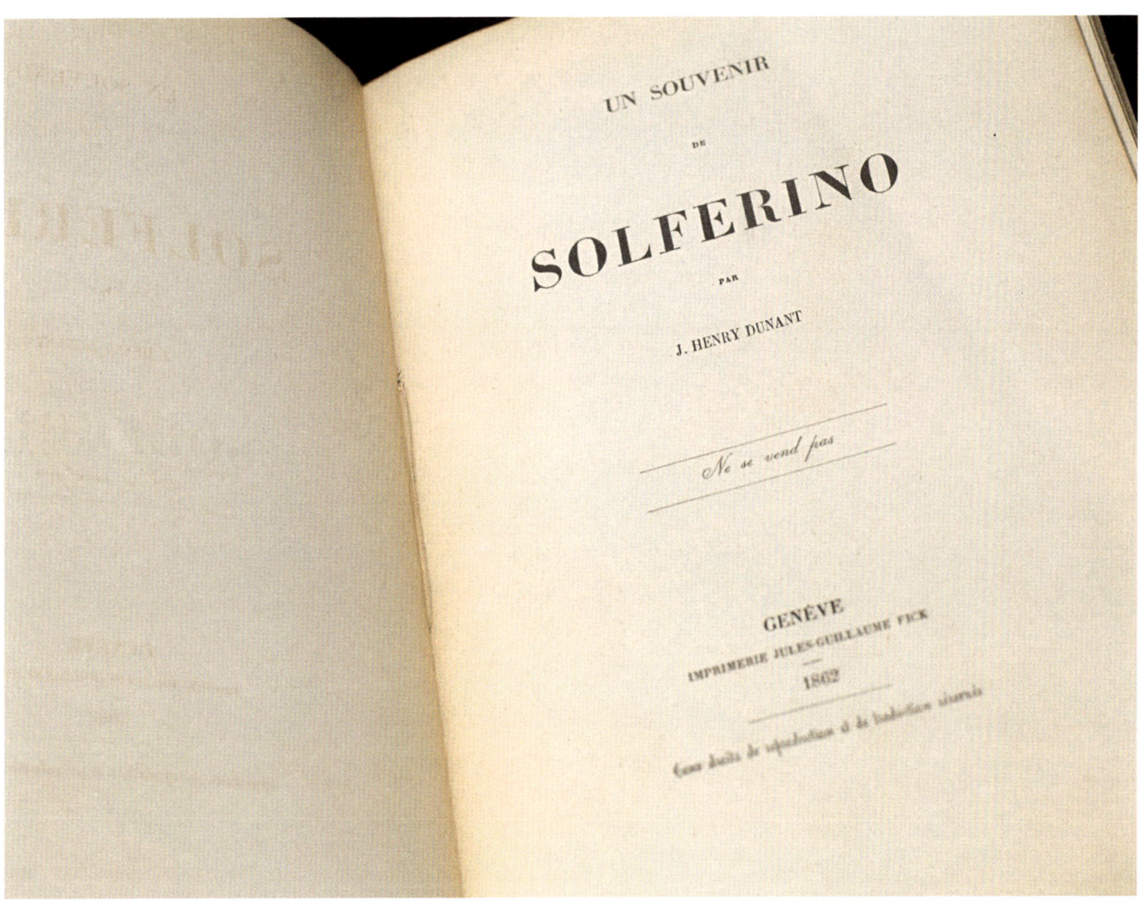

79
Henry Dunant (1828–1910)
Un souvenir de Solferino [*A Memory of Solferino*], Geneva, Imprimerie Jules-Guillaume Fick, 1862

Cologny, Martin Bodmer Foundation

The Battle of Solferino was a decisive but unplanned encounter of the Second Italian War of Independence (April–July 1859), involving more than 300,000 French, Sardinian and Austrian troops. After hours of killing, thousands of wounded soldiers from both sides were left lying on the battlefield, as there were no doctors or ambulances to care for them. Henry Dunant (1828–1910), a businessman from Geneva who happened to be in Solferino on business, joined local inhabitants in caring for the wounded with the limited means at their disposal. Dunant went on to recount this traumatic experience in his book, *A Memory of Solferino*, which was published in Geneva – at the author's expense – in November 1862. It was an immediate success, in Switzerland and internationally. More copies were quickly printed, and the book was translated into several languages. In addition to describing the battle, and his own experiences caring for the wounded soldiers, Dunant put forth two proposals: first, that a relief society for wounded soldiers be established in every country, which could be activated in the event of war; and second, that governments sign an international convention recognizing and upholding the work of these relief societies. Both proposals were discussed in 1863 by the founders of the International Committee of the Red Cross (ICRC). The first resulted in the creation of National Societies for Relief to the Wounded (which became the National Red Cross and Red Crescent Societies), while the second led to the adoption of the Geneva Convention of August 1864.   **D. P.**

80
Leo Tolstoy (1828–1910)
War and Peace, book 3, part II, chap. 25 [1865–69], autograph manuscript

Moscow, Tolstoy Museum

On the evening of 25 August 1812, the day before the decisive battle between the French and Russian armies – everyone was convinced of it, from Napoleon down to the lowliest Russian soldier – Prince Andrei, commander of a regiment, receives three battalion leaders who have come for their orders to the half-demolished barn where he is resting. They are surprised by an intruder, a civilian: Andrei's friend Pierre Bezukhov, who has come by because "it interests me". Pierre has already visited General Bennigsen and believes he has understood the plan for tomorrow's battle.

A brooding Andrei, confronted for the first time by the possibility of his own death, answers his friend's questions sardonically: general staff understand nothing, decide nothing. "A battle is won by those who firmly resolve to win it! … Me, him, all our soldiers, the measures we've taken, superior numbers, nothing determines how a war is won, when the enemy has come to kill my father, my sister, burn my house, Russia. We're going to kill and if I were commander-in-chief I would give the order: 'Take no prisoners.' War is not a game, it's an immense and repulsive lie, it's about who turns tail first."

There are many versions of this chapter. Tolstoy made drastic cuts, excising passages on war as a theatrical backdrop, on gut-wrenching fear, on the horrible "abyss of lies" and the stinking hellhole that is war. The chapter continues Tolstoy's dialogue with himself, between his two alter egos – him as the observer, him facing death – a dialogue that he started in his first tale of the Caucasus and that draws on Socrates as relayed by Plato in *Laches*. In the next chapter, a combed and feathered Napoleon gives a nonchalant order: "Take no prisoners!" A tin-soldier reply to Prince Andrei's burning rage. **G. N.**

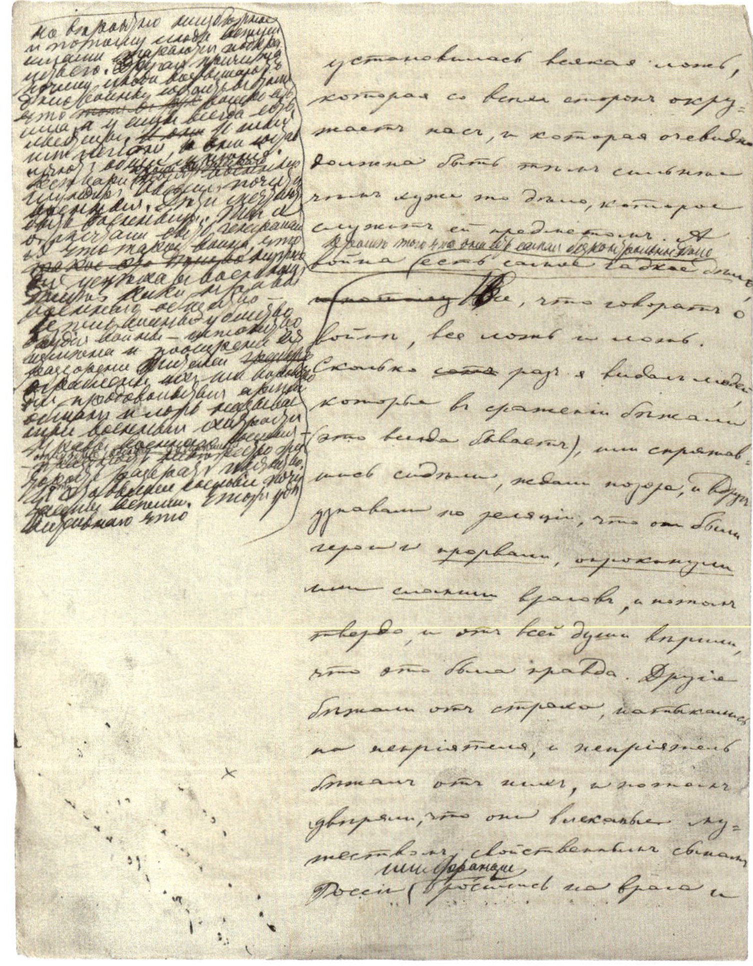

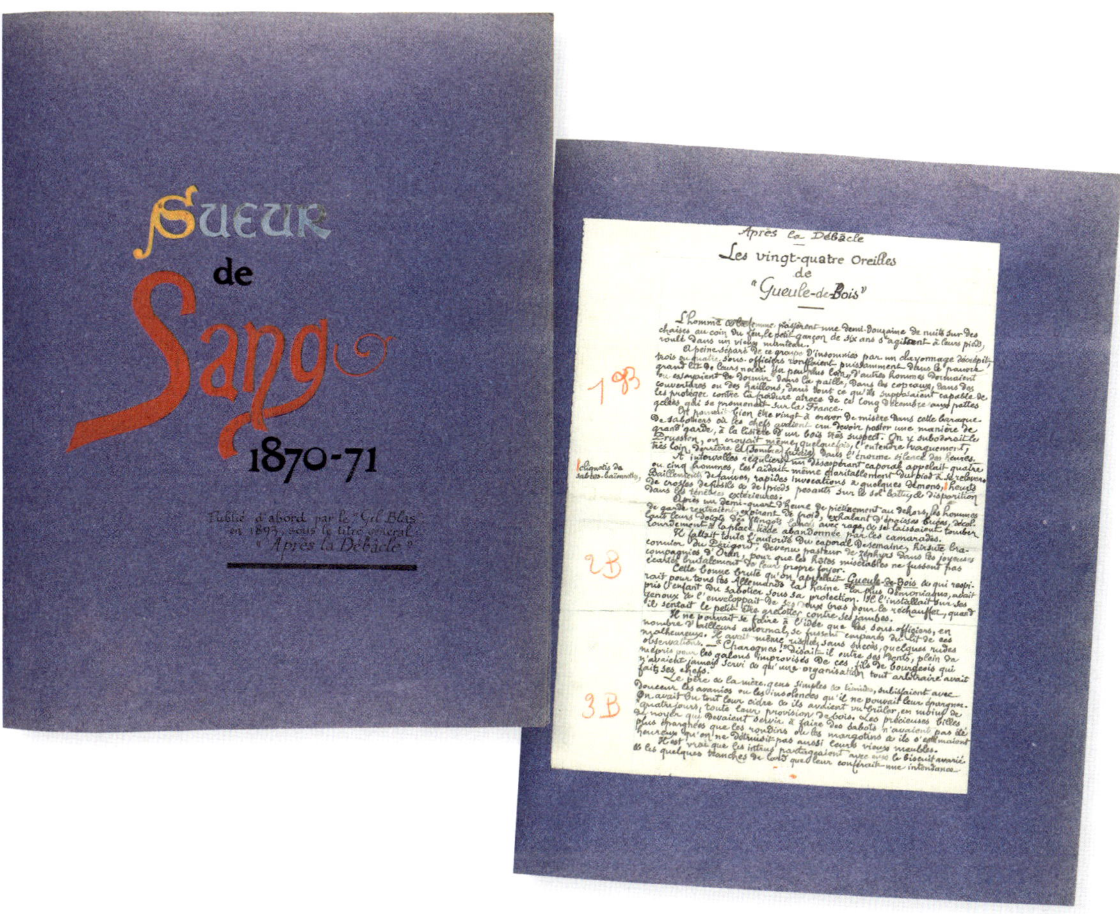

81
Léon Bloy (1846–1917)
Sueurs de sang [*Sweating Blood*],
signed autograph manuscript,
1892–93

Geneva, Jean Bonna Library

These "military tales" are based on Bloy's firsthand experience of the 1870 Franco-Prussian war. Recruited into the Mobiles de la Dordogne, promoted to corporal and later sergeant, Bloy fought near Orleans, in the Sarthe region, and at the battle of Vibraye, in January 1871, before being demobilized in early April. He was prompted to write this series of thirty searing short stories, set mainly during to the second stage of the war, by the capitulation of Metz, whose forces were in total disarray, by what he witnessed during those few months, and by his subsequent reading. They were published in the journal *Gil Blas* between November 1892 and July 1893, and then in book form by Dentu. The violence they portray is horrific and raw, exemplified by Gueule-de-Bois, a soldier who tears the ears off dead Prussians and collects them as trophies, not to mention the mother who avenges herself by killing the son of a Prussian officer and serving his flesh to the father for dinner. In Bloy's telling, Frenchmen from all walks of life, from lords to rag pickers, rose up as a single body when faced with a brutal and vulgar occupier, which he acerbically caricaturized. His stories not only exalted an injured France, but also gave voice to the nationalism and crude anti-German sentiment awakened by the war. The manuscript – written in an elegant hand on red paper, as befits the title of the book – was returned to the author after its publication in serial form (which explains why it was cut); he restored it to its original state. **N. D.**

82
Nobel Committee
Certificate of the Nobel
Peace Prize awarded to
Jean Henry Dunant, Christiana,
10 December 1901

Geneva, ICRC

The first Nobel Peace Prize was awarded in 1901 to Henry Dunant (1828–1910), the instigator the Red Cross Movement, co-founder of the International Committee of the Red Cross (ICRC), and the driving force behind the original Geneva Convention of 1864.
This distinction recognized the commitment of a man who, faced with the horrors of war, had done his utmost to succour victims and relieve their suffering. For Henry Dunant, whose humanitarian role had by then been largely forgotten, the prize contributed to restoring his reputation on the international stage, albeit belatedly.

Although Dunant's nomination received widespread support in pacifist circles, he was also criticized for being more preoccupied with humanizing war, by developing a network of Red Cross Societies, than with seeking ways to establish universal, lasting peace. That may be why the first Nobel Peace Prize was shared by Henry Dunant and the pacifist Frédéric Passy (1822–1912). The joint award thus recognized the two qualities that Alfred Nobel sought to celebrate with his prize: fraternity among nations and the promotion of peace. Henry Dunant was awarded the Nobel Peace Prize in recognition of his personal merit, rather than in honour of the institution he helped create. The ICRC had also put itself forward for the prize, but its application arrived too late to be considered! **D. P.**

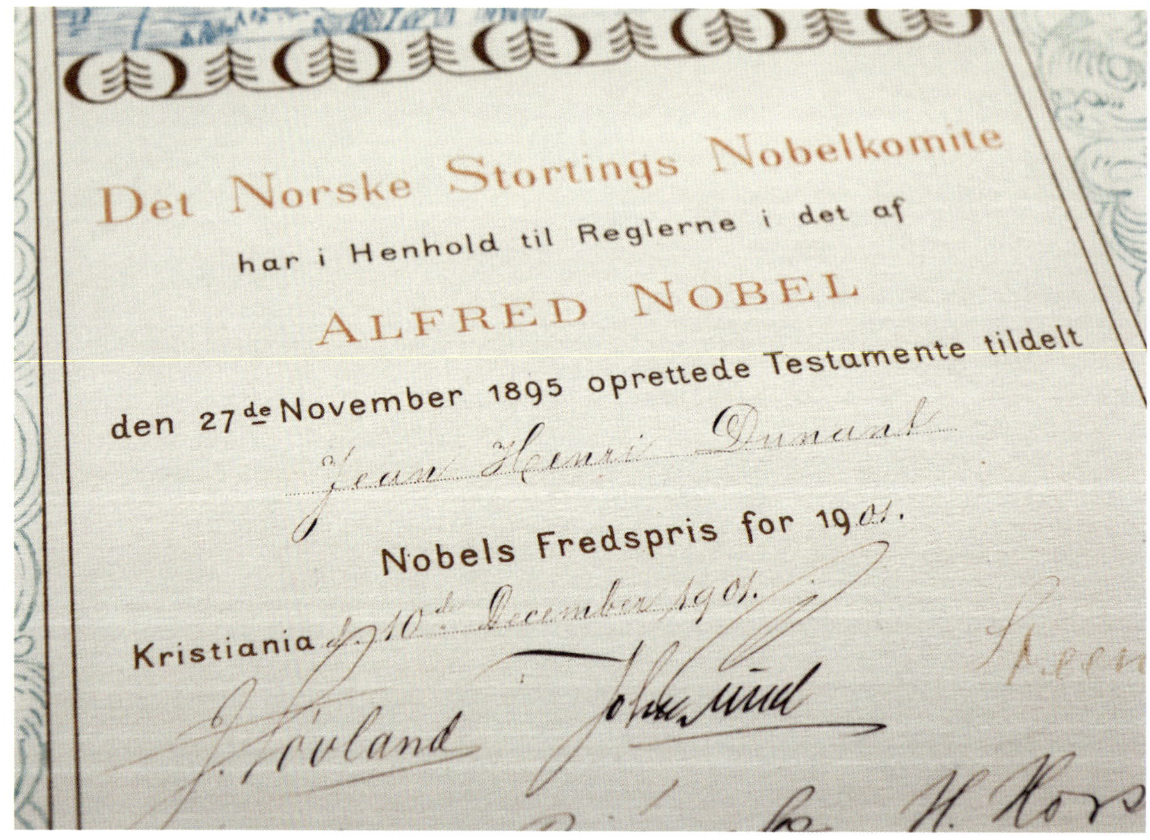

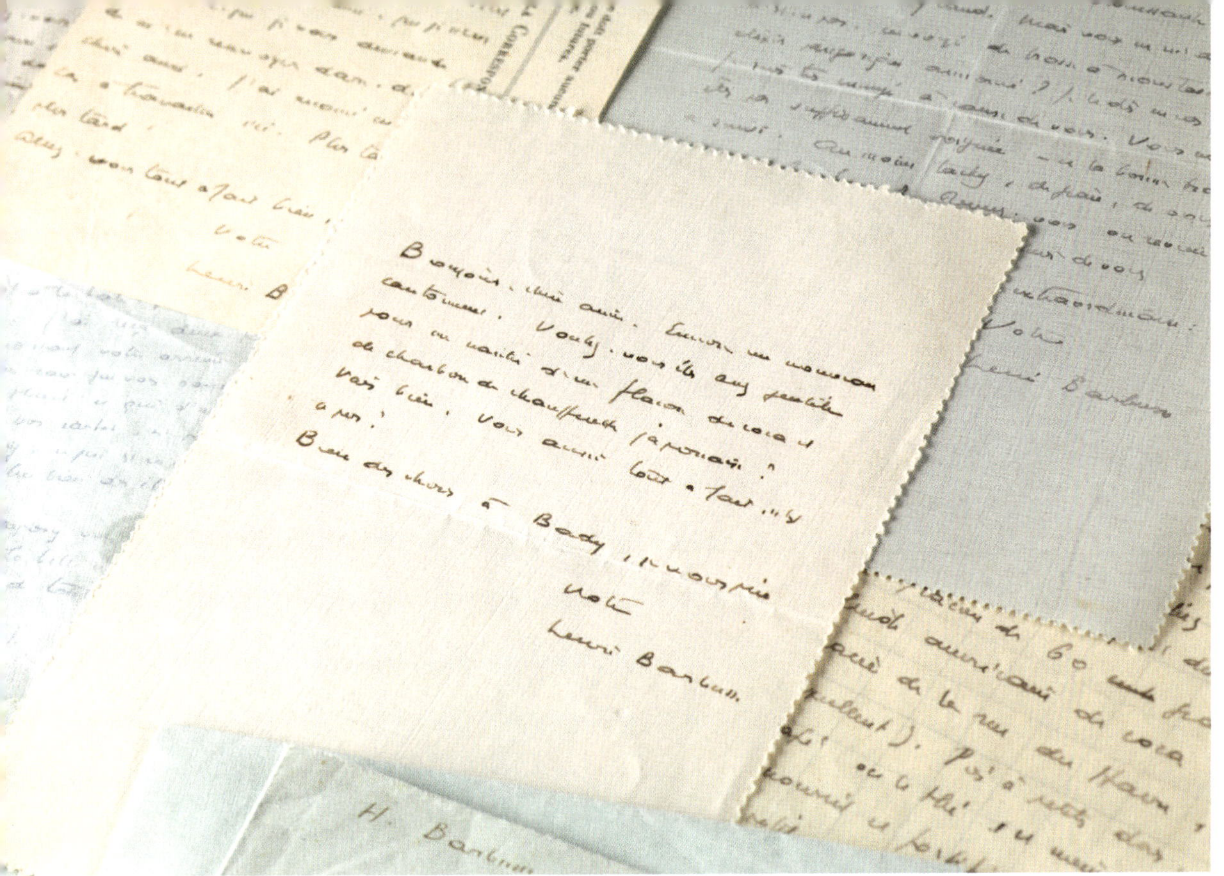

83
Henri Barbusse (1873–1935)
Signed manuscript letters to "wartime godmother" Jeanne Charrot, [from the front], January–October 1915

Nicolas Ducimetière Collection

"25 Jan. 1915. Dear friend, tomorrow, Tuesday, I will be finishing my four days in the trenches … During these quiet periods I intend to resume my novel. I shall work in a few corners of the kitchen, for an hour or two a day. I should be most obliged to you if you would be so kind as to send me a sixty-franc bottle of American fluid extract of coca every week … taken in small doses, this replaces coffee and tea … even better, it nourishes and fortifies at the same time."

"18 April 1915. Here I am back in the trenches after a long period of rest interrupted only by tedious exercises and the alerts I have told you about. Do not fear that I am growing accustomed to this coca. I take only small doses of it, from time to time, when there is an effort to be made, and I share it with those around me. That is the very reason why I have none left and why I am asking you to send me some, posthaste, dear friend. Here I stop working … Later! Later!"

During his seventeen months at the front, the writer Henri Barbusse kept up a regular correspondence with a Parisian "wartime godmother", Jeanne Charrot, a friend of his since 1910 at least. She was a journalist and, after the war, close to Dadaist circles. In his letters, Barbusse describes the physical conditions of his life as a soldier (tobacco, clothing, etc.), the "monotonous, stupid life we lead here", his need for coca extract to stimulate his exhausted body, and the omnipresence of death: "Yes, alas, many have departed. Almost every day I learn that the name of someone I knew and loved has been struck from the list of the living!" He also refers to a novel in the making, eventually published as *Le Feu* (*Under Fire*) and rewarded with a Goncourt Prize, in 1916. Some of this correspondence (forty-one letters) is conserved at the Bibliothèque de l'Arsenal (Ms. 14702); the rest is dispersed in various private collections. In 1937, Flammarion published *Lettres de Henri Barbusse à sa femme (1914–1917)* – his letters to his wife, Helyonne Mendès, daughter of the poet Catulle Mendès. (Which contain not a single mention of a bottle of coca…) **N. D.**

84
Henri Barbusse (1873–1935)
Le Feu: Journal d'une escouade
[*Under Fire: The Story of a Squad*],
Paris, Flammarion, 1916, first
edition

Nicolas Ducimetière Collection

At the outbreak of the First World War,
the writer Henri Barbusse was already
well known to the general public thanks
to the success of his novel *L'Enfer* (*Hell*),
published in 1908. Despite his age (he
was forty-one), lung problems and
pacifist views, he immediately volunteered, and in December 1914 was
assigned to the sixth battalion of the
231st infantry regiment as a stretcher-
bearer. During his seventeen months as
an ordinary soldier – a poilu – he discovered the full horror of the trenches and
observed how his comrades behaved
in combat. Gradually, he began assembling material for a novel, originally jot-
ted down in a small notebook during his
rest periods, in the uneasy calm of his
billet. A tale of the often trivial, basic,
day-to-day life of combatants whose
overwhelming desire was to survive,
Le Feu: Journal d'une escouade was
finalized in the first half of 1916, while
the writer/soldier was convalescing

in a military hospital. Publication followed almost immediately: the first
instalment appeared in the newspaper
L'Œuvre on 3 August, and by November
the novel was in bookshops. It swept
the Goncourt Prize a few days later,
securing its position as the defining
French novel of the First World War (together with Dorgelès' *Les Croix de bois*).
The novel, which was approved by the
censors at the height of the war despite

the denunciation of wartime propaganda and censorship it contains, clearly
conveys the author's pacifist convictions, already evident before the war.
A co-founder and the first president of
the Association of Republican Veterans,
Barbusse was also a founder of the
pacifist Amsterdam-Pleyel movement,
which he chaired with Romain Rolland.

N. D.

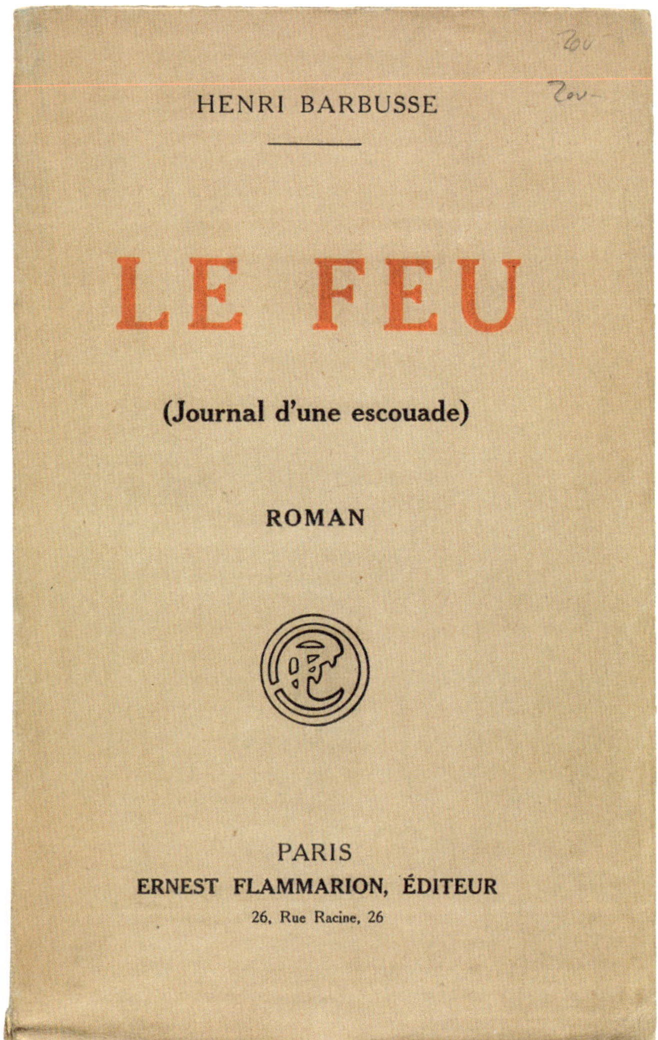

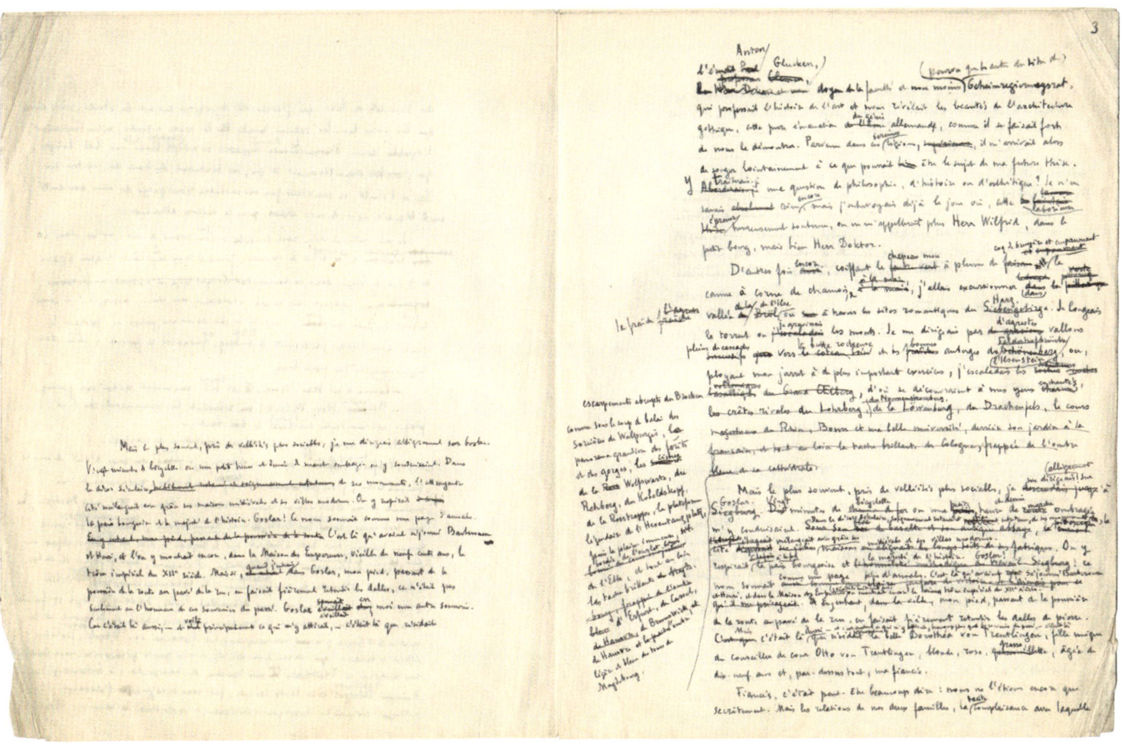

85
Louis Dumur (1863–1933)
Nach Paris! [*To Paris!*], 1919,
autograph manuscript

Lausanne, property of Cédric Dumur, Archives
of the Canton of Vaud, PP538/196-1

The first volume of Louis Dumur's wartime tetralogy *Nach Paris!* follows the adventures of Wilfrid Hering, a German officer, from the outbreak of war, in 1914, to the French victory at the Battle of La Marne. The three highlights of the novel are the violation of Belgian neutrality, the burning of the Louvain library and the "German atrocities". Though frequently criticized for its excessive realism, Dumur's work was popular with readers. First published in the magazine Mercure de France between 1 June and 1 September 1919, it appeared in book form at the end of the same year. There was even an illustrated edition "for young readers", published in 1929.

Nach Paris! stands in stark contrast to many contemporary novels devoted in part or entirely to the Great War, such as Roland Dorgelès' *Wooden Crosses* (1919) and Henri Barbusse's *Under Fire* (1916). Dumur's focus was the German *Kultur*, which, in his view, had as its natural outcome the savagery of the Kaiser's troops, deployed with special ferocity in Belgium. He had already explored this topic a few years before, in a pamphlet entitled *Culture française et culture allemande* (Lausanne, 1915). It may seem surprising that a Swiss novelist, presumably far removed from the hardships of the war due to his "neutrality" – a stance he would later mock in *La Croix rouge et la croix blanche*, aptly subtitled *La Guerre chez les neutres* (*The Red Cross and the White Cross: War among the Neutrals*) – should have chosen to side so fervently with France. Léon Daudet, writing in *L'Action française* on 5 December 1919, was delighted: "I believe that these pages were necessary, that they had to be written, and that in writing them, Dumur has set the record straight."

F. J.

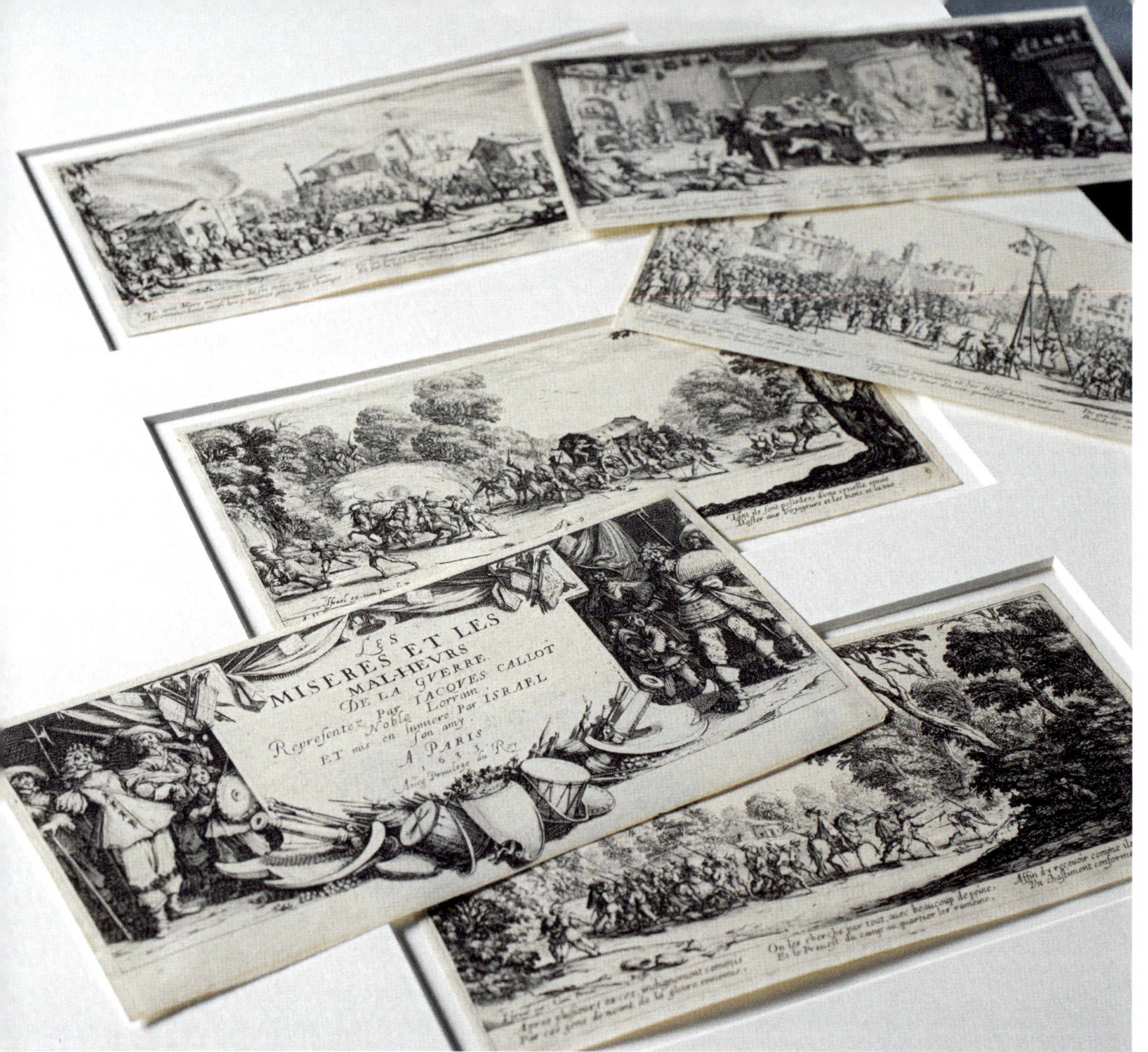

86
Jacques Callot (1592–1635)
*Les Misères et les malheurs
de la guerre* (or *Grandes misères
de la guerre*) [*Miseries
and Misfortunes of War*], Paris,
1633, Israël Henriet, series
of 18 etchings

A native of Nancy, the artist Jacques Callot addressed a broad gamut of historical, religious and popular themes in his etchings. He was especially known for his attention to beggars and the infirm. The eighteen etchings in the series *Miseries and Misfortunes of War* reflect his love of detail and interest in the sidelines of battle. In 1627, Callot sketched the siege of Breda, in the Netherlands, which offered him an opportunity to reflect upon war, military life and its misfortunes. In 1628, he drew the sieges of La Rochelle and Ile de Ré from life. In *Great Miseries of War* (and the earlier *Small Miseries of War*, so named for their size), which he "stopped out" on copper based on his drawings, he rejected official heroic imagery to focus on the humble, harsh living conditions of the "poor soldier" and his daily routine of violence – pillaging, marauding, highway robbery, executions at the gibbet, wheel or stake. He depicts the devastation that accompanied the Thirty Years War in Europe (1618–1648): the beggars, the rapes, the sacking of villages, churches and convents, the terrible wounds, the wretched hospitals. In its completed state, the series comprises a title print (cartouche) and seventeen etchings, each with a six-line caption in verse by the Abbé de Marolles, a well-known collector of prints at the time. **J. B.**

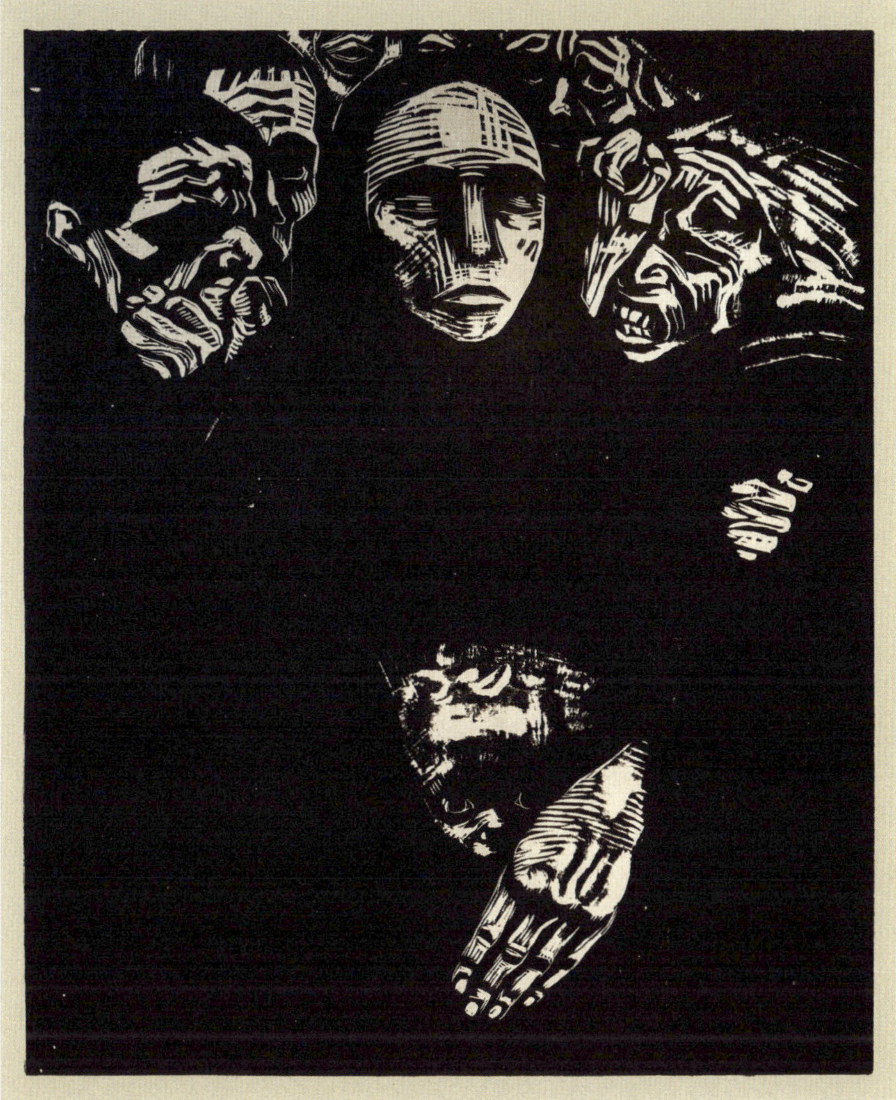

87
Käthe Kollwitz (1867–1945)
Krieg [War], 1920, series
of woodcuts

Geneva, United Nations Archives

This series of woodcuts from the early 1920s, by the German artist Käthe Kollwitz (1867–1945), is entitled simply *Krieg (War)*. Kollwitz was shattered by her son's death at the front during the First World War. Already politically active, she became a committed pacifist. The *Krieg* cycle depicts the suffering inflicted on both the combatants and the women and children at the rear. Her work aims to show that the indirect consequences of armed conflict, although generally less visible, are just as devastating as those on the battlefield. **P.-E. B.**

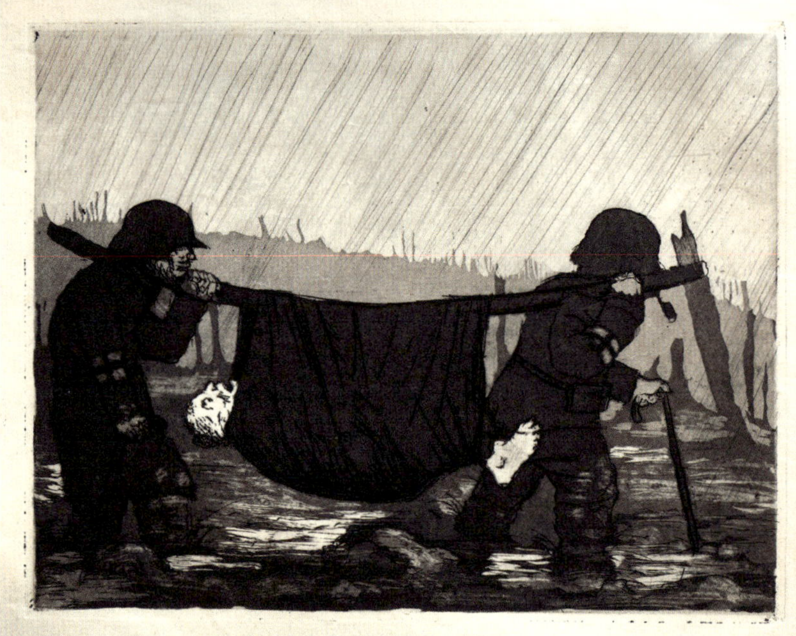

88
Otto Dix (1891–1969)
Der Krieg [*The War*], 1924,
series of etchings

Geneva, United Nations Archives

These etchings by the German artist
Otto Dix are part of a series entitled *Der
Krieg* (*The War*), created in 1924. At the
start of the First World War, Dix enlisted
in the German army as a volunteer,
firmly believing that war was a natural
phenomenon and a catalyst for change.
On returning to civilian life, he became
close to the Dadaists before joining the
New Objectivity movement. He started
work on the fifty plates of this series in
1923. His aim was to convey an uncompromising, unfiltered view of the war,
and to depict the front in all its macabre
and chilling horror, at the risk of shock-
ing the public. The etchings were published ten years after the start of the
Great War. To this day, they bear powerful witness to the trials endured
between 1914 and 1918 by millions of
soldiers on both sides. More broadly,
they offer a glimpse of war's more far-
cical aspects, a constant of every armed
conflict. **P.-E. B.**

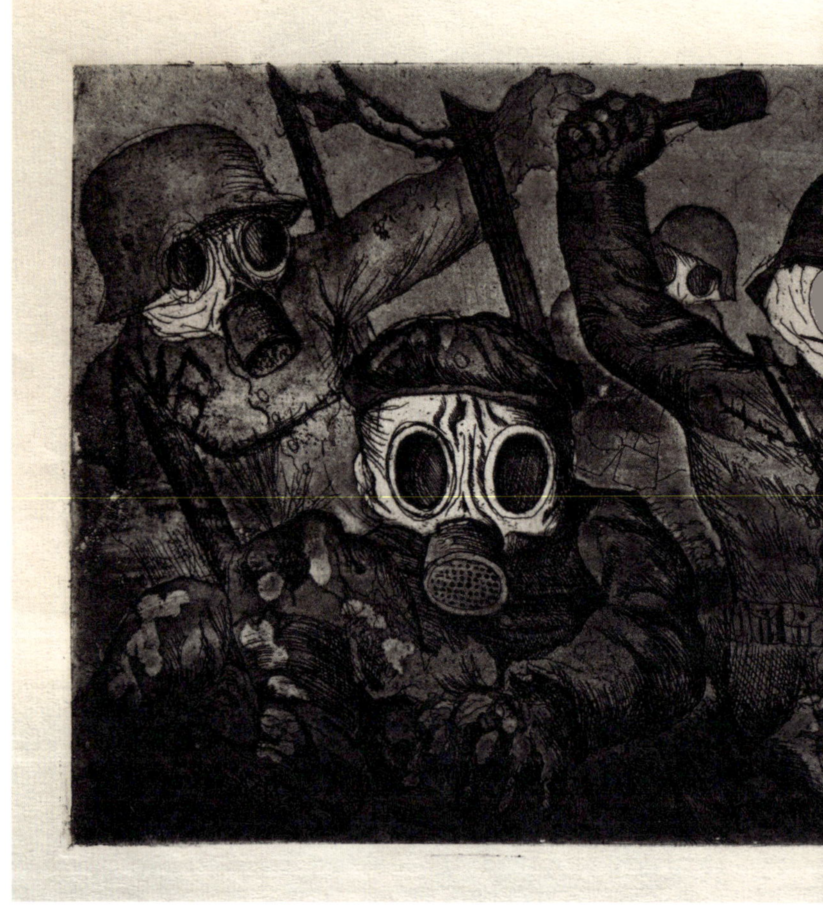

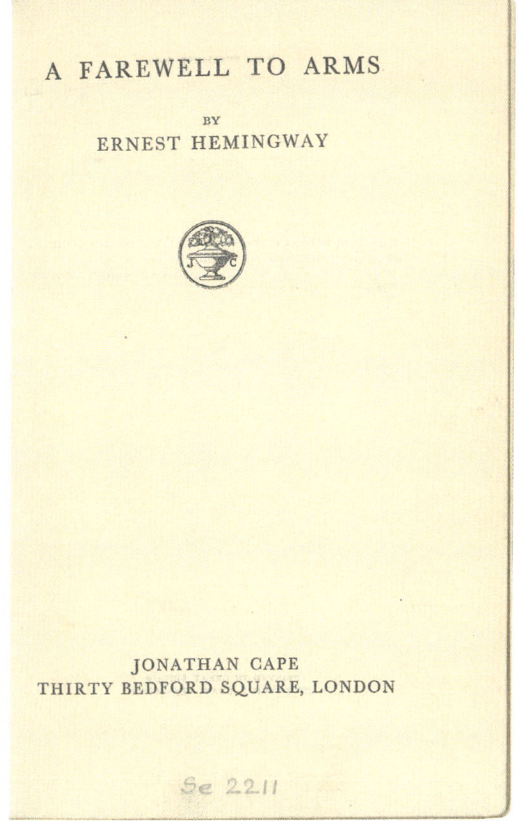

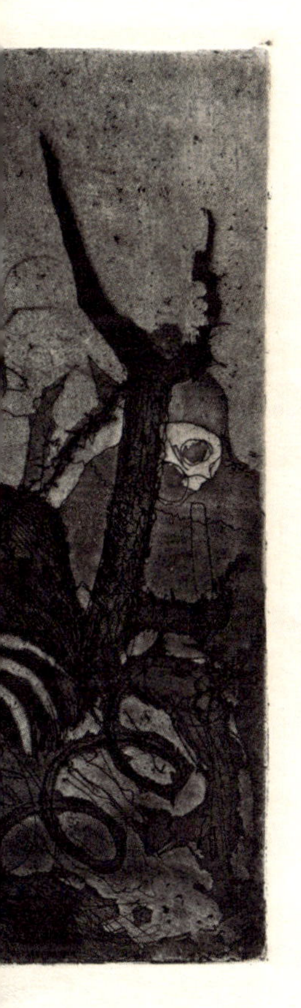

89
Ernest Hemingway (1899–1961)
A Farewell to Arms, London, Cape, 1929

Geneva, Bibliothèque de Genève, Se 2211

A Farewell to Arms is an autobiographical novel by the American writer Ernest Hemingway (1899–1961). Divided into five "books", the novel is set in Italy, during the First World War, and narrated by Frederic Henry, an American officer and paramedic. Hemingway vividly portrays a destructive conflict, and the harshness, futility and chaos of war. War, in his telling, arises in an absurdly cruel world; he does not denounce it, but instead shows it to be a continuation of a dark and deadly universe, where there is no place for love. His description of the retreat of the Italian army is justly famous. He wrote from personal experience, having joined the Italian Red Cross in 1918, in an effort to reach the front. He was wounded, and spent time in hospital in Milan, where he met the American nurse on whom the character of Catherine Barkley is based. Later, Hemingway visited other theatres of war in Europe: *For Whom the Bell Tolls* (1940), about the Spanish Civil War, is inspired by his experience as a journalist, and he was an eyewitness to both the Normandy landings and the liberation of Paris during the Second World War. **J. B.**

Arnold Zweig (1887–1968)
Erziehung vor Verdun [*Education before Verdun*], Amsterdam, Querido Verlag, 1935

Aged twenty-six at the start of the First World War, Arnold Zweig (1887–1968) enlisted despite his poor eyesight. Sent to the Western Front in the spring of 1916, he spent fifteen months near Verdun. His initial enthusiasm – he saw military service as an opportunity to reconcile his dual identities as a Jew and a German – soon turned to disenchantment. Patriotism, he observed, not only failed to curb anti-Semitism, but also served as a justification for the sacrificial slaughter of masses of soldiers and as a cover for the arrogance and corruption of the higher ranks. Zweig returned from the war a changed man: he was now an ardent pacifist, socialist and supporter of the Zionist cause.

Zweig experienced his ordeal at the front as a brutal "education", one that he repeatedly postponed turning into a novel. He returned to the task only after Hitler's rise to power, at which time he was living in exile in Haifa, in Palestine. Published in 1935, *Erziehung vor Verdun* can indeed be read as an indirect denunciation of Nazism, which in many ways was a more extreme version of Prussian militarism. But this novel of intrigue, with a large cast of characters – some endearing, some cartoonish – also explores the gamut of passions, both noble and vile, exacerbated by war. It offers a deliberate contrast with two other major German First World War novels, both published in 1929: Ludwig Renn's *War* and Erich Maria Remarque's *All Quiet on the Western Front*.   **J. K.**

ARNOLD ZWEIG

ERZIEHUNG VOR VERDUN

ROMAN

*Erkenne deine Lage,
Erkenne deine Feinde,
Erkenne dich selbst.*

1 9 3 5

QUERIDO VERLAG N.V. AMSTERDAM

91
Curzio Malaparte (1898–1957, Kurt Suckert, know as)
Kaputt, Naples, Casella, 1944, first edition

Lausanne, Bibliothèque cantonale et universitaire de Lausanne-Dorigny

In *Kaputt,* Curzio Malaparte (born Kurt Suckert, 1898–1957) recounts his experience as a war correspondent for the *Corriere della Sera* in Eastern Europe during the Second World War. Most of the events he describes (acts of savagery by the Germans) are based on fact, but some are fictional. *Kaputt* is at once funny, realistic, cruel, morbid, nightmarish and sarcastic. Europe is depicted as a sad burlesque, mired – yet again – in self-inflicted violence and dysfunctional cruelty. The tone is acerbic, the settings varied: the Iași pogrom (a Jewish massacre in 1941); the Warsaw ghetto and the poverty that lurked behind its barbed wire-topped walls (an indictment of Governor-General Frank, later convicted at Nuremberg); the bombing of Belgrade by the Luftwaffe without a declaration of war, killing seventeen thousand; the execution of educated workers in a Ukrainian *kolkhoz* – Malaparte was an eyewitness to all these events. He started writing in Ukraine, in the summer of 1941; the book follows his movements between May 1941 and August 1943 (Poland, Finland, Lapland, Germany, Italy, etc.). That the manuscript survived in such circumstances is nothing less than a miracle: he kept it safe from Gestapo searches in the lining of his uniform, in makeshift hiding spots or by asking friends to hide it for him. He finished writing *Kaputt* in Capri, publishing it in 1944, in Italian, as an "autobiographical novel" (he took considerable liberty with the facts). **J. B.**

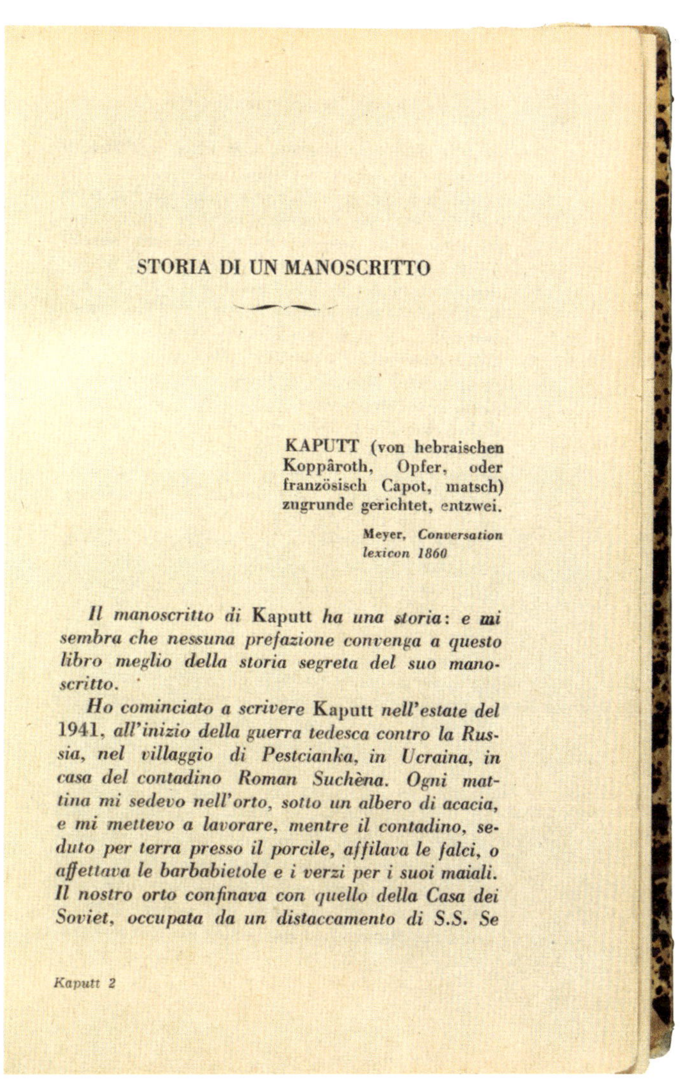

92
Julien Gracq (1910–2007)
Le Rivage des Syrtes
[*The Opposing Shore*; 1951],
autograph manuscript (first draft)

Paris, National Library of France, NAF 28515 (7)

In the opening pages of *Le Rivage des Syrtes* (*The Opposing Shore*), Julien Gracq describes the situation in the Lordship of Orsenna. "Orsenna was at war", he writes, adding immediately: "What lessened the gravity of the matter somewhat was the fact that it had been at war for three hundred years". He refers to a state of "widespread numbness" in which "there was as little desire to end the conflict legally as there was to prolong it by taking up arms".

The entire novel is an in-depth examination of the very idea of war. What does "being at war" mean? How do you enter a war, and how do you get out of one? From the first chapter, Gracq contrasts two major registers that result in markedly different answers to these questions. On the one hand there are the historians, and on the other, the poets. Historians stick to the facts, and therefore cannot spend much time on this war, in which nothing ever happens. In the imagination of poets, however, and even in folk tales, it takes up a disproportionate amount of space. Readers understand what a foundational role is played by this fantastical construction of the land on the other shore, Farghestan, of which so little is known, but which inspires so many dreams and stories.

The question at the heart of this novel, which is not set in a specific historical period, but should instead be read as a great poem about history, is whether or not to step over the border that symbolically separates the two states. In crossing this line, the main character appears as a "condenser … through which millions of scattered, unconfessed desires are turned into monstrous objects of the will". And no one will ever know whether it is for better or for worse that he takes it upon himself to make the word "war" chime, once again, with the tangible reality of weapons.   **C. I.**

93
Claude Simon (1913–2005)
La Route des Flandres
[*The Flanders Road*], Paris, 1960,
autograph manuscript,
preparatory documents

Paris, Sorbonne University, Bibliothèque littéraire
Jacques Doucet, SMN Ms 5

The novel "is no longer the writing of an adventure but the adventure of writing" – this incisive statement issued from the pen of Jean Ricardou, in 1963, at the height of the *Nouveau Roman* movement. Claude Simon might have seen this as a fairly accurate description of his own journey as a writer. His first novels followed a classical format. With *The Wind* (1957), however, he began experimenting with assembling fragments of memories analogically. Bits and pieces of text collected over several months also constitute the raw material of *The Flanders Road* (1960). To keep things straight, Simon came up with the idea of assigning a specific colour to each theme and character. He then grouped the fragments according to a predefined colour sequence, which determined the novel's "assembly plan", transforming it into a work of art in and of itself, a repository for the adventure of writing.

Yet Simon's novel is far more than that. Its account of a cavalry squadron's retreat following the French defeat, in May 1940, was based on the author's experience. He returned to that traumatic week again and again, in greater depth, in his later books. At the request of a British professor, he minutely documented the events, including in topographical sketches; this helped to firmly anchor his writing in the harshest of realities. In Claude Simon's writing, the adventure of writing and the writing of an adventure are inextricably linked, a fellowship that is the hallmark of all great books. **J. K.**

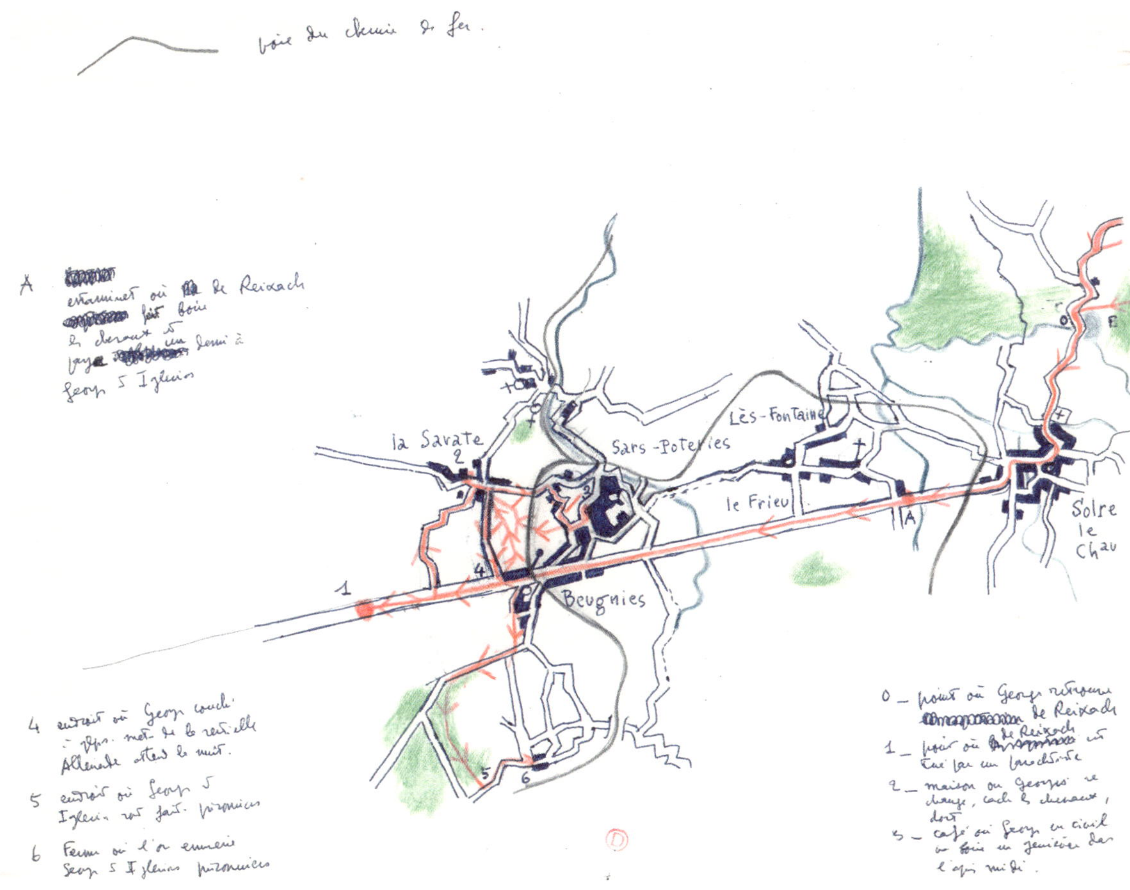

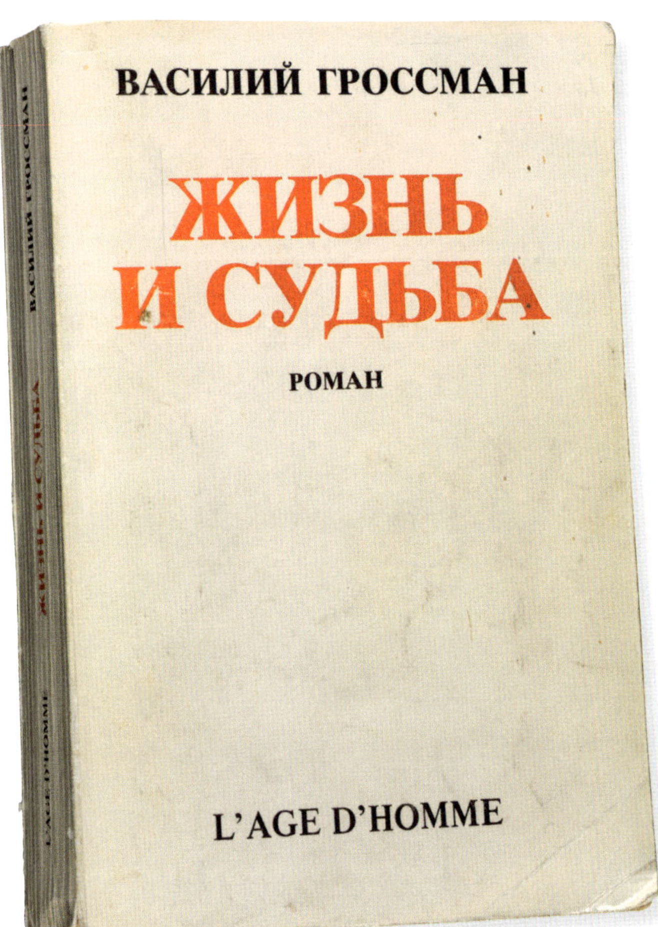

94
**Vassili Semyonovich Grossman
(1905–64)**
Zhizn'i Soud'ba [*Life and Fate*],
written in 1962, Lausanne, L'Âge
d'Homme, 1980, first edition
Geneva, Georges Nivat Collection

Who has not heard of the Battle of
Stalingrad? As a war correspondent,
Vassili Grossman reported from the
warrens dug by the combatants to
defend the pockets of resistance holding up under intense fire on the west
bank of the Volga. Grossman's son was
killed in combat, and he himself spent
two years (1942–43) in the hell that was
Stalingrad. As the siege neared its end,
he was recalled by Stalin: it would not
do to have a Jew reporting on the victory. Grossman set off for Treblinka,
where he discovered an even worse
nightmare.

Immediately after the war, Grossman
began work on an epic novel set in the
twin hells of Stalingrad and Treblinka.
The first part, *For a Just Cause*,
appeared in late 1952. In February 1953,
however, the novel was panned in
Pravda; a second instalment was now
out of the question. *Life and Fate*, written in 1962 and kept hidden by
Grossman, is indeed a sequel to *For a
Just Cause* and features the same cast
of characters. But it lays bare the
anti-Semitism of Soviet Russia and the
Shoah perpetrated at gunpoint by the
Germans, denouncing the kinship
between the two forms of totalitarianism. The vastness of the Battle of
Stalingrad is rendered through a sort of
poetic unanimism: everything in sight
– land, people, animals, insects – is
burned, crushed in a gigantic "labour of
Beelzebub". The most moving episode
is that of "house 6/1", which withstands
the German assault for three months
and sees love blossom between the
soldier Serioja Shaposhnikov and the
radio operator Katya – Daphnis and
Chloe in a rain of bullets.

Grossman naively submitted the novel
to the magazine *Novy Mir*, whose
director forwarded it to the KGB.
Grossman escaped arrest, but his type-
writer ribbons were confiscated in a
subsequent raid. A microfilm copy, kept
by the writer Vladimir Voinovich, survived; it was later smuggled to the
West and ended up in the hands of Efim
Etkind, who, with the help of his friend
Shimon Markish, tried to fill in the
"gaps" where the text was illegible.
Grossman's novel was published in
Russian by L'Age d'Homme, in
Lausanne, complete with these moving scars, as if the text had been cen-
sored. Many years later, the KGB
released the full text from its archives.
In the words of Mikhail Bulgakov,
"Manuscripts don't burn".   **G. N.**

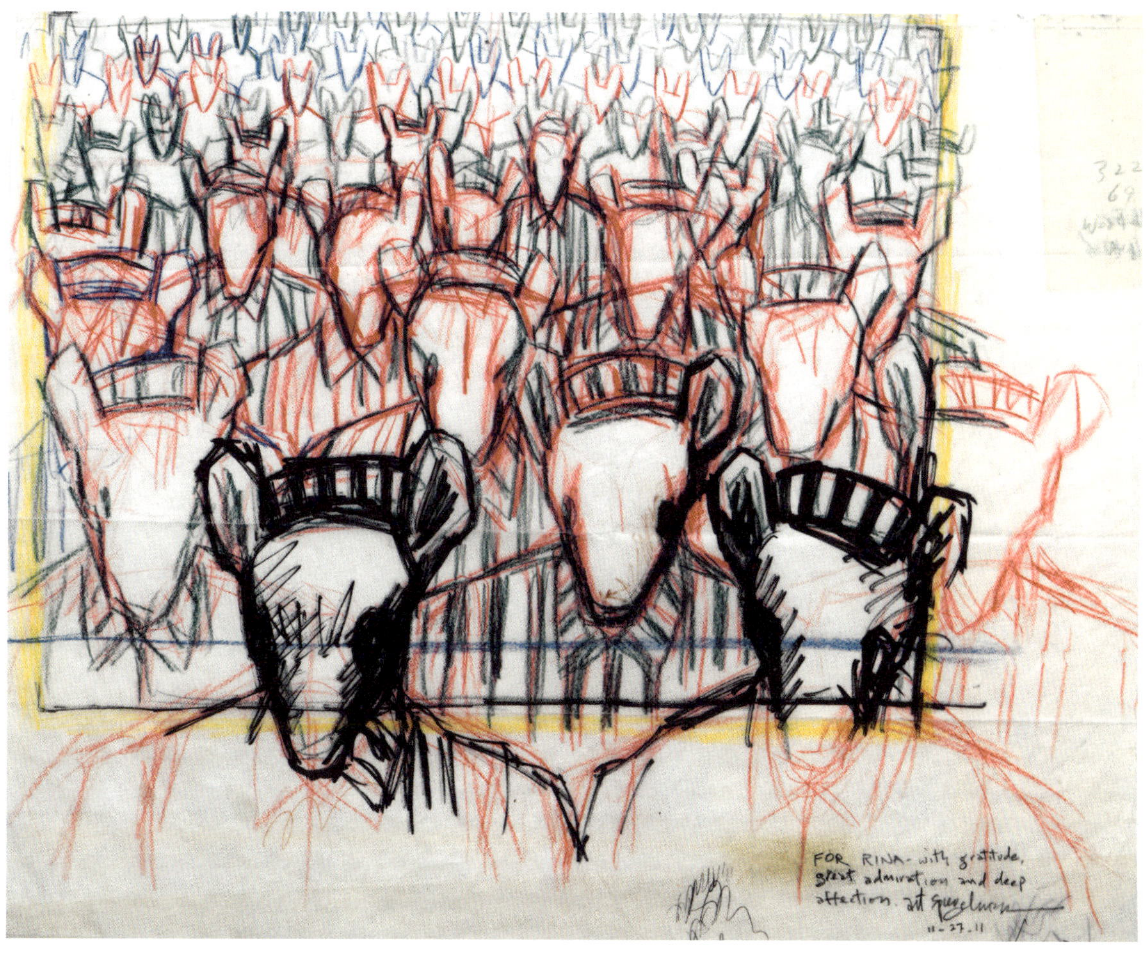

95
Art Spiegelman (b. 1948)
Preliminary drawings for *Maus*, 1980

Paris, Galerie Martel

This exceptionally colourful plate for the graphic novel *Maus* (1980) is the work of Art Spiegelman, an American writer, cartoonist and the son of Polish Jews who were survivors of Auschwitz. *Maus* shows the author in the 1970s, dutifully recording the recollections of his father, Vladek, about the nightmarish period between the mid-1930s, in Częstochowa, Poland, and the end of the war, in 1945. *Maus* contains 292 black-and-white plates, divided into 1,500 panels. Each double page presents two scenes: the left-hand page shows Art and his father talking; on the right we see Vladek's memories of that time, in particular the humiliations inflicted on the starving Jews and their fear of persecution at the hands of the SS torturers and Auschwitz *kapos*. Each community is given a distinct animal identity. Spiegelman opted for animal heads on human bodies: cruel, menacing cats in military uniform, suffering mice in civilian clothing and prison uniforms, Polish *kapos* as pigs. This device allows the author to distance himself somewhat from the inhumanity of the events depicted, while underlining the power differential between the communities. Three first plates appeared in *Funny Animals* in 1972 and the rest were serialized in the "graphix magazine" Raw between 1980 and 1991. The novel was published in book form, in two volumes, in 1986 and 1991. **J. B.**

× ×

peace,
an absence of war?

Should one remember
or draw a line under
crimes of the past?

**Why is war
retold?**

Can one forgive?

BETTING ON PEACE

RECONCILIATION: FROM FORGETTING TO REMEMBRANCE

PIERRE HAZAN
The Centre for Humanitarian Dialogue,
Geneva

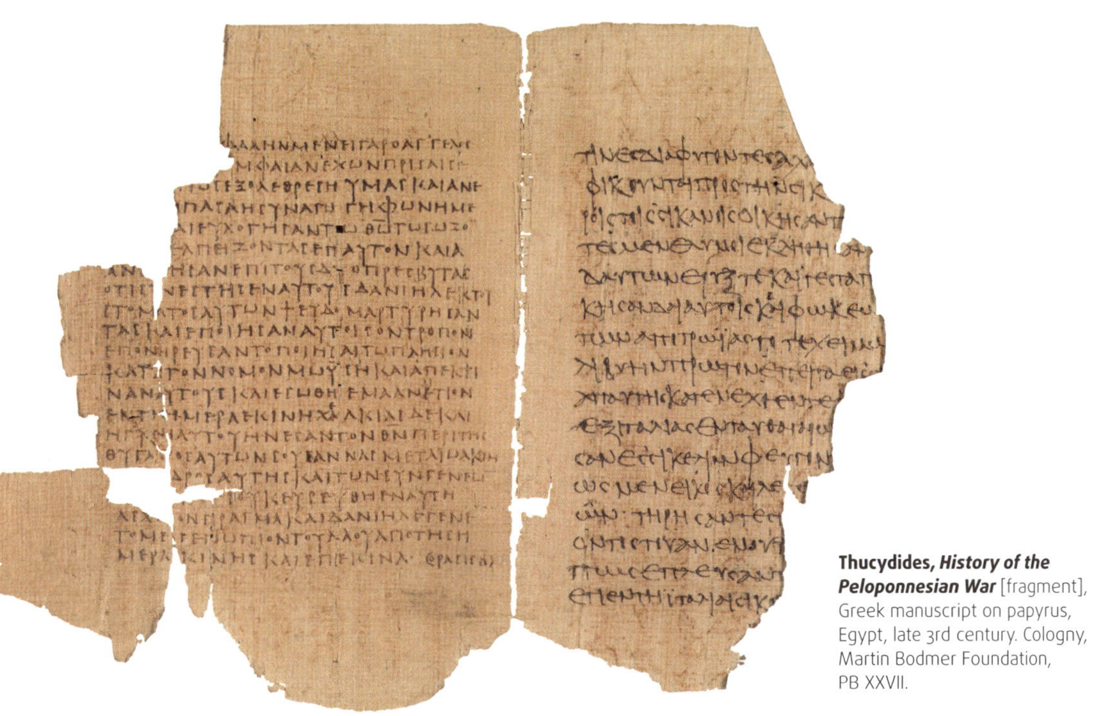

Thucydides, *History of the Peloponnesian War* [fragment], Greek manuscript on papyrus, Egypt, late 3rd century. Cologny, Martin Bodmer Foundation, PB XXVII.

n the name of reconciliation, is it better to insist on remembrance or, conversely, to draw a line under the crimes of the past? The age-old question of whether it is best to forget or best to remember has usually been answered by drawing a veil over the past. In the twentieth century, however, opinion gradually shifted, and, today, the right to remember takes precedence in processes of reconciliation. What prompted this psychological, cultural and political revolution in our relationship to the memory of conflict, and what are its implications?

For centuries, remembrance of past conflicts was perceived as a threat: it sowed the seeds of division and triggered a desire for revenge. Hence, the temptation to opt for the policy of oblivion by enacting amnesty laws. The oldest known amnesty law was drawn up in 405 BC, during the Peloponnesian War. That same approach prevailed throughout the French Wars of Religion (1562–98): each successive conflict ended with an edict of pacification, which invariably included an amnesty clause. The aim of this exhortation to forget was to dull the memory, and thus break the cycle of vengeance. The first article of the Edict of Nantes **[cat. 121]** ordered both sides to ignore the past to the extent of acting as if no violence had ever occurred:

First, that the recollection of all things done by one party or the other between March 1585 and our accession to the crown, and during all the preceding period of troubles, remain obliterated and forgotten, as if no such things had ever happened. And neither our prosecutors-general nor any other persons, public or private, shall be entitled or permitted, at any time or on any occasion whatsoever, to refer to them or to try or prosecute them in any court or jurisdiction whatsoever.

For the sake of reconciliation, the state adopted a policy of negationism: amnesty went hand-in-hand with the injunction to forget, under pain of punishment. Article two of the same edict strikes an ominous, threatening tone towards anyone who acts otherwise:

> Let our subjects be prohibited, no matter their status or quality, to remember them, to attack each other, to be affected, to insult, to provoke each other with reproaches for what happened, no matter the cause or pretext, to engage in argument, contestation or quarrel on the subject, nor let them be outraged or offended at act or word, but rather they should contain themselves and live peacefully together as brothers, friends and fellow citizens, on pain of punishment for offenders as disrupters of the peace and disturbers of public order.

Legal oblivion and social memory loss – amnesty and amnesia, in other terms – were mutually reinforcing. Both words derive from the Greek ἀμνηστία, meaning forgetfulness.

In the nineteenth century, against those who wanted to punish the Communards, Victor Hugo fervently advocated amnesty. In his writings and in the French senate, he urged parliament to adopt amnesty legislation, in 1879 and 1880 **[cat. 136]**, telling the senators that "Only in forgetting do we forgive … The wound must be closed. All hate must be extinguished."[1] It was a startling paradox: forgiveness through oblivion. But can one forgive what one has forgotten or wants to forget?

Victor Hugo's speech of 22 May 1876 calling for amnesty for the Communards [cover page] autograph manuscript. Paris, Bibliothèque du Sénat.

> Gentlemen, at times of discord, justice is invoked by all the parties. It belongs to none of them. It knows only itself. It is divinely blind to human passions. It is the guardian of all and the servant of none. Justice never involves itself in civil wars, but it is aware of them, and it intervenes. And do you know when it does that? Afterwards. It allows the special tribunals to do their work and, when they have finished, it begins. That is when it changes its name and calls itself clemency.[2]

But while Victor Hugo saw amnesty as an expression of tolerance, the acceptance of a diversity of ideas and the necessity of reconcilition through forgiveness, his political adversaries saw a need to bring the Communards to justice, to purify society, eradicate evil, and effect "a redemptive lustration".[3] At the beginning of the "Bloody Week", Thiers told the National Assembly:

> We are respectable people; justice will be done through the regular channels. The law alone shall speak, but it shall be rigorously executed ... atonement shall be complete, but it shall be – I repeat – atonement such as respectable people must inflict it when justice requires, atonement in the name of the law and by the law.[4]

That tension between the call for amnesty as a precondition of forgetting and forgiveness, on the one hand, and the injunction to remember in order to uphold a right to justice, on the other, shifted profoundly during the twentieth century. With the emergence of psychoanalysis, it became more difficult to ignore the dangers of repressed memories and the trauma that can be passed down from generation to generation like a time bomb, liable to suddenly awaken the thirst for vengeance.

Psychoanalysis was one reason for this change in perspective. But historical circumstances, more specifically the human disaster of the Second World War, were central in forcing a complete re-thinking of the dialectic between remembrance and forgetting, again in terms of the role of forgiveness.

Reflecting on the "pure wickedness" exemplified by the Shoah, Vladimir Jankélévitch wrote in *L'imprescriptible* (1967): "Forgiveness died in the death camps." For Jankélévitch, the only way to forgive the unacceptable and the unforgivable was to imagine a sort of pure, mad pardon unbound from all contingencies. Forgiveness on the moral plane in no way precluded legal sanctions, however, if neither pardon nor amnesty were possible.

This awareness of the unforgivable resulted in the development of the law of war in the wake of the Second World War. The Convention on the Prevention and Punishment of the Crime of Genocide (1948), and later the Rome Statute of the International Criminal Court (1998), prohibit amnesty for the perpetrators of international crimes. Memory, on the other hand, was reinstated, and even held sacred. Not to remember – in other words, to forget – was to betray the dead. For some, that was tantamount to killing the victims a second time, even to "committing another genocide".

Remembrance became key when, for the first time in history, the tragedies of Auschwitz and Hiroshima made humanity aware of its finiteness. As Albert Camus pointed out: "Our technical civilization has just reached its greatest level of savagery. We will have to choose, in the more or less near future, between collective suicide and the intelligent use of our scientific conquests."[5] **[cat. 115]**

It was in that context that the concept of international criminal justice took shape. Breaking with traditional constraints of place and time, this new form of justice would have no borders and, when the circumstances required, no time limit. By means of a philosophical and legal revolution that started with the Nuremberg Trials and culminated in the establishment of the International Criminal Court, in 2002, the tyranny of forgetting was replaced with the tyranny of remembrance, requiring punishment by criminal justice.

However, the imperative of criminal punishment soon hit a stumbling block: the need for people in profoundly divided societies to live alongside each other. To what extent was bringing perpetrators of mass violence to account a moral imperative, one that societies everywhere must bow to? Might doing so pave the way for a fresh cycle of violence in fragile states?

Echoing the words of Victor Hugo – "Combatants! Combatants! What is it you want? What of France on the one side and France on the other! Stop, your conquests spawn grief"[6] – Archbishop Desmond Tutu, the head of South Africa's Truth and Reconciliation Commission, in 1999 wrote a book evocatively titled *No Future without Forgiveness* **[cat. 141]**. He asserted that, in negotiated transitions, where there are no clear losers or winners and where yesterday's enemies are obliged to share the same geographical space, civil peace has a price: forgiveness. Tutu defended forgiveness at the societal and interpersonal level;[7] he justified this on cultural grounds, citing *ubuntu*[8] and Christian pardon, both of which were ultimately based on the necessity for former enemies to live side by side.

But where Victor Hugo saw forgiveness in forgetting, Desmond Tutu and, more broadly, South Africa's experience of transition in the 1990s, argued for forgiveness through remembrance. From that perspective, memory was delinked from the necessity of criminal justice, even as amnesty was decoupled from amnesia. There was no forgetting. Instead, crimes were recognized. Forgiveness was not granted for free: it was the outcome of a bargain, with amnesty conditional on the perpetrator confessing to the crime. Amnesty without amnesia fulfilled a political goal: it created the conditions necessary for people to live together by inventing an inclusive citizenship in the new South Africa, the "Rainbow Nation", and, with it, a new identity that opened the door to reconciliation.

The legacy of Vladimir Jankélévitch and Desmond Tutu lives on in the approach to mass violence adopted in the early twenty-first century by their spiritual heirs, namely, the concept of transitional justice. This form of justice strives to be all-encompassing, both punitive for the perpetrators of international crimes and restorative for the victims and for society. It is based not on forgetting the crime but on knowing the circumstances of the victims' deaths and identifying the culprits. It acknowledges and even enshrines remembrance as both an individual and a collective right for societies riven by mass violence.

That is a momentous change: remembrance is no longer the enemy of reconciliation it once was. Quite to the contrary, it is concealment, repression and denial of the past that are perceived as limiting people's capacity to live together, thus perpetuating the vicious cycle of violence. The modern world may well be rediscovering the wisdom of the ancient Greeks, who built battlefield memorials of wood to show that only the passage of time can erode memory.

Notes

[1] "Victor Hugo et l'Amnistie des Communards", *Journal officiel de la République française*, 23 May 1876, p. 3533. https://www.senat.fr/fileadmin/Fichiers/Images/archives/HUGO/debat_JO.pdf

[2] *Ibid.*

[3] Stéphane Gacon, "L'amnistie de la Commune (1871–1880)", in *Lignes*, 2003.

[4] Adolphe Thiers, "Séance du 22 mai 1871 à l'Assemblée nationale", *Journal officiel de la République française*, 23 May 1871, p. 1108

[5] Albert Camus, *Between Hell and Reason: Essays from the Resistance Newspaper* Combat, *1944-1947*, trans. Alexandre de Gramont, Wesleyan University Press, Hanover (NH), 1991, p. 110.

[6] Victor Hugo, *L'Année terrible*, Paris, 1985.

[7] He was widely criticized for this stance.

[8] *Ubuntu* means "humanity" in Bantu, in the sense that all humans are connected by their shared humanity.

ROUSSEAU, KANT AND THE ENLIGHTENMENT PROJECT FOR PERPETUAL PEACE

JACQUES BERCHTOLD

Martin Bodmer Foundation

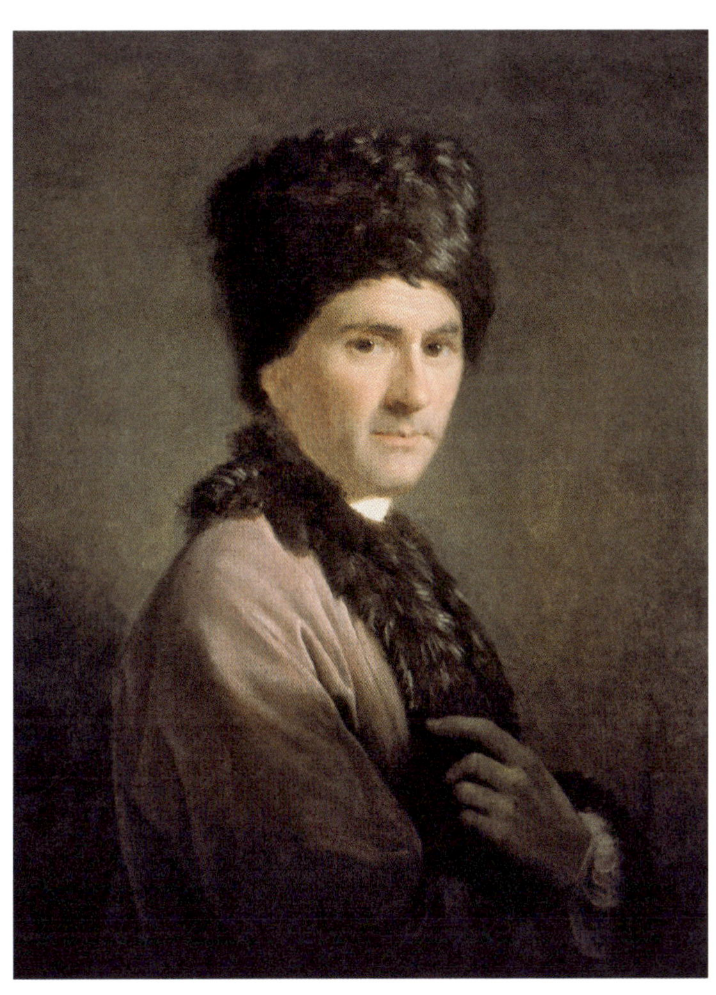

Jean-Jacques Rousseau,
by Allan Ramsay, oil on canvas,
1766. Edinburgh, National Gallery
of Scotland.

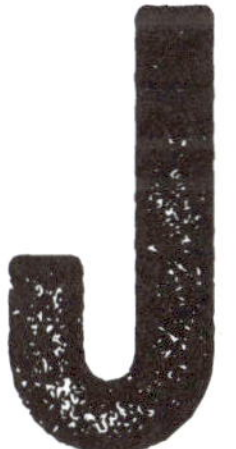

ean-Jacques Rousseau admired the soldiers of Sparta and Rome in Plutarch's *Lives of the Noble Greeks and Romans,* giving their lives for their city. He watched in awe as French troops marched through Chambéry on their way to Italy during the war with Austria (1733–37). An avid reader of Brantôme's *Vies des hommes illustres et grands capitaines* (*Lives of Distinguished Men and Great Captains),* he considered enlisting. A republican from Geneva, he was fascinated by builders of fortifications, including Vauban, du Crest and his own uncle Bernard. Once he began to frequent elite circles, however, he contributed to Enlightenment thinking about peace. Today, Rousseau's *Abstract* of the Abbé de Saint-Pierre's *Project for Perpetual Peace* (this *Abstract* was first published in 1761) is viewed through the retrospective prism of Kant's *Perpetual Peace* **[cat. 102]**: *A Philosophical Sketch*, when it should really be understood in a pre-Kantian context, before the latter work had become influential.

× ×

Having started working on the *Abstract* in 1754, Rousseau proposed several avenues for achieving a measure of peace in international relations, as well as a hypothetical model grounded in a re-examination of the social bond. The ideas put forth in his vulgarization of Saint-Pierre's thesis and in the *Social Contract* (published in late 1762) appear as part of his work on the *Institutions politiques*, in which he set out to reflect on international relations (only fragments of this unpublished work have survived). How did he convey Saint-Pierre's pacifism, despite his misgivings about many of its premises? The "Citizen of Geneva" was far removed in time from the Abbé who, born in 1658, was writing in the context of the Peace of Utrecht. Trusting in reason, the latter imagined a "League of Kings" through which princes would put an end to war. Written in the demonstrative mode, Saint-Pierre's *Project for Perpetual Peace in Europe* (originally issued in 1713 and later supplemented) is a difficult read. It is organized into principal axioms, secondary proposals and responses to objections, in the manner of Spinoza's philosophical treatises and Grotius' legal writings (*On the Law of War and Peace*, 1625) **[cat. 8]**.

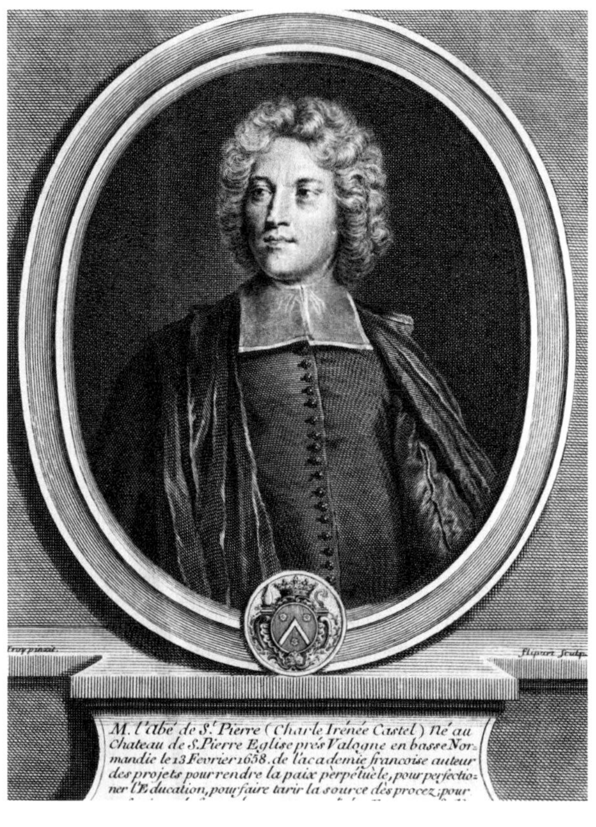

This *mos geometricus*, while appropriate for a mathematical theorem, was, in Rousseau's estimation, ill suited on its own for dealing with reality (the intuition of the heart combined with reason).

Saint-Pierre nursed a deep hatred for Louis XIV, claiming that his appetite for conquest drove him to wage war on the pretext of making peace. The Abbé favoured a peace that would enshrine the existence of a multitude of states, fixed the geopolitical map of Europe, and established treaties of unification on the empirical basis of the historical moment. Rousseau took issue with the combination, in Saint-Pierre's pacifism, of a theoretical approach to long-term questions, and the premise that certain aspects of the current situation be taken as a given – in particular the existence of principalities, whose legitimacy went unquestioned, as well as the assumption that these princes-turned-philosophers, by negotiating over contested territories, would rid themselves of their lust for conquest (their defining characteristic, in Rousseau's view). For the Genevan philosopher, Grotius had already been guilty of excessive indulgence towards his protector, Louis XIII, when he argued that *libido dominandi* was consubstantial with monarchy. Saint-Pierre, for his part, optimistically believed that those same rulers could be persuaded by the *Project's*

Abbé de Saint-Pierre,
by Jean-Baptiste Scotin the Younger, copperplate engraving, 1716.

irresistible logic to renounce their bellicose ways and conclude a lasting peace on the basis of his twelve articles. With pedantic thoroughness, he described the drawbacks of war and laid out the terms of his proposed League. The signing of the Treaty of Vienna in 1738 (War of the Polish Succession) did little to shake his conviction that the time was ripe, and that the elites could not fail to convert to his views. In 1740 (at the age of eighty-two), the progressive Abbé still insisted that he was, thanks to his *Project*, the "grand apothecary of Europe", who heralded the demise of the superfluous "physician" of armament.

The young Rousseau met Saint-Pierre at the home of their common protector, Dupin, in 1742. After the Abbé's death in 1743, the Duping asked Rousseau to write a more approachable adaptation of Saint-Pierre's ponderous treatise, whose reception had been disappointing. Rousseau completed the onerous task and his summary was published in 1761, in the form of a forceful pamphlet. In the interval, however, the dream of peace in Europe had grown increasingly distant.

In 1745, Louis XV won a resounding victory over the Dutch and English at Fontenoy. This was followed by defeat against Prussia and England in the Seven Years War, which saw the rationalization of the Prussian military art. The French debacle at Rossbach (1757) rekindled anti-militarist sentiment. In the period preceding the treaties of Paris and Hubertburg (1763) that ended the war, the ranks of those who admired Frederick II for his optimal organization grew thinner. The "enlightened monarch" and his innovative approach to war were met with mounting disapproval. Voltaire's thinking also evolved: after sycophantically praising Louis XV at Fontenot then growing close to the hypocritical "Solomon of the North", he denounced the "heroic butchery" of war in *Candide* (1759) **[cat. 75]**. Rousseau, too, was uncomfortable with Frederick's ambiguous stance: turning down the king's generous offer of support with the words: "Remove from my sight this sword that dazzles and wounds me." (letter to Frederick; 30 October 1762)

This represents a remarkable shift. A propos of painting, Diderot noted the anachronistic nature of images of the victorious Louis XV "clad in lace" (as opposed to the compassion evoked by Callot's series of engravings, *Les misères de la guerre* **[cat. 86]**) and recommended that one visit the battlefield to witness its horrors and the cries of the dying. At the

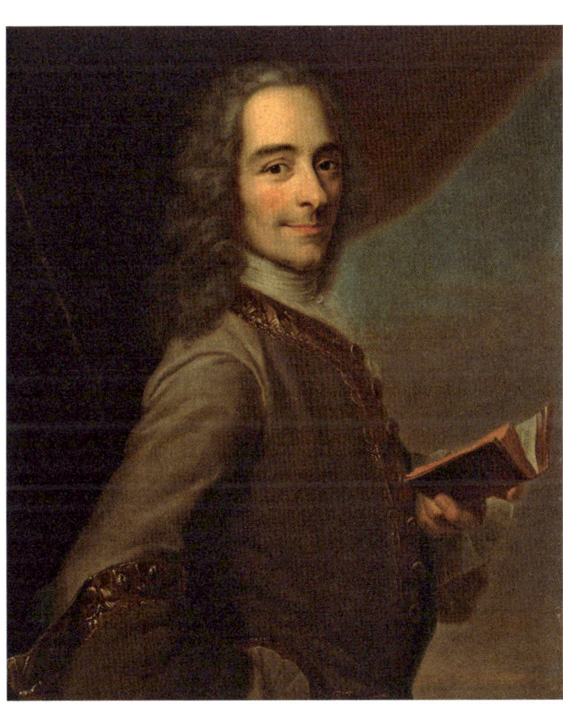

François Marie Arouet de Voltaire holding a copy of "La Henriade",
by Maurice Quentin de La Tour,
oil on canvas, 1736. Versailles,
Palaces of Versailles and Trianon.

opera, Rameau's *Zoroastre* (1749) celebrated the radiance of peace after the darkness of war. Rousseau, for his part, rejected the Hobbesian original jungle and argued that in the beginning there was good (rather than a Manichean conflict); goodness was an essential attribute of natural man, who was corrupted only after becoming politicized and civilized. In his summary of Saint-Pierre, Rousseau was thinking of his own *Institutions politiques;* he described his *Social Contract or Principles of Political Right* as a "a treatise of friendship and public peace", choosing as its epigraph the words of the pacifist king in the *Aeneid*, who would have preferred to welcome the Trojans to Latium rather than wage war against them.[1] Rousseau's understanding of the relations between the members of a community is the cornerstone of his political philosophy. Setting aside his writings on inter-state relations, he commented on Saint-Pierre. First, he published his adaptation of Saint-Pierre's work, the *Abstract* (1761). Although he completed the task entrusted to him, he was unfaithful both to the structure and the spirit of the original. He then exposed his reservations in a severe *Judgement on the Project for Perpetual Peace,* presented as a "complement" to the *Abstract* so as to avoid any possible confusion. Intended as a diptych, they were never issued together, and the *Judgement* was published only posthumously, in 1782. Since that time, we have been able to read the two texts side by side, but Rousseau's contemporaries could not.

To understand Rousseau's position, it is important to distinguish five levels of analysis. First, the *Abstract* was a milestone – as Madame Dupin had foreseen – because it was read, in particular by Kant. Its thirty pages served as a persuasive ambassador for an unreadable treatise, and rekindled discussion of the ideal of "perpetual peace", turning it into a fashionable subject ("On the Benefits of Peace" was the topic of the French Academy Prize in 1766). Rousseau served the Abbé's ideas well, even though he radically disagreed with many of his anthropological and political premises. Grimm, in his *Correspondance littéraire,* lucidly avoiding amalgamating the author with the vulgarizer, wondered how the misanthropic commoner had become the aristocratic and utopian Abbé's mouthpiece...

Second, Rousseau disagreed with Saint-Pierre. He was neither as optimistic nor as dogmatic, and his summary evinces a profound scepticism towards some of the latter's arguments. He strays from the original, for instance, when asserting: "Let us admit then that the Powers of Europe stand to each other strictly in a state of war, and that all the separate treaties between them are in the nature rather of a temporary truce than a real peace." Amused by the contrast between Rousseau's flights of idealism and his reticence, the Geneva pastor Théodore Vernes wrote to him, in 1761, that he hoped the war would cease "in spite of" the *Project for Perpetual Peace*... Yet Saint-Pierre's position was often confused with Rousseau's own. Voltaire, for one, mocked the *Abstract* in his *Rescrit de l'Empereur de Chine, à l'occasion du "Projet de paix perpétuelle"* (1761). As the *Project* sealed the vision of a pacified Fortress Europe, Voltaire, whose vision encompassed a globalized world, set out to ridicule the "citizen of Geneva's" Eurocentric focus. The emperor of vast, august China admonishes the upstart from tiny Geneva for presuming to define the eternal rules of the universe. Upon receiving the *Project* – a document predicated solely on the moral weight of Geneva – he begs, in the most reverential terms, to be allowed to join the effort for world peace. How did the political might of the venerable empire compare with the small dot at the tip of Lake Geneva? Commenting on this *Project* directed against the Ottoman world, the forgotten emperor reminds "the Citizen" (where is Geneva?) of the existence of his empire and states his willingness to extend the planned union of nations by joining it. He opines that the League's first president should hail from Geneva (which is where, again?). Voltaire thus uses comic exaggeration to cruel effect, highlighting the contrast in geographical and political scale. He also accuses Rousseau of plagiarism, noting that the *Project* glosses over the fact that Sully once proposed a similar plan to the great pacifist king Henry IV. The Emperor of China thus crushes the upstart Genevan, the transcriber of a peace plan first formulated at the highest levels of the state.

Third, the *Judgement* offers a commentary on the *Abstract* while making clear Rousseau's disagreement with its ideas. The philosopher casts a critical, Machiavellian eye on what he sees as a naïve text. He contrasts the *actions* of Henry IV with the impotence of a well-meaning utopian who flattered princes in his books. Henry was a patient manipulator, determined to build peace by means of a thousand diplomatic manoeuvres and provisional arrangements. It was that pragmatic approach – and not some vacuous idealism – that brought him within touching distance of perpetual peace in Europe. Rousseau iconoclastically contrasted the actions of the duplicitous Henry with the laughable impotence of the Abbé's theoretical system, thus disparaging the latter's efforts. The *Judgement* strikes a tone of resignation: history provided *one* opportunity (as Rousseau's description of Henry's Machiavellian genius shows), which failed by a narrow margin; a similar figure was unlikely to appear again, and there would be no second chance. However, Rousseau seemed untroubled by that pessimistic conclusion (in terms of the lessons of history and the establishment of peace on the basis of international conditions).

Fourth, the lessons of political history are fraught with inanity. Rousseau delivers his message on peace through the optimistic means of a fundamental reassessment. He suggests that one start by reconsidering the premises of the social bond upstream from the historically contingent situation. Enshrining the existence of the principalities would be a mistake, in that their ruling dynasties were founded by bandit chiefs who gained ascendance by virtue of a "law of the fittest", which was later institutionalized. Rousseau's scepticism as to the prospect for world peace hinges on his refusal to accept that corrupted bond between citizens and rulers. His project is predicated on a realignment of the notion of community. Otherwise, the demonstrative trick falls flat (Grotius' definition of just war, Saint-Pierre's utopian prescriptions, Vattel's enumeration of the correct ways to conduct war), in the sense that its rationality enshrines the validity of the proverb "man is a wolf to man", and because inter-state rivalries are worse than the reality of interpersonal relations. According to the *Social Contract,* kings are slaves to their passions and therefore bent on acquiring more power. Where Saint-Pierre writes of kingdoms, the *Abstract* refers to republics (of which the Abbé was deeply mistrustful). Because small size is a guarantee of virtuous proximity, Rousseau suggests starting with the Netherlands, the Swiss Confederation and the Republic of Geneva. He takes issue with Hobbes, arguing that the disposition to war emerged only in evolutionary stages following the state of nature. Hence, the organization of human nature into established nations masks a consubstantial state of war. Treaties are little more than a bandage on a wooden leg and war is the embodiment of "civilized evil", since national boundaries are not found in nature.

Fifth, only in a second phase – after exposing his observations on the establishment of small communities ("renatured" because they were politically rooted in the *Social Contract*) in both theoretical and programmatic terms – does Rousseau address the other aspect of the question (that is, how to account for reality) and explicitly endorse autarchy (the Corsicans) and defensive nationalistic patriotism (the Poles). He was

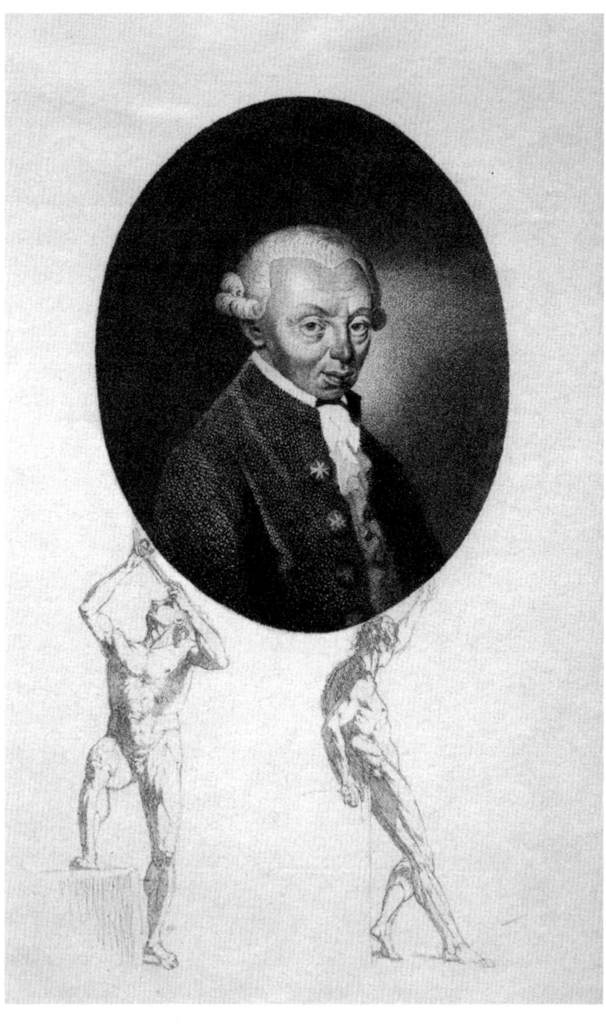

Immanuel Kant, by Johann Friedrich Bolt, copperplate engraving and drawing after a miniature by Carle Vernet, 1795.

against trade, and did not share the belief of Kant and the Physiocrats that growth in the international circulation of goods and money would foster peace. He advocated small, secluded units, autarchichal micro-communities. At a later stage, these inward-looking units could establish relations with each other if they wished. Even at the final level of political analysis – that of established nations – his model is essentially a fictional and hypothetical one, providing an approach to thinking about an order distinct from the art of grappling with contingent reality. In this way, Rousseau bolstered the cause of Enlightenment pacifism. His forceful appeal to renew society and reconsider the human bond – by returning to its natural, original purpose and focusing on individual freedom – were foundational. His contribution lies in that call to freedom.

Inspired in part by Rousseau, Immanuel Kant penned his major work, *Perpetual Peace: A Philosophical Sketch*, in 1795, the year that the Peace of Basel and the Treaty of The Hague were signed **[cat. 103]**. The Prussian philosopher starts by observing that states, jealous of their sovereignty, remain mired in a situation of potential conflict: either they go to war with each other, or they strike a precarious, *de facto* peace without basis in law. Remember that the state of nature is replaced for individuals by a "social contract"; Kant combines Rousseau's idea with insights from theology (peace as a transcendental and providential order) on the one hand, and from legal theory (institutions as artificial constructs of human reason), on the other. One must acknowledge, he writes, that war is inherent to the nature of the state and, therefore, look for a way to withdraw the question of inter-state relations from the law of the fittest, in order to approach it instead from the standpoint of the legitimacy of justice. That calls for a moral argument: one must seek to transform a peace treaty into a state of peace rooted in the law. To that end, it is necessary to develop a law-based approach to inter-state relations. Kant thus formulated the underlying principles for the conditions (i.e., a rational state of law) that would enable the emergence of an institutionalized "perpetual peace" in place of the temporary "cease-fires" that prevailed when the default mode between states was a Hobbesian state of nature. Kant's *Sketch* soon gained recognition and influence. His innovative approach went on to inspire twentieth-century pacifists, in that it called for the creation of institutions dedicated to the moral, equitable and law-based management of international relations, on the model of the League of Nations and the Charter of the United Nations.

Notes

[1] In his *Sketch*, Immanuel Kant stressed another quote from the *Aeneid* (book I): "Imprisoned fury roars with bloody mouth".

THE NANSEN PASSPORT AND THE BIRTH OF REFUGEE ASSISTANCE

PIERRE-ÉTIENNE BOURNEUF
United Nations Library

STEFAN VUKOTIC
United Nations Library

COLIN WELLS
United Nations Library

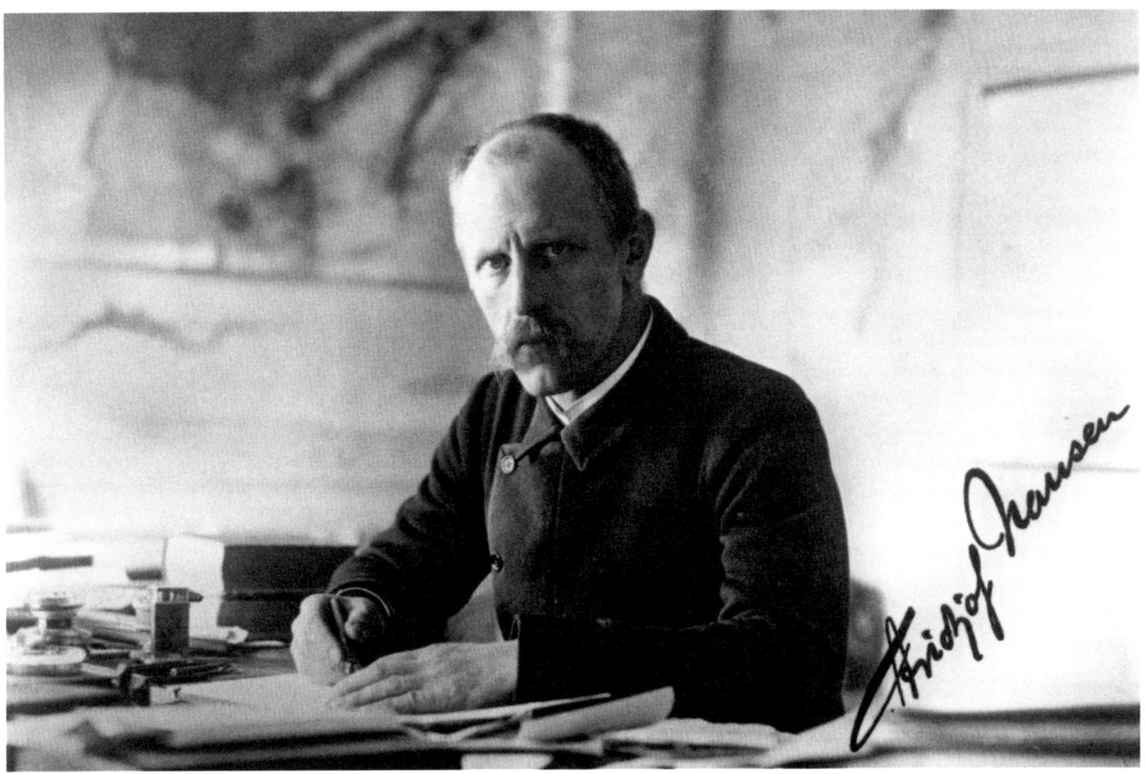

Fridtjof Nansen (1861–1930),
photograph, c. 1900.

By the end of the First World War, more than a million and a half Russians had fled civil war, famine and the Bolshevik regime to seek refuge abroad. Stripped of their nationality, and often unable to meet their own needs, many found themselves trapped in countries on Russia's borders – in Europe, Asia and even the Far East. While some governments and private entities endeavoured to help them, the scale of the crisis was such that a coordinated international response was called for. Recognizing this, in June 1921 the Council of the League of Nations decided to appoint Fridtjof Nansen, a Norwegian, High Commissioner for Russian Refugees. This decision marked the start of the League's activities on behalf of refugees which, despite political and financial obstacles, would continue to develop for almost twenty-five years. The present article describes the refugee work carried out by the League up until its dissolution in 1946.[1]

On taking office, in September 1921, Nansen had already been charged with supervising the repatriation of prisoners of war **[cat. 50]** and coordinating international aid to combat famine in Russia. His mandate as High Commissioner, and the means at his disposal, were lim-

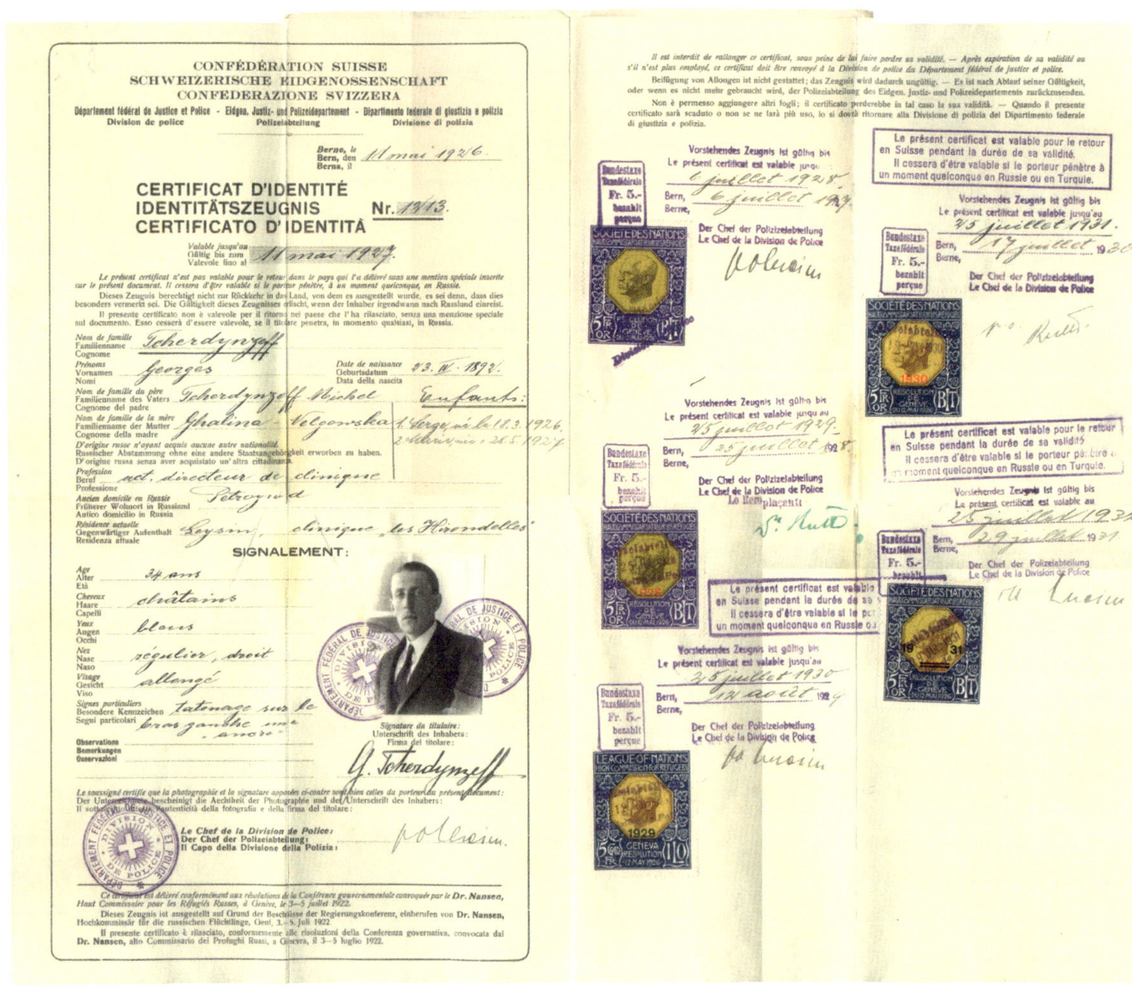

ited. With only a handful of staff, he had to coordinate the efforts of governments and private organizations to assist Russian refugees. His brief did not include material assistance: states did not regard it as being a matter for the League, and, in any case, the refugee issue was perceived as being merely temporary. The budget allocated to Nansen was approved every year and covered only the administrative cost of running the Office of the High Commissioner.

Despite these conditions, Nansen undertook substantial efforts to help the Russian refugees. He relied in particular on donations from governments, individuals and private organizations, and sometimes exceeded his mandate by providing material aid directly. He worked closely with private entities and the International Labour Office (ILO). To register and assist refugees, offices were also opened in several European cities. The Office of the High Commissioner had to overcome

Nansen Passport,
dated May 11, 1926.

logistical, administrative and political obstacles in order to facilitate aid, allocate refugees to host countries and settle them there. The adoption of the "Identity and Travel Certificate" by an international conference convened by Nansen in Geneva, in 1922 was an important step forward in affording refugees legal protection **[cat. 51]**: the certificate, later named the "Nansen passport", enabled its holders to cross borders legally and to regularize their presence within the country where they intended to settle. It enabled paperless refugees stripped of their nationality to leave a country at the Russian border in which they had found refuge but which did not have the capacity to take them in permanently. It also restored their lost dignity: without papers, refugees are invisible and cannot be born, marry, obtain a divorce or die without causing legal problems. [2]

The League's work for refugees expanded over the following years, largely in response to fresh crises. Following the Greek-Turkish war, Nansen intervened on behalf of refugees from "Central Asia", in particular in Constantinople and Greece. The League facilitated an international loan to Greece, to finance the settlement of refugees there. Bulgaria, confronted with a large influx of refugees, subsequently obtained similar assistance. In 1924, both the Nansen passport and assistance from the High Commissioner's office were granted to Armenian refugees who had fled Turkey and were unable to return home. In the following years, Nansen supported an ambitious plan to settle them in the Yerevan region, but this was frustrated by the reluctance of some League members to finance a project on Soviet territory. Other projects were carried out, however, in Lebanon and Syria. In 1926, the identity certificate system was improved, to clarify the status of Russian and Armenian refugees. In 1928, the protection of the High Commissioner was extended to Assyrians, Chaldo-Assyrians and assimilated refugees, and to Turks outlawed by the Ankara government. The extension of assistance to new categories of refugees was resisted in Geneva by states that wished to confine the League's work to certain well-defined categories and rejected a comprehensive approach.

At the administrative level, after approving the division of refugee duties between the High Commissioner and the ILO (between 1925 and 1928), and after a transition period overseen by the Secretariat, in 1930 the League's Assembly approved the creation of a new body: the International Nansen Office for Refugees, christened in honour of the Norwegian High Commissioner who had died some months previously. Under the umbrella of the League, this autonomous body was responsible for assisting refugees, facilitating their placement and settlement, and coordinating the work of the "relief agencies". Administrative and running costs were financed by the League, while other expenditure had to be covered by donations. The "Nansen Office" was intended to be a temporary body whose work was expected to end in December 1938, when it was thought the refugee issue would have been resolved. Far from winding down, however, in 1935 the Nansen Office extended its protection to people fleeing the Saar after the territory's return to Germany.

At the legal level, the progress on refugee protection made in the 1920s culminated, in October 1933 in the signing of the Convention Relating to the International Status of Refugees. Although it applied only to "Nansen refugees", the 1933 Convention was the first legally binding instrument for the protection of refugees. It clarified their personal status and socio-economic rights and, for the first time, contained a reference to the principle of *non-refoulement*. Its application remained limited, however: by 1939, only eight states had ratified it. The fact was, in the political and economic context of the 1930s, governments were reluctant to enter into binding commitments. A 1934 Nansen Office report notes that, among the issues discussed, the expulsion of refugees was "a daily concern".[3] Despite the difficulties, four years later the Office was awarded the Nobel Peace Prize.

The 1930s were also marked by a new crisis. The coming to power of Adolf Hitler, in 1933, drove tens of thousands of Germans to leave their country, fleeing political and religious persecution. In September 1933, the issue was raised in the Assembly of the League of Nations as a technical question, to avoid upsetting the Nazi government, which was still a member. This led to the establishment of a new body: the High Commissioner for Refugees (Jewish and Other) Coming from Germany. The American James McDonald was appointed High Commissioner, with a mandate to "negotiate with and direct" governments and private organizations working together to assist German refugees, in particular by facilitating their immigration to, and settlement in, host countries.[4] For political reasons, the High Commissioner's office was kept administratively and financially separate from the League: it even had its headquarters in Lausanne, to avoid being in any way associated with the Secretariat. At a time when it was still hoped that links with Germany could be mended, the refugee question was causing a certain amount of awkwardness in Geneva. Lack of political support drove McDonald to resign in December 1935. In his view, the issue of German refugees could not be resolved without a change in Nazi policy, which he described as a "challenge to the conscience of mankind".[5] Although McDonald's gesture did make waves, it did not radically change the work on behalf of German refugees.[6] His successor, the Briton Sir Neill Malcolm, was officially on the staff of the League and knew that it would both provide technical support and defray the cost of running the High Commissioner's office. And some progress was made. In 1938, the Convention relating to the status of refugees from Germany, drafted under the auspices of the League, made it possible to issue identity papers similar to the Nansen passport and to grant legal protection comparable to that afforded by the 1933 Convention. Its application was restricted, however: it was signed by only seven governments, only two of which ratified it.

Realizing that the refugee issue was far from being resolved (especially after the crisis sparked by the Anschluss in 1938), the Assembly approved the establishment of a new body, an amalgamation of the High Commissioner's Office for German refugees and the Nansen Office – and so was born the Office of the High Commissioner for Refugees, under the protection of the League of Nations. Its headquarters were established in London, and, in January 1939, Sir Herbert Emerson, a Briton, took charge of it. His task was to ensure that the "Nansen refugees", and those coming from Germany, were protected, by monitoring the application of the 1933 and 1938 Conventions and coordinating the relief provided by governments and private associations. The outbreak of the Second World War, however, severely hampered his work. The authorities in the occupied countries broke off contact, and the High Commissioner's office was unable to prevent refugees from being arrested and deported. During the war, Emerson continued his work as best he could, centralizing information about the situation of the people under his protection in Europe, giving administrative assistance in the free countries, supporting the work of private organizations and facilitating emigration (notably from Portugal). As the conflict wore on, his work gradually expanded. As he himself acknowledged, in his 1944 annual report, it was becoming harder and harder to separate the work done under the High Commissioner's mandate from the overall refugee problem.[7] Emerson was also appointed head of the Intergovernmental Committee on Refugees (IGCR), an independent body set up in 1938 on the initiative of the United States to assist German refugees and organize emigration for them; during the war, its mandate was broadened to include all refugees. Emerson also worked with allied bodies. When the League was dissolved, in 1946, the responsibilities of the Office of the High Commissioner were transferred to the IGCR. In December 1946, the United Nations General Assembly approved the creation of the International Refugee Organization (IRO), a temporary United Nations agency tasked with assisting European refugees. In 1951, the IRO was replaced by the Office of the United Nations High Commissioner for Refugees (UNHCR), still active today. The League thus left an important, if sometimes underrated, legacy. For, despite the administrative, financial and political constraints it had to contend with, the League of Nations was unquestionably an international pioneer when it came to assisting refugees.

Notes

[1] See https://libraryresources.unog.ch/c.php?g=462663&p=3162760. This article highlights the importance of the Total Digital Access to the League of Nations Project (LONTAD) to digitize the League's entire archives. Thanks to a donation by a private Swiss foundation, in the coming years the project will enable both researchers and the general public to access over fifteen million pages on the organization's activities. In developing new research methods, it will give us a better understanding of what Lord Robert Cecil described as the "great experiment" of the League. See also https://www.unog.ch/80256EE60057D930/(httpPages)/EFBEE574FFB575BEC1257DF-6003B333A?OpenDocument.

[2] See Claudena Skran, *Refugees in Inter-War Europe: The Emergence of a Regime*, Oxford, Clarendon Press, 1995, p. 103.

[3] League of Nations, A.12.1934.

[4] *Official Journal of the League of Nations*, December 1933, p. 1617.

[5] League Archives, C1614.

[6] *Official Journal ... ibid.*

[7] League of Nations, C.23.M.23.1944.XII.

CHINA, KOREA, JAPAN AND THE SCARS OF THE SECOND WORLD WAR

CONSTANCE SERENI
University of Geneva

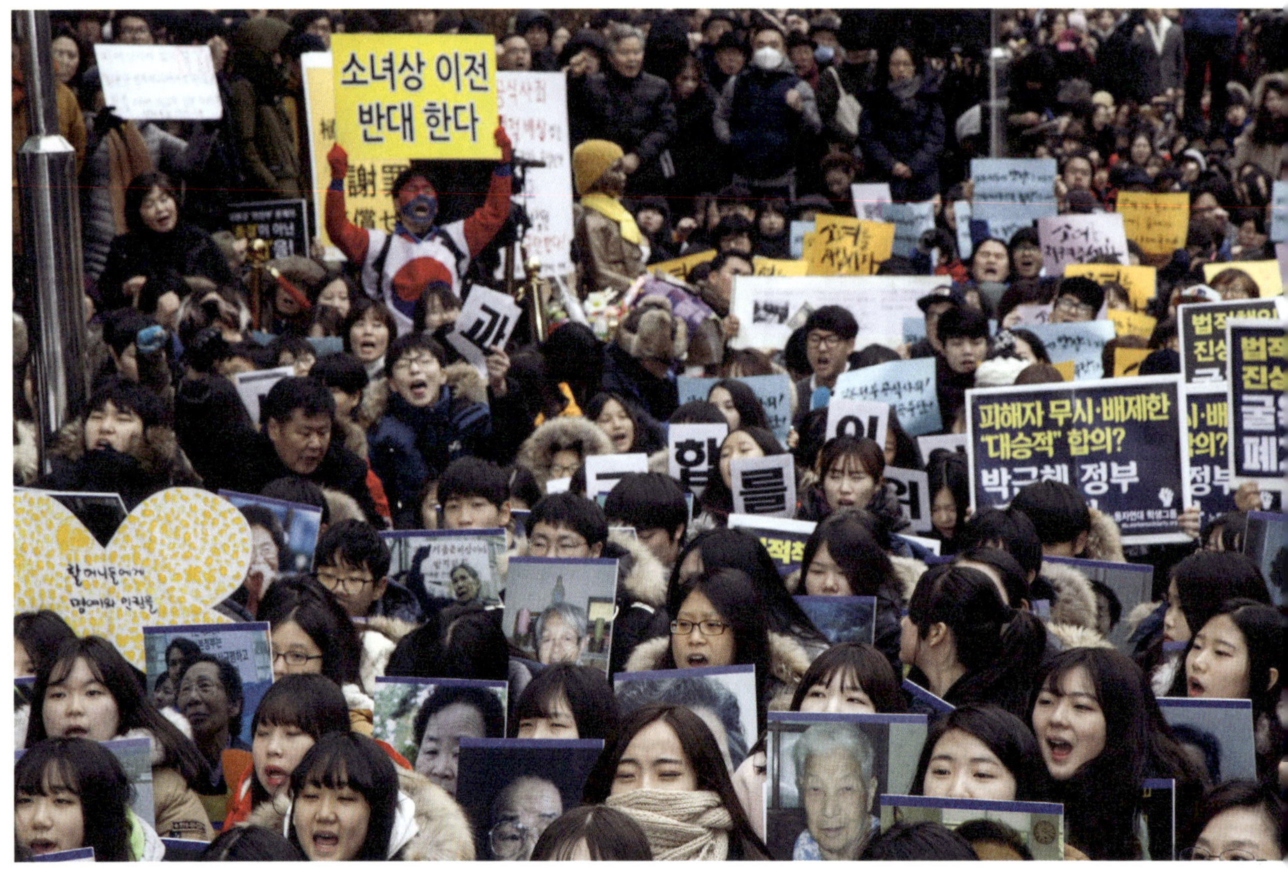

ven at a distance of almost seventy-five years, the handling of the memory of the Second World War in Asia is still a source of conflict. East Asia is currently in the throes of a deep diplomatic crisis. Between Japan, China, South Korea and even Taiwan, lines of tension are appearing – a legacy of the scars left by the war. Despite the work of historians, despite the apologies and the efforts at rapprochement and reconciliation, shadows still linger, and half-stifled resentments are re-emerging amid accusations of amnesia and the rewriting of history. How the war is perceived in Japan and its neighbouring countries lies at the root of the strain and hardening nationalist attitudes that are causing problems today.

History itself is the problem here: the history of the war waged by Japan (regarded by most historians as a war of aggression); that of Korea's lengthy, painful colonial experience; and that of the crimes committed on Chinese soil. There is no need to look elsewhere for the causes of present-day tensions between Japan, China and Korea. The

South Korean protesters holding photos of former "comfort women" gather in front of the Japanese embassy in Seoul, on 30 December 2015. During the Second World War, countless Korean women were subjected to a system of mass sexual slavery set up and operated by the Japanese army.

territorial claims to the Senkaku/Diaoyu and Takeshima/Dokdo Islands (under dispute since the early 2000s with China and South Korea, respectively) are merely a pretext that masks a far more crucial issue: who bears responsibility for the war, and how to handle its memory. The ways in which the war is viewed in different countries pose challenges to historiography that go far beyond a simple question of scientific method or epistemology. Their implications are strategic, too: they threaten the security of the Asian region, and the global balance of power, and they have far-reaching economic consequences. [1]

So profound is the disagreement that no consensus can be found over the definition of war itself. Most people would agree that it was Japan's colonial expansion from 1931 onwards that engendered the conflicts on the Asian mainland which, in Japan, came to be called the Fifteen-Year War. [2] But interpretations differ. Take the conflicts between Japan and China during the 1930s, for example: do they form part of the Japanese war of aggression on the continent or were they merely skirmishes triggered by issues over borders or the security of Japanese trading interests **[cat. 23 et 54]**? Was the 1910 annexation of Korea lawful or was it violently imposed by an imperialist nation, forcibly relegating a neighbouring country to the rank of a colony? As Japan sees it, there was never a war with Korea in the first half of the twentieth century. For Korean historians, on the other hand, the entire colonial period was one long fight against the Japanese invader.

Indeed, the legitimacy of the annexation of Korea – an issue raised in the colonial era by the independence movements – remains one of the big question marks in historical research in South Korea today. Japanese historians have, admittedly, taken postcolonial issues on board, and scrutinized the making of the nation-state. But Korea became a state through its struggle against colonization, only to be rocked again by the trauma of the Korean War and the communist dictatorship. As Arnaud Nanta writes, Korea "does not seem able, today, to tolerate murky areas in its modern or contemporary history", and co-opts remembrance-related claims for subjective, and sometimes nationalist, purposes. [3] To this day, the trauma of colonialism continues to fuel anti-Japanese feeling, as evidenced by the ongoing debates around the content of Japanese schoolbooks and how they portray Korea, its colonization and the crimes Japan committed there – the most emblematic being that of the "comfort women" taken from Korea by the Japanese army to be used as military prostitutes. [4] Whether these women went voluntarily or not is still a contentious issue in Japan, despite Japanese historical studies suggesting that they were indeed kidnapped and sexually enslaved.[5] In August 2014, the Japanese daily newspaper *Asahi Shinbun* was forced to back down after being fiercely criticized by the Japanese right for using an untrue account to substantiate the claim that the women had been recruited by force. The current prime minister, Shinzō Abe, has himself spoken about the issue several times, declaring that there is no proof that violence was used in the recruitment of comfort women.[6]

The approval by the Japanese government, in 2001, of a schoolbook produced by the Society for History Textbook Reform (Atarashii rekishi kyôkasho o tsukuru-kai) that considerably minimized Japan's responsibility for the war, as well as the importance of the Nanking Massacre,[7] provoked strong reactions in China, thereby reigniting a debate on schoolbooks first sparked in the early 1980s by the terms chosen to describe the Japanese push into China.[8] More recently, against the backdrop of a rapidly militarizing China that is increasingly affirming its desire to take its place among the leading world powers,[9] the provocative actions of Shinzō Abe's government, and in particular his own visits to the Yasukuni Shrine, have once again brought to the fore the question of how the war is remembered.

In Japan, the current crisis in Asia has prompted strong reactions from the government. Territorial integrity is a mounting concern for the Liberal Democratic Party, and Shinzō Abe has made it a priority of his second term as prime minister. On 1 July 2014, his office reaffirmed his intention to reinterpret Article 9 of the Japanese Constitution[10] to allow limited exercise of Japan's collective right to self-defence, and to enable it to more easily mobilize its self-defence forces in the East China Sea, if needed.[11] On 19 September 2015, despite opposition from the general public, the Japanese parliament adopted legislation authorizing it to send soldiers into conflicts abroad in support of an ally in difficulty. The fact that it was able to do so can be ascribed to the anxiety caused by Chinese and Korean demands.

The inability to communicate or to agree on the causes and consequences of war is thus at the heart of the tensions besetting East Asia. And yet, this stalemate is not inevitable. The memory of the war was a relatively minor problem until the 1980s and 1990s; in fact, prior to that time, it was in the political and economic interest of both China and Korea not to revisit these issues. The Japan-Korea treaty of 22 June 1965, which normalized relations between Japan and South Korea, was designed to put an end to Korea's demands for reparations;[12] and following the resumption of diplomatic relations with China, in 1972, and the signing of the Sino-Japanese Treaty of Peace and Friendship, in 1978, it seemed fair to assume that the problems resulting from the war were on a path to resolution.

But the opposite is true. Since the 1980s we have witnessed a resurgence of problems of remembrance in connection with the defence of strategic interests in the region. Rather than dwindling over time, feelings of resentment towards Japan in China and South Korea have been growing, fuelled by hardening nationalism, domestic political interests and economic needs.[13] In Japan, too, there is rising tension around war-related issues, as evidenced by its unhappiness at the addition of documents about the Nanking Massacre to UNESCO's Memory of the World Register, in 2015.[14]

The historian Oguma Eiji divided the post-war period in Japan into two distinct phases: a first, running from the defeat in 1945 to 1955, characterized by the American occupation and the reconstruction effort, and a second, characterized by the economic success of high growth and the development of a consumer society.[15] Today, we are entering a new phase, in which the post-war system is collapsing. It is therefore more vital than ever to go back to the roots of the problem: the traces that the war in Asia has etched in people's memories, and the sore points beneath the fault lines now separating the countries of East Asia.

Notes

[1] South Korea has agreed, for example, to join the Asian Infrastructure Investment Bank (AIIB) proposed by China to rival the IMF and the World Bank, whereas Japan prefers to continue backing an Asia-Pacific dominated by the United States, rather than an East Asia consisting of China, Japan and Korea.

[2] See, *inter alia*, Pierre-François Souyri, "La colonisation japonaise: un colonialisme moderne, mais non occidental", in Marc Ferro (ed.), *Le Livre noir du colonialisme*, (1st ed. 2003), Paris, Hachette, 2005, pp. 543–74.

[3] Arnaud Nanta, "Le Japon face à son passé colonial", in Olivier Dard and Daniel Lefeuvre (eds), *L'Europe face à son passé colonial*, Paris, Riveneuve éditions, 2008, pp. 129–46.

[4] Samuel Guex, "La controverse nippo-coréenne au sujet des manuels d'histoire", *Cipango*, 2012.

[5] Yoshimi Yoshiaki, *Jūgun ianfu* [Army Comfort Women], Iwanami shoten, 1995, 247 pp.

[6] See *Le Monde*, 09.03.07, "Tollé après les déclarations de Shinzo Abe: Tokyo tente de calmer la polémique sur les 'femmes de réconfort'", and Christine Lévy, "Le Tribunal international des femmes de Tokyo en 2000. Une réponse féministe au révisionnisme?", *Clio* 1/2014 (No. 39), pp. 129–150. URL: www.cairn.info/revue-clio-femmes-genre-histoire-2014-1-page-129.htm.

[7] The majority of Japanese academics do not minimize the Nanking massacre. See for example Hora Tomio, *Nankin Jiken* [The Nanking Incident], Jinbutsu Ōraisha, Tōkyō, 1972.

[8] Samuel Guex, "Les manuels d'histoire japonais vus de Chine", *Ebisu*, No. 38, 2007, pp. 25–54.

[9] John W. Dower, "The San Francisco System: Past, Present, Future in U.S.-Japan-China Relations", *The Asia-Pacific Journal*, Vol. 12, Issue 8, No. 2, February 24, 2014.

[10] Cabinet Decision on Development of Seamless Security Legislation to Ensure Japan's Survival and Protect its People, 1 July 2014.

[11] Article 9 of the constitution, which was proposed (some would say imposed) by the American occupying forces in 1946 and came into force in 1947, stipulates that Japan formally renounces its right of belligerency.

[12] Japan on this occasion paid Korea the sum of 300 million dollars, not as war reparations, but as development aid, in addition to a 500 million dollar loan.

[13] Despite some joint initiatives between the three countries to find a scientific solution to these historical controversies that would be acceptable to all. Lionel Babicz, "Japon, Chine, Corée: vers une conscience historique commune?", *Ebisu*, No. 37, spring-summer 2007, pp. 19–43.

[14] http://www.lemonde.fr/asie-pacifique/article/2015/10/10/le-japon-deplore-l-inscription-du-massacre-de-nankin-au-registre-de-la-memoire-du-monde_4786772_3216.html#1HtYRrYsezV6sxpS.99.

[15] Oguma Eiji, *Minshu to aikoku – sengo nihon no nashonarizumu to kōkyōsei* [Democracy and Patriotism: Nationalism and Solidarity in Post-War Japan], Shin'yōsha, Tōkyō, 2002, pp. 11–12.

THE RELEVANCE OF THE "APPEAL FOR A CIVILIAN TRUCE IN ALGERIA"

ANTOINE GARAPON
Institut des Hautes Études sur la Justice,
Paris

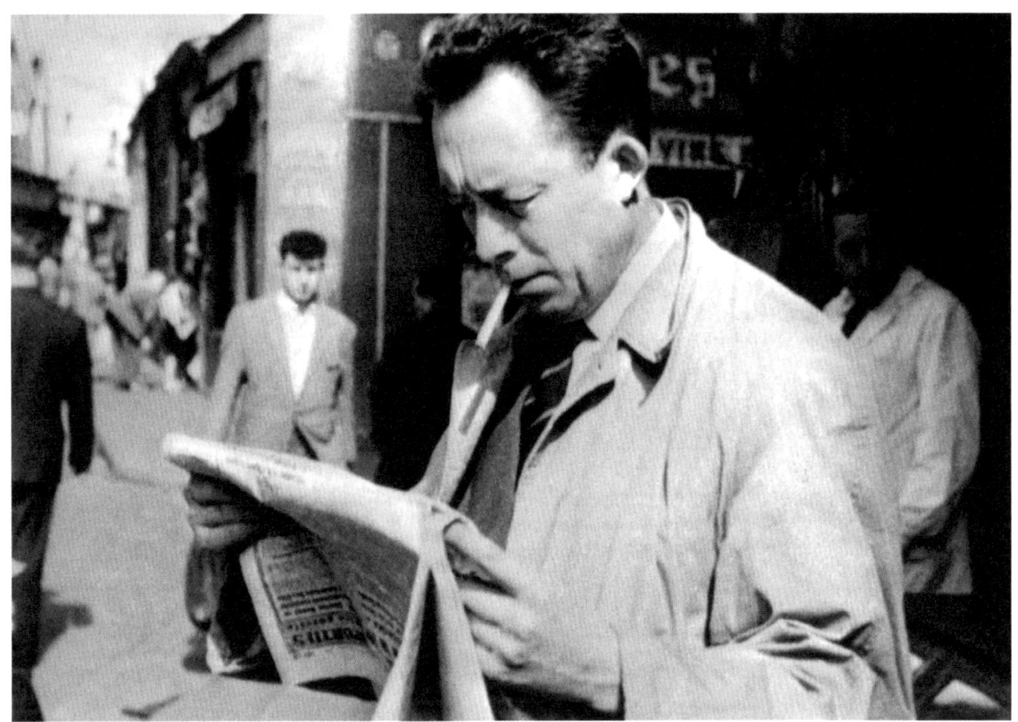

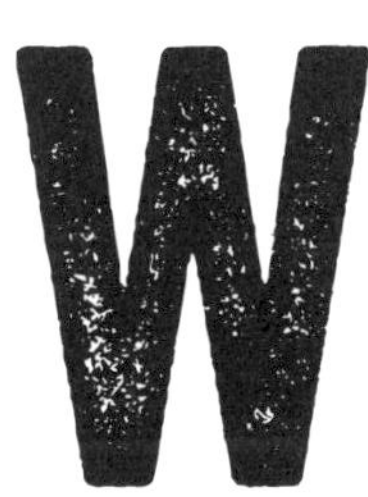
Albert Camus in Paris, 1953.

When Albert Camus returned to Algiers, in January 1956, to deliver his famous "Appeal for a Civilian Truce in Algeria", few people still believed that the carnage that was starting to grip the country could have a peaceful outcome. The Arab participants, Mohammed Lebjaoui and Amar Ouzegane, were themselves divided; to start with, they had not told the others that they were leading members of the FLN (Front de libération nationale), which was providing security to protect the event from the European ultras who had surrounded the fall-back building (the mayor having refused the use of the municipal hall) and were shouting hostile slogans. The atmosphere was so fraught that Camus delivered his text in some haste.

His speech was mocked by the Paris intellectuals, who saw in it additional proof of his lack of understanding of the meaning of history. We all know what happened next: Algeria gained independence, in a bloodbath **[cat. 44 et 132]**. History had decided: it would be "total" victory for one side, with all the terrible implications that word can have. The Appeal called for a transition to a secular, pluralistic Algerian state that would guarantee the rights of the Jewish and European minorities. Instead, as of 1963, a religious definition of nationality rapidly gained the upper hand in the newly independent state. Since then, history has followed its course: more than sixty years after the Appeal, Algeria is run by a corrupt military dictatorship, following a horrific civil war, and

Trêve pour les civils

par ALBERT CAMUS

IL n'y a pas de jour où le courrier, la presse, le téléphone même, n'apportent de terribles nouvelles d'Algérie. De toutes parts, les appels retentissent, et les cris. Dans la même matinée, voici la lettre d'un instituteur arabe dont le village a vu quelques-uns de ses hommes fusillés sans jugement, et l'appel d'un ami pour ces ouvriers français, tués et mutilés sur les lieux mêmes de leur travail. Et il faut vivre avec cela, dans ce Paris de neige et de boue, où chaque jour se fait plus pesant !

Si, du moins, une certaine surenchère pouvait prendre fin ! A quoi sert désormais de brandir les unes contre les autres les victimes du drame algérien ? Elles sont de la même tragique famille et ses membres aujourd'hui s'égorgent en pleine nuit, sans se reconnaître, à tâtons, dans une mêlée d'aveugles.

Cette tragédie d'ailleurs ne fait pas pleurer tout le monde. On en voit qui exultent, quoique de loin. Ils sermonnent, mais sous leurs airs graves, c'est toujours le même cri : « Allons ! encore plus fort ! Voyez comme celui-ci est cruel, crevez-lui donc les yeux ! » Hélas, s'il est encore en Algérie des hommes qui aient du retard dans cette course à la mort et à la vengeance, ils le rattraperont à toute allure. Bientôt l'Algérie ne sera peuplée que de meurtriers et de victimes. Bientôt les morts seuls y seront innocents.

★

JE sais : il y a une priorité de la violence. La longue violence colonialiste explique celle de la rébellion. Mais cette justification ne peut s'appliquer qu'à la rébellion armée. Comment condamner les excès de la répression si l'on ignore ou l'on tait les débordements de la rébellion ? Et inversement, comment s'indigner des massacres des prisonniers français si l'on accepte que des Arabes soient fusillés sans jugement ? Chacun s'autorise du crime de l'autre pour aller plus avant. Mais à cette logique, il n'est pas d'autre terme qu'une interminable destruction.

« Il faut choisir son camp », crient les repus de la haine. Ah ! je l'ai choisi ! J'ai choisi mon pays, j'ai choisi l'Algérie de la justice, où Français et Arabes s'associeront librement ! Et je souhaite que les militants arabes, pour préserver la justice de leur cause, choisissent aussi de condamner les massacres des civils, comme les Français, pour sauver leurs droits et leur avenir, doivent condamner ouvertement les massacres répressifs.

Quand il sera démontré que les uns et les autres sont incapables de cet effort et de la lucidité qui leur permettrait d'apercevoir leurs intérêts communs, quand il sera démontré que la France, coincée entre ses machines à sous et ses appareils à slogans, est incapable de définir une politique à la fois réaliste et généreuse, alors seulement nous désespérerons. Mais cela n'est pas encore démontré, et nous devons lutter jusqu'au bout contre les entraînements de la haine.

★

DU moins, il faut faire vite. Chaque jour qui passe ruine un peu plus l'Algérie et voue ses masses à des années de misère supplémentaires. Chaque mort sépare un peu plus les deux populations ; demain, elles ne s'affronteront plus de part et d'autre d'un fossé, mais au-dessus d'une fosse commune. Quel que soit le gouvernement qui, dans quelques semaines, abordera le problème algérien, il risque alors de se trouver devant une situation sans issue.

Il revient donc aux Français d'Algérie eux-mêmes de prendre les initiatives nécessaires. Ils craignent Paris, je le sais, et ils n'ont pas toujours tort. Mais que font-ils pendant ce temps, que proposent-ils ? S'ils ne font rien, d'autres feront pour eux, et pourquoi se plaindraient-ils ensuite ? On me dit que certains d'entre eux, éclairés d'une brusque lumière, ont choisi de soutenir Poujade. Je ne veux pas encore croire à ce qui serait un suicide pur et simple. L'Algérie a besoin d'esprit d'invention, non de slogans périmés. Elle meurt, empoisonnée par la haine et l'injustice. Elle se sauvera seulement en neutralisant sa haine par une surabondance d'énergie créatrice.

★

C'EST pourquoi il faut s'adresser une fois de plus aux Français d'Algérie pour leur dire : « Tout en défendant vos maisons et vos familles, ayez la force supplémentaire de reconnaître ce qui est juste dans la cause de vos adversaires, et de condamner ce qui ne l'est pas dans la répression. Soyez les premiers à proposer ce qui peut sauver l'Algérie et établir une loyale collaboration entre les fils différents d'une même terre ! » Aux militants arabes. Au sein même de la lutte qu'ils soutiennent pour leur cause, qu'ils désavouent enfin le meurtre des innocents et qu'ils proposent, eux aussi, leur plan d'avenir !

A tous, il faut enfin crier trêve. Trêve jusqu'au moment des solutions, trêve au massacre des civils, de part et d'autre ! Tant que l'accusateur ne donne pas l'exemple, toutes les accusations sont vaines. Amis français et arabes, ne laissez pas sans réponse un des derniers appels pour une Algérie vraiment libre et pacifique, bientôt riche et créatrice ! Il n'y a pas d'autre solution, il n'y a aucune autre solution que celle dont nous parlons. Au-delà d'elle, il n'y a que mort et destruction. Des mouvements se constituent partout, je le sais, des hommes de courage, arabes et français, se regroupent. Rejoignez-les, aidez-les de toutes vos forces ! Ils sont le seul, et le dernier espoir, de l'Algérie.

A. C.

(Copyright L'Express.)

France has fallen prey to attacks committed, for the most part, by young people from the North African community in the name of radical Islam. Neither country has succeeded in banishing terrorism from its territory. So who's laughing now?

History seems to come down – albeit belatedly – on Camus' side. In 1955, he wrote: "French and Arab solidarity is inevitable, in death as in life, in destruction as in hope." Death may have won the first round of this forced solidarity, but can hope not emerge from the words of an Appeal that continues to resonate among some listeners on both shores of the Mediterranean?

Camus never thought twice about using the word "truce", his only hesitation being whether to describe it as a "blood truce", a "truce for humanity" or "a truce for civilians", before settling on "civilian truce". The phrase refers to a temporary suspension of hostilities, the spatial equivalent of which would be asylum – in other words, a safe haven or "sanctuary". We know that the family of words derived from the root *deru* in Indo-European languages also encompasses concepts such as trust. Indeed, the actual moments or spaces preserved from violence are less important than the shared commitment of the belligerents to respect them. And why would they make that commitment? Out of

Albert Camus, "For a Civilian Truce", *L'Express*, 10 January 1996. At the invitation of his liberal friends in Algeria, Camus launched his "Appel pour une trêve civile en Algérie" [Appeal for a Civilian Truce in Algeria] on 22 January 1956. Catherine and Jean Camus Collection, Fonds Albert Camus, Bibliothèque Méjanes, Aix-en-Provence. All rights reserved.

respect for civilians and, through them, out of a concern to preserve civility among people, and, ultimately, to choose civilization over barbarity. All three concepts appear to be contained in Camus's choice of "civilian" to describe the truce.

Camus's overriding wish was to preserve civilians from the growing hostilities, not only to spare their lives, but also to preserve civility as a way of life. Through the Appeal, the European liberals, the various religious authorities and several well-known Arab dignitaries wanted to prefigure the possibility of cohabitation and voice their opposition to the use of terrorism on both sides of the conflict, so as to maintain the conditions for negotiation. Through its assault on the body, the scars it sears on the mind and the bleakness it leaves in people's hearts, removing all hope of peaceful cohabitation, terrorism basically targets civility. Civil society was the main victim of the dark years of the Algerian Civil War (1992–2002), forcing people to choose between Islamists and soldiers, or to renounce their status as "free men – in other words, as men who refuse either to practise or to suffer terror".

Civility is a state: it designates the state of living in peace, within just institutions. Civilians wear no uniforms; the values they embody are not represented on any shield but rather expressed through their lives, their occupations, their pastimes and the freedom of their minds. Those values have to be embodied, not proclaimed. Civility is always practised incognito; it has no need to announce itself as such. The explanation is forthcoming only later, when the absurdity of death reveals the richness of what has been lost. The victims are random, and it is only after the event that one understands what brought them together in the same place, on the same soil. That is as true of those who gathered at the "Cercle du Progrès", in January 1956 as it is of the people sipping coffee at the cafés in Paris one November evening in 2015 or watching the Bastille Day fireworks in Nice, on 14 July of the following year. Who was not surprised to learn that one third of the victims in Nice were Muslims, a proportion much higher than that of the French Muslim population as a whole? Can there be a better example of the nameless desire to live together?

Not by chance did the perpetrators of the Milk Bar attack in Algiers, on 30 September 1956, or those who attacked Le Carillon, Le Petit Cambodge and La Bonne Bière, as well as the Bataclan concert hall in Paris on 13 November 2015, choose places of peaceful assembly. But whereas in Algiers, the attack was intended to precipitate an abrupt end to a war of independence, in Paris, the jihadists targeted civilians purely and simply because they were civilians, as it were. The students in the cafés and the spectators at the Bataclan were not singled out as representatives of a government or to exert pressure on one, nor were they targeted as members of a particular community. Much to the contrary, they embodied a dangerous diversity, which needed to be exorcized. The victims of the Strasbourg terrorist attack in December 2018 – an Italian journalist, an Afghan refugee and auto mechanic, a Thai tourist, a Polish artist – were significant because of their diversity. Perhaps they had to die to tell us, here in France, that we can be proud of the hospitality that we were unable to safeguard in these circumstances, much to our despair. Civilians are worthy not as a segment of a mass constituting a whole, nor as reluctant ambassadors of a policy, but because they embody a way of life. What exactly does that way of life consist of? Freedom, nonchalance even, pleasure, social diversity? At a deeper level, whether in terms of *otium* (i.e. leisure activities, conversations with friends, sports, music) or *negotium* (i.e. trade, the global business world targeted in New York), in every case what was attacked was the notion of exchange itself. Death became a way to exact vengeance on that symbolic exchange.

Camus understood this, seeing civilians – defined in the broadest sense of the term, that is, in the plural, as befits their plurality, and in their diversity, which underpins all policy – as an incarnation of innocence. In his eyes, no cause could justify the death of an innocent person. With their carefree attitude, civilians personify happiness and the innocence of life and their inherent right to be protected. This was not true for everyone in Algeria in 1956, which is why the Appeal sought to make true civilians of all the country's inhabitants. Nor did Camus adopt a pacifist stance (he was never a pacifist); his aim was to encourage the opening of negotiations on the basis of a shared refusal to sacrifice innocent people.

Camus did not require supporters of the Appeal to follow a common political line; rather, he wanted to awaken what unites us despite our differences. His message was aimed at those who agreed "on a single definite point", namely, that one must start by meeting, in order to save human lives and to lay the groundwork for a discussion "that will at last be reasonable". All the foundational values of democracy are encapsulated in those few simple words: assembly, rejection of violence, deliberation, reason. Several lines further down, he defines civility as "an element... that will not indulge in murder and hatred, and that dreams of a happy Algeria", in other words, an element that refuses the dictatorship of blood and that remains capable of dreaming.

Front page of the French daily *L'Écho d'Alger*, I October 1956.

Front page of the French daily *Libération*, 16 November 2015.

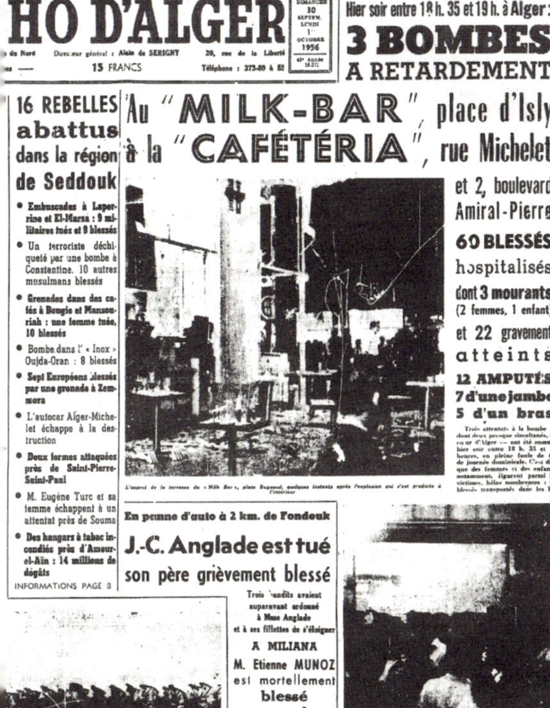

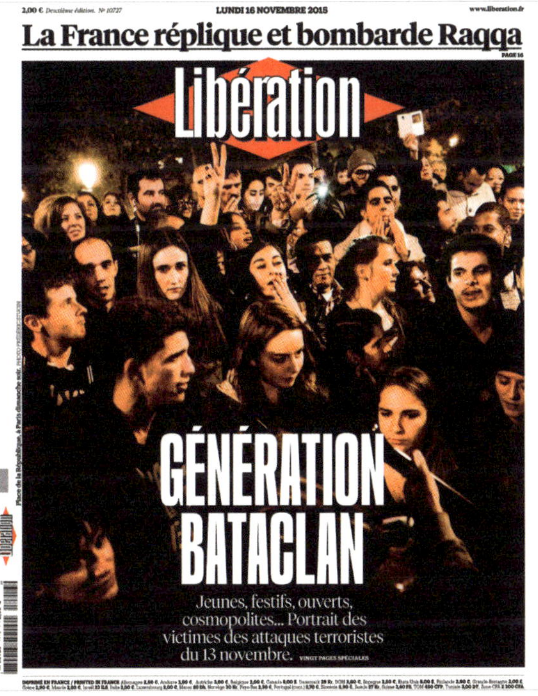

"The intentional modesty of this objective" elicits a feeling that is stronger than conviction: the will to invoke what Aristotle called political friendship, or *philia*. This is a physical phenomenon, which is why Camus ultimately located it in the land. For Camus, what unites people is love for a shared place. The land – *justissima tellus* – is the greatest source of justice, its condition, even, in the words of Virgil. To love diversity, to recognize a common fate assigned by some accident of history, which has brought people together in the same land, does not imply acceptance of the acute injustices that subsisted in Algeria in 1956. Camus knew that better than anyone, having himself denounced those injustices as early as 1938.

At the time of its reading, the Appeal was politically unrealistic, but, as we have seen, that did not prevent it from delivering a message that transcends time. That may be why it continues to resonate today. And that may also be the hallmark of major political texts: their greatest impact occurs not in the moment, in the whirlwind of history, but rather in the inner silence of those who truly seek peace and do not harbour a disturbing fascination with violence. The Appeal's message is a humanist one – I use the word advisedly – and remains as searingly topical as ever.

The violence and cries of hatred that arose outside the Cercle du Progrès where Camus read his Appeal, the mockery of intellectuals with their acute awareness of the meaning of history, the oblivion into which the text has fallen since then, have all been powerless, I believe, to weaken its message. On the contrary, they have enhanced it. Through one of those curious shifts that only history seems capable of, has time not given it as much power and relevance today, if not more, than in that tormented country at the start of the war? The Appeal was right; its timing was wrong. It came both too late and too early, after too many injustices had been committed by the colonizers, but before we could gauge the woes of the postcolonial societies that Algeria and France would eventually become, each in its own way.

Neither "truce" nor "innocence" can stand on its own; they can be understood only in opposition to their shared opposite concept, the state of nature. Innocence is not an initial state, but rather the fruit of just, even military institutions, and a constant struggle to preserve civility. Therein lies the timeless meaning of the Appeal. Life is a truce, a fragile window between the violence from which our states emerge, and which threatens to overwhelm them at any moment. The "Appeal for a Civilian Truce" is an appeal to keep that window open for as long as possible. It outlines a political programme that is still alive today, and justly so; it reminds us what the purpose of any self-respecting policy should be, namely, to construct innocence so that humans can enjoy it in peace and find happiness, at the risk of forgetting the price they have to pay.

Notes

[1] At the time of writing, there appears to be a revival of hope in Algeria, thanks to the massive, peaceful and responsible reaction of the Algerian people. May they remember the words of Friedrich Hölderlin, quoted by Camus in the epigraph of his *Summer*: "Yet you, you have been born to brilliant daylight".

[2] "Appeal for a civilian truce in Algeria", Lecture given in Algiers in February 1956, in *Resistance, Rebellion and Death*, trans. Justin O'Brien, New York, Knopf, 1969.

[3] Agnès Spiquel-Courdille, "Six récits pour un 'appel'", in Charles Poncet, *Camus et l'impossible trêve civile – suivi d'une correspondance avec Amar Ouzegane*, texts written, annotated and commented by Yvette Langrand, Christian Phéline and Agnès Spiquel-Courdille, Paris, Gallimard, 2015, p. 252.

[4] The Indo-European root *deru* initially designated wood and more generally a tree (*The American Heritage Dictionary of the English Language,* fifth edition, Indo-European Roots, Appendix 1, Houghton Mifflin Harcourt, 2019: https://www.ahdictionary.com/word/indoeurop.html.

[5] "Appeal", *op. cit.*

[6] *Ibid.*

[7] *Ibid.*

[8] Virgil, *Georgics*, II, v. 460.

100 YEARS OF MULTILATERALISM IN GENEVA

BLANDINE BLUKACZ-LOUISFERT
United Nations Library
PIERRE-ÉTIENNE BOURNEUF
United Nations Library

n 1919, the cataclysm that was the First World War gave rise to the League of Nations, the first intergovernmental organization founded to maintain peace and promote cooperation between nation-states. Its founding text, the Covenant, was adopted by the Paris Peace Conference and incorporated into the Treaty of Versailles, which was signed on 28 June 1919.

The idea of ensuring lasting peace had a long intellectual tradition, from Grotius to Jean-Jacques Rousseau **[cat. 8, 102 et 103]** and Immanuel Kant, and the "Concert of Europe" that emerged from the Congress of Vienna in 1815 provided the building blocks for the international system. But it was the trauma of 1914–18 that prompted the institutionalization of a multilateral system aimed at preserving peace.

Backed by the president of the United States, Woodrow Wilson **[cat. 127]**, Geneva was selected to host the League's seat. Wilson, the "father of the League of Nations", was convinced that Switzerland's neutrality and Geneva's tradition of hospitality offered the ideal conditions for representatives of the nations of the world to overcome the antagonisms of the Great War and meet as equals.

Although often referred to as "collective" or "concerted action" at the time, multilateralism, now as in 1919, describes a diplomatic approach aimed at maintaining relations between international actors based on adherence to a shared political project founded on the respect for a common system of norms and values. [1]

The political project set out in the Covenant had three main dimensions: disarmament, the peaceful settlement of disputes and the establishment of international solidarity (termed "collective security" in 1924 by the delegate from Czechoslovakia, Eduard Beneš). In addition, diplomatic relations were to be openly conducted on the basis of international law. The League's members were to be represented on an egalitarian basis, and all decisions would be adopted unanimously. The entire undertaking was predicated on the concept of state sovereignty.

The questions that then arise are the degree to which such an institution can act independently and the tensions that may emerge over time between national interests and multilateral cooperation. [2] As the history of the League of Nations and the United Nations has shown, the dynamics of multilateralism are complex and cannot be dissociated from the context in which the organization operates.

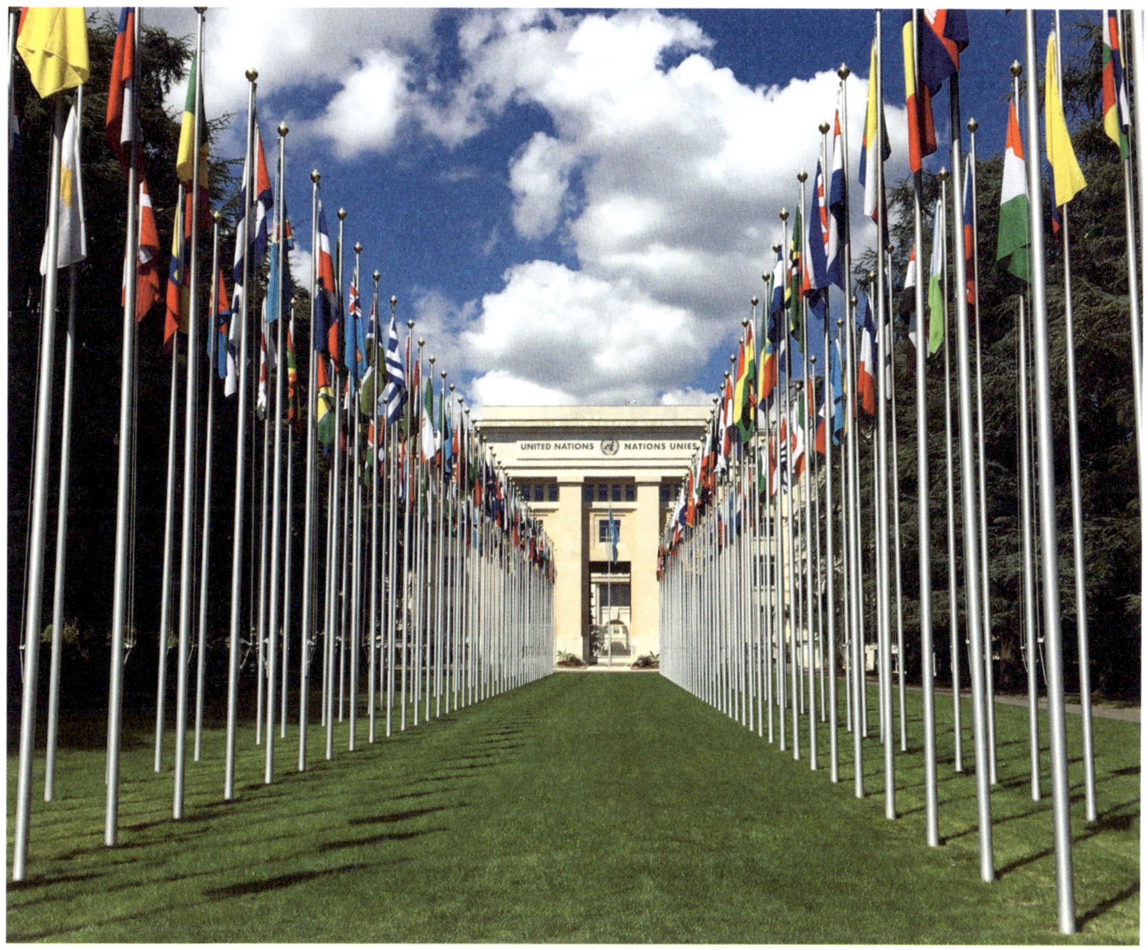

**The European headquarters
of the United Nations**,
Place des Nations, Geneva.

Uneven political results
and fruitful technical cooperation

From the outset, the League of Nations suffered setbacks, not least the
failure of the United States to join the League due to the Senate refusing to ratify membership of the organization. Despite the difficulties,
the League achieved notable success. One example was the settlement
of the Åland Islands dispute in 1921, which remains a benchmark for the
resolution of international issues involving both minority rights and territorial disputes. With a view to strengthening the Covenant, the General
Assembly adopted the "Geneva Protocol" in 1924 **[cat. 110]**. This document was intended to make arbitration mandatory: should one of the
parties refuse to abide by it, the signatories undertook to apply

collective sanctions automatically. The British government, fearing the establishment of an overly rigid system of penalties, ultimately refused to sign. That episode illustrates the latent tensions between the spirit of multilateralism and the interests of sovereign states.

The League's efforts nevertheless had encouraging results. The second half of the 1920s is associated with the "Spirit of Geneva",[3] which took the form of a series of positive developments for world peace: the Locarno Treaties (1925) **[cat. 129]**, Germany's admission to the League (1926) and the Kellogg–Briand Pact (1928) **[cat. 130]**. The draft "Memorandum on the Organization of a System of Federal European Union", submitted to the General Assembly by the delegate from France, Aristide Briand, in 1930, probably marked the high point of that spirit of cooperation **[cat. 111]**. However, the effects of the global economic crisis were already showing themselves. The draft's rejection would be a harbinger of the inward-looking approach that was to characterize the world in the 1930s.

It was in that context that the first World Disarmament Conference opened in Geneva in 1932. Eagerly anticipated by civil society, the Conference rapidly stalled, in particular because of opposition between France and Germany. Hitler's rise to power poisoned the negotiations, and Berlin withdrew from the Conference **[cat. 18]**, and from the League of Nations itself, in 1933. That failure weakened the League, which proved ineffectual when Manchuria was occupied, in 1931 **[cat. 54]**, and Italy annexed Ethiopia in 1936 **[cat. 55]**. The multilateral system put in place in 1919 had been dealt a serious blow and the League of Nations was powerless to stem the tide of events that would lead to the Second World War.

Its political failure notwithstanding, the League met with greater success when it came to "technical" cooperation. The subject is covered in only three articles of the Covenant (23 to 25), but they contain the seeds of one of the most innovative and important elements of the multilateralism the League embodied: the idea that peace could not last in a world that did not take account of social and economic concerns.

Besides establishing the International Labour Organization (ILO), in 1919, to promote social peace, the League of Nations set up a system of subsidiary bodies – on social issues, communications, health, protection of minorities and refugees, and intellectual cooperation – that would give multilateralism one of its most fruitful outlets. It was already clear that questions that went beyond national borders, and were as multidimensional as they were complex, had to be solved through heightened international cooperation within the framework of an international organization.

The experience of the League of Nations also showed that multilateralism had to be open, not just to government delegates, but also to players such as experts and civil society representatives. That multilateral dynamic created complex networks between states. [4] During the period between the wars, Geneva thus became a genuine ecosystem, a fertile breeding ground for the multilateralism that would emerge in the wake of the League of Nations.

After 1945: the time of the United Nations

Although the League of Nations was unable to maintain peace, multilateralism had taken firm root. The Charter of the United Nations echoed the collective security principles set out in the Covenant, supplementing them to give fresh impetus to multilateralism **[cat. 114]**. Drawing on the lessons of the League, the Charter prohibited recourse to force and conferred coercive authority on the Security Council. [5] The experience of the Second World War gave rise to the conviction that human rights had to be safeguarded and promoted if humanity was to progress. The structure of the new organization also incorporated economic and social development, with the establishment of the Economic and Social Council (ECOSOC). The concept of positive and lasting peace (the elimination of the causes of disagreement between peoples), as opposed to negative peace (the absence of war), was the order of the day. [6]

The United Nations established its headquarters in New York. The Palais des Nations hosted its centre in Europe, which was to become the United Nations Office at Geneva in 1966. Even though it long denied the fact, the United Nations was broadly constructed on the experience of the League. Thanks to the multilateral ecosystem inherited from the League, and to the heightened role it played in the context of the Cold War, Geneva provided a unique space for the development of United Nations activities. The city is currently home to the headquarters of many United Nations bodies, several of which continue League activities, notably the World Health Organization (WHO, the successor to the Health Organization) **[cat. 116]**, the Office of the United Nations High Commissioner for Refugees (UNHCR, whose precursor was the Nansen International Office for Refugees), and the World Intellectual Property Organization (WIPO), which has its roots in the International Committee on Intellectual Cooperation. The ILO and the International Telecommunication Union (ITU), for their part, survived the League of Nations and have continued to work within the United Nations system.

While New York is the United Nations centre for political affairs, Geneva has steadily expanded its position as a global centre for diplomatic conferences and for the negotiation and drafting of treaties. The city's name is often associated with peace talks held at the Palais des Nations. The Disarmament Conference, which has met there since 1979, has produced numerous agreements limiting and even banning the use of certain weapons. Thanks to the United Nations bodies headquartered there, Geneva is also an essential hub for humanitarian action, with the United Nations Office for the Coordination of Humanitarian Affairs (OCHA), and human rights, with the activities of the Human Rights Council and the Office of the United Nations High Commissioner for Human Rights.

United Nations multilateral activities in Geneva also focus on improving the well-being of peoples through economic cooperation and development. The United Nations Economic Commission for Europe (UNECE) facilitates economic cooperation across the continent by promoting dialogue on subjects such as climate change, gender and road safety. The work of the United Nations Conference on Trade and Development (UNCTAD) promotes and supports the economic development of the least developed countries.

The end of the Cold War saw the emergence of a complex world in which the concept of development has gradually been enhanced with criteria that take account of countries' progress on the global, human and social fronts simultaneously. The ecosystem of "international Geneva" is the ideal setting for the implementation, by 2030, of the 17 Sustainable Development Goals, which are based on a multilateral approach encompassing not only the Member States, but also civil society, the private sector and the scientific and academic communities.

Geneva, the home of multilateralism

As Michael Møller, director-general of the United Nations Office at Geneva, is wont to say, "Everything that is done here, in Geneva, has a direct impact on every person on this planet, in any twenty-four-hour period."[7] That impact, which is often unacknowledged, is the outcome of the process started by the League of Nations. Although it was unable to discharge its principal mission, the organization founded in 1919 marked a fundamental stage in the development of multilateralism.

Today, "international Geneva" and multilateralism are indissociable and mutually reinforcing. The commemoration of the hundredth anniversary of the founding of the League of Nations and of "One hundred years of multilateralism in Geneva" provide a perfect opportunity for coming to grips with the changing nature of a phenomenon that has always had to adapt in the face of collective challenges. Its fragility is not to be underestimated. The experience of the late 1930s showed that multilateralism could not be taken for granted. In a world marked by the effects of globalization and by the growing interdependence of international players, it is today – more than ever before – an indispensable instrument.

Notes

[1] See Alexandra Novosseloff, "L'essor du multilatéralisme", *Annuaire français de relations internationales*, vol. 3, 2002, pp. 303–12.

[2] Philippe Braillard and Mohammad-Reza Djalili, *Les relations internationales*, Paris, PUF, 2016, p. 39.

[3] See Robert de Traz, *L'esprit de Genève*, Grasset, Paris, 1929.

[4] *Ibid.*, p. 80.

[5] Robert Kolb, *Commentaire sur le Pacte de la Société des Nations*, Brussels, Bruylant, 2015, p. 1340.

[6] *Ibid.*, p. 1339.

[7] See unog.ch/80256EE600583A0B/ (httpPages)/728D8525F-E578883C1257DD9003716F6?OpenDocument&cntxt=74E08&cookielang=fr.

THE TRUTH COMMISSION: AN INNOVATION FOR PEACE

MARK FREEMAN
Institute for Integrated Transitions (Barcelona)

RON SLYE
Seattle University School of Law

ruth commissions have become a standard part of the arsenal of transitional justice: a body of theory and practice focused on confronting legacies of mass abuse, when wars end or tyrants fall.

Transitional justice encompasses a broad array of attempts to make sense of a whole series of national wounds – moral, legal, political and psychological. When done well, it offers a chance to begin the national healing process on an honest, humane footing.

Transitional justice provides a nuanced response to the perennial debate confronting societies in transition: is it better or worse for a society to actively confront a legacy of abuse during the transition, given so many other priorities and so many potential risks?

A number of competing, and sometimes contradictory, goals are at play. First, there is strong insistence on the need for some form of criminal sanction against the main architects of mass violence. Second, there is an expectation to provide some form of accountability and reintegration for foot soldiers and others who participated in the violations of the past. Third, there is a need to provide acknowledgment and reparations to victims and survivors. Fourth, these and other goals must be furthered in a way that is sensitive to the practical complications in transitions that limit the scope for the sanctions and other justice mechanisms, which, in more ordinary times, would be applied.

Truth commissions can, and often do, play a fundamental role in balancing these and other important societal goals during a transition. While some view truth commissions as an alternative to criminal trials, they are generally more effective as supplements to such trials.

In addition to any trials that may take place, truth commissions can offer a custom-built, non-judicial vehicle for reckoning with contested narratives. They may help to overcome false narratives of victimizers and victims; provide a reckoning with respect to a past of mass violence; and further reconciliation and national unity. However, in other cases, they may reinforce sectarian splits by conducting investigations that lack the basic hallmarks of independence and objectivity, or collapse early due to political interference.

It is important to be clear about what a truth commission is not. It is not a formal judicial tribunal; rather, it is a commission of inquiry with more flexibility and a broader mandate than a traditional tribunal. In a truth commission, there is no courtroom and there are no plaintiffs. There is no prosecution, no defence, no trial, and there are no sentences.

There have been over forty truth commissions since the first genuine one was created in 1983, in Argentina. Between 1990 and 2004, a critical mass of influential commissions operated globally (for example in Chile, El Salvador, South Africa, Guatemala, Sierra Leone, Timor-Leste, Peru and Morocco).

To this day, South Africa remains the most internationally influential commission **[cat. 141]**. In operation during the 1990s, it changed forever how people think about truth commissions. Its work involved taking individual statements from survivors and witnesses; providing public and private spaces for victims to engage with their perpetrators; using the media to publicize its activities; and holding national hearings on a variety of themes, including the role of the business community, the legal profession and the medical profession in supporting and opposing apartheid.

Previously, the final report was viewed as the primary outcome of a truth commission. After South Africa, the process took centre stage.

One of the most prominent, and controversial, aspects of the South African truth commission was its power to grant amnesty to perpetrators for their crimes. The result is that many people wrongly associate amnesties with truth commissions. For example, armed groups often express initial support for truth commissions because of the legal closure it is presumed to offer through an amnesty. Yet South Africa is the only example of a commission empowered to grant individual amnesties – a necessity of its particular transition. Other commissions lack this attribute, while a few have merely had the power to recommend amnesty.

Truth commissions are victim-centred. Their principal task is to put victims' voices and experiences under the national spotlight, to humanize the costs of past war or repression. Yet, commissions must do more. If they are unable to attract the participation of a conflict's main political and armed actors – in the form of document-sharing, private meetings, and public hearings – they will fail to contribute to a more informed and inclusive history of the past, and probably end up producing new resentments and new problems.

"Truth" is obviously a central objective of any truth commission. But it is also a precarious one. In countries where violations have occurred on a massive scale over several decades, there is no way for a truth commission to "resolve" more than a tiny percentage of the global pool of cases. The smart solution is to focus, primarily, on *patterns* of violations and *emblematic cases* in order to illuminate the main impacts

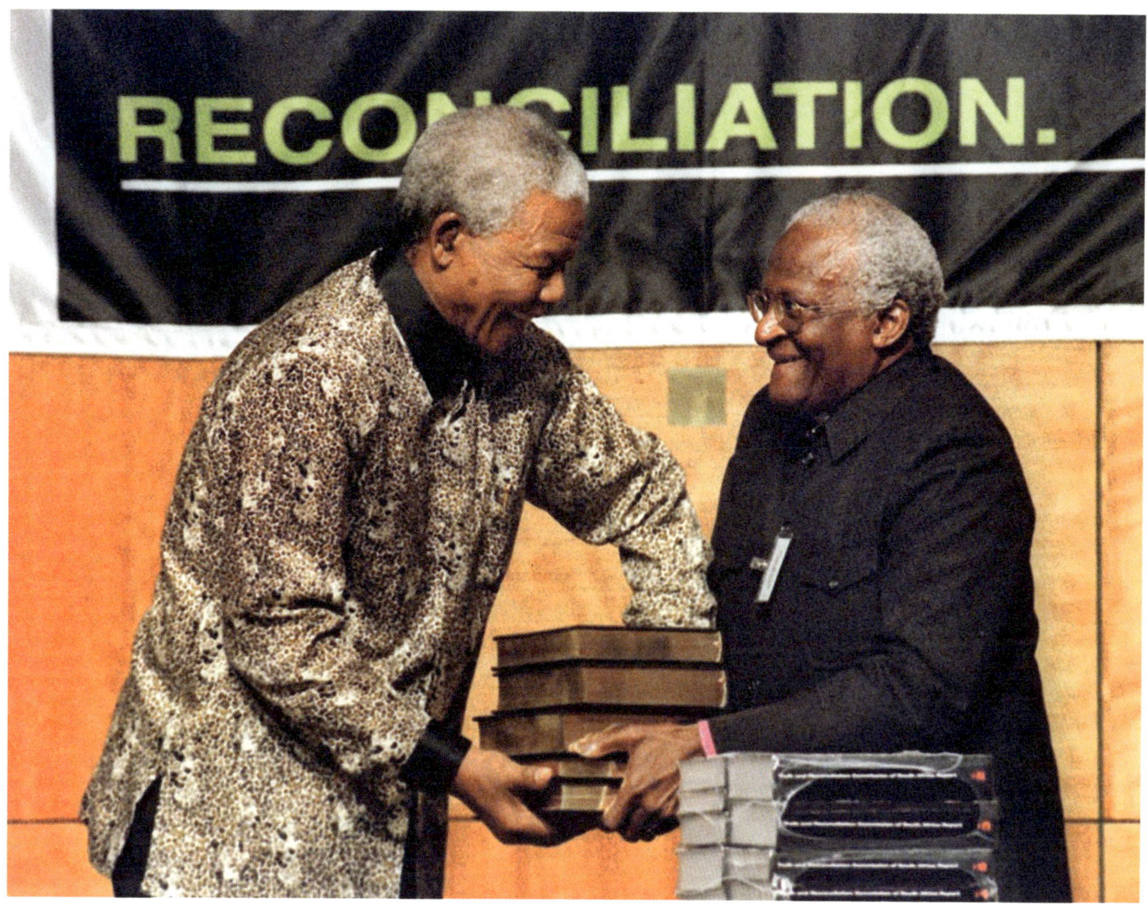

Archbishop Desmond Tutu presents Nelson Mandela with the final report of the Truth and Reconciliation Commission, on 29 October 1998, in Pretoria (South Africa). The report detailed the human rights violations committed by many political parties while the country was ruled by the National Party. Upon receiving it, Mandela acknowledged that the wounds inflicted during the time of political repression were too deep to be resolved by the Commission alone.

produced on victims and the society as a whole. A good commission should provide a master narrative – macro truths – based on a multitude of carefully investigated micro-truths drawn especially from victims' stories and accounts.

While establishing the truth is a logical end goal, it is also the means to a higher end. *Acknowledgment* of the truth – by those whose actions produced the worst atrocities – should be the first-order objective. However, such a result often comes years later. Thus, a second-order objective, more realistic in the short term, is to "reduce the number of lies that can be circulated unchallenged in public discourse".[1]

To achieve this, truth commissions must work with the greatest care, multidisciplinarity and impartiality possible; failing that, they can generate pretexts for new conflict, by making it easy for demagogues to politicize their results.

No truth commission activity has more impact than its public hearings. These are platforms for the truths that "must be heard". Victim hearings, in particular, reach beyond statistics and facts. They convey emotions and hard truths that give everyone pause. They make the public wonder "how did we ever tolerate this?" and "how can we ensure that this never happens again in our country?" At their best, public hearings have the power to penetrate the deepest reaches of the individual and collective conscience – something no final report can achieve.

Serious and continuous media coverage – TV, radio, and print – is also essential. Truth commissions must build and sustain cordial, active relationships with the media, sharing information as openly as circumstances permit, ensuring privileged access to all public hearings and encouraging news agencies to designate reporters for the commission's duration. Such measures do not contradict the media's prerogative to remain critical, but they help make the media critical partners, rather than critical adversaries.

Time is another factor: a truth commission should ideally operate for a maximum of three years, otherwise it will lose the attention of the public. The commission needs to serve as a brief, but deep, inquiry into "what happened", "why", "how" and – just as importantly – "where do we go from here". Rather than producing conditions for deeper dwelling on the past, a truth commission should primarily function as a springboard to the future.

Part of the appeal of truth commissions is that, in the midst of division and trauma, they can be vehicles for meaningful public interaction of a wide and creative variety. Beyond public hearings for individual victims or perpetrators, commissions can organize national vision exercises (as in Sierra Leone), photography exhibitions (as in Peru), thematic round tables (as in Morocco) and more. A commission can be the centre of gravity for the conversations that a society needs to both turn the page and begin writing a new one, offering a passageway to dignified debate, and ultimately, greater acknowledgment.

A good truth commission will actively publicize its mandate, incentivize participation and decentralize operations into the most violence-affected zones. It will facilitate participation with all available means, so that afterwards no essential actor can seriously claim "you never gave us a chance to tell our story". A commission must model the inclusive society that, sooner or later, it is bound to call for.

Most of the work of a commission nevertheless remains invisible to the public. It involves taking statements, in private, from victims and other deponents who choose to come forward. Typically, this is the

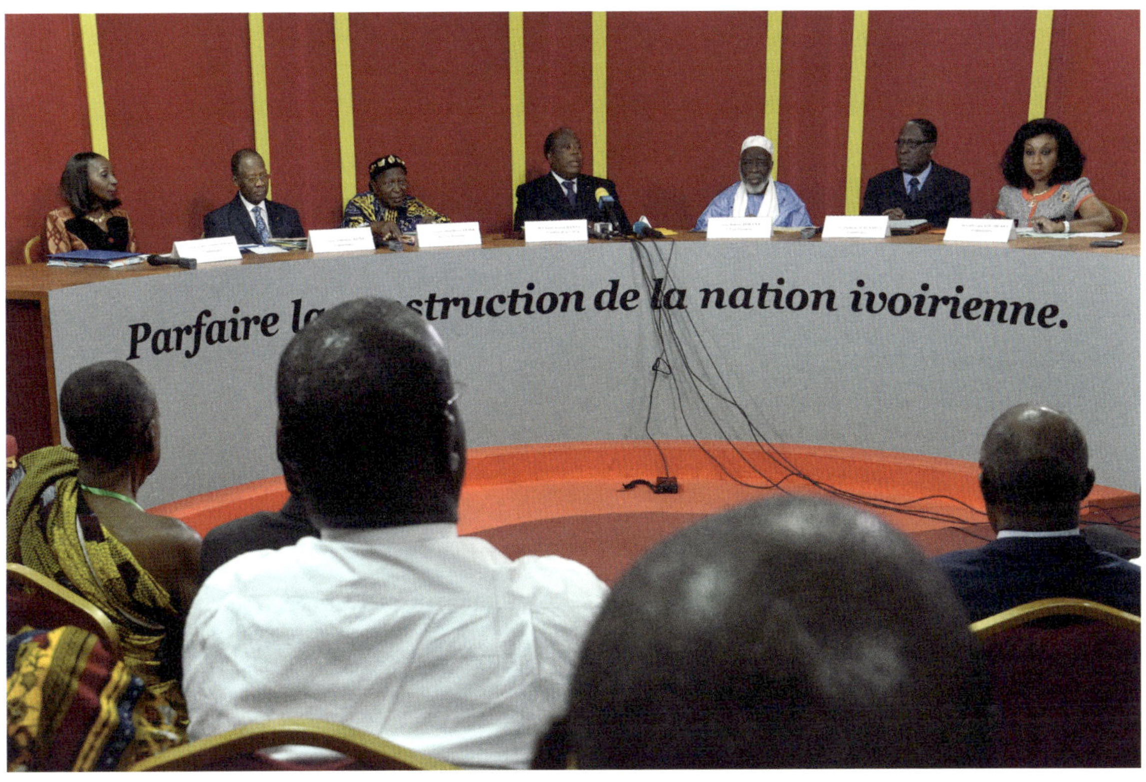

On September 8, 2014, in Abidjan, Charles Konan Banny, president of the Dialogue, Truth and Reconciliation Commission, attends the opening session before the start of the hearings of perpetrators and victims of acts of violence that took place during the various political crises that rocked the Ivory Coast from 2000 to 2011.

only moment of direct contact between a victim and the commission, since only a small percentage of those interviewed will have the opportunity to present their testimony at a public hearing. For this reason, a truth commission must make the moment count.

But public insecurity sometimes gets in the way, as fears of coming forward with testimonies persist. As such, a state committed to truth-telling must be prepared to respond rapidly and robustly to any acts of violence or intimidation during the transition. Otherwise the truth will be a thin patchwork that precludes the deeper debate and recovery a commission can bring about.

However, by far the most interesting thing about truth commissions is this: the *less* a truth commission resembles a court, the *more* benefits (legal, political and psychosocial) it will deliver to everyone, and the *less* it will cost.

Unlike criminal trials, which by their nature are perpetrator-centred, truth commissions put victims' voices and experiences under the national spotlight, to humanize the costs of past war or repression. In doing so, they can serve as vehicles for public reflection and interaction of a far wider variety (for example, through public hearings, traditional reconciliation ceremonies and more).

As such, in conflict-affected societies, in which institutions still lack the legitimacy to generate these kinds of interactions, a truth commission – by nature a transitional body – can become an epicentre for the conversations that a society needs to have. It can serve as a platform for dignified debate and help generate a minimal consensus about key events of the past and inclusive directions for the future.

Yet even a good truth commission risks producing a national depression, as its testimonies are mostly devastating. It is surprising, therefore, that nearly every commission mandate fails to put a spotlight on positive stories. For conflict-affected states in transition, it would be a welcome innovation if, along with the stories of victims, a commission was directed to pay attention to the roles and stories of ordinary citizens and leaders who at great personal risk crossed sectarian lines and acted honourably in the haze of war or tyranny.

A final frontier is impact. Although some of a truth commission's actions can certainly be measured – for example, truth-seeking involves

Managua, Nicaragua, 11 May 2018. A young man gazes at a banner portraying representatives of the Truth Commission charged with investigating the murders of young protesters during anti-government demonstrations. The social and political crisis resulted in about fifty deaths over twenty-four days, most of them between 18 and 22 April 2018.

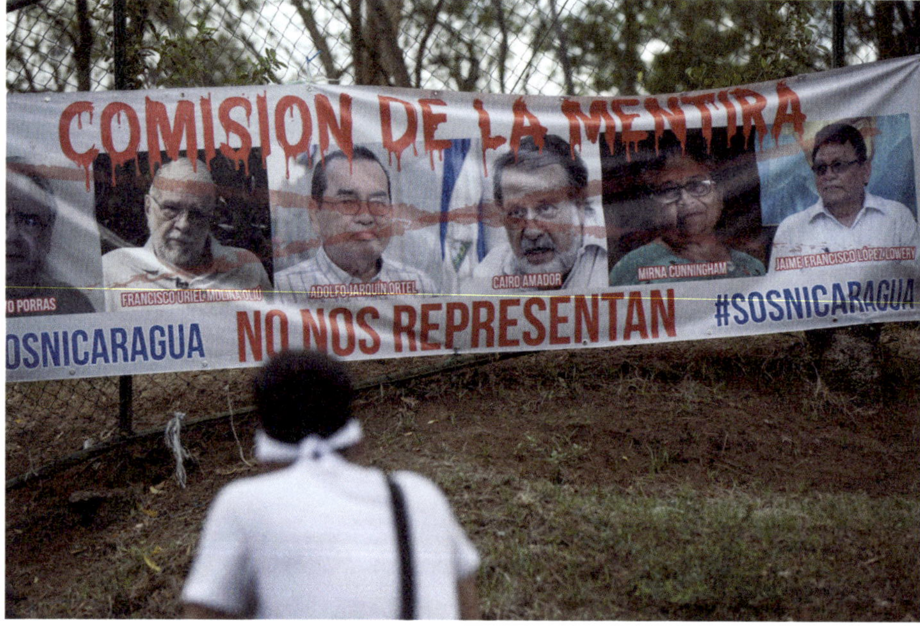

quantifiable forms of testimony, investigation, exhumation and so on, while truth-telling involves quantifiable exercises of public hearing, reports, etc. – the qualitative impact on victims, perpetrators and society is necessarily more difficult to distil. Yet it is qualitative impact that will define the most important legacy of a truth commission.

As such, if the full potential of these innovative mechanisms is to be measured and realized, there is no escaping the task of developing meaningful tools for qualitative assessment. Without that, any conclusions based upon a truth commission's legacy and impact constitute little more than guesswork and conjecture.

Notes

[1] Michael Ignatieff, "Articles of Faith", in *Index on Censorship 5*, (1996), p. 113.

THE ORESTEIA IN THE TWENTY-FIRST CENTURY: THE SNAKE IN THE BELLY

LEÏLA KILANI
Film-maker

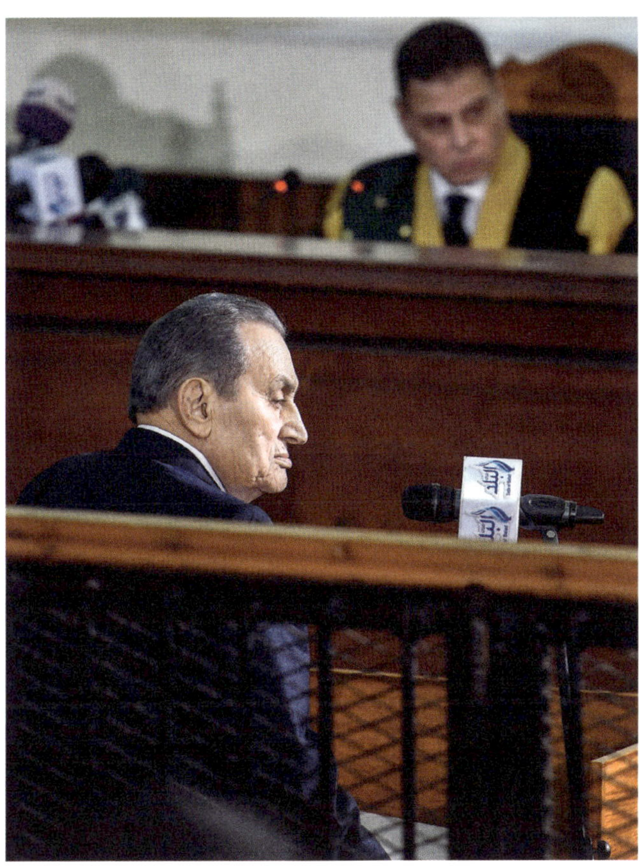

**At a trial of members
of the Muslim Brotherhood**
on 26 December 2018, in Cairo,
Judge Mohammed Shirin Fahmi
listens to the testimony of former
president Hosni Mubarak, ousted
following the popular uprising
of 2011.

The action takes place in Cairo. The time is the present, 26 December 2018. Two former presidents find themselves facing one another in court. Hosni Mubarak, the former *raïs*, is giving evidence for the first time against Mohamed Morsi, former head of state and a member of the Muslim Brotherhood, who has been in prison since his overthrow in 2013. Cameras are allowed at the hearing, and state television shows images of the pair: Mubarak, a mummified old gent, ninety years of age, in make-up and a dark suit, facing Morsi, in a metal-and-glass cage, wearing prison overalls. Morsi is accused of having orchestrated prison escapes and infiltrations across the eastern border of the Sinai during the uprising that forced Hosni Mubarak to resign, in February 2011.

"Injustice is silent, justice cries out."

Mubarak himself had been sentenced to life imprisonment for his crackdown on demonstrations, but in 2017 he was acquitted and then released. In the verdict that cleared him, the judge cited "a procedural error". One by one, all the charges against the former president were dropped. Only the evidence favourable to him, given by security agents and former regime officials, was admitted – the evidence from the victims was dismissed. The crimes committed by the security forces were reduced to mere "individual acts committed by the police officers in view of the exceptional circumstances and the large number of demonstrators". The show must go on!

Justice must not only be done, it must be seen to be done. That is its *raison d'être:* to lay down, or to reaffirm, a norm for the whole of society. And at the hearing where Mubarak gave his evidence, the proceedings were visible. The hearing's significance for the regime, however, and their intentions for it, were elusive. At issue were the roots of "the evil" of an imported war, the fights against the internal and external enemy that split the Egyptian psyche – believing in justice, in the way a person believes in the theatre, also means you have to believe in its cathartic properties, its political essence, its relationship with history and myth. And who believes in that kind of justice?

Vertigo. Dizziness. Widespread sluggishness.
Hundreds of kilometres from Cairo, stuck in the Sinai desert in a centre that no tourist ever visits any more, two caretakers, two *baouabs,* half-heartedly comment on the scene. What will Mubarak's evidence mean for everyday life in Egypt? What break with the past might Morsi's sentence represent? The theatre of justice? A parody. The lesson of justice? Vanished into thin air. The courtroom as a place for exploring evil? Laughter. *Al waqi qatala al mantiq*, "Reality has killed Reason": a slogan from the Tahrir Square revolution, sold to tourists on bits of wood. The holy alliance between spectacle and merchandise predicted by Guy Debord has come to pass: "Mubarak's testimony won't even rate a *nokta* [a joke] on Facebook", jeer the *baouabs* – liberated spectators, critical and dissatisfied. Will it all end in tears? Post-modern punk disillusionment in the Egyptian street, from *ma'alesh* to *malou* – translation: doesn't matter. SO WHAT? Fuck it. It's like a tragedy: suspension of disbelief doesn't work any more in that cardboard theatre of a courthouse over there.

This grim disillusionment had been preceded, eight years earlier, by feverish zeal. Ben Ali had been brought down in Tunisia, followed by Mubarak in Egypt. The fuse had been lit, something was happening, something was brutally challenging the paradigm of the "Arab street" condemned to live forever by the personality cult of its leader. Whether he had called himself supreme sovereign (*'ahil*), leader (*za'im*), president (*rais*), guide (*qa'id*) or even brother (*akh*), the caricature of the Eastern potentate was toppling. The Arab world was allowed to fanta-

× ×

size about bringing the Father, the Power, to trial.

Then comes a strange confession, murmured with lowered eyes by one of the caretakers: "My nephew is being detained unjustly in an army jail. Our martyrs are our sons, and our *Takfiris*[1] are our neighbours. Who will give us justice? An eye for an eye – the law of talion?" Despite the evidence, mounting since 2015, of violations, torture and other forms of repression, most local and international players have given Egypt their unconditional support. Of prosecution for the abuses committed by the army, of justice, there is no sign.

At the heart of the discussion lies the question of impunity. In a single regime, how are individual and collective responsibilities linked? Can we still dream of ascribing every serious breach of the law to a category of political violence? For political crimes, can we aspire to judicial proceedings – can we determine what the circumstances were, what methods were used, who was responsible? Can we still fantasize about justice and reconciliation in Egypt?

War and peace

The international community has never had so many opportunities to judge its dictators as it has since the Arab Spring. But the chambers of the International Criminal Court, which punishes the perpetrators of the most heinous war crimes, have so far not heard any proceedings against "Arab" dictators. Among those notable by their absence are the Syrian president, Bashar al-Assad, even though the United Nations High Commissioner for Human Rights has publicly accused him of committing crimes against his own people. One who was charged, by the International Criminal Court, with acts of genocide and crimes against humanity – Sudanese president Omar al-Bashir – is more than enjoying his freedom: he puts himself forward as the go-to person of Arab diplomacy. Saddam Hussein was tried and hanged in his own country for some of his crimes. His trial, however, was tainted by irregularities, and became a parody of justice, culminating in the hanging of the dictator amid taunts and cries of joy. After fifteen years of existence, the International Criminal Court has a lacklustre record, with barely a handful of seconds-in-command convicted. The acquittal of Laurent Gbagbo, former president of Côte d'Ivoire, was the last straw. The Court now appears to have lost credibility in the eyes of the general public, and the international arena seems bereft of the great mythical narratives so badly needed by international justice.

Death and life of a utopia: the snake is in the belly

I grew up in Morocco during the "Years of Lead", in an outwardly peaceful-looking country that was paralysed by the fear of political repression – a country silenced. As a child, as a teenager, like all Moroccans, I learned to keep quiet. Like all Moroccans, I learned to be afraid. As an adult, as a film-maker, at the heart of my questions and obsessions, the political is intertwined with the domestic; violence and crime are fused together by the forces of law and order. In 2004, the King of Morocco set up an Equity and Reconciliation Commission to inquire into state violence during the Years of Lead. How could society be reconciled if the truth were told and yet, at the same time, the torturers went unpunished? Morocco answered this question in its own way, by refusing to allow the torturers into the public arena, and by organizing public hearings for the victims in what were intended to be cathartic moments for society as a whole. From one personal account to another, from one tale of suffering to another, the power of words stifled for so long spread throughout the public space. And every Moroccan was duty-bound to commune with the victims. Nothing was said about responsibilities, as it was forbidden to name any torturers, up to the highest echelons of the state. By centring solely on the victims, this mechanism put the public in the position of voyeur, looking on as one personal tragedy followed another without ever becoming a political fact. What did this story-telling performance by victims really contribute to the building of a new nation, purified of its political crimes? The trials that will never be held – might they have healed the victims? Was justice still capable of preventing the repetition of a crime? Is it possible to mend history? Did the victims feel that financial reparation brought them the recognition they had been seeking?

Believing. Creating forms. My film accompanied four families for three years in their quest for clarification. Everyone was faced with the edict dropped from heaven, *aka* the state: bring memories back up to the surface, say what has been walled off in silence, understand the enigmas, grasp the fate of the elders, and their commitment, and one's own. Mourn the departed; mourn, too, one's own errant existence. Every secret unveiled opened onto another, falling like dominos until it was the family – with its links, its provisional legends and its comforts – that was teetering towards the abyss. At the same time, it seemed possible to gamble on rebuilding. That is probably what transitional justice means: the possibility of a story. That speech is possible does not mean it will be fluent – the path to reappropriating a language, using a mechanism as catalyst, is a painful one. The very young utopia of transitional justice is an incomparable "medium" for reinventing links

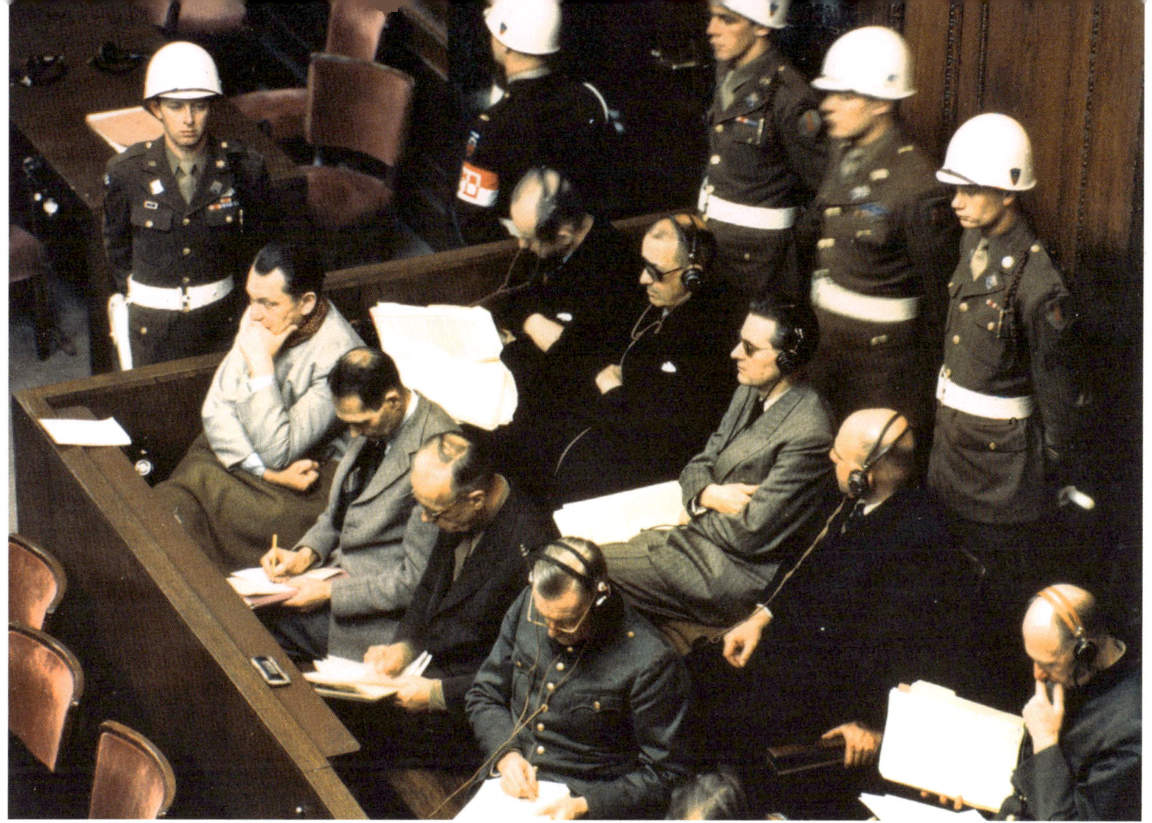

The Nuremberg trials, organized by the Allied forces after World War II to try Nazi war criminals, took place between 20 November 1945 and 1 October 1946. Sitting in the dock are Goering, Hess, von Ribbentrop, and Keitel (front row) and Dönitz, Raeder, von Schirach, Sauckel and Jodl (back row).

and social fictions; for looking at the stories and forms that might be used to describe an individual's relationship with society; for staging, in a performance, the adversarial relationship that can exist between laws that are transient, situation-bound, and those that are eternal. This conflict makes one aware of belonging to a humanity that goes beyond the limits of society. From the political to the domestic – once forcibly intertwined, their ties now loosened in the public arena – the film shows destinies, not one of which is safe from the legacy of history.

Going back to the sources of this utopia of justice, of law in the face of barbarism. And unspooling the thread of a genealogy rooted in the Nuremberg Trials: the Eichmann trial, the Barbie trial, the trial of Milošević for the former Yugoslavia, the Duch trial for Cambodia, the Mubarak trial... How can contemporary society still continue to believe it can contain the barbarism of the world within the precincts of the International Court? How, today, can societies confront their criminal past? Can the quest for justice be sacrificed in the name of other social aims, such as reconciliation? Can we introduce the rule of law while glossing over the crimes of the past? And on the other hand, should the perpetrators be punished if doing so might jeopardize a burgeoning democracy? With its truth commissions and redress mechanisms, transitional justice frees our legal imagination. It invents other ways of dispensing justice. In devastating situations – after war crimes or genocide – countries haunted by ethical and political fears have set up a new judicial arena. A new kind of justice has been invented: one with a different definition of the role of the judge, the function of punishment (no longer necessarily penal) and the place of victims and emotions. Transitional justice is not a model, but further proof that, for responding to political violence, a different "staging matrix" is possible.

Judging/creating: two inextricably linked paradigms

Creating new forms to meet new requirements of justice. There is no special vantage point from which to look at the world. "A map of the world that does not include Utopia is not worth even glancing at", said Oscar Wilde. In Diffa, Niger came up with its own solution: dozens of men and women suspected of belonging to the armed group Boko Haram were tried in the area where they had committed their crimes. It was the first attempt at this type of procedure in the region, which was also where the accused were from. This was in July 2018. It was a time when people were trying for reconciliation and making efforts to build a sustainable peace. Diffa is a small town, in a country that is not one of those power brokers whose sword hovers over the international community: here was a history lesson, and faith in humanity. When Africa reinvents the world... Niger takes its lost children by the hand, and they return home repentant. While France and other countries have become bogged down in the impossible task of integrating former ISIS "returnees or renegades", Niger – emotionally fractured, most certainly – tries to deliver a valuable message of concord. But how to escape "an eye for an eye" and go back to the law? How to avoid mistaking impunity for amnesty?

On the eve of the mobile court hearings, lengthy discussions take place between the NGO mediator and the head of a family, sitting on a mat, protected from the heat behind the walls of a refugee camp with no furniture. A mother of seventeen children, most of whom had joined the ranks of Boko Haram, kidnapped by their own brother. Two of her sons had escaped being forcibly enrolled in the armed group by the same brother. Unjustly imprisoned by the army, they were getting ready for their trial. Their mother's voice is heard, describing the barbarism of which the family's children have been both victims and perpetrators: "Whether they be a criminal or victims, they are all our children. The snake is in the belly." Mysterious, enigmatic words – but they create a meaning, they make history, they teach a lesson. And we find ourselves believing. Believing in the heady possibility of a form of justice and reconciliation. In public, the mother will explore no further her lost memories, her spoiled moments. What cannot be imagined is the emotion stirred by listening to those few words from that mother, looking at justice from inside her belly, in the white light of the African summer sky. The gentle cruelty, both ancient and contemporary, dissolving the judicial structure in the landscape by engaging it in a quasi-spiritual dialogue with the elements. An African *Oresteia* is in progress. Restorative justice. A healing justice that binds together the perpetrator, the victim and the community to involve all the parties in rehabilitation and in making reparation for the crime. The snake is in the belly.

War, peace, court proceedings – we are at the core of the issues facing the contemporary world. "A story is a mirror held while walking along a path." So we cannot but be illuminated by the *Oresteia*, so obviously a godsend. The work begins at the dawn of time with ancient killing laws and ends with the (perhaps utopian) birth of democracy.

The *Oresteia* is the only one of Aeschylus' trilogies to have come down to us complete. In *The Libation Bearers*, the second play, Aeschylus narrates the death of Clytemnestra and Aegisthus at the hands of Orestes, the son of Clytemnestra and Agamemnon; spurred on by his sister Electra, Orestes avenges the death of their father. In *The Eumenides*, the last of the three plays, Aeschylus tells how Orestes flees, pursued by the Erinyes – furies acting as the hounds of Clytemnestra, who wants him put to death. And that is when everything abruptly changes.

The goddess Athena, protector of the Athenian city-state, rises up to interrupt the cycle of vengeance. She intercedes, and orders the setting up of a tribunal of elected citizens – it is they who will try Orestes. In so doing, she ends the exercise of private, personal justice, where bloodshed leads to further bloodshed. She creates public justice, and establishes a democratic society.

Aeschylus tells the story of this transition. He feels astonishingly close, and his questions seem familiar. Greek tragedy remains acutely relevant because it asks about the links between the political and the religious, about reason, and violence, and justice, about the interconnections between the individual and the community, and how society is organized. "Neither anarchy nor tyranny."

Utopia is not dead. The debate between that old law and a new one that is both beautiful and problematic – the law of discussion and persuasion – remains an ancient memory, while at the same time perfectly fitting contemporary reality. In this ferment, the constant reinvention of transitional justice, and its story, is a challenge that must be tackled. It is a work in progress, open and uplifting.

Note

[1] *Takfiris*: Islamic extremists who accuse other Muslims or adherents of another Abrahamic faith of apostasy.

× ×

*When religions preach peace and people
commit to building a more peaceful world.*

96
Confucius (551–479 BC)
[*Works*] (Chinese), [China],
[unnamed], 1684
Cologny, Martin Bodmer Foundation

In Chinese cosmology, peace is the natural order of things. War is an exceptional situation, a measure that the emperor or one of his emissaries may resort to for one purpose only: to *restore* the peaceful order of things. According to *the Book of Odes (Shijing* – xıᵉ-vııᵉ, eleventh to seventh century BC), traditionally believed to have been compiled by Confucius (500 BC), all the lands in the world were initially entrusted to the emperor of China: "under the wide heaven, there is no land that is not the Emperor's and within the sea boundaries of the land, there is none who is not a subject of the Emperor." Under these terms, and pending the emperor's benevolent peace and world order, war could be waged only to quell internal rebellion or to repel an invasion of China or its vassals by the barbarians.
Only if the barbarians refused to accept the benefits of Chinese culture and continued their attacks, must the emperor "deal with the tribes of the West and the North and … punish them", Confucius wrote. In the Chinese tradition embodied by Confucius, war was thus tantamount to unwarranted, wrongful intervention. Invading barbarians were best dealt with by subjugating and integrating them into the Chinese world system. So long as they did not bother China, the emperor would not attempt to persuade them of their cultural inferiority. Coercion was neither noble nor necessary in Chinese eyes. **G. B.-N.**

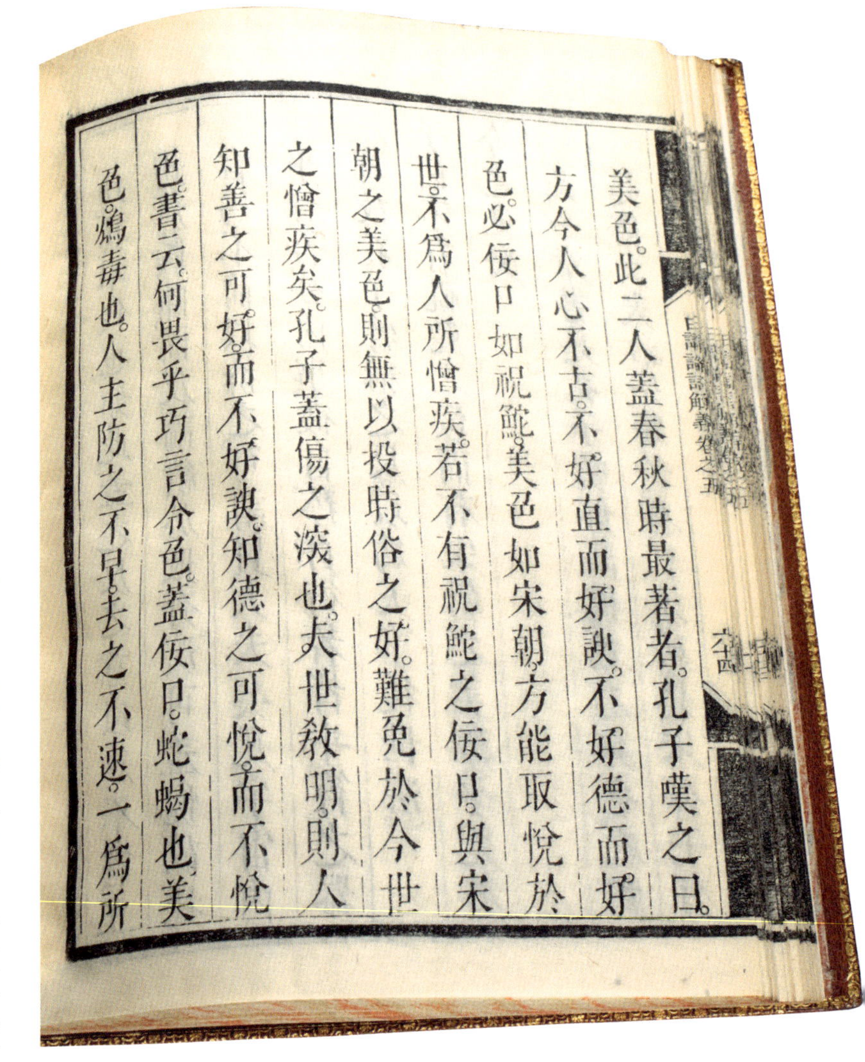

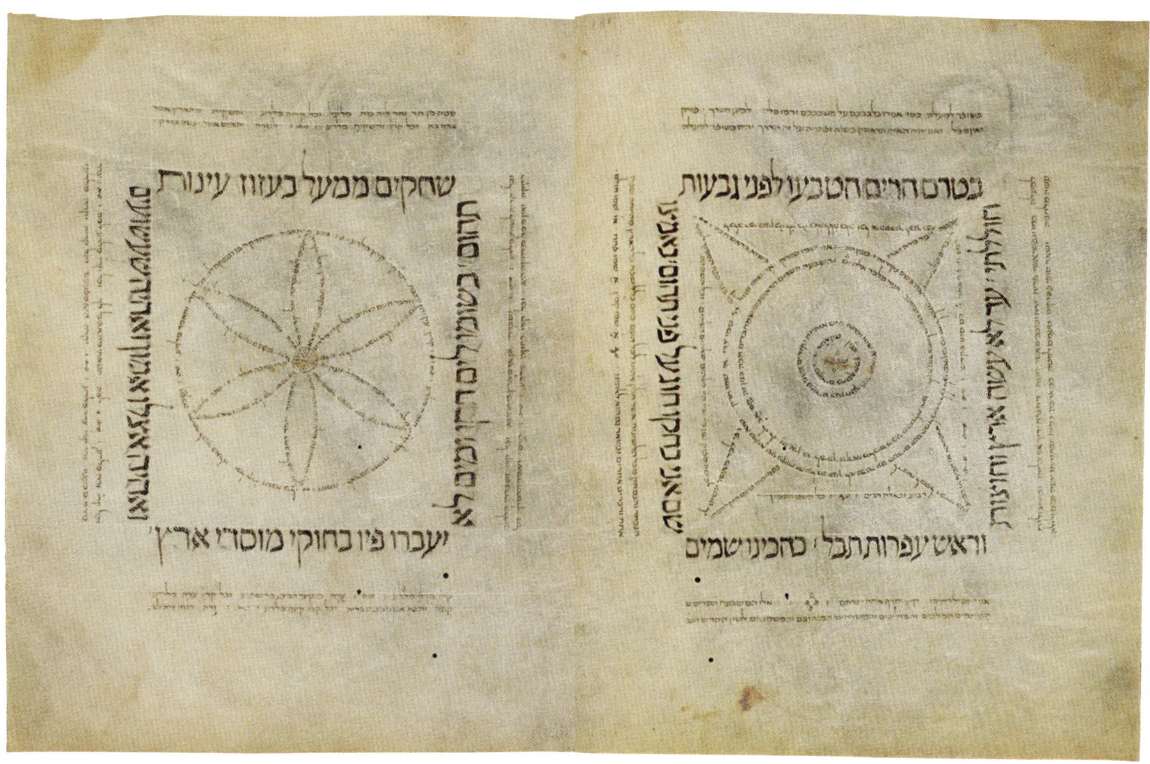

97
Tanach, Spain, 13th century,
Hebrew manuscript on parchment
Cologny, Martin Bodmer Foundation, CB 21

The most ancient of the Abrahamic religious texts, the Torah is a compilation whose elaboration spanned well over 2,500 years. The law of Moses, as laid down in the Pentateuch, the oldest text in Judaism, makes no mention of the word "Messiah". Nor does it put forth a specific vision of the end of days, aside from the idea that Jews will return from the diaspora to gather again in Israel (Deut. 30:3–5). The association of perpetual peace with the end of days was crystallized by the prophets, first among them Isaiah: "and they shall beat their swords into ploughshares, and their spears into pruning hooks; nation shall not lift up sword against nation, neither shall they learn war any more." (Isa. 2:4) The semiotic power of this verse, which is inscribed in stone in front of the United Nations building in New York, has resonated strongly throughout the ages. Nevertheless, it is worth noting that Isaiah's end-of-days depended upon the coming of the Jewish Messiah ("a shoot out of the stock of Jesse"), ushering in a world where "the wolf shall dwell with the lamb, and the leopard shall lie down with the kid ... and a little child shall lead them." (Isa. 11:6) The idea that religious supremacy was the precondition of perpetual peace was thus already outlined in this ancient Jewish text. Christianity and Islam would unfortunately take this premise to its logical conclusion, making peace conditional on the acceptance of the supremacy of their respective faiths.

G. B.-N.

98

Bible, Old Testament,
France (region of Paris?),
mid-14th century, Latin
manuscript on parchment

Cologny, Martin Bodmer Foundation, CB 29

Christianity's vision of peace is at the heart of the message of Jesus. In the Sermon on the Mount, one of the most foundational of all Christian texts, Jesus prohibits not only war but also defensive retaliation: "You have heard that it hath been said, 'An eye for an eye, and a tooth for a tooth.' But I say unto you … whosoever shall smite thee on thy right cheek, turn to him the other also." (Matt. 5:38–39) Jesus starts his sermon by elevating peacemakers to the highest possible moral level: "Blessed are the peacemakers, for they shall be called the children of God." (Matt. 5:9) Peace was pervasive in the message of early Christianity: Jesus explicitly referred to it in his final exhortation to his disciples: "Peace I leave with you; my peace I give you." (John 14:27) His early followers quickly propagated this idea across the entire holy codex. Against the bellicose Jewish mindset of the second temple period, particularly evident in Josephus Flavius' *Jewish Wars*, St Paul urged his followers to "Make every effort to live in peace with everyone and to be holy" (Heb. 12:14). Jesus' brother James, who according to the Greek Orthodox tradition was the author of the Epistle bearing his name, reiterated: "Peacemakers who sow in peace reap a harvest of righteousness." (James 3:18) Christian peacemakers have drawn on these sources ever since, from Bartolomé de las Casas' support for the rights of indigenous peoples at the Valladolid debate in the sixteenth century to Northern Ireland's Good Friday Agreement, in 1998.

G. B.-N.

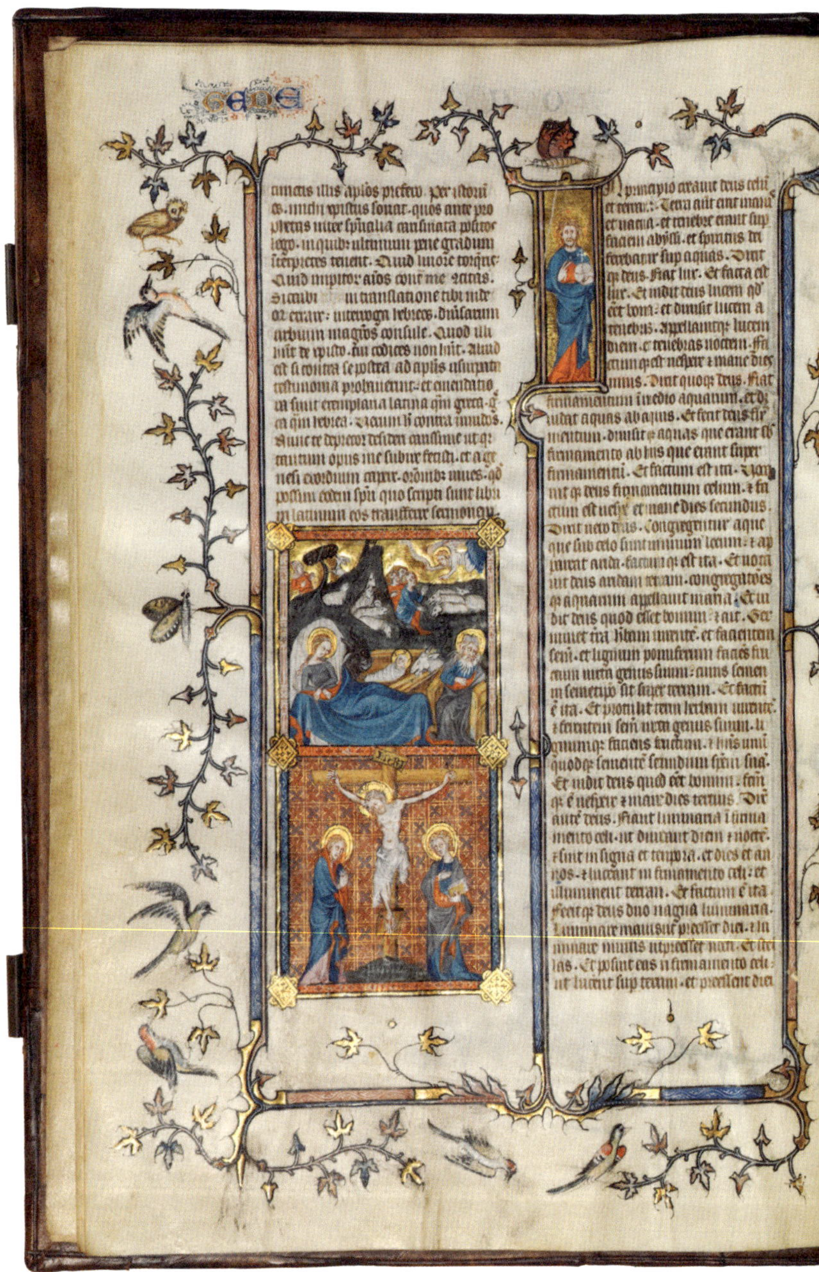

99
Quran, Arab manuscript on paper, with interlinear Persian translation, Persia, 1679, copied by Hadji Haydar Ali

Cologny, Martin Bodmer Fondation, CB 543

The Islamic vision of the unification of the world under God's word had one critical implication: war was not an objective in itself, but rather an intermediate step in a quest for perpetual peace under Islam. Hence, *jihad* was not included in the five pillars of Islam – faith, prayer, charity, fasting (*Ramadan*) and pilgrimage (*Hajj*) – which made up the bedrock of the faith. In the meantime, until the day of its eventual triumph, Islamic doctrine divided the world into two categories: the house of Islam, *Dar al-Islam*, and the house of war, *Dar al-Harb*.

Exceptions to this dichotomy were Ethiopia, Nubia and Cyprus. These countries enjoyed a position of neutrality in Islamic jurisprudence, known as *Dar al-sulh*. *Sulh*, meaning "treaty", referred to a non-Muslim land that had established treaty relations with Islam. By doing so, it became part of the *Dar al-sulh*, "the house of the treaty". For Islam, peace was thus inextricably linked to treaty-making. Although polytheists posed the greatest theological threat to the faith, the sanctity of treaties overrode all other considerations: "as for those idolaters who have honoured the treaty you have made with them, and who have not supported anyone against you: fulfil your agreements with them to the end of their term." (Quran 9:4) Peace was not the product of chance; it required long and careful effort on behalf of all belligerents, Muslims and non-Muslims alike.

G. B.-N.

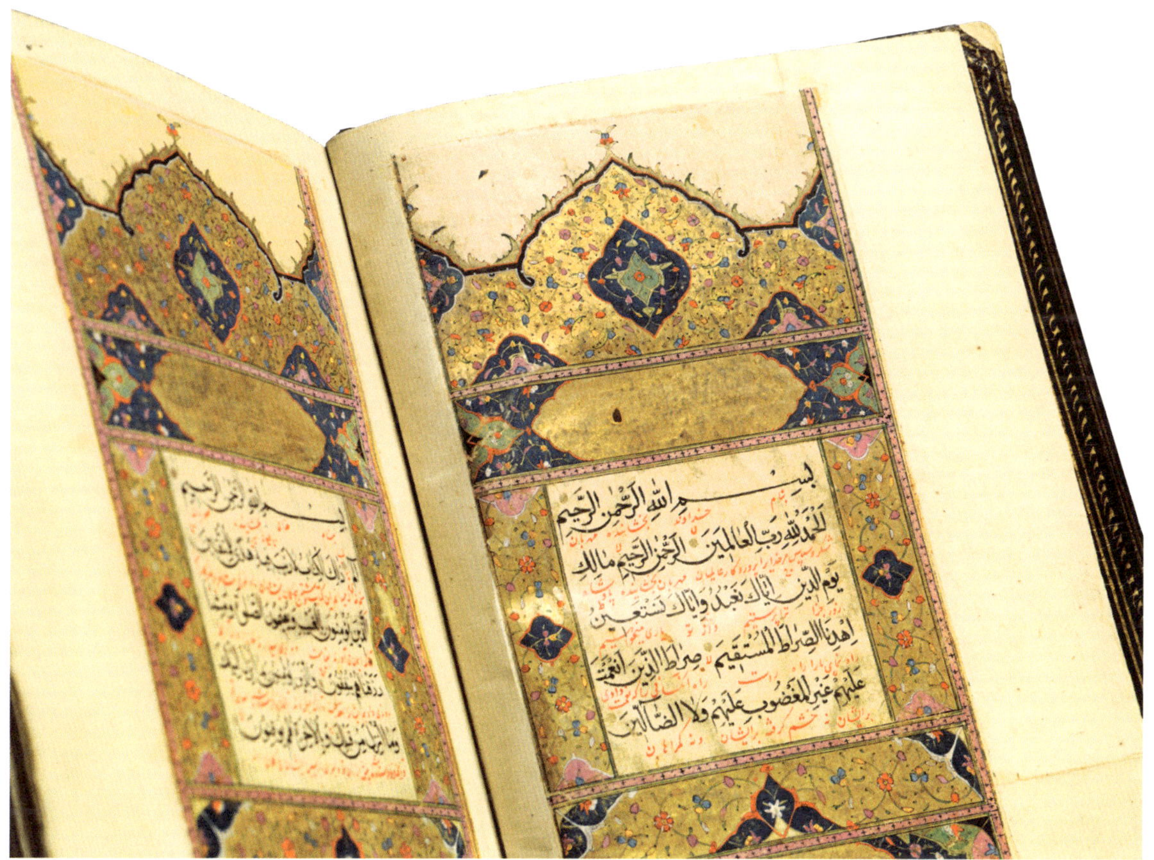

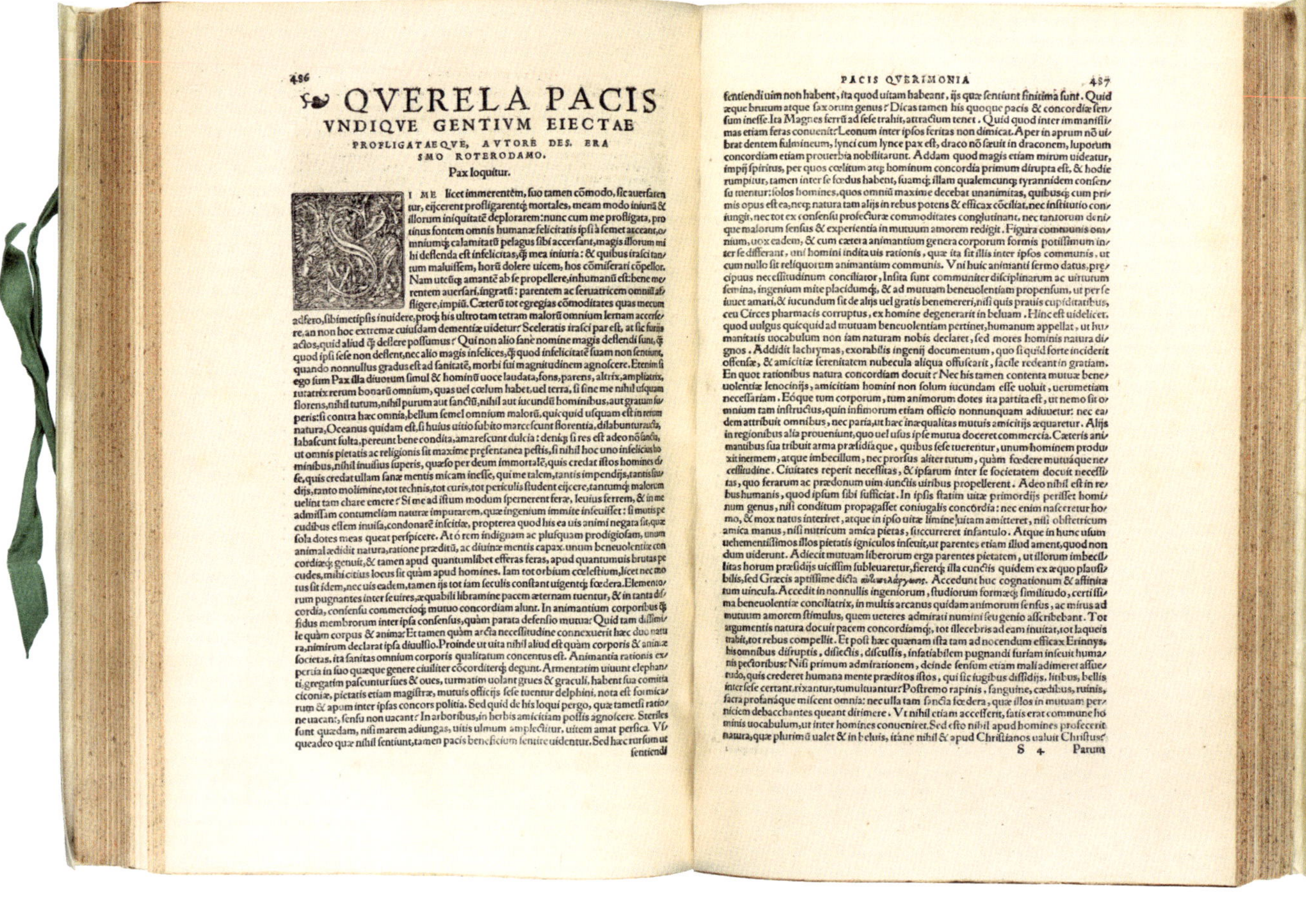

100
Erasmus (1467?–1536)
Querela pacis [*The Complaint of Peace...*], in *Opera Omnia*, Basel, Froben, 1540, first collective edition

Cologny, Martin Bodmer Foundation

Published for the first time on 1516, *The Complaint of Peace* is a political treatise by Erasmus on the diplomatic situation in Europe. It denounces the folly of power and identifies the root causes of war: anger, insults, stupidity, greed and ambition. Nature teaches us peace and harmony, yet men are divided by a tangle of demonic passions that fill their bosoms with an "insatiable rage for war". Armed with the teachings of Isaiah ("the work of righteousness shall be peace", Isa 32:17) and of Christ ("My peace I give you", John 14:27), the great humanist proposed to wage "war against war". After a lengthy "lament" on past failures, Erasmus revisits the idea of a perpetual, pan-European "robust peace" – provided that hateful passions can be soothed... An adviser to the future King Charles of Spain, Erasmus had excellent relations with the pacifist Pope Leo X, who had succeeded the bellicose Julius II. He envisioned the dawn of a genuine epoch of peace, "in the near future, as in a golden age" (letter to Francis I). Introducing the *Complaint*, "Peace" condemns military spending and seeks to move and persuade the reader of the absolute benefits of peace for humanity, by means of a series of arguments grounded in the principles of humanism (the fruits of peace are infinitely superior to those of war) and of Christianity (forgiveness is better than vengeance, appeals to the reader's conscience and the morality of the Gospels).

J. B.

101
Bartolomé de Las Casas (1484–1566)

Aqui se contiene una disputa o controversia entre el Obispo don fray Bartholome de las Casas… y el doctor Hines de Sepulveda… [*Containing a Dispute or Controversy between Bishop Bartolomé de Las Casas… and Doctor Hines de Sepulveda…*], Sevilla, Sebastian Trugillo, 1552, first edition

Cologny, Martin Bodmer Foundation

Few conquests in history have exacted a greater human toll than the subjugation of the Americas and its peoples by Spain in the sixteenth century. The wholesale slaughter of indigenous Americans and the arrival of European diseases caused unthinkable demographic tragedy. Mexico's population declined from sixteen million in 1532 to three million in 1568, to one million by 1608. Bartolomé de las Casas, a Dominican friar and the son of one of Columbus' captains, published his *Short Account of the Destruction of the Indies* (1552) following the savage conquest of Cuba in 1514, after which he was named bishop of Guatemala and "protector of the Indians" by the Spanish crown. Las Casas, who had helped stop the system of *encomienda* that legalized the mass enslavement and expropriation of indigenous Americans, agreed to debate Juan de Sepúlveda against the reinstatement of this policy in a public dispute at the University of Valladolid (1550–51). Las Casas argued that indigenous people had a right to their own freedom and to the land they cultivated. He clearly had the upper hand at Valladolid, as afterwards Sepúlveda was forbidden to circulate his reactionary anti-indigenous writings. Las Casas' arguments thus paved the way for the present-day recognition of indigenous people's right to self-determination and the criminalization of territorial aggression.

G. B.-N.

Jean-Jacques Rousseau (1712–78)

"Extrait du *Projet de paix perpétuelle* de l'abbé de Saint-Pierre" ["Abstract of the *Project for Perpetual Peace* of the Abbé de Saint-Pierre"], in *Œuvres complètes*, vol. 12, Geneva, 1782

Cologny, Martin Bodmer Foundation

The thinking of the Genevan philosopher Jean-Jacques Rousseau (1712–1778) on the question of international relations was largely based on the pacifist ideas of the Abbé de Saint-Pierre. In his *Project for Perpetual Peace* (1761), Saint-Pierre proposed the establishment of a "League of Kings", through which the rulers of Europe might put an end to war and tame their lust for conquest. His plan would serve as the "apothecary of Europe", heralding the disappearance of the "physician" of armament, he wrote in 1740, at the age of eighty-two. Rousseau, who believed that natural man had been corrupted as he became politicized, wrote an influential *Abstract* of Saint-Pierre's work. In it, Rousseau focuses instead on republics, suggesting a new approach inspired by the example of Netherlands, the Swiss Confederation and the Republic of Geneva, whose small size was a guarantee of virtuous proximity. Saint-Pierre's *Project* later inspired Immanuel Kant's *Perpetual Peace: A Philosophical Sketch* (1795). Kant combined Rousseau's ideas with insights from theology (peace is a transcendental, providential order) and law (institutionalization is an artificial construct of human reason). His thinking was highly influential, inspiring twentieth-century pacifists as well as the birth of institutions such as the League of Nations and the Charter of the United Nations. **J. B.**

EXTRAIT
DU
PROJET
DE
PAIX PERPÉTUELLE
DE MONSIEUR L'ABBÉ
DE SAINT-PIERRE.

Tunc genus humanum positis sibi consulat armis,
Inque vicem gens omnis amet. LUCAIN.

LETTRE
DE M. ROUSSEAU à M. DE BASTIDE.

A Montmorenci , le 5 Décembre 1760.

J'AUROIS voulu , Monsieur , pouvoir répondre à l'honnêteté de vos sollicitations , en concourant plus utilement à votre entreprise ; mais vous savez ma résolution , & faute de mieux , je suis réduit , pour vous complaire , à tirer de mes anciens barbouillages le morceau ci-joint , comme le moins indigne des regards du Public. Il y a six ans que M. le Comte de Saint-Pierre m'ayant confié les manuscrits de feu M. l'Abbé son oncle , j'avois commencé d'abréger ses écrits , afin de les

Pieces diverses.   A

103
Immanuel Kant (1724–1804),
Zum ewigen Frieden [*Perpetual Peace*], Königsberg, Friedrich Nicolodius, 1795, First edition
Cologny, Martin Bodmer Foundation

Kant's vision of peace amongst nations differed starkly from Hobbes' deterrence-based stability. While also premised on the existence of nation-states (like Hobbes), for Kant, the only way to achieve a permanent cessation of armed conflict and war was to unite all the states of the world in a single entity. This collectivization (which would have seemed entirely utopian to Hobbes), when accompanied by the disbandment of permanent armies, would in turn be entrusted to: "a league of a particular kind, which can be called a league of peace [*foedus pacificum*]" (*Perpetual Peace: Second Article*).

For Kant, whose *Metaphysics of Morals* is credited with inventing modern, liberal legal theory, the term "international law" was a misnomer. A law could only be considered as such if it could be enforced: "Hugo Grotius, Pufendorf, and many other irritating comforters have been cited in justification of war, though their code [i.e. international law] … has not and cannot have the least legal force, because states as such do not stand under a common external power." (*Perpetual Peace: Second Article*) Kant's idea for a "League of Nations" – a term he coined in the *Second Article* – became a reality some 120 years after he first theorized it. That alone would not suffice to prevent states from going to war against each other. Collective security required measures to enforce it, such as those laid down in chapter VII of the United Nations Charter.

G. B.-N.

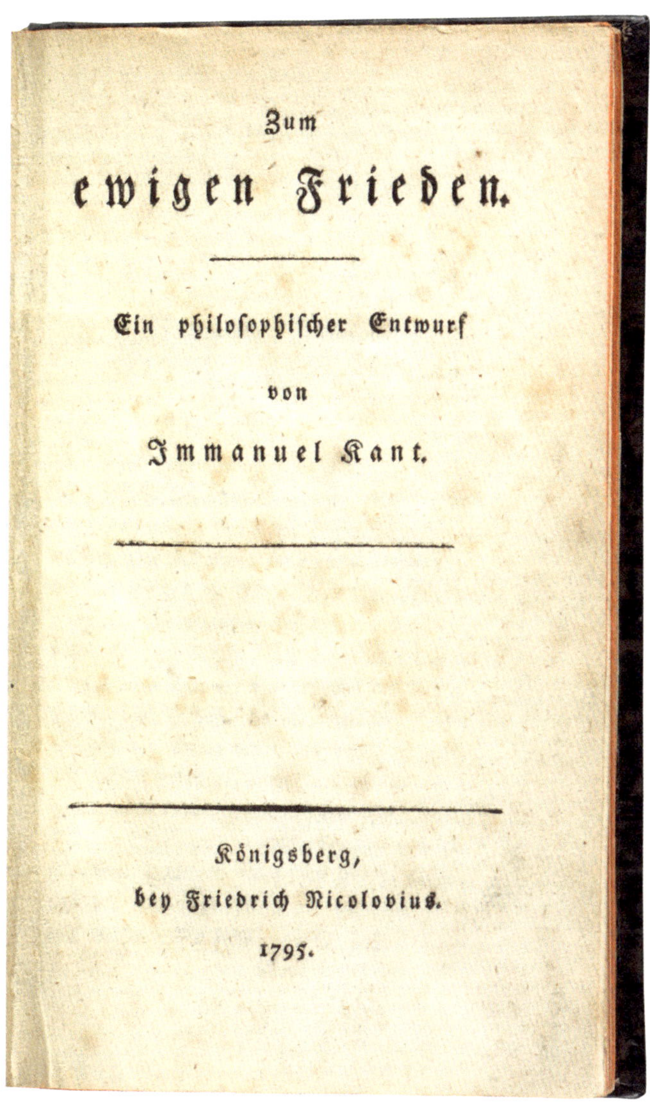

Friedrich Hölderlin (1770–1843)
"Friedensfeier", autograph
manuscript, 1802

Cologny, Martin Bodmer Foundation, Aut. H-51.9

This great poem is about the history of Germany from 1789 to 1802, but also, and more importantly, about its timeless and universal values. It was written between 1801 and 1802 – a decisive year in European history, during which Hölderlin travelled to France. The poem is organized in four groups of three stanzas, containing twelve, twelve and fifteen lines each, for a total of twelve stanzas, symbolizing the twelve disciples. A room has been decorated for the guests; the "prince of the feast" is a demi-god and long-awaited saviour – Napoleon perhaps? Interpretations differ. The poet invites Christ, who has abruptly disappeared from history; humanity has suffered in his absence. The arrival of a peace-loving and powerful son marks the culmination of a process begun in 1789. After centuries of war, the poet rejoices in this new start, extolling reconciliation with nature and the peace that fills mankind with joy through images of happiness. Peace is similarly celebrated in many other poems of the period. In the first fragmentary drafts from 1801, Hölderlin alludes to the Peace of Lunéville between France and Austria (9 February). In June 1802, France, Spain and Portugal signed a new treaty. Europe hailed Napoleon as the "prince of Peace", "the immortal peacemaker", even as negotiations were moving ahead between France and England (the "general peace" signed at Amiens was euphorically received). Incredibly, Hölderlin's great poem then disappeared for 152 years. In late 1802, realizing that the peace was fragile, the poet opted not to publish it: it made no sense to celebrate peace now that war had broken out again. However, he did not destroy the poem. The rediscovery of his autograph manuscript, in 1954, caused a sensation. It was purchased by Martin Bodmer in June 1954.   **J. B.**

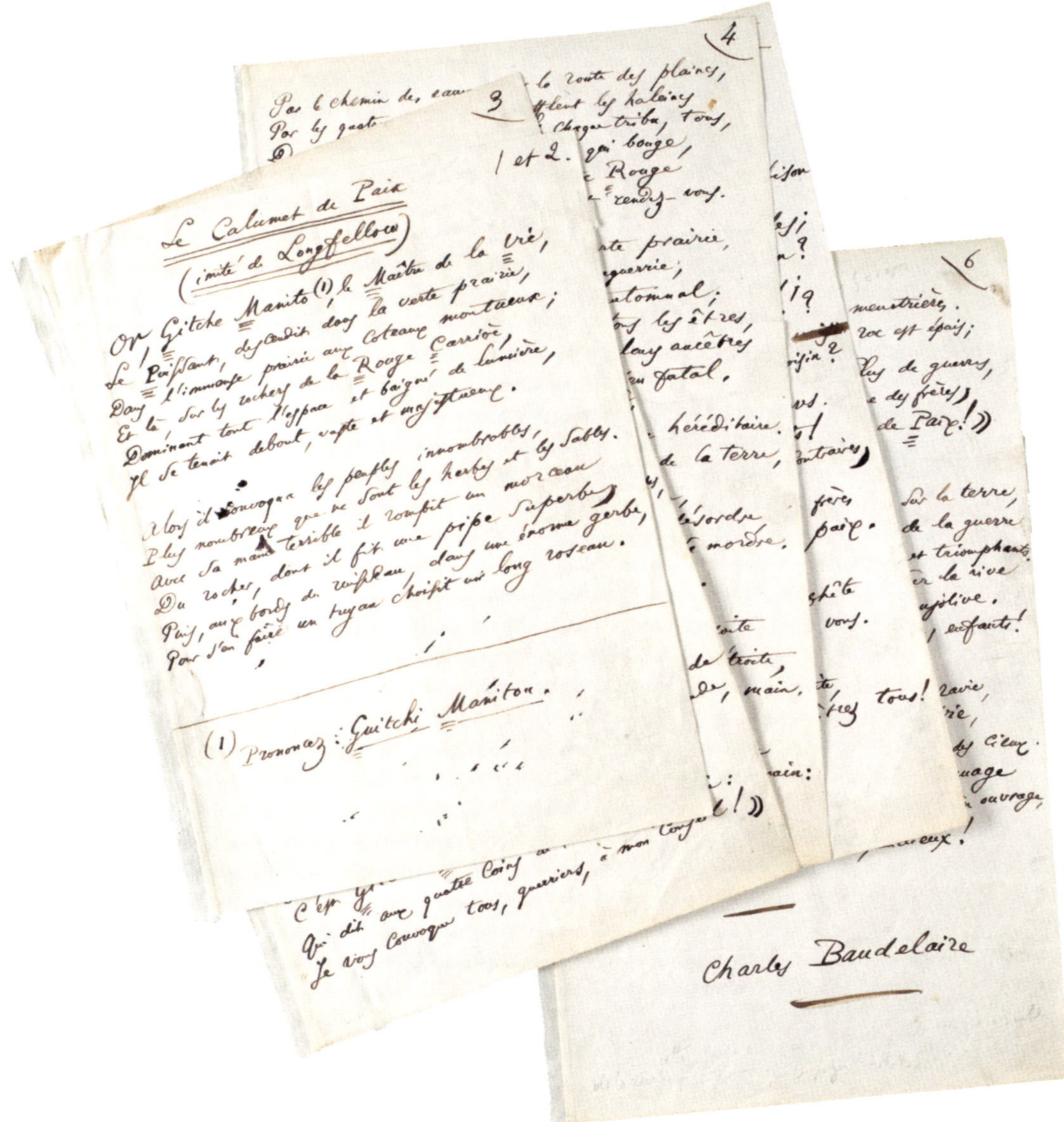

105
Charles Baudelaire (1821–67)
"Le Calumet de la paix"
[The Peace Pipe], 1860, signed
autograph manuscript

Cologny, Martin Bodmer Foundation, Aut. B-21.4

In 1860, a heavily indebted Baudelaire accepted a commission from Robert Stoepel, the German composer of *Hiawatha, an Indian Symphony*. The poet was to translate around eighteen passages from Henry Wadsworth Longfellow's epic poem, which would be read by the actress Julie Bernat at intervals during performances of Stoeopel's symphony. They agreed on a fee of 1,500 francs. But then the composer vanished. With *The Song of Hiawatha* (1855), Longfellow, who fashioned himself as "the Homer of the Redskins", gave the indigenous nations of North America their great epic. Hiawatha was already a legend among the Algonquin at the time when the ethnographer Henry Rowe Schoolcraft was studying them. Longfellow's epic is organized around two well-known episodes: "The Peace Pipe" and "Picture-writing". Baudelaire published "Le Calumet de la paix, imité de Longfellow" in *La Revue contemporaine*, in 1861. Removed from the flow of the epic, the free-standing pacifist poem, comprising 102 alexandrines, was included in the 1868 French edition of *The Flowers of Evil*. Baudelaire's fair copy was acquired by Martin Bodmer in 1955. Such manuscript excerpts of *The Flowers of Evil* are rare. **J. B.**

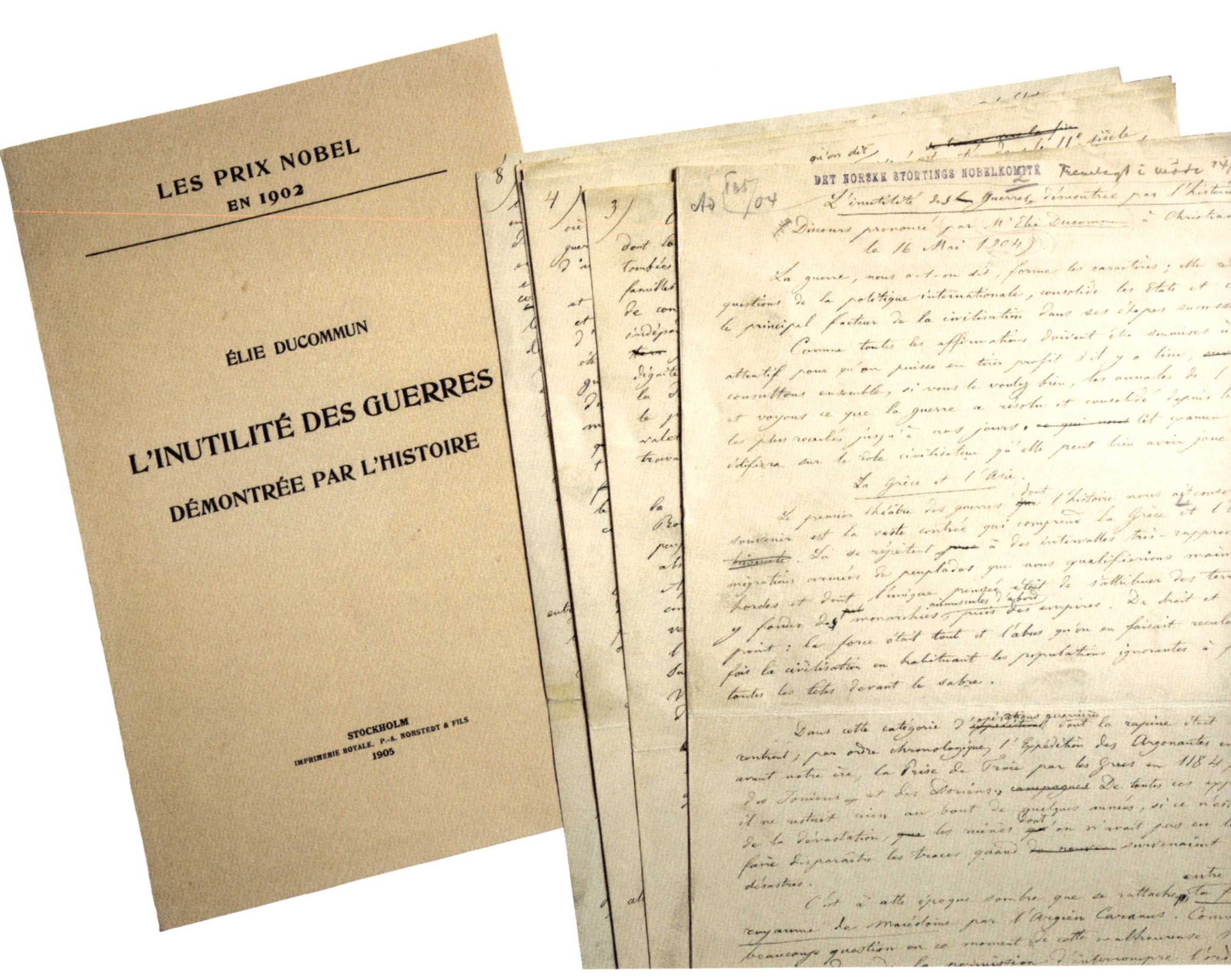

106
Elie Ducommun (1833–1906)
"L'inutilité des guerres démontrée par l'histoire", signed autograph manuscript, 1904

Geneva, United Nations Archives

Elie Ducommun (1833–1906) was the first secretary-general of the International Peace Bureau, a federation of pacifist associations founded in 1891 to forge ties between national associations and coordinate their activities. Ducommun remained in the post for twelve years, helping to organize the international pacifist movement. Devoted and determined, he worked tirelessly to spread the message of the "friends of peace". In 1902, he was awarded the second Nobel Peace Prize, along with Albert Gobat, secretary-general of the Inter-Parliamentary Union. In the speech he sent to the Nobel Committee in 1904, Ducommun observed that, while some people believed that war "builds character, … resolves grave matters of international politics, consolidates States and constitutes the principal factor of civilization in its successive stages", history had shown that, in reality, it brought only destruction and injustice, and over time generated more conflicts. The objectives sought through armed conflict could be achieved by peaceful means as well. Ducommun concluded by stating that war was a pointless evil and that arbitration was the best means of breaking the vicious cycle it created. Instruments designed for the peaceful settlement of international disputes ensured that concord would endure, by establishing it "on the unshakeable rock of justice, law and solidarity among nations!"

P.-E. B.

107
Romain Rolland (1866–1944)
"Aux peuples assassinés",
autograph manuscript, 1916

Cologny, Martin Bodmer Foundation, Aut. R-37.2

This article by Romain Rolland appeared in the November 1916 issue of the pacifist, social-anarchist and internationalist magazine *Demain*, published in Geneva by Henri Guilbeaux. From his home "above the fray", in Switzerland, the fifty-year-old Rolland denounced the horrors committed by European nations, the poisoning of China by the British opium trade and the slaughter of the Armenians by the "Red Sultan" between 1894 and 1896. "These injustices that revolt us, because we are their victims … European civilization has been perpetrating them – or allowing them to be perpetrated around it – for fifty years." He wrote eloquently of the "martyrdom of Belgium, Serbia, Poland", adding, "Who will protest the suffering of peoples given up as prey to rapacious colonial expeditions? Who looked on and was not horrified? … The stench of death hangs over European civilization." Rolland's outrage and disgust with war and colonialism chimed with the views of the Bengali poet Rabindranath Tagore, who condemned Europe in similar terms, in an article dated 18 June 1916: "The civilization of Europe is a grinder. It consumes the peoples it invades, it exterminates and annihilates the races standing in the way of its conquering advance, it is a civilization of cannibals." For Rolland, disgust was compounded by shame and guilt: "We are all partly to blame for today's evils … Who among us is not guilty? Who among us has the right to wash the blood of murdered Europe from his hands? Everyone should see where his fault lies and try to make amends!" *Demain* was banned in France, and in February 1919 the French authorities sentenced Guilbeaux – its publisher – to death *in absentia* for "conspiring with the enemy". Rolland's text was re-issued in the collection *Les Précurseurs*, in 1923.

J. B.

108
Mohandas Karamchand Gandhi (1869–1948)

La Jeune Inde [*Young India*], trans. Hélène Hart, introduction by Romain Rolland, Paris, Stock, 1924

Cologny, Martin Bodmer Foundation

Having engaged in lively correspondence with Tolstoy in the years leading up to 1910, Gandhi put his experience of non-violence in the service of the weakest members of society, India's undernourished peasants and serfs. Looking ahead to potential independence from the United Kingdom, he wrote numerous professions of faith in the power of non-violence, which he published in his weekly paper, *Young India* (1919–1931). His philosophy – "Nonviolence (*ahimsa*) implies voluntary submission to the penalty for non-cooperation with evil" – inspired many intellectuals worldwide in the wake of the First World War, chief among them Romain Rolland, the author and founder of the militantly pacifist magazine *Europe*. Rolland published an essay on the Mahatma's acts of civil disobedience (*satyagraha*), in 1924, and maintained a steady drumbeat of news about his activities. Gandhi described Rolland as "the wisest man of Europe", after visiting him at his home in Villeneuve, in 1931. **J. B.**

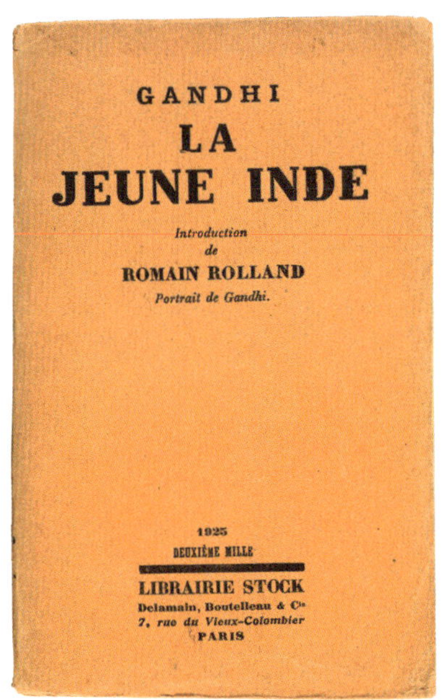

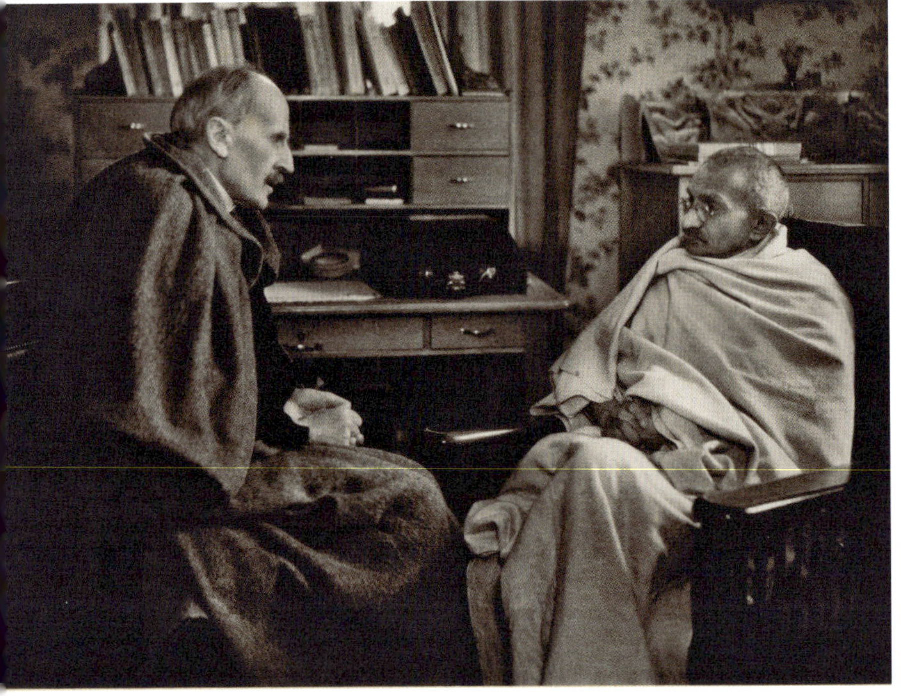

109
Rudolf Schlemmer (1878–1972)
Photograph of Romain Rolland and Mohandas Karamchand Gandhi, Villeneuve, 1931

Lausanne, Musée de l'Elysée, Schlemmer Collection

For the pacifist Romain Rolland, the First World War had demonstrated that the Western nations were capable of unparalleled savagery. Only by adopting a completely new mindset, based on Eastern pacifism, could the return of evil ideologies be prevented. As part of his endeavour to keep evil at bay and kindle greater hope for peace, Rolland correspondended with his wise friends in India, wrote essays about Ramakrishna and Vivekananda, and invited Indian partners – including Tagore and Gandhi – to his home in Villeneuve-sur-Léman, promoting a historically unpredented cultural exchange between the Rhone River and the Ganges. This collaboration also extended to the political and religious arenas. By positing mutual openness, Rolland established a dialogue between the European and Indian ways of thinking. **J. B.**

110
*Protocol for the Pacific Settlement
of International Disputes*, 1924
Geneva, United Nations Archives

The Protocol for the Pacific Settlement of International Disputes, often called the "Geneva Protocol", was unanimously adopted by the Assembly of the League of Nations in October 1924, in the atmosphere of international détente created by the arrival in power of Ramsay MacDonald in Great Britain and Édouard Herriot in France. At the opening of the Assembly, the statements by the two heads of government revealed converging views on the need to bolster the system of collective security on the basis of the three-pronged "arbitration, security and disarmament" approach. The Geneva Protocol – the work in large part of the Greek Nicolas Politis and the Czechoslovak Edvard Beneš – strengthened the mechanisms for the peaceful settlement of international disputes provided for in the Covenant, making arbitration mandatory and specifying the criteria for defining an "act of aggression". It authorized the Council to determine whether the Covenant had been violated and to "enjoin" the states to apply sanctions "as soon as possible". The entry into force of the 1924 Protocol was compromised by the fall of the MacDonald government a few weeks after the Assembly's vote: the new Tory government deemed it too constraining and refused to ratify it. The 1924 Protocol was one of the greatest missed opportunities for strengthening the collective security system of the League of Nations.   **P.-E. B.**

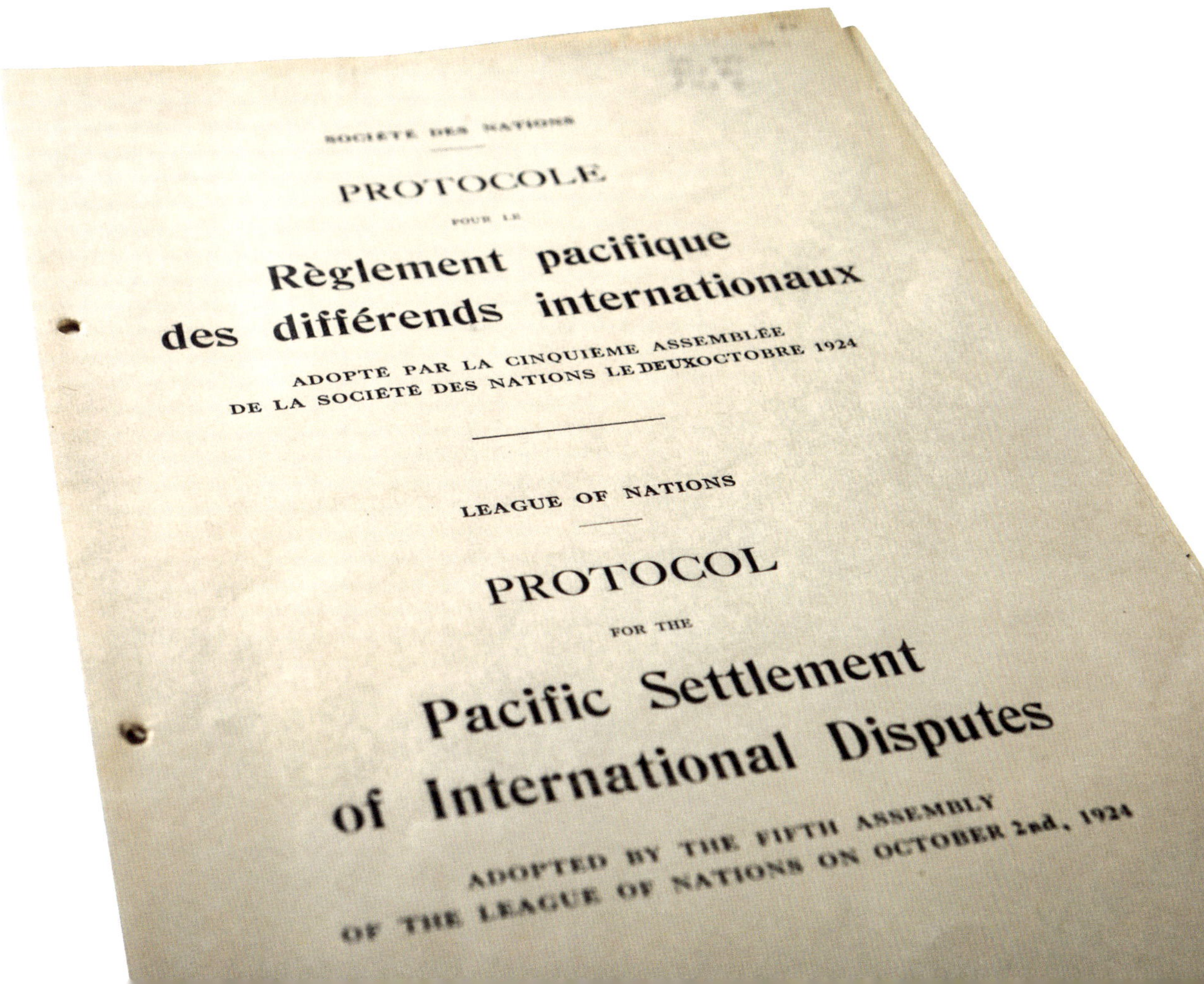

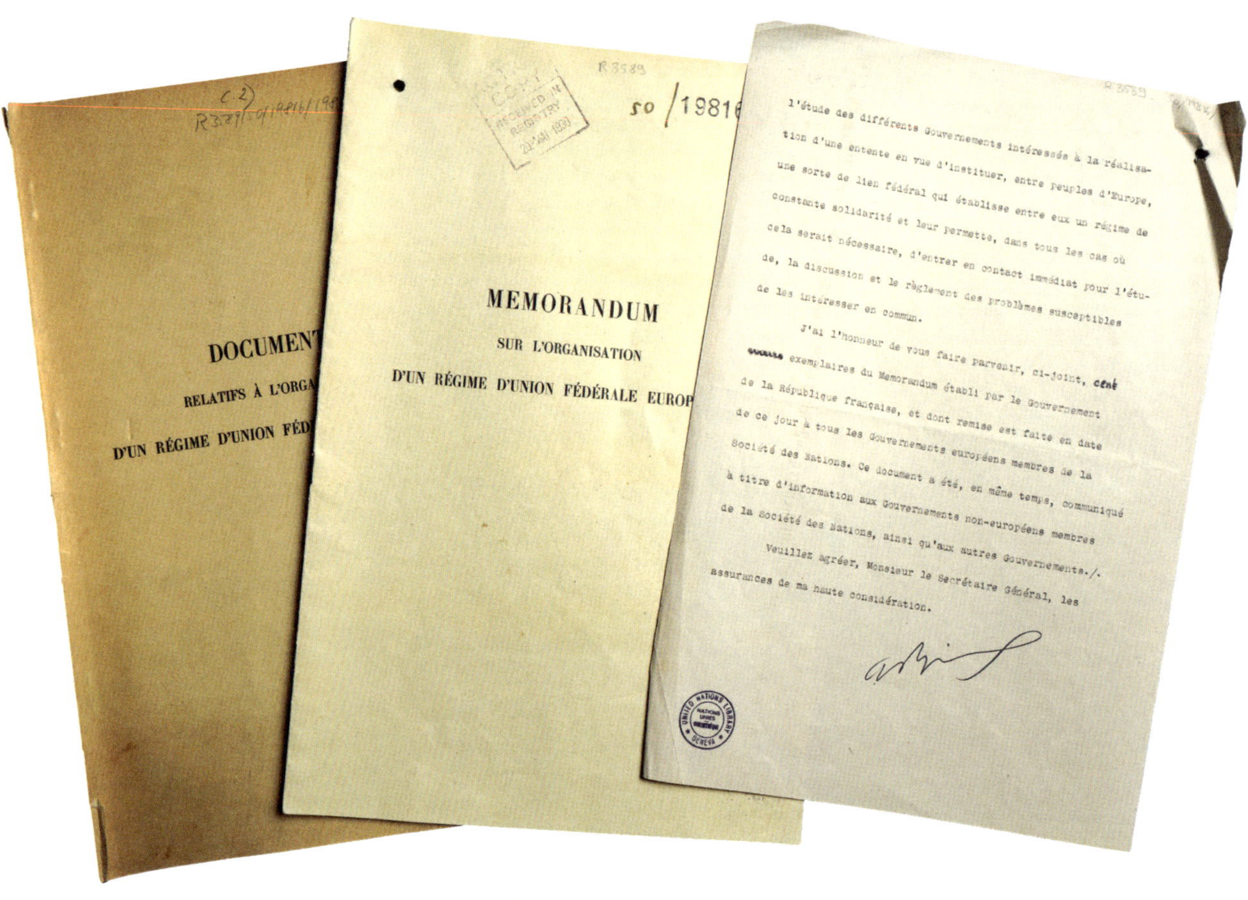

111
Aristide Briand (1862–1932)

Mémorandum sur l'organisation d'un régime d'union fédérale européenne [*Memorandum on the Organization of a System of Federal European Union*], May 1930

Geneva, United Nations Archives

In his statement to the Assembly of the League of Nations in September 1929, Aristide Briand, the French minister for foreign affairs, proposed the establishment of a "sort of federal link" between European peoples. The League's European Member States welcomed that proposal, and asked him to send it to them in writing for their consideration. His *Memorandum on the Organization of a System of Federal European Union* was submitted in May 1930. It led with the observation that "lack of cohesion" was "the most serious obstacle" to the establishment of peace in Europe. Therefore, while acknowledging "the absolute sovereignty" and "total political independence" of members, it proposed the constitution of a "European Union" endowed with a variety of bodies to coordinate the action of European governments in the political, economic and social realms. It referred in particular to the possibility of a common market and of cooperation in the fields of transportation, infrastructure and education.

At the time of publication, in 1930, the *Memorandum* – which Alexis Léger, more commonly known as Saint-John Perse, helped to draft – was met with scant enthusiasm. The deteriorating political and social climate had chilled the interest expressed several months earlier. While the plan for a European Union continued to be discussed until 1937, it was never carried through for want of political will. **P.-E. B.**

112
Documents relating to the origins of the term "collective security": Edith Williamson, *Mémorandum*, 25 June 1937; letter from Gerald Abraham to Stephen Heald, 28 June 1937

Geneva, United Nations Archives

The League of Nations is often considered the first sketch of a system of collective security. Its Covenant established a bond of solidarity between members: if any one was subject to an external aggression, all the others undertook to provide it with collective assistance.

Although this principle was set out in the League's constituent document, the term "collective security" did not appear. Indeed, it was not until 1924 that it was used for the first time in an official document. According to research carried out by the League Secretariat, the term was the brainchild of Edvard Beneš, the representative of Czechoslovakia, who, in a preparatory report on the Protocol for the Pacific Settlement of International Disputes, wrote that article 8 of the Covenant encapsulated all the problems that the League Assembly had to resolve in order to consolidate international peace, namely, "The problems I refer to as those of collective security and arms reduction." In comments on the results of the research, a League official noted that, while it was possible that the term had been used earlier, "the combination of 'collective' and 'security' is probably the product of a mind formed in the Germanic world, which appreciates complicated combinations of this kind". Today, the principle of collective security remains the cornerstone of the Charter of the United Nations.

P.-E. B.

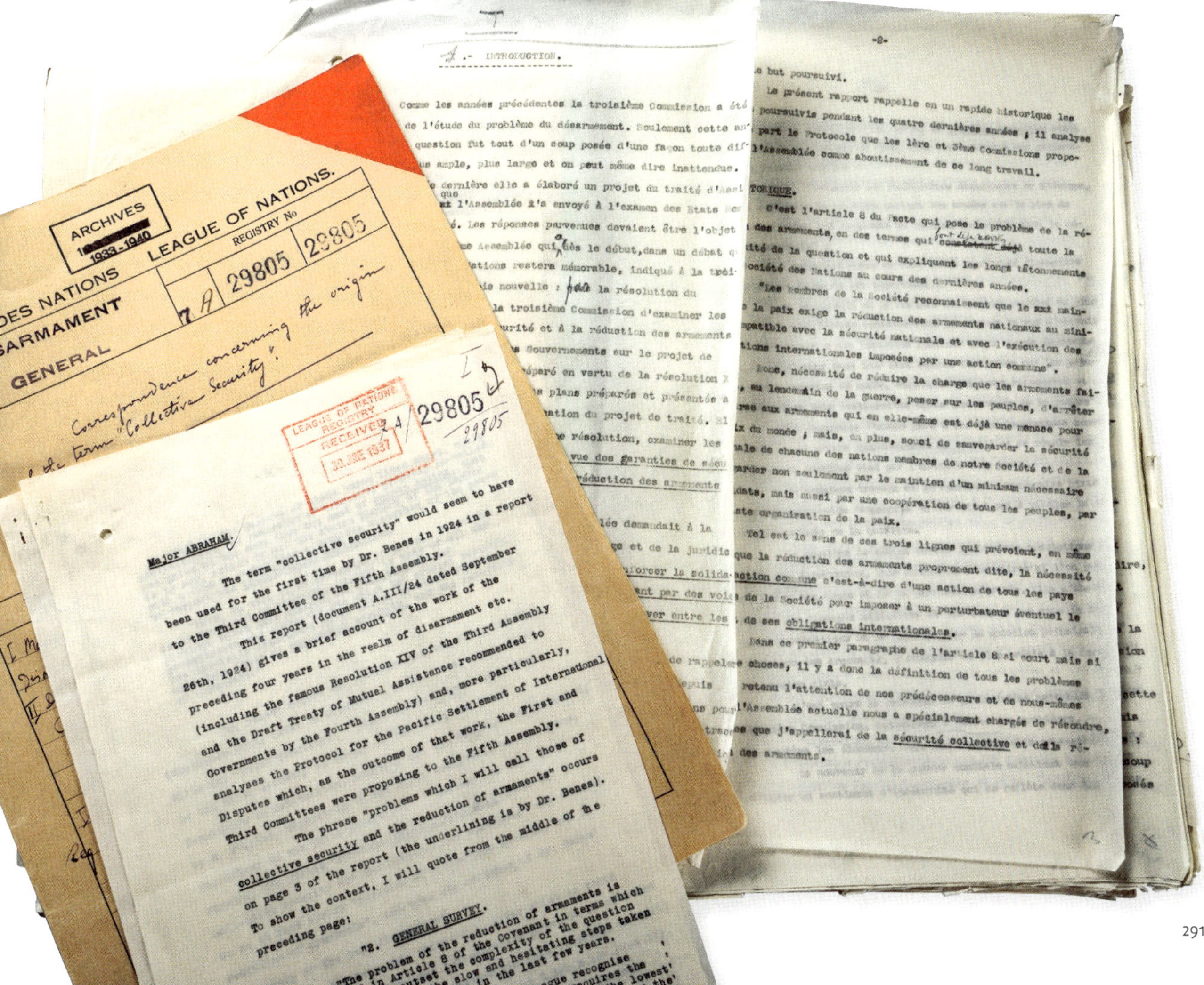

D. 19/42

Parties	Titre / Title	Nature du document / Kind of document	Présenté à l'enregistrement par / Presented for registration by	Présentation / Presentation	Signature
États-Unis d'Amérique, Royaume-Uni de Grande-Bretagne et d'Irlande du Nord, Union des Républiques Soviétiques Socialistes, …	Déclaration des Nations Unies et documents y relatifs: 1) Déclaration de principes, connue sous le nom de Charte de l'Atlantique, promulguée par le Premier Ministre du Royaume-Uni et par le Président des États-Unis d'Amérique, le 14 août 1941, et Pacte tripartite entre l'Allemagne, l'Italie et le Japon signé à Berlin, le 27 septembre 1940.	Déclaration (Politique)	Le Secrétaire d'État aux Affaires étrangères de La Majesté en Grande-Bretagne	29 octobre 1942	Washington le 1ᵉʳ janvier 1942.

113
League of Nations, register of treaties, registration of the Declaration by United Nations, 1 January 1942

Geneva, United Nations Archives at Geneva

In order to ensure transparent international relations, the Covenant of the League of Nations instructed the Member States to register with the Secretariat "any treaty or international engagement" they concluded. The League thus received over 4,500 international instruments during its existence. The outbreak of the Second World War in 1939 did not put an end to its activities. Despite the difficulties created by the conflict, the League maintained certain technical functions, in particular in the field of health, anti-drug action and economic and financial matters. In particular, the Secretariat continued to receive and register international agreements. The Declaration by United Nations is one such. Adopted on 1 January 1942 by the United States, the United Kingdom, the Soviet Union and China, it was signed the next day by twenty-two other governments. The signatories undertook to work together and pit all their resources against the members of the "Tripartite Pact" and not to make a separate armistice or peace. It was the first official document to use the term "United Nations", which was coined by United States President Franklin Delano Roosevelt. In 1945, only the states that had adhered to the Declaration and declared war on Germany and Japan were invited to participate in the San Francisco Conference. It was in honour of President Roosevelt, who had died a few weeks earlier, that the new organization, founded on 26 June 1945, when its Charter was signed, was called the "United Nations".

P.-E. B.

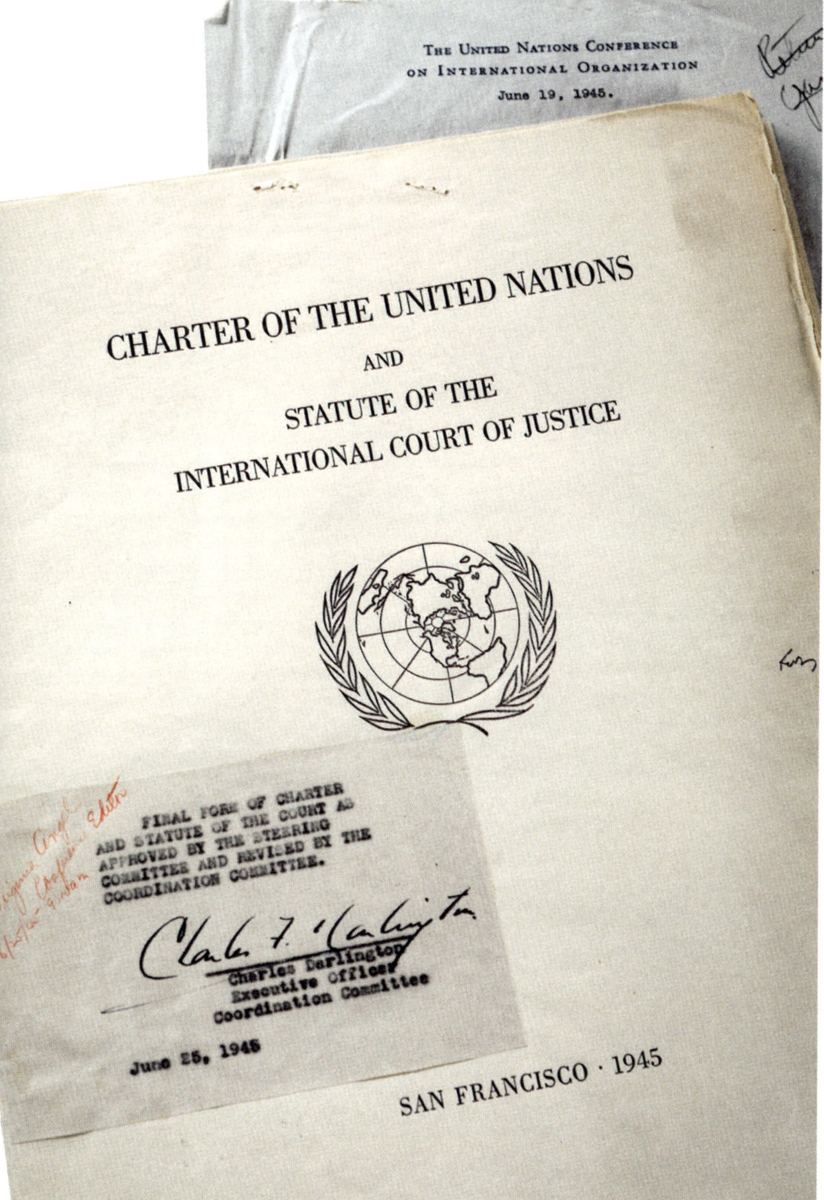

114
**United Nations, Charter
of the United Nations (certified
copy), 25 June 1945**
New York, United Nations Archives (ARMS)

On 25 April 1945, the representatives of fifty governments convened in San Francisco for the opening of the United Nations Conference on International Organization. The outcome of the deliberations, two months later, was the signing of the Charter of the United Nations, the organization's founding treaty. The discussions were intense. The Conference commissions and committees held almost four hundred meetings, and roughly 500,000 pages were printed on average per day. The most hotly debated questions included the composition of the Security Council, the right of veto – a term that does not appear in the Charter – and the prerogatives of the General Assembly. Consisting of a preamble and 111 articles, the Charter of the United Nations was signed on 26 June 1945. The Statute of the International Court of Justice, which was also approved at the Conference, was appended. On 15 October, Poland, which had been unable to attend the Conference owing to differences of opinion between the United States and the Soviet Union about the recognition of its government, signed as a founding member. The Charter entered into force on 24 October, signed by fifty-one founding states.   **P.-E. B.**

MERCREDI
8 août 1945

100, rue Réaumur, Paris-2e
Téléphone : GUT. 80-60

ABONNEMENTS
3 mois .... 140 francs
6 mois .... 260 francs
12 mois .... 500 francs
Compte chèque postal : 32-64

DERNIÈRE ÉDITION

ABONNEMENTS DE VACANCES
50 fr. pour un mois ou 2 fr. par jour pour une durée minimum d'une semaine. Règlement par mandat-poste ou chèque postal. En raison des frais divers de transmission, l'envoi du chèque postal est obligatoire pour les abonnements de vacances.

5e ANNÉE

Numéro 38

Le n° : 2 fr.

COMBAT
DE LA RÉSISTANCE A LA RÉVOLUTION

Trois anciens ministres de Vichy actuellement détenus à Fresnes ont déposé hier en faveur de Pétain

COMBAT

L E monde est ce qu'il est, c'est-à-dire peu de chose. C'est ce que chacun sait depuis hier grâce au formidable concert que la radio, les journaux et les agences d'information viennent de déclencher au sujet de la bombe atomique. On nous apprend, en effet, au milieu d'une foule de commentaires enthousiastes, que n'importe quelle ville d'importance moyenne peut être totalement rasée par une bombe de la grosseur d'un ballon de football. Des journaux américains, anglais et français se répandent en dissertations élégantes sur l'avenir, le passé, les inventeurs, le coût, la vocation pacifique et les effets guerriers, les conséquences politiques et même le caractère indépendant de la bombe atomique. Nous nous résumerons en une phrase : la civilisation mécanique vient de parvenir à son dernier degré de sauvagerie. Il va falloir choisir, dans un avenir plus ou moins proche, entre le suicide collectif ou l'utilisation intelligente des conquêtes scientifiques.

En attendant, il est permis de penser qu'il y a quelque indécence à célébrer ainsi une découverte, qui se met d'abord au service de la plus formidable rage de destruction dont l'homme ait fait preuve depuis des siècles. Que dans un monde livré à tous les déchirements de la violence, incapable d'aucun contrôle, indifférent à la justice et au simple bonheur des hommes, la science se consacre au meurtre organisé, personne sans doute, à moins d'idéalisme impénitent, ne songera à s'en étonner.

Ces découvertes doivent être enregistrées, commentées selon ce qu'elles sont, annoncées au monde pour que l'homme ait une juste idée de son destin. Mais entourer ces terribles révélations d'une littérature pittoresque ou humoristique, c'est ce qui n'est pas supportable.

Déjà, on ne respirait pas facilement dans ce monde torturé. Voici qu'une angoisse nouvelle nous est proposée, qui a toutes les chances d'être définitive. On offre sans doute à l'humanité sa dernière chance. Et ce peut être après tout le prétexte d'une édition spéciale. Mais ce devrait être plus sûrement le sujet de quelques réflexions et de beaucoup de silence.

Au reste, il est d'autres raisons d'accueillir avec réserve le roman d'anticipation que les journaux nous proposent. Quand on voit le rédacteur diplomatique de l'Agence Reuter annoncer que cette invention rend caducs les traités ou périmées les décisions mêmes de Potsdam, remarquer qu'il est indifférent que les Russes soient à Koenigsberg ou la Turquie aux Dardanelles, on ne peut se défendre de supposer à ce beau concert des intentions assez étrangères au désintéressement scientifique.

(Lire la suite en 2e page)

Les quotidiens parisiens vont-ils devoir cesser de paraître ?

A l'ouverture du procès Pétain, le Syndicat de la Presse Parisienne a décidé que les quotidiens éclateraient chaque jour un grand format pour pouvoir rendre compte aussi complètement que possible des audiences de la Haute Cour. Aucun tonnage supplémentaire de papier n'ayant été attribué depuis lors à la presse par les ministres responsables, les quotidiens étaient nécessairement menacés de me...

Depuis deux jours, « Combat » a dû maintenir sa publication...

Compte rendu d'audience par Georges ALTSCHULER

O N dit de M. Caujolle qu'il est le plus qualifié des experts français. C'est lui qui a rédigé un document de cinq cent cinquante pages sur l'activité du C. O. A. pendant l'occupation. C. O. A.? c'est-à-dire Comité de l'Organisation de l'Automobile. Ce document apporterait la preuve que l'industrie française a beaucoup travaillé pour les occupants. C'est en somme la politique économique du gouvernement de Vichy qui est en cause.

Contrairement à ce que l'on pourrait penser, cet aspect du problème Pétain ne sera pas examiné publiquement par la Haute Cour, pendant l'audition de M. Caujolle. On espérait voir répondre à l'intérêt de plus en plus décliné des audiences; mais, après les généraux, on assiste au défilé des ministres de Vichy, cités par la défense.

La quatorzième audience commence avec un sérieux retard. Un homme s'est jeté sous une rame du métro, la circulation est arrêtée, et M. Patrus Faure, juge ancien ministre, s'est trouvé en panne sous un tunnel. C'est pourquoi M. Mongibeaux ne peut ouvrir les débats qu'à quatorze heures.

La plupart des ministres de Pétain qui défilent à la barre, s'ils sont des témoins de moralité, sont également internés à Fresnes, inculpés de complot contre la sûreté de l'État.

« Incompatibilité d'humeur » entre Laval et Pétain

M. Peyrouton, premier témoin de la journée, est dans ce cas. Son feutre marron et ses gants en peau de chevreau attirent tous les regards, aussi celui de l'accusé qui ne daigne pas répondre à son salut. Pétain aurait-il conservé un mauvais souvenir de son ministre de l'Intérieur.

La défense a cité M. Peyrouton pour lui demander des éclaircissements sur les événements du 13 décembre 1940. C'est une occasion pour l'ancien ministre de brosser un sombre tableau, dans lequel Laval n'est pas présenté à son avantage.

— Le 13 décembre il y eut une abolition de crédit, le témoin pour commencer.

Et d'évoquer dans quelles conditions le gouvernement Pétain devait travailler : Laval, seul bénéficiaire d'un laissez-passer (sauvez) permanent ; des ministres qui ne peuvent se déplacer et qui ne sont pas renseignés sur ce qui se passe de l'autre côté de la ligne de démarcation ; ils sont presque séparés (une zone presque séparée (l'une l'autre) la presse de Paris aux ordres (de l'occupant)...

L'arrestation de Laval

Au même moment, des bruits assez précis courent : d'accord avec les Allemands, Laval projette une action contre le Tchad, colonie ralliée à de Gaulle.

MM. Chevalier, Bouthillier et moi-même considérions qu'en acceptant cette grave éventualité le gouvernement opérait une espèce de renversement des alliances qui entraînerait inévitablement la guerre avec l'Angleterre.

Le 13 décembre, Peyrouton se rend auprès de Pétain, déjà alerté par deux personnes qui confirment ces bruits, lui expose la gravité de la situation et lui dit son intention de faire arrêter Laval...

Peyrouton se fâche

M. Peyrouton a terminé sa déposition. Mais il n'a pas fini d'être questionné. M. Pierre Bloch lui demande, par exemple, sur l'ordre de qui ont été arrêtés MM. Vincent-Auriol, Jules Moch et Marx Dormoy.

— Je n'avais pas l'initiative de l'arrestation des anciens ministres. M. Marquet pourrait vous donner sur ce point quelques précisions, alors, au bon vieux de la Garde des Sceaux de cette époque.

Le témoin se fâche : « Ce n'est pas mon procès, tout de même ». Mais il reconnaît que « toutes les arrestations importantes ont été décidées en Conseil des ministres, présidé par le Maréchal ».

Un juge remarque que le témoin...

M. Malvy, caution morale

Quelques juges applaudissent voudraient abuser à cette époque comme les gendarmes reprochent au témoin d'avoir suspendu des municipalités. J'avais interdit aux Conseils généraux et de se réunir et d'avoir donné à la préfecture un préfet qui, en fait, « détruisaient tout ce qui était républicain ».

Peyrouton se montre de M. Malvy, ancien président de la Commission des finances de la Chambre.

— J'appartiens par alliance à une famille républicaine, s'écrit-il. Je pense peut qu'on puisse dire que M. Malvy soit antirépublicain.

Les décrets portaient votre nom. Vos décisions étaient-elles prises en accord avec le maréchal ?

Le témoin lui répond avec directement. Il dit qu'il a jamais pris l'initiative d'une suppression ou d'une suspension.

— Je n'ai pas accepté les propositions des préfets.

Un juge non parlementaire, M. Poupon lui pose une question : « Le maréchal était-il au courant de ce qui se passait dans les camps d'internement d'Afrique du Nord où des enfants, femmes, jeunes gens, vieillards, etc. sont rigoureusement maltraités ? »

— Je ne pense pas qu'il ait été au courant, répond le témoin. Malombre n'était pas au courant. J'ai quitté le ministère le 12 février 1941.

M. Poupon fait remarquer que le premier navire amenant des étages part lequel il se trouvait était arrivé à Alger le 5 février 1941.

— Vous devez bien être au courant.

— C'est mon procès que l'on fait.

(Lire la suite en 2e page)

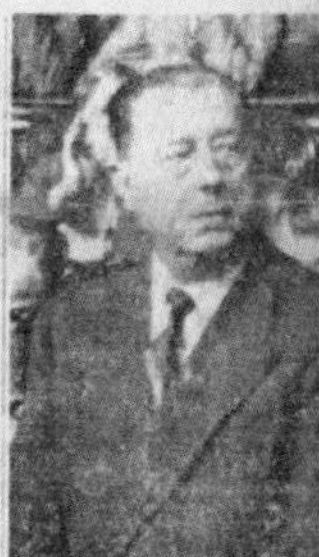

M. PEYROUTON :
« C'est ce mon procès ? »

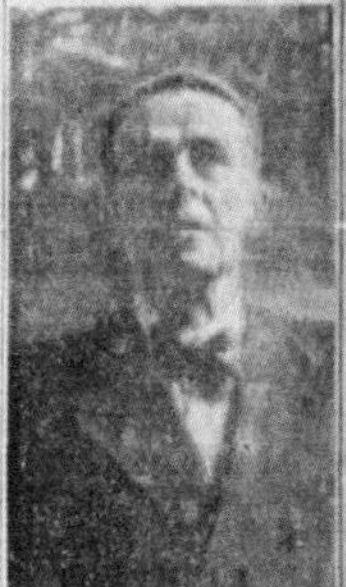

Le vice-amiral FERNET

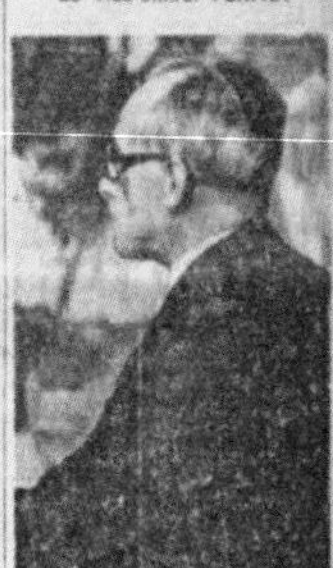

M. CHEVALIER :
« Je suis philosophe de profession »

L'ALSACE DIVISÉE
par la question des spoliations

Seize cents procès sont déjà engagés entre « rentrants » et « restants »

De notre envoyé spécial Roger GRENIER

S TRASBOURG, août. — L'Alsace est la province où se posent le plus de problèmes humains. Son destin tourmenté en est la cause, et, dès l'abord, la désolation de ses villages totalement rasés se fait présentir. Car on n'évoque pas devant ces ruines les pertes matérielles, mais on pense que l'homme a vécu là où il n'y a plus que le silence et les murs écroulés.

Il est accablant de traverser l'après-midi cette bourg martyre, dans laquelle on perçoit peu à peu le décombre où se nichent quelque clarté. Et si disloquante reste de bout, c'est en dissimulant ces plaies numériques. Il n'est pas une rue qui n'ait été tragédie.

Comment étonner que le problème du logement ait ici des répercussions considérables et, ajouté à celui des spoliations, finisse par diviser les Alsaciens en deux clans ? ceux qui...

LE PROBLÈME constitutionnel et le mode du prochain scrutin étudiés en Conseil des ministres

Les délibérations gouvernementales commencées hier reprennent ce matin

Le Conseil des Ministres, qui s'est réuni hier sous la présidence du général de Gaulle, n'a pas achevé ses délibérations et va les reprendre ce matin.

Son ordre du jour comportait l'examen des différents projets concernant la question constitutionnelle et le prochain mode de scrutin. Le Conseil a siégé durant plusieurs heures, il n'a pas douteux qu'une partie du prochain mercredi n'ait été résolue. On croit qu'en matière de référendum serait « actuel (?) l'approbation du Conseil », à l'exception toutefois des deux représentants du parti communiste et d'un ministre radical, qui ont ainsi marqué le point de vue de leur parti, hostiles à toute forme de référendum.

Les questions posées au suffrage resteront scellées celles qui ont été formulées à plusieurs reprises par le président du Gouvernement, et qui donnent le choix à l'électeur entre : 1. La Constitution de 1875, 2. l'élection d'une Constituante par l'élection d'une Constituante qui aura pleins pouvoirs ou un nouveau mandat.

Sur ce point, le Conseil des ministres aurait examiné le projet soumis par l'Assemblée consultative et écarté par elle à la justesse par MM. Vincent et Bastid. On eût été en vain le texte du Gouvernement soumis responsable devant l'Assemblée, mais de certaines dispositions réglementaires autoriseront sa stabilité. L'Assemblée voterait les lois et le budget... et des dépenses.

Comment votera-t-on ?

Les dispositions complémentaires examinées, il restera encore un Français à décider le mode du scrutin selon lequel seront élus la prochaine assemblée constituante.

Il est probable que le scrutin unanime d'arrondissement sera écarté au profit de la liste départementale avec répartition proportionnelle pour laquelle s'est prononcée la majorité de l'Assemblée consultative. L'adoption de ce système de scrutin offrira différentes modalités entre lesquelles il revient au Gouvernement de choisir.

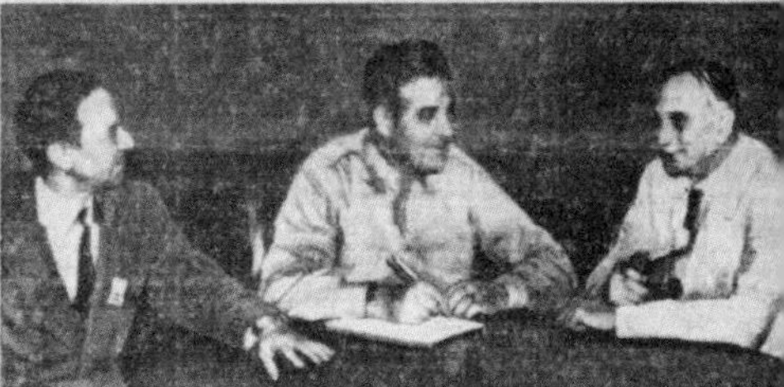

Trois des hommes qui travaillèrent à la mise au point de la bombe atomique : Sir James Chadwick, le général Groves et le Dr Richard Tolman.

L'emploi de la puissance atomique suscite les spéculations les plus hardies
sur le développement futur des industries et les rapports entre les peuples

De notre correspondant particulier Jean-Paul de DADELSEN

L ONDRES, 7 août (par téléphone). — La première bombe atomique lâchée sur Hiroshima a eu en Grande-Bretagne un formidable retentissement. L'effet produit sur les imaginations est, dès maintenant, bien plus profond que celui d'une information sensationnelle concernant un fait de guerre. Ce n'est pas seulement la révolution technique dans le domaine de la destruction avec ses conséquences stratégiques, mathématiques, morales, qui frappe les esprits, ce qui impressionne l'opinion peut être le tirage encore, c'est de deviner le point de départ possible d'une prodigieuse révolution industrielle avec toutes les répercussions politiques et sociales qu'elle peut avoir sur l'équilibre général du monde et sur la structure intérieure des nations.

L'ensemble de la presse britannique contribue fortement à donner à l'opinion l'impression qu'il y a là une date, dans l'histoire générale de l'humanité, comparable au passage de l'âge de pierre à l'âge de fer ou à l'apparition de la première machine à vapeur.

Un point d'histoire

En ce qui concerne l'histoire de la présente guerre, le correspondant diplomatique du journal du soir affirme que la première décision d'employer la bombe atomique a été prise par MM. Truman et Churchill au cours du mois dernier pour le cas où l'ultimatum adressé à Tokio ne provoquerait ni même l'intervention ni même simplement diplomatique de la Russie pour hâter la défaite japonaise.

Moscou, selon le correspondant, n'aurait pas été mis au courant de l'existence de la nouvelle arme. L'accord Truman-Churchill sur...

" LES DECISIONS STRATEGIQUES DE POTSDAM SONT PERIMEES "
écrit le rédacteur diplomatique de Reuter

Londres, 7 août. — « La bombe atomique a d'ores et déjà rendu périmées les décisions stratégiques de Potsdam, aussi bien que de Téhéran ou de Yalta », écrit John Kimche, rédacteur diplomatique de l'agence Reuter.

C'est du moins l'avis de cet expert. La stratégie prend un aspect nouveau avec cette découverte. La sécurité ne se définit plus par la réalité des Dardanelles ou de Suez. La possession du port de Kœnigsberg par la Russie ou de telle ou telle rivière ou chaîne de montagnes comme frontières n'ajoutera rien aux avantages stratégiques possédés par les adversaires.

Ainsi, par exemple, la frontière du Rhin ou la possession de Cologne sont désormais privées de frontières stratégiques. Il est parfaitement probable que la production des bombes atomiques, placée sous le contrôle de certaines puissances dominantes, soit réservée à quelques grandes puissances pour le protection des rapports de dépendance des petites puissances envers les grandes. S'il est certain que la bombe atomique est une arme sera un gage de compétition entre les grandes puissances, il est certain également qu'il faudra réviser les conceptions anciennes qui ont fait l'objet des discussions entre « Trois Grands » et qui, dans les circonstances actuelles, ne se justifient plus. (A.F.P.)

POUR METTRE AU POINT ET FABRIQUER des bombes atomiques, les Américains édifièrent une cité nouvelle

C'est à bord de l'« Augusta » que le président Truman a annoncé l'utilisation de la bombe atomique. Les membres de l'équipage accueillirent la nouvelle avec enthousiasme et exprimèrent l'espoir de rentrer bientôt chez eux à la victoire.

Le président rendit grâce à M. Stimson qui lutta à bénéficiâmes » pour obtenir les crédits nécessaires à la fabrication du nouvel engin, crédits se montaient à deux milliards et demi de dollars. Il a en outre révélé que le secret au sujet de cette arme que M. Stimson était allié le suivi à Potsdam au cours de la Conférence.

La bombe atomique, dont une colonne relativement réduite « le dixième des plusieurs pouces » brisera comme à le remporter (...) explosive une arme que 20.000 tonnes de dynamite. Les premiers essais de l'engin eurent lieu le 16 juillet dernier. La bombe fut placée en haut d'une tour d'acier, tandis que des observateurs se plaçaient respectueusement à 10 kilomètres de la tour. Les signaux annoncent l'imminence de l'explosion, furent faits par radio. C'est le docteur Bainbridge du Massachusetts, qui commandait l'explosion. 45 secondes avant l'instant « x » signalé à la réception...

« La puissance de feu fut telle que dix-sept des observateurs, qui suivaient l'explosion, furent projetés à terre; d'autres, malgré leurs verres colorés, furent aveuglés quelques instants. Pour un instant, il fut minuit en plein jour. La colonne de feu monta à 3.000 mètres de hauteur... »

Par qui fut découverte la nouvelle arme ?

L'Agence a apporté une contribution à l'élaboration de la bombe atomique. MM. Anderson, Robert Oppenheimer et le Comité de la bombe atomique du « Manhattan » ont collaboré...

Comment a été fabriquée la bombe atomique

Une cité spéciale fut construite pour mettre au point et produire les bombes atomiques à Oak Ridge, dans l'État de Tennessee...

Le général de Gaulle se rendra à Beauvais et à Béthune samedi et dimanche prochains

Le directeur de l'I.G. Farben est arrêté

Le Vatican condamne la bombe atomique

Cité du Vatican, 7 août. — Selon une déclaration recueillie par l'Associated Press, l'« Osservatore Romano » a condamné l'emploi de la bombe atomique...

« La recherche de nouvelles alliances ne s'impose plus avec la même force »

Londres, 7 août. — La bombe atomique rend sans valeur tout le système des accords politiques et des alliances militaires...

Avec parachu...

Une tour volati...

RADIO-TOKIO RECONNAIT QUE DES « BOMBES » D'UN NOUVEAU GENRE ont provoqué à Hiroshima des dégâts considérables

115
Albert Camus (1913–1960)
"Le monde est ce qu'il est,
c'est-à-dire peu de chose",
Combat, No. 366, 8 August 1945

Geneva, private collection

On the morning of 6 August 1945, the B-29 Superfortress *Enola Gay* dropped an atomic bomb on Hiroshima. The bomb, called *Little Boy*, was three metres long and weighed 4.5 tonnes (64 kg of which were enriched uranium-235). The impact on the Japanese city was devastating: seventy thousand were killed, most of them in fires ignited by the wave of heat. Several tens of thousands sustained serious burns and many more would die years later from the effects of the radiation. Going against the mainstream view at the time, on 8 August Albert Camus wrote an editorial – acclaimed to this day – for the magazine *Combat* that began, "The world is what it is, which is to say, nothing much." He was one of the few to immediately grasp the event's significance: "the civilization of the machine has just reached its ultimate degree of savagery. We will have to choose, in the relatively near future, between collective suicide and the intelligent use of scientific conquests." The author of *The Plague*, while not displeased that the atomic bomb had no doubt hastened Japan's defeat, focused on "the terrifying prospects now available to humanity", considering that the only alternative to more destruction was the search for peace. That peace, he hoped, will be concluded within "a genuine international organization in which the great powers will have no more rights than medium-sized or small nations, and in which war, a plague that has become terminal by the fruits of the human mind alone, will no longer be decided by the appetites or doctrines of any one state". He ended the editorial by calling on humans to choose between "hell and reason".   **P. H.**

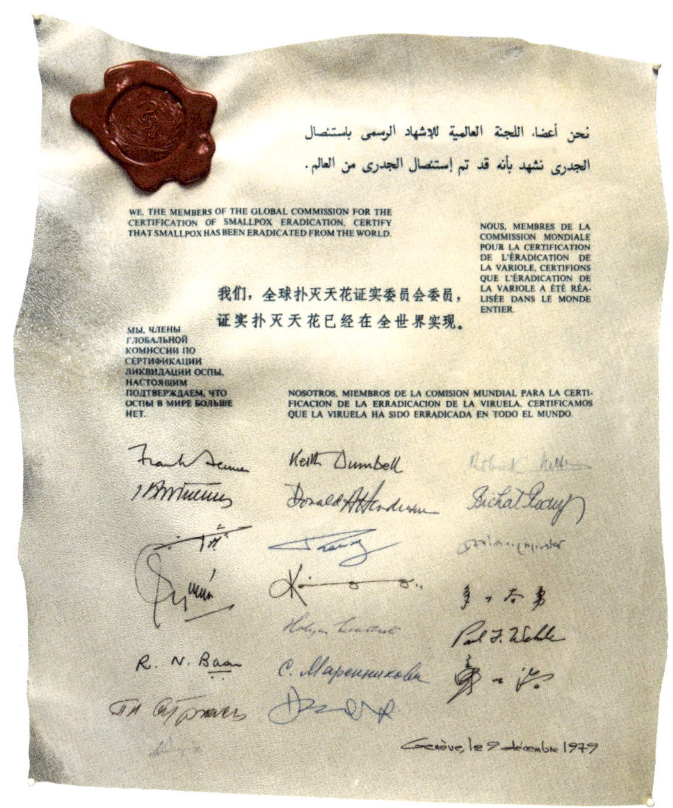

116
Global Commission for
the Certification of Smallpox
Eradication, parchment certifying
the eradication of smallpox,
9 December 1979

Geneva, Archives of the World Health Organization

Maintaining peace involves more than establishing political mechanisms to avoid or resolve conflicts. It implies, above all, the creation of conditions conducive to international peace and security. That preventive element lies at the heart of the work of the United Nations, the founding treaty of which, the Charter of the United Nations, recognizes respect for international law and human rights, alongside economic and social progress, as essential factors of peace. Today, the entities making up the United Nations system work in a host of fields, contributing to a global approach to the maintenance of peace. Continuing on from the principles enshrined in the Charter, the Constitution of the World Health Organization (WHO), which entered into force in 1948, recognizes that the "health of all peoples is fundamental to the attainment of peace and security". From that perspective, the eradication of smallpox, attested by the parchment signed by the members of the Global Commission in 1979, is an extraordinary victory that is worth highlighting: the first disease to be vanquished thanks to concerted action by states.   **P.-E. B.**

Peace is a matter of treaties as well as symbols.

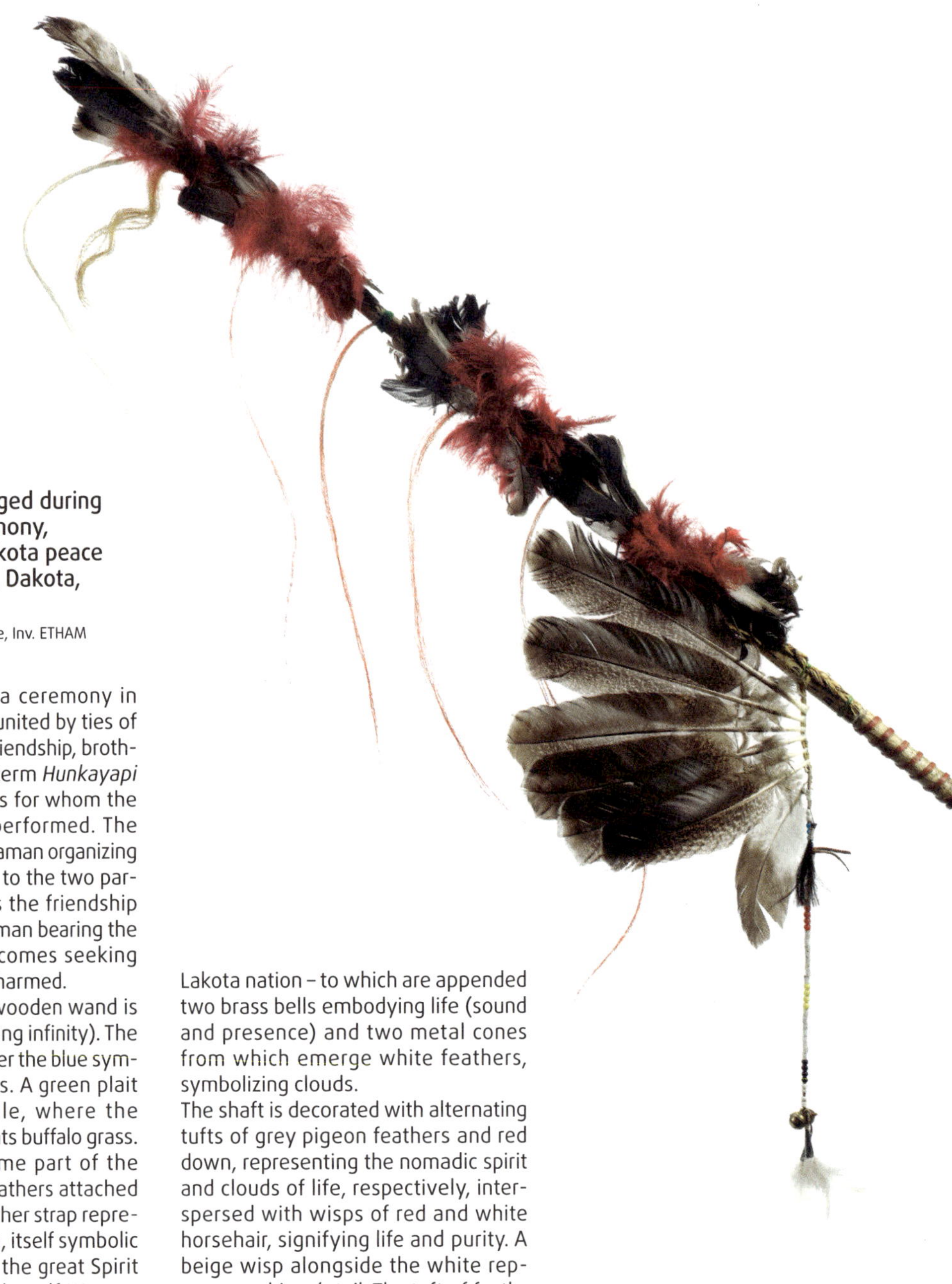

117
Hunka wand exchanged during the *Hunkayapi* ceremony, forerunner of the Lakota peace pipe, North America, Dakota, date unknown

Geneva, Musée d'ethnographie, Inv. ETHAM 027915

The *Hunka* is a Lakota ceremony in which two people are united by ties of fidelity stronger than friendship, brotherhood or family. The term *Hunkayapi* designates the persons for whom the ceremony has been performed. The wand belongs to the shaman organizing the ceremony. Handed to the two participants, it represents the friendship between two tribes. A man bearing the wand shows that he comes seeking peace and may not be harmed.

This feather-covered wooden wand is painted blue (symbolizing infinity). The black marks painted over the blue symbolize bison hoofprints. A green plait just above the handle, where the feathers start, represents buffalo grass. Hanging from the same part of the wand, seven turkey feathers attached to a loose-hanging leather strap represent the number seven, itself symbolic of the four directions, the great Spirit (Wakan Tanka), Buffalo Calf Woman and the son of the creator. The band ends in a string of white, red, yellow and blue beads – the colours of the Lakota nation – to which are appended two brass bells embodying life (sound and presence) and two metal cones from which emerge white feathers, symbolizing clouds.

The shaft is decorated with alternating tufts of grey pigeon feathers and red down, representing the nomadic spirit and clouds of life, respectively, interspersed with wisps of red and white horsehair, signifying life and purity. A beige wisp alongside the white represents a bison's tail. The tuft of feathers at the very top symbolizes the *orenda*, the spirits of space.

C. D.

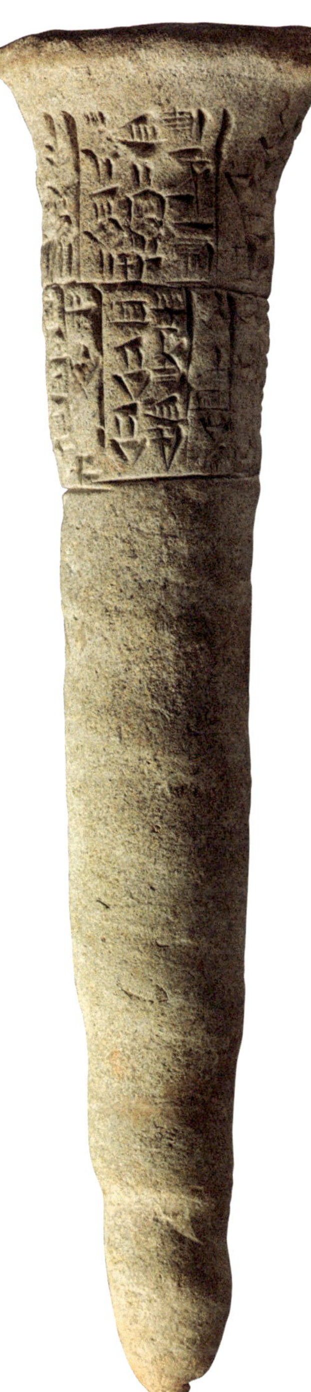

118
Entemena (third millenium BC)
[Treaty of alliance with Uruk]
Sumerian cuneiform inscription on
clay nail, Tell el-Medain, near Tello
(ancient city of Girsu), *c.* 2430 BC

Cologny, Martin Bodmer Foundation, inv. 32

"For Inanna and for An, king of the
temple of Inanna, Entemena, governor/
king of Lagash, has built the temple of
Inanna, their beloved temple … On this
day, Entemena, governor/king of
Lagash, and Lugal-ki-ni-she-du-du,
governor/king of Uruk, have formed an
alliance [literally: made [a treaty of]
fraternity]." Inscribed on a clay nail used
in the foundations of the E-Khu temple,
dedicated to the goddess of fertility and
war (the Sumerian manifestation of the
Mesopotamian goddess Ishtar), this

text is known today thanks to forty-six
complete or fragmentary copies, in the
form of nails, cylinders or bricks; it is the
oldest surviving diplomatic text in the
world. The son of the great warrior-king
Eannatum, Entemena completed the
subjugation of the rival city-state of
Umma begun by his father. He likewise
won a war against the king of Uruk,
Lugal-kigin-dudu, and signed a treaty
of peace and fraternity with him in
order to strengthen his political position
in Sumer. Although widely publicized
(as evidenced by the number of extant
copies), the treaty nevertheless reflects
the decline of the kingdom of Lagash,
forced to negotiate on equal terms with
Uruk, its former vassal, which in the following decades became the dominant
regional power. **N. D.**

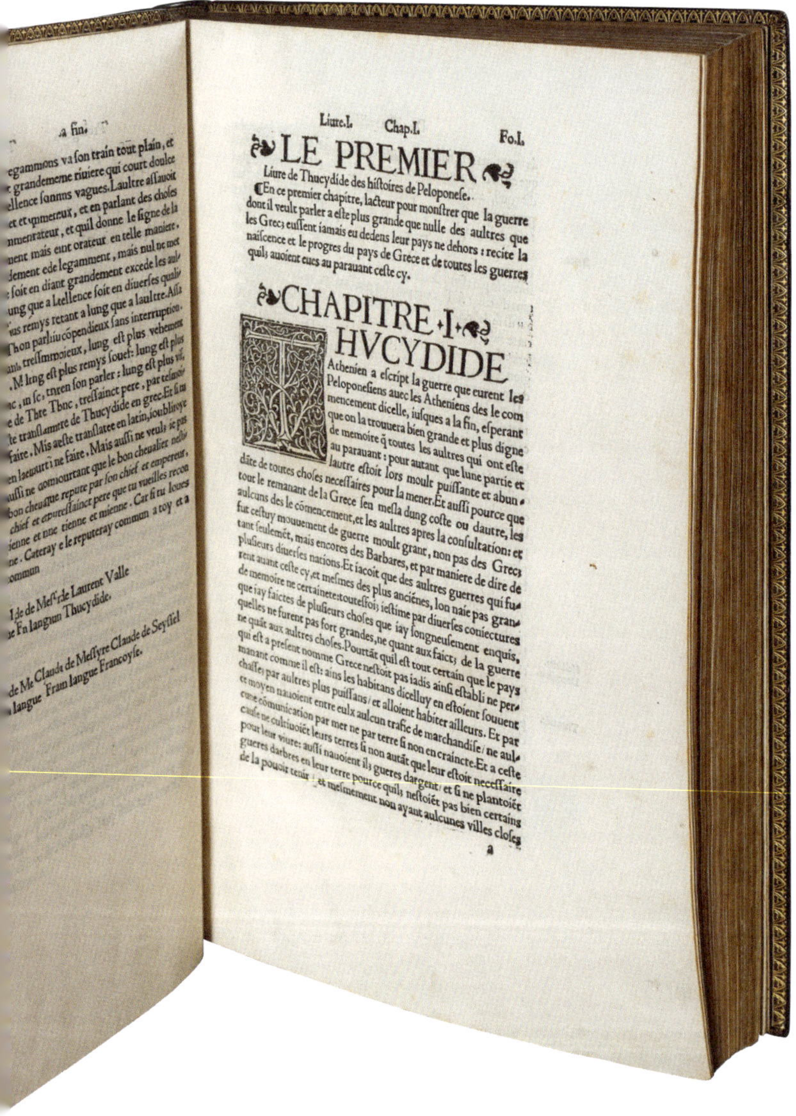

119
Thucydides
(465–400 or 395 BC)
La Guerre du Péloponnèse
[*The Peloponnesian War*],
trans. Claude de Seyssel,
Paris, Conrad Bade, 1527,
first French edition

Cologny, Martin Bodmer Foundation

The peace treaty concluded in 421 BC between Athens and Sparta is named after the Athenian general Nicias, its main advocate to the Athenians, although it was in fact initiatied by Sparta in 425, not least with the aim of recovering the three hundred elite Spartan warriors captured by the Athenians at Pylos. The treaty (of which Thucydides transcribed the official text, kept in the Athenian archives) brought to an end the first phase of the Peloponnesian War, begun in 431 BC. It was signed by the two belligerents on an equal footing, and was to remain in place for fifty years. The treaty was thus meant to establish a long-term truce rather than a lasting peace, leaving open the possibility of resuming the struggle for hegemony once the two cities had reassembled their forces. The adversaries agreed in essence to revert to the pre-war situation: they undertook to guarantee access for all Greeks to the Panhellenic shrines, to return prisoners and strongholds captured during the conflict, and to settle their disputes through arbitration. The treaty was reinforced by a defensive military alliance, also limited to fifty years. The peace broke down soon afterwards, however, for three principal reasons: first, Sparta's main allies refused to observe it; second, the issue of restitution was not resolved satisfactorily; and third, the Athenians, urged on by Alcibiades, immediately sought to damage their rivals by sowing discord in Peloponnesian affairs, while avoiding open confrontation. In 415 BC already, Sparta repudiated the treaty in retaliation for the Athenian decision to attack their ally Syracuse.

P. S.

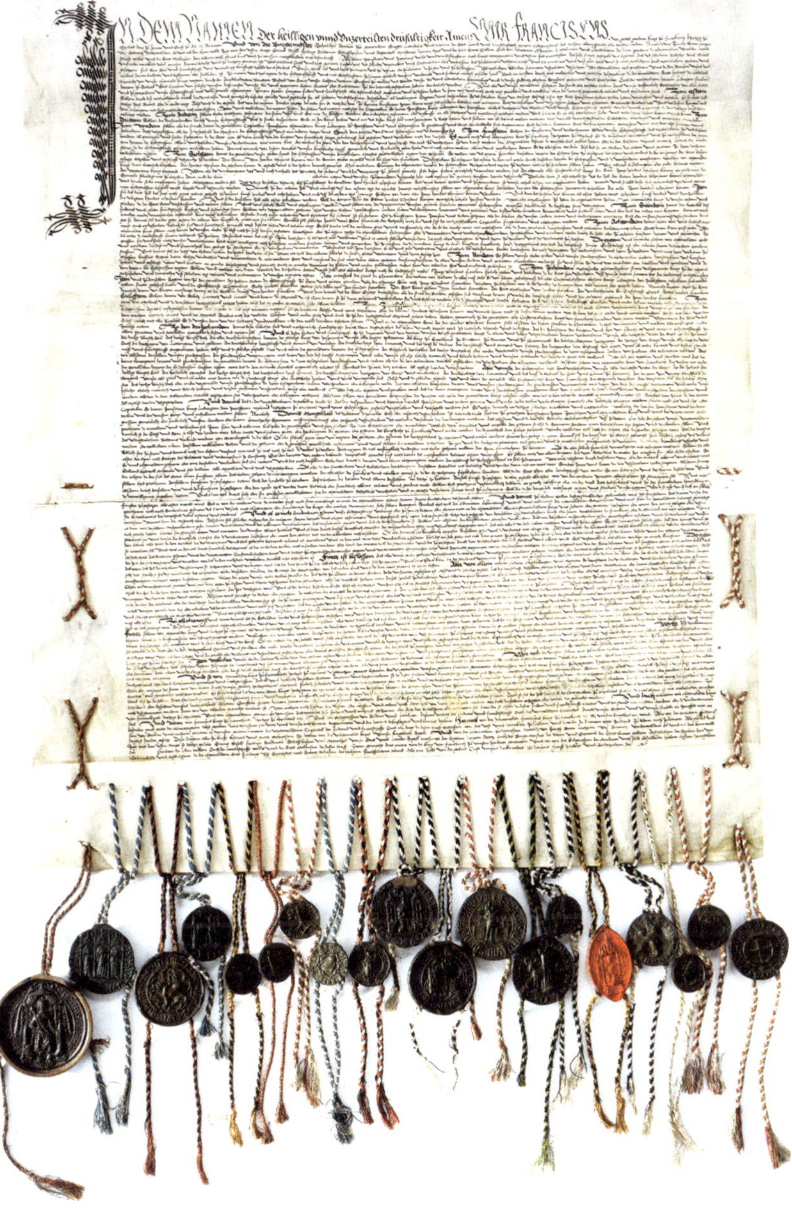

Treaty of Perpetual Peace between the Swiss Confederacy and France, 1516, original document

Fribourg, State Archives

The 1516 Treaty of Perpetual Peace between the Swiss Confederacy and the king of France marked the end of Swiss expansionism south of the Alps during the Italian Wars. Supplemented with a periodically renewed treaty of defensive alliance (1521), it stabilized bilateral relations until the French Revolution. After a series of victories and territorial conquests, the Swiss mercenaries in the service of the duke of Milan were defeated by Francis I at Marignan, in September 1515. A first treaty of peace between the two sides, concluded in November in Geneva, never entered into force owing to the objections of several cantons, in particular to the cession of Locarno and Lugano to France. Following lengthy negotiations, a new text was approved in Fribourg, on 25 November 1516: a "Treaty of Peace and Friendship between Francis I, King of France, and the Confederation of Thirteen Cantons and its Allies" (abbot and city of St Gallen, Three Leagues, Valais and city of Mulhouse). The nineteen wax seals – that of the king, followed by those of the Swiss cantons by order of precedence – are affixed to the bottom of the document, which is written in German and conserved in Fribourg. There is a Latin version, without the king's seal, in Paris. Under the terms of the treaty, the Confederacy renounced its claim to Milan but kept the entire territory of the present-day canton of Tessin. Francis I paid it a one-time compensatory sum and an annuity. The parties also granted their citizens trade privileges. The Treaty of Perpetual Peace, as it was known, was of huge significance to the Old Swiss Confederacy, both domestically and diplomatically. The 500th anniversary of its signing was commemorated in a celebration attended by ministers.

F. W.

121
Henry IV (1553–1610)
Edict of Nantes and Secret Articles, apograph manuscript, 22 May 1599

Geneva, Bibliothèque de Genève, Ms. fr. 413, fol. 1-40

Signed in the final days of April 1598, the peace treaty known as the Edict of Nantes marked the end of the eighth and final War of Religion, after ten years of deadly fighting that saw Henry IV, the Protestant prince, reconquer his kingdom and his subjects both by the sword and through his clemency, using his conversion to reconcile the country. Concluded in the last rebel bastion of the ultra-Catholic League after its surrender, the treaty was largely based on previous edicts of tolerance. It granted Protestants fundamental rights such as freedom of religion and of conscience, safe havens, respect for legal rights and property and the right to hold public office, but prohibited them from offering communion in Paris and other cities in a series of secret (or particular) articles. As the basis of religious and civil peace, the Edict remained in force until its revocation in 1685. The two original copies have disappeared, the one in the possession of the Protestant negotiators having gone up in flames during the siege of La Rochelle in 1627–28. The only surviving record of the original wording is this contemporary apograph, copied from the Huguenot original. The Edict was modified several times after being submitted for registration by the Parliament of Paris, in early 1599, and it is this modified version that appeared in the first print edition, under the title *Edit du Roi et déclaration sur les dits de pacification faits à Nantes au mois d'avril 1598...* ("Attached the copy printed in Paris", 1599).

N. D.

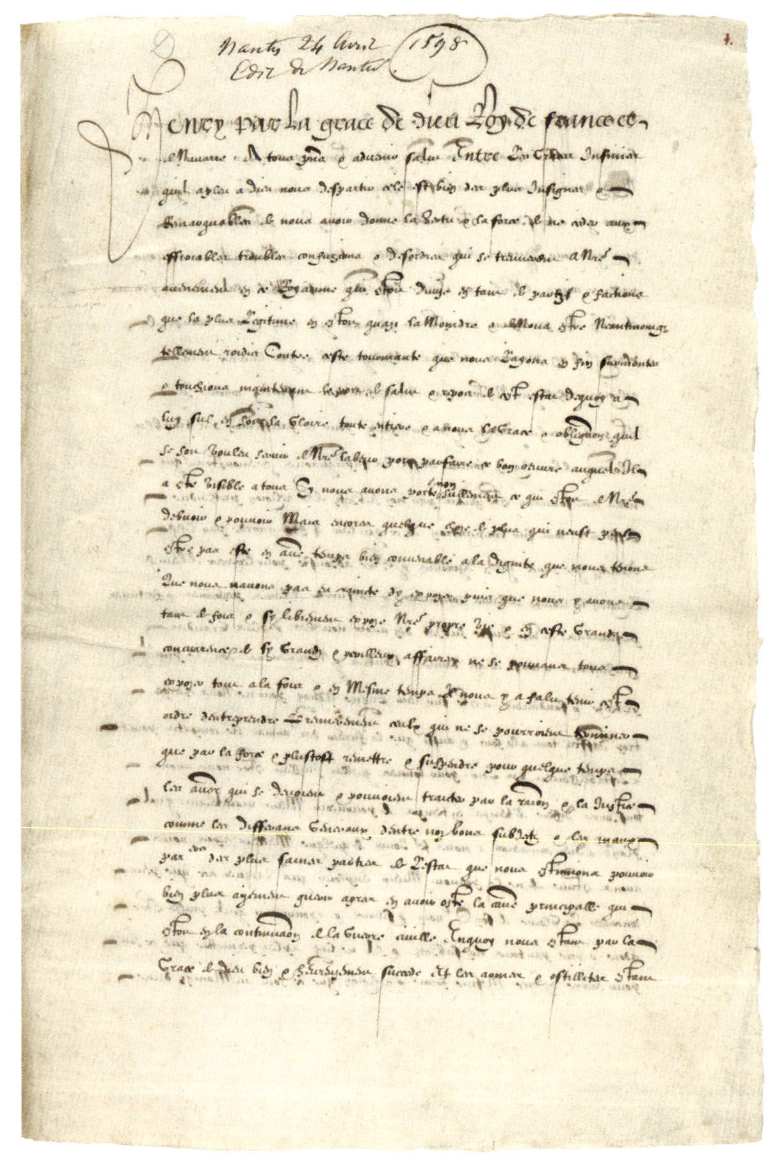

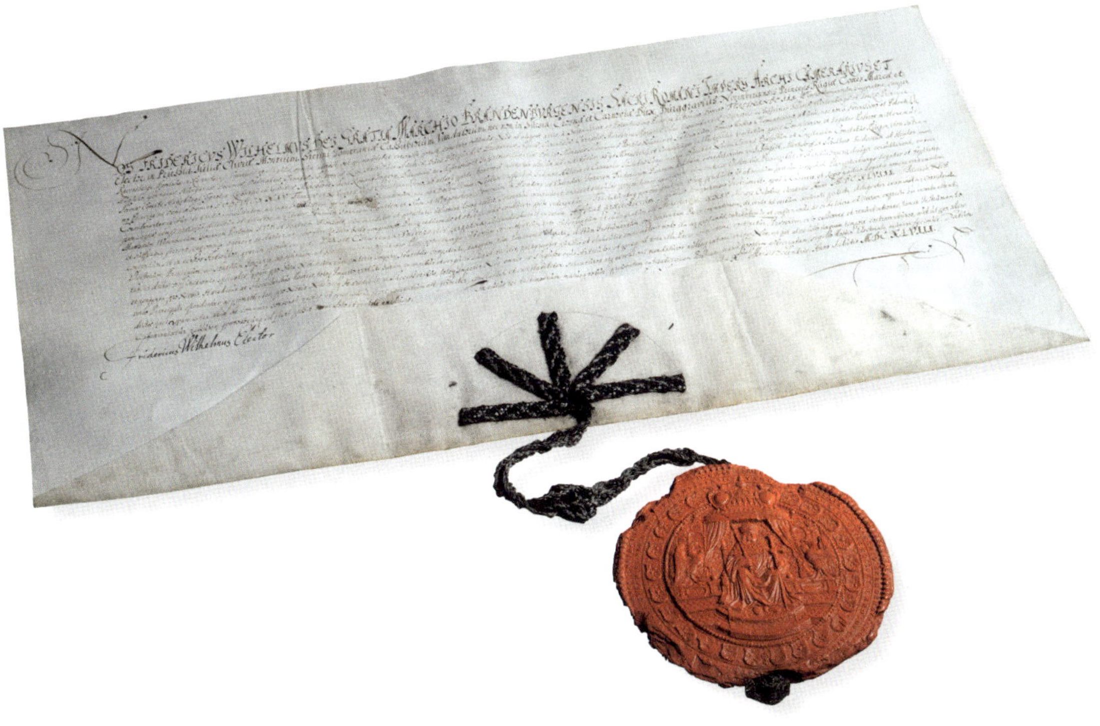

122
**Peace of Westphalia, decree
of ratification by Frederick William
I, Margrave of Brandenburg,
Cleves, 10 December 1648**
Original parchment, with red wax
seal affixed on a cord of silk
and silver thread

La Courneuve, Archives du ministère des Affaires
étrangères, TRA 16480001/005

Considered a turning point in the history
of modern Europe, the Peace of Westphalia spelled the end of a particularly
long and painful conflict, the Thirty
Years' War (1618–48), which, though
opposing France and the Holy Roman
Empire, set much of Europe aflame. The
treaty was exceptional for the length of
the negotiations leading up to it (1644–
48) and the number of diplomats (nearly
three hundred) who took part in them,
both in Münster and Osnabrück, where
the delegations of the Catholic and the
Protestant powers where quartered.
Containing provisions on territorial matters, religious observance and the constitution of the empire, the Peace came
to be seen as the cornerstone of order
in Europe. Its significance for French and
German history, and its place in the
national memory of both countries, cannot be understated. On the German
side, it was generally viewed in a
favourable light – both at the time and
by subsequent generations, well into
the eighteenth century – for establishing
lasting order in the empire after years of
horrific fighting. Others, however, saw
1648 as a dark year, and blamed
Richelieu and Louis XIV for the misfortunes that befell the German states.
That view was also widespread among
nineteenth-century Prussian and
Austrian historians. After the Second
World War, the Peace of 1648 was
restored to the curriculum as a chapter
in the common history of the various
Christian European nations.
A table of the decrees of ratification of
the treaties of Münster and Osnabrück,
published in *Acta Pacis Westphalicae*,
lists 250 for Germany and fifty for
France (thirty-six in the National
Archives and fourteen in the archives of
the Ministry of Foreign Affairs). The latter include this decree signed by
Frederic William I, prince elector of
Brandenburg, who skilfully negotiated
the same rights for members of the
Reformed church as had been enjoyed
until then by the Lutherans. Equally
keen to advance his territorial interests,
he annexed the bishopric of Minden,
after the ecclesiastical principality was
secularized. **I. R.**

123

Act of accession by the kingdom of France to the Acts of the Congress of Vienna and to the treaty between Prussia and Saxony of 18 May 1815, Paris, 18 September 1815

La Courneuve, Archives du ministère des Affaires étrangères, TRA 18150001/040

Convened under the presidency of Austria, in November 1814, to reshape Europe after twenty-five years of upheaval, the Congress of Vienna closed on 9 June 1815 with the signing of a "Final Act" reflecting the will of the powers to "embrace, in one common transaction, the various results of their negotiations". As such, the Final Act is often considered the first multilateral treaty in the history of international law. It instituted a new order that was grounded in constant dialogue between the powers and that was brought to a halt by the First World War. In its original version, the Final Act comprised 121 articles and seventeen annexes (copies of various agreements negotiated during the congress), which together redrew the map of Europe. It focused in particular on the reorganization of Germany, with the constitution of the German Confederation and a map altered for the benefit of Prussia, which obtained almost two-fifths of the Kingdom of Saxony. The annexes thus included the contemporaneous copy, in French, of the treaty signed in Vienna on 18 May 1815 between Prussia and Saxony, establishing the border and recording the king of Saxony's renunciation to all claim to Poland, which was divided up between Prussia and Russia.

Speaking for a vanquished power, Talleyrand was nonetheless able to promote the interests of France to the four major powers – Austria, Great Britain, Prussia and Russia – and his authority to sign the treaty was not contested, even though he represented, at the close of the congress, a king who had fled to Ghent in an episode known as the "flight of the Eagle". After Waterloo and the return to power of Louis XVIII on 8 July 1815, matters proceeded as though the treaties signed during the Hundred Days would need to be confirmed by the king. Hence the need to draw up an act of accession by the kingdom of France to the Final Act and to the treaty between Prussia and Saxony, towards which imperial France had been the best of allies. Again, it was Talleyrand who was called on to place his signature next to that of the Duke of Schulenburg, representing Saxony, on the bilateral treaty of accession, whereby the king of France undertook to be bound by all the clauses of the treaty of 18 May 1815.

I. N.

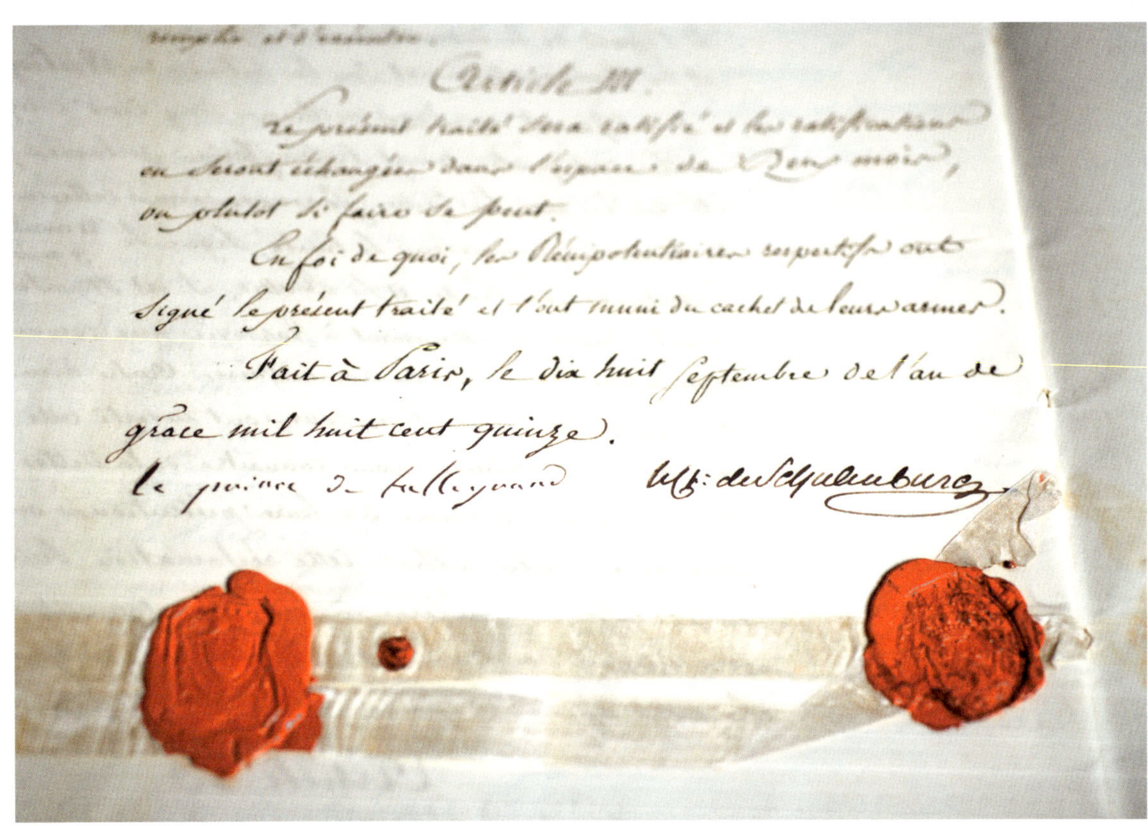

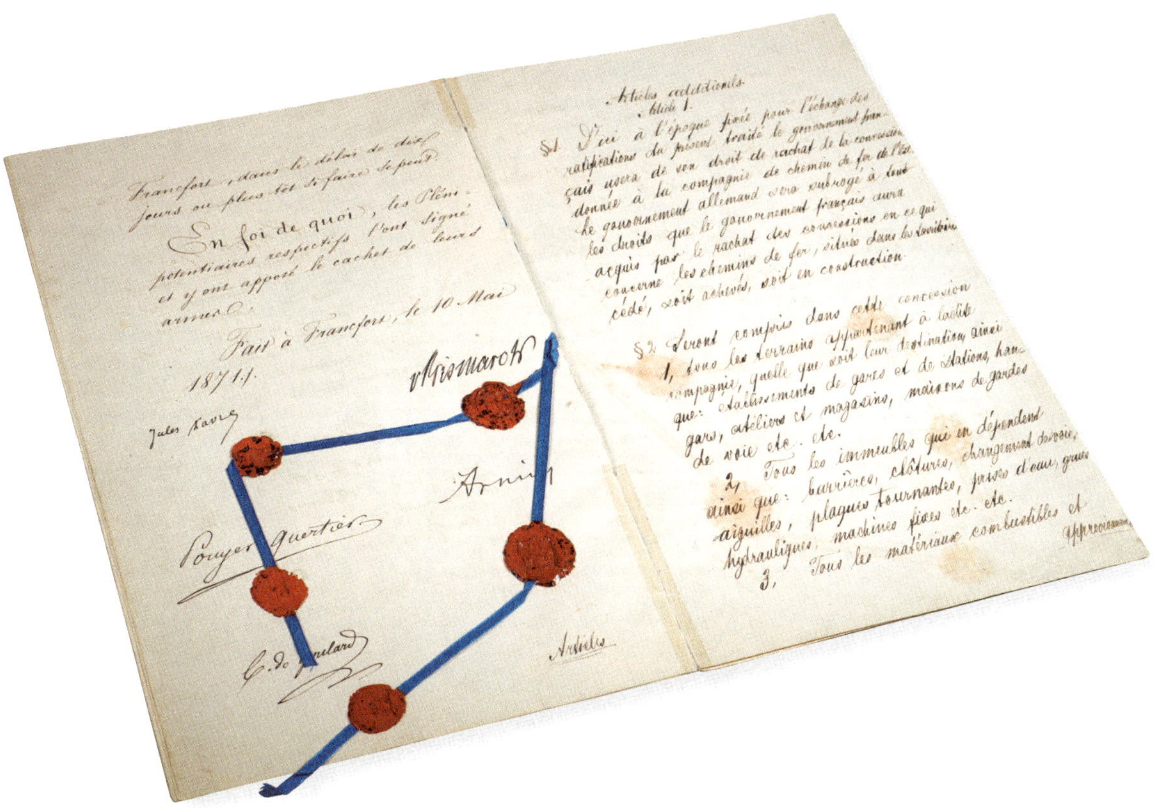

124
Peace treaty between France and Germany, Frankfurt, 10 May 1871, original document in French

La Courneuve, Archives du ministère des Affaires étrangères, TRA 18710015/001

The eighteen articles of the Treaty of Frankfurt put an end to the Franco-Prussian War of 1870–71. One of the signatories was the French minister of finance – as would again be the case at the end of the First World War – with a view to settling the heavy economic consequences of the conflict. Augustin Pouyer-Quertier, a graduate of the École polytechnique and minister for finance from 25 February 1871 to 5 March 1872, was thus seated next to Jules Favre (minister of foreign affairs in the government of Adolphe Thiers, who had just been elected president of the French Republic), Eugène de Goulard (member of parliament), the German chancellor, Prince Otto von Bismarck, and Count Harry von Arnim (German envoy to the Holy See). He played an important part in the negotiations that followed the signing of the provisional armistice on 26 January 1871 (published on 28 January), from the preliminaries for peace on 26 February to the payment of the war reparations demanded by the German empire, founded on 18 January of the same year, in the Hall of Mirrors at Versailles. By raising a series of new taxes, he obtained parliament's approval for a bond issue totalling 2.5 million francs (law of 20 May 1871) which, paid in two tranches, served to liberate nine occupied departments at the end of 1871. He signed two conventions after the treaty of 10 May, the first at Frankfurt on 21 May, "relating to the modalities for the payment of the sum of 500 million stipulated in the peace treaty", the second on 12 October, in Berlin, on "the evacuation of six departments and the payment to Germany of an amount of 650 million". Thanks to his efforts in particular, the reparations of five billion gold francs were paid off much earlier than anticipated and the last German soldier left France on 16 September 1873.

The peace treaty also redefined the borders of the belligerents, expanded the territory around Belfort, which remained French, provided for freedom of navigation on the Moselle and the canals, granted most-favoured nation status to Germany for trade and navigation, gave the inhabitants of Alsace-Lorraine the right to opt for French nationality by declaring their intention to do so before 1 October 1872, and stipulated that no inhabitant of a ceded territory could be prosecuted, troubled or sought in respect of his person or property owing to political or military acts carried out during the war. It was the first treaty to lay down rules for the protection of soldiers' graves. It also dealt with the organization of church services, which, depending on the religion, would cease to be governed by the French religious authorities.
A. L.

125

Tribunal of arbitration on the *Alabama* claims, decision handed down by the tribunal of arbitration established under article I of the treaty concluded in Washington on 8 May 1871, original documents in French and English

Geneva, State Archives, Alabama 1

On 15 September 1872, a tribunal of arbitration, sitting in Geneva, ordered Great Britain to pay the United States of America a particularly high amount in damages ($15.5 million in 1872 dollars) for having failed to abide by its international obligation of strict neutrality during the American Civil War. The decision stipulated that her majesty's government had acted with culpable negligence in tolerating the delivery, from its territory, of about twenty armored vessels, including the sloop CSS *Alabama*, to the Confederate rebels. That covert military aid, which London granted the Confederates in violation of the British Neutrality Act, caused enormous damage to the North's merchant marine. The British government accepted the decision, as did the United States, which had demanded compensation of two billion dollars or the cession of Canada.

This case is the first example of recourse to a supranational jurisdiction and laid the foundations of public international law. It is well known for a number of reasons: it paved the way for a new mode of peacefully settling disputes in international relations; it opposed two major powers full of their own might and prestige; and lastly, it gave the city of Geneva international stature, as a result of which it would subsequently be chosen to host the headquarters of the League of Nations. **P. H.**

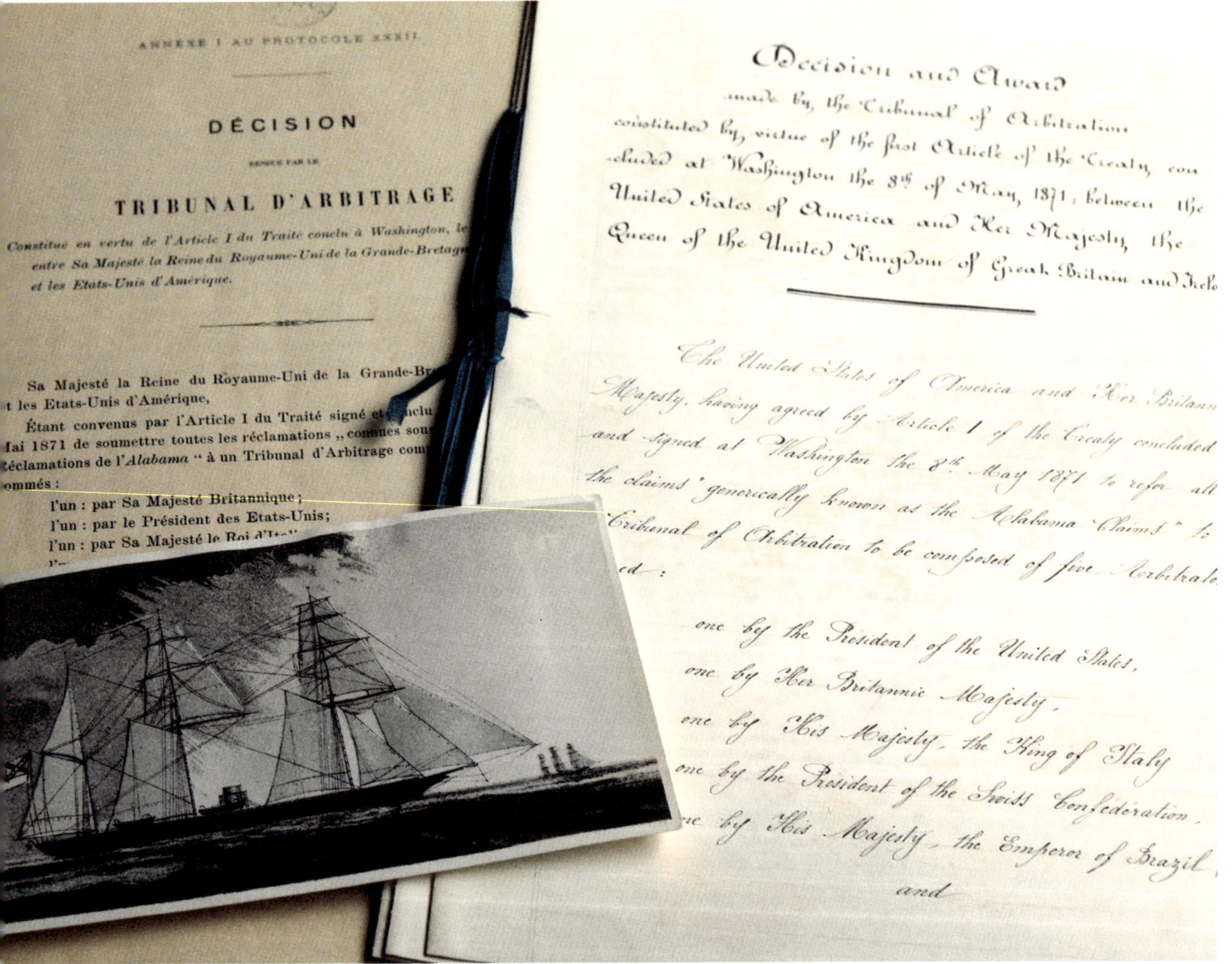

126
Alfred Nobel (1833–1896)
Letter to Bertha von Suttner,
7 January 1893

Geneva, United Nations Archives

In his letter of 7 January 1893 to Bertha von Suttner, a major figure in pre-war Austrian pacifism, Alfred Nobel spoke of his intention to set aside an amount in his will to create a peace prize. "I would like," he wrote, "… to provide that part of my fortune shall be distributed as a prize … to the man or woman having done the most to advance the cause of peace in Europe." Nobel considered that the prize should be awarded "every five years", "shall we say, six times in all", "for if in thirty years we have not succeeded in reforming the current system we shall have to return to savagery". The inventor of dynamite, Nobel acknowledged that the cause would not be advanced through disarmament, "which would happen but timidly and slowly", nor through "absolutely compulsory arbitration". He nevertheless considered that "we should attain this result if all states jointly commit to attack the state that attacked first". "That would be tantamount to making war impossible and forcing even the most brutal and unreasonable of powers to have recourse to arbitration." Two years after he wrote the letter, Nobel signed his will. Since 1901, the Nobel Peace Prize has been awarded ninety-nine times. Bertha von Suttner was the first woman laureate, in 1905.

P.-E. B.

2340 S STREET N W

WOODROW WILSON
WASHINGTON D C

2nd October 1923

My dear Sir Eric,

Your letter of September seventh was very welcome and has gratified me very much.

I share your satisfaction in the record already made by the League and your confidence that its future is assured. I personally have no doubt that no nation that wishes to play a satisfying part in the affairs of the world will find it possible to remain long outside of the League. The enemies of the League are proving as impotent as they are ignorant and the mills of the gods are proceeding to grind them exceeding fine.

I warmly appreciate your generous assurances of friendship and approval and hope that you may gain increasing satisfaction in the performance of the great duties which have fallen to you. I am sure that you can count upon the confident support of all who have been competent to observe the administration of the General Secretariat.

With sincere personal regard,

Faithfully Yours,

Woodrow Wilson

Sir Eric Drummond.

127
Woodrow Wilson (1856–1924)
Letter to Eric Drummond,
2 October 1923
Geneva, United Nations Archives

After the First World War, the president of the United States, Woodrow Wilson, played a decisive role in the founding of the League of Nations. Had he not been so determined, even obstinate, the first international organization aimed at maintaining peace and promoting international cooperation would never have been established by the Paris Peace Conference. However, the American Senate refused to ratify the Treaty of Versailles, which incorporated the Covenant of the League of Nations. Several weeks later, the Republican victory in the 1920 presidential election marked a return to American isolationism.

In the letter that he sent in October 1923 to the League secretary-general, the British diplomat Eric Drummond, Wilson expressed satisfaction at the results achieved by the Geneva-based organization and confidence for its future. He personally had no doubt that "no nation that wishes to play a satisfying part in the affairs of the world will find it possible to remain long outside the League". Cooperation between Washington and the Geneva organization evolved over the years – and culminated in a significant rapprochement on technical cooperation matters – but the United States would never become a member of the League, which was deeply marked by that absence and never realized its vocation to be universal.   P.-E. B.

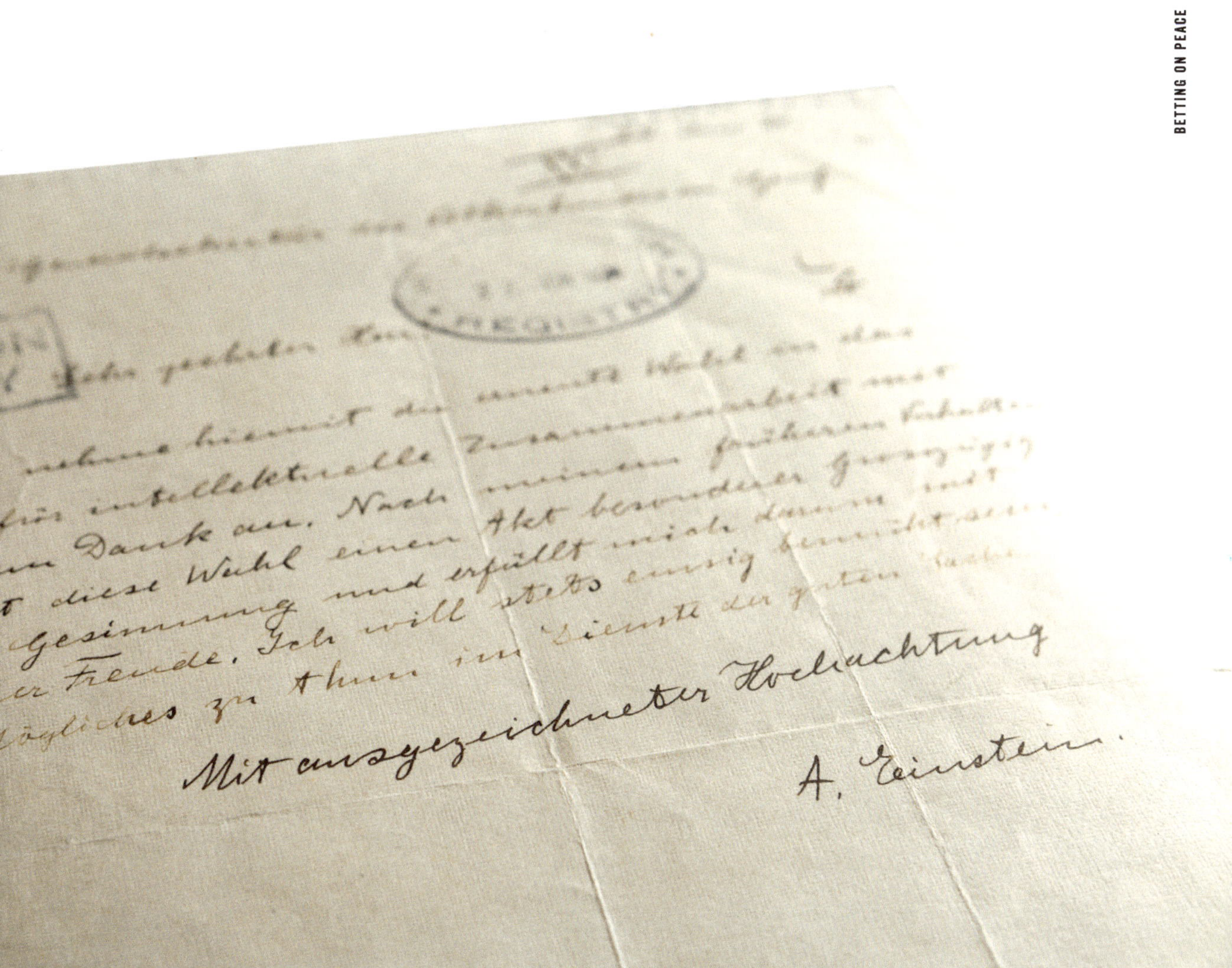

128
Albert Einstein (1879–1955)
Letter to Eric Drummond,
25 June 1924

Geneva, United Nations Archives

In this letter dated 25 June 1924, Albert Einstein thanked Eric Drummond, secretary-general of the League of Nations, for appointing him to the International Committee on Intellectual Cooperation. "In view of my past behaviour," he wrote, "this appointment represents an act of special generosity." Einstein had first been a member of the committee in 1922, but had resigned in 1923 in protest against the League's passivity in the face of the French occupation of the Ruhr. Einstein was no doubt one of the best-known figures to participate in the League's work in the field of intellectual cooperation. His colleagues included other scientists, such as Marie Curie and Hendrik Lorentz, but also writers such as Paul Valéry, Thomas Mann and Hélène Vacaresco, philosophers such as Henri Berstein, composers such as Béla Bartók, and university professors such as Sarvepalli Radhakrishnan, James Shotwell, Gilbert Murray and Johan Huizinga. The committee was part of the Intellectual Cooperation Organization, which gradually emerged within the League of Nations. Its objective was to bring peoples together by promoting better knowledge of the world. In addition to creating connections among intellectuals, the organization was active in numerous fields, such as education, academic cooperation and intellectual property protection. Most of its activities were later taken up by the United Nations Educational, Scientific and Cultural Organization (UNESCO).

P.-E. B.

129

"Rhineland Pact" of the Locarno Treaties, arbitration agreement between France and Germany, 26 October 1925

Geneva, United Nations Archives

This arbitration agreement, signed by Aristide Briand and Gustav Stresemann, is one of several treaties agreed in Locarno, in October 1925, at a conference attended by representatives of seven countries: Belgium, Czechoslovakia, France, Germany, Italy, Poland and the United Kingdom. In the Rhineland Pact, Germany recognizes its borders with France and Belgium as decided at Versailles, and accepts the demilitarization of the Rhineland. The three countries renounce war as a means of changing the status quo, while the United Kingdom and Italy agree to guarantee the implementation of these commitments. The Locarno Treaties paved the way for Germany's accession to the League of Nations. The Franco-German arbitration agreement defined processes for resolving issues that it "[might] not be possible to settle amicably by the normal methods of diplomacy". Any dispute between the two countries would be submitted to a Permanent Conciliation Commission, the Permanent Court of International Justice or an arbitration commission. If no agreement could be reached, the issue was to be brought before the Council of the League of Nations. Despite some ambiguities, the Locarno Treaties seemed like the fulfilment of hopes for a lasting peace in Europe. As Briand, the French foreign minister, solemnly declared in September 1926: "No more wars, no more brutal solutions to our disputes ... Like individuals who go before a magistrate to settle their difficulties, we too will settle ours through peaceful proceedings. Away with rifles, machine guns and cannons! In their stead, conciliation, arbitration and peace!" A few weeks later, Briand and Stresemann, his German counterpart, were awarded the Nobel Peace Prize.

P. E. B.

130
French ratification of the Kellogg-Briand Pact of 27 August 1928, decree of deposition signed by Paul Claudel, French ambassador to Washington, 22 April 1929

La Courneuve, Archives du ministère des Affaires étrangères, TRA 19280028/010

Forty years after starting his career as vice-consul in New York and acting consul in Boston, the writer Paul Claudel returned to the United States as ambassador to Washington. He was posted for seven years, from 1927, during the presidency of Calvin Coolidge, to 1933 and the election of Franklin Delano Roosevelt. In the summer of 1927, he wrote the libretto for an opera, *Le Livre de Christophe Colomb*, which expresses a hope for greater unity between Europe and America in almost programmatic fashion. While in Washington, Claudel negotiated the settlement of France's First World War debts to the United States. He lectured frequently on the historical ties between the two cultures. In a report from May 1928, he emphasized the fault lines in America's prosperity, an observation borne out by the Wall Street crash. Lastly, he supported and actively monitored the drafting of an international treaty to renounce war. The outcome of these efforts was a short text, comprising just three articles, which was signed on 27 August 1928 and ratified by France on 6 April 1929.

On 22 April, Claudel signed the decree of deposition on behalf of the French government, in accordance with article III of the "Kellogg-Briand Pact", as it came to be known: "The present Treaty shall be ratified by the High Contracting Parties named in the Preamble in accordance with their respective constitutional requirements, and shall take effect as between them as soon as all their several instruments of ratification have been deposited at Washington." The fifteen signatory countries (including the British dominions) who gathered in the formal Clock Room of the French Ministry of Foreign Affairs were all members of the League of Nations, except for the United States. In the following years, forty-eight other nations, including the Soviet Union, in September 1928, joined to the treaty, pledging not to settle their disputes by recourse to war except in self-defence. Contrary to the Locarno Treaties – which it did not abrogate – the Kellogg-Briand Pact did not stipulate any legal penalties or require signatories to disarm, and its effect was therefore limited. Far from offering guarantees of peace, it was essentially approved by parliaments for its moral effect. It expressed the desire for a new international order, which the United Nations would begin to realize, with more success, in the wake of the Second World War. **A. L.**

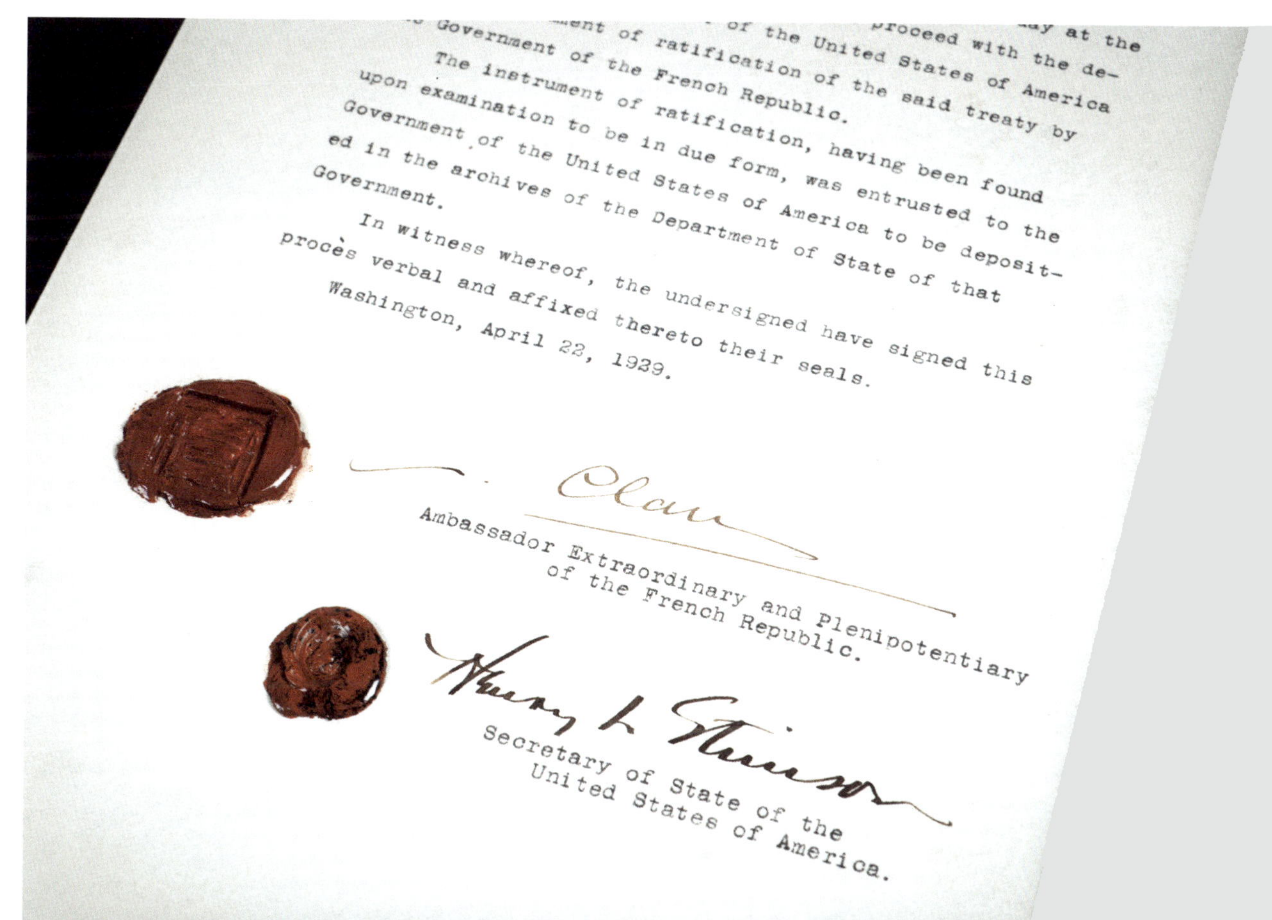

Haile Selassie (1892–1975)
Speech to the Assembly of the League of Nations, 30 June 1936

Geneva, United Nations Archives

On 30 June 1936, Haile Selassie, emperor of Ethiopia, approached the rostrum at the Assembly of the League of Nations to make one of the most stirring speeches of the interwar period. Several weeks earlier, his country had been annexed by Italy, despite the sanctions adopted eight months previously by the League, after having determined that Rome had had recourse to war in violation of the Covenant. The representatives of the Member States convened in Geneva to decide on the measures to take. As soon as he opened his mouth to speak, Selassie was interrupted by Italian journalists and members of the public present in the room. Order was swiftly restored and, after a few words in French, the emperor addressed the Assembly in Amharic. "The question is not simply to find a solution to the problem of the Italian aggression," he said. "It is collective security, it is the very essence of the League of Nations that is at stake … Placed by the aggressor face to face with a *fait accompli*, are states going to set the terrible precedent of bowing to force?" Selassie's cry of distress was not heard. In the end, the League Assembly voted to suspend the sanctions against Italy. National interests and the political myopia of the great powers trumped the principles enshrined in the Covenant. That decision completely undermined the League's political credibility.

P.-E. B.

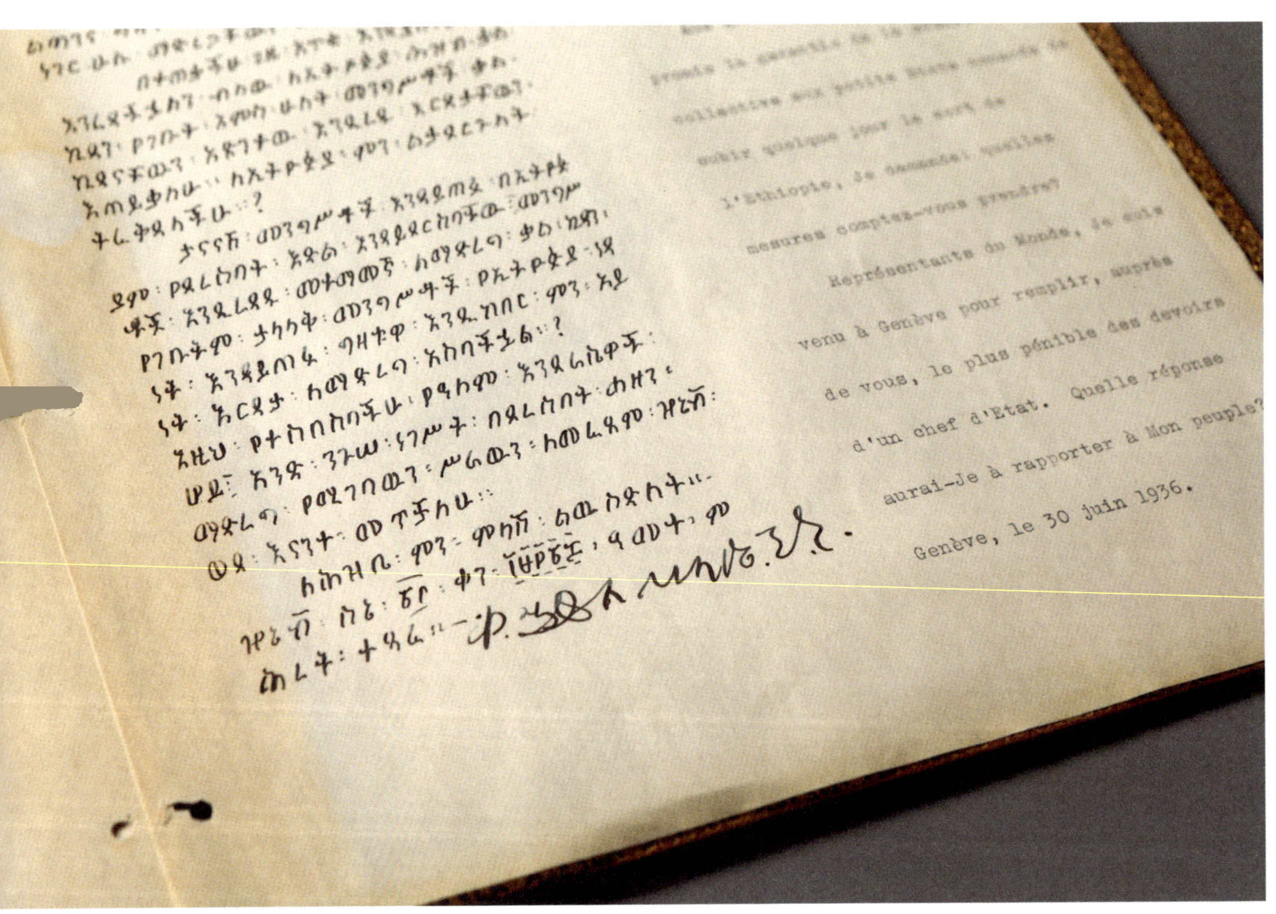

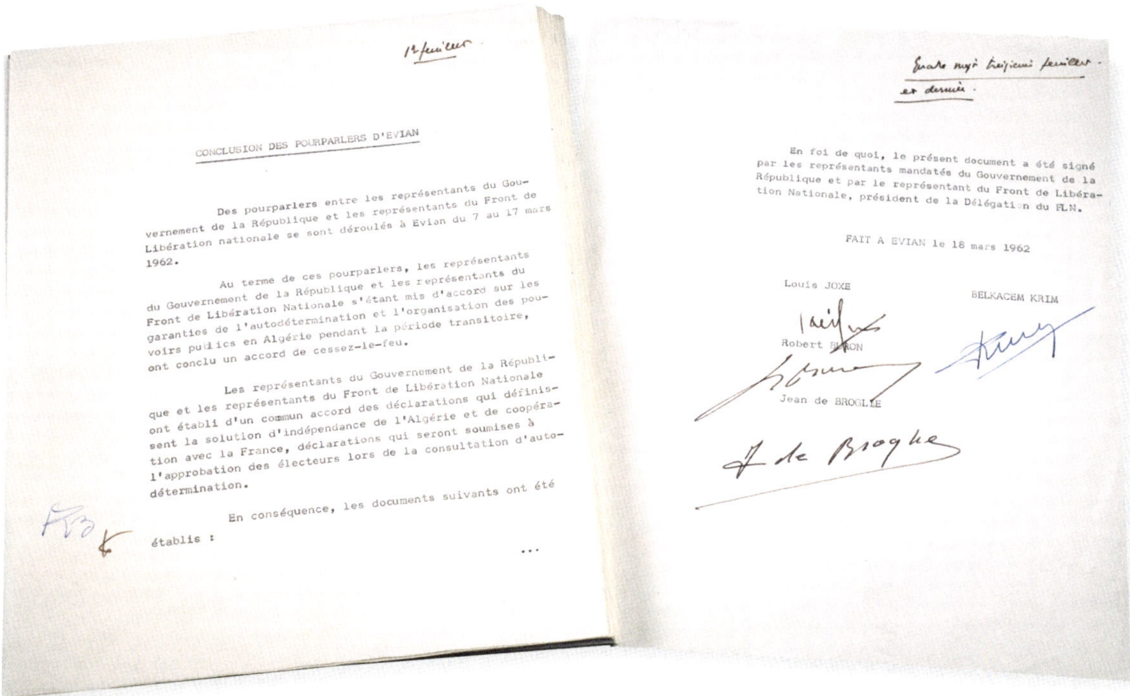

CONCLUSION DES POURPARLERS D'EVIAN

Des pourparlers entre les représentants du Gouvernement de la République et les représentants du Front de Libération nationale se sont déroulés à Evian du 7 au 17 mars 1962.

Au terme de ces pourparlers, les représentants du Gouvernement de la République et les représentants du Front de Libération Nationale s'étant mis d'accord sur les garanties de l'autodétermination et l'organisation des pouvoirs publics en Algérie pendant la période transitoire, ont conclu un accord de cessez-le-feu.

Les représentants du Gouvernement de la République et les représentants du Front de Libération Nationale ont établi d'un commun accord des déclarations qui définissent la solution d'indépendance de l'Algérie et de coopération avec la France, déclarations qui seront soumises à l'approbation des électeurs lors de la consultation d'autodétermination.

En conséquence, les documents suivants ont été établis :

...

En foi de quoi, le présent document a été signé par les représentants mandatés du Gouvernement de la République et par le représentant du Front de Libération Nationale, président de la Délégation du FLN.

FAIT A EVIAN le 18 mars 1962

Louis JOXE   BELKACEM KRIM

Robert BURON

Jean de BROGLIE

132
Conclusions of the Evian Talks, 18 March 1962

La Courneuve, Archives du ministère des Affaires étrangères, TRA 19620009/001

After the collapse of the Melun talks between France and two emissaries from the National Liberation Front (FLN), in the summer of 1960, General de Gaulle endeavoured to end the war in Algeria by holding fresh – and secret – negotiations in Switzerland. Max Petitpierre, the head of the Federal Department of Political Affairs (the Swiss ministry of foreign affairs), agreed to act as mediator, in line with the "active policy of neutrality" he advocated. As reported by diplomat Olivier Long, the discreet intermediary between the Provisional Government of the Algerian Republic (GPRA) and the French government, in his 1988 book, *Le Dossier secret des accords d'Évian: une mission suisse pour la paix* (*The Secret File of the Evian Accords: A Swiss Mission for Peace*), "After a good start in Luzern, the talks deadlocked in Neuchâtel." Officially, however, several conferences took place in 1961 and 1962 in the Lake Geneva area: in Evian from 20 May to 13 June 1961 (with no results), and later in Lugrin (20 to 28 July) and Les Rousses (11 to 18 February 1962). Subsequent talks in Evian, on 7 to 18 March of the same year, resulted in the Evian Accords, also known as the "Conclusions of the Evian talks". From a legal standpoint, the Accords did not have the standing of a bilateral treaty between sovereign states, since Algeria was at the time still a French department; they were merely a text ending the war in the country. Ninety-three pages long, it was signed by the members of the French government delegation (Louis Joxe, minister for Algerian affairs; Robert Buron, minister for public works, transport and tourism; Jean de Broglie, minister for the Sahara and overseas territories and departments) and the FLN representative (Belkacem Krim, GPRA vice-president). It contained arrangements for a cease-fire, which entered into force the following day; for independence, which would be proclaimed on 3 July 1962; for the future relationship between the two countries; and for safeguarding the property rights and interests of both parties. On 20 March 1962, the *Journal officiel de la République française* published part of the conclusions, including the cease-fire agreement. Algeria never implemented the text, however, as the FLN preferred the revolutionary Tripoli Programme, secretly drafted in June 1962 and intended to erase all vestiges of colonialism. In the ensuing months, domestic political upheaval and terrorism resulted in the massacre of thousands of *Harkis* (Algerians who served as auxiliaries in the French army), as well as the country's rapid "defrancization", with the repatriation of 800,000 *Pieds-noirs* (French settlers) to mainland France by the end of 1962.   **A. L.**

Document attesting to the dissolution of the Basque armed group ETA, 3 May 2018

Geneva, Centre for Humanitarian Dialogue

On 3 May 2018, the Basque armed group ETA sent an official statement to the Geneva headquarters of the Centre for Humanitarian Dialogue announcing its definitive dismantling, thereby ending sixty years of armed confrontation: "ETA, the Basque socialist revolutionary organization … hereby informs the Basque people that, following the ratification by its members of the proposal to conclude the Organization's historical cycle and function, its journey has ended." The statement, which was issued in four languages (Basque, Spanish, French and English), concluded: "ETA was formed from the people, and to the people it returns."

At the ceremony announcing ETA's dissolution, David Harland, Director of the Centre for Humanitarian Dialogue, stressed that the statement ended "a confrontation in which ETA killed over 850 people and injured thousands more, in which torture was used against some detainees sympathetic to ETA, and several alleged ETA members were murdered by mercenaries obeying members of a government." [Editor's note: the Spanish government]. For several decades, violence in the Basque Country not only killed and injured hundreds of people, it also polarized society, divided families and communities, disrupted people's daily lives and undermined democracy. The dissolution of ETA came after a lengthy process marked by occasional confidential negotiations with the Spanish authorities, a conversation among ETA leaders that gradually came to favour the idea of abandoning the armed struggle, and the arrest of many of the group's members. In 2011, ETA had announced its decision to resort to political violence no more. **P. H.**

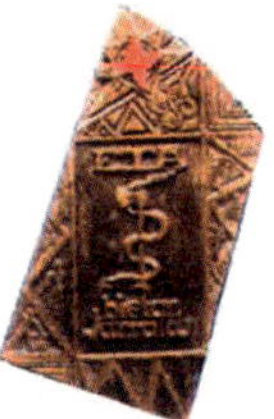

Déclaration finale d'ETA au Peuple Basque

ETA, organisation socialiste révolutionnaire basque de libération nationale, souhaite informer le Peuple Basque de la fin de sa trajectoire, après la ratification par ses militants de la proposition de mettre un terme au cycle historique et à la fonction de l'Organisation. En conséquence de cette décision

- ETA a entièrement défait l'ensemble de ses structures.
- ETA a mis un terme à toute son activité politique. Elle ne sera plus un acteur qui exprime des positions politiques, engage des initiatives ou interpelle d'autres acteurs.
- Les ex militants et militantes d'ETA poursuivront la lutte en faveur d'un Pays Basque reunifié, indépendant, socialiste, euskaldun et non patriarcal dans d'autres champs, chacun dans le domaine qu'il considère le plus opportun, avec la responsabilité et l'honnêteté de toujours.

ETA est née alors que le Pays Basque agonisait, étouffé par les serres du franquisme et assimilé par l'État jacobin, et maintenant, 60 ans plus tard, un peuple vivant existe et veut décider de son avenir, grâce au travail réalisé dans différents domaines et la lutte menée par plusieurs générations.

ETA veut mettre un terme à un cycle dans le conflit qui oppose le Pays Basque aux Etats, caractérisé par l'usage de la violence politique. Malgré cela, les États s'entêtent à perpétuer ce cycle, conscients de leur faiblesse dans la confrontation strictement politique et craignant la situation qu'engendrerait la résolution complète du conflit. En revanche, ETA n'a pas du tout peur de ce scénario démocratique, et c'est la raison pour laquelle elle a pris cette décision historique, pour que le processus en faveur de la liberté et de la paix continue à travers d'autres voies. C'est la conséquence logique de la décision adoptée en 2011 d'abandonner définitivement la lutte armée.

Dorénavant, le principal défi sera celui de construire en tant que peuple un processus axé sur l'accumulation des forces, la mobilisation populaire et les accords entre différents acteurs, tant pour aborder les conséquences du conflit que ses causes politiques et historiques. La concrétisation du droit de décider afin d'obtenir la reconnaissance nationale sera l'élément clé. L'indépendantisme de gauche va œuvrer pour que cela ouvre la voie à la constitution de l'État Basque.

Cette ultime décision, nous l'avons adoptée pour favoriser une nouvelle phase historique. ETA est née du peuple et, à présent, elle se dissout en lui.

GORA EUSKAL HERRIA ASKATUTA! GORA EUSKAL HERRIA SOZIALISTA!
JO TA KE INDEPENDENTZIA ETA SOZIALISMOA LORTU ARTE!

Pays Basque, 3 mai 2018

Euskadi Ta Askatasuna
E.T.A.

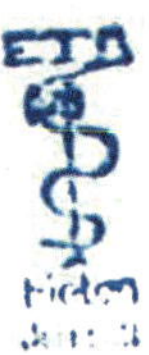

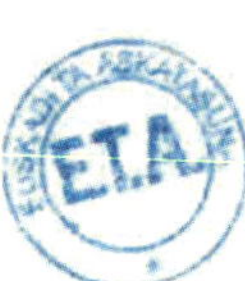

134
Dogon–Fula Communal Peace Agreement, 28 August 2018
Geneva, Centre for Humanitarian Dialogue

This peace agreement has the distinction of having been concluded between two ethnic groups in Mali. On 28 August 2018, in Sévaré, the Fula (or Peul) and Dogon groups living in the Mopti region of central Mali signed a peace agreement ending the hostilities between them – at least in theory. Under the aegis of the Geneva-based Centre for Humanitarian Dialogue, thirty-four Dogon and Fula village chiefs from the Koro administrative area signed this document, which refers to the causes of the violence affecting this part of Mali since 2016.

In the agreement, the two communities undertake to jointly condemn any acts of violence committed by a member of their community, to turn to the relevant military authorities in the event of threats or attacks, and to ask all the armed groups to end their confrontations. The agreement also aims to raise awareness among young people and opinion leaders, encouraging them to commit to living peacefully, to prioritize the use of traditional mediation to prevent and manage their disputes, and to mobilize jointly for access to natural resources without recourse to violence. In the Mopti region, clashes between the two communities since 2016 have resulted in the destruction of villages and in summary executions, looting and

the theft of livestock. According to UN reports, armed jihadist groups, self-defence militias and armed forces have committed serious human rights violations, even since the peace agreement. The causes of the conflict are rooted in the competition for control of resources (which are dwindling, due to global warming), an explosion in population size and the lack of a state presence. This situation has been playing into the hands of jihadist groups, who exploit the tensions in the area while posing as guarantors of social order. According to the Malian authorities, this communal conflict has left hundreds of people dead and thousands displaced. **P. H.**

**Accord de paix entre les communautés
Dogon et Peule du cercle de Koro**

Août 2018

Les représentants des chefs de village du cercle de Koro

**Les représentants des chefs
de village peuhls**

Souleymane O BARRY

Chef de village de Diankagabou

Boucari O BARRY

Chef de village Gondogourou

Gouro Issiaka BARRY

Chef de village de Banguel

Sekou B BARRY

Chef de village de Sourindé

Daouda A BARRY

Chef de village Dioungani

de village dogons

Les représentants des chefs

Moctar NIANGALY

Chef de village de Koro

Yessa ONGOIBA

Chef de village Kombogourou

Seydou NIANGALY

Chef de village Bondo

Hama TOGO

Chef de village de Birga Dogon

Diakaridia DAME

Chef de village Sobangouma

Souleymane DOUGNON

Chef de village Dagaténé

7

Which is most likely to pacify hearts: criminal punishment or amnesty?

135
Gustave Moynier (1826–1910)
"Institution judiciaire internationale propre à prévenir et à réprimer les infractions à la Convention de Genève" [An International Judicial Institution Capable of Preventing and Punishing Breaches of the Geneva Convention], *Bulletin international des sociétés de secours aux militaires blessés*, No. 11, 1872

Loan of Valentin Zellweger

The International Criminal Court was founded on 17 July 1998. The need for an international tribunal to prosecute the most heinous infractions – genocide, crimes against humanity, war crimes – emerged from the horrors of the Second World War. The Court is currently recognized by two-thirds of the world's countries.

It was a Geneva lawyer who first suggested such an institution. Reacting to the general lack of respect for the 1864 Geneva Convention evidenced during the Franco-Prussian war of 1870–71, Gustave Moynier, writing in 1872 in the *Bulletin international des Sociétés de secours aux militaires blessés*, proposed the establishment of an "international legal institution capable of preventing and punishing breaches of the Geneva Convention". At the time, however, his idea attracted little interest.

This copy of Moynier's essay has a story of its own. It was intended as a gift to a colleague by a group of diplomats in New York. When they picked it up from the bookbinder, though, they noticed that the book had been bound in gilt-embossed Morocco leather – to their chagrin, as they had specifically asked for a more inexpensive binding. Asked to explain why, the bookbinder said that he had decided to offer them the more luxurious binding, hoping that it would go some way towards making up for the wrong that his government had done to the International Criminal Court, which the United States still does not recognize. **V. Z.**

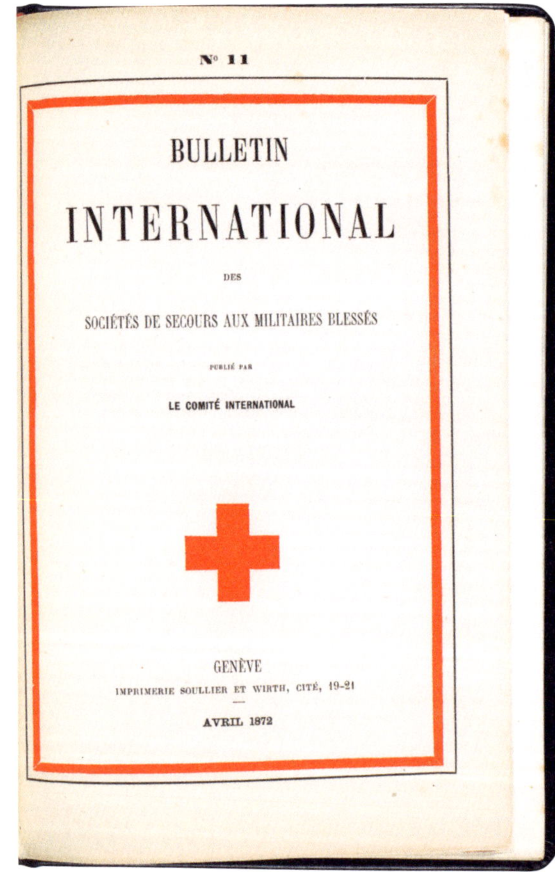

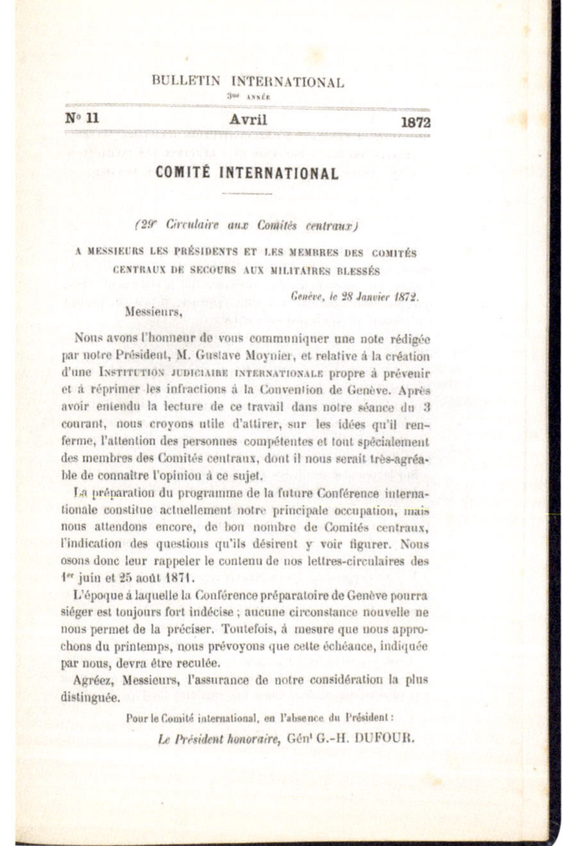

BULLETIN INTERNATIONAL
3ᵐᵉ ANNÉE

Nº 11   Avril   1872

COMITÉ INTERNATIONAL

(29ᵉ Circulaire aux Comités centraux)

A MESSIEURS LES PRÉSIDENTS ET LES MEMBRES DES COMITÉS CENTRAUX DE SECOURS AUX MILITAIRES BLESSÉS

Genève, le 28 Janvier 1872.

Messieurs,

Nous avons l'honneur de vous communiquer une note rédigée par notre Président, M. Gustave Moynier, et relative à la création d'une INSTITUTION JUDICIAIRE INTERNATIONALE propre à prévenir et à réprimer les infractions à la Convention de Genève. Après avoir entendu la lecture de ce travail dans notre séance du 3 courant, nous croyons utile d'attirer, sur les idées qu'il renferme, l'attention des personnes compétentes et tout spécialement des membres des Comités centraux, dont il nous serait très-agréable de connaître l'opinion à ce sujet.

La préparation du programme de la future Conférence internationale constitue actuellement notre principale occupation, mais nous attendons encore, de bon nombre de Comités centraux, l'indication des questions qu'ils désirent y voir figurer. Nous osons donc leur rappeler le contenu de nos lettres-circulaires des 1ᵉʳ juin et 25 août 1871.

L'époque à laquelle la Conférence préparatoire de Genève pourra siéger est toujours fort indécise ; aucune circonstance nouvelle ne nous permet de la préciser. Toutefois, à mesure que nous approchons du printemps, nous prévoyons que cette échéance, indiquée par nous, devra être reculée.

Agréez, Messieurs, l'assurance de notre considération la plus distinguée.

Pour le Comité international, en l'absence du Président :

Le Président honoraire, Génᵗ G.-H. DUFOUR.

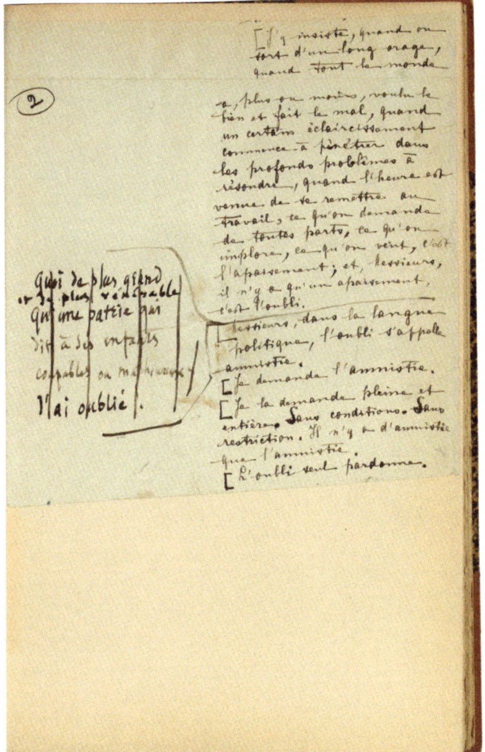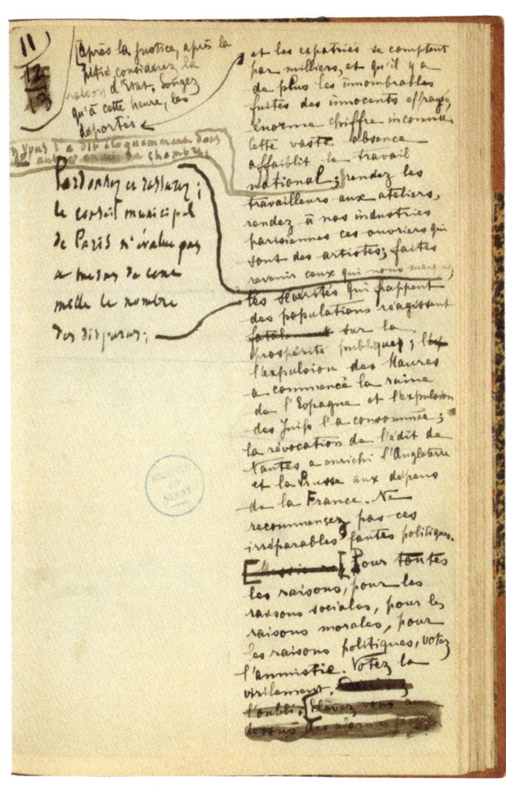

136
Victor Hugo, Speech to the French Senate urging an amnesty for the Communards, 22 May 1876, autograph manuscript

Paris, Bibliothèque du Sénat

On the margins of his prodigious career as a writer, Victor Hugo frequently lent his voice to political issues. Hugo, initially a staunch royalist, had been a peer of the realm (from 1845 to 1848) and, later, after he came to support the republican model, an elected member of various assemblies (between 1848 and 1851). Following his return from exile, in 1871, he became a French senator in 1876.

As soon as he was elected, he began to use his position to raise an issue he had been passionately championing for five years: an amnesty for the Communards.

Five years after the violent clampdown against the Paris Commune, thousands of activists were either in prison or in exile, mainly in New Caledonia, where convicts were still being deported. Utterly revolted by this unyielding refusal to forgive and forget, Hugo put his considerable rhetorical skill to work in arguing for an amnesty. After a lengthy storm, everyone yearns for appeasement, he writes, "yet there is only one appeasement, and that is forgetting". Which, in political terms, means amnesty: "I call for it to be whole and complete. No conditions. No restrictions. The only true amnesty is amnesty. The only pardon lies in forgetting", he adds. He continues by contrasting sovereignty with fraternity and justice with clemency ("clemency finds justice unjust"), and follows this with a descrip-

tion of his visits to the hovels where the families of deportees live, their wives valiantly struggling to ward off destitution. In passing, he aims a jab at the reviled Napoleon III, whom he accuses of having "in Sedan, on 2 December, crowned betrayal with ineptitude, and the overthrow of the Republic with the fall of France."

Despite the strength of Hugo's conviction, his plea had no immediate effect. But he brought it back to the table again and again, and could be justifiably proud of his role in securing the acceptance by the senate, in March 1879, of a law of partial amnesty, followed by full amnesty on 11 July 1880 . **C. I.**

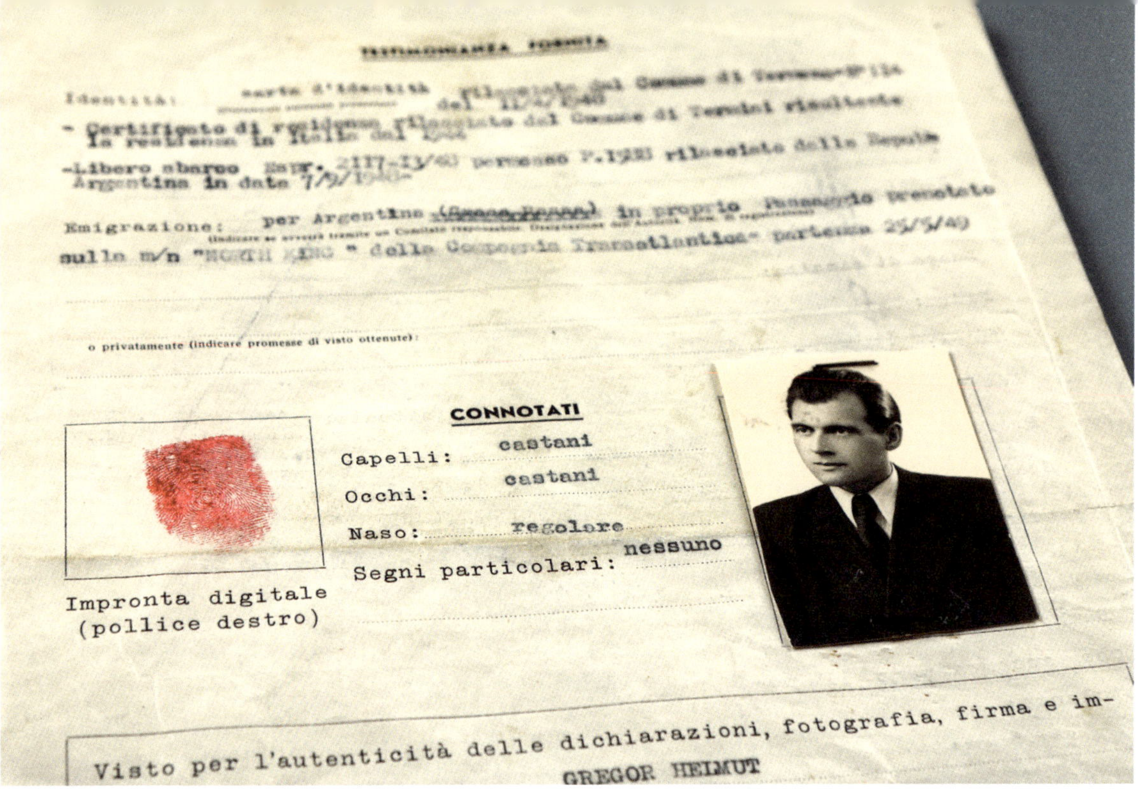

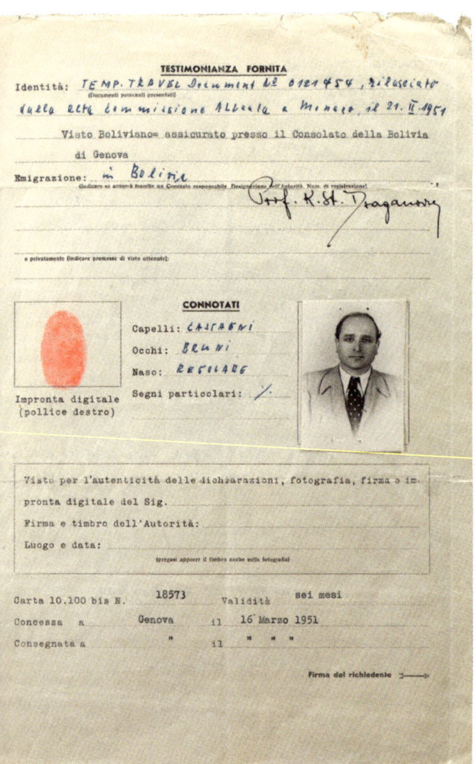

TESTIMONIANZA FORNITA

Identità: TEMP. TRAVEL Document N° 0121454, rilasciato dalla Alta Commissione Alleata a Monaco, il 21.II.1951

Visto Boliviano assicurato presso il Consolato della Bolivia di Genova

Emigrazione: in Bolivia

Prof. R.St. Draganovic

o privatamente (indicare promesse di visto ottenute):

CONNOTATI

Capelli: CASTAGNI
Occhi: BRUNI
Naso: REGOLARE
Segni particolari: /

Impronta digitale
(pollice destro)

Visto per l'autenticità delle dichiarazioni, fotografia, firma o impronta digitale del Sig.

Firma e timbro dell'Autorità:

Luogo e data:

Carta 10.100 bis N.	18573	Validità	sei mesi
Concessa a	Genova	il	16 Marzo 1951
Consegnata a	"	il	" "

Firma del richiedente

137
Application form for an ICRC travel document, Genoa, 1949–51

Geneva, ICRC, ICRCA, C TVCR 1994 18.573; 100.501; 100.940

With the end of the Second World War, millions of people sought to flee Europe. Former prisoners of war, survivors of the camps, civilians fleeing communism or expelled from their countries, stateless people – all hoping for a better life, often abroad. While many obtained help from international organizations, some – often those from the losing side – were left to fend for themselves or languished in camps.

Against this backdrop, in 1944, the International Committee of the Red Cross (ICRC) created a travel document that would be accepted by a number of governments. Originally intended to enable former prisoners of war and civilian internees without identity documents to cross borders to return home, it soon came to be issued to former deportees and forced labourers who lacked a means of proving who they were. In summer 1945, a new travel document was introduced, which could be issued to any person who had not received international assistance or protection, and who wished to emigrate. Although the travel document was intended as a temporary measure until an international agreement could be reached, it continued to be a central part of the ICRC's work well into the early 1950s, at the insistence of the affected countries. The only concession made to the ICRC was that, starting in the spring of 1947, the task of checking applicants' personal information was entrusted to third-party agencies.

These travel documents helped thousands of destitute people, but were also used by war criminals to escape.

– Travel document of Adolf Eichmann (1906–62), alias Ricardo Klement, SS officer in charge of implementing the "final solution"

– Travel document of Josef Mengele (1911–79), alias Helmut Gregor, SS "doctor" at Auschwitz-Birkenau concentration camp

– Travel document of Klaus Barbie (1913–91), alias Klaus Altmann, SS officer and head of the Gestapo in Lyon

D. P.

138
Index cards for the documents of the United Nations War Crimes Commission

New York, United Nations Archives (ARMS)

Established during the Second World War, the United Nations War Crimes Commission is considered one of the first international initiatives to punish such infractions. Founded in October 1943, following a conference attended by representatives of the seventeen Allied governments, it started work in January 1944 and remained active until 1948. The Commission's mandate was to collect information about, and investigate, war crimes committed in Europe and Asia. It was also charged with identifying war criminals and helping national governments prosecute them. The nearly 37,000 cases handled by the Commission included those of the Nazi leaders, such as Adolf Hitler, Heinrich Himmler, Joseph Goebbels and Joseph Mengele. In terms of legal doctrine, the Commission's members, all of whom were eminent jurists, were instrumental in defining concepts that emerged as central in the wake of the war, such as the recognition of aggression as a war crime, the "just following orders" defence, the issue of collective responsibility and the definition of crimes against humanity. Although less well known today than the international military tribunals of Nuremburg and Tokyo, the Commission nevertheless played a pioneering role in the field of international criminal justice.

P.-E. B.

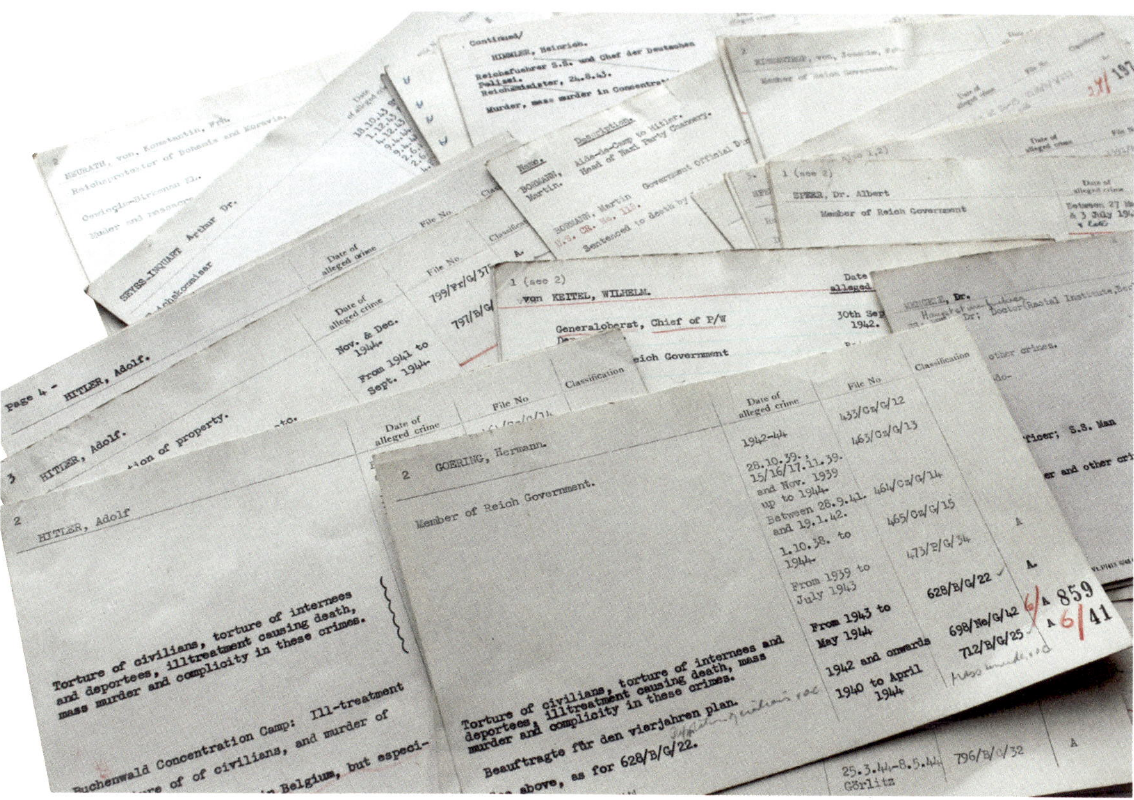

139

Hannah Arendt (1906–75)
*Eichmann in Jerusalem: A Report
on the Banality of Evil*, New York,
Viking Press, 1963

Cologny, Martin Bodmer Foundation

Is it possible to do evil without being profoundly evil? That is the question that Hannah Arendt tried to answer during the trial of Adolf Eichmann, the mastermind behind the deportation of millions of Jews to the death camps. Born in Hanover in 1906, Hannah Arendt studied philosophy, theology and philology, under the tutelage of Martin Heidegger. In 1933, after the Nazis' rise to power, she fled Germany, first to France and later to the United States, where she arrived in 1941, after a difficult journey. In 1960, Israeli agents kidnapped Adolf Eichmann and brought him to Israel to be judged. Hannah Arendt covered the trial for *The New Yorker*. Her five articles for the magazine were published in book form under the title *Eichmann in Jerusalem: A Report on the Banality of Evil* (1963). Arendt saw Eichmann as a man who was "neither perverted nor sadistic", but rather "terrifyingly normal". This prompted her to borrow the concept of "the banality of evil" – the title of her book – from Raoul Hilberg. For Arendt, Eichmann was not amoral, but, rather, incapable of independent thought, a bureaucrat who, thanks to his organizational and logistical skills, actively contributed to the largest genocide of the twentieth century, without ever measuring the extent of his responsibility. Arendt's book sparked an international controversy. She was criticized in particular for her psychological reading of Eichmann: as historians would later show, he was far from being an ideologically agnostic bureaucrat, having joined the Nazi party very early on. Her thinking on totalitarian systems and the banality of evil nevertheless continue to inform the debate today.   **P. H.**

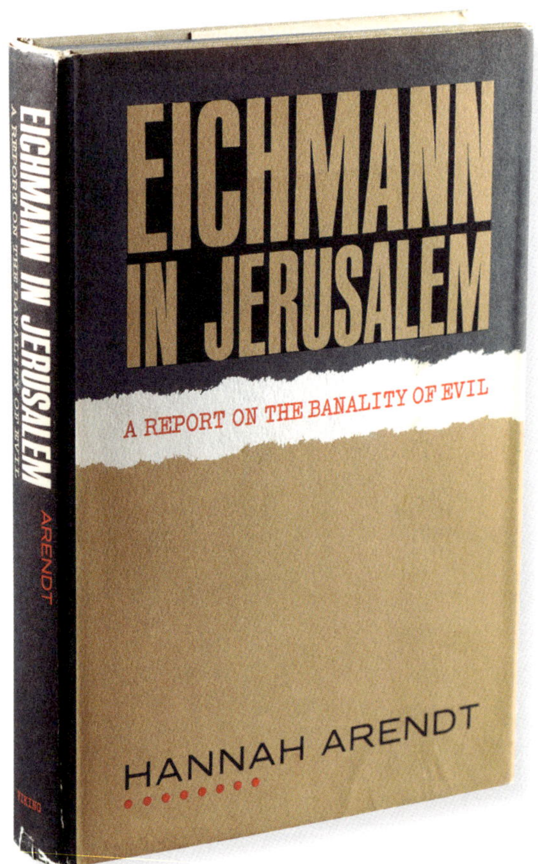

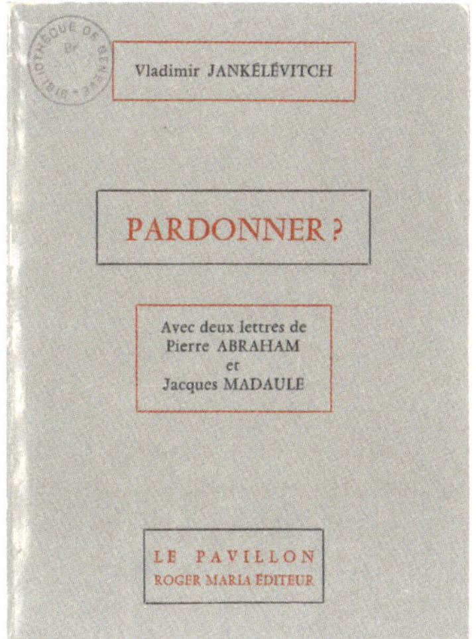

140
Vladimir Jankélévitch (1903–85)
Pardonner? [*Should We Pardon Them*], Paris, R. Maria, 1971

Geneva, Bibliothèque de Genève, Br 2838/4

Until what point are human beings capable of forgiving? Is there an insuperable limit beyond which forgiveness is no longer possible? As a survivor of the Second World War, these were the questions that Vladimir Jankélévitch, the author of *Traité des vertus* (*Treatise on Virtues*, 1949), sought to answer. A musicologist, philosopher and eminent professor at the Sorbonne, Jankélévitch refused to speak German, read books in German or listen to German music ever again after the war, because the genocide against the Jews was a crime "against the very essence of humankind". In his *Pardonner?* (1971; an preliminary version appeared in 1965), a short, incisive essay with a pamphleteering tone, he wrote: "When an act denies the very essence of man as man, a prescription that would tend to absolve him in the name of morality itself contradicts morality. Is it not contradictory, even absurd, to speak of forgiveness? Forgetting this gigantic crime against humanity would constitute a new crime against humankind." In the epigraph, he quotes Paul Eluard: "There is no salvation on earth for as long as executioners can be forgiven." Nevertheless, in another philosophical essay, *Le Pardon* (*Forgiveness*, 1967), Jankélévitch raised the possibility of a pure, hyperbolic forgiveness: "instant grace", an "imperceptible blink of charity". Commenting on the tension between these two approaches, he explained: "Evil is stronger than forgiveness, and forgiveness is stronger than evil. That is something I cannot escape. It is a kind of oscillation, which in philosophy would be described as dialectical and which to me appears infinite." **P. H.**

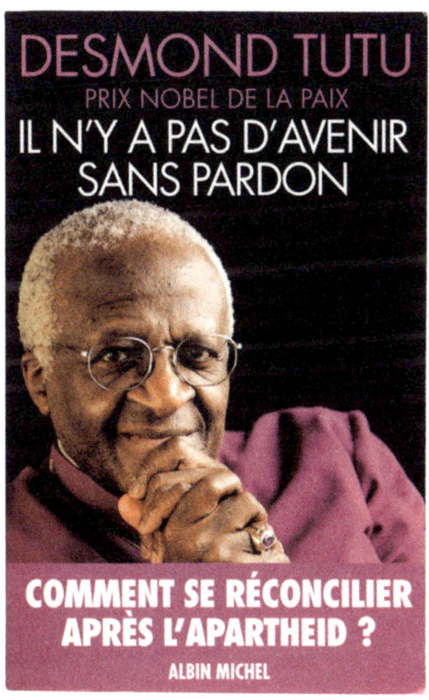

141
Desmond Mpilo Tutu (b. 1931)
Il n'y a pas d'avenir sans pardon [*No Future Without Forgiveness*], trans. J. and A. Deschamps, Paris, A. Michel, 2000

Cologny, Martin Bodmer Foundation

Desmond Mpilo Tutu is a South African Anglican archbishop who was awarded the 1984 Nobel Peace Prize for his non-violent struggle against the racist regime in his country. After the transition to democracy, President Nelson Mandela appointed him head of the Truth and Reconciliation Commission, in 1995. The commission was charged with shedding light on the crimes and atrocities committed in the apartheid era, both by the South African authorities and by the national liberation movements. In public hearings, which were broadcast in the media, and which symbolized the transition from the apartheid regime to democracy in the new South African rainbow nation, victims and executioners told the often harrowing stories of what they had lived through.

In his book *No Future Without Forgiveness* (1999), Desmond Tutu vigorously defends his approach in the name of both Christian forgiveness and the African culture of *ubuntu*. He justifies the non-prosecution of those who committed political crimes by the need to prevent a bloody civil war and to build a new South Africa, finally at peace with itself. He has made an impression on people all over the world with his assertion that forgiving is not the same as forgetting. This approach differentiates between judicial amnesty and social amnesia, whereas, traditionally, judicial oblivion went hand in hand with social oblivion. For Desmond Tutu, remembering does not put the brakes on reconciliation – rather, it is essential for achieving it. Since the book's publication, this legacy has inspired the creation of truth and reconciliation commissions in many other countries. **P. H.**

Pierre Hazan
Guest curator of *War and Peace*
Pierre Hazan is Transitional Justice advisor to the Centre for Humanitarian Dialogue (Geneva), which is specialized in armed conflict mediation. He also is professor at the Media Academy in the University of Neuchâtel. Previously, was a research fellow at Harvard Law School and at the United States Institute of Peace in Washington D.C., and has worked with the United Nations Office of the High Commissioner for Human Rights (UNHCR). Hazan has covered numerous conflicts as a journalist for *Le Temps* and *Libération* before specializing in justice in divided societies. He is the author of several books on international criminal justice, including *Judging War, Judging History: Behind Truth and Reconciliation* (Stanford University Press, 2010), and *La paix contre la Justice? Comment reconstruire un État avec des criminels de guerre* (GRIP/André Versaille, 2010).

Jacques Berchtold
co-curator of *War and Peace*
Jacques Berchtold is the director of the Bodmer Foundation and a professor of French literature at Sorbonne University. Since 2018, he also teaches at the University of Geneva. He is the author of numerous articles, including "Rabelais, Voltaire et les rois belliqueux" (*Campus*, 25, 1994); "Rousseau et la paix des Lumières", in *Genève et la paix* (Geneva, 2005); "Le souvenir des guerres de Religion", "Voltaire et *La Henriade*" and "*La Henriade travestie*, éclairage sur les violences", in *La Mémoire des guerres de Religion* (J. Berchtold and M.-M. Fragonard eds, vol. I-II, Droz, 2007–09); "Rousseau visiteur de Vauban" (Annales Rousseau, 2008); "Guéhenno lecteur de Rousseau", in *Jean Guéhenno: Guerres et Paix* (J. Guérin et al., Presses universitaires du Septentrion, 2009).

Nicolas Ducimetière has been vice-director of the Bodmer Foundation since 2012. Previously, he was a curator at the Barbier-Mueller Museum in Geneva, where he presented the treasures of Jean-Paul Barbier-Mueller's library of French Renaissance poetry in *Mignonne, allons voir...* (Hazan, 2007). A historian by training, he is the author and editor of studies on the poetry of the Renaissance, including *Poètes, princes et collectionneurs* (Droz, 2011), and has curated several exhibitions at the Martin Bodmer Foundation, including *Frankenstein: Creation of Darkness* (2016) and *The Roads of Translation* (2017). He is vice-president of the Barbier-Mueller Foundation at the University of Geneva and is a member of the Swiss Commission for UNESCO. He was recently named Chevalier de l'ordre des Arts et des Lettres of France.

Christophe Imperiali is a research associate with the Martin Bodmer Foundation. His PhD research led to two publications: *Perceval en question: Éloge de la curiosité* (Classiques Garnier, 2015) and *En quête de Perceval: Étude sur un mythe littéraire* (Champion, 2017). His current research focuses on the relationship between music and poetry during the 19th century. He was the curator of the exhibition *Wagner, l'opéra hors de soi* at the Martin Bodmer Foundation in 2013.

Gilad Ben-Nun is a professor of world history and modern international law at the Centre for Area Studies at Leipzig University. A former UN official, Ford Foundation scholar at UNIDIR, and EU Marie Curie individual fellow, he is the author of a monograph on the history of the 1951 Refugee Convention which was recognized with the 2017 US National Jewish Book Award. His most recent book explores the writing of history, and the biographies of the delegates to the Fourth Geneva Convention on the Protection of Civilians, in 1949.

Blandine Blukacz-Louisfert heads the Institutional Memory Section of the United Nations Library Geneva and is the director of the Total Digital Access to the League of Nations Archives Project. She graduated in history from the University Paris-IV-Sorbonne and in archival science from the École nationale des chartes, Paris. From 1992 to 1997, she worked as a UN volunteer and a UNESCO consultant on developing the National Archives of the Republic of Yemen. She joined the UN Geneva in 1999.

Pierre-Étienne Bourneuf is a scientific adviser at the UN Library's Institutional Memory Section in Geneva, responsible for overseeing the organization of the exhibition *100 Years of Multilateralism in Geneva*. He is the author of several publications, including *Bombarder l'Allemagne: l'offensive alliée sur les villes pendant la Deuxième Guerre mondiale* (PUF, 2014), and is currently working on a book on the history of the League of Nations.

Lindsey Cameron heads the Unit of Thematic Legal Advisers in the legal division of the International Committee of the Red Cross (ICRC). She holds a

PhD in public international law from the University of Geneva and has published numerous books and articles on international humanitarian law. Prior to joining the ICRC, Lindsey worked as a researcher at the University of Geneva. She has also worked for the United Nations High Commission for Refugees (UNHCR) in the Balkans and at the Court of Appeal for Ontario in Canada.

Mark Freeman is the founder and executive director of the Institute for Integrated Transitions (IFIT) in Barcelona. Before founding IFIT, Freeman served as Chief of External Relations at the International Crisis Group (ICG). He helped launch and direct the International Center for Transitional Justice (ICTJ), in New York and Brussels. He is the author of *Necessary Evils: Amnesties and the Search for Justice* (Cambridge University Press, 2010) and of *Truth Commissions and Procedural Fairness* (Cambridge University. Press, 2006). He is currently co-editing a new book: *Negotiating Transitional Justice* (Cambridge University Press, to be published end of 2019).

Antoine Garapon is a lawyer and the secretary-feneral of the Institut des Hautes Études sur la Justice (IHEJ) in Paris. Previously, Garapon served for several years as a juvenile court judge. He is the co-editor of the journal Esprit and editor of the "Bien commun" collection published by Michalon, and hosts a weekly radio program on the French national radio station France-Culture. His most recent book is *Justice digitale: Révolution graphique et rupture anthropologique* (with Jean Lassègue, PUF, 2018).

Solange Ghernaouti is a professor at the University of Lausanne (UNIL) and internationally recognized expert in the fields of cyber security and cyber

defence. A former auditor at the French Institute of Higher National Defence Studies, she holds a PhD in Computer Science from Sorbonne University in Paris. Cited as one of the twenty most influential women in Switzerland, Solange Ghernaouti is a member of the Swiss Commission for UNESCO and the Swiss Academy of Engineering Sciences. She currently heads the Swiss Cybersecurity Advisory and Research Group (SCARG) and is president of the SGH Foundation Cyberworld Research Institute. She has been awarded the French Legion of Honour.

Jean-Charles Giroud is the former director of the Bibliothèque de Genève and the former curator of its poster collection. An art historian, he is the author of several books, studies and exhibitions on poster art.

António Guterres became secretary-general of the United Nations in January 2017, after serving as the United Nations High Commissioner for Refugees from 2005 to 2015. His tenure at the head of one of the world's largest humanitarian organizations coincided with migratory flows of unprecedented magnitude: the number of people displaced by armed conflict or persecution almost doubled from 38 million in 2005 to over 60 million a decade later. Prior to joining the UNHCR, António Guterres spent more than twenty years in public service. He was prime minister of Portugal from 1995 to 2002, during which time he played a key role in international efforts to end the crisis in East Timor. As President of the European Council in the early 2000s, Guterres was instrumental in the adoption by the EU of the Lisbon Strategy for growth and employment. He was also co-chair of the first European Union–Africa summit. From 1991 to 2002, he was a member of the Portuguese Council of State.

André Hurst is a hellenist, professor emeritus and the former rector of the University of Geneva. He is the author of numerous books on Greek epic poetry and theater, as well as publisher about papyrus. He has been a visiting professor at McGill University in Montreal; at Babeş-Bolyai University in Cluj, Romania; at the University of Lausanne; and at the École normale supérieure (ENS) in Paris. He has been a member of the Senior Common Room of St John's College in Oxford; the International Committee for Strategic Direction of ENS; and the Scientific Committee of the École pratique des hautes études (EPHE) in Paris.

Jean Kaempfer is professor emeritus of French literature at the University of Lausanne. He is the author of *Poétique du récit de guerre* (Corti, 1998) and numerous articles on literary representations of the First World War. He directed an interdisciplinary research project on the "practices of Jesus" in the 20th century and regularly publishes studies on contemporary authors.

Leïla Kilani is a film-maker who always dreamed of being a clown. She studied history, and worked on a thesis at EHESS in Paris. She began working in film-making in the early 2000s, directing several well-received documentaries, including *Tangier: The Burners' Dream* in 2002 and *Our Forbidden Places* in 2008. Her first feature film, On the Edge (2011) was screened during the Director's Fortnight, a sidebar to the Cannes Film Festival. She is currently finishing her second feature, *Indivision*.

Jean-Paul Marthoz is a political columnist for the Brussels-based newspaper *Le Soir* and a guest professor at KU Leuven. He is the author of numerous books, including *Objectif Bastogne: Sur les traces des reporters* *de guerre américains* (GRIP, 2014), *Les Médias face au terrorisme* (UNESCO, 2017) and *En première ligne: Le journalisme au cœur des conflits* (GRIP, 2018). He has served as Human Rights Watch's European director of information and as the European correspondent of the Committee to Protect Journalists.

Peter Maurer has been president of the International Committee of the Red Cross (ICRC) since 2012. Under his leadership, the ICRC has pursued its humanitarian mission in over eighty countries, with major operations in Syria, Yemen, Iraq, South Sudan, Lake Chad and Myanmar. Peter Maurer's priorities for his presidency have included strengthening humanitarian diplomacy, engaging states and other actors to support international humanitarian law, and improving the effectiveness of humanitarian action through innovation and new partnerships. Prior to his appointment to the ICRC, Maurer served as Switzerland's minister of foreign affairs and as the Swiss ambassador and permanent representative to the United Nations in New York.

Georges Nivat is professor emeritus at the University of Geneva, specializing in Slavic languages and the history of ideas. He was the head of the European Institute in Geneva and chair of the Rencontres internationales de Genève. He was awarded the Legion of Honour (France) and the Pushkin Medal (Russia). Prof. Nivat holds honorary degrees from the Russian Academy of Science and University of Kyiv-Mohyla Academy. He has curated several exhibitions at the Martin Bodmer Foundation and is the author of a trilogy about Russian culture, published by L'Âge d'Homme: *Vers*

la fin du mythe russe (1982), *Russie-Europe, la fin du schisme* (1993) and *Vivre en russe* (2007). Among others, his research addresses Russian symbolism (studies and translations of Andreï Biely) and moral resistance or "dissidence", particularly on Alexander Solzhenitsyn (*Phénomène Soljénitsyne*, Fayard, 2009). He has also published diaries of his travels in Russia (*Impressions de Russie and Regards sur la Russie de l'an VI*, Éditions de Fallois, 1993 and 1997), and articles magazines in both France (*Le Débat*, Esprit) and Russia (*Znamia*, *Zvezda*, *Kontinent*).

Daniel Palmieri has been a historical research officer at the International Committee of the Red Cross (ICRC) since 2002. He is the author of numerous works on the history of the ICRC, its humanitarian work and the history of war. His recent articles include "Humanitarianism on the Screen: The ICRC Films, 1921–1965" in *Humanitarianism and Media: 1900 to the Present* (Johannes Paulmann ed., Berghahn Books, 2018) and "Se souvenir pour oublier: la politique mémorielle du CICR" in *Normer l'oubli* (Vincent Négri and Isabelle Schulte-Tenckhoff, eds, IRJS, 2018).

David Sander is professor of psychology and director of the Interfaculty Center for Affective Sciences at the University of Geneva. Having studied mathematics, psychology and cognitive science in Paris and Lyon, Sander joined the University of Geneva in 2002 to research the mechanisms of emotional triggers and how they regulate emotional response, attention span, memory and decision-making.

Constance Sereni is an assistant professor in the Department of East Asian Studies at the University of Geneva. Her research focuses on twentieth-century Japan, more specifically the history of World War II and the Japanese defeat. Her publications include *Kamikazes: Missions suicides au Japon* (1944–1945) (with Pierre-François Souyri, Flammarion, 2015).

Ronald Slye teaches law at the Seattle University School of Law. He is an internationally recognized expert in international criminal law, transitional justice and international human rights law. He is the co-author of a best-selling casebook in the United States, *International Criminal Law and Its Enforcement* (Foundation Press), and *The Kenyan TJRC: An Outsider's View from the Inside* (Cambridge University Press, 2018). He serves on the board of directors of the Documentation Center of Cambodia, and is a member of IFIT's Law and Peace Practice Group.

Pierre-François Souyri is professor emeritus at the University of Geneva, where he taught Japanese history for many years. Souyri has also taught at the National Institute of Oriental Languages and Civilization in Paris, and was the director of the Maison Franco-Japonaise in Tokyo. He is the author of *Nouvelle Histoire du Japon* (Perrin, 2010), *Histoire du Japon médiéval, le monde à l'envers* (Perrin, 2013) and *Moderne sans être occidental, aux origines du Japon d'aujourd'hui* (Gallimard, 2016), as well as several works on Japanese samurai and kamikaze pilots. .

Stefan Vukotić is chief of archives
management at the UN in Geneva.
He is responsible for communications
and relations with researchers and
is in charge of the UN Museum
Geneva, as well as secretary of the
Centenary Coordination Committee
for the *100 Years of Multilateralism
in Geneva project*. He served as head
of international communications for
the government of Montenegro and
was press and information officer for
the EU Delegation to Montenegro. His
academic background is in the history of
international relations and international
law.

Colin Wells is the project manager of
the Total Digital Access to the League of
Nations Archives Project at the United
Nations Library Geneva, where he
was previously chief of the Archives
Management Unit with the Institutional
Memory Section.

AUTHORS OF THE CATALOGUE PART

Éric Anceau (E. A.) (lecturer in history,
Sorbonne University, Paris): cat. 15.

Gilad Ben-Nun (G. B.-N.): cat. 1 to 9, 11,
12, 96 to 99, 101, 103.

Jessica Beasley (J. Bea.) (curator, The
Ann & Gabriel Barbier-Mueller Museum):
cat. 26.

Jacques Berchtold (J. B.): cat. 68 and 69,
71 to 75, 78, 86, 89, 91, 95, 100, 102, 104
and 105, 107 to 109.

Pierre-Étienne Bourneuf (P.-E. B.):
cat. 16 to 18, 24, 39, 50 to 55, 58, 87 and
88, 106, 110 to 114, 116, 126 to 129, 131,
138.

Vérène de Diesbach (V. de D.) (Curator,
Jean Bonna Library): cat. 76.

Nicolas Ducimetière (N. D.): cat. 14, 21,
23, 25, 28 and 29, 30 to 33, 46 and 47, 57,
59, 61, 77, 81, 83 and 84, 118, 121, 137.

Carine Durand (C. D.) (curator, Musée
d'ethnographie de Genève): cat. 117.

Mélanie Exquis (M. E.) (research
assistant, Martin Bodmer Foundation):
cat. 64.

Pierre Hazan (P. H.): cat. 22, 34, 60, 66
and 67, 115, 133 and 134, 139 to 141.

Christophe Imperiali (C. I.): cat. 10, 20,
70, 92, 136.

François Jacob (F. J.) (former director,
Institut et Musée Voltaire): cat. 85.

Jean Kaempfer (J. K.): cat. 90, 93.

Anne Liskenne (A. L.) (head of the
Treaties Division, Direction of the
Diplomatic Archives, Ministry of Foreign
Affairs, France): cat. 124, 130, 132.

Floriane Morin (F. M.) (curator, Musée
d'ethnographie de Genève): cat. 13.

Isabelle Nathan (I. N.) (head of the
Public Awareness Section, Direction
of the Diplomatic Archives, Ministry
of Foreign Affairs, France): cat. 123.

Georges Nivat (G. N.): cat. 80, 94.

Daniel Palmieri (D. P.): cat. 35 to 38, 40
to 45, 48 and 49, 56, 59, 61 to 63, 65, 79,
82, 137.

Isabelle Richefort (I. R.) (assistant
to the director, Diplomatic Archives,
Ministry of Foreign Affairs, France):
cat. 122.

Pierre Sánchez (P. S.) (professor of
ancient history, University of Geneva):
cat. 119.

François Wisard (F. W.) (head of the
History Unit, Federal Department
of Foreign Affairs): cat. 19 and 120.

Valentin Zellweger (V. Z.) (ambassador
and permanent representative of
Switzerland to the United Nations):
cat. 135.

Nicolas Zufferey (N. Z.) (professor of
Chinese studies, University of Geneva):
cat. 27.

The exhibition *War and Peace* was organized in collaboration with the United Nations Office (UN) and The International Committee of the Red Cross (ICRC).

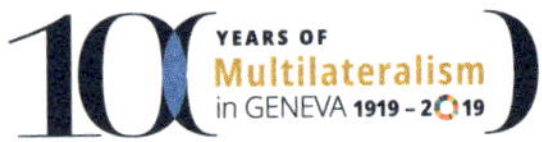 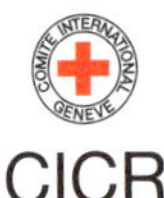

Acknowledgements

The Martin Bodmer Foundation wishes to thank very warmly its direct interlocutors with the partner institutions: Guy Thomas and Daniel Palmieri (ICRC) as well as Francesco Pisano, Blandine Blukacz-Louisfert and Pierre-Etienne Bourneuf (UN).

We also thank for their help and collaboration:
Gilad Ben-Nun, Josep Bosch, Paola Ceresetti, Olivier Coutau, Ella Duc Cemetery, Jean-Charles Giroud, Anne Liskenne, Georges Nivat, Brigitte Vast, Boris Wastiau, François Wisard and Valentin Zellweger.

The Martin Bodmer Foundation is deeply grateful to its institutional partners: the Republic and Canton of Geneva, the municipality of Cologny and a private foundation in Geneva; and to the many sponsors and benefactors whose support made this exhibition possible: the Loterie Romande, the Neva Foundation, the Swiss Confederation (Federal Department of Foreign Affairs, FDFA), the Yves and Ines Oltramare Foundation, the SIG Patronage Fund, de Pury Pictet Turrettini & Co. S.A., a Zurich-based philanthropic foundation, as well as the Leenaards Foundation for its contribution to the catalogue.

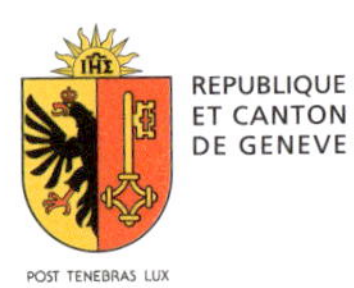 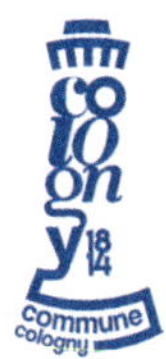 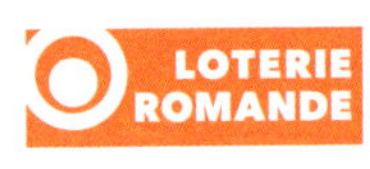

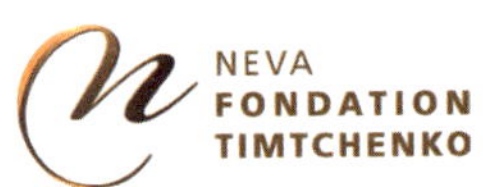 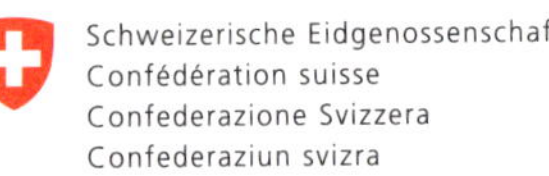

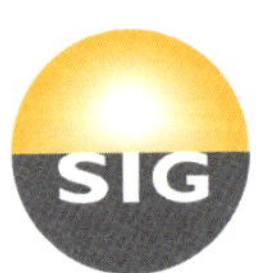 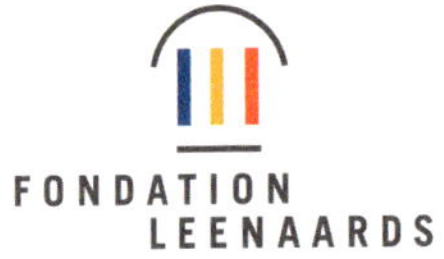 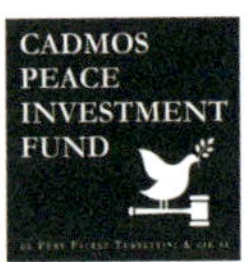

NEWSPAPER HEADLINES
Josep Bosch Collection, Geneva

Inside front cover: *Le Matin*,
31st year, no. 11116, 4 August 1914.

Page 1: *Le Petit Journal*, Illustrated supplement, 26th year, no. 1278,
20 June 1915.

Page 2: *America at War*, no. 58,
14 July 1943.

Page 3: *Los Angeles Times*, vol. 64, 15 August 1945.

Page 4: *La Vanguardia*, 20 September 1936.

Page 5: *New York Herald Tribune*,
vol. 105, no. 36059, 7 August 1945.

Page 6: *The Washington Post*, 98th year, no. 146, 30 April 1975.

Page 7: *Le Courrier*, 135th year, no. 32, 10 February 2003.

POSTERS
Private Collection

Page 330: Burkhard Mangold, *Gegen den Bolschewismus* [*Against Bolshevism*],
1919, color lithograph, 41.5 x 31.5 cm.

Page 331: Jean Carlu, *Pour le désarmement des nations*
[*For the Disarmament of Nations*], 1932, photomontage, 161.5 x 118 cm.

Page 332: Anonymous, *Jo-Jo-la-Colombe* [*Jo-Jo the Dove*],
1951, color lithograph, 77.5 x 58.5 cm, published by Paix et Liberté in 1951.

Page 333: Hans Erni, *Atomkrieg Nein* [*No to Nuclear War*],
1954, black and white offset, 128 x 90.5 cm.

Page 334: Connie Keelan, *Flower Love*, 1967, colour offset, 85 x 64 cm.

Page 335: Tran Nguyen Dung,
[*Urban Youth, Proudly Take to the Road and Give your Life for your Country*],
1971, colour offset, 78 x 54 cm.

Page 336: Anonymous North Korean Poster, [*To this day, rice is our life!*],
c. 2000, gouache on paper, 77.5 x 55 cm.

Recto 4th cover : Anonymous, *Egitto. Compendio di religioni*
[*Egypt, compendium of religions*], c. 1950, color lithograph, 102.5 x 74.5 cm.

Composite work in Daxline OT and Veneer
Paper: Magno natural 140 g
Photogravure: IGS-CP
Printed in September 2019 on Indice presses, Barcelona, Spain.

Legal deposit: September 2019
ISBN: 978-2-07-285734-8
Edition Number: 355907

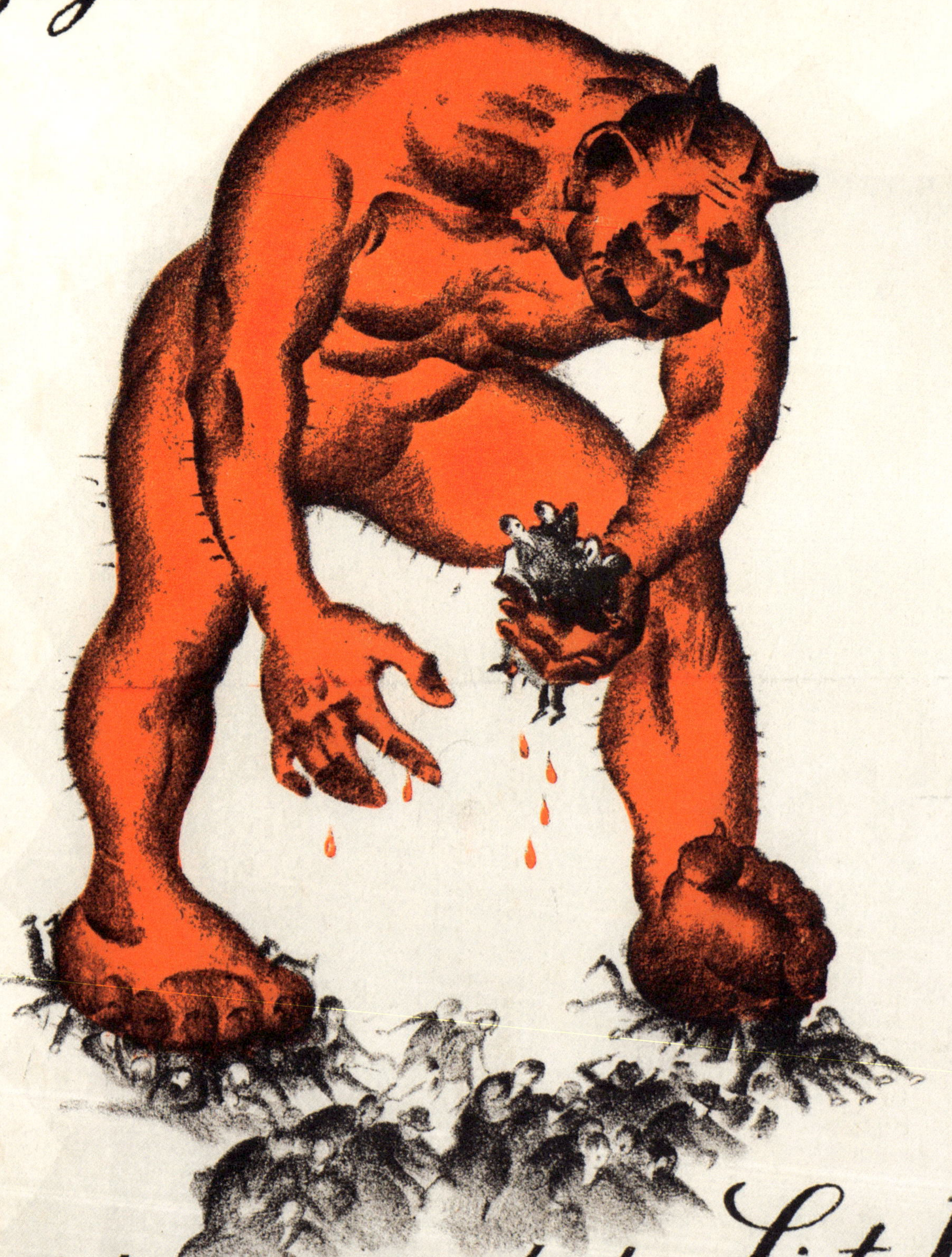

Gegen den Bolschewismus
mit der unveränderten Liste I
FREISINNIGE PARTEI. Alle zur Urne!
J. E. WOLFENSBERGER ZÜRICH

POUR LE
DÉSARMEMENT
DES NATIONS
JEAN CARLU
PHOTOG. ANDRÉ VIGNEAU
"Succès" 7.sup Marie-Blanche, H.CHACHOIN imp Paris
ÉDITÉ PAR L'OFFICE DE PROPAGANDE GRAPHIQUE POUR LA PAIX, 17, AVENUE CARNOT, PARIS
AVEC LE CONCOURS DU COMITÉ D'ACTION POUR LA S.D.N. 3, RUE LE GOFF, PARIS

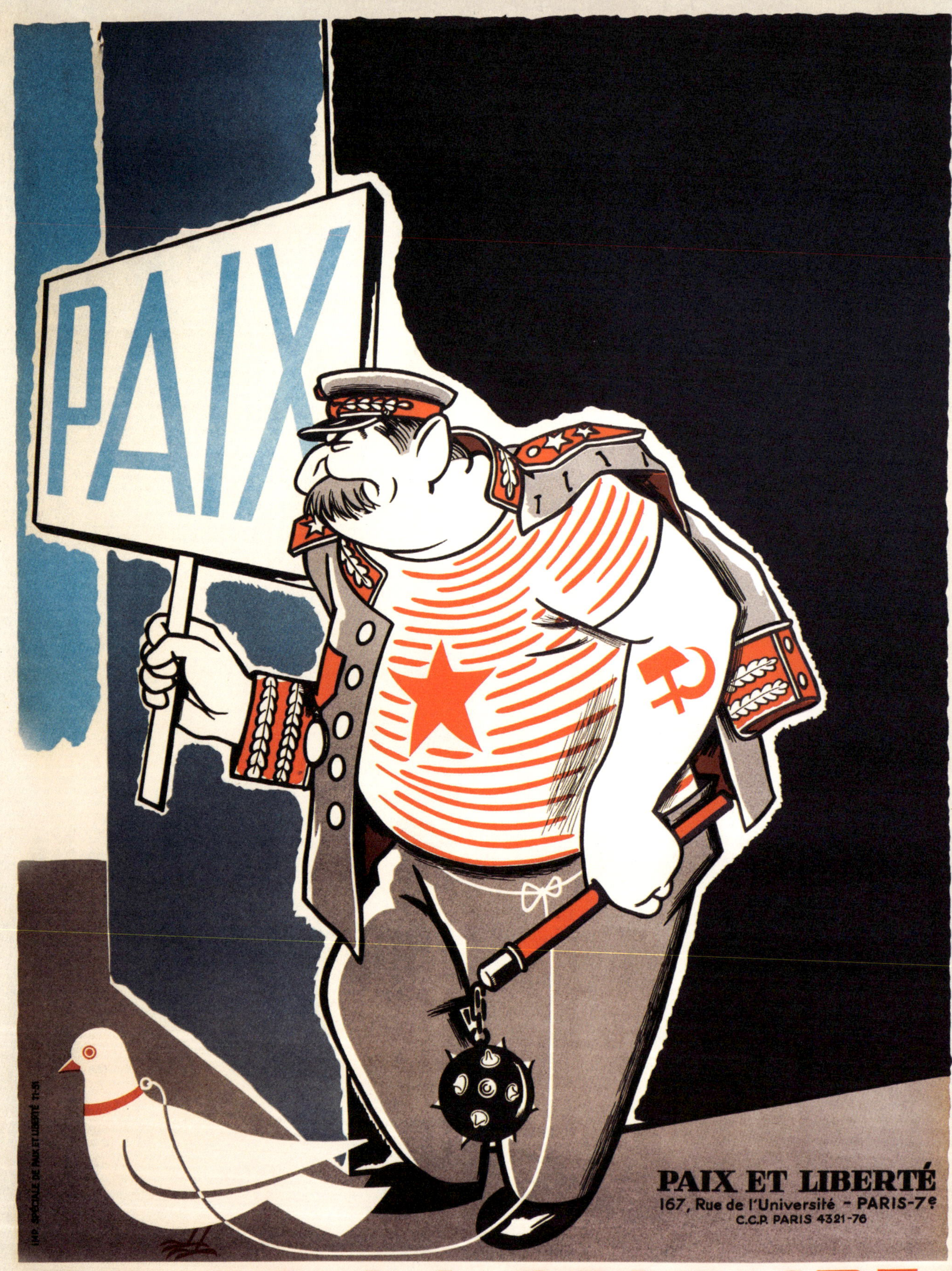

PAIX
PAIX ET LIBERTÉ
167, Rue de l'Université - PARIS-7e
C.C.P. PARIS 4321-76
JO-JO-LA COLOMBE
IMP. SPÉCIALE DE PAIX ET LIBERTÉ 37-51

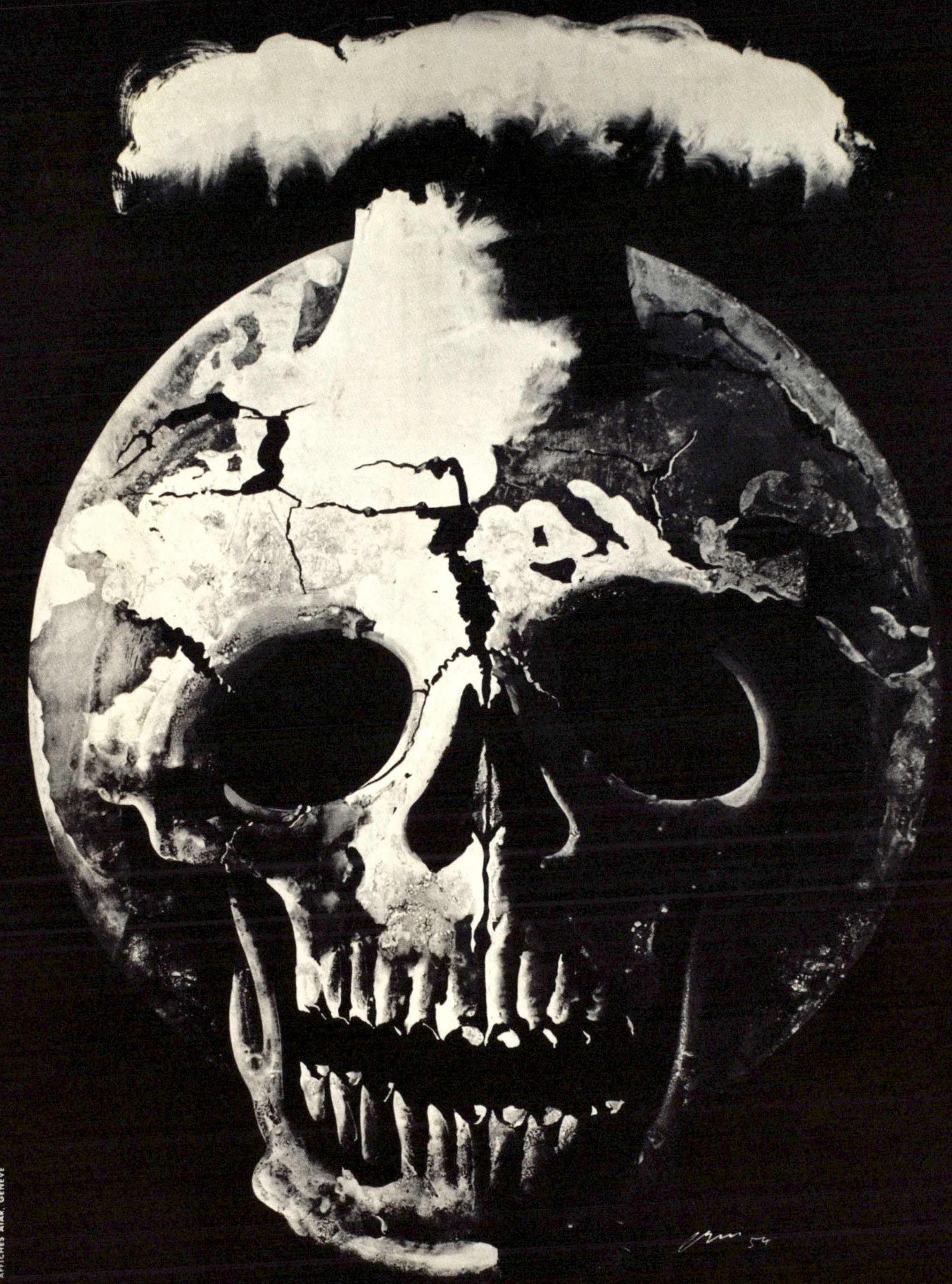

ATOMKRIEG NEIN

MOUVEMENT SUISSE DE LA PAIX · SCHWEIZERISCHE BEWEGUNG FÜR DEN FRIEDEN · MOVIMENTO SVIZZERO PER LA PACE

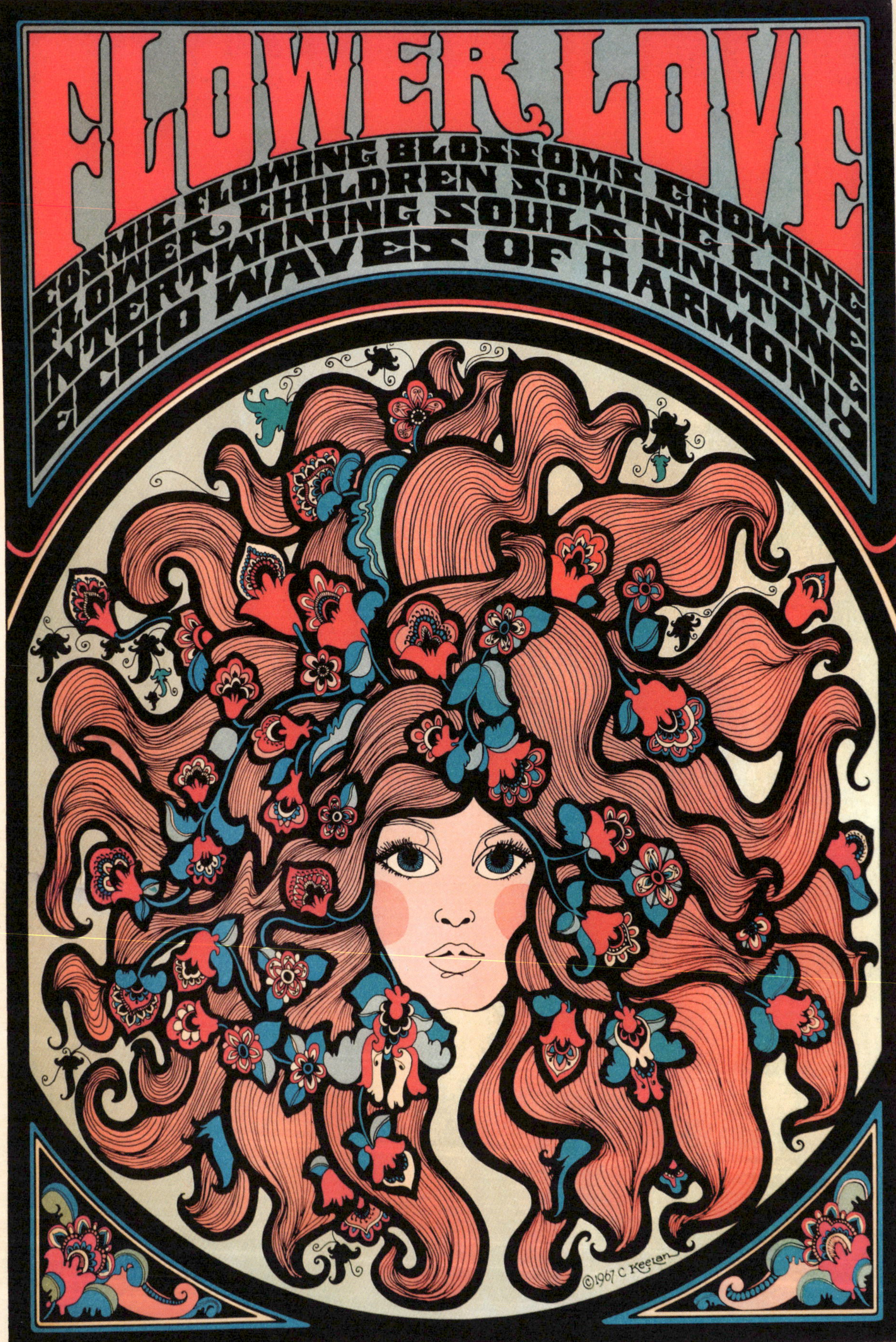

FLOWER LOVE
COSMIC FLOWING BLOSSOMS GROWING
FLOWER CHILDREN SOWING LOVE
ENTWINING SOULS UNITING
INTO WAVES OF HARMONY
ECHO
©1967 C Keetan

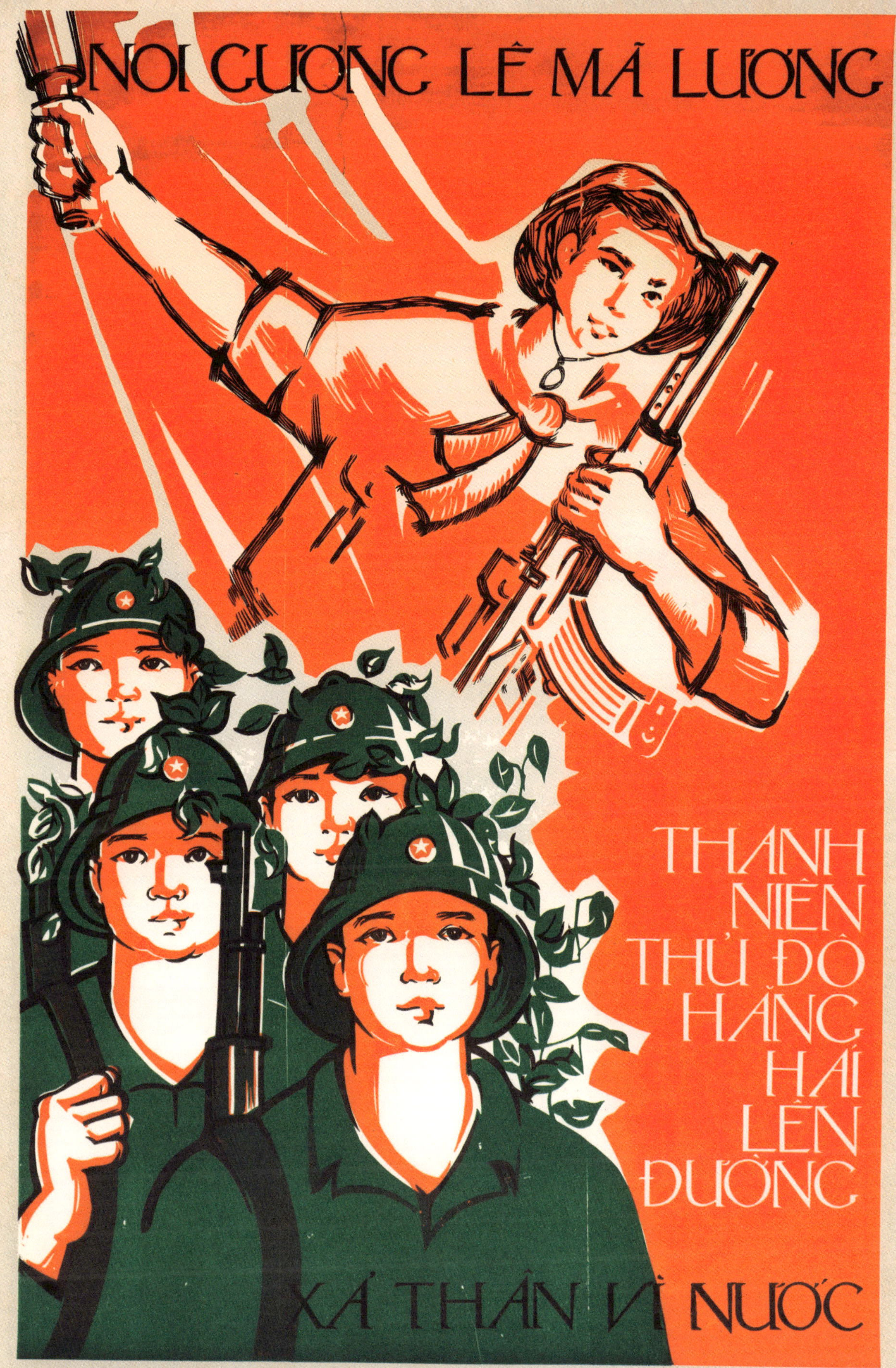
NOI GƯƠNG LÊ MÃ LƯƠNG
THANH NIÊN THỦ ĐÔ HĂNG HÁI LÊN ĐƯỜNG
XÁ THÂN VÌ NƯỚC
Tranh cổ động của Sở Văn hóa thông tin Hà Nội — IN 5000 BẢN TẠI XÍ NGHIỆP IN HÀ NỘI — THÁNG 12-1971
TÁC GIẢ: TRẦN NGUYÊN DŨNG

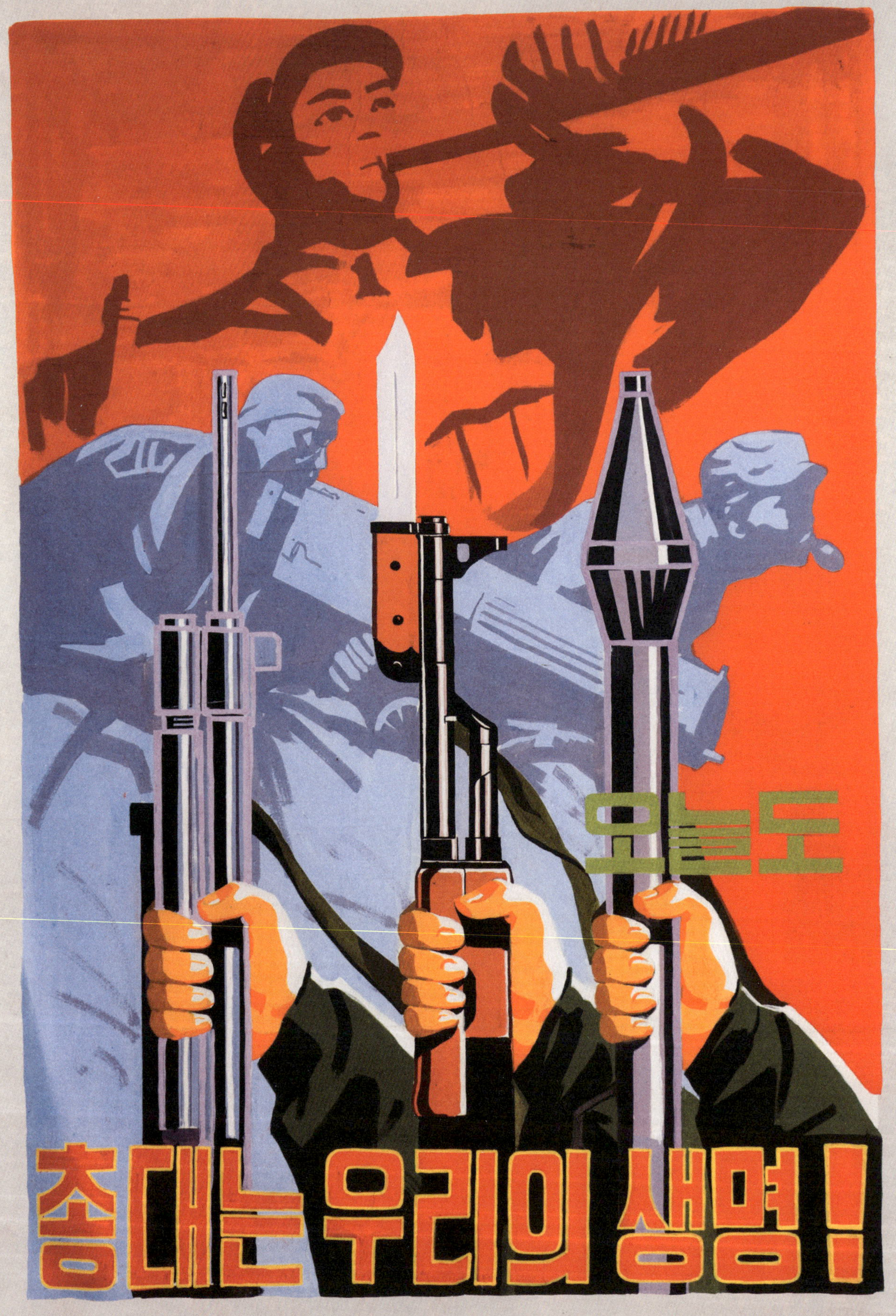

오늘도
총대는 우리의 생명!